BLACKWELL CRITICAL BIOGRAPHIES

General Editor: Claude Rawson

This acclaimed series offers informative and durable biographies of important authors, British, European, and North American, which will include substantial critical discussion of their works. An underlying objective is to re-establish the notion that books are written by people who lived in particular times and places. This objective is pursued not by programmatic assertions or strenuous point-making, but through the practical persuasion of volumes which offer intelligent criticism within a well-researched biographical context.

Also in this series

The Life of William Shakespeare

A Critical Biography

Lois Potter

WILEY-BLACKWELL

A John Wiley & Sons, Ltd., Publication

This edition first published 2012
© 2012 Lois Potter

Blackwell Publishing was acquired by John Wiley & Sons in February 2007. Blackwell's publishing program has been merged with Wiley's global Scientific, Technical, and Medical business to form Wiley-Blackwell.

Registered Office
John Wiley & Sons Ltd, The Atrium, Southern Gate, Chichester, West Sussex, PO19 8SQ, UK

Editorial Offices
350 Main Street, Malden, MA 02148-5020, USA
9600 Garsington Road, Oxford, OX4 2DQ, UK
The Atrium, Southern Gate, Chichester, West Sussex, PO19 8SQ, UK

For details of our global editorial offices, for customer services, and for information about how to apply for permission to reuse the copyright material in this book please see our website at www.wiley.com/wiley-blackwell.

The right of Lois Potter to be identified as the author of this work has been asserted in accordance with the UK Copyright, Designs and Patents Act 1988.

Library of Congress Cataloging-in-Publication Data

Potter, Lois.
  The life of William Shakespeare : a critical biography / Lois Potter.
   pages cm
  Includes bibliographical references and index.
  ISBN 978-0-631-20784-9 (cloth) – ISBN 978-1-118-28152-9 (pbk.)
  1. Shakespeare, William, 1564-1616. 2. Dramatists, English–Early modern,
  1500-1700–Biography. I. Title.
  PR2894.P68 2012
  822.3′3–dc23
                                                               2011043348

A catalogue record for this book is available from the British Library.

Set in 10/12pt Bembo by Thomson Digital, Noida, India

Printed in Singapore by Ho Printing Singapore Pte Ltd

1   2012

Contents

List of Illustrations

Preface and Acknowledgments

What differentiates one Shakespeare biography from another is the kind of context (and therefore speculation) within which it locates the available facts. This biography does not have a great deal of local color, and there isn't much sex either. Other people can and will write better on these subjects; the only Shakespeare I can imagine is one whose imaginative life was fed essentially by words. Though the chapters follow a chronological sequence, with occasional overlapping, each one begins with the discussion of the words in its epigraph, which are not necessarily part of the chronology. These mini-critiques are meant to remind both me and the reader that my subject is a writer whose words, more than most people's, have taken on a life of their own. As "Seeds spring from seeds, and beauty breedeth beauty" (*Venus and Adonis* 167) words, I believe, spring from the memory of other words. Memory is crucial: actors cannot function without it, and the Greeks made Mnemosyne the mother of the Muses. This book, then, will focus mainly on Shakespeare's literary and theatrical world. Its most unusual feature may be its stress on his relation to his fellow-dramatists and actors, particularly as collaborator and reviser. These activities have been the focus of a great deal of ongoing research, and some of my suggestions may be proved wrong by the time the book is out, but no biography of Shakespeare can remain cutting-edge for long. Though the final chapters in this Critical Biographies series normally give an exhaustive account of the subject's afterlife, in the case of Shakespeare this is simply not possible, and I am well aware that I have been selective and impressionistic.

If this book shows any of the theatrical awareness that I consider essential to an understanding of Shakespeare, this is due to many years of attending plays in rehearsal as well as in performance, particularly at the University of Leicester and the University of Delaware's Professional Theatre Training Program. I have also learned from the biennial Blackfriars Conference in Staunton, Virginia, which focuses on performance in the early modern theater, from the different versions of "original practices" in productions there and at "Shakespeare's Globe" in London, and from many foreign-language productions. Though I always wanted to be a good teacher,

I suspect that whatever success I had came not from anything I said, but from the play readings that I held throughout my teaching career. By the end, I had come to feel that simply reading a play aloud was more valuable than any amount of talking *about* it. Some of my speculations are the result of this experience.

I have always believed that writers are entitled to any delusions, however self-aggrandizing or silly, that enable them to continue writing; I have even speculated about which of these Shakespeare might have indulged in. Having the encouragement of others, however, is even better. The University of Delaware provided a pleasant environment, a good library, good students, and several sabbaticals that helped in the writing of this book, though I had to retire in order to complete it. At various stages I spent happy months at both the Folger Shakespeare Library and the Henry E. Huntington Library – which, I am sure with a full sense of the irony involved, gave me a Francis Bacon Fellowship in 2002. Throughout the final stages of this project I benefited most from the excellent electronic databases that the University of Delaware Library had the foresight to acquire, especially the online *Oxford Dictionary of National Biography*, a wonderful resource. Though I've never worked at the Chapin Library of Rare Books at Williams College, I am very grateful to Assistant Chapin Librarian Wayne G. Hammond for taking the trouble, at the last minute, to scan a Middleton portrait for me.

In its semi-final state, the manuscript was read by David Bevington, Lena Orlin, and Laurie Maguire. I cannot say how grateful I am for their comments at a time when I seemed to be writing from and into a black hole. Still later, Alan H. Nelson generously made criticisms and suggestions that saved me from many errors of detail. None of them should be blamed if this book is not as good as the one they could have written. It is difficult to know where other acknowledgments should begin and end, since it is the nature of Shakespeare's writing to seem relevant to everything else and for everything else to seem relevant to it. I have worried both about putting too much into the bibliography and about leaving out major influences that I have absorbed so completely that they are now forgotten. I probably owe something to anyone who has ever talked with me about Shakespeare, whether or not in connection with this project. The following names are the tip of an iceberg: Debby Andrews (who got me to discuss *The Birthplace* with her class), Jim Dean, Pavel Drábek, Lindsay Duguid, Richard Dutton, Reg Foakes (who suggested I should think about the magus), Martin Hilský, John Jowett, David Kathman, Lawrence Normand, Jay L. Halio, Angela Ingram, Roslyn Knutson, Lena Orlin, Kristen Poole, Richard Proudfoot, Angela Smallwood, Zdeněk and Majka Stříbrný, Ann Thompson, Lyn Tribble, Roger Warren, Michele and Raymond Willems, Julian Yates, and Georgianna Ziegler. I should also mention all of my former research assistants at the University of Delaware: Pamela Vasile, Mark Netzloff, Rebecca Jaroff, Barbara Silverstein, Paige Harrison, Bradley Ryner, Michael Clody, Kelly Nutter, Darlene Farabee, Michael Edson, Kevin Burke, Matthew Sauter, and Hannah Eagleson.

Some were more involved in the biography than others – I didn't start on it until this century – but all of us talked about Shakespeare.

Much earlier versions of parts of this book came out of the conference on "Early Modern Lives" organized by Sarah Hutton (Middlesex University, London, 2002); several "Setting the Scene" talks at the Globe Theatre; the conference on "Shakespeare and His Collaborators over the Centuries" organized by Pavel Drábek (Masaryk University, Brno, 2006); the Folger seminar on "The English Grammar School", taught by Lynn Enterline in 2007; and presentations at the Huntington Library, the University of Delaware, Temple University, the Columbia Renaissance seminar, King's College London, and the Modern Language Association. A research seminar at the University of London in 2008, chaired by Brian Vickers and featuring a presentation by Marina Tarlinskaya, got me interested in the possible role of Kyd in this story. I have relied a great deal, as will be obvious from my notes, on valuable work done by other biographer-critics – J. Leeds Barroll, E. K. Chambers, Mark Eccles, Park Honan, Dennis Kay, Alan H. Nelson, Charles Nicholl, Samuel Schoenbaum, James Shapiro, René Weis, and of course Stanley Wells. Katherine Duncan-Jones's studies of Shakespeare in relation to his contemporaries have been a great help to me, as has the Gary Taylor – John Lavagnino edition of Middleton's *Complete Works*. I am grateful to my editors at Wiley-Blackwell, particularly Emma Bennett, for helpful advice and, still more, for encouragement. Claude Rawson has been a sympathetic and supportive general editor. Ben Thatcher shepherded the book through production, with lots of good suggestions. I cannot imagine a better copy editor than Janet Moth. Linda English compiled the index. The oldest hath borne most: my mother, who reached her 101st birthday as this book went into production, has been wonderfully patient about the time it took away from her.

Shakespeare quotations, unless otherwise noted, are taken from the *Complete Works* by David Bevington (New York: Longman Pearson, 5th edition, 2004). I have modernized quotations from other early modern literary works, even when using old-spelling editions. Occasionally, however, I have left documentary material in the original spelling, when modernization would conceal its ambiguity.

List of Abbreviations

Works are cited in the notes by author name followed by a short title; full details are given in the bibliography. The following abbreviations have also been used:

Bullough	Geoffrey Bullough, ed., *Narrative and Dramatic Sources of Shakespeare*. 8 vols. London: Routledge & Kegan Paul, 1957–75.
Chambers, *ES*	E. K. Chambers, *The Elizabethan Stage*. 4 vols. Oxford: Clarendon Press, 1923.
Chambers, *WS*	E. K. Chambers, *William Shakespeare: A Study of Facts and Problems*. 2 vols. Oxford: Clarendon Press, 1930
Companion	Stanley Wells and Gary Taylor, with John Jowett and William Montgomery, *William Shakespeare: A Textual Companion*. Revised edn. New York: W. W. Norton, 1997
Cox and Kastan	John D. Cox and David Scott Kastan, eds., *A New History of Early English Drama*. New York: Columbia University Press, 1997
Honan	Park Honan, *Shakespeare: A Life*. Oxford: Oxford University Press, 1998
Herford and Simpson	*Ben Jonson*, ed. C. H. Herford and Percy and Evelyn Simpson. 11 vols. Oxford: Clarendon Press, 1925–52
Minutes	*Minutes and Accounts of the Corporation of Stratford-upon-Avon and other records 1553–1620*. Transcribed by Richard Savage. Introduction and notes by Edgar I. Fripp. Vol. 1 (1553–1566), Oxford: Dugdale Society, 1921. Vol. 2 (1566–1577), London: Dugdale Society, 1924. Vol. 3 (1577–1586), London: Dugdale Society, 1926. Vol. 4 (1586–1592), London: Dugdale Society, 1929. Vol. 5 (1593–1598), ed. Levi Fox. Hertford: Dugdale Society, 1990

N&Q	*Notes & Queries*
ODNB	*Oxford Dictionary of National Biography*. Oxford: Oxford University Press, 2004. Online edition
RES	*The Review of English Studies*
Schoenbaum	Samuel Schoenbaum, *William Shakespeare: A Compact Documentary Life*. Oxford: Oxford University Press, 1977
SQ	*Shakespeare Quarterly*
SS	*Shakespeare Survey*
TLS	*Times Literary Supplement*
Wickham	Glynne Wickham, ed., *English Professional Theatre 1530–1660*. Cambridge: Cambridge University Press, 2000

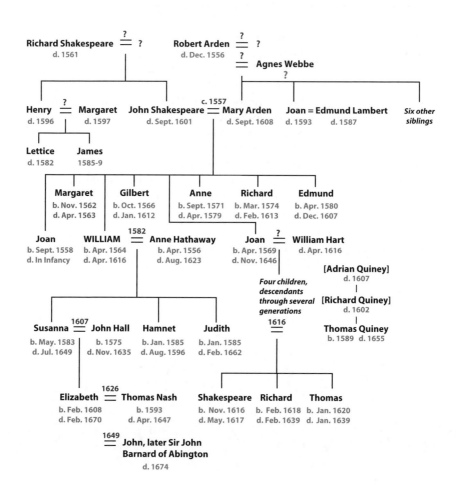

1

"Born into the World"
1564–1571

A woman when she travaileth hath sorrow, because her hour is come. But as soon as she is delivered of the child, she remembereth no more the anguish for joy that a man is born into the world.
(John 16: 21, from the Gospel lesson for 26 April 1564, Book of Common Prayer 1559)

Birth and Baptism

The Stratford-upon-Avon parish register states that William Shakespeare was baptized into the Church of England on Wednesday 26 April 1564. The register does not give his date of birth, and it does not show how committed his parents were to the church into which they brought him, one that would have been heretical only six years earlier. The Book of Common Prayer does, however, give the words that would have been read on the occasion. Some of them appear above as the epigraph to this chapter.

The children baptized on the 26th would have been those born between the 22nd and the 25th, if they were considered strong enough to be brought to church. Traditionally, Shakespeare's birthday has been 23 April, which was the feast of St. George, the patron saint of England. A major holiday after 1415 (the year of Henry V's victory at Agincourt), St. George's Day was once celebrated with pageants depicting his most famous act, the killing of a dragon. For the select few belonging to the Order of the Garter it was an important feast, at which their attendance was required. St. George was the Red Cross Knight of Spenser's *Faerie Queene* and his red

The Life of William Shakespeare: A Critical Biography, First Edition. Lois Potter.
© 2012 Lois Potter. Published 2012 by Blackwell Publishing Ltd.

cross on a white background is the official flag of England. He is now considered a mythical figure, and when 23 April is celebrated it is because of Shakespeare, who sometimes seems almost equally mythical.

It is natural to be suspicious of the too convenient link between national poet and national saint, especially since 23 April is also the day on which Shakespeare died in 1616. Still, it may well be right. In the sixteenth century, Catholics and some Protestants believed that infants who died unbaptized could not go to heaven, so clergymen were supposed to warn parents to perform the ceremony no later than "the Sunday or other holy day next after the child be born."[1] The Sunday before the 26th was 23 April. The next holy day, Tuesday 25 April, was the feast of St. Mark, which had the reputation of being unlucky.[2] There may have been another reason why it was not chosen. Since the minister was required to use the Book of Common Prayer, finalized in 1559, the congregation on St. Mark's day would have heard a Gospel reading in which Jesus tells his disciples that "If a man bide not in me, he is cast forth as a branch, and is withered. And men gather them, and cast them in the fire, and they burn" (John 15: 5–6).[3] This reading would have been particularly divisive in 1564, only a year after the publication of John Foxe's *Acts and Monuments* (usually called "Foxe's Book of Martyrs"), with its vivid woodcuts of Protestants being burned at the stake by Catholics. It was a time when many still remembered those on both sides who had been burned for their faith.

John Bretchgirdle, vicar of Stratford for the past three years, had every reason to be tactful. When Elizabeth I succeeded her sister Mary in November 1558, the incumbent Catholic vicar refused either to conform to the Protestant religion or to resign from his post, so the Corporation of Stratford forced him out by withholding his salary. His departure left the town with no resident clergyman for some time. The local congregation must have been divided and perhaps resentful. Bretchgirdle, an unmarried man with an Oxford MA, was the kind of well-educated preacher that the Reformation leaders wanted to establish in every parish, and would not have offended those who disapproved of married clergy. He died only a year after this christening, requesting in his will that his possessions should be sold, and the proceeds given to various charities.[4] This learned and charitable man was no doubt perfectly capable of gloating over the burning of those outside the true faith. Still, he does not sound like someone who would provoke his congregation by baptizing the son of a leading citizen on a day when the readings were bound to antagonize supporters of the old religion. He had some reason to like the baby's father in any case: as chamberlain or acting chamberlain of Stratford-upon-Avon from 1561 to 1565, John Shakespeare had been heavily involved with maintenance and improvement of Corporation buildings, including the vicar's house.[5] Bretchgirdle might also have felt sympathy for a man about to witness the baptism of his first son after losing his first two children in infancy.

So it was on 26 April, at the end of either morning or evening prayer, that the baptismal party gathered round the font. It was probably the midwife who held the baby.[6] Mary Shakespeare would be confined to her house for about a month, and then, in a special ceremony known as the Churching of Women, would come to the church to give thanks for a safe delivery and present the "chrisom" cloth in which the child had been wrapped, along with a sum of money. The Prayer Book put the desire for baptism into the mouth of the baby's godfather, who said, on its behalf, that he renounced the world, the flesh, and the devil with all his works, that he believed in all the articles of the Creed, and that he wished to be baptized in that faith. It was to the godparents that the priest directed his questions; until 1552 the child had been questioned directly, though someone else gave its answers, a kind of play-acting of which the Reformers disapproved.[7] The godparents' task was to name the child, though they had probably discussed the choice with the parents. John and Mary Shakespeare did not give their own names to any of their children. A child was often named after a godparent, someone trusted by the parents and perhaps someone they hoped would be of financial as well as moral help. Possible godfathers include William Smith, a haberdasher who lived, like the Shakespeares, in Henley Street, and served on the town council alongside John Shakespeare,[8] and William Tyler, a butcher in Sheep Street (John Shakespeare was a glover, and butchers provided the hides that glovers used).[9] William may even have been named after a relation, if William Shakespeare of Snitterfield, mentioned in a document of December 1569, was an otherwise unknown brother of John Shakespeare.[10] As the map (Figure 1) shows, the church was at the far end of town from the Shakespeares' house, and from most Stratford residents.

The relatives of the parents probably attended as well. John's father had died in 1561, but Henry Shakespeare, John's one identifiable brother, lived in the next village. Mary Shakespeare's relatives were more numerous. She was born Mary Arden, a family name derived from the forest of Arden, which contains the villages in which all the pre-1500 Shakespeares lived.[11] Her father Robert had recently died, but she had numerous siblings from her father's two, or possibly three, marriages. Robert Arden had owned the land that John's father had farmed, so the Shakespeares and Ardens must have seen something of each other while Mary was growing up. When Robert Arden made his will he may well have known and approved of the impending marriage between his daughter and his ex-tenant's son. Among Mary's siblings, her sister Joan and Joan's husband Edmund Lambert are the most likely to have attended this baptism. All the Shakespeare daughters were named after Mary's sisters, but Joan's name was reused for a younger girl after an older one died, so the family must have felt particularly close to her.

The group may have included colleagues, friends, and neighbors, since by 1564 John Shakespeare had lived in Henley Street for at least ten years and was a member of Stratford's governing body. Those most likely to come were this year's bailiff, George Whateley, also of Henley Street, and his chief alderman, Roger Sadler of

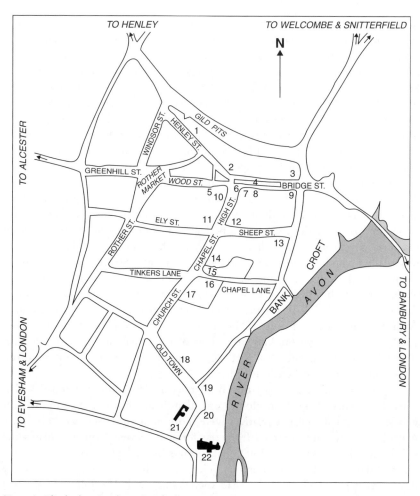

Figure 1 Elizabethan-Jacobean Stratford-upon-Avon

1. Two of John Shakespeare's houses (WS was probably born in one of them). JS also owned rental property in Greenhill St.   **2.** Bridge Street. House of Henry Field, tanner, father of the printer Richard Field   **3.** Swan Inn. This, and the Bear Inn across the street, are where prestigious guests were entertained. Its owner, Thomas Dixon/ Waterman, a glover, may have been JS's master   **4.** Middle Row, where most shops were located   **5.** Wood Street, where Richard Hill and Abraham Sturley lived   **6.** High Cross, where markets were held   **7.** The Cage, a former prison, now a house; home, after 1616, of Thomas and Judith Quiney   **8.** Crown Inn   **9.** Bear Inn   **10.** High Street, where the Quiney family lived   **11.** House of Thomas Rogers (butcher): now called Harvard House after his grandson John Harvard   **12.** House of Roger Sadler (baker), then of Hamnet and Judith Sadler   **13.** House of William Tyler (butcher)   **14.** House of July Shaw (later witness of WS's will)   **15.** New Place   **16.** Guild Chapel   **17.** Guild Hall and grammar school   **18.** Hall's Croft, possible residence of John and Susanna Hall from 1608 to 1616 (though they may have lived continuously at New Place)   **19.** House of William Reynolds, one of WS's legatees   **20.** Thomas Greene, town clerk of Stratford, lived here from 1612 to 1616, after moving out of New Place   **21.** The College, formerly a religious institution, then the Stratford home of Thomas Combe, father of William and Thomas, WS's friends   **22.** Holy Trinity Church, where the Shakespeare family are buried

4

Church Street. Some of the twenty-seven other councilors might also have found time to attend the baptismal service, particularly Adrian Quiney, who had already served as bailiff of Stratford and would do so on two more occasions. He lived in the High Street, round the corner from John Shakespeare's house, and their two families would be closely connected for over fifty years.

A healthy child was dipped in the holy water, while a sickly one might be gently sprinkled on the head. The heavy font cover was designed to prevent people from stealing the water, which was normally replenished and blessed at Easter in Catholic times. Health-conscious parishes changed the water regularly; perhaps a child born three weeks after Easter – it fell on 2 April in 1564 – had an advantage in being exposed to relatively fresh water. Bretchgirdle probably made the sign of the cross on the child's forehead, to show that William was not ashamed of the faith of the crucified Christ; this was a controversial gesture, a relic of Catholicism, and some parents refused to allow it. The priest then exhorted the godparents to teach the Creed, the Lord's Prayer, and the Ten Commandments in English as soon as the child was capable of learning them, and the group went back to Henley Street for a celebratory feast. Some guests would have visited the child's mother, who was supposed to remain in a quiet, dark room for several days after giving birth. They brought her their christening gifts, usually silver spoons or, from the more affluent, pieces of plate.[12] Sometimes these celebrations became rowdy. They were also expensive, since the mother was supposed to be given sweet, strengthening food and drink, as well as ointments, and many delicacies were also provided for guests.

William would have heard the words of the baptismal ceremony on many occasions. He may have been too young to go to the christening of his brother Gilbert in 1568 or that of Joan in 1569, but he probably attended those of his siblings Anne (1571), Richard (1574), and Edmund (1580). By the time Edmund was born, Shakespeare himself was about to father a child. The language of the Bible and Prayer Book is the first stratum of the many strata that make up the so-called Shakespearean style.

William Shakespeare's Name

Whether or not Shakespeare's godfather William turned out to be a profitable choice, his name was a gift to a boy with a taste for puns. According to Camden, "This name hath been most common in England since king *William* the Conqueror,"[13] an association that would inspire one of the few contemporary anecdotes about Shakespeare (see Chapter 7). "Will" is a crucial word in Christian doctrine, since the extent to which human beings had free will was one of the main Reformation controversies. "Will" was also a slang term for the penis, the physical means by which men commit sexual sin. The name, in full, can be broken down into "Will I am," as in the seventeenth-century riddle:

> My lovers will
> I am content for to fulfil;
> Within this rhyme his name is framed;
> Tell me then how he is named?

Solution. – His name is William; for in the first line is *will*, and in the beginning of the second line is *I am*, and then put them together, and it maketh *William*.[14]

The poet would later pun on it obsessively in his sonnets, giving some point to his admission "That every word doth almost tell my name" (76.7).

Shakespeare's surname, too, lent itself to sexual symbolism. A fifteenth-century fellow of Merton College, Oxford, is recorded as having changed his name from Shakespeare to Saunder because the earlier name was "*vile reputatum*" – perhaps "vulgar" is the best translation, since it has been interpreted as both "vile" and "common."[15] The dramatist's contemporaries usually emphasized its military meaning (Jonson punned on shaking a lance – to rhyme with "ignorance" – in his verses for the 1623 Folio). Thomas Fuller jokingly suggested, in *Worthies of England* (1662), that Shakespeare had been channeling the classical writer Martial in "the warlike sound of his surname (whence some may conjecture him of a military extraction) Hasti-vibrans, or Shake-speare."[16] When his contemporaries referred to Will as "gentle Shakespeare" they may have intended a paradox: one does not expect a spear-shaker to be gentle.

Odd as the surname was, it was surprisingly common. The existence in Warwickshire of a second John Shakespeare, a shoemaker who lived both in Warwick and in Stratford, has complicated the search for relations,[17] and the Stratford records show that the same person could be known by more than one name. People sometimes assumed the name of someone from whom they expected a legacy. In a culture that was still largely oral, people wrote down what they heard or remembered and did not ask how to spell it. The Hugh Saunder who was once Hugh Shakespeare is named elsewhere as "Saunder alias Shakespere alias Brakespere," and Richard Shakespeare, the poet's grandfather, is recorded as Shakstaff in 1541–2.[18] A "Thomas Greene, alias Shakspere" was buried in Stratford in 1589/90,[19] and a later Thomas Greene would call himself Shakespeare's "cousin."

John and Mary Shakespeare

The long genealogical tables of traditional biographies make one valuable point: family and ancestry were important to all classes, not just to the aristocracy. People looked first to their family for friends and allies; they looked to their ancestors for models. The poet had many relations in the Midlands, though he probably did not know as many of them as later scholars have found in the parish registers and civic records of Warwickshire and beyond.[20] Through his mother and the Ardens he could claim long descent and distinguished military service. The Ardens descended from men who had fought in the Wars of the Roses, and a distant branch of the family lived in Park Hall, in Castle Bromwich, near present-day Birmingham. The application for a coat of arms made on behalf of John Shakespeare in 1596 refers to valiant service on the part of his ancestors on behalf of Henry VII, presumably at Bosworth. Despite his military name, John Shakespeare's side of the family lacked this history of wartime service. The poet's grandfather, Richard Shakespeare, was a farmer in Snitterfield, nearly four miles from Stratford on the way to Warwick. He rented his property, as opposed to owning it, but it was substantial: at his death in 1561 his goods were valued at "almost £5 more than the vicar's."[21]

His son Henry, Shakespeare's uncle, also farmed. Most of what survives on paper from the sixteenth century consists of legal documents and court records, so Henry is known mainly for the trouble he got into: he was accused of "making a fray" or fighting, excommunicated in 1580 for refusing to pay tithes on crops in Snitterfield, and fined in 1583 for wearing a hat to church, thus disobeying the Statute of Caps, which was intended to help the declining industry of wool knitting.[22] This statute was apparently widely resented; the Stratford historian Edgar I. Fripp discovered that in 1596 the whole population of a nearby village was accused of disobeying it.[23] As this case illustrates, it was easy to accumulate a criminal record. Since fines were used to raise money for the borough (and for the person who informed against the delinquent), every possible offense was carefully followed up: failing to clean the gutters or the pavement in front of one's house, letting animals run loose, reviling one's neighbors.[24] As one historian puts it, "where there were so many laws to break, lawlessness was not the prerogative of the poor, and not necessarily a shameful thing."[25] This is the context in which to note the first mention of John Shakespeare in 1552, when he – along with two other highly respectable residents of Henley Street – was fined a shilling for having an unauthorized muck-heap.

At some time before then, clearly, either John Shakespeare or his father decided that the young man should leave the Snitterfield farm to seek a career in the nearby market town. Young men often left home in their teens – to study, to go into the service of another family, or to learn a trade. It has been suggested that this practice was a way of dealing with "the adolescent peer-group problem" by displacing the natural rebelliousness of teenage males onto a surrogate family, whether as apprentices or students.[26] It was also a practical necessity. This may have been an era of social mobility, but communities regarded as a foreigner anyone who arrived without connections to an existing social group. In order to have the rights of citizenship in another town, which included the right to buy and sell, a man had to have been apprenticed there or to show that he was part of some corporate entity, a craft guild, or a religious fraternity.

Apprenticeships were essential for aspiring craftsmen, but they were also popular with their masters, as they provided cheap labor, often for much longer than the training process required. Since there were limits on the number who could be apprenticed to any one master, they were in relatively short supply, and not normally available to farmers' children. Stratford had had a cluster of leather-workers since the thirteenth century,[27] and John Shakespeare learned the skilled trade of whittawyer (or white-tawyer) – working with alum and salt to soften the white leather (deerskin, horsehide, goatskin, sheepskin, and even dogskin) that was used for making gloves, belts, and other small leather goods. It is unlikely that he could have turned up in Stratford without some previous arrangement. Among the various possible master glover-whittawyers who might have trained him, historians suggest Thomas Dickson, alias Waterman, whose wife came from Snitterfield.[28] The fact that Dickson became an alderman in 1553 might have helped his former prentice's rapid rise in the borough.

Since John Shakespeare was able to buy Stratford property in the early 1550s, his apprenticeship must have ended some years before that date. Mary was still single in March 1556, when her father died, and was married by the time their first child was born in September 1558, but her exact marriage date is not known. Some complications may have gone unrecorded. In June 1557 John was fined for missing three of the fortnightly sessions of the court of record; he was also excused jury service in April of that year. On the other hand, he was very much present in September/October, when he served on a jury and brought three lawsuits.[29] The evidence suggests either that he was away from Stratford in the spring, perhaps on Corporation business, or that some event required his full attention – perhaps Robert Arden's will and its implications for the marriage settlement. Mary and her sister Alice had been made joint executors of their father's estate. In Alice's case, this task included another responsibility – she was to live with her widowed mother – but Mary received not only the same share of her father's wealth as her brothers and sisters, but also a substantial amount of land and a house in Wilmcote. Perhaps John, seen as a desirable marriage prospect, drove a hard bargain. If she was her father's favorite, the rest of her family may have resented this arrangement, but there is no evidence of the fact except perhaps what happened later when the Shakespeares got into a controversial financial entanglement with Mary's sister and brother-in-law.

Shakespeare's parents were born before the start of the Stratford parish registers, but John must have been considerably older than his wife, even allowing for the fact that most sixteenth-century women married late. In the early years, Mary may have helped her husband with his work – for instance, as one of the "stitchers" who made up the leather goods after he had tawyed the skins. He continued to farm in Snitterfield until 1561, but he soon realized that selling the work of one's own hands was less profitable than buying goods and reselling them at a profit. He also found that what people most wanted was ready money, and that they were prepared to pay for it. In the early 1570s he would be accused both of illegal dealing in wool and of charging excessive interest for money-lending. It has been argued that few medieval tradesmen could have made a living if they had practiced only the craft for which they had been trained.[30] The same seems to have been true in the early modern period.

It seems unlikely that either John or Mary could read, since there was no school in Snitterfield or Wilmcote. John's usual signature was a mark that probably symbolized his trade as a glover: a pair of compasses or, on one occasion, something that Samuel Schoenbaum interpreted as "a glover's stitching-clamp"[31] and another biographer took rather optimistically as evidence of literacy.[32] Park Honan, looking at Mary's "SM," saw evidence that she was used to holding a pen and might have been capable of teaching her son.[33] Inability to write did not necessarily mean illiteracy. Children who had spent only a short time in school were often able to read but signed with a mark, as did even literate men like Adrian Quiney, to save time.[34] Reading and writing were taught separately, with a writing master who worked with individual students. Schoolmasters were reluctant to teach writing too early, not only because they felt that the pupils might not be ready for it, but also because some parents pulled their children out of school once they had this knowledge.[35] What John clearly did have was basic numeracy, since at several points in his career he was given important tasks that required it.

The year itself had two alternative birthdays, because the Elizabethans were using a calendar established by Julius Caesar and modestly rectified by his successor Augustus. A number of alternative calendars had used dates in the Christian year to replace the Roman ones, but the most important reform of the system, by Pope Gregory XIII in 1582, was not adopted in the British Isles until 1752, apparently because it would have meant changing the Prayer Book, which contains elaborate tables for finding the date of Easter.[36] In the late sixteenth and the seventeenth centuries, most countries on the European continent, even the Protestant ones, gradually adopted the Gregorian calendar, with the result that their dates were some ten days ahead of those in Britain. Increasingly, too, Europe was beginning the year on 1 January (a practice that Scotland also adopted in 1600), while in England commercial records and many others still started on 25 March (Lady Day, the Feast of the Annunciation).[37] This is why dates are often given as "February 1601/2."

Thus the year was still new on 23 April, and up-to-date almanacs were just appearing. As usual, they tried to stay on the safe side by predicting disaster, assuming that the eclipses of the moon in June and July of the previous year would continue to have after-effects. The almanac that exclaimed over "the goodness of God that warneth us by the heavens, his ministering angels,"[38] was right in predicting plague in 1564. Stratford saw the first cases in June of that year and the sickness, exceptionally virulent, continued through the late fall, possibly killing as many as one-sixth of the population.[39] The Shakespeare household was fortunate to be spared, particularly as John Shakespeare had taken on a number of civic duties that compelled him to stay in the town. Though no one knew this, the epidemic was to be the last one for twenty years, a period "remarkably free of serious epidemics and harvest failures, during which life expectancy reached its highest level in all of the sixteenth and seventeenth centuries."[40]

At the time of William's birth, the couple had been married for at least seven years, and had had two other children, Joan and Margaret. Margaret had died after only a few weeks, and Joan must have died early as well, since another daughter would be christened Joan in 1569. As William was the first son, the first child to outlive infancy, and the only child for his first two years, it is natural to assume that he would have been loved and even spoiled by parents still grieving for two early deaths. Moreover, he was born just before plague struck the town, and his survival would have made him all the more valued. There is considerable evidence that being the eldest child is a common factor among unusually successful adults,[41] and William was in effect the eldest in his family. Joan, five years younger than her brother, survived all her siblings, dying just before the outbreak of the English Civil War. The rest of the family, by contrast, was relatively short-lived, especially considering that both John and Mary had long life-spans for their time. Joan and William were, moreover, the only ones to marry and have children. Remaining single was, however, a surprisingly common choice. Despite the closure of monasteries and convents and extensive Protestant propaganda in favor of the godly married household, popular literature generally depicted marriage as an unhappy state, especially for men. By the time a young man had become financially able to think of it, he may well have become afraid that it would mean a change for the worse.

There is considerable evidence that highly creative men, in common with dictators and military heroes, tend to have "dominating, possessive, or smothering mothers."[42] All anyone can deduce about Shakespeare's mother is that she must have been healthy, since she survived the births of eight children, not counting possible miscarriages that would not appear in the parish records. Germaine Greer, annoyed by biographers' tendency to idealize this woman, suggests that she was probably "spoiled rotten" by her father and may have ruined her husband's life by encouraging him to give up the messy but reliable trade he had learned for "cleaner" and more prestigious activities that would eventually get him into legal and financial trouble.[43] Mary might have felt that she had married beneath her, like Mrs. Morel in D. H. Lawrence's *Sons and Lovers*, and become obsessed with getting her eldest son to make the most of himself. Since the connection with the old and distinguished Arden family would later be an important part of the claim for the family's right to bear arms, it might have been discussed at home as well. Some scholars have imagined that she resembled Volumnia, the terrifying mother of Coriolanus. On the other hand, there may not have been so much of a gap between the status of husband and wife as used to be thought. It was recently discovered that her family home at Wilmcote was not the same place identified since the eighteenth century as "Mary Arden's house," but a somewhat smaller one nearby.[44] John's father was not poor and, though some of John's prosperity probably came through his marriage, his rapid rise in Stratford was due to his own efforts.

Stratford

Stratford was the most substantial borough in its district, with an important market. The town's government had originally been a religious foundation – the Guild of the Holy Cross, Blessed Mary the Virgin, and St. John the Baptist – which dated from the thirteenth century. Like other religious guilds, it provided insurance to cover the cost of burial for its "brothers" and "sisters" and encouraged solidarity among them. The many gifts and legacies from its members made it the wealthiest and most important local institution before the Reformation. Its chapel, conveniently located in the center of town, was reconsecrated in 1428 and further beautified after a bequest in 1496 from Stratford's most famous benefactor, Sir Hugh Clopton.[45] The walls of the chancel were painted with stories relevant to the guild, including the Last Judgment and the legend that gave the guild its name, the finding of the True Cross by St. Helena. The nave had wall paintings of the Dance of Death: a skeleton seized partners from all ranks of life – king, merchant, minstrel, artificer – and scrolls emerging from their mouths reminded those who could read that death comes to everyone. Next to the chapel were an almshouse and a free grammar school, both of which dated from the mid-fifteenth century.

Shortly before Edward VI's death in 1553, he granted a charter to the Corporation of Stratford, which replaced the guild as the town's governing body. The town retained the privileges to which it had been accustomed: a market every other week, two annual fairs, a perpetual vicar in the church and a perpetual free school. Funds originally used for candles and prayers for the dead were redirected to the grammar school and to the maintenance of Sir Hugh Clopton's other major gift, Clopton Bridge. Stratford became part of the diocese of the Bishop of Worcester, who was responsible for ensuring that the vicar and schoolmaster were teaching appropriate doctrine. Each was to have an annual salary of £20 – double what it had been, to show the reformers' seriousness about the value of education.[46] The borough when it was chartered belonged to John, Earl of Northumberland, who went to the block in 1553 after his unsuccessful attempt to place the Protestant Lady Jane Grey on the throne in place of Mary Tudor. It then passed to a series of other aristocrats, until the Earl of Warwick (Ambrose Dudley, brother of the Earl of Leicester) became its Lord of the Manor between 1562 and 1590. He had the right to choose the vicar and schoolmaster, though he often left the task to the Corporation.

The Corporation consisted of a bailiff (the equivalent of a mayor), fourteen aldermen, and fourteen capital burgesses (chief citizens). The minutes of its meetings show it making more and more rules: citizens were forbidden to engage in bowling in their own homes and were fined if their servants played cards; to the laws against unmuzzled dogs, sheep and pigs in the streets, it added one against ducks in 1555.[47] Special attention was given to punishing anyone who sheltered unmarried pregnant women – partly for fear that these women were trying to prevent their children from being baptized by Protestant clergymen, but mostly from anxiety that a fatherless child would be a charge on the parish.[48] Both the midwife and parish priest were supposed to persuade the mother to divulge the name of the child's father so that the sinner could be suitably punished. It was a society that believed in controlling all aspects of life in the interest of the general good, but also one in which individuals strongly resisted such control. Some of the council meetings must have become heated: reviling other members and refusing to go forth "in brotherly love" was punishable by a fine of 6s. 8d.[49]

By the time of William's birth John Shakespeare had become a solid and respectable member of this governing body. His first official post, in 1556, was as one of its two ale-tasters, inspecting the two most important foodstuffs, ale and bread, whose price, weight, and quality had been centrally regulated since the thirteenth century.[50] He moved on to other appointments in 1558 and 1559, and at some point before 1564 was elected a capital burgess. His chief service at this time was as the borough's chamberlain, administering its property and finances. In 1565 a vacancy occurred among the aldermen. William Bott, who lived in New Place, was reported "by credible persons" to have spoken evil words of the bailiff and to have added that "there was never a honest man of the Council or the body of the corporation of Stratford." Bott refused to attend the election meeting to clear himself, so he was expelled from the council.[51] In his place, John Shakespeare became an alderman, and hence "Master Shakespeare," with a special ring and a black gown trimmed with fur.[52] Two years later, he was one of three candidates for bailiff, the town's equivalent of mayor. He nearly had to take on the role, as the alderman who received the most votes refused to serve. John's own refusal was, however, accepted, possibly after he promised that he would accept the job in the following year. In 1568–9 he was duly elected as the sixteenth bailiff of Stratford. At the age of 5, William Shakespeare would have been known as the bailiff's son.

This election may have been the high-water mark of John's career, but any satisfaction it brought him was probably short-lived. Local government was time-consuming, since meetings took place at 9 a.m. on working days. There were fines for missing meetings, and the entire council had to attend the funeral of every alderman or burgess, or of his wife; there must have been resentment, since in 1557 the regulation was expanded to say that members should wear appropriate clothing and remain until the end of the service.[53]

The Imaginative World

Is it worth attempting to reconstruct what Wordsworth called "the growth of a poet's mind"? All normal children use metaphorical language and engage in imaginative activity, often in the form of games or story-telling. Yet, as Howard Gardner acknowledges, "a central mystery" remains: "These aspects of literary imagination seem to be universal. But it is an entirely separate matter to determine which of the millions of children who engage in these activities will later in life somehow be impelled, on their own, once again to create new worlds, to invent new realms of fiction into which other people can be invited and about whose reality they may be convinced."[54] It may be difficult to draw conclusions from developmental research that focuses on children in developed societies with resources unavailable even to the wealthiest sixteenth-century child, such as plentiful supplies of paper and tools for writing and drawing. Perhaps a closer analogy would be with the opening of Joyce's *Portrait of the Artist as a Young Man*, which shows young Stephen Dedalus's pre-literate mind being planted with the seeds of his later literary career: a story told by his father in baby-talk; dancing and singing "his song" while changing the words a little; making up a rhyme to words that he hears older people use; hearing a ballad sung by the maid. In addition, he is present at family arguments over politics and religion. A sixteenth-century child could have been exposed to the same kinds of stimulus, including bitter religious arguments. There might have been more music than in most families today. On the other hand, John and Mary Shakespeare may have been too busy to sing songs and too cautious to discuss public events. By the 1570s William, as the eldest of five, might have taken over the task of making up stories for his siblings. Being starved of imaginative food might have been as important to a gifted child as being glutted with it.

Imagination literally means the ability to create images. One of the most passionately felt differences between Catholics and Protestants was their interpretation of the commandment, "Thou shalt not make unto thee any graven image." Although it is the second commandment in Catholic bibles, in Protestant translations it was often merged with the first, "Thou shalt have no other gods before me," thus equating images with false gods. While the early Christian church had been hostile to the depiction of the supernatural, the rules had relaxed, especially in the west, several centuries before the Reformation. In defense of religious images it was sometimes argued that stained-glass windows and wall-paintings were "layman's books": a way of teaching the illiterate. The Reformers, however, seized on the prohibition of idols in the Commandments and, especially in England, took it as a command for wholesale destruction.

The Reformation in Stratford had its most visible results in the borough's treatment of its Guild Chapel paintings. The town's famous benefactor, Hugh Clopton, was still honored in local memory. Thus, even though the royal injunctions of 1559 ordered the removal of idolatrous images on "walls, glasses, windows," and so on, it was only in 1564 that they were covered with whitewash, and even then the whitewashing was confined to the most obviously Catholic images.[55] John Shakespeare was one of the members of the Corporation who saw this task carried out. Like many other acts of this period, it can be read either as enthusiastic rejection of an idolatrous past or as half-hearted placating of the government – whitewashing did not damage the work underneath and could be removed if religious policy changed again. The Dance of Death, with its grim message, was apparently not considered explicitly Catholic. The paintings remained in the nave, where a visitor saw them in 1574, and later disappeared under paneling.[56] They may already have been hard to read by the 1560s, but Shakespeare might have been able to see the minstrel's farewell to his harp, pipe, lute, and fiddle, among other reminders that death strikes all classes and professions.

The Reformers saw idolatry not only in inanimate images of artists and craftsmen but also in the impersonations of divine figures by living actors. Performances of the scriptural story from Creation to Doomsday had been a highlight of the church year in many communities. The "riding" on St. George's Day was particularly popular in the Midlands. Stratford in the sixteenth century had both a dragon costume and a set of armor. The procession was suppressed under Edward VI, like other events not based directly on the Bible, but revived during the reign of Mary Tudor. It probably had its last showing in 1557. John and Mary Shakespeare could have seen this show, and John might even have made a little extra money – the records show that someone did – by "Scouring the harness," or repairing the leather costume.[57] With Elizabeth's accession, the procession was suppressed again. The inextricable connection between traditional drama and repudiated beliefs meant that, after some attempts to "reform" the guild plays, most city fathers eventually banned them altogether.

Even so, Shakespeare's childhood probably included a good deal of theatrical experience, since Stratford was large enough to be a venue for traveling players. The Statute against Rogues and Vagabonds (1572), designed to control the mobility of unattached travelers, required touring performers to prove (with a license) that they were someone's servants. Since an aristocratic patron often preferred that his players, when not needed, spent their time living at someone else's expense rather than his, many of them existed primarily to tour the provinces. There were thirty-five such companies, with patrons, in the period between 1572 and 1583. Touring routes were well worked out and companies were licensed to perform in both public and private locations. Arriving in a town with drums and trumpets, the players would send their representative to show the license to a city official and get permission to perform. Some offered plays, others tightrope walking, tumbling, and other circus-like entertainment.[58] According to Sir John Harington, traveling actors got themselves an audience by going "up and down with visors [masks] and lights ... till all the town is drawn by this revel to the place ... and all be packed in together so thick, as now is left scant room for the Prologue to come upon the stage."[59]

A number of the noblemen most active in theatrical patronage (such as the Dudley brothers, Earls of Leicester and Warwick) had properties in Warwickshire and were therefore likely to offer hospitality to players. Elizabeth's favorite, the Earl of Leicester, had players from 1559 on and they benefited from their patron's position on the Privy Council: James Burbage is among those named in a patent in 1574, exempting them from the Statute against Vagabonds.[60] Shakespeare, who would be associated with the Burbage family in the 1590s, could thus have known them from much earlier. Before 1570 it was customary for the mayor and council of each town to view the play before deciding whether to license it for general viewing. Licensing eventually became the prerogative of the Master of the Revels at court, but the custom of the mayor's private showing died out slowly. When the council chose not to give the company its support, the actors performed in coaching inns; sometimes they were paid not to play.[61] The first performances of traveling players in Stratford took place in 1568. A 4-year-old was probably too young to see a play in this year, although another writer later recalled standing between his father's knees at the mayor's performance in Gloucester of a moral play, *The Cradle of Security*, which made an unforgettable impression on him.[62] That was in about 1572, the year when Leicester's Men played in Stratford. William, at 8, might have attended with other council members on this occasion. Two other companies came in 1574, Leicester's Men returned in 1576, and four others performed in Stratford between 1578 and 1579. Later, Shakespeare may have seen plays in Coventry – a city with a population more than twice the size of Stratford's, about twenty miles away. It was the most popular touring venue in Warwickshire because it paid better than anywhere else.[63]

That players first acted in Stratford in the year that John Shakespeare was bailiff may be a coincidence, but it is possible that he took some interest in the profession. As a man with connections in the clothing and leather trades, he might have made a little extra money by helping with costume repairs or replacements. Gloves, his speciality, were an important accessory for performances, especially at court.[64] If Shakespeare attended not only the mayor's performance but also the one given for the general public, he could observe how a play changes in harmony, or in conflict, with the audience's response to it; he could also watch actors respond to this response and – effectively or not – to other contingencies. As a space for performance, the Guild Hall at Stratford resembled many others – college dining halls or the largest rooms in inns and country houses – to which players were accustomed. Typically, there was a raised platform at one end where the most distinguished guests could see and be seen while they dined. At the opposite end were two doors, allowing servants with dishes of food to enter by one and leave by the other. Above the doors was a gallery for musicians. The actors may have performed in front of the two doors, possibly using the gallery as well, but they may also have played on the floor of the hall, so as to be closer to the spectators at the high table, in which case the actors made their entrances through the audience.[65]

Even a child might become aware of the rhythm of entrances and exits and the changes in the theater space created as characters enter and leave the stage – what Emrys Jones has called "scenic form."[66] The importance of this rhythm is easy to miss if one is accustomed mainly to the conventions of film, which rarely shows how characters get from one place to another. Most public events, however, were about movement to or from a place, and processions were as important a part of civic life as the dramatizations that sometimes accompanied them. The sight of fine clothes, whether on an ambassador and his train or on the cast of a play, was a pleasure in its own right. Actors began a play by "going about the stage" to let the entire audience see them before they began the story itself. The first appearance of an actor in costume had the potential to surprise and delight. Sometimes it was heralded by other speakers on stage ("Look where he comes!"). Sometimes the audience was kept in suspense waiting for him, especially if he was a popular character like the clown, and sometimes (if the audience was as "packed in" as Harington claimed) he had to fight his way into the acting space. Sometimes the entering character and those already on stage were imagined to occupy separate spaces, unable to hear or see each other. Entrances and exits could be used to make a point about characters' social status, if one insisted on preceding the other, or to waive that precedence (as when Prince Hamlet says, "Nay, come, let's go together"). Since the stage was unlocalized, actors came and went when they needed to, without explaining why. Even in performances of modern plays with representational scenery, the audience normally assumes that actors, once they leave the stage, cannot hear what is said there. This is a vestige of a theatrical tradition in which the actors entered, not into a room, but into a space for acting, and went out (or rather "within"), not into another room, but into a space for something else. A theater audience absorbs these "conventions" unconsciously, as it learns a language.

The typical mid-century touring company was small, judging from the number of plays that say on their title page (not always truthfully) that they can be performed by five actors. The five actors were usually four men and a boy who played female roles as well as children. They probably acted moral interludes, a genre that had existed before the Reformation, adapted to reinforce Protestant doctrine. These plays usually incorporated a good deal of comedy in the behavior of the bad characters, who demonstrated their worthlessness by crowd-pleasing songs and dances before finally repenting. To ensure that the story was properly understood, a presenter, sometimes costumed as a doctor, explained the moral at the beginning and end. By the late 1560s, however, there are records of plays on classical and romantic subjects, some of them calling for larger casts.

The sort of spectator who becomes an actor or playwright will be thrilled by the theatrical experience but will also want to understand how it works. If Shakespeare took advantage of his status as the son of an alderman, it is likely that he talked to the boy actors in the company and asked what their life was like. Unique to English theater (though boys had played in Spain until recently), they represented an uneasy compromise.[67] Letting men play women's roles, as in Greece and Rome, was considered better than allowing women to display themselves in public, but, as preachers had said for centuries, it was a transgression of Deuteronomy 22: 5, which forbade men to wear women's clothes and women to wear men's. Boys in school plays were used to taking male and female roles of all ages. Thinking of them as sexless or androgynous was a way of evading the prohibition. The small-cast moral interlude could manage without them, but they must have been a great asset to the plays based on romance material, with their exquisite and virtuous heroines. Depending on the company and its leaders, they may have been cosseted and admired or they may have led a miserable life. They were sometimes the children of company members, but often they were orphans or at least fatherless children. Shakespeare would have felt no temptation to become one of them.

He would soon, however, have something in common with the boy actors: literacy and the ability to memorize and recite. The craftsmen who performed in the biblical plays may sometimes have learned their roles through constant repetition with the help of a literate organizer, but a professional theater company had no time for something so labor-intensive. (Even the craftsmen actors in *A Midsummer Night's Dream* are told to memorize their parts in time for rehearsal on the next evening.) By definition, then, the theater was a world of literate people. Literacy was also important to Protestants, who aspired to a church in which everyone would be focused on the words of the Scriptures. Although they often attacked Catholicism for its theatricality, they insisted on the importance of public speaking. The 1559 Prayer Book specified that "all Ministers and Readers of public Prayers, Chapters, and Homilies shall be charged to read leisurely, plainly and distinctly, and also such as are but mean readers shall peruse over before once or twice the Chapters and homilies, to the intent they may read to the better understanding of the people, and the more encouragement of godliness."[68]

At the age of 7, assuming that he and his family conformed to the practice of the Church of England, Shakespeare would have had to do a substantial amount of memorizing for his first public performance, Confirmation. On this occasion, he had to "confirm" the promises that had been made for him at his baptism by demonstrating his knowledge and understanding of basic Christian beliefs. The parish priest, if he was conscientious, had already prepared the children by drilling them in the catechism. Now they were questioned by the bishop. After the boy had recited the commandments, he was asked the most important thing he had learned from them, to which he replied," My duty towards God, and my duty towards my neighbour." The dialogue continued:

Question. What is thy duty toward thy neighbour?
Answer. My duty towards my neighbour is to love him as myself: And to do to all men as I would they should do unto me. To love, honour, and succour my father and mother. To honour and obey the King, and his ministers.

17

> To submit my self to all my governors, teachers, spiritual pastors and masters. To order my self lowly and reverently to all my betters. To hurt nobody by word, nor deed. To be true and just in all my dealing. To bear no malice nor hatred in my heart. To keep my hands from picking and stealing, and my tongue from evil speaking, lying and slaundering. To keep my body in temperance, soberness, and chastity. Not to covet nor desire other men's goods.

The children may not have understood what they recited, but words memorized at an early age tend to stay in the memory and to explode into meaning at a later date. They may have joked among themselves about the picturesque phrase about "picking and stealing"; Hamlet would later refer to his hands as "these pickers and stealers" (3.2.334).

The petty (*petit*, or small) school offered a mixture of written and oral learning, including regular catechizing. Shakespeare probably learned basic reading there, and perhaps writing and ciphering. He would have learned from a primer, usually a single sheet containing the alphabet and then the syllabary (the five vowels, then a consonant affixed to each of them, as "ba, be, bi, bo, bu," and so on), followed by the Lord's Prayer, which could be "spelled out" (read aloud) by this method. According to John Brinsley's *Ludus Literarius or, The Grammar School* (1612), children started school at the age of 7 or 8; if they were sent earlier, it was "to keep them from troubling the house at home."[69] Being able to recite the Commandments, the Lord's Prayer, and the Creed, and to answer questions on them, was considered evidence that a child was rational, so Shakespeare probably entered the King's Free School in Stratford in the same year that he was confirmed. As he had said at the end of his confirmation speech on the message of the Ten Commandments, Shakespeare's task was to "learn and labour truly to get mine own living, and to do my duty in that state of life, unto which it shall please God to call me." The object of both religion and education was to ensure uniformity of belief and practice. The boy who would become a classic example of "original genius" was about to receive an education designed to prevent him from being original in any way.

Notes

1. *Book of Common Prayer 1559*, 277. For attitudes to unbaptized infants, see Bromley, *Baptism and the Anglican Reformers*, 49–59.
2. Schoenbaum, 25.
3. *Book of Common Prayer*, 226.
4. His will is reprinted in Fripp, *Shakespeare Studies, Biographical and Literary*, 23–9.
5. Ibid.,17.
6. Cressy, *Birth, Marriage, and Death*, 165.

7. Bromley, *Baptism and the Anglican Reformers*, 130.

8. Suggested by Edgar I. Fripp in *Minutes*, I: lii.

9. Katherine Duncan-Jones argues that confusion of "godfather" with "father" would explain the belief of early biographers that Shakespeare was a butcher's son. See Duncan-Jones, *Shakespeare: Upstart Crow*, 3.

10. M. Eccles, *Shakespeare in Warwickshire*, 12. The godparent did not necessarily give his own name. Laurie Maguire draws attention to Regan's words to Gloucester in *King Lear*: "What, did my father's godson seek your life? / He whom my father named? Your Edgar?" (2.1.91–2): Maguire, *Shakespeare's Names*, 26–7.

11. M. Eccles, *Shakespeare in Warwickshire*, 3.

12. Cressy, *Education in Tudor and Stuart England*, 152–66.

13. Camden, *Remains Concerning Britain*, 79, lines 22–3.

14. Riddle 51 in *The Book of Merry Riddles* (1629), first cited by J. O. Halliwell, in *The Sonnets and A Lover's Complaint*, ed. Kerrigan, 367–8, also note to 121: 9 ("I am that I am"), 342.

15. Chambers, *WS*, 2: 375, quoting the college register of 23 June 1487: *mutatum est istud nomen eius, quia vile reputatum est*. Chambers speculates that the scholar may have been a bondman who fled his village to take orders. Schoenbaum (13 and 324n.) thinks that he changed his name because it was "so commonplace."

16. Fuller, *The Worthies of England*, 590.

17. Fripp, *Shakespeare's Haunts*, 67–8.

18. Chambers, *WS*, 2: 375; Schoenbaum, 112, 114. The roll has to do with property in Snitterfield, recorded in the College of St. Mary, Warwick.

19. M. Eccles, *Shakespeare in Warwickshire*, 11.

20. e.g. ibid., 3–23.

21. Schoenbaum, 228, 15.

22. M. Eccles, *Shakespeare in Warwickshire*, 9–10.

23. Fripp, *Shakespeare's Haunts*, 61–2.

24. *Minutes*, I: xxii.

25. Collinson, *The Religion of Protestants*, 220.

26. See Stone, *The Family, Sex and Marriage in England 1500–1800*, 376.

27. Veale, *The English Fur Trade in the Later Middle Ages*, 36.

28. *Minutes*, I: xxxiii.

29. M. Eccles, *Shakespeare in Warwickshire*, 25.

30. Swanson, *Medieval Artisans*, 6.

31. Schoenbaum, 37.

32. *Minutes*, IV: xl.

33. Honan, 14.

34. Schoenbaum, 37.

35. Brinsley, *Ludus Literarius*, F3^v–F4^v.

36. Sohmer, *Shakespeare's Mystery Play*, 20.

37. See C. R. Cheney, ed., *A Handbook of Dates for Students of British History*, esp. ch. 1, "Reckonings of Time," and appendix (p. 236).

38. Cunningham, A *Prognostication for the Yeare of our redemption, 1564*.

39. Schoenbaum (p. 26) agrees with Edmond Malone's deduction, based on the burial register for 1564.

40. Muldrew, *The Economy of Obligation*, 36.
41. Simonton, *Genius, Creativity and Leadership*, 26.
42. Ibid., citing V. Goertzel and M. T. Goertzel, *Cradles of Eminence* (Boston: Little, Brown, 1962), 29.
43. Greer, *Shakespeare's Wife*, 27–9.
44. Alcock, with Bearman, "Discovering Mary Arden's House."
45. Davidson, *The Guild Chapel Wall Paintings at Stratford-upon-Avon*, 3.
46. *Minutes*, V: xv.
47. *Minutes* I: 26–7, 43.
48. René Weis stresses the anti-Catholic motive, while David Cressy emphasizes the need to avoid a charge on the parish. See Weis, *Shakespeare Revealed*, 15–17, and Cressy, *Birth, Marriage, and Death*, 74–9.
49. *Minutes*, I: 65.
50. *Minutes*, I: 30, 58.
51. *Minutes*, I: 144–5
52. M. Eccles, *Shakespeare in Warwickshire*, 27.
53. *Minutes*, I: 68
54. Gardner, *Art, Mind, and Brain*, 183.
55. Davidson, *The Guild Chapel Wall Paintings*, 10.
56. They were rediscovered in the 1950s, in very poor condition, only to be hidden again behind restored paneling (Davidson, *The Guild Chapel Wall Paintings at Stratford-upon-Avon*, 11, 13–14).
57. Davidson, *The Guild Chapel Wall Paintings*, 4–5, 30–1, 5.
58. Ingram, *The Business of Playing*, 237–41.
59. [Harington], *An Apologie for a new discourse of a stale subiect, called the metamorphosis of Aiax*, Bb1ᵛ.
60. Wickham, 206.
61. Gurr, *The Shakespeare Company, 1594–1642*, 64.
62. R. Willis, *Mount Tabor* (1639), in Chambers, *ES*, 1: 333.
63. Tiner, "Patrons and Travelling Companies in Warwickshire."
64. Chambers, *ES*, 1: 225.
65. See Burkhart, "The Playing Space in the Halls of the Inns of Court," and Arlidge, *Shakespeare and the Prince of Love*, 118–19.
66. Jones, *Scenic Form in Shakespeare*.
67. Thacker, *A Companion to Golden Age Theatre*, 130.
68. *Injunctions given by the Queenes Maiestie anno Dom. 1559*, 53.
69. Brinsley, *Ludus Literarius*, C1.

2

"Nemo Sibi Nascitur"

1571–1578

Parentes ama. Love your parents.
Mundus esto. Be clean [or neat].
Foeminae sunt inconstantes. Women are inconstant.
Nemo sibi nascitur. No one is born for himself alone.

These "sentences" – sententiae – were among the first Latin phrases that grammar-school children were taught. After starting with simple two- and three-word sayings, the pupils moved on to longer ones and then to distichs (two lines of verse). They usually learned one or two each night and had to repeat them the following morning. Shakespeare remembered some of them. In *The Comedy of Errors* the slave Dromio, who thinks his master is about to whip his wife and servants, warns Adriana: "*respice finem*, respect your end, or rather . . . respect the rope's end" (4.4.41–2). The Latin phrase is one that every schoolboy would have learned as either *Respice futurum* or *Respice finem*; both mean that you should look to the future, or be conscious of the brevity of life, but Dromio is making an obvious pun on the English translation of "end." In *The Winter's Tale*, Leontes, having told his son Mamillius, "We must be neat," a translation of *Mundus esto*, hastily corrects himself – "not neat, but cleanly" (1.2.123). Anyone who had been to grammar school would have understood why this jealous husband suddenly jumped from the adjectival meaning of "neat" to the noun meaning cattle – in other words, horned beasts or cuckolds. Mamillius is 7 years old, precisely the age at which he would have begun to learn such phrases.

Learning meant the possession of words and sentences – sometimes inscribed on the inside of a ring, on the beams of ceilings, or above fireplaces – and the ability to spend this verbal wealth. In a French conversation textbook, a father calls on his 9-year-old son to recite "some fair saying or sentence, that we may see what you have learned." In the interest of vocabulary-building, the boy offers a range of genres from

The Life of William Shakespeare: A Critical Biography, First Edition. Lois Potter.
© 2012 Lois Potter. Published 2012 by Blackwell Publishing Ltd.

which to choose: "a sentence, a proverb, a fable, an epigram or an apophthegm."[1] Of these, the fable would have been the longest, since it was a story with a moral. An apothegm was a saying attributed to some historical personage, often occurring as the climax of an anecdote. Allowed to choose for himself, the textbook boy comes up with, "For one pleasure, a thousand sorrows," to which the father replies, "It is very well and truly said." If John Shakespeare enjoyed watching his sons show off their grammar-school learning in public, he might have been pleased with the saying *Nemo sibi nascitur*. The words explained his involvement in the Stratford Corporation, while it lasted.

Grammar School

The Stratford grammar school was next door to the Guild Hall and its chapel (see Figure 2), which would have made it easy for Stratford's council members to drop in on lessons. The master was given £20 a year and free accommodation. Out of that salary he paid £4 a year to an usher whose task was to arrive an hour earlier than the master, get the classroom ready, and teach the younger pupils. The salary was good enough to attract well-qualified, Oxford-trained teachers, many of whom moved on to still better jobs after only a few years at the school. Simon Hunt was the schoolmaster from 1571 until early 1575, but if Shakespeare started school at 7 he would probably have been taught by the usher during most or all of that period – probably Hunt's successor, Thomas Jenkins, an Oxford MA (1570). Despite his Welsh name, Jenkins was born in London, the son of a servant to Sir Thomas White, who founded St. John's College, Oxford, in 1554 and apparently sent the children of all his servants and apprentices there. Jenkins was thus a good example of the kind of upward mobility available to an educated man. T. W. Baldwin, the great expert on Stratford education, points out that the schoolmaster's room, above the council chamber in the Guild Hall, was still called "Mr Jenkins' chamber" in 1587, as if he had been the most memorable of the teachers.[2] If Shakespeare was still at school in 1579, he would also have been taught by John Cottom, who took his BA at Oxford in 1566. Cottom's brother, a Jesuit, accompanied the famous Edmund Campion on his illegal mission to England in the early 1580s and, with him, was put to death. Probably as a result, the schoolmaster was asked to leave his post. Though he may have been a Catholic, he would probably not have had much chance to indoctrinate his pupils, since schoolmasters were closely watched by the town and church authorities, and the boys were encouraged to report any suspicious comments to their parents.[3]

A grammar school was exactly what its name implies. As with the Prayer Book, everyone was expected to use the same grammar book and, since the curriculum and method of instruction were largely the same from one school to another, it is possible to know a good deal about the educational system of the period. Its ideal product was

Sam Ireland delt

Shakspere's House, New Place, Chapel, & Grammar School.

Figure 2   Drawing of (*left to right*) New Place, the Guild Chapel, and the grammar school, by Samuel Ireland (1795). By permission of the Folger Shakespeare Library

a young man who could give a grammatical analysis of a Latin sentence and write imitations of Cicero, Ovid, and Virgil indistinguishable from the originals.[4] This is the view stated in John Brinsley's *Ludus Literarius* (1612), a fascinating book in which a confident and successful teacher gives advice to another teacher who feels burned out. The two teachers, between them, describe both good and bad teaching methods, the ideal classroom, and the often inadequate reality.

Teachers preferred to have their pupils literate on arrival, though apparently this was not always possible. Young children spent a lot of time on the alphabet, sounding out letters, syllables, and even words. They were taught rules of orthography, although with an element of permissiveness: one author comments, for instance, that the silent "e" is optional and that it does not matter whether one writes "madde" or "mad."[5] Brinsley recommends that the teacher pronounce syllables distinctly in order to ensure that the children spell correctly.[6] He does not say what the teacher should do when, as was already the case, words were not spelled as they were pronounced. Arithmetic was making considerable advances in the second half of the sixteenth century but it was not taught in grammar school; a scholar needed to learn only how to read out a number or to write one down. This, and the difference between Roman and Arabic numerals, was all that the schoolmaster had time to teach; the student who wanted more would need to study in private or at "the ciphering school."[7] The result, not surprisingly, was that many students, even in their last year of school, were unable to find the right chapter and verse in church or use the index in their books.[8] The exchange between the page Mote and his master Don Armado in *Love's Labour's Lost*, a play permeated with school language, is less incredible than it might seem:

> Mote. How many is one thrice told?
> Armado. I am ill at reckoning; it fitteth the spirit of a tapster.
>
> (1.2.39–41)

Armado, who not only cannot multiply one times three but regards this kind of knowledge as beneath him, is not much different from the speakers in *Ludus Literarius*, one of whom apologizes for asking his friend so many questions about arithmetic, "in itself so very a trifle."[9] It is hardly surprising that so many scholars in this period found themselves trapped in complicated financial bonds whose implications they had never been taught to understand.

Because so much of the education was in Latin, it is easy to imagine that the educated Elizabethan was something of a linguistic prodigy. While reading and speaking classical languages may have become second nature among those who lived in Oxford and Cambridge colleges, or at the highest levels in the church and civil service, it was probably not true of the typical grammar-school product or even the ordinary clergyman. Something of the true state of affairs can be seen in another of John Brinsley's publications. Since its first publication in 1564, "Corderius" had been a standard text for beginning schoolboys. It was a series of dialogues, skillfully introducing increasingly difficult vocabulary and grammar, written by the Calvinist schoolmaster Mathurin Cordier (Corderius) for use in his school in Geneva. Brinsley translated them in 1614, intending that English schoolboys would translate his translations back into Latin and then compare their versions with the original. The fact that these dialogues were now fifty years old did not worry him; apparently the school experience had changed very little over time. The little boys are depicted for the most part as exemplary in their desire to practice Latin conversation, but the dialogues also reveal the difficulties of an education that separated them from their peers: one boy says that other children make fun of those who speak Latin in the streets and even attack them physically.[10] Stratford schoolboys were perhaps supposed to speak Latin to each other outside the classroom, but in *Ludus Literarius* the two schoolmasters ruefully agree that this probably happens only when the master is within hearing.[11] Nevertheless, the surviving letters of some of Shakespeare's Stratford acquaintances, such as Abraham Sturley and Richard Quiney, show that they could read and quote Erasmus and Cicero in the original.[12]

Despite the curriculum's emphasis on Latin, *Ludus Literarius* also recommends some kind of English practice daily (writing familiar letters, translating from Latin, summarizing Aesop's fables, reporting on sermons).[13] English grammar posed its own problems. Young children found it difficult to understand the "you/thou" distinction, which was becoming less and less clear.[14] Some grammatical constructions still used in the country were disappearing in the city: "hath," for instance, was being replaced with "has"; "did take" was becoming less common as an alternative to "took." Though Shakespeare continued to use the older forms throughout his career (a fact that distinguishes him from younger, city-based writers), he eventually started to adopt the newer ones. His preference for constructions with "do" or "did" may have been pragmatic, since, especially with a one-syllable verb, they often made rhyming easier or provided an easy iambic foot. Over time, "did" and "do" have taken on an emphatic sense ("I *do* think") and modern actors sometimes stress them accordingly, thus undoing the musical effect as well as creating an unnecessarily argumentative tone.

The standard practice was to learn words or lines one at a time and then to repeat the entire series. In one of Corderius's early dialogues, the master asks Latin vocabulary questions on "the head; the top of the head; the forepart of the head; the hinder part of the head." It was easy to point to these features, thus avoiding the need to lapse into English. After putting the questions individually, the master challenges the pupil to say them all and, pleased with the result, tells him to go have breakfast.[15] Claudius Holyband's French phrasebook, similarly, shows a boy giving the entire list of French measuring terms: "Escoutez si je les nommeray bien: un demy sestier, un sestier, une pinte, une quarte, un broc, trois quartes."[16] In *Henry V*, when the Princess of France tries to learn English she too learns the words for parts of the body, repeating them first individually and then all together ("Écoutez si je parle bien"); however, since she is the social superior of her teacher, it is she who then declares, "C'est assez pour une fois. Allons-nous à diner" (3.4.59–60).[17]

It was a very competitive system. Brinsley advises the master to make everyone read the same sentence, ridicule the ones who do it badly, and praise the ones who get it right.[18] The master probably asked for homework every night, to be handed in by 9 a.m. the next day. Part of every Saturday was supposed to be devoted to the catechism. On Sundays the children were led to church by the usher and were examined later to make sure they had paid attention to the sermon.[19] There may have been some frantic note-taking and whispered discussions, since the older children were supposed to recognize the scriptural sources of quotations. The psalms and proverbs were normally the first works that pupils translated into Latin, which explains why the psalms are the part of the Bible most often alluded to in Shakespeare.[20]

Since there was only a limited selection of available books, note-taking was very important. Early on, pupils were told how to compile a commonplace book. Rather than writing the details of the source at the top of the page, the pupil would write the subject on which he was making the notes – perhaps God, or Faith, or Death. He would then look out for short, pithy sayings. It did not always matter who had said them, unless the author's name added to the weight of the saying. It was not even

25

important to quote the exact words; in fact, sometimes it was better to change anything in the original that might prevent the quotation from being universally applicable. Pagan quotations might, for instance, be made more Christian. The pupil was encouraged to use published collections of *sententiae* or, for the more sophisticated, *florilegia* ("flowers" of speech gathered from the best writers). Some editions indicate the presence of *sententiae* in longer works through typography or a pointing finger in the margin.

The Books

Learning Latin was the key to almost all earlier literature. Virtually no one could read the Germanic language of pre-Conquest England and only a few scholars had ever heard of *Beowulf*. Gower and Chaucer were only as far from Shakespeare as Byron and Sir Walter Scott are from a reader in the first quarter of the twenty-first century, but, because of changes in pronunciation, Middle English verse may have been as hard to read as Latin. This was even truer of verse written according to the Old English system, which, to readers not trained in its pattern of alliteration and stress, looked primitive and clumsy. The admiration that Shakespeare still inspires, after 500 years, pales in comparison to what Shakespeare and his classmates were taught to feel for Cicero, Virgil, and their countrymen, some 1,600 years after the death of Julius Caesar. Their works were still the basis of education, not merely in language and literature but in nearly all subjects.

Though the saying *Nemo sibi nascitur* is credited to Erasmus, it is implicit in Cicero's writings, with their stress on public duty. Cicero was important for Renaissance readers not only in himself but also because he quoted and described so much earlier (and now lost) literature. Without learning Greek, one could know Platonic thought, since he quoted and discussed it, with attractive aesthetic analogies derived from Plato. He wrote, for instance, that the soul was like music, that the good life should be harmonious, and that there was no conflict between "virtue" and "profit" (to use the terms of a sixteenth-century translator) because virtue was natural, and living according to nature – which is already moral – was the source of a happy life. However, one sometimes had to choose among different virtues, and his anecdotes, often attached to famous people, demonstrate how these choices are to be made. Mere wealth, health, and other worldly goods – things that benefited only one's self – were subordinate to friendship and loyalty to one's family. But above these was the good of one's country, since its welfare benefited everyone. The complexity of this ethical framework emerges in a series of hypotheses. Suppose a man discovers that his father is plotting against the state. Provided that the father is not actively seeking to destroy the state, the man's first duty is to his father, whom he should take all possible steps to dissuade but should not betray. Why not? Because it is good for the state that men should revere their fathers.[21] Such reasoning may have been helpful to children whose parents were still Roman Catholic, or who feared that their Catholic grandparents might have been damned for their beliefs.

Virgil's Aeneas was the age's model hero: fleeing from the burning city of Troy, he makes a long voyage like Odysseus and then, on arrival in Italy, is obliged to wage war on its inhabitants, as the Greeks did in Troy. The fact that the *Aeneid* combined the subject matter of the two great Homeric epics showed how a truly gifted poet can build on existing work to create something still greater. Those who met his work in school particularly loved such elaborations of the original as Aeneas's carrying his old father on his back out of the burning city and the conflict between his love for Dido, the Queen of Carthage, and his destiny as the founder of a great nation. The hero's most important encounter is with his father's ghost, which prophesies the future greatness of Rome. British history, as it had been told for centuries, claimed that another Trojan hero, Brute, had fled from Troy to settle in Britain. For those who still accepted this myth, the Romans were distant relatives, and London was poetically called Troynovant, New Troy.

Sidney's *Apology for Poetry* (published in 1595, but probably written at about the time Shakespeare was finishing school), argued that literary figures were better models than the less exemplary historical reality. "Let Aeneas be worn in the tablet of your memory," he wrote.[22] Analogies with the Trojan diaspora constantly sprang to people's lips. The Earl of Oxford aptly referred to Protestant refugees from the St. Bartholomew's Day Massacre in 1572 "as a number of French Aeneases in this city."[23] The massacre, which took place at the time of a royal wedding, recalled the Trojans' tragically misplaced celebrations when they brought the wooden horse into their city. The memory of these events haunted early modern drama, which is full of weddings that turn to funerals and feasts, masques, and plays that end in murder. An anonymous author, recounting the fall of Troy, added that it was

> Like to our time, wherein hath broken out
> The hidden harm that we suspected least.
> Wombed within our walls and realm about,
> As Greeks in Troy were in the Greekish beast.[24]

The subject matter of the *Aeneid* was important to Shakespeare, but so was its poetry. Its most quotable lines were spoken by the hero himself, a character whose sensitivity and sadness had already inspired much medieval literature. *Forsan et haec olim meminisse iuvabit* (Perhaps one day we will remember even these things with pleasure; *Aeneid* 1.203) is Aeneas's consolation to his sailors during a storm at sea. It may be echoed when Romeo answers Juliet's "Oh, think'st thou that we shall ever meet again?" with "I doubt it not, and all these woes shall serve/ For sweet discourses in our times to come" (3.5.51–3). Looking forward to a time when the present will become the past is a characteristic Shakespearean theme. When Dido asks Aeneas about his history, he begins his tale with the words, *Infandum, regina, juves renovare dolorem* (O queen, you command me to renew an unspeakable sorrow; *Aeneid* 2.3). Aegeon answers a similar request in *The Comedy of Errors*: "A heavier task could not have been imposed/ Than I to speak my griefs unspeakable" (1.1.31–2). Virgil could also be dramatic. For instance, the forsaken Dido, surrounded by friends who want to save her life, ends her speech with S*ic, sic, iuvat ire sub umbras* (Thus, thus, I am pleased to go down to the shades; *Aeneid* 4.660): the *sic* (thus) is spoken as she stabs herself. Shakespeare's readers quickly learn that "thus" often indicates an unwritten stage direction that has to be inferred from the context. In Othello's last scene, he, like Dido, lulls his hearers with words and, on the final line – "I took by th' throat the circumcisèd dog / And smote him, thus" (5.2.365–6) – illustrates what he means by "thus" as he stabs himself with a concealed weapon.

Ovid, a generation later than Virgil, was perhaps polarized by him, and critics conventionally treated him as the opposite of his serious and moral predecessor. His *Art of Love* and *Elegies*, unlikely to be part of any school curriculum, give an inside view of the young Roman man about town, visiting brothels, arranging an abortion for his mistress, laughing at her for using damaging cosmetics, and ridiculing the husbands whose wives he is seducing. For young readers, saturated with the patriotic and rational idealism of the classical canon, it was probably a relief to read his depictions of passion failing to be ruled by reason. Ovid's unexplained banishment from Rome was attributed to love, particularly his supposed affair with Augustus's daughter Julia. If Shakespeare read Philip Stubbes's popular *Anatomie of Abuses*, which went through four editions between 1583 and 1595, he could have learned that Ovid was also punished for "making books of love, interludes, and such other amorous trumpery."[25] The mention of interludes is apparently unique to Stubbes, but Ovid was supposed to have written a play called *Medea*, lost except for a couple of lines. Frequently pleading, in vain, for a reprieve, he lamented his exile in a poem called *Tristia* (sorrows, or regrets) and finished the *Fasti*, a poem on the significant dates in the Roman calendar, which he had begun before his exile. It is Shakespeare's main source for the story of Lucretia.

In his most famous work, the *Metamorphoses*, Ovid uses the idea of change as his main structural device, retelling virtually every classical myth. Adonis becomes a flower, Daphne a laurel tree, the incestuous Myrrha the bitter myrrh tree. One mythical character tells the story of another, only to be interrupted by the arrival of someone with yet another story to tell. Near the end, Ovid takes a wider view, insisting that these transformations are part of a larger pattern of change and renewal. Shakespeare absorbed the philosophy, expressed most memorably in his sonnets. In Ovid's *Heroides* (heroines), the fluctuation is psychological. The wives and lovers of classical heroes are imagined writing letters filled with every shade of grief, reproach, anger, longing, teasing, and emotional blackmail – perfect models for the dramatic monologue. Shakespeare probably knew by heart at least part of the epistle in which Penelope grieves that Ulysses is so late in returning from Troy.

He used two lines from it as Lucentio's Latin lesson to Bianca in *The Taming of the Shrew*:

> *Hic ibat Simois, hic est Sigeia tellus,*
> *Hic steterat Priami regia celsa senis.*

It is Penelope who speaks, but she is imagining, and ventriloquizing, a soldier just back from the conquest of Troy, at a feast with his family. Tracing a map on the table with spilled wine, he shows the different locations in the war zone: "Here flowed the Simois; this is the Sigeian land; here stood the lofty palace of Priam the ancient" (*Heroides* 1.33–4). Nestor, she imagines, will tell his sons, who will tell their sons. Here, as in Aeneas's speech to his men, the present (imaginary, this time) is becoming the future. As Henry V tells his followers before Agincourt, "This story shall the good man teach his son" (4.3.56). In *The Two Gentlemen of Verona*, the clown Launce tries to use props to describe a much less heroic event, his parting from his family: "I'll show you the manner of it. This shoe is my father. No, this left shoe is my father. No, no, this left shoe is my mother" – and so on (2.3.13–15).

Although the educational system was focused on the cultivation of "masculine virtue," the works most imitated were those that dealt with love and women, like the story of Dido and the *Heroides*. The "complaint" was one genre in which it was permissible for women to speak at great length, because it was understood that words replaced actions: a copiously lamenting woman would be unlikely to take vengeance on anyone but herself. Within the developing Protestant martyrology also, suffering women were important figures: Foxe's *Acts and Monuments* emphasized that even women and children – like Lady Jane Grey – had suffered for their faith.

Role Models

Voyeuristic interest in the private lives of famous people was widespread in the sixteenth century. Lyly's Prologue to *Campaspe* (1584) admits that, although the play deals with awe-inspiring historical figures, it is going to treat them lightly: "we, calling Alexander from his grave, seek only who was his love."[26] Marlowe mocked this fixation on gossip in *Doctor Faustus*, when the hero, who has conjured up spirits representing Alexander the Great and his mistress, lets his patron find out for himself the only thing he really wants to know: whether the lady had a wart on her neck. For Shakespeare and his fellow-students, the lives of Roman writers were as important, and as exemplary, as their works. If he was beginning to see the flaws in his own father, the Roman writers, being dead, could not disappoint him. To Renaissance readers, Cicero was not only a writer and orator who achieved political eminence but also a high-principled martyr, murdered by Mark Antony's soldiers during the civil wars that followed the death of Caesar. Whether or not the Seneca who wrote tragedies was also the philosopher Seneca who tutored the emperor Nero and eventually committed suicide on his orders, the fact that he was thought to be the same man inevitably affected the way his plays were read. That Ovid ended his life in exile was important to sixteenth-century readers, many of whom knew someone who had lived abroad as a Protestant under Mary I or as a Catholic under Edward VI and Elizabeth I.

It was Virgil's life, above all, that had been transformed into legend, the only way posterity could deal with his inexplicable genius. Any writer whose work is so extensively memorized and analyzed will reveal patterns and prophetic statements. His fourth eclogue predicted the birth of a child who would bring back the golden age. Because the poem also referred to the return of the virgin Astraea (goddess of justice, who had abandoned earth at the end of the golden age), this linking of virgin and miraculous child convinced Christian readers that the pagan poet had been granted a vision of the true religion. The belief that all human knowledge was contained in the *Aeneid* led to the practice of the *sortes virgilianae*: opening the epic at random and pointing at a line, which was then interpreted and acted on. By the end of the first century CE, the poet was being credited with near-magical abilities, and in the Middle Ages he acquired a history as a necromancer. His life, probably first written by Suetonius in the second century and retold by the fourth-century biographer Aelius Donatus, was printed in every edition of his works.[27] Whether or not Virgil was self-conscious about his literary career, his admirers and imitators certainly were. Donatus interpreted the sequence of his works as an allegory of the history of the human race: first shepherds (the *Eclogues*), then farmers (the *Georgics*), then warriors (the *Aeneid*). Though the movement from pastoral to epic could be seen simply as a way of saying that a young writer should begin with the less ambitious genres, Spenser offered *The Shepheardes Calender* (1579) as a first step towards the epic poem that he planned to produce, and when his *Faerie Queene* appeared in 1590 everyone recognized that he was trying to be the English Virgil. The sequence left no room for drama, but Donatus's life makes clear that Virgil was thought of as a dramatist as well as an epic poet. The *Aeneid*, though an epic, has an oral context: Virgil read it aloud at the court of Augustus; it was recited in theaters, and plays based on it were popular for centuries after his death. According to Donatus, an entire theater audience rose and applauded on one occasion when it discovered that Virgil was present.

English writers, too, may have been as important to schoolboys for their lives as for their works. By the time Shakespeare started school, it was possible to buy contemporary, or near-contemporary, English poetry. In 1557 Richard Tottel published a volume of poems – *Songs and Sonnets*, usually known as *Tottel's Miscellany* – and this famous collection was revised and enlarged several times. Tottel's title page gave pride of place to Henry Howard, Earl of Surrey, printing forty of his poems, and in the same year published Surrey's translations of two books of the *Aeneid*. They are historically important because they use blank verse (a five-foot line, unrhymed) – possibly the first example of the form in English – as an equivalent to the classical hexameter (six feet, unrhymed). As some English writers were beginning to be ashamed of their need for rhyme, the example of this prestigious figure was important. Only four years later, two Inns of Court men wrote *Gorboduc*, the first blank verse play in English.

The largest number of poems in both the first and second editions of Tottel were by an author not named on the title page: Thomas Wyatt, who was believed to have been one of Anne Boleyn's lovers. Tottel played up the author's sensational background by inserting "Anna" in poems that were otherwise ambiguous about their object. The authorship of many other poems in the collection is unknown, since names, even initials, are rarely given, but Tottel's headings turn them into dramatic statements: "The lover, accusing his love for her unfaithfulness, purposeth to live in liberty" (no. 214). Tottel sometimes notes that a poem is put into the mouth of a woman, or that it answers a previous one. In other words, the poems in his collection, like those read aloud or sung in plays, were presented, not as self-contained aesthetic artifacts, but as part of an ongoing dialogue in the "real world." The *Songs and Sonnets* created a sense of intimacy with famous figures whose lives and deaths were highly public. They re-established writing as an adventurous profession that gave status to men of talent, though these tended to be mainly aristocrats and their protégés.

When Shakespeare had access to a more recent anthology, *The Paradise of Dainty Devices*, first published in 1576, he would have seen that it was compiled by "Master Edwards, sometimes of her Majesty's Chapel," with other contributions from "sundry learned Gentlemen, both of honor and worship." Some of these learned gentlemen must have completed the work for Richard Edwards, since he died at the age of 41, but the prominence given to his name shows that he was thought of as a prestigious figure, though his ancestry is obscure and his success seems to have been due entirely to his remarkable combination of literary, theatrical, and musical gifts. In the year of his death, 1566, he directed a cast of Oxford undergraduates in a spectacularly successful production, before the queen, of his own play, *Palamon and Arcite*. Edwards's death is mentioned in a French conversation textbook that Shakespeare might have used when he started to teach himself the language: "Truly it is pity: he was a man of a good wit, and a good poet: and a great player of plays."[28] Perhaps "player" means "actor," but it might also mean something more like impresario. The comic schoolmasters who appear in early modern drama are usually not only the author but the producer-director of the play-within-the-play, and they frequently speak the prologue as well. Shakespeare, who quoted one of Edwards's songs in *Romeo and Juliet*, needed to look no farther for evidence that poets and theater men could achieve the highest recognition.

Becoming a Writer

No one went to school or university in the sixteenth century with the aim of becoming a creative writer. Yet the background given by the heavily classical education now seems, with hindsight, an almost ideal training. It is usually an advantage to have started early on any activity in which one wants to excel, since it is thought that expertise takes some ten years to acquire. Though rhetoric was essentially a university subject, students acquired its basic principles when they translated Latin into English, and, after a day or so, put their English back into Latin and compared their own Latin with the Roman model. Elegant variation, abundance – or *copia*, to use Erasmus's term – were valued then as conciseness is now.[29] Repetition was a key principle of Renaissance education, and in his earlier plays Shakespeare is particularly given to it, almost as if he was trying to make his works easier for future schoolmasters to analyze.

The flexible word order of Latin offered many models for experiment. Even though early modern English had lost its case endings, which allowed words to be grammatically identified wherever they were in a sentence, it was still much freer with word order than modern English. Two Latin models, completely different in kind, were popular. The Ciceronian orator prided himself on being able to develop a long, grammatically intricate sentence, with embedded parenthetical clauses. On the other hand, Tacitus used the minimum number of words, often to devastating effect, as in *capax imperii, nisi imperasset*, which takes only four words to say what modern English needs many more to convey: "[he would have been thought] capable of being emperor, had he not been emperor." In verse, the order could be still more unusual. For instance, the second of the lines that Lucentio pretends to teach Bianca, *Hic steterat Priami regia celsa senis*, is, word for word, "Here stood of Priam the kingdom lofty of old [that is, of old Priam]." One of the schoolmasters in Brinsley's dialogue notes that some children seem unable to grasp the rules of Latin word order: "the more confusedly that they can transpose or disorder the words of a sentence, the more excellent they think it to be."[30] Shakespeare might have been one of those children, since his word order became increasingly ingenious (or maddening) in the course of his career.

Brinsley's schoolmaster, while admitting that verse writing is only an ornament, recommends that students develop the ability since it can be useful, as in writing elegies, and it wins praise for those who can do it well.[31] If William had gone farther with his studies, his literary works might have consisted of Latin elegies on Stratford aldermen. Writing verses in English required different skills, especially the ability to rhyme. W. H. Auden has described the process by which the young writer develops this expertise: "As he scribbles on he is beginning to get the habit of noticing metrical quantities, to see that any two syllable word in isolation must be either a *ti-tum*, a *tum-ti* or, occasionally, a *tum-tum*, but that when associated with other words it can sometimes become a *ti-ti*; when he discovers a rhyme he has not thought of before, he stores it away in his memory, a habit which an Italian poet may not need to acquire but which an English poet will find useful."[32] The ability to rhyme is largely, as Auden indicates, the result of memory and practice. Elizabethan teachers made pupils aware of the sounds of words: one teacher urged pupils to work out the spelling of a difficult word by trying each syllable with a series of vowels: the person trying to spell "brush," for example, was to work through "brash," "bresh," "brish," "brosh," "brush."[33] Brinsley found that it was possible to "make children to take a delight in spelling" by having them "spell many syllables together, which differ but only in one letter, as hand, band, land, sand, &c."[34]

Many children, even those who do not go on to be writers, create imaginary countries in which idealized characters undergo as many adventures as their creator can imagine; in other words, they invent romances. Shakespeare obviously liked this genre, in which he was writing up to the end of his career. Tales like that of the local hero, *Guy of Warwick*, were widely sold as chapbooks. Originally based on saints' lives and moral in intention, they had turned into adventure stories. Guy, for instance, won his lady by killing monsters. In one version, the monster is a cow, and the story told by Aubrey of how Shakespeare would kill a calf "in a high style, and make a speech" has sometimes been thought a garbled allusion to his performing in this play.[35] Shortly after his marriage Guy left his pregnant wife, deciding that it was his duty to take part in the Crusades, and single-handedly saved Jerusalem for the Christian army. Returning to England, he decided that it was *now* his duty to spend the rest of his life as a hermit and was reunited with his wife and son only on his deathbed. Heroism, renunciation, a family reunion after many years of separation – they remained appealing subjects to Shakespeare. If he wrote romances as a boy, they may well have been in verse, since English prose was still relatively undeveloped as a literary medium. Playing with the sounds of words must have been ingrained in him. The Latin verse quantities – where length of syllables rather than stress determines the meter of a line – never seem to have tempted him to imitation as they did Sir Philip Sidney, but something that C. S. Lewis noted in the sonnets – "There is a high percentage of lines in which every second syllable is not merely stressed but also long" – creates a musical effect that might derive from an awareness of Latin vowel lengths.[36]

Becoming an Actor

Among the earliest works studied in school were those of the Latin dramatists, especially Terence, because they were relatively easy. Both Plautus and Terence have a great deal to teach any playwright about the timing of entrances and exits, cross-purpose dialogue, and actor–audience rapport. In particular, they know when to shatter the theatrical illusion to produce metatheatrical humor – as when a clever slave in Plautus's *Pseudolus* admits that he is giving information only because the audience needs to know it. Their character types – old men and young lovers, braggarts, clever and stupid slaves, prostitutes, and parasites – are the basis of much Renaissance comedy, both through direct influence and that of the Italian *commedia* that derives from it. They intersperse their stories with sententious remarks, often at odds with the amoral behavior of the characters. These lines were sometimes learned separately, as were the sententiae of Publilius Syrus, a mime artist and dramatist, whose didactic and witty sayings are the only part of his plays that have survived. So, Shakespeare might have deduced, anyone who wants to be famous as a dramatist must be sure to say quotable things.[37]

If Brinsley's *Ludus Literarius* is typical, schoolmasters thought oral presentation even more important than writing, since public speaking and the ability to argue effectively would be important skills for most of their students. The result was a close relation between writing and acting. Imitating the styles of various authors introduced children to the art of creating character through speech. Their first exercise in composition was usually writing a letter in the manner of Cicero, for which they were supposed to imagine both the situation of the writer and the needs and feelings of the hypothetical recipient. Brinsley also recommended that they should read Corderius's dialogues aloud, not just with the correct Latin pronunciation, but "lively, as if they themselves were the persons which did speak in that dialogue." Since Corderius's speakers were children like themselves, this might not be too difficult, but Brinsley expects the same thing when they get to Virgil's eclogues; they should "express the affections and persons of shepherds; or whose speech soever else, which they are to imitate."[38] Though a staunch Puritan, Brinsley apparently had no problem with schoolboys trying to imagine and perform the loves and griefs of pagan shepherds. He was probably drawing on Quintilian, who insisted that the effective orator, like a good actor, must convince his listeners that he is genuinely moved.[39]

Performance had a large place in the educational system. Putting on plays, often those written by the schoolmaster, was required at some grammar schools.[40] Rehearsal and performance could be an important part of the school year, and the great London grammar schools were already giving plays at court in the 1560s. Though Brinsley does not discuss the practice of boys playing women's roles, it is evident that in the classroom they must frequently have read lines written for women, like the speeches of Dido in the *Aeneid*, and played women's roles in the comedies of Plautus and Terence. For the most part, the Latin plays depicted only immodest women, keeping the virtuous ones out of the public gaze on stage as in life. English writers, imitating the classics at second hand, created female roles even though they knew that these would be acted by boys. It is evident that teachers were not worried about anyone moving on to the commercial stage. The schoolboy was being trained for public performance as a lawyer or preacher or member of the borough council, and much of the interest of school performances must have derived from trying to spot which of the young actors, many from distinguished families, were likely to become influential figures at court or in the church.[41]

How much training the children got in acting depended on the schoolmaster. It might consist simply of making them understand their lines and speak them with the appropriate expressions and gestures. They could have found other advice in Quintilian, though he was writing for orators. One of his suggestions – that the ability to visualize what one is describing will move the orator and therefore enable him to move his audience – is not unlike Stanislavsky's concept of "emotional memory."[42] At least one of Quintilian's other recommendations – that gestures be made exclusively with the right arm – is known to have been adopted by eighteenth-century actors and may therefore have been taken seriously by earlier ones as well,[43] even though the reason for the rule – that the left arm was needed to hold the toga in place – had long since become irrelevant.

Shakespeare, then, by his teens, might not only have seen visiting players, but also have acted in classical or neoclassical plays. He would also have had a strong motive for writing them, since an author can give himself large parts in his own plays. The opening of Aegeon's speech in *The Comedy of Errors*, with its echo of Virgil, might at one time have been part of a Latin composition, probably a collage of phrases from Roman authors. To see what a play was meant to look like on paper, Shakespeare might have turned to examples in English. If he was able to get hold of either George Gascoigne's *Supposes* (1566) or George Whetstone's *Promos and Cassandra* (1578), he would have found, first, that Italian writers are a good source of plots, and second, that, at a time when most reading was reading aloud, dramatists worried about controlling the interpretation of their text. Gascoigne added marginal notes to enlighten readers about the kinds of confusion in his plot. Whetstone's printer, Richard Jones, advised in a prefatory epistle: "if by chance thou light of some speech that seemeth dark, consider of it with judgment before thou condemn the work: for in many places he is driven both to praise and blame with one breath, which in reading will seem hard, & in action appear plain."[44] He seems to mean that it is hard to understand irony ("to praise and blame with one breath") when one cannot *hear* the actor's tone of voice.

Recognition

Though it is possible to know more about Shakespeare's education than about any other aspect of his life, what remains opaque is his response to it. He could have been the "whining schoolboy" of the "seven ages" speech in *As You Like It*, who goes "creeping like snail/ Unwillingly to school." However, this image, like the others in Jaques' speech, is a familiar cliché. Posthumus in *Cymbeline* is the opposite: offered "all the learnings that his time/ Could make him the receiver of," he is said to have absorbed them, "As we take air, fast as 'twas ministered, / And in's spring became a harvest" (1.1.43–4, 46). Shakespeare could have fitted either description. Much of a child's sense of identity is acquired at school. Even his own appearance may become clear to him only through the words of other children, and conditions like myopia are often diagnosed in the classroom. For many children the ability to read depends on their eyesight: myopia makes it easier to focus on small print; children who are praised for reading well are likely to read more. Stanley Wells thinks that both the "Cobbe portrait" (Figure 24; recently identified by him as Shakespeare's) and the

p. 437

frontispiece to the 1623 Folio (Figure 19; which he thinks is based on it) show that the poet had a cast in his left eye.[45] It is not clear how much this feature – which no one else seems to have noticed – would have affected Shakespeare, but there are references in his works to double vision (*Venus and Adonis* 1070; *Midsummer Night's Dream* 4.1.188; and perhaps *Merchant of Venice* 5.1.243–5). His fondness for miniaturization, though characteristic of the aesthetic of the 1590s, is compatible with vision that sees better at close range than at a distance. Cassius in *Julius Caesar* recognizes one character by his voice (1.3.41), another "by his gait" (1.3.132). Shakespeare had read Plutarch's reference to the character's short-sightedness, which is finally mentioned in his last scene. In *Troilus and Cressida*, similarly, Ulysses recognizes Diomedes from "the manner of his gait" (4.5.14). E. A. J. Honigmann has suggested that Othello, who often asks who is approaching, might also be depicted as short-sighted.[46] Some of these moments may, however, be designed to convey the sense of stage darkness or to ensure that audiences know who is entering. Much drama of the period seems to spell out what is happening on stage, perhaps because many spectators themselves had difficulty seeing it or in knowing where to look.

The advantage of being recognized as exceptionally gifted at an early age is that one is likely to be given more opportunities.[47] At a grammar school, these might come once or twice a year, when a distinguished visitor arrived: the brightest boys would be asked to pronounce an oration in his honor (probably in Latin) or to read verses, sometimes of their own composition. The reward might be praise and a piece of money; it might be more, if the visitor was someone with the power to award scholarships. None of the stories told about Shakespeare in the seventeenth century include an episode like the one John Aubrey tells about Ben Jonson. As the future dramatist was serving his apprenticeship by laying bricks at Lincoln's Inn, "a knight, a bencher, walking through and hearing him repeat some Greek verses out of Homer, discoursing with him, and finding him to have a wit extraordinary, gave him some exhibition to maintain him at Trinity College in Cambridge."[48] Some kinds of ability are more likely than others to attract attention. If Shakespeare was an exceptional actor in school plays the fact would probably have been noted, but no one would have imagined him as university material simply for that reason. His gifts as a writer might not have been obvious if most of his compositions were in Latin and were judged mainly on their grammar and their ability to sound like someone else.

Although Quintilian, like Cicero, admires young students who have "an ardour that leads at times to ideas bordering on the extravagant,"[49] it was for slow but thorough learners that the repetitious Elizabethan teaching methods were designed. The great schoolmaster Roger Ascham distinguished between quick wits and slow ones, preferring the latter because, although it took them a long time to acquire knowledge, they did not lose it quickly. George Gascoigne's play *The Glass of Government* (published 1575) dramatizes this distinction. Two sets of brothers are sent to study with a tutor. As homework, he tells them to put some pious precepts into verse. The older boys ignore the assignment and write love sonnets and martial

36

verses, while the younger ones plod away and do what they were asked.[50] The schoolmaster is not at all impressed by the boys who display precocious creative originality, and the play justifies his view, since they both fall into debauchery and come to a bad end, while their hard-working younger brothers rise to important positions in the state and church.

Shakespeare probably read this play, since one scene, involving an illiterate messenger who has to carry a list of the addressees of his letters for others to read, seems to be echoed in *Romeo and Juliet* (1.2.57–63). Which kind of pupil was he? Given that his mature writing is usually copious and exuberant in style, using terse understatement mainly for the sake of contrast, it is natural to imagine him as a fluent, easy writer, likely to arouse suspicion rather than admiration in his teachers. Perhaps, however, he was clever enough to cultivate the image of inconspicuous reliability that seems to have characterized his adult working life. He may even have been alarmed by his own fluency, if he internalized the moral that "things soon got, are lost again as fast."[51] He knew the concept of *Furor Poeticus*, which Theseus draws on when, in *A Midsummer Night's Dream*, he lumps together "the lunatic, the lover and the poet" as victims rather than masters of imagination (5.1.7). Yet Charles Lamb argued that "It is impossible for the mind to conceive of a mad Shakspeare [*sic*],"[52] and others have echoed his phrase about "the sanity of true genius." Most studies of the relationship between genius and mental illness are flawed because they belong to a post-Romantic period in which geniuses were expected to demonstrate emotional vulnerability. However, research published in 1970, based on the study of a relatively closed society in Iceland, revealed that highly creative people tended to come from families containing a high proportion of schizophrenics.[53] Subsequent studies have seemed to confirm that "creativity and psychopathology feature a common genetic component."[54] The reasons for this apparent link, and for its apparent privileging in the process of natural selection, are still mysterious. One suggestion, however, is that attenuated versions of mental disorder may be beneficial to writers or composers, since the manic phase of psychosis, the "sustained high mood" – may enable them to persevere through the otherwise solitary and unrewarding period of creation.[55] It is, then, quite possible that serious mental instability was present in other members of Shakespeare's family (perhaps the otherwise invisible brother Richard?), and that he might have distrusted his own imagination when he saw the distorted version of it in someone else. A strong ego is, however, another necessity for the creative artist, and Shakespeare's education probably gave him that, along with much else.

Notes

1. Holyband, *The French Schoole-maister*, K5^v–K6.
2. Baldwin, *William Shakespeare's Small Latine & Lesse Greeke*, 1: 478.
3. Cressy, ed., *Education in Tudor and Stuart England*, 25.

4. Brinsley, *Ludus Literarius*, S4^v.
5. Clement, *The Petie Schole*, A8^v.
6. Brinsley, *Ludus Literarius*, D1.
7. Ibid., E1–E1^v.
8. Ibid., E1.
9. Ibid., E2.
10. Cordier, *Corderius Dialogues*, II. 35 (p.109).
11. Brinsley, *Ludus Literarius*, Ff2.
12. See Kathman, "Shakespeare's Stratford Friends," at http://shakespeareauthorship.com/
13. Brinsley, *Ludus Literarius*, D2^v–D3^v.
14. Ibid., P3^v.
15. Cordier, *Corderius Dialogues*, I. 2 (p. 3).
16. Holyband, *The French Littelton*, 49.
17. The modernized text cleans up the French of F1. Q1 has "Aloues a diner."
18. Brinsley, *Ludus Literarius*, Ee3.
19. *An Act to Retain the Queen's Majesty's Subjects in Their Due Obedience* (1581: 23 Eliz. I, c.I), in Cressy, ed., *Education in Tudor and Stuart England*, 50–1.
20. Baldwin, *William Shakespeare's Small Latine & Lesse Greeke*, 1: 144.
21. Cicero, *Marcus Tullius Ciceroes thre bokes of duties*, Book III, p. 179.
22. Sidney, *An Apology for Poetry, or the Defence of Poesy*, 99.
23. Nelson, *Monstrous Adversary*, 87.
24. "Of the troubled comon welth restored to quiet by the mighty power of god," lines 20–3, in *Tottel's Miscellany* (1557–1587), vol. 1, no. 279 (pp. 227–9).
25. Stubbes, *The Anatomie of Abuses*, p. 201, lines 5461–3.
26. Lyly, *Campaspe*, Prologue at Court, lines 10–13.
27. An English version was published along with Thomas Phaer's translation of the *Aeneid* (1573).
28. Holyband, *The French Schoole-maister*, K3^v–K4^v.
29. For *copia* see Trousdale, *Shakespeare and the Rhetoricians*, esp. ch. 3, "The Criterion of Richness" (pp. 39–64).
30. Brinsley, *Ludus Literarius*, X3^v.
31. Ibid., S4^v, Bb3^r.
32. Auden, "Making, Knowing, and Judging," in *The Dyer's Hand*, 36.
33. Clement, *The Petie Schole*, B1^v–B2.
34. Brinsley, *Ludus Literarius*, C4^v.
35. Aubrey, *Brief Lives*, 2: 225. See Duncan-Jones, *Shakespeare: Upstart Crow*, 11–15, and Richmond, *The Legend of Guy of Warwick*.
36. Lewis, *English Literature in the Sixteenth Century*, 505.
37. C. G. Smith, *Shakespeare's Proverb Lore*, 14.
38. Brinsley, *Ludus Literarius*, Ee2^v, Ee3.
39. Mack, "Early Modern Ideas of Imagination," 63.
40. Fripp, *Shakespeare: Man and Artist*, 118–21.
41. See Astington, *Actors and Acting in Shakespeare's Time*, 68–9.
42. Quintilian, *The Institutio Oratoria*, 2: vi.30–1.
43. Ibid., 2: iii.114. For eighteenth-century practice, see Roach, *The Player's Passion*, 53–4.

44. Whetstone, *Promos and Cassandra*, in Bullough, 2: 444.
45. Wells, ed., *Shakespeare Found!*, 13.
46. *Othello*, ed. Honigmann, 17–19.
47. Howe, *Genius Explained*, 137.
48. Aubrey, *Brief Lives*, 2: 11.
49. Quintilian, *Institutio Oratoria*, 2: iii.114.
50. Gascoigne, *The Glasse of Government*, 4.1, in *Complete Works*, ed. Cunliffe, 60.
51. Ibid., 88.
52. Lamb, "The Sanity of True Genius," 212.
53. J. I. Karlson, "Genetic Association of Giftedness and Creativity with Schizophrenia," (*Hereditas* 66 (1970), 177–82), cited in Simonton, *Origins of Genius*, 104–5.
54. Simonton, *Origins of Genius*, 105.
55. Nettle, *Strong Imagination*, 150–1.

3

"Hic et Ubique"
1578–1588

Hic et Ubique? Then we'll shift our ground
(*Hamlet* 1.5.165)

Hamlet's joking use of the phrase *hic et ubique* (originally part of the theological definition of God) has been brilliantly connected by Stephen Greenblatt to a traditional Roman Catholic prayer.[1] Shakespeare uses the phrase with surprising frequency in works written soon after his father's death in 1601: the purgatorial ghost is an "extravagant and erring spirit"; Othello is called "An extravagant and wheeling stranger/ Of here and everywhere" (*Othello* 1.1.139–40); and, as Greenblatt also notes, Sebastian in *Twelfth Night* has to assure everyone that he does not have "that deity in my nature/ Of here and everywhere" (5.1.227–8). If the phrase stuck in Shakespeare's mind, it might be because, by the turn of the century, he was drawn into thoughts of the afterlife.

On the other hand, especially in the phrase about Othello, he may also have been thinking of his own earlier wanderings ("extravagant" implies an out-of-bounds, vagabond existence). The opening of Sonnet 110 –

> Alas, 'tis true, I have gone here and there,
> And made myself a motley to the view
> Gored mine own thoughts, sold cheap what is most dear,
> Made old offences of affections new
>
> (1–4)

– sounds like a description of the life of an actor on tour, either literally or figuratively playing the fool. In fact, it is a metaphor for something else, in this case faithlessness in love. Yet, when the sonnets were published in 1609, this sonnet was immediately followed by one that is often considered autobiographical in its reference to the

The Life of William Shakespeare: A Critical Biography, First Edition. Lois Potter.
© 2012 Lois Potter. Published 2012 by Blackwell Publishing Ltd.

"public means" by which the speaker is forced to live (111.4). Someone, whether Shakespeare or his editor, clearly saw a connection between the two poems. They might reflect their author's retrospective view of the early part of his career, with its travel, its necessary extravertism, and its casual sexual relationships that made him unfaithful to an older and more meaningful love, whether this was a friend, a lover, or the wife and family he had left behind him. The word "public" at this period had something of the same meaning as "common," as in "common players." When Othello calls Desdemona a "public commoner" – or paid courtesan (4.2.75) – he is combining the two words most often used to describe the actors. Public manners were what one might expect from a publican, and a surprising number of actors, including the great clown Tarlton, did in fact double as innkeepers. Shakespeare dramatized such public manners in the likeable but rather over-jolly Host of the Garter Inn in *The Merry Wives of Windsor*, who constantly performs his "humor": "What wouldst thou have, boor? What, thickskin? Speak, breathe, discuss, brief, short, quick, snap" (4.5.1–2). Perhaps this is how Shakespeare saw himself, or was afraid others saw him.

Fidelity was also a virtue in the theater, because actors were the servants of their aristocratic patron. Though they naturally moved on when a patron died and his company was disbanded, to move to another company during a patron's lifetime could be seen as disloyal. In the early 1580s, when two upwardly mobile actors went in quick succession through three other companies and into the prestigious Queen's Men, an anonymous satirist wrote that they should be called "chameleons" rather than "comedians."[2] Both the unfaithful lover and the motley fool of no fixed address are relevant to this chapter, which will deal with the years – sometimes called the "lost years" – between Shakespeare's schooling and the first reference to him in the London theater. They were the years in which he made the major decisions of his life: to marry and to be an actor. There is no evidence as to the order in which these things happened, nor is it certain whether they were connected with his father's situation at the period. But since something is known about John Shakespeare in this period, and almost nothing about his son, it seems logical to start by trying to understand the father's story.

John Shakespeare's Finances

By 1575–6, when William Shakespeare had probably learned to recite a few *sententiae* in Latin, John Shakespeare was a prosperous man with three sons and two daughters, ranging in age from 12-year-old William to 2-year-old Richard. He bought a house in Henley Street next door to the one already in his possession, and another house round the corner in Greenhill Street. By now he must have employed others to do his glove-making, since one definition of a gentleman was that he did not live by manual labor and he was about to apply for a coat of arms.

He may have been encouraged, even urged, to make this application, since he was an officer of the queen, and "For a man in public life not to have arms would be eccentric."[3] At this period, the members of the College of Arms were visiting every region of the country, trying to establish who had the right to bear arms and, of course, eager for the fees that accrued to them with each application.[4] John could claim gentry status both through his wife's descent from the old family of Arden and because of his property, annual income, and status as alderman and former bailiff. He may have had a "patierne" – a sketch for the final version – drawn up by the visiting College of Arms official.[5] John Shakespeare never took his application beyond the initial stage. Perhaps he decided that the fees were too high.

From 1576 on, the minutes of the Stratford town council show a change in John Shakespeare's behavior. Since the town clerk forgot (tactfully?) to indicate absences at the meetings of 5 October and 5 December 1576, it is not clear exactly when the alderman stopped attending, but he is consistently absent after those dates, except for one anomalous appearance at the election meeting in September 1582. In October 1577 John Whitgift, the new Bishop of Worcester, attempting to track down potential Catholic or Puritan dissidents, compiled a preliminary list of those in the diocese who were failing to attend church. It distinguishes delinquents according to their stated motives for staying away: John Shakespeare is in the category of those who alleged fear of arrest for debt, which could happen even on Sunday.[6] There is evidence of his need for cash: in 1578/9 he mortgaged some of his (or rather, his wife's) lands to his brother-in-law Edmund Lambert, and he sold and mortgaged more in the years that followed. When his last child was born in 1580 he named the boy Edmund, either in gratitude or in the hope that the godfather might be inspired to forgive the loan. He was never able to repay Lambert or to regain the land, though he and his wife went to court over the case in 1588, and continued their suit over the next decade. Land transactions in this period are complicated by the various devices used to evade taxation or to get round such vestiges of the feudal system as the "fines" payable to the lord of the manor on any transfer of land. Since it was possible to convey land to another person for the "use" of a third party,[7] one early Stratford historian argued that John and Mary Shakespeare mortgaged their property so as to avoid paying tax on it.[8] However, most of those who have worked with Stratford records, like Mark Eccles and Robert Bearman, are convinced that John Shakespeare's sales of freehold property in Stratford, Snitterfield, and Wilmcote to three or four other people mean exactly what they appear to mean, that he "was in genuine need of ready cash."[9]

It used to be thought that he had ruined his life singlehandedly, perhaps by taking to drink (and thus inspiring the creation of Falstaff and Sir Toby Belch). A family tragedy, the death of his 7-year-old daughter Anne in April 1579, must have deeply affected all the Shakespeares, but the "decline," if it was one, had started before that. Some of John Shakespeare's earlier prosperity may have been the result of illegal wool-brogging: the buying of wool outside the town, smuggling it in so as to avoid paying duty on it, and undercutting the official market (the Staple of Wool) by selling it more cheaply. It would have been easy to do, since a wool merchant, Ralph Shaw, was one of the Shakespeares' neighbors in Henley Street and the families were close (one of his sons witnessed Shakespeare's will).[10] In 1577 there was "a great outcry" against the unregulated exportation of wool, leading to legislation that required a special license from anyone who wanted to buy wool for export.[11] John Shakespeare had already been in trouble: an informer, one of the many on whom the legal system relied, accused him in 1572 of two illegal dealings in wool during the previous year, for which he was fined.[12] Like most of his contemporaries, he probably went on dealing in the forbidden commodity until the legislation of 1577 stopped him.

In 1570 he had also been accused of lending money at extortionate rates of interest. The Christian view of this subject was an uneasy mixture of pragmatism and principle. The Puritan Philip Stubbes quoted the common defense – "If no interest were permitted, no man would lend, and then how should the poor do?" – and replied that all charging of interest was evil; it would be better to give to the poor without hope of return.[13] In practice, with actual money in short supply, almost everyone lived on credit, and many people's wealth consisted largely of other people's debts to them.[14] Borrowing, necessarily, was a personal transaction, and, since many borrowers defaulted, lenders protected themselves by charging interest and seeking "sureties" (guarantors) for their debtors. For John Shakespeare, all these roles were equally risky. In June 1571 he lent £23. 13s. 4d. to a glover in Banbury and, when the glover defaulted, sued him for £50, which represents a substantial amount of interest as well as a penalty.[15] He also stood surety for two borrowers, one of them his brother Henry, who apparently defaulted and left him responsible.

One reason why John's difficulties worsened in the 1580s was that other people could not afford to be as forgiving as in the past. In 1586–7 a twenty-year period of relative prosperity came abruptly to an end, with a "dearth" in the Midlands and around most of the country. The Privy Council issued its usual orders, recommending public prayer, fasting (the money saved was to be given to the poor), regular alms-giving evenings, and the avoidance of "needless waste and riotous consumption."[16] Those to whom money was owed needed to call it in. In January 1587 John Shakespeare was arrested for Henry's debt of £10 (now raised, with damages, to £20) and released on bail from another former bailiff, Richard Hill.[17] Early in 1591 he owed money to three other members of the Stratford council, including Adrian Quiney and Hill, who were suing him between March and June. The case eventually petered out, either because John was able to satisfy his creditors out of court or because they gave up on him.[18] Being friends, they would probably not have sued him if they had not themselves been in financial difficulties. If he had been borrowing from Hill and other council members throughout the 1580s, this in itself might have given him good reason to avoid meetings. A list submitted to the Privy Council in October 1591 listed John Shakespeare again as one who did not attend church because he feared imprisonment for debt. When Henry was in debt again in the early 1590s, he was imprisoned; it looks as if John was no longer willing or able to help him out.[19]

John's arrest and virtual imprisonment in his own home might have been devastating experiences for the Shakespeare family. On the other hand, such events were becoming increasingly common. "By the late sixteenth century," Craig Muldrew suggests, there were few households "who had not witnessed or experienced the process of an arrest or attachment of goods, or who did not know someone who had been in prison or seen bailiffs distraining the material symbols of wealth for auction in satisfaction of a judgment."[20] Some of the aldermen who had been lending to John Shakespeare in the 1580s would be in difficulties themselves within a few years. Most people still find it hard to operate in a world of virtual finance, and at a time when regulation was rudimentary it is not surprising that so many fell into debt. No one who owned as much property as John Shakespeare could be called poor, but he had over-extended himself financially with his land purchases.

The evidence can, however, be read in more ways than one. Some scholars think that Shakespeare's father was avoiding church because of his religious convictions. Since recusancy – failure to attend regularly at Church of England services – was heavily fined, this in itself might explain his financial difficulties. The main piece of evidence for John Shakespeare's Catholicism is a document said to have been found in the rafters of the Henley Street house in 1757. The original is lost and what remains is a copy made in the eighteenth century. By then, the first page was already missing and had been replaced with a forgery made up by one of the souvenir sellers who were already flourishing in Stratford. However, the rest of it is a genuine example of the "Spiritual Testament" originally devised by Cardinal Borromeo in 1576, a profession of faith devised for Roman Catholics to carry on their persons in case they should happen to die with no priest to give them the last rites. John Shakespeare's name was inserted into the blanks and someone added the name of St. Winifred as a chosen intercessary. There has been extensive discussion of every aspect of this document: whether John Shakespeare really owned it, whether it was really found in the rafters of his house, and why, for that matter, he hid it there instead of carrying it on his person.

Regardless of the testament's status, it would not be strange if Shakespeare's father had been a Catholic at some point, especially during the five-year reign of Mary I. On the other hand, views changed with the times. The will of Mary Arden's father Robert, made in 1556, used Catholic formulae, but three decades later Mary's half-brother Robert called his children Elias and Prudence, names that were popular with Puritans.[21] John Shakespeare's Catholic sympathies, if any, would not have been a great problem at the beginning of Elizabeth's reign, when she and her government were still feeling their way toward a national church that they hoped would be as inclusive as possible. The government assumed that the most obstinate Catholics would die within a generation, leaving the country united in happy uniformity.

In 1570, however, the Pope excommunicated Elizabeth and released her subjects from obedience to her. Foreign-trained missionary priests began arriving in England, not only to encourage existing Catholics but also to make new converts. In retaliation, increasingly punitive laws prevented Catholics from traveling out of the country, and education was closely supervised to ensure doctrinal uniformity. Predictably, persecution hardened feelings among the Catholic population and may have won them converts.

John Shakespeare's boycotting of the guild meetings, if that is what it was, was consistent through a series of changes in the English church as well as in the Corporation itself. For much of Elizabeth's reign it seemed possible that she would marry a Catholic under whom the old religion would be tolerated if not restored. At the time when Shakespeare was probably just beginning to pay attention to public events, the most divisive issue of the day was the prospect of such a marriage. After the St. Bartholomew's Day Massacre in 1572, the English court went into mourning and ostentatiously snubbed the French ambassador – but Elizabeth I spent much of the rest of the decade in marriage negotiations with a French prince, the Duke of Alençon, who was twenty-two years younger than she was.[22] By 1579 the negotiations seemed to have become serious. A local joke in Stratford was that one clergyman had shaved off his beard in the expectation of a return to popery.[23] Protestant ministers were supposed to be bearded, to emphasize their difference from the celibate Catholic clergy.

Foreign policy reversed itself again when the Jesuit scholar and missionary Edmund Campion was executed at Tyburn in December 1581. His death, regarded by Catholics as a martyrdom, coincided with the end of the negotiations for the French marriage and also ended the period of conciliation with Catholicism. In October 1583 Warwickshire was in turmoil when the fanatical Catholic John Somerville, son-in-law of Edward and Mary Arden of Park Hall, was arrested for conspiring to kill the queen. The Ardens and their priest were quickly sent to London, tried, and found guilty. Mary Arden was pardoned, but Edward Arden was executed on 20 December, and Somerville hanged himself in prison. Their heads were set up on London Bridge.[24] Whether or not the Shakespeares knew the Park Hall Ardens well, the connection with that family had been one of the arguments used in John Shakespeare's application for a coat of arms.[25] Catholics replaced Puritans as the principal national enemy. The new Bishop of Worcester was a leading Puritan, as was the MP for Warwick elected in 1586. Since the bishop was invited by the Stratford Corporation to preach in the Guild Chapel in 1586 and 1587, the prevailing sentiment in Stratford must have been Puritan as well. This branch of Protestantism was concerned not only with external conformity but with the actual beliefs of men.[26] In practice, this might have meant that, no matter how well John Shakespeare carried out his civic responsibilities and attended his parish church, he might be the victim of informers on the lookout for evidence of subversive beliefs, noting, for example, whether he regularly took communion.

It may well be, however, that local politics and personalities were more important to him than religious issues. The most striking thing about the minutes of the Stratford Corporation is what they show about the difficulty of getting people to hold office. At the election meeting of 5 September 1576 – probably the last, with one exception, that John Shakespeare attended – the council elected an absent alderman, John Wheeler, as bailiff. He must have refused, because they ordered him to appear in person two days later, by 9 a.m., or pay a fine. He duly agreed to perform the office, but the next two council meetings (5 October and 5 December) went on into the evening, so that candles had to be brought in. These were the two meetings at which the clerk failed to record absences, so John Shakespeare may or may not have been present, and there is nothing in the minutes to indicate what made these meetings so long. After December, however, John is consistently marked as absent. Did he have strong feelings about Alderman Wheeler, who had been his deputy during his own time as bailiff, or about the practice of voting men into office in order to punish them for refusing to accept it, or about something else, too secret to record in the minutes?

In 1557 "The Book of Orders of the Chamber" had fixed a fine of £10 for anyone who refused to be bailiff "when his turn commeth," with a fine of £8 for refusing to be chief alderman, of which £4 was to be paid toward the expenses of whoever agreed to serve.[27] The phrase "when his turn commeth" seems to have been taken seriously, since the four men who held the office of bailiff between 1559 and 1563 held it again, in the same order, from 1571 to 1575. There were some disturbances to the pattern – one-term bailiffs and bailiffs who served out of sequence – but it looks as if John Shakespeare's turn was about to come again when he stopped attending meetings; the bailiff elected in 1580 was the man who had succeeded him in 1570. His motive for absence may have been simple unwillingness to take office again. At his one further appearance, on 5 September 1582, he voted for his friend John Sadler as bailiff. Sadler refused to serve and was excused on the grounds of ill health (he died in the following year), at which point the mercer Adrian Quiney, another of the candidates and one who had already served twice, agreed to take office for a third term. There is something odd about John Shakespeare's taking so much trouble to vote for someone he probably knew could not serve, and it is even odder that Richard Quiney, who had been on the council only since 1580, voted against his own father. Perhaps they were all manipulating the system in some way.

These details of local politics, though less exciting than the idea of religious persecution, could explain John Shakespeare's withdrawal from public life. The council's long tolerance of his absences suggests, not that it was persecuting him, but that it hoped that time would change his attitude or circumstances. Removal from office was generally a last resort: another alderman who also stopped attending meetings after 5 September 1576 was kept on for four years. John Shakespeare was finally expelled in 1586, as was John Wheeler, at his own request. William Smith, who was elected to one of the resulting vacancies, refused to serve. The three men were neighbors, so their withdrawal may indicate dislike of the Corporation's dominant Puritanism or a feeling that Corporation business was too expensive and time-consuming. In contrast, Adrian Quiney had been part of the original Corporation of 1553, succeeded John Shakespeare as bailiff in 1569, and held the position three times in all, attending his last meeting, as a very old man, two months before his death in 1607.[28] Many of his relatives, notably his son Richard, also held public office. But none of John Shakespeare's sons took any part in local government, and William seems mainly to have learned how general reluctance to hold office could result in the long tenure of people like the inept Constable Elbow in *Measure for Measure:*

> *Escalus.* I thought, by the readiness in the office, you had continued in it some
> time. You say, seven years together?
> *Elbow.* And a half, sir.
> *Escalus.* Alas, it hath been great pains to you. They do you wrong to put you so
> oft upon't. Are there not men in your ward sufficient to serve it?
> *Elbow.* Faith, sir, few of any wit in such matters. As they are chosen, they are
> glad to choose me for them. I do it for some piece of money and go
> through with all.
>
> (2.1.259–69)

There are attractions in the idea that the Shakespeare family was not merely sympathetic but seriously committed to Catholicism. It can explain why William kept a comparatively low profile.[29] It also introduces an element of excitement into a life that otherwise seems sadly lacking in it, connecting him with daring Catholic missionaries, an elaborate underground support organization, and a world of disguises and priest-holes. Inevitably, many of the people he knew, both in Stratford and in London, were Catholics or had links to Catholics. As under most repressive governments, punishment was applied inconsistently and it was possible to get away with a good deal, provided that one's disobedience did not become notorious or potentially treasonous – as when John Donne's brother Henry sheltered a priest and died in prison as a result.

Depending on how one reads John Shakespeare's life, he can be seen almost anywhere on a spectrum ranging from failure to heroic resistance. Meredith Skura's research on twentieth-century actors has found that the typical actor "remembered – or still felt – his mother's importance in his life, for better or for worse, and remarked on the absence – literal or emotional – of his father."[30] The relationship of father and son, especially the eldest son, is bound to be an important one, even where the legal system does not, as in Elizabethan England, make that son the father's heir. If Shakespeare thought of his father as having suffered for his religion, he might have felt for him the mixture of admiration and exasperation that fanatics of all kinds seem to inspire in his plays. He might, however, have thought of John Shakespeare as having failed because he was too trusting, too generous, or simply too improvident – a category of human being for which he shows considerable sympathy. He might have wanted to rescue and rehabilitate him, literally or vicariously – or he might simply have wanted to live down the embarrassment the old man had caused.

Shakespeare After School

If Shakespeare's family became significantly poorer after 1576, it would have meant a rethinking of the future planned for the son and heir. He did not go to university, which he could have attended as early as 1579 (15 being the youngest age admitted by the university statutes). In fact, only one of the young men born in Stratford in 1564 attended a university; he later entered the church.[31] Shakespeare and many of his fellow-students may have shared the pragmatic attitude of the boy in one of Corderius's dialogues: "I know how to read, to write, to speak Latin, at least meanly: what need I so much knowledge? I know more than three popish priests."[32] For all but the rich, attending university meant living uncomfortably, sometimes as a servant to a richer student, while preparing to "profess" divinity, law, or medicine. Fewer than half of those who attended took a degree. As T. W. Baldwin points out, Shakespeare's plays show considerable knowledge of grammar school but none of the awareness of university life that permeates Marlowe's *Doctor Faustus*.[33] By the end of the 1570s, then, he may have been wondering how to show himself a gentleman and yet avoid being a charge on his family. Nothing is known about the cause of his 7-year-old sister's death in April 1579, but his mother's last child, Edmund, born in May 1580, may have been a deliberately conceived "replacement" for Anne.[34] A new baby would have occupied much of the family's attention and might well have made a 16-year-old feel that it was high time to leave home, especially since most of the alternatives to university study would have meant living in another household.

This is one reason why a brief reference in the will of Sir Alexander Hoghton of Lea Hall in Lancashire (made on 3 August 1581) has aroused so much speculation.[35] Hoghton bequeathed his musical instruments and "play-clothes" to his heir, in case he wanted to "keep players," and urged him to be good to two servants resident in the house, one of whom was "William Shakshafte."[36] It is not clear that the reference to players means that William Shakshafte was in fact a player, but much scholarship has attempted to identify Will Shakshafte with Will Shakespeare, pointing, for instance, to passages in his works that might suggest acquaintance with northern England.[37] Hypothetically, one of Shakespeare's schoolmasters who came from the same part of Lancashire might have introduced him to the household in a secretarial or teaching role. He could have become a writer and performer when the household was called upon to supply entertainment. Hoghton was a close friend of Henry

Stanley, fourth Earl of Derby, and two successive Earls of Derby maintained acting troupes that might have taken on the promising servant. Moreover, Hoghton was a devout Roman Catholic. Some of those who think that the young Shakespeare was a Catholic also think that he was being groomed for a role in Catholic counter-espionage and was sent to Lancashire to save him from arrest in the late 1570s.[38]

The difficulties with this story have become more obvious over time. Sir Alexander came into his estate only a year before his death, and at the time when he made his will Shakespeare was only 17. Though Ernst Honigmann admits that "It would be unusual to reward a young servant so generously," he adds that "Shakespeare struck those who knew him as an unusually attractive person" – something one would like to believe but for which there is no firm evidence. Further, Honigmann suspects that Hoghton's "players" were mainly musicians, since they seem not to have traveled and the small household would not have needed plays very often.[39] And, though Shakespeare probably did act, ten years later, in a company sponsored by one of the Stanleys, its actors came from all over the kingdom; he did not need to go to Lancashire to meet them. If (which is unlikely) he was to be involved in undercover Catholic activities, it would have made more sense to send him abroad than to Lancashire, especially since Shakeshaft is not much of an alias. Those who think that he did go abroad point to the many plays set in Italy, but Italian literature was a popular source long before Shakespeare started to draw on it.

His education had given him enough Latin for other employments closer to home. It was once thought that he acquired his knowledge of the law by working as an attorney's clerk.[40] Henry Rogers was the town clerk and steward from 1570 to 1586. If Shakespeare had been in his office in 1580, he would have known about an inquest on 11 February for which Rogers acted as coroner. Katherine Hamlet had fallen into the Avon and drowned while fetching a pail of water. The inquest confirmed that she had died by accident, not suicide, and was thus entitled to Christian burial.[41] The conjunction of the name Hamlet, a "doubtful" death by drowning, and the need for "crowner's quest law" (*Hamlet* 5.1.22) probably did stay in Shakespeare's memory, but he did not need to work in a law office to know about the event, since people have always talked about fatal accidents.[42] The two lawyers who wrote *The Law of Property in Shakespeare and the Elizabethan Drama* found that Shakespeare's use of legal language was by no means exceptional in the drama of the period, and can often be traced directly to his sources. In fact, legal imagery turned out not to correlate with a writer's background: the plays of Ben Jonson, who never formally studied law, contain over 500 legal references,[43] whereas John Marston, who spent several years at the Middle Temple, rarely uses legal terms. The average person had a fair amount of experience of the law, since it was cheap to bring a lawsuit. To recover a debt of £100 in Common Pleas or King's Bench would cost between £6 and £8, which most would consider money well spent.[44]

There is a better provenance for what William Beeston told John Aubrey, some fifty years after Shakespeare's death. Contradicting Jonson's famous statement that

Shakespeare had "small Latin and less Greek," the old man declared that "he understood Latin pretty well, for he had been in his younger years a schoolmaster in the country."[45] Beeston's father Christopher had been an apprentice in the Lord Chamberlain's Men in the late 1590s, but his information might have been distorted over time.[46] A university degree was not required for the post of usher – the schoolmaster's deputy, who did the less demanding tasks before the great man arrived – or for a private tutor. A teaching position would have provided opportunities for writing and directing plays, and kept him in touch with some of the texts that were important sources for his early work. Knowing how to discipline pupils would also be important for anyone working with boy actors, but, with three younger brothers, Shakespeare probably didn't have much to learn about this.

At some point after 1577, when William turned 13, John Shakespeare might have started looking for apprenticeship opportunities in London. Several Stratford boys were stationers' apprentices, including one whom Shakespeare certainly knew.[47] In 1579, the Shakespeares' neighbor, the tanner Henry Field, sent his son Richard, nearly three years older than Shakespeare, to become an apprentice to a London printer. The number and location of presses were carefully controlled and it had probably taken the Fields some time to obtain one of these coveted places. Richard served under the French Huguenot Thomas Vautrollier, a distinguished printer. He eventually married his master's widow, thus acquiring his own shop, and went on to become a leading member of his profession. People moving to London from the provinces generally sought out their countrymen: the two Stratford men kept in touch, and, many years later, Field printed Shakespeare's first published works. It has often been noted that many of the books that Shakespeare used as sources were printed by Field.

Attending university or taking up an apprenticeship would soon become impossible in any case. It is no accident that a university graduate is called a Bachelor, since married men could not attend university or be apprenticed. Marrying before one was able to support a family was regarded as a disastrous course of action, a fact that explains why most people did not marry until their mid-twenties. Yet by the time Shakespeare was 19 he was already a married man and a father. His marriage in 1582 and the births of his children in 1583 and 1585 are the only recorded events of his life in the 1580s. If, at this time, he had not settled on a career, he was not only being amazingly feckless but also making his father's already difficult situation even worse. It is more likely that he had already begun acting by the time he married. Edward Alleyn, the most famous actor of the 1590s, was playing leading roles at 16. The entertainment and service professions, like everything else, depended on the national economy but were not so directly affected by bad harvests; they may even have benefited from weather that prevented men from working outside. Since most companies had been formed primarily for touring, the profession fulfilled at least one of the needs of the parents of adolescent boys, getting them out of the house during their most difficult years.

Theater in the 1580s

Most accounts of Shakespeare's life imagine his departure from Stratford as a life-changing moment in the mid- to late 1580s. In fact, it was probably some time before Shakespeare realized that acting was to be his career and that it would mean living away from his family for most of the year. Many provincial companies toured only a limited, fairly local area, though they sometimes played a short season in London, so it was possible to return home during the gaps in a touring schedule. Shakespeare probably knew something of London already. John Shakespeare had been there on Corporation business in 1572 and perhaps in the previous January as well, since it was in Westminster that he was said to have conducted one of his illegal wool transactions. He may have made other, unrecorded, journeys, perhaps even taking his eldest son with him. It would be useful to have someone literate in case anything had to be put into writing and, given the illicit nature of his wool-trading, it would have been better to keep the knowledge within the family.

If father and son came to town together, and took time out to see a play by one of the companies they already knew from its Stratford visits, they would have found that a major change was taking place in the entertainment profession.[48] Traditionally, performance, amateur or professional, was attached to special occasions. At Stratford and even Coventry, its availability depended on visits from a touring company and on the Corporation's willingness to allow them. Now, London had begun to offer entertainment – even a choice of entertainments – for much of the year, to anyone who could pay. It was the beginning of a continuing process by which the public has gained increasing control over what it sees, as well as when and where it sees it. The City of London, technically independent of the Crown, was hostile to the entertainment industry, but also eager to get its share of any money that anyone else was making from it. Even when actors performed in a private house, the city insisted on the right to determine whether the performance really was private. In 1569 it ruled that such performances could take place only between 3 and 5 p.m., so as not to disturb the neighbors, and householders were held responsible for the behavior of the spectators.[49] Thus, the earliest purpose-built theaters were located outside the city walls. In January 1571 or 1572, if he had been willing to walk out into the country, John Shakespeare could have treated himself to a play at the Red Lion (built in 1567) at Mile End, a mile to the east of the city. After 1575 he could have remained in the heart of London, but paid considerably more, to watch a newly established children's company in a small space to the side of St. Paul's Cathedral. By the mid-1570s there were four inns in London that offered plays (the city got its cut if admission was charged), and three of them were within easy walking distance of the Bell in Carter Lane, which may have been the inn used by the Stratford Corporation (Richard Quiney stayed there in 1598). From 1577 on, there were five companies in the city with their own playing spaces (see Figure 3). Most of these were outside the city

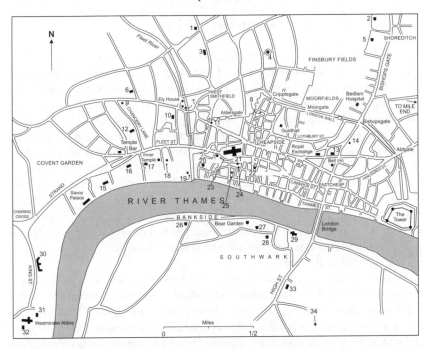

Figure 3 Elizabethan-Jacobean London: locations associated with Shakespeare and his contemporaries

1. Red Bull Theatre (*c.*1604) **2.** The Theatre (1576–98) **3.** St. John's Priory, where the Master of the Revels resided **4.** The Fortune (1600–21) **5.** The Curtain (1577–1625) **6.** Gray's Inn: where *The Comedy of Errors* was performed in December 1594 **7.** Mitre Tavern: where Jonson held court in his later years **8.** Silver Street: the Mountjoys' house and shop, where Shakespeare was living in 1604. Heminges and Condell lived nearby in Aldermanbury **9.** Southampton House: residence of the Earl of Southampton **10.** Fleet Prison: where John Donne was imprisoned in 1601 **11.** Newgate Prison: where Jonson was imprisoned in 1598 **12.** Lincoln's Inn: residence (at various times) of John Marston, John Donne, and Sir John Salusbury **13.** Merchant Taylors' School: where Thomas Kyd and John Webster were educated **14.** St. Helen's Church, Bishopsgate: Shakespeare's parish church in the early 1590s **15.** Somerset House: where the King's Men waited on the Spanish delegation in 1604 **16.** Essex House: where the attempted rebellion of 1601 began **17.** Middle Temple: where *Twelfth Night* was performed in February 1602 **18.** Whitefriars: former Carmelite priory, used as theater by several boys' companies, 1607–13 **19.** Bridewell Prison: where Thomas Kyd was imprisoned in 1593 **20.** Blackfriars, former Dominican priory: one auditorium used by boys' companies (1576–87), and another (the Parliament Chamber) by the Children of the Chapel (1597–1608), then by the King's Men (1609–42). Richard Field's home and printing house were near here and Jonson was resident nearby (1606–12). Shakespeare bought a Gate-house at Blackfriars in 1613 **21.** St. Paul's: the churchyard was occupied by booksellers; the cathedral's central aisle was a meeting place and unofficial information center; the small playhouse attached to it was used by company of choristers, from the 1550s to 1591 and from 1599 to 1606 **22.** Mermaid Tavern: location of Mermaid Club, to which Donne and Jonson belonged. Its host was a trustee for Shakespeare in 1613 **23.** Stationers' Hall: where books were registered **24.** Bell Inn, Carter Lane: where Richard Quiney (and other Stratford officials?) stayed (not to be confused with the Bell Inn, where plays were performed) **25.** College of Arms: where applications for coats of arms were processed **26.** Swan Theatre (1595) **27.** Rose Theatre (1588–1604) **28.** Globe Theatre (1599–1613), rebuilt after fire (1614–42) **29.** St. Mary Overies (now Southwark Cathedral): where Edmund Shakespeare, Fletcher, and Massinger are buried **30.** Whitehall: location of most court performances **31.** Westminster Hall: where Shakespeare gave evidence in 1612 **32.** Westminster School: where Ben Jonson was educated **33.** Marshalsea Prison: where Jonson was imprisoned for *The Isle of Dogs* (1597) **34.** Newington Butts Theatre (1576–94) walls. Newington Butts was a mile south of London Bridge, while the Theatre and the Curtain stood almost side by side in Shoreditch, to the north. Both the Theatre and Newington Butts dated from 1576, and the Curtain from 1577 (the latter was named after the pasture on which it stood, which had been bounded by a wall).[50] The two Shoreditch theaters, though they had separate owners, operated jointly and were frequently referred to together, as if they represented the London theater scene.[51]

A businessman like John Shakespeare might have been interested to know how these new buildings had been financed. They were examples of a relatively new kind of entrepreneurship. The one most relevant to Shakespeare's life, the Theatre (its Greek-derived name would have been exotic), was a joint effort by the builder of the Red Lion, a wealthy grocer named John Brayne, and his brother-in-law, James Burbage. Burbage, whom John Shakespeare might have known from his visits to Stratford in the early 1570s, persuaded Brayne to join with him on a larger and more ambitious playhouse in north London, and the two brothers-in-law fell out almost immediately. Later Burbage would be accused of using a secret key to the strongbox to steal some of the box-office receipts and of having insisted that the devil made him do it.[52] Though the theatrical profession was obviously risky, and some of its practitioners sound, at this distance, rather unsavory, it is possible that John Shakespeare might have encouraged William's inclination to the theater. The ambitious risk-taker had after all been the first bailiff to allow players to perform in Stratford. One reason for official antagonism toward the theater was precisely that it was making a good deal of money. He might have recognized that, at this particular moment, the London playhouses were the best place for a businessman to be. Families (the Burbages are an example) specialized in theater as in other trades, and it is worth remembering that not one but two of John Shakespeare's sons became actors.

How Shakespeare got into the acting profession is a matter for speculation. Like Hamlet, he may have been on friendly terms with actors who visited Stratford frequently. He may even have taken part in productions if, as is known to have happened later, the company recruited bit-part actors from the local population. Barbara D. Palmer, who found a reference to someone being paid 5 shillings to play a part in *The Knight of the Burning Pestle* in 1636, suggests that other small roles in this play were filled by "household members and guests."[53] The playwright Thomas Killigrew told Pepys that before the English Civil War, when he wanted to see a play for nothing he used to hang around the playhouse until someone came out looking for volunteers to play walk-on parts as devils.[54] Two companies that would become important, Lord Hunsdon's Men (later the Lord Chamberlain's Men) and the Lord Admiral's Men, seem to have acted mainly in the provinces during the 1580s, with occasional visits to London. They appeared at court together in 1585/6. By 1584 James Burbage, once a member of Leicester's company, was describing himself as "my Lord of Hunsdon's man."[55] The other important companies were the Earl of

Worcester's Men, who had been in existence for at least twenty years, and those of the Earl of Sussex, who was Lord Chamberlain from 1572 to 1583. Each company had at least one leading actor, the young Edward Alleyn with Worcester's and Richard Tarlton with Sussex's.

It is likely that Shakespeare started with one of the many small provincial touring companies and then moved on to one of these major ones. Opportunities would have come after 1583, when the Privy Council intervened in the theatrical world, amalgamating the best adult actors from several companies into one. The Queen's Men, probably the first officially constituted theater company, included not only actors but tumblers and fencers, and was so large that it may have been divided into two groups for touring purposes.[56] The company's size created a need for longer plays with larger casts; tumblers and fencers performed their feats of skill between the acts, and were perhaps introduced in fight scenes and comic subplots. Its most famous actors were the clowns, Robert Wilson (formerly of the Earl of Leicester's men), and, especially, Richard Tarlton (probably from the Earl of Sussex's men). Tarlton was a legendary figure, famous for having made the queen laugh until she had to beg him to stop. He left an estate of £700 at his death and Sir Philip Sidney was godfather to his son. Professionally a vintner who still kept a tavern, he was also an expert fencer who played demonstration matches. He probably performed the jigs at the end of the play (song-and-dance routines with bawdy plots), but he was so popular that it was also essential to write plays in which he could figure importantly, probably by doubling comic roles with those that required fighting. A battle scene was a sure way of winning back the attention of an unruly crowd, and Tarlton had the classic comedian's ability to buttonhole spectators, either getting them on his side or turning the audience against potential trouble-makers. It is possible that he was at least part-author of *The Famous Victories of Henry V*, and the role of Mumford in the old *King Leir* play, with its mixture of comedy and fighting, seems made for him. Wilson, like Tarlton, specialized in acting simple countrymen, but his contemporaries praised his learning, and his surviving plays are sophisticated allegories interspersed with low comedy.[57] He was still writing in the early 1590s and might have been something of a role model for Shakespeare.

If Shakespeare initially found a place in a touring company from which the best actors had been poached by the Queen's Men, it has been suggested that he would have had the opportunity to join the major company in 1587. One of their leading actors, William Knell, was killed in a fight on tour in June of that year, and the company visited Stratford shortly afterward. The 23-year-old Shakespeare would have had to be very impressive to take over from the man who played the title role in *The Famous Victories of Henry V*; it would have been easier for this large and distinguished company to promote one of its own players. Still, when Knell's widow, Rebecca, remarried in the following year, her new husband was John Heminges, aged 22, who would be one of Shakespeare's closest colleagues in the future. Heminges was born in Worcestershire, though he had just ended his apprenticeship as a grocer in London and would continue to be active as both a businessman and an actor. No one seems to know how he met Rebecca Knell – he may have been the replacement actor as well as husband – but if he already knew Shakespeare he might have introduced his countryman into the company. Shakespeare later revised several of the plays that seem to have been in their repertory: *The Famous Victories of Henry V*, *The Tragical History of King Leir*, and *The Troublesome Reign of King John*. Moreover, George Peele and Thomas Kyd (who may have been the authors of some of the anonymous plays) were two of the most important influences during his early years as a London playwright. If he did belong to the Queen's Men at any point, he might have visited Scotland, since James VI invited the company to Edinburgh to perform for his wedding with Anna of Denmark in 1589. Whether they did play before him is not known, since the wedding was delayed by the bad weather that prevented the bride from sailing and eventually led to the king's going to Denmark instead.[58] Even if Shakespeare did not belong to the Queen's Men, he would later meet some of its members and hear first-hand reports of the young king, who apparently rewarded players much more generously than Elizabeth ever did.

By 1589, however, the Queen's Men, weakened by the death of Tarlton in the previous year, were in competition with a new company under the patronage of Ferdinando Stanley, Lord Strange, the heir to the earldom of Derby. Strange had sponsored a troupe of tumblers when he was still in his teens. By 1589 his company was an acting one, which absorbed some of Leicester's Men after their patron died in 1588. Like the Queen's Men, Strange's company was large. The earl and his son, like many other aristocrats, liked to have large numbers of followers dressed in their livery, and the actors were part of their entourage when they were not performing. The company was assertive: it probably won Edward Alleyn away from Worcester's Men, and it was looking for a London base and court patronage. Its repertoire indicates that a number of its plays were meant to appeal to local patriotism. In 1593 it played *Harry of Cornwall* in the west of England.[59] Faversham was another stop on the touring circuit, and it is likely that the anonymous *Arden of Faversham*, a play about the murder that was the town's best-known event, was written initially for performance there. Some of Shakespeare's earliest works, such as the Henry VI plays and the Induction to *The Taming of the Shrew*, are dotted with names of places in the Midlands. It seems almost certain that at some point he was acting and writing for this company.

Marriage and Children

But Shakespeare's career in the 1580s must have run in parallel with a very different life in Stratford. Near the end of 1582, the 18-year old William (still a minor, and in need of his father's consent) married the 26-year-old Anne Hathaway (or possibly

Agnes, which was pronounced Annis and hence interchangeable with Anne). Their first child was born six months later, so the marriage must have taken place as soon as Anne became aware that she was pregnant. Since nothing is known about their courtship, it has naturally attracted some pleasant fantasies about Shakespeare teaching her to read and writing poems to her. She was the daughter of a friend of his father's and probably someone he had known for a long time, but there were a number of ways in which they could have been thrown together. As visitors to Stratford know, what is now called Anne Hathaway's cottage is an easy walk from the center of the town. Anne might have been living in her father's house; she might have been employed stitching gloves for John Shakespeare;[60] she might have been in service elsewhere, since young women as well as men were often sent away from home in adolescence.

They might even have met in a theatrical context. Davy Jones had been the husband of Adrian Quiney's daughter. After her death in 1579 he married Anne Hathaway's cousin, Frances. In 1583 the Stratford Corporation paid him "and his company" 13s. 4d. for a Whitsuntide pastime.[61] Celebrations of Whitsunday, or Pentecost, the day on which Christ's disciples started speaking in tongues, were a common rural practice, but this was the first such event that Stratford had financed. It may be rather far-fetched to imagine the excitement over this event beginning as early as late summer of 1582, when Shakespeare and Anne must have been making love, and there is of course no proof that either of them was involved with the production. Still, the reference to "his company" might mean that Davy Jones had already been organizing performances before 1583, in which case Shakespeare could have been part of the group, and even the author of the Whitsun pastoral. Since the theatrical atmosphere is a highly erotic one, especially for amateurs, Davy Jones might have influenced not only Shakespeare's career but his private life.

Anne's age on marriage – probably 26, assuming that her epitaph is accurate – was not unusual for the period. As noted above, except in royal and aristocratic families, where the bride and groom were often very young, most couples waited until their mid-twenties to marry. The delay was an effective form of birth control as it reduced the number of years in which a woman could bear children.[62] Since Anne's father, in his will of 1581, left her 10 marks to be paid on her wedding day, he may have known about her relationship with Shakespeare and expected the couple to marry soon. Ten marks was the equivalent of £6. 13s. 4d., probably a bit more than a playwright in the next decade usually received for a completed play.[63] Normally, when the wife provided a dowry the husband was expected to ensure that she would not be left destitute at his death. Her "dower right," under common law, was a third of his property. Alternatively, the couple could make a "jointure," which meant that they would hold all their lands jointly during their lifetimes, with the survivor enjoying the right to them until death.[64] While Shakespeare as yet owned no lands, he was the heir to his parents, whose possessions were still fairly extensive even if they were short of cash. So, while Shakespeare's wedding may have been a shotgun affair, it is equally possible that he and Anne had been planning marriage for some time, or that, if their parents were reluctant to approve, the couple deliberately forced the issue. Park Honan has even suggested that this marriage, far from being an unplanned and embarrassing mistake, may have been the result of careful thought: "A son who wed early might count on having a grown heir in his lifetime, so that heritable land would not devolve (with wardship complications) on a mere child."[65] This, of course, assumes that there was something to inherit and that John Shakespeare's financial difficulties – like William Shakespeare's apparent, and anomalous, recklessness – were more apparent than real.

Historians have estimated that a quarter of brides in the late sixteenth century were pregnant on their wedding day.[66] While unmarried mothers were stigmatized and punished, there seems to have been no hostility toward the woman who gave birth less than nine months after marriage.[67] Her child, after all, would not be a financial burden on the town. Couples seem often to have had sex as soon as they were contracted, without waiting for the formal ceremony – sometimes, perhaps, to make sure that they were capable of conceiving a child. The situation did, however, require some maneuvering. In 1582 the reading of banns, and hence marriage, was forbidden between Advent Sunday (2 December) and the octave of Epiphany (13 January). The Church of England prohibited marriage on more days – 144 in total – than any other church in Europe, Catholic or Protestant. It then exploited those in a hurry to marry by selling a license to dispense with the formalities, thus raising money for the church. The restrictions were so unpopular that some people went ahead and married anyway, pleading ignorance, but in such cases the officiating clergyman usually found himself in trouble.[68] Shakespeare and his fiancée did things properly, obtaining a license that allowed one reading of the banns instead of the usual three. Because the bridegroom was under-age, two friends of the bride's father posted the sum of £40 as surety for the validity of the marriage license. This presumably means that they trusted the bridegroom, not that they were going to drag him to the altar.

For some reason, however, the entry in the consistory court at Worcester gave the bride's name as Anne Whateley of Temple Grafton. Whateley is probably a clerical error; the clerk who recorded this entry also got other names wrong; a vicar named William Whatley had been in a court case on the day the entry was made and appears in several records for 1582–3.[69] E. K. Chambers, who examined the Worcester records, found so much confusion in them that he concluded that the surname was simply inaccurately recorded. Anne's listed domicile may also be a mistake, though she might have been residing in another village for some reason. It is interesting that John Frith, the parish priest at Temple Grafton, was later given a particularly bad report by the Puritan-leaning "Survey of the State of the Ministery in Warwickshire," dated 2 November 1586. Frith, it wrote, "can neither preach nor read well, his chiefest trade is to cure hawks that are hurt or diseased, for which purpose many do usually repair to him."[70] An unlettered clergyman with a fondness for hawks might have suited this unconventional couple, but it is equally possible that they held their wedding somewhere else, since in the bond posted by the two farmers Shakespeare and Anne Hathaway are listed as residents of Stratford. They might even have chosen to marry in Worcester, where the license was granted. In transcribing the records of this period, Richard Savage discovered "that two leaves of the marriage register of St. Martin's, Worcester, of the date of Shakespeare's wedding had been cut out, as by a collector" and he wondered whether these pages had originally recorded the wedding.[71] Yet if Anne had been present in Worcester, one would expect the clerk to get her name right.

Shakespeare's marriage choice – assuming that it was a real choice on his part – works against the view that he was a committed Roman Catholic at this period. Anne came from a family which, by the early seventeenth century, had at least one pious member of the established church: Anne's brother Bartholomew was a churchwarden from 1605 to 1609, and three of his sons also held this office. On the other hand, George Whateley of Stratford had a brother who would be described in 1592 as "an old massing priest."[72] If there really was an Anne Whateley, and if she was a Roman Catholic whereas Anne Hathaway was a devout Protestant, we have the makings of a fascinating story intertwining religious and romantic conflicts – for which, as with all the other romantic stories, there is unfortunately no evidence.

The couple's first child was born on 26 May 1583, just a week after the Whitsun pageant, and christened by Stratford's long-time minister, Henry Heicroft.[73] William and Anne gave their daughter the still uncommon name of Susanna. They may have had some godparent in mind, but perhaps they chose the name for its own sake. The Susanna of the apocryphal book of Daniel is a virtuous wife accused of adultery by two elders in revenge for her refusal to be seduced. The young prophet Daniel, an early example of the detective at work, vindicates the heroine by cross-examining the elders separately and seizing on the discrepancies between their stories. The story had been dramatized in a play published in 1578, Thomas Garter's *The Most Virtuous and Godly Susanna*, which might have been performed locally. Shakespeare had a certain taste for detective logic, as in Humphrey of Gloucester's questioning of a man who is pretending to have been cured of blindness (*2 Henry VI* 2.1) and in Dogberry's absurd attempt at cross-examination in *Much Ado About Nothing* (4.2). In *The Merchant of Venice*, Shylock praises a promising young lawyer as "a Daniel come to judgment." But, given the circumstances surrounding the wedding, the most important feature of the child's name was its association with injured innocence, which might suggest an element of defiance on the part of the young couple.

In late January 1585 Anne gave birth to twins, a boy and a girl. They were presumably conceived in May 1584, when Shakespeare might have been in Stratford in connection with another Whitsuntide performance. Twins were not an unusual sight in Stratford: two other families in Henley Street had them – in fact, two sets of twins accounted for four of the fourteen children of George Ainge, a mercer.[74]

On this occasion, the names were dictated by the choice of godparents, the couple Hamnet and Judith Sadler, who lived in the High Street. Surprisingly, Hamlet, an alternative spelling for Hamnet, is found elsewhere in Stratford; there is a Hamlet Smith in the town records.[75] Like Susanna, the twins were baptized in Stratford-upon-Avon. This time, the officiating minister was a new arrival, Richard Barton, one of the few parish priests of the diocese to be unreservedly praised by the Puritan committee in 1586.[76] Shakespeare was either a good Church of England Protestant or doing his best to look like one. Anne herself may have leaned toward Puritanism, if the epitaph written for her in 1623 can be taken literally when it says that she gave her children both life and milk.[77] At a time when most women who could afford it employed a wet nurse, "Puritan authors made it a Christian duty for mothers to nurse their own children."[78]

There would be no more children after Hamnet and Judith. Since Shakespeare's later career suggests a strong desire to perpetuate his name, it seems strange that the couple would limit their family after the birth of only one son. Perhaps the twins left Anne unable, or too fragile, to bear more children. Robert Bearman has found that Stratford had an unusually high rate of twin births, with an equally high rate of early mortality.[79] A couple who had three children within three years of marriage might well feel that they needed to take precautions against the two great dangers of excessive fecundity: financial ruin and the early death of the wife. If Shakespeare did indeed have Catholic sympathies, he might have been unable to envisage any way except separation to avoid having more children. The Shakespeares must have known that Henry Field, Richard's father, was said in 1584 to have been living apart from his wife "without order of law." The Fields had ten children at the time and do not seem to have been estranged, since his wife lived in the house after Field's death.[80] Ben Jonson would later separate from his wife for five years, apparently because he had converted to Catholicism and they were too poor to have more children.[81] Thomas Middleton, who knew and worked with Shakespeare (and who had only one child), would later create several dramatic characters who suffer from excessive fertility. Touchwood Senior in *A Chaste Maid in Cheapside* and Leantio in *Women Beware Women* abstain from sex, to the frustration of their young wives, in order to avoid having larger families than they can afford. Leantio comments, "I have such luck to flesh/ I never bought a horse but he bore double" (that is, fathered twin foals: 1.2.51–2).[82] Shakespeare, thinking of George Ainge and his two sets of twins, might have feared that he had the same kind of "luck."

Very young couples generally lived with their parents, though the English practice was for them to set up their own household as soon as possible.[83] John Shakespeare still owned a "double house" in Henley Street and had other invest-ments, but William, Anne, and their three children had no home of their own. Throughout the 1580s the Shakespeares were engaged in unsuccessful litigation to recover the land in Wilmcote that they mortgaged to Edmund Lambert in 1578–9, and the younger couple may have expected to inherit it. Instead, in 1587 mother, father, and heir agreed to sign away some of Mary Arden's inherited lands to Lambert. In 1588 they tried to argue that Lambert had not accepted their money and that they were therefore entitled to the land. Because much litigation involved discussion of the "true intent" of legal documents, it was possible for the two parties to be at cross-purposes over transactions like this. When the case was heard before the Court of Queen's Bench in London in 1588, the family acted through an attorney, but it is possible that, as Jonathan Bate suggests, he was instructed by William Shakespeare in London.[84] It is not clear what the outcome was. Nor is it known whether the Shakespeares lost the eighty-six acres in Wilmcote which in 1578 they conveyed to someone else on a lease due to revert in 1601 to Mary Arden's heirs.[85]

It is often assumed that the Shakespeares' marriage was unhappy, and it may have been. Either prolonged infertility or forced abstinence would put a strain on any marriage. But there are many stories that one could tell on the basis of the existing facts. Shakespeare and his wife may have agreed, even before marriage, that he would lead an itinerant life for a few years with a view to making enough money to buy a substantial property. The few years stretched into more as his acting and writing commitments grew, but there is no evidence that anyone thought he had deserted his family. He traveled with a company of players, or several companies in succession, probably coming to London for a short season each year and returning to Stratford when the tour ended. The period between 1588 and 1592, however, saw a change in some of the major companies. During these four years, the city of London was free from major epidemics, and hence from long playhouse closures. This period of respite meant there were greater opportunities than usual for playing an extended season in the city, and some companies began to make it their permanent base.[86] Shakespeare still acted "here and everywhere," but "Here" and "there" were now becoming specific locations, Stratford and London.

Notes

1. Greenblatt, *Hamlet in Purgatory*, 16. See p. 279 below for further discussion of the phrase in *Hamlet*.
2. Printed in Chambers, *ES*, 2: 98–9.
3. Sutherland, "The Grant of Arms to Shakespeare's Father," 382–3.
4. In his *Brief Treatise on the Right Use of Giving Arms* (1597), Henry Howard, later Earl of Northampton, commented on "heralds hungry for money." See Peck, *Northampton*, 14.
5. The statement may have been a fiction designed to expedite the grant twenty years later. For the pattern, see Figure 6 (p. 206) below.
6. *Minutes*, III: 6.
7. See Simpson, *A History of the Land Law*, 173–207 (ch. 8, "Uses and the Statute").
8. *Minutes*, III: xxxiv–xxxvi.
9. Bearman, "John Shakespeare: A Papist or Penniless?," 418. See also M. Eccles, *Shakespeare in Warwickshire*, 33–4.

10. Lane, ed., *John Hall and His Patients*, 7, 9.
11. Unwin, *Industrial Organization in the Sixteenth and Seventeenth Centuries*, 106.
12. Thomas, ed., *Shakespeare in the Public Records*, 3.
13. Stubbes, *The Anatomie of Abuses*, pp. 178–9, lines 4599–4641.
14. Muldrew, *The Economy of Obligation*, 96, 177–80.
15. Bearman, "John Shakespeare: A Papist or Penniless?," 414–15 and n.
16. Hindle, "Dearth, Fasting and Alms," 44. Hindle quotes the orders for 1596, but says that a similar set was issued for 1586–7 (pp. 50–1).
17. Bearman, "John Shakespeare: A Papist or Penniless?," 420.
18. Ibid., 427. Mark Eccles argues (*Shakespeare in Warwickshire*, 32) that these debts belong to the "other" John Shakespeare, a corvisor, who lived in Stratford until 1596. It seems more likely that Shakespeare's father would have borrowed from people he knew.
19. Bearman, "John Shakespeare: A Papist or Penniless?," 428–9.
20. Muldrew, *The Economy of Obligation*, 273.
21. M. Eccles, *Shakespeare in Warwickshire*, 22.
22. He later became the Duke of Anjou. This earlier title avoids confusion with his brother Henri, Duke of Anjou, also a suitor to the queen until 1571. When Anjou became Henri III of France in 1574, his title passed to Alençon. See Doran, *Monarchy and Matrimony*.
23. *Minutes*, IV: 3n.
24. Ibid.
25. See Honan, 417.
26. Lake, *Anglicans and Puritans?*, 48.
27. *Minutes*, I: 63.
28. Fripp, *Master Richard Quyny*, 199.
29. See e.g. Greenblatt, *Will in the World*.
30. Skura, *Shakespeare the Actor*, 23.
31. Kay, *Shakespeare*, 30–1.
32. Cordier, *Corderius Dialogues*, II.33.
33. Baldwin, *William Shakespeare's Small Latine & Lesse Greeke*, 2: 670–1.
34. Skura, *Shakespeare the Actor*, 78.
35. Schoenbaum, 113, traces the origin of this theory to Oliver Baker, *In Shakespeare's Warwickshire* (1937); E. A. J. Honigmann developed it more fully in *Shakespeare: The "Lost Years."*
36. Schoenbaum, 112.
37. e.g. Honan, 69.
38. Wilson, *Secret Shakespeare*, 65.
39. Honigmann, *Shakespeare: The "Lost Years,"* 130, 27.
40. See e.g. Fripp, *Shakespeare: Man and Artist*, 138–49.
41. *Minutes*, III: xlii–xlviii.
42. Steven Gunn's discovery of the coroner's report of the drowning of a young child picking flowers was widely reported in June 2011. It happened some 20 miles from Stratford, and in 1569, but her name, by another strange coincidence, was Jane Shaxspere. Would Shakespeare have remembered hearing such an event discussed when he was 5 years old? Only, I should guess, if the girl was a relative, which she probably was not. See Sylvia Morris's posting on http://theshakespeareblog.com/?

p=285. Morris had also been told of another possible death by drowning at Clopton House, still nearer to Stratford. As she notes, "Deaths by drowning seem to have been fairly common."

43. Clarkson and Warren, *The Law of Property*; see their conclusion, 285–6, 285.
44. Brooks, *Pettyfoggers and Vipers of the Commonwealth*, 101–3. See also Schoenbaum, 109–10.
45. Aubrey, *Brief Lives*, 2: 227.
46. Baldwin, *William Shakespeare's Small Latine & Lesse Greeke*, 1: 36.
47. Duncan-Jones, *Ungentle Shakespeare: Scenes from His Life*, 5.
48. For a more detailed account of theatre history in this period, see Gurr, *The Shakespearian Playing Companies*; Ingram, *The Business of Playing*; Wickham, ed., *English Professional Theatre 1530–1660*; and the great work that lies behind them all, E. K. Chambers, *Elizabethan Stage*.
49. Ingram, *The Business of Playing*, 73–4. Ingram suggests that this may be the origin of the idea that a play represented "two-hours' traffic."
50. Wickham, 404.
51. Ibid., 408–9.
52. Ingram, *The Business of Playing*, 196.
53. Palmer, "Playing in the Provinces," 99.
54. Samuel Pepys, *Diary*, ed. Robert Latham and William Matthews, 11 vols. (Berkeley: University of California Press, 1970), 3: 243–4, quoted in Stern, *Rehearsal from Shakespeare to Sheridan*, 77.
55. Wickham, 346.
56. See McMillin and MacLean, *The Queen's Men and Their Plays*.
57. Kathman, "Wilson, Robert," *ODNB*.
58. P. R. Roberts, "The Business of Playing," 85.
59. Maclean, "Adult Playing Companies, 1583–1593," 55.
60. Germaine Greer's suggestion (see *Shakespeare's Wife*, 73).
61. M. Eccles, *Shakespeare in Warwickshire*, 83.
62. Wrightson, *English Society 1580–1680*, 68.
63. For playwrights' earnings, see *Henslowe's Diary* and Carson, *A Companion to Henslowe's Diary*, 65–6.
64. J. H. Baker, *Introduction to English Legal History*, 229–30.
65. Honan, 82.
66. See Cressy, *Birth, Marriage, and Death*, 74, citing G. R. Quaife, *Wanton Wenches and Wayward Wives* (1979), 90–1.
67. Wrightson, *English Society*, 84–6.
68. Cressy, *Birth, Marriage, and Death*, 298–300.
69. J. W. Gray, in *Shakespeare's Marriage* (1905), summarized in Chambers, *WS*, 2: 45–6, and Schoenbaum, 85–6.
70. *Minutes*, IV: 5.
71. *Minutes*, III: lv, n.
72. *Minutes*, III: l–li, IV: 159–60.
73. M. Eccles, *Shakespeare in Warwickshire*, 50–1.
74. Ibid., 41.

75. Ibid., 44.
76. *Minutes*, IV: 2–8.
77. Duncan-Jones, *Shakespeare: An Ungentle Life*, 26.
78. Cressy, *Birth, Marriage, and Death*, 89.
79. Bearman is cited in Greer, *Shakespeare's Wife*: "Just how dangerous twinning was can be seen from the Holy Trinity registers. Robert Bearman has counted thirty-two sets of twins baptised at Holy Trinity between 1560 and 1600; he looked to see how may of these infants were buried within three months and came up with eighteen sets of twins surviving. However, the burial register also contains records of twins who were never publicly baptised, including some who were buried as nameless" (pp. 130–1).
80. *Stratford-upon-Avon Inventories 1538–1699*, 1: 119.
81. Riggs, *Ben Jonson: A Life*, 54, 92–3.
82. Ed. John Jowett, in Middleton, *Collected Works*, ed. Taylor and Lavagnino. Jowett glosses this as "bore two riders," but Leantio has just said that if he spends any more nights with his wife he is in for forty weeks more, an obvious reference to pregnancy.
83. Stone, *The Family, Sex and Marriage in England 1500–1800*, 51.
84. Thomas, ed., *Shakespeare in the Public Records*, 5; Bate, *Soul of the Age*, 322–3.
85. M. Eccles, *Shakespeare in Warwickshire*, 30.
86. Wickham, 83.

4

"This Man's Art and That Man's Scope"
1588–1592

> *When in disgrace with fortune and men's eyes,*
> *I all alone beweep my outcast state,*
> *And trouble deaf heaven with my bootless cries,*
> *And look upon myself and curse my fate,*
> *Wishing me like to one more rich in hope,*
> *Featured like him, like him with friends possessed,*
> *Desiring this man's art and that man's scope,*
> *With what I most enjoy contented least;*
> *Yet in these thoughts myself almost despising,*
> *Haply I think on thee, and then my state,*
> *Like to the lark at break of day arising*
> *From sullen earth, sings hymns at heaven's gate;*
> > *For thy sweet love remembered such wealth brings*
> > *That then I scorn to change my state with kings.*
> > (Sonnet 29)

Whether one thinks the author of this sonnet really meant the first part of it (especially line 7) must be a major factor in any interpretation of Shakespeare's character. Of course, the lines only *seem* to be personal; their real purpose is to create the darkness from which the next six can be born. The reader's voice soars upward, like to the lark, as it makes the transition from the unpunctuated eleventh line to the twelfth, coming to rest in the final couplet, where, as usual, the solution turns out to be love.

Since Sonnet 29 could have been written at any time before its publication in 1609, many different situations might explain the complaint of "disgrace" and an "outcast state." The situation of a traveling player, especially one whose father was still in danger of arrest for debt, might have been one of these. Moreover, the 1609

The Life of William Shakespeare: A Critical Biography, First Edition. Lois Potter.
© 2012 Lois Potter. Published 2012 by Blackwell Publishing Ltd.

edition places Sonnet 29 after two others that complain of weariness, apparently connected with work and travel, so someone, possibly the author, thought that they belonged together. Everyone sometimes feels that someone else has more of the attributes mentioned here: appearance, wealth, ancestry, prospects, and circle of friends. "Art" did not necessarily have to mean artistic ability;[1] it could be skill of any kind, and it could also be education, and even, possibly, something more like "deviousness."[2] "Scope" could be "opportunity." Still, it is worth asking, with whom would Shakespeare have been comparing himself, and what did he "most enjoy" (in the sense of possess)? A reader in 1609 would have taken him to mean his status as a leading member of the leading company of actors of his day. But what would his first readers, or hearers, have thought he meant? His wife and family? His verbal facility? His acting talent?

Like many of the sonnets, number 29 reflects the competitive nature of Shakespeare's life. Touring players needed to be good in order to be selected for performance in towns or houses which had a choice of companies, and they were probably aware of each others' activities.[3] This competition, however, was mainly on the level of production and acting: when their visits were only once a year and they gave only one or two performances in each location, they could offer the same small group of plays over and over. On the other hand, when they started playing for longer seasons in London, the competition among them was concurrent rather than consecutive. Shakespeare might, for the first time, have seen what other companies were playing and had a chance to meet other playwrights. As a result, he might have felt, or remembered when he wrote Sonnet 29, a strong sense of inadequacy.

The stakes were higher in London, both for actors and authors. The outdoor theaters built in mid-sixteenth-century London were designed not only to hold a much larger audience than the marketplace but also to allow the company to collect money before rather than during the play. Since nothing makes people angrier than being disappointed in their expectation of pleasure, requiring payment in advance put the audience into a potentially hostile relationship with the players. After a year or two on the road, Shakespeare would have known something about the situation of a human being surrounded by an angry crowd. In front of the still larger audiences in London's public theaters, he might have recognized the resemblance between acting and another popular activity, and identified himself, as some of his characters do, with the baited bear.[4] He might even have agreed with the satirist John Cocke, who in 1615 described "The Character of a Common Player" as one who "hath been so accustomed to the scorn and laughter of his audience, that he cannot be ashamed of himself."[5]

The ostensible justification for the existence of actors in London was to provide solace and recreation for the queen so as to ensure her long life, something that every good subject ought to desire. The solace would obviously be greater if the performance was perfect; hence the need for public "rehearsals." The City of

London authorities frequently pointed out the flimsiness of this argument, since royal recreation was provided mainly at the Christmas season, whereas public performances went on for much of the year. Why, they asked in 1584, should the queen be offered entertainment that had previously been seen by "all the basest assemblies in London and Midd[lesex]" and by players who might be carrying diseases from those places? Why could they not confine themselves to performances in private houses?[6] But the presence of theater patrons on the Privy Council usually protected the players. There were in fact other opportunities to perform before a select audience. As in the country, the players were sometimes invited to private houses by spectators who preferred not to make the long and dirty journey to the playhouse and mix with an audience that might be carrying disease. Sometimes there were spontaneous events in the private rooms of taverns, often immediately after a performance, when well-off spectators were willing to pay in order to see favorite scenes again and socialize with the players.[7]

The most desirable audiences were also the most demanding. The honor of a court performance brought with it not only a substantial fee but a lot of hard work. Elaborate lighting arrangements had to be made for these late-night performances; the visual and musical elements also needed to be re-rehearsed, and perhaps added to. Costumes were a greater problem. The cleaning of silks, velvets, wools, and laces was a nonstop operation for the laundresses employed by the theater, when performances took place by daylight and with some of the audience only a few feet away. When the actors played at court, they sometimes had to replace worn-out costumes, since it was a breach of decorum to appear before a royal audience with shabby clothes, whatever the social status of the characters.[8] The university actors who performed during a royal visit to Queens' College, Cambridge, in 1632 recognized the absurdity of their lavish costuming of the characters in a play with a rustic setting: "But that they hope the Court will excuse, for, had it not been here, they had been forced (they say) to keep the true *decorum*."[9]

The court audience was particularly difficult. Men and women who had spent years learning to fence and dance would be critical of inadequate performance from characters purporting to be royal or aristocratic. Foreign ambassadors and their entourages attended frequently, enjoying the music and dancing and taking special interest in the boys playing women's roles, a feature unknown in continental Europe. Since most of them did not understand English, they were given a written synopsis, but this was not always enough. A Spaniard who saw a play in 1564 wrote to his king that "I should not have understood much of it if the Queen had not interpreted, as she told me she would do."[10] The simultaneous translation must have been audible to everyone, since the queen was proud of her linguistic skills. The actors had to ignore the running commentary on their action, or (as the clowns probably did) incorporate it into their dialogue without seeming impertinent. A further problem was that the play often began after the spectators had already seen several other entertainments. They were likely to be tired, and on some occasions an exhausted

Elizabeth simply canceled a performance on which a great deal of time and trouble had been spent.

To be successful in this environment, Shakespeare and his colleagues had to avoid resembling the stereotypical strutting players. He was able to recite Latin correctly; if he had not already started to study French and Italian he probably did so now, since some writers threw in a few lines in these languages in order to compliment those members of the audience who understood them and, perhaps, to provide some relief for those who knew no English. Spending longer periods in London allowed him to work on skills like dancing and fencing that would make him convincing in the part of a gentleman. As an actor, he could probably mimic real-life examples of good and bad behavior, but there were also books aimed at upwardly mobile young men. He almost certainly read George Pettie's *Ciuile Conuersatione*, translated from Stefano Guazzo (1581, with an enlarged version in 1586). In what begins as a philosophical doctor's attempt to encourage his melancholy patient to take part in society, the book discusses the fine points of social interaction, the importance of courtesy and "gentle speech," and the delicate balance between excessive formality and excessive bluntness that makes up good manners. The fourth book, purporting to be an account of a conversation among men and women, allows the precepts of the other books to be put into practice, as the speakers engage in verbal games, riddles, and versifying. Shakespeare seems to have learned from Guazzo's advice that "civil conversation ought to vary according to the variety of the persons" and that the reader should take notes even on "comedies and posies" for later use. Some think that Shakespeare returned the compliment by borrowing from Guazzo. Many so-called parallels are commonplaces, but their general tone is in accord with his interests: "to play the foole well, it behoueth a man first to be wise"; meaningless "Ceremony" is exemplified in courtiers who refuse to let their duke go bareheaded, not realizing "that he was not bare in respect of them, but because of the heat."[11] By 1601, as an established writer, Shakespeare may have been relaxed enough to draw on these two examples when he wrote *Twelfth Night* 3.1.60–8 and the scene between Osric and Hamlet. The earlier plays, however, are full of self-consciousness about manners. Among those who are given lectures on "behavior" are Berowne in *Love's Labour's Lost*, Gratiano in *The Merchant of Venice*, Benedick and Beatrice in *Much Ado About Nothing*, and Hotspur in *1 Henry IV*.

The Playwriting Business and Henslowe

It is likely that Shakespeare's first lodgings in London were in the neighborhood of the Theatre and the Curtain, the two most important theater buildings. They were located outside the city walls, where there was still a good deal of open country, but once the visitor entered the city, via Bishopsgate, he was in an overcrowded maze. As John Fisher writes, "Visitors to Elizabethan London must have experienced difficulty finding their way around the city, as there were no horse-drawn vehicles for hire, and it was not possible to purchase pocket-maps to guide one through the maze of narrow, twisting streets."[12] Shakespeare may have lived first in an inn, then rented a room in one of those streets. By 1596 he was being taxed in the parish of St. Helen's, Bishopsgate, inside the city walls but still close to the theaters. Bishopsgate, the main street leading to the north, was a district that attracted theater people. Charles Wallace, who first examined the tax records, noted that an exceptionally large number of foreigners also lived in St. Helen's.[13] Although they never comprised more than 4 or 5 percent of the London population, the fact that they tended to congregate made them seem more numerous than they were and encouraged the xenophobia of their neighbors.[14] It may have been Shakespeare's first opportunity to see the French, German, and Dutch residents of the city and to recognize the cultural antagonisms that emerged in difficult economic times.

From reading the life of Virgil, Shakespeare knew the rewards that were available for a successful writer in ancient Rome. On arrival in London, he had his first opportunity to see what life was like for a writer in his own time. As Charles Nicholl points out, Marlowe at his death was not described as a dramatist, because there was no such occupation.[15] The only professional writers in Elizabethan London were scriveners. Writing, like painting, was a combination – or confusion – of intellectual and manual labor. Renaissance theories of painting emphasized the importance of the *idea* of the picture, as opposed to the mere business of slapping paint on a canvas. There was no such theorizing of the distinction between the scrivener and the author, though Hamlet's remark about having once thought it "a baseness to write fair" (5.2.34) suggests that some people cultivated bad handwriting so as not to be mistaken for scriveners. Some London-based dramatists took advantage of the opportunity of belonging to the livery companies for the sake of the status and security they provided. Ben Jonson, for example, though others mocked him for having worked in his stepfather's profession as a bricklayer, kept up his membership of the guild for years, and was thus entitled to be called a freeman of London.[16]

In the pre-Elizabethan era, when few playscripts were printed, they were hard to obtain and expensive.[17] As early as the 1570s, when a London theater scene was beginning to develop, it had already become obvious that actors needed to ensure themselves a regular and rapid supply of plays. In the summer of 1572 the brothers Lawrence and John Dutton, with another actor named Thomas Goffe or Gough, made what may have been the first attempt to create a formal link between author and actors. They committed themselves to act *only* plays by Rowland Broughton, for a period of two and a half years, on condition that he keep them supplied at a regular rate, with a total of eighteen plays during that period. The actors specified the financial terms in some detail: Broughton was to bear a sixth of the charges of putting on his plays and in return would receive a sixth of the profits. The Duttons and Gough evidently intended to include two other actors in their company and to hire boys to play the women's roles as needed. The plan was totally unrealistic and it is hard to see how anyone could have expected it to work. Broughton, described in the contract as a gentleman, may have been quite young and probably had no idea how long it takes to write even an interlude for a company of five; he was eventually sued for defaulting after writing the first play.[18] The Duttons were prominent figures in the theater world from the 1570s to the early 1590s and had toured with the Queen's Men. There is a good chance that Shakespeare met them either in the provinces or on his arrival in London, where both were living by the 1590s (John in fact kept an inn in Bishopsgate).[19] He might have learned from them that a writer able to turn out high-quality work at speed could be at least as indispensable to actors as they were to him.

By the early 1590s one theater manager, Philip Henslowe, was operating a much more successful version of what the Duttons had tried to set up. Though he is best known today for his theater connections, Henslowe came from a family that held a number of court appointments – his father was Master of the Game in two parks – so he may have seen himself primarily as a courtier, just as James Burbage saw himself as "Lord Hunsdon's man." By 1592 he was a Groom of the Queen's Chamber.[20] Like other ambitious men, he operated several ventures at once, running a pawnshop, investing in a starch business, and acting as landlord for at least two theaters, the Rose in Southwark and Newington Butts at Mile End Green.[21] Because his account book (usually called *Henslowe's Diary*) has survived, with details of his payments to writers, his expenses on productions, and his receipts from them, he is the main source of information about theater management in the 1590s. Other theater companies may have followed the same practices; on the other hand, it is possible that Henslowe was more efficient, or more ruthless, than his competitors. Moreover, since the *Diary* covers only part of his working life, mostly from 1592 to 1603, it is not certain that it can be used as evidence of earlier or later periods. Shakespeare was never a member of Henslowe's team of writers, but he probably acted at his theaters. He also began his London career by working in collaboration, so it is worth looking at the methods recorded in the *Diary*.

It was both for reasons of speed and because a writer needed to learn the basic requirements of the company for which he wrote that as many as four or five of Henslowe's playwrights were sometimes paid for a single play. Not only did collaboration enable inexperienced playwrights to learn from others, it also provided a clear plan of action, deadlines, a fixed rate of payment (to which Henslowe sometimes added a bonus for an exceptionally successful play), and perhaps a sounding board for ideas. Henslowe usually authorized payment only after someone he trusted had read part of the play, or heard it read aloud. He then paid in installments as the different acts arrived and were approved. He had obviously discovered the risks of letting writers have their money too soon, though occasionally he sent an advance payment to someone in desperate straits. By the end of the 1590s, some writers had signed contracts promising to write only for Henslowe. He said nothing about what kind of writing they would have to do, and there is nothing in the *Diary* to suggest that he was annoyed when a writer chose to go solo.

Someone must have made sure that the authors suited their play to the company personnel. Ideally, they knew the actors well enough to know just how much they could ask of each of them, but they also needed to know what kinds of doubling were and were not possible, how to alternate scenes with only a few characters with others that needed the rest of the cast, how long it took an actor to make an elaborate costume change, and how to get the clown offstage before the end so that he could come back dressed for the jig after the play. Anthony Munday is called "our best plotter" in 1598,[22] and this may refer to a recognized theatrical function, though it is also a possible glance at Munday's past career as a spy. Writers who were used to working together probably did not need a plotter. Henslowe set aside money for a meeting in a tavern when the final version was read to the entire company. This was presumably the author's or authors' opportunity to answer actors' questions about the characters. Minor revisions could be made at this point and, if there was time, someone may have sorted out any glaring inconsistencies in the plot. Or they may have been corrected during rehearsal. If they were not, the audience probably would not have noticed.

The fact that his authors often had to be bailed out of debtors' prison may suggest that Henslowe exploited them. But a collaborator in the early 1590s could receive £1 for one act of a play, and £5 for a complete play, rising to £6 for the more experienced writers. If the actor and writer Thomas Heywood was earning 5 shillings a week for acting when the playhouses were open and making an additional £5 or £6 for each complete play that he wrote, with additional earnings from dramatic piecework, he should have had a decent income. However, life in London was expensive if one was not a Londoner. Writers who wrote mainly for publication, such as Gabriel Harvey and Thomas Nashe, sometimes lived with their publishers, apparently receiving room and board in exchange for a prolific output of pamphlets.[23] Most playwrights, however, probably lived in rented rooms where they had to pay for a fire and candles. It was easier to work in a tavern, which is where most production meetings took place, but this meant the temptation to drink and gamble. In *1 Henry IV* the bill for Falstaff's drinking in one evening is 5*s.* 8*d.*, more than Heywood's weekly takings as a actor. Admittedly, this is for 2 gallons of sack, represented as a "monstrous" amount, and Falstaff is expecting someone else to pay for it. Still, an author who drank every night in a tavern could easily spend his entire wage there. The fashionable new habit of smoking tobacco also cost money. Clothes were proportionately very expensive, since there were few cheap fabrics, and a good appearance mattered to one's status. Most people could afford only one or two outfits and could easily be described and identified by them. In *Poetaster* (1602) Jonson described the clothes of two characters: these may well have been the ones really worn by his satiric targets, the playwrights Dekker and Marston.[24]

There were also, of course, the expenses that resulted from the sex trade. It is hardly surprising that this was thriving: as Gary Taylor notes, London probably had 115 men for every 100 women, and 15 percent of its population were apprentices, forbidden to marry.[25] To judge from the plays about London life that Middleton and others wrote later, some men sought out married women who were less likely than prostitutes to be diseased, to expect payment, or to make paternity claims; others preferred the brothel, wanting to avoid relationships that might become emotionally involving. Some believed that sexual intercourse was necessary to one's health, others that each act shortened one's life by a day.[26] The one contemporary anecdote about Shakespeare's sex life (see below, p. 140) links him with a citizen's wife who makes the first advances. This was probably the dream situation for most men and sounds too good to be true. Those less fortunate paid for sex, and often had to pay later to be cured of sexually transmitted diseases.

Because Henslowe's playwrights are less well known than Shakespeare, there has been a tendency to think that collaboration denotes inferior status. In fact, many dramatists went on collaborating throughout their careers, even when they had become well known in their own right. In some contexts, as in plays by the gentleman writers at the Inns of Court, collaboration was something to be proud of. In 1587 Thomas Hughes published an Inns of Court play, *The Misfortunes of Arthur*, of which he had been the main author. The title page shows the care with which he discriminated between his own contribution and those of others, even indicating "certain words and lines, where some of the Actors either helped their memories by brief omission; or fitted their acting by some alteration." He added "a note in the end of such speeches as were penned by others,"[27] which included two choruses, dumb shows, and several speeches. This of course was an amateur group of gentlemen, whose feelings had to be taken into consideration. Professional dramatists seem to have been quite different: it was only for the purpose of payment, or when the play got them into trouble, that they needed to state what each of them had written.

There were other kinds of collaboration. The repertoire of the Queen's Men, as early as 1585, included *Five Plays in One* and *Three Plays in One*. Such mixtures continued to be popular into the seventeenth century, partly because they allowed the company to adjust the length of a theatrical performance as needed. In some cases, the plays were on related topics, but by different playwrights. One of the most intriguing comments on play writing was made by Margaret, Duchess of Newcastle, when in 1662 she published her "plays" – short conversations, sometimes involving action, with no necessary connection between them. In a preface she says she has heard that the best playwrights "seldom or never join or sew the several scenes together; they are two several professions," and compares this division of labor to that of the master tailor and his apprentices.[28] This idea must have come from her husband, who collaborated before the Civil War with James Shirley, and with Davenant and Dryden after the Restoration. Apparently, Newcastle provided isolated episodes and then expected a professional playwright to link them in some sort of plot. That others may have followed the same practice is evident from the compliment Leonard Digges paid to Shakespeare in verses published in 1640:

> Nor begs he from each witty friend a scene
> To piece his acts with; all that he doth write,
> Is pure his own, plot, language, exquisite . . .[29]

By then, clearly, any collaborative history behind Shakespeare's plays had long since been forgotten.

Since none of Shakespeare's early plays were published before the plague watershed of 1594, it has traditionally been assumed that they were written not long before then. However, Ernst Honigmann and Eric Sams, among others, have argued forcefully that the dramatist started writing in the mid-1580s, not the early 1590s. They also believe, however, that he revised his works throughout his career. So, although some of the plays may have first been written in the 1580s and performed on tour, these were probably very different from the published versions, which represent the expansion and enrichment that Shakespeare undertook between performances – perhaps, in fact, in the intervals between one company and another. The fact that he was willing to learn from the experience of seeing the plays in performance, and to improve even plays that had already been successful, is part of what made Shakespeare Shakespeare. So is the fact that he was able to learn from the other playwrights whose works he was now able to see.

Playwrights of the 1580s

Because the company's main purpose was to travel, and its season in London was relatively short, the Queen's Men did not need a large repertory. Two of their actors, the clown Robert Wilson and (probably) Richard Tarlton, were also playwrights. By the mid-1580s, however, Thomas Kyd and George Peele were writing for the company. Both came from the middle class and could call themselves gentlemen, but, though neither man acted professionally, both had some background in theater. Peele's father, the bursar of Christ's Hospital, kept a stock of costumes and properties for the annual Lord Mayor's Show, and the Hospital had a tradition of musical and theatrical performance which must have been of high quality, since in 1580 Sebastian Westcote, the famous Master of the Children of Paul's, had taken one of its boys into his own company.[30] The bursar managed to send Peele to Oxford, where he earned an MA, usually mentioned on the title pages of his published works. His *Arraignment of Paris* was performed before the queen in the early 1580s. In 1583 he was invited back to Oxford to help with the production of William Gager's Latin play about the loves of Dido and Aeneas for an audience that included Sir Philip Sidney and a Polish prince. It was probably Peele who devised its special effects, such as sweetmeats falling from the sky, offstage hunting sounds, and – something Shakespeare would have found fascinating – a marzipan model of Troy which Aeneas explained in the Ovidian lines that recur in *The Shrew* (see pp. 28–9 above).[31] Though Peele hovered around the edges of the court, by the end of the 1580s he was in financial difficulties. He probably started writing for the public theaters when his income from patronage, and from his wife's dowry, had dried up. Kyd, about whom much less is known, may have begun writing while he was still a pupil of the Merchant Taylors' School in London. Since the school often gave performances, he may also have acted in them.

Some of the other gentlemen who began writing plays in the 1580s did so less out of love for the theater than because they had discovered that their education in foreign languages gave them an advantage in finding stories with which to supply its demands. They were among the large number of clever, over-educated young men who had emerged from the universities expecting to be important court officials or public intellectuals, only to find that there was already too much competition for these attractive roles. For a short while at the end of the 1580s – probably at the time when Shakespeare was becoming a part-time resident in London – some of them seemed to be achieving their ambition, thanks to the controversy associated with "Martin Marprelate" and his attacks on the church hierarchy. Since 1586 the conservative John Whitgift, Archbishop of Canterbury, had been in charge of licensing for the press, a fact that enabled him to spot the most talented pamphleteers and recruit them to answer Martin. Like the Martinist tracts, the anti-Martin pamphlets were published anonymously or pseudonymously, and some of their authors have never been identified. However, they included at least three dramatists: John Lyly, Robert Greene, and Thomas Nashe.

Lyly had become an overnight success in 1578 when he published the novel *Euphues*, with its mannered, easily imitated prose style and its mixture of bad behavior and moralizing comment. Its title is the name of its hero (meaning "beautiful"), but it was also applied to a deliberately artificial style characterized by balance and elaborate comparisons. By 1583 Lyly had transposed that style to the stage, where it worked even better: actors must have welcomed its easy-to-remember patterned phrases. As the Earl of Oxford's secretary he wrote for, and apparently directed, a company of boys taken from the choirs of St. Paul's and the Chapel Royal. Perhaps there was already a tradition of mannered acting in the boys' companies. His style at any rate encouraged that kind of acting and helped to exploit the boys' charm. Some of the anti-Martinist plays were apparently performed by his company.

Robert Greene was the best-known writer of the decade, mainly because he was so willing to exploit his own personality, or persona. He wrote everything –romances, epistles, moralizing tracts. Several of his pamphlets carried his name in the title, sometimes claiming to be autobiographical. They follow the Prodigal Son formula, first inviting the reader to enjoy the wicked behavior of the hero and then milking his repentance for all possible emotional value. Later, Greene extended the formula to his "cony-catching pamphlets" describing how cheaters prey upon their victims. A young man newly settled in London might have felt that such works had educational value. Thomas Nashe, a precocious and self-advertising writer, was the sort of young man who gets noticed at university and whose friends expect him to have a brilliant career. On arriving in London, he wrote prefaces to Greene's romance *Menaphon* (1589), and to an unauthorized edition of Sidney's *Astrophil and Stella* (1590), thus positioning himself, in his early twenties, as an arbiter of the literary scene. He also threw in anti-Martinist references, suggesting that he was ready to be employed in this cause, as Greene apparently was.

If Shakespeare was in London early in 1588 he would have known that the most prestigious theatrical events of the year were the court performances by the Children of Paul's, who gave Lyly's *Gallathea* on New Year's day and *Endymion* on 2 February (Candlemas Day). Perhaps he managed to see one of the public "rehearsals." There is no doubt that he read *Gallathea* after it was published in 1592. Its plot requires two girls to dress up as boys, and each falls in love with the other. Their equivocal dialogue –

> *Phyllida.* But, I pray, have you ever a sister?
> *Gallathea.* If I had but one, my brother must needs have two.
>
> (3.2.35–6)

– soon leads them to suspect the truth, but one "boy" asks the other to "let me call thee mistress" (4.4.26–17). These scenes stayed in Shakespeare's mind at least until he wrote *As You Like It* and *Twelfth Night*. The plot of *Endymion* – a shepherd is in love with Cynthia, the chaste goddess of the moon – was obvious praise of the queen, now 55 years old and no longer involved in marriage negotiations. Lyly's treatment was a model of how to combine graceful courtship and delicate hints at larger political issues such as the threat of invasion from Spain and the recent threats from Catholic supporters of Mary Queen of Scots, who had been executed the previous year. Its numerous roles for the very young boy actors, who were presumably cast as pages to contrast with the slightly taller boys who played grown men and women, seem to have delighted female spectators. The play's main comic character is the braggart Sir Tophas, probably played by an adult actor. He is paired with a tiny page whose main role is to puncture his master's absurd pretensions with sarcastic asides and double-edged comments. Boys' companies were favorites with the queen and frequently invited to court performances in the 1580s. Though Shakespeare had worked with boy actors since his schooldays, this may have been the first time that he saw really accomplished children – the children's choirs were after all drawn from a nationwide talent search – who were encouraged to make the most of their youthful good looks and singing talents, and to show off their education by quoting Latin at each other.

In 1590, however, Lyly's company stopped acting, for reasons that are still not clear. It is sometimes thought that they were suppressed because of their involvement in political satire. The anti-Martinist pamphlets, firmly on the side of the church authorities, used the same irreverent language that Martin had used. Authors on both sides also mention the existence of anti-Martinist comedies (or perhaps jigs), though none of these were printed.[32] This was the first time that there had been official sanction for plays on topical issues since the reign of Henry VIII, when Thomas Cromwell subsidized anti-Catholic plays. The Marprelate episode effectively ended in 1592 with the discovery of its secret press, and its printer was hanged the following year. The pamphlets and plays created an appetite for satire that later writers would try to satisfy, but they also revealed a good deal of official uneasiness about the genre. Since an anonymous anti-Martinist writer wished in 1589 that "these comedies might be allowed to be played that are penned,"[33] it seems that Whitgift eventually suppressed plays even by writers on his own side. Perhaps he discovered that the responses of crowds at a public entertainment are hard to predict or control. Shakespeare, watching from the outside, may have been intrigued by what this episode showed about the difficulty of writing to please those in authority.

One other writer of this period, a friend of Greene's, would have had much in common with Shakespeare. Though Thomas Lodge was an Oxford graduate and member of Lincoln's Inn, his father had been a city official (a former lord mayor of London) and, like John Shakespeare, imprisoned for debt, the result, apparently, of financial speculation.[34] Lodge was not involved in the Marprelate affair; he had already been abroad, and would leave England again in 1591. In 1588 he was working on a narrative poem, *Glaucus and Silla*, which he published in 1589. It was apparently the first of the short Ovidian epics, a genre of the 1590s to which Shakespeare would eventually contribute. In 1590 Lodge published the work for which he is now best known, the novel *Rosalynde*, which became the basis for *As You Like It*.

The most famous writer of this period, Christopher Marlowe, stands outside this group. He and Nashe seem to have gone straight from university to London, probably in 1587, and apparently collaborated on a classical tragedy, *Dido, Queen of Carthage*. Nashe may even have been involved with Marlowe's first success for the public theater, *Tamburlaine the Great* (1587): its publisher Richard Jones said in his preface that he was omitting what he considered "fond and frivolous jestures," which might mean either comic subplots or (if "jestures" means *gestus*, the thing done) irrelevant episodes. The play was such a success as to acquire a second part, and in 1589 both parts appeared in print, inspiring a rash of imitations.

Marlowe was not the first to base a play on a vicious, non-Christian foreign ruler: in the 1560s Thomas Preston's *Cambyses* had depicted a Persian king who flayed one courtier alive and murdered many others until he accidentally wounded himself and died. One difference in Marlowe's play was the absence of any obvious divine retribution. Although most other characters are outraged by Tamburlaine's behavior, his career in the two plays is one of unbroken success, both in conquering armies and in winning the love of the beautiful Zenocrate. Part One in fact ends with him in triumph, crowning the woman he loves, defeating her father in battle, and then getting his consent to their marriage. In Part Two he continues to defeat every opponent and, although he is finally defeated by death – first his wife's, then his own – the only moral that emerges is that everyone must die. Because Tamburlaine is not a Christian, he can utter the otherwise unspeakable blasphemies that audiences had once heard from Herod and Pilate in the biblical drama and absorb the inchoate emotions of audiences in the late 1580s toward their many distant enemies. The play's other distinctive aspect is its grandiose language (lines such as Tamburlaine's phrase about the human mind "still climbing after knowledge infinite" can still thrill listeners). Most of Tamburlaine's antagonists share his desire for power; the exceptions are comic cowards, unable or unwilling to speak and act heroically. They may get some sympathy from the audience, but they are killed all the same, even though one of them is Tamburlaine's son. There is no interesting virtuous character to oppose the hero. His beloved Zenocrate sometimes expresses compassion: it is seen as appropriate to a woman but irrelevant to the action. The Prologue to Part Two of *Tamburlaine* refers to "The general welcome Tamburlaine received" meaning the character rather than the play.[35]

If Tamburlaine's violence and atheism made spectators uneasy, this may have been because, for the first time, they were made aware of the difference between what they ought to want as Christians and what they wanted as theatrical experience. The Vice character had dominated the moral interlude, but he was also a spokesman for conventional morality, well aware of his own wickedness; his gloating over it made him funny. In *The Jew of Malta* Marlowe drew on this tradition. His grotesque central character comes to a bad end through his own cleverness, but the fact that the other characters are either corrupt or naive (again, one female character is a carefully gendered exception) allows the audience to enjoy watching Barabas outsmart them. Its brilliantly constructed plot, in which an initial wrong leads to revenge, which leads to further crimes to cover up the initial one, became the model for later revenge tragedies. *Doctor Faustus* lacks this kind of construction, because of the basic simplicity of its narrative. The hero sells his soul to the devil at the beginning; it is claimed at the end. Between these two moments there can be as many intrigues, jokes, and spectacular magic displays as the actors can manage. Thus it is not surprising that the two published versions of the play (1604 and 1616) are so different. Scholars and theater directors try to distinguish "genuine" Marlowe from supposedly inferior comic material by others, but the play's source – a translation of a German biography of the magician first published in 1587 – is itself episodic and often comic. The dominant personalities of Marlowe's plays lent themselves to performance by a star actor – in this case, the tall and powerful Edward Alleyn, who by now was acting for the Admiral's Men. If he created the role of Tamburlaine he would have been only about 21 at the time. The famous lines of the plays were the ones that he spoke, and some of them were obviously meant to be branded on the memory, as when, in Part One, Tamburlaine lets the magic phrase "and ride in triumph through Persepolis" (2.5.50) carry him to attack the man he has just put on the throne of

Persia, or when, in Part Two, he turns the name of the dying Zenocrate into an incantation (2.4.15–37). Alleyn was to be equally famous in *Doctor Faustus* and *The Jew of Malta*, and probably played the Duke de Guise in *The Massacre at Paris*, which dramatized the St. Bartholomew's Day Massacre. Shakespeare could learn from Marlowe that audiences will listen to long speeches if they are spoken by a great actor; in *Doctor Faustus* Marlowe had even undertaken to make a speech seem longer than it was, by having Faustus experience his last hour of life in the presence of the audience, vacillating among horror, rage, faint glimpses of hope, and final despair.

Kyd may have been even better known than Marlowe, if only because he was a Londoner and may have been writing since the formation of the Queen's Men. By the end of the sixteenth century *The Spanish Tragedy* had already been adapted into German and performed by English actors all over Europe. Kyd's only other acknowledged works are translations from the French and Italian. There is no agreement as to the authorship of *Soliman and Perseda*, a full-length version of the play given in condensed form by characters in *The Spanish Tragedy*. My view, which will be relevant to later chapters, is that Kyd did write the Soliman play and that its success resulted in his reuse of it, perhaps parodically, as a play-within-a-play.

In the 1623 Folio, Ben Jonson named Kyd, along with Lyly and Marlowe, as one of the contemporaries whom Shakespeare had surpassed. Curiously, he called him "sportive Kyd." Jonson was not so fond of puns as to choose the worst possible adjective for a tragic dramatist; he and Shakespeare probably knew Kyd also as a comic writer. Despite the bloodiness of *The Spanish Tragedy*, one of its most popular features was the black comedy episode, sometimes referred to as "the play of Pedringano," in which the killer Pedringano, tricked by his aristocratic employer into thinking that he will receive a last-minute pardon, clowns his way to the gallows, while a boy who knows the truth delivers a mocking commentary on his folly.[36] The relationship of boy and braggart (already noted in Lyly's *Endymion*) recurs in *Soliman and Perseda*, another example of Kyd's sportiveness, which contains the funniest braggart soldier role before Shakespeare's Falstaff.

More recently, Kyd has been credited with a number of Queen's Men plays, including the old *King Leir*, on the basis of internal evidence, mostly word groupings and parallel passages.[37] It is more generally agreed that he was the author of a lost Hamlet play. The only evidence for this is Nashe's preface to Greene's *Menaphon* (1589) which, after giving a few sentences of praise to the pastoral romance it was supposedly introducing, spends most of its time satirizing the contemporary literary scene. Unfortunately, Nashe's determination to be witty makes him hard to interpret. One passage in particular has been analyzed in minute detail. It starts as a satire on bad playwrights:

> Mongst this kind of men that repose eternity in the mouth of a player, I can but engross some deep-read grammarians, who, having no more learning in their skull than will serve to take up a commodity, nor Art in their brain than was nourished in a serving

man's idleness, will take upon them to be the ironical censors of all, when God and Poetry doth know they are the simplest of all. . . . It is a common practice nowadays amongst a sort of shifting companions, that run through every Art and thrive by none, to leave the trade of *Noverint*, whereto they were born, and busy themselves with the endeavours of Art, that could scarcely Latinize their neck-verse if they should have need. Yet English Seneca read by candlelight yields many good sentences, as *Blood is a begger*, and so forth; and if you entreat him fair in a frosty morning, he will afford you whole *Hamlets*, I should say handfuls of Tragical speeches. But O grief! *Tempus edax rerum*, what's that will last always? The sea exhaled by drops will in continuance be dry, and Seneca, let blood line by line and page by page, at length must needs die to our Stage; which makes his famished followers to imitate the Kidde [kid] in *Æsop*, who, enamoured with the Fox's newfangles, forsook all hopes of life to leap into a new occupation; and these men, renouncing all possibilities of credit or estimation, to intermeddle with Italian translations . . .[38]

Though Nashe criticizes others who want to be "the ironical Censors of all," that role is the one he adopts here, with pretended slips of the tongue ("*Hamlets*, I should say handfuls") and an ironic pretense of concern: how sad for the hack dramatists that all the Senecan plots and speeches have been used up! His attack is supposedly directed at a whole group of ignorant writers, but the pleasure for its early readers, and the puzzle for everyone else, is how to put names to the descriptions. Could "the Kidde in *Æsop*" be Thomas Kyd, who happened also to be the son of a scrivener and perhaps trained to write legal documents that began with *Noverint* ("let it be known to all")? Is Nashe also implying that Kyd has leaped into a new occupation, probably translating Tasso's prose work, *Padre di Famiglia* (1588) because he has run out of Senecan sources from which to steal his plays – such as, perhaps, one called *Hamlet*? There is other evidence of the existence of such a play. Henslowe's *Diary* records a performance of *Hamlet* on 9 June 1594, and Thomas Lodge in 1596 describes someone "as pale as the Visard of the ghost that cried so miserably at the Theater like an oysterwife, *Hamlet Revenge*."[39] If a single writer is really the target of all this sarcasm, it is possible that Kyd wrote a Hamlet play that was the basis of Shakespeare's. Much of Nashe's attack is of course unfair: Kyd may have been only a grammarian – the product of a grammar school – but that school was the famous Merchant Taylors'. He certainly did not need to read his Seneca in translation and he had a good knowledge of French and Italian as well. Either Nashe was attacking Kyd at random or he was writing about someone else at least part of the time. In either case, he is an unreliable source of information about a Hamlet play. Yet Kyd would be a likely author for such a play, since *Hamlet*, where a son avenges his father, inverts the plot of *The Spanish Tragedy*, where a father avenges his son. If he was not its sole author, the other most likely explanations are that the early *Hamlet* was by Shakespeare himself, or that it was a Kyd–Shakespeare collaboration, heavily revised later on.[40]

The importance of these writers is not simply that Shakespeare must have known them, since the theatrical world was a relatively small one. It is that he probably worked closely with most of them. Many scholars agree that Nashe probably wrote the first act of *1 Henry VI* and that Peele wrote the first act of *Titus Andronicus* and one or more later scenes. After that, despite the extensive recent computer tests of vocabulary and grammar, the authorship of early "Shakespeare" is still uncertain. Gary Taylor attributes *1 Henry VI* to Nashe, Shakespeare, and two unidentified playwrights; Brian Vickers and Marina Tarlinskaya think that one of the latter was Thomas Kyd; MacDonald P. Jackson is more skeptical about Kyd but does not rule him out, as Hugh Craig does; Craig also assigns the Joan la Pucelle scenes of Part One to Marlowe, though no one else has accepted this attribution.[41] Understandably, many biographers have preferred to suspend judgment, meanwhile treating all the plays as one man's unaided work. However, the likelihood of collaboration is so strong – certain, I think, in the cases of *1 Henry VI* and *Titus Andronicus* – that it seems impossible to ignore it. While Shakespeare was working with them, these men were the most important people in his life, just as, when the plays moved into rehearsal, the actors were the people he cared about most. It is frustrating that, for the most part, we know as little about their personalities as we do about his. Nashe, the youngest, gives the impression of trying out poses and wanting to become famous quickly; Peele was perpetually hard up and may, like Greene, have had a reputation for unreliability and procrastination. Marlowe's history included not merely the usual financial irregularities but episodes of violence. An anonymous Cambridge playwright's quick summing up, perhaps on the basis of personal acquaintance – "Wit lent from heaven, but vices sent from hell" (*The Second Part of the Return from Parnassus*, 1.2.286–9) – shows that he retained his reputation nearly ten years after his death. About Kyd's personality we know nothing except that later, after describing Marlowe as "intemperate and of a cruel heart," he claimed that even his worst enemies could never accuse him of either quality.[42] No one has found a criminal record for him, which suggests that he was at least law-abiding. All the best-known writers of the period can be said to have ended tragically except Lodge, who had stopped writing plays by the end of the century and retrained as a physician.

Eric Sams thinks that the other playwrights would have condescended to Shakespeare and that there were "clear lines for battle: Wits versus Grammarians."[43] Shakespeare and Kyd might have roomed together in the early years, he argues, presumably to protect each other from the sneers of the Wits. The only actual evidence of shared rooms (which would become very important in 1593) was that Kyd and Marlowe worked in the same space in 1591. Too much, however, can be made of the difference between the two groups. Of the Wits, only Peele was a Londoner. Marlowe was from Canterbury; Greene and Nashe were both from East Anglia and may have had stronger regional accents than Shakespeare's. In any case, according to linguistic historian Jonathan Hope, his culture "did not stigmatize regional varieties of English."[44] The university degree automatically conferred the rank of gentleman, but Kyd, as the son of a gentleman, had that status anyway, and Shakespeare could claim gentle status on the basis of his father's civic function. All these writers, including Shakespeare, could be accused of showing off their knowledge of foreign languages. Marlowe's *Tragedy of Dido Queen of Carthage* breaks into Latin at its two most moving moments (5.1.136–40 and 5.1.310–13), as if to acknowledge that Virgil's words cannot be improved upon. Peele's *The Arraignment of Paris* includes songs in Latin and Italian. Even in his *Edward I*, written for the public theater, two characters, in a moment of high emotion, quote Ariosto's *Orlando Furioso* in Italian. In *The Spanish Tragedy,* characters speak at length in Latin, and perhaps – no one is sure about this – the play at the end was meant to be given in four different languages. That play's supposed author, Hieronimo, says that when he was at the university he wrote a tragedy that was intended "to have been acted/ By gentlemen and scholars too,/ Such as could tell what to speak." The prince Lorenzo answers, "And now it shall be play'd by princes and courtiers,/ Such as can tell how to speak" (4.1.101–5).[45] The irony is that the actors speaking these lines were professionals, not princes and courtiers. The exchange draws attention to the ability of good actors to impersonate both the most educated and the most aristocratic of performers. In this status-obsessed world, what was being shown off was not so much the author's knowledge of foreign languages as the actor's ability to remember and speak them correctly.

Art and Scope and Shakespeare

According to Henslowe's *Diary*, "*Harey the VI*" was acted by Lord Strange's Men between February 1592 and late June, the time of plague closure. It was evidently a popular play, and it is usually assumed that it was one of Shakespeare's history plays (probably the one now called Part One, since it is given no number). It seems likely, then, that he was acting with Strange's Men at the time. When the theaters reopened on 29 December 1592 the same repertory was revived, with new additions, and played until 1 February 1593. It included *The Jew of Malta* and *Jeronimo* (probably *The Spanish Tragedy*). Shakespeare could, then, have acted in what were, judging from Henslowe's receipts, two of the three most popular plays of the 1590s. (The third was *The Wise Man of Westchester*, which is either a now lost play by an unknown author or an alternative title for Anthony Munday's disguise play, *John a Kent and John a Cumber*. It is important to remember how partial and arbitrary our knowledge of this period is.) As an actor, he would have been given only his own lines and cues, intuiting from these – and perhaps from conversations with the author – what kind of part he was to play. This is why the dramatists who influenced him most were his elder contemporaries in the 1590s, whose cadences became part of his own internal rhythms. The spectators watching their plays may not have cared who had written them; Shakespeare, hoping to rival the authors, would certainly have wanted to know.

80

Many plays of the period, especially the tragedies, sound very much alike after four centuries, since individual voices are less obvious than the requirements of the high style. Everyone had read the same texts at school and had imitated and copied the same Latin authors. It seemed natural to do the same with English authors. The first three books of *The Faerie Queene* were published in 1590 but had been circulating in manuscript before then. Marlowe adapted part of a stanza from Book I in the second part of *Tamburlaine* (4.3.119–24), retaining a version of the final alexandrine as if to acknowledge his source – or, as Roma Gill suggests, to show that Tamburlaine is quoting.[46] The borrowings could even have been a concerted publicity campaign for Spenser, who was known to be eager for promotion. After *Tamburlaine* the theaters were full of plays about barbarous rulers in exotic places. In Greene's *Alphonsus King of Aragon* (1587–8, published 1599), a Turk reminds his followers that they are facing foes vastly inferior to "mighty Tamburlaine," and, whereas Tamburlaine famously enters in a chariot drawn by four kings, Alphonsus enters under a canopy with the heads of conquered kings hanging over each corner. In *Selimus* (probably at least partly by Greene), one character claims descent from Bajazet, who was caged by Tamburlaine, another from Usum-Casane, Tamburlaine's companion.[47]

Sometimes writers sound alike because a stock situation produces a stock verbal response. A gracious if reluctant abdication occurs in *Selimus*, where the emperor tells his son that he

> Resigns the crown as willingly to thee
> As ere my father gave it unto me
> (1659–60)

In *2 Henry VI* Humphrey of Gloucester delivers up his Protector's staff of office to Henry VI with the words:

> As willingly do I the same resign
> As ere thy father Henry made it mine
> (2.3.33–4)

Though both couplets say the same thing, neither author was stealing the other's words or rhymes. Such repetition occurs most often in formulaic epic contexts, such as descriptions of battles.

Emrys Jones's *Scenic Form in Shakespeare* has shown that Shakespeare remembered not only the words of other plays but their visual effects, including those that gave shape to a scene through a pattern of entrances and exits. A striking line often coincided with a striking stage picture for a star actor. Entrances were particularly famous: Hieronimo with a torch,[48] Tamburlaine in a chariot drawn by four kings. The visual effect was linked with the lines that accompanied it, whether Hieronimo's

"What outcries pluck me from my naked bed?" (2.5.1) or Tamburlaine's "Holla, ye pampered jades of Asia!" (*2 Tamburlaine* 4.3.1). The entrance of Muly Mahomet in Peele's *Battle of Alcazar* is equally unforgettable. His wife Calipolis is fainting with hunger in their desert exile; he goes offstage vowing to find food for her and comes back with a chunk of bleeding raw flesh on his dagger:

> *Moor.* Hold thee, Calipolis, feed and faint no more.
> This flesh I forcèd from a lioness –
> Meat of a princess, for a princess meet.

Calipolis understandably finds this meat revolting, however "meet" it may be for her, but he insists:

> ... Feed and be fat that we may meet the foe
> With strength and terror to revenge our wrong.

Like Tamburlaine's entrance line, this one would be parodied later by Shakespeare's most stage-struck character, Ancient Pistol.

What Shakespeare remembered about Kyd was not only his memorable, heavily patterned, lines ("O eyes, no eyes, but fountains fraught with tears," etc.) but his use of stage space and significant props, like the bloodstained handkerchief that Hieronimo carries with him until the end of the play. A crucial scene early in *The Spanish Tragedy* juxtaposes the formal but sensual love-making of two characters with the angry comments of two eavesdroppers, an effect that Shakespeare used in the very different eavesdropping scenes of *Twelfth Night* and *Troilus and Cressida*. Kyd also demonstrated the principle of parallels and contrasts in following Hieronimo's mad scenes with those of his wife Isabella. Like Hieronimo, she runs in and out, and returns carrying either real or imaginary herbs:

> So that you say this herb will purge the eye,
> And this the head?
> Ah, but none of them will purge the heart.
> (3.8.1–3)

In her final appearance she is mad with grief, hallucinates a vision of her son's angry ghost, and stabs herself. Kyd may have influenced, or been influenced by, a scene in the first part of *Tamburlaine*: Bajazet's wife Zabina, before killing herself, has a brief but harrowing prose speech in which she tells imaginary servants to "Make ready my coach, my chair, my jewels" (5.1.316–17). Shakespeare's most famous madwoman, Ophelia, would echo both of these characters.

Although a number of biographers think that Shakespeare's most life-changing experience was a performance of *Tamburlaine*,[49] the scene that affected him most, to

judge by its influence on his later work, was *The Jew of Malta* 2.1. It begins in
darkness, indicated both by the fact that Barabas enters carrying a lantern and by his
somber tone:

> Thus like the sad presaging raven, that tolls
> The sick man's passport in her hollow beak,
> And in the shadow of the silent night
> Doth shake contagion from her sable wings,
> Vexed and tormented runs poor Barabas
> With fatal curses towards these Christians ...
>
> (2.1.1–6)

Into this darkness, suddenly, comes a voice from a window above, that of the
boy actor playing his daughter Abigail. Not hearing or seeing each other, father
and daughter continue with parallel soliloquies. At last they catch sight of each
other. and she throws down the bags of money that he had hidden in the house.
Ecstatic, he cries,

> O my girl,
> My gold, my fortune, my felicity,
> Strength to my soul, death to mine enemy! ...
> O girl, O gold, O beauty, O my bliss!
>
> (47–9, 54)

The comedy depends on rapid switches from fatherly love to love of money, until
it is not clear which is which: the stage direction to line 54 says that he "*Hugs his bags*"
and then tells Abigail that he wishes he had her there too. This extraordinary mixture
of tones is like nothing else in the play, which rapidly escalates into a series of complex
and entertaining intrigues.

While both the language and content of this scene were echoed later in *The
Merchant of Venice*, they were not all that caught Shakespeare's imagination. It was
probably not until he came to London that he could see and hear the effect created by
placing one actor on the upper stage and the other below. Perhaps it impressed him
too much: Park Honan comments that in the Henry VI plays "the device of having
actors speak aloft from galleries seems artificially over-used."[50] There must have
been something exceptionally beautiful about the high-pitched voice of the boy,
when heard from that angle. When Romeo hears Juliet calling him back from above,
he cries, "How silver-sweet sound lovers' tongues by night,/ Like softest music to
attending ears!" (2.2.166–7). Portia in *The Merchant of Venice*, equally sensitive,
notices how much more beautiful the music from her house (presumably the tiring
house gallery) sounds by night. Musical effects in this period are often created by
positioning instruments and singers in different parts of a venue, so that they are heard

but not seen. Shakespeare's later reworkings of Marlowe's scene show how strongly he was influenced by its visual and verbal rhythm, as well as by its conflation of love and wealth, always a crucial theme in his work.

Perhaps no one can remain a dramatist without a high degree of tolerance, even liking, for the contingent – the influence of factors that have nothing to do with personal feelings about what one is writing. Shakespeare, who seems to have preferred to work from a source and was willing to write parts for particular actors and incorporate allusions to topical events, probably did not object to writing in collaboration either. Moss Hart, who wrote six plays with actor-playwright George Kaufman, quoted the view that "collaboration is like a marriage,"[51] and Shakespeare's relationships with his literary partners must have been as important to him as the one with his wife. There may have been friction, there may have been snobbery. But he probably discovered that a playwright who was also an actor had advantages that outweighed the greater "art" of the university-educated dramatists, and the greater "scope" of those who had access to court costumes and city properties.

Notes

1. *Shakespeare's Sonnets*, ed. Duncan-Jones, 168.
2. *Shakespeare's Sonnets*, ed. Booth, 180.
3. Palmer, "Playing in the Provinces," 90.
4. Leggatt, "Shakespeare and Bearbaiting," and Skura, *Shakespeare the Actor*, 203–10.
5. From *Essays and Characters, Ironical and Instructive*, quoted in Wickham, 180.
6. Letter of the Corporation of London to the Privy Council *c.*1584, in Chambers and Greg, eds., "Dramatic Records from the Lansdowne MSS," 172.
7. Preface to Beaumont and Fletcher, *Comedies and Tragedies*.
8. Chambers, *ES*, 1: 224–5.
9. Hausted, *The Rival Friends*, B2^v.
10. *Calendar of State Papers Spanish, 1558–1567*, 367, quoted in Steele, *Plays and Masques at Court*, 16.
11. Pettie, trans., *The Ciuile Conuersation of M. Stephen Guazzo*, 12, 114, 159, 165.
12. John Fisher, introduction to Prockter and Taylor, *The A to Z of Elizabethan London*, x.
13. Huntington Library: C. W. Wallace papers, Box 4, File II.20A, PRO 146/369: Lay Subsidies, 146/369.
14. Yungblut, *Strangers Settled Here Amongst Us*, 25–9.
15. Nicholl, *The Reckoning*, 38.
16. Donaldson, "Jonson, Ben," *ODNB*.
17. Streitberger, "Personnel and Professionalization," 339.
18. Benbow, "Dutton and Goffe versus Broughton." Interestingly, the kinds of work Broughton was expected to write are listed as "history, comedy, or tragedy" (p. 8), the same categories into which Shakespeare's colleagues divided his works in the 1623 Folio.
19. Ingram, "Laurence Dutton, Stage Player," 123. For the Duttons, see also Richard Dutton, "Shakespearean Origins."

20. See Cerasano, "Philip Henslowe and the Elizabethan Court."
21. *Henslowe's Diary*, xxv.
22. Meres, *Palladis Tamia: Wits Treasury*.
23. Newcomb, *Reading Popular Romance in Early Modern England*, 54.
24. Jonson, *Poetaster*, ed. Cain, 9.
25. Taylor, "Lives and Afterlives," in Middleton, *Collected Works*, ed. Taylor and Lavagnino, 47.
26. The most famous expression of the latter view is the poem "Farewell to Love," attributed to Donne.
27. See Greg, *A Bibliography of the English Printed Drama to the Restoration*, 1: 88–9.
28. *Plays written by the thrice noble, illustrious and excellent princess, the Lady Marchioness of Newcastle*, A5^v.
29. Commendatory verses to *Poems* (1640), repr. in Chambers, *WS*, 2: 232.
30. M. Shapiro, *Children of the Revels*, 12.
31. Gager, *Complete Works*, ed. Sutton, 1: 242.
32. Chambers, *ES*, 2: 229–33, prints extracts from pamphlets on both sides.
33. *Pappe with an Hatchet* (1589), quoted from R. W. Bond's edition of Lyly (3: 408) in Chambers, *ES*, 2: 232.
34. Sisson et al., *Thomas Lodge and Other Elizabethans*, 17–19.
35. Marlowe is quoted from *Doctor Faustus and Other Plays*, ed. Bevington and Rasmussen.
36. See the appendix on "Hieronimo's Afterlife" in *The Spanish Tragedie*, ed. Smith, 133–59.
37. For arguments pro and con, see Vickers, "Thomas Kyd, Secret Sharer," and Jackson, "New Research on the Dramatic Canon of Thomas Kyd."
38. Preface to Robert Greene, *Menaphon*, in Chambers, *ES*, 2: 235.
39. Lodge, *Wit's Miserie*, H4^v.
40. Sams, *The Real Shakespeare*.
41. Taylor, "Shakespeare and Others: The Authorship of *Henry the Sixth, Part One*"; Vickers, *Shakespeare, Co-Author*; Jackson, "New Research on the Dramatic Canon of Thomas Kyd," 126–7; Craig, "The Three Parts of *Henry VI*," in Craig and Kinney, eds., *Shakespeare, Computers, and the Mystery of Authorship*, 59–77.
42. The phrase comes from Kyd's letter to the Lord Keeper Puckering in 1593, printed in full in Freeman, *Thomas Kyd: Facts and Problems*, 181.
43. Sams, *The Real Shakespeare*, 60. Cf. Greenblatt, *Will in the World*, 200.
44. Hope, *Shakespeare and Language*, 99.
45. Kyd, *The Spanish Tragedy*, ed. Edwards.
46. Gill, "Christopher Marlowe," 453.
47. *Selimus*, ed. Bang, lines 1753–8, 2344–6.
48. For the echoing of this visual effect in *Othello* see Hattaway, *Elizabethan Popular Theatre*, 122.
49. See e.g. Greenblatt, *Will in the World*, 189.
50. Honan, 143.
51. M. Hart, *Act One*, 274, quoted in *The Two Noble Kinsmen*, ed. Potter, 18.

5

"Tigers' Hearts"

1592–1593

York. Oh, tiger's heart wrapped in a woman's hide!

(*3 Henry VI* 1.4.137)

Yes, trust them not: for there is an upstart crow, beautified with our feathers, that with his tiger's heart wrapped in a player's hide, supposes he is as well able to bombast out a blank verse as the best of you: and being an absolute Iohannes fac totum, is in his own conceit the only Shake-scene in a country.

(*Greene's Groatsworth of Wit*)

Greene's Groatsworth of Wit (1592) is an important document, both because it provides a limiting date for the first plays with which Shakespeare is known to have been involved and because it shows that he was already creating stage moments that could be remembered and parodied. Unlike the great entrance lines of Hieronimo, Tamburlaine, and Muly Mahomet, York's words are not accompanied by action; in fact, he is virtually immobile, captured and surrounded by enemies. Queen Margaret has just taunted him in a speech of forty-two lines, a mixture of sarcasm, mockery, and unholy joy that horrifies even her own followers. York remains silent while she insults him, tantalizes him with the question "where is your darling Rutland?," shows him a cloth soaked in the child's blood, and invites him to react. His silence provokes her to mock him further by placing a paper crown on his head. On the page, the speech that he makes in reply may seem too long (fifty-five lines, followed by another nineteen after Northumberland's brief exclamation of pity). But in the theater one does not know from the beginning how long a speech will be, and spectators who have watched a character endure so much must passionately want to hear him speak. In *Richard III* the scene, with its movement

The Life of William Shakespeare: A Critical Biography, First Edition. Lois Potter.
© 2012 Lois Potter. Published 2012 by Blackwell Publishing Ltd.

from contempt to rage to grief, is recalled again by characters who were not present but who have heard that even York's enemies wept.

The reason why York compares Margaret of Anjou to the exotic tiger, as well as to a "she-wolf of France," is that he is echoing Dido's famous reproach to Aeneas (*Aeneid* 4.365–7), which Marlowe had translated:

> Thy mother was no goddess, perjured man,
> Nor Dardanus the author of thy stock,
> But thou art sprung from Scythian Caucasus,
> And tigers from Hyrcania gave thee suck.
> (*Dido Queen of Carthage* 5.1.156–9)

Tigers belong to the world of the Henry VI plays and *Titus Andronicus*, the harshest world that Shakespeare would depict until *King Lear*, where Goneril and Regan are called "Tigers, not daughters" (4.2.41). What makes these worlds so horrible is that it is women who behave like tigers.

If what is now called *3 Henry VI* was well enough known to parody in 1592, then both the second and third parts of the play must have been in existence by then. They may, however, have looked very different. Both were published with titles meant to identify them to those who had seen them in the theater. *The First Part of the Contention of the Two Famous Houses of York and Lancaster* was licensed on 12 March 1594, with no indication of who had acted it. The second play was published, unlicensed, in 1595 as *The True Tragedy of Richard Duke of York and the Death of Good King Henry the Sixth*, attributing it to the Earl of Pembroke's Men. The play that is now known as Part One of the sequence was published, apparently for the first time, in the Folio of 1623.

That *Greene's Groatsworth* quotes a line from the *True Tragedy* and also mentions a player who writes would seem to make this a clear allusion to the actor-dramatist to whom the play was attributed in the 1623 Folio of Shakespeare's works. In context, the passage demonstrates a distrust of actors in general as much as of the one particular actor who wrote or spoke the "tiger's heart" line. It reflects the tensions of that brief plague-free period when actors were again able to make good money by playing long seasons in London and writers envied their prosperity. The pamphlet seems to see the "Shake-Scene" as a *new* threat, even though Shakespeare must already have written at least two ambitious plays. This may mean that the *Contention* and *True Tragedy* had already been performed in the country, but only recently in London. The 1594 publication may have been unattributed because the play originally belonged to Lord Strange's Men, who had probably disbanded by the fall of that year. Shakespeare may have progressed from a touring company (perhaps 1587 to 1589) to Strange's Men (1589–93) and then Pembroke's (1593–4). He may have initiated the transfer or – since good playwrights have always been in much shorter supply than good actors – he may have been recruited.

The Early Quartos: Competing Theories

The relation of *The First Part of the Contention* and *The True Tragedy* to the plays that were published in the 1623 Folio as the second and third parts of *Henry VI* is confusing. They contain some passages that must be shortened or garbled versions of an already existing play. The best-known example, first pointed out in 1929, is the speech in which the Duke of York sets out his claim to the crown.[1] In *The First Part of the Contention,* York claims that he is a direct descendant of Edward III's third son, while Henry VI is descended only from the fourth son. If that had been true, the justice of his claim would have been obvious and there would have been no Wars of the Roses. The longer account in the Folio (*2 Henry VI* 2.2.10–52) shows, accurately, that his claim was much more tortuous. His grandfather on the mother's side was *fifth* son to Edward III, but he claims the throne through his grandmother, the *daughter* of Edward's *third* son. No one would have deliberately written an inaccurate summary of this important topic, since the spectators that the company most wanted to please were the ones most likely to know these facts. So York's original speech must have been inaccurately recorded, either in a shorthand transcript or in a text put together on the basis of the parts and memories of one or more actors. Ironically, the actor in the best position to do this would have been the one playing the Earl of Warwick, who obviously did not understand the lines to which he had replied, "What plain proceedings can be more plain?" This is understandable, since he probably never saw the text of York's speech; his part would have contained only his own lines and brief cues. If this account is right, it must also be clear that, whatever part Shakespeare took in this play, it wasn't Warwick. Perhaps, then, as Roger Warren suggests, Q is an inaccurate version, and F a revised version, of the original script.[2]

If *The Contention* and *The True Tragedy* were originally written for performance by a touring company in the Midlands, they might have needed rewriting as Shakespeare moved from one company to another. Playwrights obviously had to be careful (as Shakespeare would find out a few years later) in their depiction of families whose descendants were still living. Strange's Men needed to be tactful about their patron's ancestors. Warwick's role as kingmaker is crucial to the plays: he was an ancestor of Lord Strange and the current Earl of Warwick was the brother of the Earl of Leicester, so there was every reason to praise him. Stanley's mother, the Countess of Derby, had been accused of treasonable activity similar to that of the Duchess of Gloucester in *2 Henry VI.*[3] The Sir John Stanley who escorts the duchess into exile and the Lord Stanley whose two-faced dealings helped win the Battle of Bosworth for the future Henry VII were also among his ancestors, as was the "butcher" Clifford of Cumberland, who murders York's young son because York killed his father in battle. In his account of those who have died in the Civil War – a speech that is the same in the *True Tragedy* and *3 Henry VI* – Edward IV draws attention to the number of characters with the same title, something that audiences often find confusing:

> Three Dukes of Somerset, threefold renowned
> For hardy and undoubted champions;
> Two Cliffords, as the father and the son;
> And two Northumberlands . . .
>
> (5.7.5–8)

The father of the first of these "two Northumberlands" was the Hotspur of *1 Henry IV* and one of his descendants would support the Earl of Essex at the end of Elizabeth's reign. Northumberland was only one of a number of members of the Percy family whose names could hardly be avoided in the history plays. Since there were no living dukes of Gloucester, the future Richard III could make a point about the bad luck which (as Holinshed noted) seemed to go with the title:

> *Richard.* Let me be Duke of Clarence, George of Gloucester;
>   For Gloucester's dukedom is too ominous.
> *Warwick.* Tut, that's a foolish observation.
>   Richard, be Duke of Gloucester.
>
> (*3 Henry VI* 2.6.106–9)

The plays are almost comically full of praise for "brave Oxford, wondrous well-beloved/ In Oxfordshire," "sweet Oxford," and "valiant Oxford" (*3 Henry VI* 4.8.17, 4.8.30, and 5.1.1). An Earl of Oxford also helps (unhistorically) to escort the young Earl of Richmond out of England (*3 Henry VI* 4.6.96), thus preserving the life of the first Tudor king. Since Oxford was a patron of players, and holder of the oldest earldom in the kingdom, playwrights evidently felt that it was safe – and flattering – to assume that his ancestors had played a major role in every reign.

Other differences between Q and F may have arisen from casting changes. When (in *2 Henry VI* 1.4) York and Buckingham capture the conjuror and witch who have just answered the Duchess of Gloucester's questions about the kingdom's future, they also capture the paper on which the questions and answers are written. In Q, Buckingham takes these to the king, who reads them aloud in the presence of his court. In F, York himself reads them, with acerbic comments. Both versions are dramatically effective and either could be claimed as an improvement on the other. Q has the advantage of separating the two readings, allowing the characters most affected to respond in characteristic ways. In F, York is a more dominant figure. Demonstrating a surprising scholarly bent (but one consistent with his unhistorical residence at an Inn of Court in Part One), he notes that one of the prophecies is only an English version of a Latin one that he already knows, presumably from its use in Cicero's *De Divinatione*.[4]

That it was a line from York's final speech that Greene/Chettle thought memorable enough to quote must say something about the performance of the actor who played this role. Chettle may have been lying when he said in *Kind-Heart's Dream* that he had only recently had a chance to see Shakespeare acting. What if the author of the "tiger's heart" speech was also its actor? This would explain why the pamphlet chose one of his lines rather than Margaret's to epitomize the upstart crow. That Shakespeare should have played such a major scene might seem to contradict the usual view that he was much better known as a playwright than as an actor, but the play is full of major roles, and York's, though impressive, ends with the first act.

History and the Henry VI Plays

For a sixteenth-century reader, English history was still an exciting topic. It was not taught in schools, and the Reformation had encouraged a suspicion of traditional histories by "monkish" chroniclers. A massive project, begun under Henry VIII, had produced a number of revisionist histories, but one reason why most early historical plays are so unhistorical is that their authors did not have access to reliable source material; perhaps they also preferred to draw mainly on folk tradition and anecdote to avoid getting themselves into trouble. Anyone who went to see Greene's *History of James IV of Scotland* expecting to learn about his death at the Battle of Flodden would have been startled to find that the confrontation between England and Scotland was caused by the king's attempt to murder his wife and marry another woman, and that it ended, without a battle, through the couple's happy reunion. The anonymous *Fair Em* purports to be about William the Conqueror but confines itself to his imaginary love life. *The Famous Victories of Henry V* draws on widely accepted notions about the king's wild youth, and his military successes in France are interspersed with numerous scenes of clowning.

The "harey the vi" play at the Rose in 1592 was quite different. Edward Hall's history, *The Union of the Two Noble and Illustre Families of Lancaster and York* (1548), provided the basic design. As Hall shaped events, the deposition of Richard II and the later rebellion of Richard Duke of York led to a period of devastating civil war, but the defeat of the monstrous Richard III and the marriage of the heirs of the two enemy houses resulted in the unquestioned legitimacy of the Tudors and the peace that audience and actors could unite in celebrating. Hall dedicated the first edition to Henry VIII, son of that marriage, making the point explicitly: "for as King Henry the Fourth was the beginning and root of the great discord and division, so was the godly matrimony, the final end of all dissensions, titles, and debates" (p. vii). Richmond's final speech in *Richard III* (first published 1597) echoes his moral:

> Oh, now let Richmond and Elizabeth,
> The true succeeders of each royal house,
> By God's fair ordinance conjoin together!
> (5.5.30–2)

The advantage of Hall's structure was that it allowed dramatists to merge historical material with the romantic plots that their audiences expected and loved. Whether the dissension in question was that of two families, two countries, or two sexes, marriage was offered as the harmonizing of discords, and audiences can still be counted on to want every marriageable couple, however apparently unsuited, to be united by the end of a play.

1 Henry VI

Because Part One, a Folio-only play, appeared so much later than the other two Henry VI plays, there has been considerable argument about the order in which they were written. Still more than Parts Two and Three, Part One looks like a collaboration. Not only does the versification differ from one scene to another – something that is not very noticeable in the theater – but there are obvious inconsistencies in the time-scheme, and the wicked churchman, usually known simply as Winchester, is called both a bishop and a cardinal (perhaps references to bishops were being removed in the light of Marprelate's attacks on them). The view at the time of writing is that Shakespeare was responsible for only a small part of this play – perhaps only 2.4, the plucking of red and white roses in the Temple Garden, and some of the Talbot scenes in Act 4. I agree with those scholars who think that Part One in its present form was either written as a prequel to the other two or adapted from an existing play to become a prequel.[5] Shakespeare's revisions were extensive enough for John Heminges, who had acted with Strange's Men and must have known the early history of the plays, to consider all three eligible for inclusion in the Folio of 1623.

Nashe has been considered a possible co-author for some time, because of a passage in *Pierce Penniless* (1592): "How would it haue joyed brave *Talbot* (the terror of the French) to think that after he had lain two hundred years in his tomb he should triumph again on the stage, and have his bones new embalmed with the tears of ten thousand spectators at least (at seueral times) who, in the Tragedian that represents his person, imagine they behold him fresh bleeding!"[6] Nashe was not incapable of praising works by other people, but recent attribution studies seem to confirm the suspicion that this enthusiasm is a typical example of self-promotion.[7] Nashe's emphasis on the role of Sir John Talbot may mean that the play was initially focused on the wars in France, where the heroic soldier, victim of his country's quarreling nobility, is forced to encounter the French without the promised reinforcements and not only dies himself but witnesses the death of his son. The French, utterly without dignity or shame, are led by Joan la Pucelle, better known to history as Joan of Arc. By the end Joan is revealed as a witch and, threatened with death, disgraces herself by pleading pregnancy and claiming one after another of the French lords as the father of her unborn child, before being dragged off to the stake. This story of events in France is skillfully interwoven with the intrigues in England, where Humphrey of Gloucester, the brother of the dead king Henry V, squabbles with his uncle, the

Bishop of Winchester, while the animosity between York, Regent of France, and his rival Somerset results in their failure to send reinforcements to Talbot. A truce is finally signed with the French and there is some attempt to make the ending look like an English victory, though the French are already planning to break the treaty when the time is right.

This clear and self-contained plot may be that of the play that Nashe and others originally wrote, building the story around a single dominant protagonist and offering plenty of spectacle. A Marlowe–Nashe collaboration is possible, since the two men apparently collaborated on *Dido Queen of Carthage*, but Nashe, according to the *Groatsworth*, also worked with Greene. Kyd's hand has also been suggested. The play begins with the funeral of Henry V, includes the coronation of Henry VI in France, and may have ended, in the original version, as the Dauphin and his nobles pledged their allegiance to the crown of England. A taste for the grotesque – perhaps Nashe's – is often in evidence. In the opening lines the Duke of Bedford, shouting in despair at the sky, tells the comets to turn their "crystal tresses" into scourges with which to whip the stars that allowed the death of Henry V (1.1.2–5). Another speaker reacts to the sight of the dead Talbot by telling the French, "Oh, were mine eyeballs into bullets turned,/ That I in rage might shoot them at your faces!" (4.7.79–80). From the start there is a tension between the oratorical and the plain style, between ceremony and its interruption (usually, as in the opening scene, by bad news).

Other scenes, however, point forward to the story that will continue into the next two plays, one with which Talbot has nothing to do. They may have been part of the play as first written, or they might belong to the revision stage. Perhaps because Shakespeare had friends at the Inns of Court, York and Somerset make their first appearance in the Temple Garden, a setting that would have been familiar to much of the London audience. The scene includes two other characters who will be important in Part Two, the Earls of Suffolk and Warwick. As with other "prequels," the scene depends on our knowledge of what these characters will do later in the story. Each has an opening speech that establishes his nature. Warwick describes himself as a bluff, energetic type, uninterested in the fine points of legal issues, while Suffolk, in a callous joke, says that, instead of framing his will to the law, he prefers "to frame the law unto my will" (2.4.9). York (as he will soon be called) shows the sarcastic humor that is usually the marker of a villain, a trait that is intensified in his son Richard. Though the red and white roses were historically the badges of Lancaster and York, it was Shakespeare's idea to make them visible as fresh flowers in a garden. When, in the next scene, York visits his dying uncle Mortimer and resolves to take up his claim to the throne against the house of Lancaster, he is less humorous and intelligent than in the garden scene – perhaps an indication that a different playwright is now depicting a more conventional avenger, though lines may have been inserted to recall the previous scene.

The French and English plots come together in a battle scene. York captures La Pucelle, effectively ending the French military threat, but the Earl of Suffolk captures Margaret of Anjou and decides to persuade the young Henry VI to marry her so that he himself can make her his mistress. Their wooing scene – patterned, like most of the male–female dialogues in this sequence – plays wittily with the convention of unheard asides by letting the characters hear and comment on each other. First, Suffolk, despite his attraction to Margaret, conducts a debate with himself about how to achieve his desires; when he finally turns to her, she reciprocates by soliloquizing aloud instead of answering him. The final scene is a quiet one, quite unlike the bitter confrontation between the French and English that ends in the forced truce of 5.4. Thanks to Suffolk's persuasions, Henry makes the first of many bad decisions by agreeing to marry Margaret. In the play's final moments Suffolk, left alone, announces what will be – until it slips from his control – the action of much of Part Two:

> Margaret shall now be Queen and rule the King,
> But I will rule both her, the King, and realm.
> (5.5.107–8)

If these episodes are not by Shakespeare, they are certainly by someone who, like Shakespeare, was envisaging a continuation of the story. They place an unusual emphasis on human relationships, something from which the French characters are deliberately isolated. (Joan la Pucelle contemptuously refuses to acknowledge her old peasant father.) Admittedly, the Talbot play includes one episode that could be called romantic. The Countess of Auvergne invites Talbot to her castle with a view to taking him prisoner, but he foresees her intention and brings his soldiers out of hiding to turn the tables on her, while never failing to treat her with courtesy. The consistent treatment of female characters (all of them dangerous) could be seen as the result of single authorship, but it probably results from several writers' consistent belief in French, and female, inconstancy.

Some of the excitement of the play had to do with the smallness of the space in which it was staged. In 1587 the Rose was a fourteen-sided polygon, with a stage of $36'\,9''$ at its widest point, tapering to about $26'\,10''$ as it projected into the yard.[8] In 1592 Henslowe made substantial changes and improvements to this theater, raising and extending the stage area, and it is possible that his intention was to enable more effective presentation of battle scenes. Both *Tamburlaine* and the Henry VI plays were filled with action.

2 and 3 Henry VI

If Lodge had not already used the title for a play about Roman history, the second and third parts of *Henry VI* might have been called *The Wounds of Civil War* or, as they were in a Restoration adaption, *The Miseries of Civil War*.[9] Unlike Part One, they focus entirely on England and on the Wars of the Roses. Though they seem to require the elaborate staging of a purpose-built London theater, they may have begun as touring productions, and they sometimes give the impression of being aimed mainly at spectators in the Midlands and the south of England. The Earl of Warwick in particular often embodies local pride, leading the "southern power/ Of Essex, Norfolk, Sussex [and] Kent" (*3 Henry VI* 1.1.155–6). Some of the ardent praise for specific regions of England is put into the mouths of characters who are about to impress the men of those regions into their armies. York plans to raise troops among "the Kentishmen":

> In them I trust, for they are soldiers,
> Witty, courteous, liberal, full of spirit
> (1.2.42–3)

and Warwick, seeking supporters for Henry VI's cause, declares,

> In Warwickshire, I have true-hearted friends,
> Not mutinous in peace, yet bold in war,
> Those will I muster up.
> (4.8.9–11)

Other noblemen set off for other regions, with the same intention, and they all promise to meet at Coventry, a theatrical hub that was certain to be part of any tour Shakespeare's company made. The scene in which Warwick appears on (supposedly) the city's walls indicates detailed knowledge of the area. It also introduces a messenger who, surprisingly, is given a name. In the Folio it is Somerville, and it was John Somerville's wild bragging of his plan to murder the queen that had led to the Park Hall arrests and executions in 1583.[10] There is something tantalizing in the juxtaposition of his name with Warwick's confidence in the loyalty of Warwickshire people. On the other hand, the Quarto gives the character's name as Sommerfield. Perhaps the name was altered for safety's sake before publication; perhaps, also, the apparent connection is only a coincidence.

The Henry VI plays show the difficulty of making a coherent story out of material that has no single character on whom to focus. The title page of *The Contention* names five major characters: Humphrey of Gloucester, the Duke of Suffolk, the Bishop/ Cardinal of Winchester, Jack Cade, and the Duke of York – and this leaves out both Richard of Gloucester and the Earl of Warwick.[11] The good Duke Humphrey was well known because of his tomb in St. Paul's – those who had no money to dine and spent their dinner hour walking there were said to "dine with Duke Humphrey." He is brought to life in Part Two as the virtuous if hot-tempered Protector of England. The hostility between him and his uncle, Winchester, already sketched in Part One, is central in the first half of this play. Horrified at the treaty giving away many of Henry V's conquests in exchange for a French bride, Margaret of Anjou,

Humphrey tries in vain to contain her malice, the growing factions among the nobles, and the plots against his own rule. What finally destroys him is the ambition of his wife. He fights off her urgings that he reach out and grasp the vision of "King Henry's diadem" that, like Macbeth's dagger, seems to dangle just before him. Like Joan la Pucelle, she resorts to witchcraft, but those with whom she deals have already been suborned by Gloucester's enemies, who catch her in the act. Her disgrace makes her husband too wretched to resist the elaborate schemes of Winchester, the queen, and her lover Suffolk, while York, though he knows Gloucester's innocence, cynically lets him be destroyed, realizing that the conspirators are bound to destroy themselves in the process. Gloucester is murdered offstage, halfway through the play. His body is brought onstage to serve as the basis of an early example of dramatic detection, as Warwick uses the appearance of the corpse to prove that he died a violent death. Winchester himself dies soon afterwards, in a horrific scene that leaves no doubt of his guilt.

After Gloucester's death there is a change of focus. A popular uprising gives Henry a justification for banishing Suffolk, who is captured at sea and beheaded (his is the first of several severed heads to be shown in the play). York disappears on a mission to pacify Ireland, which, like most actions set in Ireland, takes place entirely off stage. Depicting Ireland was beyond the imagination of most writers (apart from Spenser, who lived there) and was potentially dangerous. Thus, four of the five characters mentioned in the play's 1594 title disappear from the action and only York will return. While he exploits his position to raise an army on his own behalf, the plebian Jack Cade, whom York sees as his substitute, temporarily takes over the play with his own popular uprising. A nineteenth-century adaptation of the plays allowed the great actor Edmund Kean to double the roles of York and Cade and it is possible that the play might at some point have been intended to offer a star actor like Tarlton a virtuoso double role exploiting his skills as both fighter and clown. The scenes of rebellion, both comic and horrific, have often been seen as the quintessentially Shakespearean part of the play, since Shakespeare later dealt rather similarly with crowds in *Julius Caesar, Coriolanus*, and *Sir Thomas More*. Cade's defeat and death are immediately followed by York's open rebellion, and the play moves quickly into the first battle of the Civil War. While the Yorkist victory at St. Albans suggests some sort of finality, the main effect is one of open-endedness, "a deliberate feature of the history plays" as John D. Cox has argued.[12]

The action is continuous from the end of Part Two to the opening of Part Three, *in medias res*: the opening line, "I wonder how the king escaped our hands," clearly assumes an audience that has seen the earlier play. York is dead by the end of Act 1 and York's three sons, who appear only briefly in Part Two, become the central characters of Part Three. In particular, the younger Richard seems to announce his taking over of the leading role when he says, "Richard, I bear thy name. I'll venge thy death" (*3 Henry VI* 2.1.87). If the actor had played Humphrey of Gloucester as well, there would be a metatheatrical joke in his reluctance to accept such an unlucky title.

For audiences who had seen all three plays, Henry VI and Margaret would now be the dominant figures. Although the ineffectual Henry seems to grow in wisdom, this may be simply because he is the only character with enough moral credibility to be a mouthpiece for ideas about the unhappiness of great men and the fickleness of the common people; nevertheless, his moments of reflection, even bitterness, make the part rewarding for the actor. What is *not* in the text – the failure of his marriage, the birth of his son, and the question of whether he suspects his wife's fidelity – lends itself particularly well to productions emphasizing subtext. When he faints after hearing of Gloucester's death, and revives to hear Suffolk saying, "Gracious Henry, comfort!," his outraged "What, doth my lord of Suffolk comfort me?" (3.2.38–9) seems not only an instinctive revulsion from a possible murderer but also a release of pent-up feelings that he has tried to ignore.

Margaret has become a popular role precisely because, as is constantly stressed, she is not like a woman. Her unnaturalness is summed up in York's diatribe:

> Women are soft, mild, pitiful and flexible,
> Thou stern, obdurate, flinty, rough, remorseless.
> (*3 Henry VI* 1.4.141–2)

It may be thanks to Edward Hall that (by this definition) there are almost no women in the Henry VI plays. Hall is consistently harsh with Joan of Arc, perhaps trying to counter the arguments for her sanctity that were already being made in France. In his account, she is ugly, "a shepherd's daughter, a chamberlain in an hostelrie, and a beggar's brat." Her lack of "womanly behaviour" is obvious: "she clad herself in a man's clothing, and was conversant with every losel, giving occasion to all men to judge and speak evil of her and her doings."[13] Writing of Margaret, Hall had to be more careful, since after all she was a queen of England. She is introduced as a lady who "excelled all other, as well in beauty and favour, as in wit and policy, and was of stomach and courage more like to a man than a woman." Later, as she becomes the de facto leader of Henry VI's army, she is still "this manly woman, this courageous queen."[14] But by now the terms are more ambiguous, and there is a possible double meaning in "queen" (which, spelled quean, could mean whore). The dramatists developed this view, making explicit what is only hinted in Hall about Margaret's love for Suffolk. The York faction even accuse her of being the main cause of their rebellion.

If Joan of Arc and Margaret of Anjou were the first roles that Shakespeare wrote for boy actors, they reflect the fact that he knew more boys than girls. Boys in fiction were not generally depicted as lovably childish but as sharp-witted "peevish" brats determined to have the last word, and these characteristics carried over into many of the female characters that they were asked to play. The only really pathetic children in these early histories are Rutland, who pleads with Clifford for his life, and the elder prince in *Richard III*, who looks forward to being a great king. His pert younger brother is described as "all the mother's from the top to toe" (*Richard III* 3.1.156), and Gloucester had already made a similar comment on Prince Edward in *3 Henry VI*, with a characteristic jibe about the boy's legitimacy:

> Whoever got thee, there thy mother stands,
> For well I wot, thou hast thy mother's tongue
> (*3 Henry VI* 2.2.133–4)

Boys could be boys even when they were playing women: Joan of Arc fights impressively; Margaret takes over as "general" from her weak husband. The other women in the Henry VI plays are a witch, an ambitious woman who deals with witches, and, late in the story, Elizabeth Woodville, another woman of relatively humble origins, who marries Edward IV. Edward's wooing of Elizabeth recalls that of Suffolk and Margaret, and foreshadows not only the scene between Richard of Gloucester and Lady Anne in *Richard III* but also the wooing of Katherine and Petruchio in *The Taming of the Shrew* and some of the male–female exchanges in *Love's Labour's Lost*. These scenes are often written in "stichomythia," a series of parallel one- or two-line speeches, which are particularly suited to exchanges of insults. Actors who had gone to grammar school – probably including many of the boys in the company – would have known this kind of repartee from classical drama. The mysterious comment in *Hamlet* about the child actors "who cry out on the top of question and are most tyrannically clapped for't" (2.2.340–1) might refer to the popularity of actors whose training (much of it musical) made them quicker at this give-and-take than most adult actors.

It is only when women become maternal figures that the boy actor is required to display something more than boyishness. Elizabeth, Edward IV's queen, is probably visibly pregnant in Part Three, 4.4, whereas Margaret in the same play is not seen as a mother until her son is a teenager. It is in Part Three that the murdering of children becomes a central theme: Clifford takes revenge for York's killing of his father by killing York's young son; York prays that Margaret may be as wretched as he is, and his curse is fulfilled when the Yorkists murder Prince Edward after the Battle of Tewkesbury. In the aftermath of that crime, Edward IV looks forward to his own fatherhood, and the final scene shows him with a son and heir, but Richard Gloucester's muttered asides foreshadow the child's death in the famous sequel.

Actors vs Playwrights

Greene's quarrel with the actors was only partly related to the ancient argument about the morality of theater in general. As William Webbe wrote in his *Discourse of English Poesie* (1586), there had always been a debate about whether to emphasize "The profit or discommodity which ariseth by the use of these Comedies and

Tragedies" and it had become a "sore" issue again recently.[15] Most attacks on the commercial theater focused on the potentially erotic effect of boys playing women and on the depiction of immoral behavior as comic. However, by the end of the 1580s, even playwrights themselves were expressing hostility. Stephen Gosson (who published *The School of Abuse* in 1586) and Anthony Munday (who may have written *The Third Blast of the Retreat from Plays and Theatres* in 1580) were also playwrights. Nashe's more favorable view of the stage in *Pierce Penniless* contrasts with his apparent contempt for it in his preface to *Menaphon* (1589); perhaps his attitude had changed when he saw the success of the Henry VI play that he had helped to write. He added praise of other actors to what he had already said of Alleyn, and distinguished the English stage from that of Europe, where lewd women played female roles. Plays, he insisted, could be "a rare exercise of vertue" when they dramatized "our English Chronicles," bringing our heroic ancestors back from the grave in an implicit reproach to "these degenerate effeminate days of ours." Almost immediately after Nashe's pamphlet, another attack appeared. Robert Greene had died, at 34, in August 1592. Since he had a reputation for being dissolute and unreliable, his death inspired several pamphlets purporting to describe his last days and his repentance. Greene had already written several public repentances of his former life, but the public was presumably not expected to believe in the genuineness of works with titles like *Greene's Vision, written at the instant of his death* and *Greene's News Both from Heaven and Hell* (1593), which Barnaby Rich claimed to have received from the ghost of Greene in person.

    Greene's Groatsworth of Wit, which Henry Chettle registered on 20 September 1592 and printed himself, is another supposed deathbed pamphlet, but it begins, oddly, with a third-person account of the sordid life of one Roberto. His shady past includes a period of writing for the theater, after he meets a rich player who has been a success in the country despite his voice that is "nothing gracious."[16] Though he despises the players and cheats them, he also resents their unwillingness to support him in his poverty, since he considers himself the cause of their success. Suddenly the story breaks off and Roberto speaks of himself in the first person, clearly identifiable now as Robert Greene himself. From his deathbed, he addresses three scholars who are also friends, almost certainly Marlowe, Nashe, and Peele. All three are warned not to trust the players, who will abandon them likewise. The Greene-persona then adds his famous comment on the most dangerous player: "an upstart Crow, beautified with our feathers." Though the pamphlet was printed in black-letter, the quotation, "*Tiger's heart wrapped in a Player's hide,*" in Roman type, leaps out to catch the eye of the most casual reader.[17] It has also been thought that there are other veiled allusions to Shakespeare elsewhere in the pamphlet, as the country actor with the bad voice and, in the concluding fable, the prudent ant who refuses to help the spendthrift – and greene –grasshopper.[18] As with Nashe's "kid" in the preface to *Menaphon*, the allusive and punning attack can be read in a number of ways. What exactly was the upstart crow being accused of? It used to be thought that it was plagiarism. But the dramatists of this period echo each other so frequently that they all lived in glass houses. The image of a crow decked out with other birds' feathers means simply that actors are unfairly given the credit that ought to go to the author of the words they speak. This is certainly a view that Greene would have shared. One difference between elite and popular culture is that, while the former tends to focus on the creator of a work, the latter is much more interested in its performer. Greene, who had been a famous pamphleteer, may have been startled, when he turned to writing plays, to discover that he was now less important than his actors. He struck back in his pamphlet *Francisco's Fortunes, or, the Second Part of Greene's Never too Late* (1590), by quoting Cicero's claim that the actor's art was only "a kind of mechanical labour" – which meant that no actor could be a gentleman. The players' dependence on the language of others made them, he said, resemble Aesop's crow, "being pranked with the glory of others' feathers."[19] The *Groatsworth* reused that image.

Even at the time, its authorship was suspected. Nashe, in the preface to a second edition of *Pierce Penniless*, quickly denied having written it. Within a few weeks, Henry Chettle had published a pamphlet called *Kind-Heart's Dream* (Kind-Heart was a locally famous tooth-drawer), adding a preface in which he insisted that the *Groatsworth* was Greene's work, not his. He recognized that two people had recognized themselves as the targets of its accusations: "With neither of them that take offence was I acquainted, and with one of them I care not if I never be": this is usually assumed to be Marlowe. But he apologized to "The other, whom at that time I did not so much spare, as since I wish I had," saying that "I am as sorry as if the original fault had been my fault." This other is probably Shakespeare, of whom Chettle adds, "myself have seen his demeanor no less civil than he excellent in the quality he professes: besides, divers of worship have reported his uprightness of dealing, which argues his honesty, and his facetious grace in writing, that approves his art."[20] Assuming that Chettle was telling the truth, Katherine Duncan-Jones has argued that the only play in which he could have seen Shakespeare act during the plague period was Nashe's *Summer's Last Will and Testament*, privately performed at the Croydon residence of the Archbishop of Canterbury.[21] I suspect, however, that Chettle had in fact seen Shakespeare in the role from which he quoted in *The Groatsworth*, and was pretending otherwise because he was still claiming that the pamphlet was by Greene. Stephen Greenblatt suggests that there was some coercion behind this apparently gracious comment, and that "divers of worship" means "people who have it in their power to make my life miserable."[22] If Shakespeare had such connections as early as 1592, he probably acquired them through the patrons of the companies in which he had performed.

At present, many scholars doubt that the *Groatsworth* was written by Greene, on his deathbed or otherwise. Internal evidence tells against Chettle's denial. Given the vile nature of some of the things of which Roberto accuses himself and the extremity of his punishment, it seems unlikely that even such a public self-flagellator as Greene would have wished to be identified with the character. External evidence includes the fact that Chettle had already admitted his own authorship of an epistle signed T.N., which was obviously meant to be taken for – and does in fact sound like – the work of Thomas Nashe.[23] Even the pamphlet in which he denied counterfeiting Greene's style contains a mock-epistle from the dead Greene in a good imitation of precisely that style.[24] In 1933 Chauncey Sanders argued plausibly that *Greene's Groatsworth* is based on a work still in manuscript that Greene had promised earlier, *The Repentance of a Cony-Catcher*, adapted to make it look like Greene's autobiography.[25] The attack on Shakespeare and the direct address to easily recognizable contemporary writers might have been Chettle's idea of what Greene would have wanted to say.[26] Or perhaps Chettle was expressing his own frustrations. Though trained as a printer, he would soon become one of the most prolific and talented dramatists in Henslowe's team. His name had not yet appeared in the famous diary, but he may have been writing plays as a freelance, jealous, like Greene, of the attention and admiration given to actors and eager, like Nashe, to make himself known by plunging into a controversy. Perhaps he had intended to reveal the *Groatsworth* as his own work after exploiting its success, only to be frightened off when he found that it had given offense.[27] Yet he was always to be an invisible writer. As Alfred Hart has pointed out, Henslowe's *Diary* shows that Chettle later had a hand in forty-eight plays, "and his name does not appear on the title page of one!"[28]

So far, no one has produced evidence for Greene's or Chettle's involvement in any of the Henry VI plays, least of all in *3 Henry VI*, so the comments in *Groatsworth* do not look like a co-author's anger at having his lines rewritten by Johannes Fac-Totum. If the *Groatsworth* author was better informed than he claimed to be, there may be some significance in the fact that he addressed his warnings to Marlowe, Nashe, and Peele, since all three may have been among Shakespeare's earliest collaborators. The controversy shows that, although the plays about the Wars of the Roses were well known, the author of the "tiger's heart" speech was not yet a well-known personality. Chettle, on the margins on the literary world, obviously did not know that Shakespeare had friends and patrons.

If Shakespeare was acting with Lord Strange's Men in 1592 he might not have seen the *Groatsworth* for some time, since in late June the company left for an extended tour of southern England and the pamphlet appeared in late September.[29] A number of writers have believed that he was deeply offended by its attack and that he later alluded to it twice. The first suggested allusion, Polonius's "'Beautified' is a vile phrase" (*Hamlet* 2.2.111–12), seems far-fetched: how many spectators would have remembered "beautified with our feathers," in a pamphlet now some eight or nine years old? The second occurs in the opening lines of Sonnet 112:

> Your love and pity doth th' impression fill
> Which vulgar scandal stamped upon my brow;
> For what care I who calls me well or ill,
> So you o'ergreen my bad, my good allow?

For this allusion to make sense, "o'ergreen" must mean "cancel out what Greene wrote." Greene and his contemporaries constantly pun on his name, and the context is relevant here as it is not in *Hamlet*. Yet the quatrain does not say that something else will cover over the green but rather that love and pity will smooth the wrinkles of a furrowed brow as new green growth fills the furrows of a plowed field.[30] The best context for this sonnet is that of the two others which precede it in the 1609 edition. In both, the speaker says that he has suffered in public estimation because his profession depends on "public" and therefore "vulgar" activity: that is, the life of an actor. That the profession was considered vulgar may be indicated in the fact that Chettle, even while praising Shakespeare, seemed to feel that it was more tactful not to name "the quality he professes." Looking back on his own vulgar behavior, Shakespeare might have recalled that there was a time when, like Greene and Nashe, he thought that any publicity was good publicity. The gratuitous attack on him, followed by the fulsome making of amends in *Kind-Heart's Dream*, might even have been his own idea.

Titus Andronicus

As observers saw signs that the plague was weakening its hold on London, Shakespeare began working on other plays for presentation when playing resumed. *Titus Andronicus* is first mentioned in January 1594, assuming that it is the play that Henslowe's *Diary* calls *Titus & Ondronicus*. It may have existed before the plague closures. Scholars once hoped that they could prove that this blood-soaked play was not by Shakespeare, or that it was a very early work, or that it was a parody. In the late twentieth century, however, it became popular, thanks to a taste for horror and black comedy, the attractions of the leading role, and the contemporary relevance of its raped heroine and the racial pride of its black villain. Ironically, this was just when computer tests began to confirm a longstanding suspicion that the first act, at least, was probably the work of George Peele – innovative, gifted, theatrically experienced, and perpetually in need of money. But such a hand-to-mouth writer as Peele would never have worked on *Titus Andronicus* unless there was a real likelihood of prompt payment and thus performance. Perhaps he wrote the first act and left it unfinished when the theaters closed, after which Shakespeare may have taken it up. It is equally possible that he worked closely with Peele, who was resident in London and perhaps already suffering from the long illness which, by 1595–6, made him unable to work.

The play might date from even later. As the next chapter will show, writers after the summer of 1593 would have been especially nervous about charges of atheism. Marlowe and Kyd were vulnerable because they had set their major plays in the Christian era, and depicted amoral and blasphemous characters achieving worldly success. Peele too seems to have been interested in religious and cultural conflict. His first venture may have been a play about the tragic love between a Turkish sultan and a Greek woman, though it is known only by its title, *The Turkish Mahomet and Hiren the Fair Greek*. His first surviving play, *The Battle of Alcazar* (performed 1588–9), made innovative use of recent history (the battle took place in 1578) and dramatized the complex political and religious motives that brought Catholic troops from several countries into this dynastic quarrel between members of the Moroccan royal family. The advantage of the Roman setting of *Titus* was that the characters could question the gods without questioning the established religion of England. It is likely that Peele and Shakespeare identified Titus's son Lucius with the legendary first Christian emperor of Rome, but religion enters the story only briefly, when the atheist Aaron makes Lucius swear by the god in whom he believes, and whom, according to Aaron, he worships "With twenty popish tricks and ceremonies" (5.1.76). This recalls the episode in Part Two of *Tamburlaine* (2.1, 2.2), when a Muslim king calls on Christ to avenge the perjury of a Christian king and, when the latter has been defeated, decides henceforth to honor Christ alongside Mahomet.

Peele, as his previous career had shown, was good at devising occasions for spectacle. *Alcazar* had featured many dumb shows, including a banquet scene in which dishes of blood, bones, and skulls were served to the participants. As Jonathan Bate has shown, the dramatists also recalled *The Spanish Tragedy*: *Titus* too opens with a triumphal return from battle, shows the corruption of the conquest by intrigue, depicts the revenger as feigning madness to achieve his ends, and ends with a celebration that destroys the ruling family.[31] Both Kyd and Shakespeare had already used the image of the blood-dipped cloth. Hieronimo keeps a "handkercher besmeared with blood" to remind him to take revenge (*The Spanish Tragedy* 2.5.51–2) and produces it at the end to show the horrified court the reason for his actions. Margaret, taunting York, gives him a similar handkerchief to prove that his son has been murdered. His response,

> How couldst thou drain the lifeblood of the child
> To bid the father wipe his eyes withal . . .?
> (*3 Henry VI* 1.4.138–9)

alludes to a still more horrible idea from Ovid and Seneca, where the blood drained from a murdered child is made into a meal and fed to its parent. Nashe's reference to plays based on Senecan themes as "English Seneca, let blood line by line and page by page,"[32] makes English writers metaphorically do to Seneca what Seneca himself had done when he opened his veins after receiving Nero's suicide order. Seneca's *Thyestes* discovers that he has eaten his own sons, murdered by his brother; Procne, in Ovid's *Metamorphoses*, kills her own children and feeds them to her husband as punishment for his rape of her sister. In *Titus Andronicus*, the blood of the two rapists becomes part of Titus's recipe for a meat pie. Some of the pleasure of these outrageous episodes must have come from recognition of their sources. Lavinia reveals the crime committed against her by showing the others a passage from the *Metamorphoses*, and Titus's quotations from classical authors hint to the rapists that he knows their identity. Though one of them sees that his line is "a verse from Horace; I know it well./ I read it in the grammar long ago" (4.2.22–3), only Aaron is clever enough to understand that it is being used for a purpose. The literary references are not anachronistic, since the play is set in the final years of the Roman empire, with its great writers far in the past. Even Titus's murder of Lavinia has a text to support it, Livy's story of Virginius. The play does not refer to the parallel story, which Shakespeare may have been writing at the same time: the suicide of Lucretia after her rape by Tarquinius.

Since there is no logical reason for a Moor in the army of Goths, the creation of Aaron was a rather obvious repetition of a previous success. The most famous character in *The Battle of Alcazar* was Muly Mahomet, played by Edward Alleyn. Despite the presence of several other moors in the play, he is always called "the Moor" in stage directions, and, until Shakespeare's *Othello* reached the stage, anyone who mentioned a Moor in drama would have meant this one. Ben Jonson's *Poetaster* (1602) offers a rare glimpse of how Alleyn played the part. When a boy actor offers to "do the Moor," he borrows a scarf (presumably for his Muslim headgear), then rides in on someone's shoulders while his bearer "stalks" in an imitation of the tall Alleyn's distinctive walk.[33] In the first instance, Peele probably thought of Aaron as a part for Alleyn, but, if the play was intended for the two companies performing jointly at the Rose, Titus and Aaron would have been designed for the two leading actors, perhaps with Alleyn as the raging and grieving Titus and Burbage as Aaron, who, from the point at which Shakespeare takes over the writing, is more sophisticated and intelligent than Muly Mahomet had been. When the birth of a black baby makes his adultery with Tamora obvious to her sons he mocks their horrified reactions:

> *Demetrius.* Villain, what hast thou done?
> *Aaron.* That which thou canst not undo.
> *Chiron.* Thou hast undone our mother.
> *Aaron.* Villain, I have done thy mother.
> (4.2.74–7)

Titus is, however, the part that Burbage must have played once the play moved to the company that he headed, because it requires a much greater range of emotion: grief, rage, feigned madness, and ironic humor. Although he is – or has been – a highly successful general like Tamburlaine, the play is not concerned with his conquests, only with his suffering. Seneca was a model not only for exhaustive expressions of grief but also for simple and telling understatements. The play contains both. Marcus Andronicus, when he brings the raped and mutilated Lavinia to her father, recognizes the total destruction of her former identity by speaking of her in the past tense: "This was thy daughter." The sight requires a moment of horrified silence. Then comes Titus's movingly simple reply: "Why, Marcus, so she is" (3.1.63). As further unspeakable events follow – Titus's self-mutilation to buy the lives of his condemned sons, the discovery that it has been useless since they are already dead – the scene becomes an argument between Marcus and Titus about the appropriate way in which to respond to this piling up of horrible events: "Now is a time to storm," Marcus insists, but Titus laughs, because, he explains, "I have not another tear to shed" (3.1.263–4). These quieter moments make it possible to bear the constant stress on grief and anger.

It is Titus who first uses the image of the tiger when he realizes that the city for which he has sacrificed his family has turned into something else:

> Why, foolish Lucius, dost thou not perceive
> That Rome is but a wilderness of tigers?
> Tigers must prey, and Rome affords no prey
> But me and mine.
> (*Titus Andronicus* 3.1.50–4)

In the final scene, Lucius calls Aaron "that ravenous tiger" (5.3.5) as he orders the Moor's punishment. He later applies the same term to Tamora:

> As for that ravenous tiger, Tamora,
> No funeral rite, nor man in mourning weed,
> No mournful bell shall ring her burial;
> But throw her forth to beasts and birds to prey.
> Her life was beastly and devoid of pity,
> And being dead, let birds on her take pity.
> (5.3.195–200)

These harsh words are the last lines of the play in the Quarto published in 1594. When the play was reprinted in 1600, however, it was followed by four other lines. Lucius repeats his command that Aaron be punished and then speaks of the next task:

> Then afterwards to order well the state,
> That like events may ne'er it ruinate.

Most editions and productions omit these rather bathetic lines, which may or may not be Shakespeare's. They show, however, that, only a few years after the play's first publication, the theater for which Shakespeare was writing felt the need to suggest some alternative to the wilderness of tigers.

Notes

1. Alexander, *Shakespeare's Henry VI and Richard II.*
2. Warren, "The Quarto and Folio Texts of *2 Henry VI*," 206.

3. Manley, "From Strange's Men to Pembroke's Men," 272–5.

4. Note to 1.4.62 in the Arden 3, ed. Knowles.

5. *Companion,* 112–13; *1 Henry VI,* ed. Burns, 69–73.

6. *Pierce Penniless his Supplication to the Devil* (1592), quoted from Chambers, *ES,* 2: 238–9.

7. See Vickers, *Shakespeare, Co-Author,* and Taylor, "Shakespeare and Others: The Authorship of *Henry the Sixth, Part One.*"

8. Orrell, "The Theatres," 106–7.

9. John Crowne's version (1680) draws many parallels with the recent civil wars in England.

10. See Martin and Cox, "Who is 'Somerfille' in *3 Henry VI?*".

11. Perhaps there was some fear that "Warwick" would be taken to mean Ambrose Dudley, brother to the Earl of Leicester, who died in 1590.

12. *3 Henry VI,* ed. Cox and Rasmussen, 103.

13. *Hall's Chronicle,* 159.

14. Ibid., 205, 209.

15. Quoted in Chambers, *ES,* 2: 227; the full text is printed in *Elizabethan Critical Essays,* ed. Smith, 1: 236.

16. *Greene's Groatsworth of Wit,* ed. Carroll, 68.

17. Ibid., 84.

18. Bradbrook, *The Rise of the Common Player,* 85–6.

19. Quoted in Chambers, *ES,* 2: 236–7.

20. Quoted from Chambers, *WS,* 2: 189.

21. Duncan-Jones, "Shakespeare the Motley Player," 723–43.

22. Greenblatt, *Will in the World,* 215.

23. Carroll, "Who Wrote *Greenes Groats-worth of Witte?*," 71.

24. *Greene's Groatsworth of Wit,* ed. Carroll, 3–4; Sanders, "Robert Greene and His 'Editors'," 401–2.

25. Sanders, 'Robert Greene and His 'Editors'," 415–16.

26. *Greene's Groatsworth of Wit,* ed. Carroll, 3–4.

27. Jowett, "Notes on Henry Chettle," 517–18.

28. A. Hart, *Shakespeare and the Homilies,* 91.

29. For a map of their touring stops, which included Cambridge, Canterbury, Bath, and Bristol, see Maclean, "Adult Playing Companies 1583–1593," 47.

30. See David Bevington's gloss on this line: "cover as with green growth."

31. *Titus Andronicus,* ed. Bate, 86–7.

32. Preface to Robert Greene, *Menaphon* (1589), in Chambers, *ES,* 2: 235.

33. Jonson, *Poetaster,* ed. Cain, 3.4.270 (p. 343).

6

"The Dangerous Year"
1593–1594

"Oh, thou didst kill me; kill me once again!
Thy eyes' shrewd tutor, that hard heart of thine,
Hath taught them scornful tricks and such disdain
That they have murdered this poor heart of mine;
*   And these mine eyes, true leaders to their queen,*
*   But for thy piteous lips no more had seen.*

Long may they kiss each other, for this cure!
Oh, never let their crimson liveries wear!
And as they last, their verdure still endure,
To drive infection from the dangerous year,
*   That the stargazers, having writ on death,*
*   May say the plague is banished by thy breath!"*
                              (*Venus and Adonis* 499–510)

It was with lines like these that Shakespeare first appeared under his own name to the reading public, most of whom did not know that he also wrote plays, still less that he was an actor. Anyone reading the poem simply for content might find the lines distasteful, partly because they are a plea for sex, spoken by a goddess to a mortal boy who is completely indifferent to her, and partly because a glance down the page of a modern double-columned *Complete Works* makes it obvious that there is going to be much more of the same. As published in 1593, the poem would have been viewed eight stanzas at a time, with four fitting neatly onto each page (a characteristically nice printing job by Richard Field), and probably read aloud. Approached this way, it offers different pleasures: the surprising change of tone in the first line, the effort that it takes to say the next two consonant-packed lines, and the delayed and inverted final line which completes the meaning ("thy eyes, taught by thy heart, haves murdered

The Life of William Shakespeare: A Critical Biography, First Edition. Lois Potter.
© 2012 Lois Potter. Published 2012 by Blackwell Publishing Ltd.

my heart, and my eyes, but for [if it hadn't been for] thy piteous lips, had seen [would have seen] no more"). The ecstatic second stanza, by contrast, is musical; its surprises lie in the imagery. A livery is the clothing given by a master to his servants: who has given the crimson color to Adonis's lips? How can the speaker wish them to remain an unfading red ("wear" means "wear out"), and yet wish also that their "verdure" (the fresh green of youthful nature) shall last forever? Those who carried sweet-smelling herbs as a protective against the plague understood the paradox that makes red and green the same.

Venus and Adonis is one of the most intensely erotic poems of a decade in which much of the best writing was erotic. Ovid is usually credited with this explosion, because most of the narrative poems are based on his works. But the Ovid/Virgil contrast has been overemphasized. Virgil's pastorals were about love more than about sheep, and his second eclogue was responsible for the most controversial poems of the period, those about the love of men for boys. The works that made sensuality fashionable in the 1590s were those of the two most prestigious English writers of the decade, Spenser and Sidney. Skillful advance publicity and manuscript circulation meant that dramatists were quoting Spenser's poem even before the first three books of *The Faerie Queene* appeared in 1590. Its moral allegory is embodied in highly sexualized figures, such as Book I's arch-schemer and seductress, Duessa, based on the Scarlet Woman of the Bible, and the Circe-like Acrasia of Book II, "greedily depasturing delight" – that is, almost literally devouring the young knight who has fallen asleep in her arms. The central figure of Book III is a cross-dressed woman, Britomart, whose disguise as a knight in armor leads to equivocal situations with both men and women. The songs and sonnets of Sidney's *Astrophil and Stella* (1591), obviously meant to be read as autobiographical, depict an adulterous love affair in which reason constantly fights with sexual desire. Astrophil often advises himself to behave sensibly, only to end the poem with a passionate outcry: "But ah! Desire still cries, 'Give me some food'" (Sonnet 71.14). After 1593, Shakespeare would be famous for expressing devouring desire: female in *Venus and Adonis*, male in *The Rape of Lucrece*.

He might have written *Venus and Adonis* in the second half of 1592, when the playhouses were closed, or in February 1593, after acting at the Rose Theatre in *Henry VI*. This brief season ended with Lent; then, in early April 1593, a theater-starved public was offered eight days of the most popular plays, with two perfor-mances each of *Friar Bacon and Friar Bungay*, *The Jew of Malta*, and *King Leir*. A more serious outbreak of plague – the worst one since 1564 – soon followed, with official prohibitions of events likely to attract crowds. There was no more playing in London for the rest of 1593, but Lord Strange's Men were licensed, on 6 May, to perform "anywhere free from plague and outside a 7 mile radius of the capital."[1] If Shakespeare went with them, he had some sort of employment but it is unlikely to have covered the whole period. He might have returned to Stratford in order to avoid paying the high London rents. On the other hand, this would have meant writing in his parents' overcrowded house, with his wife and three young children and perhaps his brothers and sister as well. The ideal situation would be to find a patron to provide accommodation outside London.

Some writers had managed rather well. John Lyly was living on his wife's estates in the north. Marlowe found patronage with Sir Thomas Walsingham. Nashe spent some of the plague period in the house of the Archbishop of Canterbury, for whom in 1592 he wrote *Summer's Last Will and Testament*, with its haunting song ("I am sick, I must die; Lord have mercy on us"). Peele, always in financial difficulties, was simply writing anything for which he could be paid quickly. Thomas Lodge, another chronically hard-up writer, had sailed in 1591 on what was meant to be Thomas Cavendish's second round-the-world voyage, and returned to London, probably late in 1592, to find his friend Greene dead.[2] As usual, Kyd is untraceable, but he seems to have had a patron and may have been living in his household.

Marlowe may have had other plans, since he was later accused of trying to persuade others to go to Scotland. At a time when it was forbidden even to discuss the succession, it would have been treasonous to desert the aging queen in order to curry favor with her most likely successor, James VI of Scotland.[3] Despite this fact, many courtiers were already anticipating her death and secretly corresponding with him. Marlowe may, however, have been less interested in James's closeness to the throne than in his reputation as a patron of poets. In the 1580s the young king's court included many Scottish poets and even some English ones. He exchanged poems with his courtiers and urged them to translate his favorite authors. James took an interest in drama, had at least one actor in his pay,[4] and in 1589 had invited the Queen's Men to his court.[5] His first volume of poems, *Essayes of a Prentise, in the Divine Art of Poesie*, was published in 1584 when he was only 18. It included an essay giving "rules" for Scottish poetry and a series of twelve sonnets related to the four seasons, one of the earliest sonnet sequences in English and certainly the first to be widely known.

In *Hero and Leander*, which he was writing at this time, Marlowe devised a fable to explain why Fortune was hostile to scholars, concluding that "Gross gold from them runs headlong to the boor" (1.471–2).[6] That riches were unfairly valued above learning was a common complaint. What followed might have had more specific meaning:

> And fruitful wits, that in aspiring are,
> Shall discontent run into regions far.
> (1.477–8)

Perhaps he too intended to "run into regions far" – that is, to be in Scotland by the time these lines were published. Other writers, equally distressed at the drying up of sources of income in England, may have wondered what rewards might await them there. Shakespeare probably knew about Marlowe's poem, which was based on a late fifth-century Greek epyllion, or short epic, available in Latin translation. In the wake of the Marprelate controversy, translations and adaptations from the classics were relatively safe from topical interpretations. Without the regular income that Spenser received from his government appointment, most writers were hardly in a position to write an epic, but these short love stories, written in the highly decorative style associated with Ovid, were within their reach. It was important, however, to be able to associate a poem with a patron.

Shakespeare looked for an aristocrat who had money but who was not already being besieged by authors. He knew better than to follow the example of Spenser, who in 1590 had dedicated the first three books of *The Faerie Queene* to Elizabeth I and filled the volume with sonnets in praise of members of her court. There was too much competition for the patronage of the spectacularly famous Earl of Essex. The playwright may already have been a "servant" of the Earl and Countess of Pembroke, if he acted in their company. Their sons would later be joint dedicatees of the 1623 Folio, but in 1593 they were only 13 and 9 years old and the countess, though a generous patron, favored the translators of classical and continental works. Samuel Daniel – well connected, recently returned from travel in Italy, and the author of *Delia* (1592), a much-admired sonnet collection – was the kind of writer she encouraged. He was now living at Wilton, perhaps as a tutor, and writing a closet drama, *Cleopatra*, as a companion piece to the countess's translation of a French tragedy on Antony.

Shakespeare finally targeted the Earl of Southampton, with a poem so perfectly fitted to its dedicatee that he may have chosen the patron before the subject. His brief dedication to *Venus and Adonis* has been minutely analyzed for evidence of the relationship between poet and patron, and this is not inappropriate, since he probably took as much trouble over the dedication as over the poem itself.

To the Right Honorable Henry Wriothesley, Earl of Southampton, and Baron of Titchfield:

I know not how I shall offend in dedicating my unpolished lines to Your Lordship, nor how the world will censure me for choosing so strong a prop to support so weak a burden; only if Your Honor seem but pleased, I account myself highly pleased, and vow to take advantage of all idle hours, till I have honored you with some graver labor. But if the first heir of my invention prove deformed, I shall be sorry it had so noble a godfather, and never after ear so barren a land, for fear it yield me still so bad a harvest. I leave it to your honorable survey, and Your Honor to your heart's content, which I wish may always answer your own wish and the world's hopeful expectation.

> Your Honor's in all duty,
> William Shakespeare.

The modest tone is to be expected in this genre, and there is no reason why the poet should allude to previous writings or theatrical successes. He does, however, seem eager to erase his status as an actor-playwright. In calling the poem "this first heir of my invention," he may mean simply that it is his first published work.[7] None of his plays had yet been published, and many had been collaborations where the "invention" (choice of subject and treatment) was at least partly that of another person. Besides, no one thought of dedicating a play to a patron until 1598.[8] The promise that he will write "some graver labor" in his "idle hours" seems intended to suggest that he belongs to a social class that has idle hours. James VI's latest book, registered though not printed by Richard Field, was called *His Majesties Poeticall Exercises at vacant houres*.

The final sentence of the dedication may or may not refer to Southampton's personal situation, but undoubtedly Shakespeare knew about it. Southampton had been extremely visible in the two years since he came to court. He had become a favorite of the queen and a friend of the Earl of Essex, at a time when the Essex faction was most influential; its chief rival, Sir Walter Ralegh, was barred from court between 1592 and 1597. Now aged 19, Southampton was given to displays of lavish generosity, a fact well known among writers. Shakespeare researched the earl's interests with some care. He knew that, because of his father's early death, Southampton had become a ward of Lord Burghley. He had been well educated, first under Burghley's supervision, then at Oxford and Gray's Inn. He was well read in Latin and Italian and loved poetry and plays.

What must also have been known was that Burghley at this time was using his privilege as guardian to force Southampton to marry the woman chosen for him or else pay a fine for his refusal. Burghley's choice was his own granddaughter, and Southampton was known to be unwilling. The young man's refusal may have been more prudent than it seems. Elizabeth Vere was also the daughter of the Earl of Oxford (another former ward of Burghley's), notorious for his lavish expenses and gigantic debts, and for having at one point refused to believe that she was his child.[9] Southampton, whose father had separated from his mother after accusing her of adultery, may have recoiled from the prospect of being married into another unhappy family. Southampton was also a friend of Essex, another Burghley ward, who may already have been interested in Elizabeth Vere; he had a fairly public affair with her in 1596–7, soon after she had married someone else. Faced with two ways of ruining his fortune, Southampton seems to have chosen the more honorable.

Shakespeare knew better than to equate Elizabeth Vere with the lovesick Venus and Southampton with the petulant Adonis. On the other hand, since Southampton clearly cultivated the androgynous good looks that were fashionable at the period, wearing his hair long, it would be flattering rather than insulting to suggest that he was so beautiful that women would court him rather than expecting courtship from him. One portrait (Figure 4), believed for centuries to be that of a woman, was in fact recognized only in 2002 as that of the young Earl.[10] Southampton would later be accused of homosexuality, though by an extremely unreliable witness;[11] he was also to be happily married, a father, and a successful military leader. The fusion of female

Figure 4 The Earl of Southampton, attributed to John de Critz (Cobbe collection). Dating from the early 1590s, and thus contemporary with *Venus and Adonis* (1593), until 2002 this portrait was thought to be that of a woman. Cobbe Collection (reproduced under copyright held by a private trust)

beauty and masculine valor in a very young man was particularly titillating to both sexes.

Venus and Adonis

Poems based on the *Metamorphoses* generally tell of lovers who suffer some misfortune and undergo a transformation into something appropriate: a flower, bird, tree, or star. Lodge's 1589 imitation, *Scylla's Metamorphosis*, or *Glaucus and Scilla* in its running title, depicts a conventional male–female courtship, but Lodge blurs the gender roles by giving each lover in turn the role of rejected wooer. When the

111

sea-god Glaucus loves the nymph Scylla she despises him; when she falls in love with him, he no longer cares for her. Her despair turns her into a monster and Lodge ends the poem by warning women not to reject offered love in case they too become monsters. Glaucus at the beginning compares his unhappiness to that of three women: among them is Venus, vividly imagined as she weeps over the dead Adonis.

Shakespeare used the same form (sixaines – quatrain plus couplet) as Lodge. The first part of his poem is a debate between the passionately sensual goddess and the young mortal Adonis, who is neither ready nor willing to return her love. During a brief interval in their struggle, they watch as Adonis's horse couples with a mare, not only preventing the boy from making his escape but also setting Venus's desire in a context that can be seen as either natural or bestial. The rest of the poem describes her longing for Adonis, her fears the next day when she hears the sounds of a hunt, her horror when she finds his body, her lament, and her curse on all lovers. Because the story is told mainly through Venus's eyes, there is no description of the hunt itself or of Adonis's fatal wounding by the boar.

Ovid had not depicted Adonis as a reluctant boy. Some verses in Robert Greene's *Perimedes the Blacksmith* (1588) had, however, stressed Adonis's youth. Venus first overcomes his shyness by assuring him that "he was but young, and might be wanton yet," but Greene follows the poem with one saying that Adonis's early death proves that "the spring of age" should be decked with flowers of virtue. While Shakespeare's Adonis is hardly virtuous, he differs from most prototypes in that his youth makes him resistant to desire. In Euripides' *Hippolytus*, Theseus's son is Adonis's mirror-image, dedicated to Artemis, goddess of the hunt. For his refusal to worship her, Aphrodite punishes him with a horrible death; Artemis appears to the dying boy and promises to avenge him by killing Adonis, Aphrodite's mortal lover. This story, which most Elizabethans knew from the version by Seneca or from Latin translations of Euripides, is an attack not only on blind sexual passion but also on the equally cruel behavior of the goddess of chastity, and perhaps on the frustration caused in human beings by the antagonism of these two goddesses. Shakespeare, though not primarily interested in the allegorical aspect of Venus, sometimes refers to her as Love for the sake of the paradox that results: "She's Love, she loves, and yet she is not loved" (610).

The poem often seems to be in dialogue with *Hero and Leander*, which puts the arguments for sex where they are usually found, in the mouth of a man courting a woman. Leander tells Hero that women have no value except as sexual objects:

> Base bullion for the stamp's sake we allow;
> Even so for men's impression do we you,
> By which alone, our reverend fathers say,
> Women receive perfection every way.
>
> (1.265–6)

This is the Ovid not of the *Metamorphoses* but the *Amores* which Marlowe had translated and which John Donne was currently imitating in his own *Elegies*. Marlowe's narrator is given to deliberately provocative misogyny ("Women are won when they begin to jar," "All women are ambitious naturally") and to generalizations about love:

> Love is not full of pity (as men say)
> But deaf and cruel where he means to prey.
> (2.287–8)

Shakespeare's Venus also generalizes about love in quotable couplets:

> Love is a spirit all compact of fire,
> Not gross to sink, but light, and will aspire.
> (149–50)

> Oh, learn to love; the lesson is but plain,
> And once made perfect, never lost again.
> (407–8)

> Were beauty under twenty locks kept fast,
> Yet love breaks through, and picks them all at last.
> (575–6)

This idealism is like nothing in Marlowe. It is, however, contrasted with the comic insensibility of Adonis:

> "I know not love," quoth he, "nor will not know it,
> Unless it be a boar, and then I chase it . . ."
> (409–10)

> "Your treatise makes me like you worse and worse"
> (774)

Yet the sulky boy's main point – that he is simply too young for love – is not unreasonable. The poem exists for the sake of the argument between these two unpersuadable people. What finally happens is caused neither by the intervention of another deity nor by anything that Venus herself does. This is presumably why Shakespeare gives the boy's killing by the boar such cursory treatment that the reader can almost miss it. Venus thinks that she hears the sound of a hunting horn and rushes in the direction of the sound:

> As falcon to the lure, away she flies –
> The grass stoops not, she treads on it so light –
> And in her haste unfortunately spies

113

> The foul boar's conquest on her fair delight;
> Which seen, her eyes, as murdered with the view,
> Like stars ashamed of day, themselves withdrew.
>   (1027–32)

Though the situation is tragic, the tone is not. The poem, constantly stressing what is beautiful, such as the lightness of Venus's running feet and her star-like eyes, turns the bloody and mutilated Adonis into an abstraction, and, like Venus herself in the final couplet, refuses to look at the corpse.

Death is present throughout the poem, but always in an aestheticized form. It has been suggested that the dominant red and white colors in *Venus and Adonis* – always, of course, a symbol of beauty – might also carry associations with the plague: "those infected with the plague in the city carried red wands to warn passers-by; in the country they carried white."[12] As Shakespeare knew, the bawdy stories of Boccaccio's *Decameron* are told by aristocrats who have fled Florence to escape the plague. Even Venus, praising the sweetness of Adonis's breath, says that it can "drive infection from the dangerous year" (508) and in her last, most desperate plea to him she dwells at length on the enemies to beauty:

> As burning fevers, agues pale and faint,
> Life-poisoning pestilence and frenzies wood [insane],
> The marrow-eating sickness, whose attaint
> Disorder breeds by heating of the blood;
>   Surfeits, imposthumes, grief, and damned despair
>   Swear Nature's death for framing thee so fair.
>   (739–44)

Though she urges him to light the world with the beauty of his descendants, the final lines of the poem show that his beauty will be preserved only in the purple flower, which she promptly plucks. Since "flowers" could also be extracts from literary works, Adonis's metamorphosis mirrors his transformation into the poem that the reader has just finished.

Shakespeare's promise to Southampton of "some graver labor" corresponds to the ending of *Glaucus and Sylla*, where Glaucus makes his author promise "To write no more of that whence shame doth grow." Whether or not Shakespeare at this time seriously thought of abandoning the theater, he may well have thought, like Lodge, about how he would have wished to be remembered if he had been among the 10,000 people who died of the plague. The famous Puritan preacher William Perkins, calling the sickness God's warning to sinners, pointed out many sins that one could commit without realizing it. For example, one could break the commandment against stealing if one made one's living "by casting of figures and by playes."[13] In linking actors, playwrights, and astrologers, Perkins was emphasizing the element of fantasy and deception in their professions. The theater encouraged poor people to part with money that they should not be spending and to seek entertainment instead of salvation. In choosing to take the subject of his next poem from a story of sin and repentance, Shakespeare was responding to the mood of his time.

Summer 1593

Venus and Adonis was finished by April 1593, when Richard Field entered it in the Stationers' Register, and it was bought on 12 June, probably for sixpence.[14] The publication of one's first book, and the response of one's first readers, are great moments in a writer's life. Shakespeare was still under 30, the age at which young men are expected to settle down, and he had finally produced something that he considered to be of literary value. He probably expected his poem and Marlowe's to appear within the same year, and to be compared.

Suddenly everything changed. In the spring of 1593, even though the playhouses were closed, the authorities were nervous about the effect of the dismal economic situation on Londoners. There had been riots against foreign residents at least once in every decade of Elizabeth's reign; riots had already closed the theaters in spring 1592; and feelings were exacerbated in March 1593 by the failure of Parliament to pass a bill forbidding "strangers" to engage in retail trade in London.[15] On 5 May, verses threatening death to foreigners appeared on the wall of the Dutch churchyard, ominously signed "Tamburlaine." Other allusions in the verses indicated a knowledge of Marlowe's plays, so those searching for the author began, it seems, by seizing the papers of people with theatrical connections. The search widened to include not only anti-alien but anti-religious views, like those of which Marlowe had been accused by the informer Richard Baines. Baines had confessed to similar opinions, after torture, when he was caught spying on the Catholic seminary in Rheims,[16] and many of the same charges had been laid against the Earl of Oxford almost ten years earlier.[17] There may have been a standard list of questions in connection with accusations of atheism, and witnesses would have reason to agree whenever possible.

The first person arrested, on 12 May, was Thomas Kyd. His papers included a manuscript, possibly though not certainly in his fine italic hand, expressing skepticism about the Trinity.[18] It had been copied from *The Fall of the Late Arian* (1549), by the clergyman John Proctor, who had quoted the views of an imprisoned Arian piecemeal, giving his own triumphant replies at great length. Someone may have wanted to have a brief summary of Arianism without the long-winded refutation. Proctor considered these anti-Trinitarian beliefs damnable, and the owner of such a document, despite its origins, might well be suspected of atheism – "a deadly thing" as Kyd said in his letter from prison.[19] He may have known that in 1579 three men had been executed in Norwich for denying the Trinity.[20] He insisted that the document had belonged not to him but to Marlowe: they had been using the same room for writing and their papers had become mixed up. Torture was probably used to get Kyd to corroborate the devilish views that other witnesses had already ascribed to Marlowe, and he was eventually released from prison. His patron, however, had repudiated him and he was left destitute as well as broken by his experiences.

Marlowe himself was arrested on the 18th, examined by the Privy Council, and, surprisingly, released on bail on 20 May. On 30 May he was killed. The inquest declared that the killer had stabbed him in self-defense during a fight over the bill in an eating house. Since the others present on this occasion were servants of Essex and Robert Cecil, both of whom operated intelligence networks, Marlowe's fellow-dramatists probably doubted the official story, as have many recent scholars,[21] but there is no evidence for the conspiracy theories that have developed around the episode. If Shakespeare knew that Marlowe (only 29) was almost exactly his age, he might have been still more disturbed. He may have thought first of the unfinished *Hero and Leander*. Was the manuscript among the confiscated papers? Somehow, it was entered into the Stationers' Register on 28 September. Marlowe's patron, Sir Thomas Walsingham, may have had a copy; or perhaps the poem was already in the possession of Edward Blount, though he waited five years before publishing it. It is possible that it was always "designed to be a fragment."[22] Marlowe was interested in the beauty of the two lovers and their erotic fulfillment, not in their deaths.

Everyone in the literary world must have been deeply disturbed at what happened to Kyd and Marlowe. The fact that they were the two most successful playwrights of their age had not protected them. Marlowe, clearly the stronger personality, was remembered for some time. Though Kyd was occasionally mentioned among major authors of the previous generation, his authorship of *The Spanish Tragedy* is known only from a reference in Thomas Heywood's *Apology for Actors* (1612), and the clue was not picked up until the eighteenth century. In his official statements Kyd had done his best to distance himself from Marlowe, but Jeffrey Masten has suggested that his words can also be read as testimony to a lost friendship.[23] Whether Shakespeare remembered the two men as friends or enemies – his own, or each others' – their influence is pervasive. It may even be present in the motto on the title page of *Venus and Adonis*:

> *Vilia miretur vulgus; mihi flavus Apollo*
> *Pocula Castalia plena ministret aqua.*
> (Ovid, *Amores* 1.15)

That is, in Marlowe's translation, "Let base conceited wits admire vilde things;/ Fair Phoebus lead me to the Muses' springs."[24] The lines have been read as "an implicit renunciation of the 'low' art of playwriting."[25] Yet the elegy from which they come is Ovid's passionate defense of his writing against those who want him to practice law or war, in keeping with "the line from whence I sprung." Perhaps Shakespeare, in view of his name, felt that the rejection of a military career had a particularly personal meaning for him. More importantly, he probably knew that Ovid's elegies had been translated by Marlowe. The translation finally appeared – in the same volume as the epigrams of "I.D." (Sir John Davies) and with an obviously false imprint on the title page – only to be condemned and probably burned in 1599. In view of the April date of the Stationers' Register entry of *Venus and Adonis*, it is possible that Shakespeare chose the motto before the events of May 1593, but he might also have added it at the last minute. To use a passage from a work translated by Marlowe, in the immediate aftermath of Marlowe's death, may have been as far as Shakespeare dared to go; there is no motto to *Lucrece*.

Despite the background against which it appeared, he could take pride in the success of *Venus and Adonis*, probably his best-known work until the publication of the 1623 Folio. It went into fourteen more editions before 1636 and was widely quoted both in manuscript commonplace books and in printed anthologies – and even in commonplace books copying from the printed anthologies.[26] Perhaps he was somewhat uneasy about the nature of his success. It is evident from most of the allusions and borrowings that the poem was enjoyed simply as a luscious piece of amorous writing. At times Venus appears to be on the verge of raping Adonis:

> Forced to consent, but never to obey,
> Panting he lies and breatheth in her face.
> She feedeth on the steam as on a prey,
> And calls it heavenly moisture, air of grace ...
>
> (61–4)

One of the most popular passages was a condensed version of the familiar topos of the sexualized landscape:

> "Fondling," she saith, "since I have hemmed thee here
> Within the circuit of this ivory pale,
> I'll be a park, and thou shalt be my deer.
> Feed where thou wilt, on mountain or in dale;
>   Graze on my lips; and if those hills be dry,
>   Stray lower, where the pleasant fountains lie.
>
> (229–34)

Some readers have preferred the descriptions of the natural world, such as the descriptions of the two horses mating (258–324) or Venus's sensitive account of a hare vainly trying to escape the pursuing hounds (679–708). In context, however, both the horse and the hare are simply analogues for the experience of the goddess and the boy, images of a Nature in which everything is in pursuit of its desires.

A typical early reaction came from 20-year-old Thomas Heywood, who left Cambridge early and must have started writing his *Oenone and Paris* (1594), almost as soon as he finished reading *Venus and Adonis*. It uses the same stanza form, compares Paris to Adonis, and makes Oenone plead for his love. Michael Drayton responded to

Venus and Adonis – and to Marlowe's *Edward II* – in 1593 with the first of his many poems on English history: *Peirs Gaueston, Earle of Cornwall, his life, death, and fortune.* The speaker, Gaveston, compares Edward II to "Love-nursing *Venus* when she sports,/ With cherry-lipped *Adonis* in the shade" (stanza 41).[27] The author of the anonymously published *Licia*, a collection of songs and sonnets, Giles Fletcher, advises the reader that his mistress is "some Diana, at the least chaste, or some Minerva, no Venus, fairer far."[28] The epistle is dated September 1593, which suggests that Fletcher had read the newly published poem and wanted to distance himself from it by pre-empting most possible identifications. Especially after the intentionally autobiographical *Astrophil and Stella* and the rumors around Marlowe's death, poets may have been exceptionally nervous about misinterpretation. At least one reader, as Katherine Duncan-Jones discovered, found a way of "decoding" *Venus and Adonis*. On 21 September the soldier William Reynolds wrote to Burghley that the poem depicted Elizabeth I as a sexually rapacious Venus, though "those books are mingled with other stuff to dazzle the matter."[29] Since a goddess is ageless, the question of age does not arise in the poem, but Reynolds may have been thinking of Elizabeth's relationship with the much younger Duke of Alençon. If Reynolds's reading had been accepted as any part of Shakespeare's intention, it could have caused as much trouble as the statements that Baines made about Marlowe. Fortunately, Reynolds seems already to have had a reputation as a crackpot.

Southampton – the most important reader, from Shakespeare's point of view – apparently liked *Venus and Adonis*, and rewarded the author. The evidence for this statement is the dedication – again, very brief – that Shakespeare wrote in the following year when he published his second poem, *Lucrece*:

> The love I dedicate to your Lordship is without end, whereof this pamphlet without beginning is but a superfluous moiety. The warrant I have of your honorable disposition, not the worth of my untutored lines, makes it assured of acceptance. What I have done is yours, what I have to do is yours; being part in all I have, devoted yours. Were my worth greater, my duty would show greater; meantime, as it is, it is bound to your Lordship, to whom I wish long life still lengthened with all happiness.

Shakespeare's success contrasts with what happened to one of his equally ambitious contemporaries. Around September 1594, Nashe presented Southampton with his famous comic-grotesque novel, *The Unfortunate Traveller*.[30] The dedication seems not to have produced results, since Nashe removed it from the next edition of the novel. Perhaps Southampton was becoming aware that he would soon need to cut down his expenses, but he may also have been annoyed at the tone of the dedication, which is almost a parody of the genre: "Incomprehensible is the height of your spirit both in heroical resolution and matters of conceit."[31] This was the kind of attitude that made university graduates suspect: "your proud university princox thinks he is a man of such merit the world cannot sufficiently endow him with preferment...."[32] Shakespeare had managed to avoid suggesting that he thought he deserved anything.

Lucrece

Though usually known as *The Rape of Lucrece,* and registered as "The Ravishment of Lucrece," Shakespeare's second long poem was published in 1594 simply as *Lucrece.* It remained *Lucrece* in three reprints, becoming *The Rape of Lucrece* only in a 1616 edition with which Shakespeare had nothing to do. It is possible that the short title was Field's "dampning down" of the original in the interest of propriety,[33] but if the poem was the "graver labor" promised in the *Venus and Adonis* dedication, Shakespeare himself may have wanted to avoid sensationalism. For this poem, some 700 lines longer than its predecessor, he chose a more difficult verse form (rhyme-royal, a seven-line stanza normally used in serious works like Chaucer's *Troilus and Criseyde*).

If the poem was written at about the same time as *Titus Andronicus,* possibly before the play reached production, Shakespeare had already developed, with Peele, the horrific theme of the raped and mutilated woman in a military society. The story of a chaste wife who commits suicide rather than live dishonored made a fit pair with *Venus and Adonis* (many writers mention the two together) and might have helped to counter any accusations of immorality or misogyny in the earlier poem. Whereas in the Petrarchan culture chastity is sadistic and life-denying, in *Lucrece* the Roman (and Elizabethan) ethos of married chastity is set against what Shakespeare would later call "appetite, an universal wolf,/ So doubly seconded with will and power" (*Troilus and Cressida* 1.3.121–2).

Lucrece was prefaced by an Argument (plot summary). It is almost certainly by Shakespeare – why would he allow anyone else to insert it? – and its purpose is to highlight the political background. An anonymous pamphlet of 1590 called *The Serpent of Division* saw the rape of Lucretia as the first episode in the process that had led to the end of Roman liberty.[34] The poem, however, ends with the consequences of the first retelling of Lucretia's story, which is the oration by Brutus, "with a bitter invective against the tyranny of the King, wherewith the people were so moved that with one consent and a general acclamation the Tarquins were all exiled and the state government changed from kings to consuls." By now, Southampton and his friend Essex were probably entertaining some of the views – about the successor to Elizabeth and perhaps about ancient Greek and Roman alternatives to monarchy – that would bring them both to disaster in 1601. After what had happened to Kyd and Marlowe, Shakespeare may have sympathized with such views.

The poem, wisely, is less inflammatory than the Argument. It begins long after the usurpation of the elder Tarquin (the dedication calls it "a pamphlet without beginning") and it ends without quoting Brutus's speech or even making it clear that the banishment of Sextus Tarquinius did not mean the end of kingship in Rome.[35] The *in medias res* opening is even more rapid than that of *Venus and Adonis*:

> From the besieged Ardea all in post,
> Borne by the trustless wings of false desire,
> Lust-breathèd Tarquin leaves the Roman host
> And to Collatium bears the lightless fire
> Which, in pale embers hid, lurks to aspire
>   And girdle with embracing flames the waste
>   Of Collatine's fair love, Lucrece the chaste:
>   (1–7)

Tarquin's lust is a wild horse and a raging fire that devours (like his horse) the space between the city he should be besieging and the woman he intends to rape. The fire is also hidden beneath its embers, since Tarquin gives no hint of his intentions while Lucrece is welcoming him to her house.

Whereas *Venus and Adonis* focused on the goddess throughout, *Lucrece* divides attention between Lucrece and Tarquin. Much of the opening section takes the reader into the mind of a man debating whether he should act on his desires. Like Macbeth later on, Tarquin knows that he is committing a crime that will bring nothing but repentance:

> "What win I, if I gain the thing I seek?
> A dream, a breath, a froth of fleeting joy.
> Who buys a minute's mirth to wail a week?
> Or sells eternity to get a toy?"
>   (211–14)

Such generalizations are directed at readers looking for lines to enter into their commonplace books. Perhaps at Richard Field's suggestion, Shakespeare occasionally used double quotation marks to indicate the presence of quotable *sententiae* – for example:

> "The sweets we wish for turn to loathèd sours
> "Even in the moment that we call them ours.
>   (867–8)

Their presence may explain why the scholar Gabriel Harvey made a note that this poem, along with *Hamlet*, had qualities to "please the wiser sort." The quotation marks (often omitted in modern editions) are used sparingly and none draw attention to the more political statements, like Lucrece's bitter comment on the cause of the Trojan War:

> "Why should the private pleasure of some one
> Become the public plague of many moe?"
>
> (1478–9)

At one point, ironically, the markings actually point to Tarquin's defiance of just such moral "sentences":

> "Who fears a sentence or an old man's saw
> Shall by a painted cloth be kept in awe."
>
> (244–5)

The slowness with which the narrative leads up to the central action intensifies its horror. Tarquin moves through the silent house, forcing lock after lock on the doors between his room and Lucrece's, and gazes for some time at the sleeping woman before awakening her by placing one hand on her breast. Like Lavinia in *Titus*, Lucrece appeals eloquently to his better nature, but she "pleads in a wilderness where are no laws" (544) like the "wilderness of tigers" that Titus identifies with Rome. Tarquin's first reaction is to talk like a Petrarchan lover, blaming his mistress for causing his behavior and making a pun on "color," which Lucrece had used in the sense of "justification":

> But she with vehement prayers urgeth still
> Under what color he commits this ill.
>
> Thus he replies: "The color in thy face,
> That even for anger makes the lily pale,
> And the red rose blush at her own disgrace,
> Shall plead for me and tell my loving tale.
> Under that color am I come to scale
>   Thy never-conquered fort; the fault is thine,
>   For those thine eyes betray thee unto mine.
>
> Thus I forestall thee, if thou mean to chide:
>
> (475–84)

The ingenuity of Tarquin, indeed, lies in his ability to "forestall" whatever anyone might say against his crime: he already knows that it is a vile deed that he will regret, "Yet strive I to embrace my infamy" (504); if she refuses, he will not only kill her but also destroy her reputation after death. The pre-empting of any kind of escape means that the poem's focus is less on the rape itself than on Lucrece's determination to achieve fame on her own terms in spite of him. Once he has left her, the poem is seen almost entirely from Lucrece's point of view. She is almost excessively self-aware: in the letter she sends her husband she is careful not to anticipate what she will say when they meet ("the life and feeling of her passion/ She hoards, to spend when he is by to hear her" (1317–18). Through this non-dramatic genre, Katherine Duncan-Jones

121

argues, "Shakespeare was liberated to explore aspects of female behaviour that were beyond the reach of even the most brilliant boy actor."[36] At the same time, the poem almost cries out for dramatic interpretation. In conversation with her maid, Lucrece has trouble even speaking the name of Tarquin; she asks for pen, ink, and paper, then remembers that she has them already.

Time has to pass after she sends the letter. To distract herself until Collatine arrives, she goes to look at a painting of the siege of Troy. Her reaction to it suggests that Shakespeare himself had seen very few paintings at this time; perhaps Southampton's house and the aristocratic settings where he sometimes acted made him aware that he had been visually starved. In *Venus and Adonis*, Venus's grief makes her see double and she comments, almost comically, on seeing "two Adons dead" (1070). In *Lucrece* intense emotion again affects visual perception. Shakespeare evokes both the difficulty of seeing – something of which he is always peculiarly aware – and the parallel between his own task as a writer and that of the visual artist. The painter's "sweet observance" (careful recording of detail) allows the spectator to see the sadness even in the eyes of distant figures gazing through loopholes in the towers of Troy (1382–6). Where the artist has conveyed the sense of a crowd by what seems to be rudimentary perspective, Lucrece, or Shakespeare, does not mentally convert this image into a three-dimensional one, but describes it grotesquely, as if the individual listeners were fragments existing in the same visual plane:

> Some high, some low, the painter was so nice.
> The scalps of many, almost hid behind,
> To jump up higher seemed, to mock the mind.
> (1413–15)

The story of Lucretia was frequently cited as a test case of whether suicide might ever be condoned. Though sympathetic but troubling suicides and "doubtful" deaths would characterize much of Shakespeare's drama, the poem remains within a Roman perspective and does not question her decision. After her death, the tone changes abruptly. There has been no preparation for the important role of Brutus, who has survived under tyrannical rule by pretending to be simple-minded; he has not even been mentioned as one of Collatine's companions. His first act is to take the knife out of Lucrece's wound. Then he silences the father and husband who are debating which of them has the greater grief, urging them to revenge:

> "Thy wretched wife mistook the matter so,
> To slay herself, that should have slain her foe."
> (1826–7)

Though Lucrece will have the fame she wanted, it is as an icon that she will be remembered: Brutus will use both her knife and her "bleeding body" to rouse the

Roman people to overthrow the Tarquins. Shakespeare ends abruptly as he began, with "Tarquin's everlasting banishment," but this Brutus remains in the memory of his descendant in *Julius Caesar*, much as the ghost of old Hamlet does in *Hamlet*, and the unheard oration in *Lucrece* will become Antony's famous speech over the bleeding body of Caesar.

The parallel between the two Shakespeare poems would have been obvious if, as Colin Burrow suggests, the new poem appeared in summer 1594 in time to be sold as a pair with the second edition of *Venus and Adonis*.[37] "Who loves not Adon's love, and Lucrece' rape?" is a rhetorical question in a Cambridge play early in the seventeenth century.[38] *Lucrece* went through nine editions before 1655 – fewer than *Venus and Adonis*, but still remarkably successful.

WS and HW

Did Southampton invite Shakespeare to live for a time as one of his household servants? Literate and creative men could be useful in a number of ways to an aristocrat. The opposite was equally true, especially if the aristocrat had a good library. Southampton probably owned copies of the two most important and expensive literary publications of 1590, the *Arcadia* and *Faerie Queene*. He might also have bought the 1587 edition of Holinshed's *Chronicle*. Moreover, he knew Italian, and was a patron of John Florio, the author of two teach-yourself-Italian books and a distinguished translator. Florio would say in 1598 that he had been living for some years in the Earl's "pay and patronage."[39] Shakespeare must have been eager to read the numerous Italian *novelle* not yet translated and to make direct contact with the poetry of Ariosto and Tasso, some of which was quoted in *The Faerie Queene*. Southampton may have brought the dramatist and translator into contact, but Shakespeare could have been at least a beginner in Italian before he ever knew Southampton. In *The Taming of the Shrew* (usually dated to the early 1590s) Petruchio and Hortensio, who are of course supposed to be Italian, greet each other in phrases learned from Florio's primer ("*Con tutto il cuore ben trovato*, may I say," 1.2.24).[40] Although the *Shrew* was published only in 1623, this comic reference to the popularity of Italian language books probably belongs to the earlier period.

Still, Shakespeare, like other dramatists, could find books in other places than at Southampton House. Richard Field's printing shop, where he went to proofread his poems, had copies of the numerous works printed by Field, and a little to the northeast of the shop was St. Paul's Churchyard, where the booksellers had their shops. What is more important is that Southampton could offer "access" – contact with people and places that would otherwise have been inaccessible. One reason that the elaborate euphuistic style was so much used by writers of romances and romantic plays was that it provided a language for royal and aristocratic characters that sounded appropriately elegant yet did not presume to know how such people really talked.

For someone who wanted to depict kings and courtiers in less artificial contexts, simply hearing "real" conversation was important.

The one possible indication of a relationship between Shakespeare and Southampton is a poem that appeared late in 1594, *Willobie His Avisa*. Apparently a long paean of praise to a chaste wife somewhere in the west of England, it demonstrates how effectively, both before and after her marriage, she repels a variety of lascivious suitors – French, Germano-English, and Italo-English. The supposed editor, Hadrian Dorrell, claims to have found the papers in the study of his friend Henry Willoughby, who is now out of the country, and Willoughby (a real person who attended Oxford, whereas Hadrian Dorrell is probably a pseudonym) seems to be the HW who appears at the end of the poem as the most passionate of Avisa's suitors. Much of the volume consists of poems supposedly written by him to her. *Lucrece* is specifically mentioned, and credited to Shakespeare, in a prefatory poem where she, Susanna, and Penelope are placed alongside Avisa as heroic examples of chastity. The poem inspired at least one rebuttal in 1596, when another author claimed that Penelope, Ulysses' wife, was superior to Avisa. "Hadrian Dorrell" answered the Penelope poem with additional verses to a new edition in the same year, and the poem was reprinted several more times.[41] *Lucrece* may have inspired a small circle of friends in Wiltshire (the apparent location) to write about women who managed to retain their chastity without committing suicide. In the preface to the 1596 reprint of his poem, "Dorrell" denied that it had any hidden meaning – which, of course, has only encouraged scholars to think that it did.

In the episode of *Avisa* that has aroused the most interest, young Willoughby falls madly in love with Avisa and takes counsel of his friend WS, an "old player," supposedly more experienced than HW, the "new actor." WS, rather like Pandarus, advises, "She is no saint she is no nun,/ I think in time she may be won." WS disappears and is forgotten when HW begins his courtship. Has HW suddenly changed into Henry Wriothesley? No such episode has ever been identified in the life of the young Earl of Southampton, and the praise of Shakespeare's *Lucrece* in one of the commendatory poems seems hard to reconcile with the portrayal of WS as a cynical old misogynist. The location seems wrong; the situation seems wrong; the only reason why the poem has been associated with Shakespeare is the coincidence of the initials and the fact that WS is called "an old player." In context, this seems to mean someone experienced in the ways of courtship, or perhaps of brothels, but the double meaning could be deliberate. Shakespeare, aged 30 in 1594, probably did know a great deal more than the university student HW. As Schoenbaum has noted,[42] there is even a remote connection between Shakespeare and Willoughby, via the latter's relation by marriage, Thomas Russell, who would later be an overseer of Shakespeare's will.

The poem may be exactly what it purports to be: a warning to women not to fall for the arguments of lecherous men and a series of witty answers that they can use in return. Any poem in praise of chastity could also be associated with the queen, so

Barbara de Luna has interpreted it as a series of satires on Elizabeth's suitors (which would at least explain why one of them is French).[43] A few years later, in *A Midsummer Night's Dream*, Shakespeare made a fairly obvious allusion to the queen's rejection of marriage: Oberon describes her as "a fair vestal thronèd in the west" whose "chaste beams" quenched Cupid's fiery arrows. Shakespeare probably would not have written in this way if he thought that anyone would connect him with *Willoughby His Avisa*. If it were not for the dragged-in feel of WS's appearance, no one would be likely to read more into it than the author says is there.

The Early Sonnets

By 1594 Shakespeare clearly had a reputation for erotic poetry, with great appeal to the young in particular. Yet the language of love, in the two narrative poems, is limited. The love that loses all sense of self, that which Plato saw as leading to the creation either of new forms of beauty in children or of virtuous deeds and works of art, that which the Neoplatonists saw as a ladder leading from individual beauty and goodness to abstract beauty and goodness and finally to love of the God who was the source of all beauty and goodness – these are completely absent from the poems. All of them do, however, appear in Shakespeare's sonnets.

Since these are the most apparently personal of his works, it is important to realize that almost nothing is known about the order in which they were composed. Andrew Gurr has argued that Sonnet 145, though not published until 1609, was an early poem written for, or about, Anne Hathaway by the young Shakespeare. This unusual octosyllabic sonnet focuses on a grammatical quibble: a woman who has said "I hate" to the speaker makes him happy by turning the statement into a negative:

> I hate, from hate away she threw,
> And saved my life, saying "not you".

The idea that "hate away" was a pun on Hathaway has appealed to many (another fine critic, Stephen Booth, adds the suggestion that "And" can also be read as "Anne").[44] I find it hard to imagine Shakespeare using even a metrically unusual sonnet form in the 1580s, when very few sonnets were in print. On the other hand, *Astrophil and Stella*, first published in 1591, would have introduced him to a sonnet where Stella's insistent "No, no," leads to Astrophil's triumphant insistence on the power of "grammar rules":

> For grammar says, – oh this, dear Stella, weigh, –
> For grammar says, – to grammar who says nay? –
> That in one speech two negatives affirm!
>
> (Sonnet 63)

Although Barnabe Barnes published a sonnet collection dedicated to the Earl of Southampton only a month after *Venus and Adonis*, Shakespeare did not follow up his two poems with a sequence, and his sonnets do not appear to have been widely known until they were mentioned in print in 1598. They could have been perceived as a whole only when 154 of them were finally published in 1609. Once this book appeared – or, more accurately, once the sonnets began to be widely read, which happened only in the nineteenth century – it became possible to treat them as a "story" with specific, even identifiable, characters. At present, there is enough consensus about the approximate dates of some of them to enable a degree of contextualization. Some of the sonnets are so similar to *Venus and Adonis* that they seem like offshoots of it. Even in their appearance on the page, many sonnets of the period are indistinguishable from *Venus and Adonis*. Unlike the early translators of Petrarch, who followed his form closely, some poets of the 1580s, such as Thomas Watson and Thomas Lodge, wrote sequences of sixaines that resulted in "sonnets" of twelve lines, or eighteen, or even longer. Drayton called the poems in his first collection "quatorzaines": some had three quatrains, and some four, before the final couplet.

Thematically, Shakespeare's first seventeen sonnets also recall *Venus and Adonis*. Venus has eloquently told Adonis that it is his duty to procreate:

> Torches are made to light, jewels to wear,
> Dainties to taste, fresh beauty for the use,
> Herbs for their smell, and sappy plants to bear.
> Things growing to themselves are growth's abuse.
> Seeds spring from seeds, and beauty breedeth beauty.
> Thou wast begot; to get it is thy duty.
>
> (163–8)

Adonis retorts, rightly, that this is an "idle overhandled theme" (770). Shakespeare probably knew of the lines in *Hero and Leander* that associate hoarding love with hoarding money:

> Ah, simple Hero, learn thyself to cherish.
> Lone women like to empty houses perish.
> Less sins the poor rich man that starves himself
> In heaping up a mass of drossy pelf,
> Than such as you.
>
> (1.353–7)

This is the subject of the first sonnet in the 1609 sequence, though paradoxically its addressee is a "tender churl" who "makes waste by niggarding" (12).

It is hard to imagine any writer, without external motivation, composing seventeen sonnets urging someone else to marry and procreate. As it happens, both

Southampton and the young Earl of Pembroke, William Herbert, were, at different times in the 1590s, known to be reluctant to marry the granddaughter that Burghley was offering them. In Southampton's case, the crucial period was 1593–4; William Herbert was under pressure in the second half of the decade. John Dover Wilson suggested that the first seventeen were designed for Herbert's seventeenth birthday in 1597.[45] Any time between 1593 and 1597 would be appropriate if these were indeed topical poems, and anyone who asked Shakespeare to write a set of poems would probably have requested something as much like *Venus and Adonis* as possible.

The gender ambiguity of the early sonnets is their most controversial quality. In Sonnet 1, the genders of the writer and the imagined recipient are unknown:

> From fairest creatures we desire increase
> That thereby beauty's rose might never die,
> But as the riper should by time decease,
> His tender heir might bear his memory . . .
>
> (1–4)

Normally it is women who are compared to roses, but here the pronouns are male ("His tender heir," "his memory"). Southampton's family name, Wriothesley, was apparently pronounced enough like "rosely" for a pun on roses to be intelligible to informed readers.[46] For those less well informed, it is only in Sonnet 3 that it becomes clear that the addressee is male, and is being urged to seek immortality through procreation. The speaker delights in multiplying arguments for marriage: he prophesies immortality through the preservation of physical resemblance, accuses the recipient of selfishness toward the human race in refusing to replicate his beauty, and argues, absurdly, against the assumption that the addressee's refusal is based on "fear to wet a widow's eye" (9.1). (This makes no sense for Southampton's widowed mother, who wanted him to marry, or for his hypothetical future wife, or for William Herbert's biography.) The subject gradually becomes the poet's own role. Plato's *Symposium* defines love as the desire to perpetuate beauty, distinguishing between immortality through the birth of children and immortality through the other "births" of heroic actions or artistic creations. Though the author insists that children are better guarantors than his writing, a Platonic preference for the latter has emerged by the time Sonnet 18 arrives with its famous "Shall I compare thee to a summer's day?" which claims immortality for the poem that has just rejected poetic comparisons.

The sonnets immediately following are the ones that have provoked the most discussion. Sonnets 19 and 20 are the only ones that specifically refer to the object of their love as male and superior to a female object of love, and only 20 openly states the desire for a sexual relationship:

> A woman's face with Nature's own hand painted
> Hast thou, the master-mistress of my passion;

> A woman's gentle heart, but not acquainted
> With shifting change, as is false woman's fashion;
> An eye more bright than theirs, less false in rolling,
> Gilding the object whereupon it gazeth;
> A man in hue, all hues in his controlling,
> Which steals men's eyes and women's souls amazeth.
>
> (1–8)

Women are false both in appearance (because "painted" or made-up) and in their love, but the young man is a constant lover and his *natural* beauty is attractive to both men and women. However, the speaker's desires are frustrated by his gender:

> And for a woman wert thou first created,
> Till Nature, as she wrought thee, fell a-doting,
> And by addition me of thee defeated,
> By adding one thing to my purpose nothing.
>
> (9–12)

Nature, not bisexual as in some personifications but a female goddess, started out to make a woman but at the last minute fell in love herself and added his "thing," or penis. The final lines of the poem resolve the conflict via a pun on "prick":

> Then since she pricked thee out for women's pleasure,
> Mine be thy love and thy love's use their treasure.
>
> (13–14)

The idealized "love" of the speaker is distinguished from "thy love's use" – the sexual love leading to procreation which has been the focus of the previous sonnets but which now seems only a second best.

Probably no sonnet has been analyzed more than this one. It can be read as explicitly homosexual, and those who want to find a story need to believe that the poet who was urging the young man to marry now finds himself in love with his subject. But there is no reason to believe that these poems have the same implied recipient as Sonnets 1–17. It seems odd, for instance, that the poet who addressed Southampton as "your Lordship" in his two dedications would use the familiar "thou" in his sonnets, though the change of register might perhaps have been excused as poetic license. But neither the 19-year-old Southampton of 1593 nor the 17-year-old Herbert of 1597 is likely to have appreciated being called a "lovely boy," even though, as Jonathan Bate points out, the phrase is a translation of *formose puer* in Virgil's second eclogue.[47]

A number of writers, of whom Oscar Wilde is the most famous, have thought that "master-mistress" might refer to a boy dressed as a woman – most obviously, a boy actor, though he probably was "painted" on stage (the *Groatsworth* had attacked actors as "painted monsters"[48]), and was constantly "shifting" his costume if not his affections. Shakespeare was still writing on this theme, as on the "procreation" theme of Sonnets 1–17, in *Twelfth Night* (1601–2). Viola, a boy actor playing a woman disguised as a boy, praises the complexion of Olivia, a boy actor playing a woman:

> 'Tis beauty truly blent, whose red and white
> Nature's own sweet and loving hand laid on.
> Lady, you are the cruel'st she alive
> If you will lead these graces to the grave
> And leave the world no copy.
>
> (1.5.234–8)

The emphasis on the addressee's androgynous beauty is compatible with sixteenth-century poetry that praises male beauty by comparing it with female, as when Marlowe says of Leander, "Some swore he was a maid in man's attire,/ For in his looks were all that men desire" (*Hero and Leander* 1.83–4). The addressee of Sonnet 20 is one "that steals men's eyes and women's souls amazeth" (8), and androgyny has an appeal that cuts across gender lines: in modern Japan, for instance, the women who play male leads in the all-female Takarazuka company ("more suave, more affectionate, more courageous, more charming, more handsome, and more fascinating than a real male"[49]) have most of their following among women.[50] The child actors seem to have been particularly attractive to women because they were unthreatening both physically and sexually.[51] Dressed as women, they were equally unthreatening to men.

Any study of the homoerotic poetry of the 1590s needs to take account of the eclogues with which Virgil began his career, and particularly the famous second one, which is addressed by the shepherd Corydon to another shepherd, Alexis:

> *O crudelis Alexis, nihil mea carmina curas? ...*
> *Nonne fuit satius, tristes Amaryllidis iras*
> *Atque superba pati fastidia? Nonne Menalcan,*
> *Quamvis ille niger, quamvis tu candidus esses?*

Cruel Alexis, do you care nothing for my songs? ... Would it not have been better to put up with the sulky moods of Amaryllis and the airs she gives herself? Or with Menalcas, dark though he is – and you so fair?[52]

The alternatives of which Virgil's Corydon is so aware – the difficult woman and the beautiful man, the dark lover and the fair one – pervade Shakespeare's sonnets. Sonnet 126, a twelve-line poem written in couplets and specifically addressed to a "lovely boy," may be meant to conclude this series.

129

This Virgilian aesthetic was apparently considered acceptable, at least in some circles; in fact, it may have constituted a literary circle. Otherwise, it is hard to explain why a 20-year-old poet, Richard Barnfield, in 1594, published his first book of poems under the frank title, *The Affectionate* [passionate] *Shepheard: Containing the Complaint of Daphnis for the loue of Ganymede*. The poems themselves are equally frank:

> If it be sin to love a sweet-faced boy,
> (Whose amber locks trussed up in golden trammels
> Dangle adown his lovely cheeks with joy,
> When pearl and flowers his fair hair enamels)
>   If it be sin to love a lovely lad;
>   Oh then sin I, for whom my soul is sad.[53]

Eventually the shepherd bids farewell to "thou love-hating boy (whom once I loved)" (E1), but not before he has run the gamut of Virgilian emotions.

Barnfield and Shakespeare, the only 1590s sonneteers explicitly to address a male object,[54] seem to have been associated in readers' minds and some of their poems would be published together again in 1599. Barnfield never names the playwright, but does mention another friend, Michael Drayton, who also came from Warwickshire. Drayton's Gaveston is even more explicit than Marlowe's about his relationship with Edward II:

> My breast his pillow, where he laid his head,
> Mine eyes his book, my bosom was his bed . . .
> His love-sick lips at every kissing qualm,
> Cling to my lips, to cure their grief with balm.[55]

By comparison with these poems, even Shakespeare's Sonnet 20 only teases the reader with the possibility that it will argue in favor of homosexual love. Drayton and Barnfield seem surprisingly unworried about the reception of their poems. Barnfield, when he published his second book in 1595, began by defending his previous one, insisting that he was merely imitating Virgil's second eclogue.[56] Yet he did not really take back what he had said in *The Affectionate Shepheard*, and the motto he chose, *Quod cupio, nequeo*, (What I desire, I cannot have), may indicate that he felt coerced.

A literary circle with a taste for homoerotic verse would have had political implications. Since writers consistently depicted the queen as female in appearance but male in virtues and intellect, androgyny was a metaphor for the idealized ruler or lover. In political terms, the male favorite was less dangerous than the mistress, since bastards and their descendants were potential claimants to a throne. An intelligent and virtuous favorite, indeed, was exactly what every ruler was thought to need, and Castiglione's *Courtier* had explained how to cultivate the talents and virtues that would make one attractive to the ruler and thus an influence for good. Shakespeare could have noticed that the longest poem in James VI's 1584 volume was *Phoenix*, an allegorical elegy on his former favorite, the Duke of Lennox, who died a year after James's lairds had forced him into banishment in 1582. The Essex faction, including Southampton, were enthusiastic supporters of James's claim to the throne and patronized writers who favored classical literary models, especially those of Greece; Essex's secretary, Henry Cuffe, had been Professor of Greek at Oxford. They were aware of the Athenian idealization of Harmodius and Aristogeiton, homosexual lovers and tyrannicides. The enthusiasm for Greek continued when George Chapman began to proselytize for it, but the tolerance for homosexual love was short-lived. Drayton's later revisions to *Gaveston* suggest that he recognized the need to tone it down for general consumption, and he soon had a reputation as a serious moral writer. Barnfield, however, published nothing further after 1598, and his father disinherited him in 1600. In 1597, when Chapman dedicated the first installment of his Homer translation to Essex, William Burton dedicated to Southampton a translation of the Greek romance *Clitophon and Leucippe*, which includes a debate as to whether boys or women make the best objects of love. When another version of the romance was published in 1638 the translator omitted the entire chapter.

Meanwhile, writers must have known that time was running out for Southampton. In October 1594, when he turned 21, he would have to pay a fine for refusing to marry Elizabeth Vere, as well as a fee for the resumption of his estates, and reduce his expenses — such as literary patronage — drastically. Shakespeare, after having promised in *Lucrece* that "what I have to do is yours," never dedicated another work to him, and returned to writing for the theater shortly after its publication. Many biographers think that the end of the plague period meant that Shakespeare was forced to choose between prestigious poetry and vulgar drama. The choice was not as stark as this. Although this chapter has separated Shakespeare's writing of poems from his writing and acting in plays, the plague years did not necessarily mean a complete cessation of acting. The obvious resemblance between the subject matter of *Lucrece* and *Titus Andronicus* is as interesting as the differences between the two works (for instance, the raped Lavinia becomes a silent character, with a haunting visual presence, in the play, while the form of the poem allows the raped Lucrece, though invisible, to soliloquize at length). Whatever some writers said about the acting profession, a man who had achieved success in it would have found it hard to leave. At the same time Shakespeare continued to be in contact with other poets, and his plays immediately after 1594 were the most obviously poetic that he ever wrote.

Notes

1. Edmond, "Heminges, John," *ODNB*.
2. Lodge, *Complete Works*, ed. Gosse, 1; 25–7.

3. See Freeman, *Thomas Kyd: Facts and Problems*, appendix A, 183, and Nicholl, *The Reckoning*, 260.

4. Lawrence Fletcher accompanied him from Scotland in 1604 and became a member of the King's Men. In 1599 he and an English actor, Martin Slater, performed before the king. See M. Eccles, "Elizabethan Actors IV," 171, and P. R. Roberts, "The Business of Playing."

5. Chambers, *ES*, 2: 111, citing a letter printed in the *Athenaeum*, 21 Jan 1882. See above, p. 55.

6. Quoted from Marlowe, *Complete Poems and Translations*, ed. Orgel.

7. Gary Taylor suggests that "'heire' here means 'legitimate offspring', contrasting the poem favorably with the 'bastard' products of his theatrical career." Taylor and Lavagnino, eds., *Thomas Middleton: A Companion*, 116.

8. See Chandler, ed., *An Anthology of Commendatory Verse*, 3.

9. Nelson, *Monstrous Adversary*, 141–54.

10. See Anthony Holden in the *Observer*, 21 Apr. 2002, available online, with a link to the portrait: http://books.guardian.co.uk/departments/classics/story/0,6000,688633,00.html#article.

11. The accuser was William Reynolds. See below, p. 118, and note 29.

12. W. P. Barrett, ed., "A Learned Physician," *Present Remedies: good counsel against the Plague* (Shakespeare Association, Oxford University Press, 1933), xiv, cited in *The Complete Sonnets and Poems*, ed. Burrow, 15.

13. Perkins, *Two Treatises*, B7^v–B8^v.

14. Schoenbaum, 175–6. Since the book was one of two bought for a total of 12*d.*, its exact price is conjectural; my thanks to Alan Nelson for this point.

15. Yungblut, *Strangers Settled Here Amongst Us*, 40–1.

16. Baines's confession was first translated and published by R. Kendall in "Richard Baines and Christopher Marlowe's Milieu." See also Riggs, *The World of Christopher Marlowe*, 130–8.

17. Nelson, *Monstrous Adversary*, 209.

18. Kyd's first biographer, an expert paleographer, does not think it his. See Freeman, *Thomas Kyd: Facts and Problems*, 27.

19. Freeman, *Thomas Kyd: Facts and Problems*, 181.

20. Nelson, *Monstrous Adversary*, 210–11.

21. See e.g. Nicholl, *The Reckoning*, 324–9, and Riggs, *The World of Christopher Marlowe*, 315–37. For a more skeptical view, see Kuriyama, *Christopher Marlowe: A Renaissance Life*, 136–41.

22. Marlowe, *Complete Poems and Translations*, ed. Orgel, xvii.

23. Masten, "Playwriting: Authorship and Collaboration," 360–6.

24. Quoted from Marlowe, *Complete Poems and Translations*, ed. Orgel, Elegy 15.

25. Bate, *The Genius of Shakespeare*, 18.

26. S. Roberts, *Reading Shakespeare's Poems*, 91–3.

27. Drayton, *Peirs Gaueston, Earle of Cornwall*, C2.

28. Giles Fletcher, *Licia. Or Poemes of Loue*, B1.

29. Duncan-Jones, "Much Ado with Red and White," 488.

30. Nashe's *Choice of Valentines* (1592 or 1593) is dedicated to a 'Lord S.' Since he says in the 1594 dedication that he has been wanting for some time to dedicate something to

Southampton, the earlier dedication is more likely to be intended for Lord Strange – unless both dedications are characteristic mystifications.

31. M. Green, *Wriothesley's Roses*, 98.

32. *The Second Part of the Return from Parnassus*, 3.2.1154–9, in *The Three Parnassus Plays*, ed. Leishman. The play was acted at St. John's College, Cambridge, sometime between 1601 and 1603, and published in 1606.

33. *The Complete Sonnets and Poems*, ed. Burrow, 43.

34. *The serpent of deuision VVherein is conteined the true history or mappe of Romes ouerthrowe . . . Whereunto is annexed the tragedye of Gorboduc.*

35. Chernaik, *The Myth of Rome in Shakespeare and His Contemporaries*, 37.

36. *Shakespeare's Poems*, ed. Duncan-Jones and Woudhuysen, 32–4.

37. *The Complete Sonnets and Poems*, ed. Burrow, 41–2.

38. *The Second Part of the Return from Parnassus*, 1.2.301, in *The Three Parnassus Plays*, ed. Leishman.

39. O'Connor, "Florio, John," *ODNB*.

40. See Lawrence, *"Who the Devil Taught thee so much Italian?,"* 120–3.

41. Peter Colse, *Penelope's Complaint, or, a Mirror for Wanton Minions* (1596), claims that its purpose is to "abolish Venus Idolators." See *Willobie His Avisa*, ed. Hughes.

42. Schoenbaum, 181.

43. De Luna, *The Queen Declined: An Interpretation of Willobie His Avisa*.

44. *Shakespeare's Sonnets*, ed. Booth, 501. See the notes to *Shakespeare's Sonnets*, ed. Duncan-Jones, 406.

45. See Duncan-Jones, *Ungentle Shakespeare: Scenes from His Life*, 154–5.

46. Akrigg, *Shakespeare and the Earl of Southampton*, 3, n. 3.

47. Bate, *Soul of the Age*, 209.

48. Carroll, "Who Wrote *Greenes Groats-worth of Witte*?," 86.

49. Quoted in Robertson, "The Politics of Androgyny in Japan," 424.

50. Brau, "The Women's Theatre of Takarazuka," 81.

51. McCarthy, "The Queen's 'Unfledged Minions'," 101–2.

52. Virgil, *The Pastoral Poems*, trans. Rieu.

53. [Barnfield], *The Affectionate Shepheard*, Aiii.

54. Wells, *Shakespeare & Co.*, 95.

55. Drayton, *Peirs Gaueston, Earle of Cornwall*, C1^v.

56. Barnfield, *Cynthia, with Certaine Sonnets, and the Legend of Cassandra*, A6^v.

7

"Our Usual Manager of Mirth"
1594–1595

Theseus. Where is our usual manager of mirth?
  What revels are in hand? Is there no play
  To ease the anguish of a torturing hour?
  Call Philostrate.

                                (*Midsummer Night's Dream* 5.1.35–8)

Philostrate is Theseus's Master of the Revels, who is supposed to ensure that anything performed at court is worthy of the occasion. In answer to Theseus, he provides a substantial list of possible entertainments: a musical piece for a countertenor and harpist, perhaps illustrated in mime; an "old device," probably musical, depicting the murder of Orpheus by the Bacchanals; and a show of the nine Muses, probably imagined as similar to the pageant of the nine Worthies in *Love's Labour's Lost*. It is not clear why Philostrate even mentions *Pyramus and Thisbe*, since he has seen a rehearsal and considers the production substandard. But Theseus wants a play, and this is the only real play on offer.

Theater Companies of 1594

Between 1578 and his death in 1610, the English equivalent to Philostrate was the Master of the Revels, Edmund Tilney. Initially, he had been required to command "every player or players with their playmakers, either belonging to any noble man or otherwise," to appear before him and perform their repertory for him to evaluate.[1] *A Midsummer Night's Dream* probably alludes to this practice, though by the 1590s Tilney was more likely to read a script than to attend a rehearsal, especially if he had confidence in the company. Shakespeare would probably be a frequent visitor to his office in St. John's, Clerkenwell (see page 52 above). Tilney, a writer himself, must have been better acquainted than anyone with the theater world before the plague of 1592–3, and he probably had something to do with what happened after it. By the time the playhouses reopened early in 1594, the theater companies seem to have been in disarray, though the available court entertainment was probably less dire than Philostrate's list. Henslowe's *Diary* indicates the fluctuations. For example, it was the Earl of Sussex's men who gave the apparently new *Titus & Ondronicus* on 23 January 1594, followed on 4 February by the old favorite, *The Jew of Malta*, which had previously belonged to Lord Strange's Men. Strange's Men had briefly become Derby's Men on 25 September 1593, when Lord Strange succeeded to the earldom, but the new earl died suddenly on 16 April 1594. He had recently been visited by a Catholic plotter who urged him to pursue his claim to the throne; he reported the visit to the government, but his family believed that his sudden death a few months later was the result of poison. His company, once so successful, did not appear at court in the Christmas season of 1593/4; it had probably been dissolved.[2] Some of his actors joined a company belonging to the Earl of Pembroke. This is presumably why, when *Titus Andronicus* was published in 1594, its title page stated that it had been played by "the Right Honourable the Earl of Derby, Earl of Pembroke, and Earl of Sussex their Servants."

At some point in 1594, probably on Tilney's advice, the Privy Council recognized two new companies, each under the patronage of a privy councilor. On 14 May 1594 Henslowe recorded three performances by an apparently new company, the Admiral's Men, who now owned *The Jew of Malta*. There is a gap after 16 May, and then in the entry for 3 June Henslowe wrote: "In the name of god Amen begininge at newington my lord Admeralle men & my lord chamberlan men As foloweth." This is the first mention of the Lord Chamberlain's Men, the company with which Shakespeare was to make his whole career. They played only a short season at Newington Butts, which was demolished later that year. Back at the Rose, Henslowe recorded virtually non-stop performances into 1595, with the two companies sharing the Southwark playhouse at least some of the time. The two possible Shakespeare plays, "*Andronicous*" and "*The Taming of A Shrowe*," disappear from the repertory after 12 June, so it is possible that the Burbage company broke away at this point. It is likely that they too would have acted through the summer to make up for lost playing opportunities. Shakespeare would, then, have been in London when Thomas Kyd was buried on 15 August. Since his parents renounced the administration of his estate, the 36-year-old writer probably died destitute.[3] Would many actors and playwrights have been there, to show respect to the man who had created some of the greatest theatrical roles of the period?

In the Christmas season of 1594/5, the Chamberlain's Men gave two performances before the queen at Greenwich Palace. When they were finally paid, on 15 March 1595, the treasurer's accounts indicate that three members of the company came to collect the fee. In almost any court business, from the carrying of letters to the receipt of payments, the choice of messengers was significant. They met important people, if only briefly, and became visible in a world where visibility mattered.[4] The task obviously did not require three people; the usual payees after this date were Augustine Phillips, and, later, John Heminges. In 1595, however, they were William Kemp, Richard Burbage, and William Shakespeare. They presumably saw themselves as the leaders of the new company; they may even have been the people that someone in office wanted to meet. Kemp and Burbage were already famous, one as a clown and the other as a leading tragic and romantic actor. Shakespeare was the celebrated author of *Venus and Adonis* and *Lucrece* and the court had probably seen at least one of his plays during the Christmas season.

Though other companies did in fact exist, the council apparently meant, and on 19 February 1598 stated specifically, that only the Admiral's Men and the Lord Chamberlain's men had been licensed to give public performances in order to be ready to perform at court.[5] Each side of the river was to be allowed one playhouse. Their competition might have been friendly, since their patrons were friends. Both Charles Howard and Henry Carey, Lord Hunsdon, were military men, related to each other and to the queen, and Howard, like Hunsdon, had taken his turn as lord chamberlain. Tilney could have divided the repertory between the companies,[6] or perhaps the players themselves held on to their plays and had a say in their own reorganization.[7] Edward Alleyn certainly kept his Marlowe roles. What is less clear is whether Shakespeare's plays moved to the Lord Chamberlain's Men because of Burbage or Shakespeare. At least half of the Lord Chamberlain's Men had been members of Strange's Men. Yet Edward Alleyn, its leading actor, became the star of the Admiral's Men, while Richard Burbage went to the Lord Chamberlain's. The two stars might have found it impossible to move in one sphere, but perhaps it was their patrons who decided that each company should have its own leading tragedian. Since Alleyn's older brother John had acted with the Admiral's Men and Edward Alleyn had married the stepdaughter of Philip Henslowe, landlord of the Rose Theatre, in the fall of 1592, the arrangement may have been a family affair. Alleyn and Henslowe worked as a team from this point on, with theater as only one of their money-making ventures.

The Lord Chamberlain's Men also had a family at their head. James Burbage had been involved in professional theater from its beginnings, both as an actor and as a businessman. This fact had its disadvantages, since there were ongoing legal repercussions of his dispute with the partner with whom he had built the Theatre almost twenty years ago. In November 1590, the partner's widow and friends invaded the Theatre with her bill of complaint, demanding half of the day's takings. According to witnesses, James, his wife, and his younger son Richard attacked them with a broomstick and tried to tear up the bill. Richard was also accused of "scornfully and disdainfully playing with this deponent's nose."[8] The great tragedian of the future evidently had a gift for comedy too. Even after this dispute died down, the fact that Burbage's lease on the Theatre was due to expire in four years remained a problem.

136

While the new company probably included some dozen actors, only five of them were "sharers," entitled to a portion of the receipts for each performance. The number of shares, of course, had to be limited. If "a share in the Lord Admiral's Men in 1597 was worth fifty pounds,"[9] it is likely that shares in the Lord Chamberlain's Men had about the same value. That Shakespeare was able to buy one may mean that the company accepted his existing plays and exclusive rights to future plays as part of his payment. He may have made up the rest in cash, or perhaps the money came out of his future earnings as an actor. His colleagues were a sophisticated and experienced group. Of these, Richard Burbage is the only one whose Shakespearean roles have been identified. Contemporary anecdotes and an anonymous elegy of 1619 show that he was famous as Richard III, Romeo, Hamlet, Lear, and Othello. John Davies of Hereford, in *Microcosmos* (1603), and the author of an anonymous elegy of 1619 speak of him as a skillful painter,[10] and there is a tradition that the painting in the Dulwich College Picture Gallery is his self-portrait (Figure 5). If so, it obviously belongs to a much later period.

There is tantalizingly little information about these actors. However, Webster's Induction to Marston's *The Malcontent* (1604), offers a brief glimpse of Burbage, Condell, and a later addition to the company, John Lowin, in conversation with two stupid spectators. The actors Sinclair (or Sincklo) and Sly play the spectators, and may have been well known for this kind of comic part. The three others play themselves. Burbage speaks eloquently: "Why should not we enjoy the ancient freedom of poesy? . . . No, sir, such vices as stand not accountable to law should be cured as men heal tetters, by casting ink upon them."[11] This is Webster's characteristic satiric style, but he must have assumed that audiences would accept it as the sort of thing Burbage might say. Henry Condell is equally articulate, making witty use of a Latin quotation as a put-down. There is some evidence of his repertory, since Ben Jonson listed the actors of his plays in his 1616 Folio and an anonymous annotator matched them with their roles. Condell, it seems, was the original Mosca in *Volpone* (opposite Burbage as Volpone), Surly in *The Alchemist* (opposite Burbage as Subtle), and the 1623 edition of *The Duchess of Malfi* shows that he played the suavely sinister Cardinal (again opposite Burbage as his brother Ferdinand).[12] Both Mosca and Surly are virtuoso roles, requiring intelligence and precise diction to negotiate their long, complex speeches. As Surly, Condell would also have had to speak a little Spanish. He sounds ideally suited to fast-talking and energetic characters like Mercutio and Hotspur. Perhaps because of his onstage charisma, he married a wealthy woman and was able eventually to retire to an estate in the country.

The other actors in the company are more shadowy figures, though the Jonson evidence is helpful. John Heminges played Corbaccio, a comic old man, in *Volpone*, and is often thought to have specialized in elderly characters like Polonius, although he was two years younger than Shakespeare. He does not appear in later Jonson cast lists and may not have continued acting long after 1606. He seems to have become the company's chief trainer of apprentices and its business manager, which is

Figure 5 Portrait said to be of Richard Burbage, and possibly painted by him. By permission of the Trustees of Dulwich Picture Gallery

probably why it was he who usually received the payment for court performances. As a member of the Grocers' Company, he may have organized the refreshment concessions, an important part of the company's profits. Heminges and Condell were friends with Shakespeare and with each other. All three lived in the same neighborhood at one point; they are mentioned in each others' wills, and both Heminges and Condell had sons named William.[13]

The other members of the company did not live long enough to be documented in James I's reign. The clowns Thomas Pope and William Kemp had been in the Earl of Leicester's company and went with him in 1586 when he was commander of the English army in the Low Countries, also visiting the courts of Denmark and Saxony. Kemp's acrobatic skills had been in great demand: he performed in a show that Leicester put on to celebrate St. George's Day and was paid 5 shillings for a feat of skill described only as "leaping into a ditch."[14] He was as much the star of the company as Burbage. Augustine Phillips, a leading actor with Strange's Men, joined the company in about 1594 and may have been its business manager until his death in 1605. Both he and Kemp were known for their jigs, the comic song-and-dance routines that traditionally followed a performance. He bequeathed musical instruments in his will, and created a successful jig that was named after him, so he was probably a musician as well as actor. He was also a friend of Shakespeare, to whom he left a bequest.

Until recently, almost nothing was known about the boy actors who were probably one of the theater's main attractions, but recent research has filled in many details.[15] As David Kathman, Mary Edmond, and John Astington have shown, the acting companies, like the guilds, operated an apprenticeship system, though some boys were hired on short-term contracts as "covenant servants" (initially for very short periods, later for three years).[16] Since there was no requirement to practice the trade of one's own guild, actors who belonged to livery companies were able to bind apprentices and train them as actors.[17] John Heminges, a member of the Grocers' Company, had a total of ten apprentices between 1595 and 1628.[18] The "plot" of a lost play, part two of *The Seven Deadly Sins*, names a number of actors in the Lord Chamberlain's Men, and if David Kathman is right in dating it to 1596–7 it indicates which boys were acting for the company at this time. "T. Belt" and "Sander" (Thomas Belt and Alexander Cooke) were apprentices to Heminges who went on to act with the adult company. "Ro Go" (Robert Gough) was probably a servant to Thomas Pope, who made a bequest to him later. "Nick" was probably Nicholas Tooley, Richard Burbage's apprentice; "Kit" was perhaps Christopher Beeston, servant to Augustine Phillips. There were also the unidentified "Will" and "Ned." The last of these is tantalizing, since it might refer to Shakespeare's youngest brother Edmund (aged 16 in 1596), but only fiction can fill in the gap between his birth in 1580 and the first mention of him, in 1607, as a player.

The boys had varied careers. Nicholas Tooley, 13 in 1596, was the son of an English merchant with a Flemish wife, brought back to England after his father died in Antwerp and cared for by the City of London's Court of Orphans. Since his father's family had their home in Burmington, Warwickshire, very near Stratford, Mary Edmond has conjectured that Shakespeare was responsible for the boy's introduction into the theater world.[19] By 1605 Tooley was a full-fledged member of the company, and the parts that he played as an adult (Corvino in *Volpone* and Ananias in *The Alchemist*) indicate that he was an excellent comic actor who could have handled roles like Beatrice and Rosalind, or could perhaps have taken over as the Nurse in *Romeo and Juliet*. Alexander Cooke was bound to Heminges in January 1597, continued acting for the company as an adult, and eventually became a sharer; like Tooley, he played leading roles. Gough went on to act as an adult, though in minor roles, and Beeston became a theater manager. The quality of the acting of the female parts was crucial to the success of a play, so there must have been other, slightly younger, actors in training at the same time. Augustine Phillips, though not a member of a livery company, had two apprentices, Samuel Gilburne and James

Sands, who may have been among the next generation of boy actors. They got on-the-job training by playing the servants and waiting women whose silent presence helped to establish other characters' "gentle" status. Boys' roles are more numerous than women's, so as to give the younger actors some stage exposure. As Catherine Belsey points out, very young boys wore petticoats, and the actors who played such roles "would also have become accustomed to managing skirts in preparation for their reappearance as heroines in due course."[20] They must have been present in many scenes, although the text indicates their existence only when they are needed, as when the wounded Mercutio asks, "Where is my page?" (*Romeo and Juliet* 3.1.93). As Scott McMillin and Evelyn B. Tribble have shown, they graduated to roles in which they played mainly opposite a single actor and where their action was carefully controlled by verbal and non-verbal cues, before moving on to those that required more experience.[21]

Shakespeare the Actor

Shakespeare was also an actor in the company, and for some reason many scholars are reluctant to believe that he could have been very good. There are only a few genuinely contemporary pieces of evidence about his acting. One is Chettle's statement late in 1592 that he is "excellent in the quality he professes" – i.e., acting. This is too unspecific to be useful, especially in the context of an apology. The second is an anecdote told in 1602, which may or may not describe him as an actor. John Manningham, a law student at the Middle Temple, heard it from a lawyer at the Inner Temple:

Upon a time when Burbage played Rich[ard] 3. there was a citizen grew so far in liking with him, that before she went from the play she appointed him to come that night unto her by the name of Ri[chard] the 3. Shakespeare, overhearing their conclusion, went before, was entertained, and at his game ere Burbage came. Then message being brought that Richard the 3[d]. was at the door, Shakespeare caused return to be made that William the Conquerour was before Rich[ard] the 3.[22]

"Shakespeare's name William," Manningham helpfully added; he obviously did not know the actor personally. The story has an independent existence, since a more elaborate version was told in 1759, at a time when Manningham's *Diary* existed only in manuscript.[23] It might already have been old when Manningham heard it. Since it exists mainly for the sake of its punchline, and since the substitution may have been some sort of bed-trick in the dark, one need not assume with Katherine Duncan-Jones that Shakespeare actually had to impersonate Burbage (or Burbage as Richard III) to seduce the stage-struck woman.[24] But the retort would be even wittier if, as has been suggested, Shakespeare had actually played the role of William the

Conqueror in *Fair Em*, a romantic comedy acted by Lord Strange's Men in about 1590, or King William Rufus in Dekker's *Satiromastix* (1601). Shakespeare's retort could also be taken to mean that the author of *Richard III* should have precedence over the man who only played the part.

The third piece of evidence comes in an epigram addressed to Shakespeare by John Davies of Hereford in 1610, which says that he "played some kingly parts in sport."[25] Though the Manningham anecdote might seem to substantiate this, most of the kingly roles in Shakespeare's plays must have been written for Burbage. With Burbage as Prince Hal, however, the dramatist might have taken the role of Henry IV, whose part is long and difficult to sustain as well as to memorize. He might have played the King of France in *All's Well That Ends Well*: it is the kind of part actors like, small but always effective.

So far undiscussed, as far as I know, is Jonson's comment in his *Discoveries*, probably written at least fifteen years after Shakespeare's death:

> Many times he fell into those things, could not escape laughter: As when he said in the person of *Caesar*, one speaking to him, *Caesar thou dost me wrong*. He replyed: *Caesar did never wrong, but with just cause* and such like: which were ridiculous.[26]

In the Folio text of the play, Caesar tells the senators, "Know, Caesar doth not wrong, nor without cause/ Will he be satisfied" (*Julius Caesar* 3.1.48–9). It has sometimes been thought that Jonson was misquoting, either maliciously or because he was confusing these lines with a later exchange between Brutus and Cassius:

> *Cassius.* Most noble brother, you have done me wrong.
> *Brutus.* Judge me, you gods! Wrong I mine enemies?
>   And if not so, how should I wrong a brother?
>
> (4.2.37–9)

It has also been suggested that Jonson's ridicule embarrassed Shakespeare enough to make him rewrite the lines. What is less often noticed is that Jonson comments on what Shakespeare *said*, rather than on what he wrote. He may have been remembering Shakespeare playing Caesar (another "kingly part") and being laughed at, either because his line was deliberately self-contradictory or because he had extemporized something absurd.

Another recently discovered piece of evidence is more doubtful.[27] At some time after 1621, the Warwickshire clergyman Richard Hunt annotated his copy of Camden's *Britannia* in the section on Stratford-upon-Avon where the author says that the town owes its fame to John de Stratford and Hugh Clopton. Hunt added in the margin, "*et Gulielmo Shakespeare Roscio plane nostro*" (and to William Shakespeare, truly [or indeed, or clearly] our Roscius). Though the historical Roscius was a famous Roman comedian, his name was traditionally applied to any admired actor.

Since Hunt was probably born around 1596, he was unlikely to be writing from personal experience, but the comment may mean that Shakespeare was remembered as a man of the theater.

The two other traditions about Shakespeare's acting date from considerably later. The old man who told a post-Restoration interviewer about seeing Shakespeare carried onstage on someone's back, and wearing a long false beard, may have been recalling Adam in *As You Like It*, but if he claimed to be Shakespeare's brother, as the story says, he was lying, since none of those brothers lived to be old. The other tradition, recorded by Rowe in 1709, is that "the top of his performance was the Ghost in his own *Hamlet*."[28] The Ghost is also a king, but nothing is said about his doubling the role with Claudius, a possibility that has been exploited in some modern productions. For some reason, this attribution is often taken as evidence that Shakespeare was not much of an actor, yet contemporary allusions suggest that the ghost scenes were the most memorable part of the play, and the effectiveness of Hamlet's performance obviously depends on the Ghost's.[29] More recently, several critics have thought that the dramatist played William in *As You Like It* (an easy double with Adam), simply because the constant stress on the character's name might have been funny for those who knew that the apparently moronic yokel was the play's author. However, Manningham's anecdote seems to show that he, at least, did not know Shakespeare's first name until he realized that it was crucial to his story.

Everything else that is said about the parts Shakespeare might have played, or about the quality of his acting, is pure conjecture. Some assume, for example, that Shakespeare's Warwickshire accent, which might have been an asset in *As You Like It* and in comic roles, would have been a handicap in "kingly" parts.[30] Yet regional accents were less important than they would become in a more class-conscious era, and not all of Shakespeare's fellow-actors were Londoners: Henry Condell was from Norwich and apparently did not come to London until the early 1590s. Boy actors were recruited from all round the country, and, as late as 1631, two companies were fighting over a boy from Yorkshire.[31]

There is no evidence that Shakespeare ever played clown's roles, but, historically, the actor-playwright was more likely to be a clown than a tragedian. As Meredith Skura writes, "More than any other single group they [clowns] seem to have shaped the period's drama."[32] Before Shakespeare, the clown-playwrights were Wilson and Tarlton; in his lifetime, Thomas Heywood, Robert Armin, and William Rowley were all clowns. Even Nathan Field, who wrote and collaborated on several plays, seems to have been primarily a light comedian. Perhaps, since clowns invented much of their own material, and relied on their ability to improvise, it was natural for them to move from stand-up comedy to the writing of full-scale plays with starring roles for themselves. Though some later actor-playwrights, like David Garrick, excelled in both tragedy and comedy, it remains true that many of those who acted in their own plays – Molière, Colley Cibber, and Noel Coward – were best known for their comic roles. Indeed, Ben Jonson, like Molière and Cibber, seems to have been unsuccessful as a writer or actor of serious roles. It is possible that an actor-dramatist makes audiences uncomfortable when the roles he writes for himself are too flattering. Shakespeare might have observed this fact early in his career and sought out roles with which he would not be identified.

One piece of evidence not usually mentioned suggests that Shakespeare's acting must have been more than competent. Jonson was unusually concerned with recording details of the performance of his plays. In the 1616 Folio of his works, Shakespeare is listed first in the cast of *Every Man in His Humour* and second in the cast of *Sejanus*. This positioning presumably refers either to the order of entry or to the order of importance of the parts. Even assuming that Jonson gave prominence to Shakespeare's name as a tribute in the year of his death, it is unlikely that he would have done so if the actor had played only unmemorable roles. Jonson, who began as an actor, was notoriously fussy about the performance of his plays, and a meticulous director long before such a role came to be recognized. Some forty years later, the elderly Marquis of Newcastle, a former patron, told his wife that Jonson was the best reader he ever heard.[33] The anonymous author of verses on a forthcoming revival of *The Alchemist* in 1660–1 wondered how actors could dare to play the leading roles now that they no longer had access to a playwright who had "Taught, Line by Line, each Tittle, Accent, Word."[34] If Shakespeare had been inadequate in *Every Man in His Humour*, Jonson would not have given him a major role in *Sejanus*.

Sharers were paid out of the company's profits, but they also had to contribute to its expenses. They usually took the largest parts, though Heminges may have been an exception. The "hired men," on a weekly salary, ranged from very minor players to experienced ones who became sharers when they could buy their way into the company. The boys were paid a small weekly wage. Those who were apprentices lived and boarded with their master. Although the directives of the Privy Council indicate that playing was supposed to take place only twice a week, it is obvious from Henslowe's *Diary* that whenever possible the Admiral's Men gave performances every day. The repertory could be changed at a day's notice, allowing one play to respond to another or to exploit recent events. The main duty of the lord chamberlain's "servants" was to perform at court whenever requested, and the public "rehearsals" were supposed to ensure the quality of those performances. When their patron wanted to make an impression, they might be asked to process in his livery. They were most in demand between Christmas and Lent, the time of the annual revels. Playing stopped during Lent and during the summer, when the law courts were in recess and London's population shrank; this was the time for touring in the country. The players might be on call for other occasions: for instance, the best speakers declaimed from pageants during the Lord Mayor's Show on 28–29 October, celebrating the livery companies of London.

Shakespeare's decision to buy a share in his company seems in retrospect a wise one, separating him from the hand-to-mouth playwrights who lived off the fee for one play after another. But it was something of a gamble, since it offered a secure income only when the actors were able to perform, which depended on the weather and the plague. Buying a share meant postponing the purchase of a house in Stratford. He had now been married for over ten years, and as far as is known his wife Anne, now about 36, was still living, like her 10- and 8-year-old children, with her husband's parents. If they discussed the matter at all, Shakespeare may have had to argue for a long-term view. The theater, when it was not closed down, was a highly profitable business that might enable the family to have a finer house in a few more years.

In any case, the question of buying property was temporarily postponed when fire swept through Stratford on 22 September 1594. It destroyed over 200 houses, including those of the Quineys and the Sadlers on the High Street. Though John Shakespeare's large Henley Street house seems to have escaped, he may have had to pull down some of the structures on its west side to separate it from the burning buildings only a short distance away.[35] The fire followed a summer of disastrous crop failures, including a shortage of the barley from which many households made their malt. Members of the council were deputed to go round the neighboring towns collecting contributions toward relief.[36] If Shakespeare managed to return to Stratford to assess the damage, his visit could be only a brief one. As the Christmas season approached, his first task for the Lord Chamberlain's Men must have been either to write a new play for the court or to rework one already written. Assuming that the plague did not recur, there would also be revels at the Inns of Court, another opportunity to perform before a prestigious audience.

With an audience eager for plays after so long an absence, both companies not only commissioned new work but revived everything in their existing repertory. In the first instance, Shakespeare probably revised plays that had been performed on the road or seen in London before the cessation of playing. Claims have been made for *The Taming of the Shrew*, *The Two Gentlemen of Verona*, and *The Comedy of Errors* as Shakespeare's earliest play, even though none was published until 1623. One reason is the desire to dissociate him from these light, farcical comedies by making them works of an immature and imitative period. The *Shrew* has clear affinities with Italian *commedia dell'arte* and acknowledges this in both text and stage directions by calling some characters pantaloons and pedants, stock *commedia* types. *The Two Gentlemen* is partly based on a popular Spanish novel, the *Diana* of Jorge de Montemayor, and partly on versions of the story already used in Italian comedies. *The Comedy of Errors* is meant to be recognized as a conflation of two plays by Plautus. Imitation, however, is hardly proof of early composition. Much of Shakespeare's success in the 1590s was due to the closeness and care with which he responded to a wide range of sources.

There are better arguments for early composition. All three plays differ from those known to have been written specifically for the Lord Chamberlain's Men. They contain extensive passages in "fourteeners," fourteen-syllable lines that had once been the standard dramatic form and which were still common in the 1580s.

Although they lend themselves easily to musical comedy treatment, they actually have less music than the later plays. *The Two Gentlemen of Verona* is the only one that contains a song, which occurs in a scene closely based on the source novel. Perhaps the company had not yet acquired its most talented boy performers, since most of these appear to have joined only in 1596 or 1597. The plays were certainly performed in the early years of the new company (in one case we know the date of a performance), but all three may have been revised by the time they reached the Folio.

The Taming of the Shrew

Perhaps company rivalry explains the odd publication history of the play now known as *The Taming of the Shrew*. Both this play and one called *The Taming of a Shrew* are known to have existed before 1594, the year in which *A Shrew* was published, since a poem published in 1593 apparently contains a reference to a moment that occurs in *The* – not *A* – *Shrew*.[37] The Folio text, however, may contain later interpolations, perhaps dating from the time when the play was revived to accompany a performance of John Fletcher's *The Woman's Prize, or the Tamer Tamed* (1611).[38] Thus, whatever version was being performed in the early 1590s was at least slightly different from the one known to modern readers. Peter Short's entry in the Stationers' Register, on 2 May 1594, of *A Pleasant Conceited History Called The Taming of a Shrew* not only established his ownership of the book but, thanks to the rules of the Stationers' Company, would have made it difficult for anyone else to publish Shakespeare's play. As Peter M. W. Blayney explains, the owner of a copy could "seek the Company's protection if *any* book – not necessarily a reprint or plagiarism of his own copy – threatened his ability to dispose of unsold copies of an existing edition."[39] The two *Shrew* plays, though vastly different, had some of the same characters and were recognizably based on the same plot.

That plot is the courtship of a shrew and of her apparently meek sister (two sisters in *A Shrew*). By the end, the women's roles are reversed: the former shrew makes a long speech declaring that wives should obey their husbands, which the former saint refuses to subscribe to. *A Shrew* has an elaborate frame in which a drunken tinker is persuaded that he is a lord and invited to watch a play; he intervenes in the action at one point, then falls asleep, and, waking up after the play is over, decides to go home and use what he has learned in his "dream" to tame his shrewish wife. A performance of a play called *The Taming of a Shrew* is recorded in Henslowe's Diary on 11 June 1594, while the Lord Chamberlain's and Lord Admiral's Men were evidently sharing the same theater space. Henslowe was notoriously casual with titles, so it is not certain whether he was deliberately differentiating it from one that he already knew as *The Shrew*. Was the 1594 play *The Shrew*, and did it then get into trouble with Pembroke's Men or the publisher, because of the pre-existence of another similarly titled play? Or was it really *A Shrew*, and did Shakespeare object to the acting of a play of which he had already written his own version?

Many scholars believe that *A Shrew* is a garbled and rewritten transmission of *The Shrew*. I believe, on the contrary, that *The Shrew* is a version of *A Shrew* designed for a somewhat smaller company, with a star actor and a star clown. *A Shrew* has three sisters and therefore three wooing episodes; Shakespeare's revisions removed one of the sisters so that he had to manage only two wooing plots along with the Sly framework (the sudden introduction of a widow to marry Hortensio results from the need to test three wives in the final scene). He also made the subplot of Bianca's wooing more complex, drawing, as *A Shrew* does not, on *The Supposes*, a translation of Ariosto's comedy by George Gascoigne. He set the play in Italy rather than Athens, and emphasized its "Italian" atmosphere with allusions to the *commedia dell'arte*. His original intention was probably to rewrite all the frame scenes. The opening, when Sly is thrown out of the alehouse, is full of references to places in the Stratford area. It might have been written for performance on tour in the Midlands, with other place names substituted in other locales. But Sly disappears after Act 1. Perhaps he was removed from the play when frame scenes went out of fashion, and the survival of the Induction is an anomaly. Productions used to cut him out altogether, thus removing the metatheatrical element; when he was restored in the twentieth century, the other frame scenes from *A Shrew* were often inserted as well.

If the revised play was first performed when Shakespeare was writing for a company on tour, and the company had both plays in its possession, the new version could still be played under the old license. Once the actors reached London, it may have become necessary for Shakespeare not only to make the play look less like its source but also to find a new title. This is at least one possible explanation for the mysterious appearance of the title *Love's Labour's Won* in a list of Shakespeare's plays in 1598 and in a bookseller's catalogue of 1603. No such play exists at present, and the most likely explanation is that it is an alternative title for something else. The title might have been given after the success of *Love's Labour's Lost* (1593–7), the title of which is a familiar catch-phrase. To rename *The Shrew* as *Love's Labour's Won* might be explained by the claim that taming Katherine would be like all Hercules' labors rolled into one ("Yea, leave that labour to great Hercules,/ And let it be more than Alcides' twelve," 1.2.255–6). This comparison is present in both plays, since in *A Shrew* Ferando (the equivalent to Petruchio) declares that he would be equal to Kate even if she were "the Thracian horse Alcides tamed."[40] While *The Shrew* is by no means an allegory of the labors of Hercules, two of the others may be mentioned when Petruchio claims that a scolding woman will be nothing in comparison with his previous experiences: "Have I not in my time heard lions roar?/ Have I not heard the sea, puffed up with winds,/ Rage like an angry boar chafèd with sweat?" (1.2.199–201) The main argument against the identification of *The Shrew* with *Love's Labour's Lost* is the fact that *The Taming of a Shrew* also appears in the bookseller's catalogue.[41] However, this other *Shrew* is the one with the indefinite article.

Like many plays of the early 1590s, *A Shrew* makes frequent allusion to other plays of the period. In a scene at the house of Ferando, Katherine, complaining of hunger, pleads with her husband's servant to get her something to eat:

Sander. But what say you to a fat capon?
Kate. That's meat for a king. Sweet Sander, help me to some of it.
Sander. Nay by'r lady, then 'tis too dear for us. We must not meddle with the
    king's meat.

(D4^{r-v}, pp. 373–4)

Soon follows the stage direction, "*Enter* Ferando *with a piece of meat upon his dagger's point.*"

Ferando. See here, *Kate*, I have provided meat for thee,
    Here, take it: what, is't not worthy thanks?

(D4^{v}, p. 374)

What he has provided is indeed "meet" for her in her present wild state. Katherine and the servant, between them, have already made the pun on "meet" and "meat." It originated in Peele's *The Battle of Alcazar*, from which the play takes, and parodies, the famous image of the Moor brandishing a sword with raw flesh on it. In *The Taming of the Shrew*, the stage direction reads simply "*Enter Petruchio and Hortensio with meat*" and Petruchio is considerably politer:

Here, love, thou see'st how diligent I am
    To dress thy meat myself and bring it thee.
I am sure, sweet Kate, this kindness merits thanks.
(4.3.39–41)

A Shrew may, however, indicate how the moment was originally played, with Petruchio parodying the famous entrance of Muly Mahomet. In the final scene of *A Shrew*, when Kate proves how thoroughly she has been tamed, Ferando's line, "See where she brings her sisters forth by force," accompanies the stage direction, "Enter *Kate* thrusting *Phylema* and *Emelia* before her" (G1). In *The Shrew*, Petruchio tells Kate that if the other women deny to come she should "Swinge me them soundly forth unto their husbands" (5.2.108), but greets their entrance with "See where she comes and brings your froward wives/ As prisoners to her womanly persuasion" (5.2.123–4). Again, the stage direction in *A Shrew* probably indicates the stage business. What Shakespeare adds to the original knockabout farce is the subtler joke of having Petruchio talk politely while behaving rudely, and the further joke when Kate, in the final scene, shows that she too can play this game. The absence of specific directions in the Folio could mean that by the 1620s the play had already become more refined, perhaps discarding a parody that would no longer mean anything.

Stories about women who bully their husbands are funny because they invert what everyone knows to be the reality about the strength of men and women; stories of men "curing" such wives by outsmarting or forcibly repressing them usually make no attempt to depict the process as anything but a power struggle. Shakespeare's play complicates the roles of the two central characters. Petruchio tells Katherine that he finds her beautiful and he looks forward at the end to "peace . . . and love, and quiet life" (5.2.112). The Kates of both plays want to get married, but whereas the Kate of *A Shrew* is conventionally disruptive and rude, the Kate of *The Shrew* is angry and unhappy, frequently crying, and anything but a free spirit. She gets no sympathy or support from the other women in the play, who disagree with her at the end as Bianca did at the beginning. In neither version does Kate threaten the revenge that is most obviously in her power: cuckolding her husband. Though *The Taming of the Shrew* is one of the few comedies to treat marriage as the beginning rather than the end of a story, Petruchio's refusal to consummate the marriage until Katherine has been tamed means that neither party can be trapped in a genuinely unhappy relationship, since non-consummation was one of the few legal grounds for divorce.

Modern readings of *The Shrew* pay unwilling tribute to its effectiveness by treating it like real life – to the point where some critiques and productions make it a tragedy. As Kathleen McLuskie has pointed out, adopting a feminist reading of a Shakespeare play often means denying oneself its "narrative, theatrical and intellectual pleasures."[42] Early modern women apparently copied misogynistic verses into their commonplace books.[43] Reading such verses, especially aloud, presumably let them identify themselves with the superior speaker and distance themselves from the fictitious addressee. This is what happens when Katherine, in her final scene, lectures the other women, proving her ability to make a coherent and eloquent speech.

In fact, the modern performance experience is exactly the opposite of the early modern one. A female actor usually spends four acts demonstrating the aggressive behavior that is identified both with masculinity and with success, then recognizes, like the heroine of *Annie Get Your Gun*, that it's better not to compete with men. The boy apprentice, on the other hand, was someone for whom success meant playing a role as different from his own gender as possible. The key male–female scenes were probably rehearsed separately by an actor and his apprentice.[44] The relation is replicated in the play when both Lucentio and Petruchio act as teachers of the woman they marry. Kate begins as the kind of angry, boyish woman that the actor probably found easiest to play (and perhaps had played, as Queen Margaret or Joan la Pucelle). The final scene, in which she demonstrates how women should behave, may look like a defeat in a modern production; in the 1590s, it would have been a masterpiece in the original sense of the word, the triumphant conclusion to the boy's training.

The Two Gentlemen of Verona

If Shakespeare ever contemplated writing for a children's company, *The Two Gentlemen of Verona* is the kind of play he might have offered them. Like other plays for such companies, it offers a number of good roles (including three for women and one for a boy) rather than one or two highly demanding ones. It works well with young actors: the total selfishness of Proteus and his apparent certainty that he is entitled to sacrifice both Valentine and Julia in order to "find himself" ring particularly true, and are more forgivable, coming from a very young man. One would expect a children's comedy to contain more than one song, but these could have been interpolated.

The plot is derived partly from one of the stories in *Diana* by Jorge de Montemayor (a Portuguese writing in Spanish), and partly from Arthur Brooke's *Romeus and Juliet* (1562), which is why it opens in Verona instead of Portugal, Montemayor's locale. Bartholomew Yong's English translation of *Diana* was published only in 1598, but apparently had been completed by 1583. Yong had acted in plays in both French and Spanish during his time at an Inn of Chancery and was now a member of the Middle Temple, where Shakespeare had connections, so he might have read it before publication. A play called *Felix and Philiomena*, acted at court by the Queen's Men in January 1585 and possibly on tour before then, may have been an early adaptation of some parts of the novel. For the first part of his play Shakespeare used Montemayor's basic plot: a man deserts his mistress for one in another town; she follows him in boy's disguise and finds him serenading another woman, then becomes his page and is sent on an errand to that woman. He stopped following the story at the point where it becomes most interesting, when the second woman falls in love with the disguised page. This eventually became part of *Twelfth Night*, and it is possible that he was already thinking of it for a separate play. Or perhaps he did not yet know how the story would end? Montemayor's novel is long, and the intertwined adventures of its large cast cover many pages. The story of Felix and Felismena (Proteus and Julia) begins in Book 2 of Part One. This includes the episodes that Shakespeare followed most closely, particularly the by-play between Julia and her maid Lucetta over Proteus's letter and the scene in which Julia and her host listen to Proteus wooing Sylvia. What Montemayor then did with his story was, however, completely different. The character corresponding to Sylvia dies of her love, never learning that the object of her hopeless passion was a woman, and it is only in Book 7 that Felismena, who has been brought up as a warrior, rescues her false lover, reproaches him with his falsehood, and is happily reunited with him. Shakespeare would have had to read through a great many other stories to find out what happened to these two lovers. He may have done so: one episode in Book 5, in which a wise woman gives a sleeping potion to two rival shepherds, with the result that one of them promptly falls out of love with the woman he has been pursuing and in love with the one who loves him, may be a source for *A Midsummer Night's Dream*.

Shakespeare made two main changes to the story. One was his introduction of a second hero, Proteus's friend Valentine. Proteus in the play deceives not only his former mistress, Julia, but also his friend, who is in love with Sylvia, and whose plan to elope with her is betrayed by Proteus to Sylvia's father. Julia, in male disguise, arrives in Milan and soon discovers that Proteus is false to her. Proteus's betrayal leads to Valentine's banishment from Milan. Absurdly, he is invited to become the leader of a band of outlaws – perhaps because Shakespeare had just read Thomas Lodge's *Rosalynde*, published in 1590, in which all the major characters are exiles in the forest. (He would return to this plot later; perhaps he was keeping a notebook of ideas for plays.) The story is rather abruptly resolved when Sylvia is captured by the outlaws, then rescued – first by Proteus, then by Valentine, who arrives just in time to stop Proteus from raping her. Forgetting all about Sylvia, the two men exchange reproaches, and Valentine proves how thoroughly he accepts Proteus's apology by offering him Sylvia, without asking her views. Admittedly, his phrase, "All that was mine in Sylvia I give thee" (5.4.52), might leave open the question of just what in Sylvia *is* his to give, but the words horrify the disguised Julia as much as they do most modern audiences. She faints and the discovery of her true identity brings about a complete realignment of Proteus's desires and an ending where everyone is forgiven, even the outlaws. The ease with which Proteus changes his mind and his desires is explained by his name, just as Valentine's constancy is explained by his.

Completely forgotten in this conclusion are two other Shakespearean additions: the comic servants, Speed and Lance, who are so important in the early part of the play, though not in the plot. Speed is a boy in the tradition of Lyly's pages, and makes fun of his master's lovesickness. Lance, however, is a role for an adult actor with a dog. These characters have so little connection with the first part of the love story that they are often thought to be a late addition. Lance's scenes are easily detachable and might have been given on their own. They are funny even when performed without a dog, but funnier with one, preferably a rather large one. If the part of Lance was added after Will Kemp joined the Chamberlain's Men in 1594, the play might have been revised to accommodate him. A jestbook account of Kemp's great predecessor Richard Tarlton describes him as acting with a well-trained dog.[45] Kemp did not need to have such a dog, since Lance's reproachful comments on Crab's insensitive behavior work equally well however the dog behaves. The failure to integrate the clown into the conclusion (because he had to be ready to perform his jig) sometimes bothered later actors, and nineteenth-century adaptations occasionally reintroduced Speed and Lance in the last act.[46]

In Montemayor, the character of Felismena is rather Amazonian: she has been brought up as a warrior, like her twin brother, and sometimes uses her skill with the bow and arrow. Shakespeare got rid of her masculine characteristics, making Julia and her maid Lucetta talk self-consciously about their femininity. Asked why she admires Proteus more than Julia's other suitors, Lucetta replies,

> I have no other than a woman's reason:
> I think him so because I think him so.
> (1.2.23–4)

There is similar emphasis on the charming idiocy of women in love when Julia first refuses to read Proteus's letter, then takes it but tears it up, then, when her maid is out of sight, lovingly puts the pieces back together, blaming herself for her cruelty. Later, when Julia decides to follow Proteus to court in the disguise of a page, Lucetta brings up the need for a costume with a codpiece in order, again, to draw attention to the femininity of a character who from this point on will be dressed as a boy. The point is partly to clarify the plot, partly to titillate, and partly to show off the boy actor's ability to impersonate a woman.

When *Romeo and Juliet* joined the company's repertory, *The Two Gentlemen of Verona* was probably dropped from it. Shakespeare's use of Arthur Brooke's poem for both plays makes them too much alike in details such as the woman speaking from a window, the rope ladder, the lover's banishment, and even the strange reference in the earlier play to a Friar Lawrence who is supposed to have seen Sylvia "as he in penance wandered through the forest" (*Two Gentlemen* 5.2.41). Brooke says at the end of his poem that, although Friar Lawrence was pardoned, he chose to go into a hermitage and died five years later. It is possible that the reference in *The Two Gentlemen of Verona* was introduced when Shakespeare was revising his plays for publication, emphasizing an interconnectedness like that of Ovid's tales.

The Comedy of Errors

The performance of *The Comedy of Errors* at Gray's Inn on 28 December 1594 is one of the best-documented events of Shakespeare's life. This is because it formed part of the Inn's Christmas revels, which were even more elaborate than usual since it was the first time in four years that the sports had not been cancelled. The festivities lasted from 27 December to 6 January – the full twelve days of Christmas – and the most elaborate offering, the masque of Proteus, belongs to early March, when it was given at court in a Shrove Tuesday performance before the queen.[47] An account, written up in mock-heroic style by some of the organizers, was published much later under the title *Gesta Grayorum* (the feats of the Gray's Inn men).[48]

The Comedy of Errors was probably acted by the Lord Chamberlain's Men, but since the chronicler did not think it necessary to mention the performers it is possible that at this point it still belonged to a different company. The play may well have been written some years earlier; its jokes about the French civil wars make more sense in the context of 1589–93, before Henri IV was finally accepted as king of France. It lacks the songs and the emphasis on female characters and boys that characterized drama for the boys' theaters before 1591, but it is less star-centered than most of the plays Shakespeare wrote with the Chamberlain's Men in mind. Like *The Two Gentlemen of Verona*, it is built around two leading men (which might fit the brief period when Burbage and Alleyn were acting in the same company), and also has two comic servants and four fairly substantial roles for boys. The two plays would thus have been easy for a single company to cast, and might have been the ones that the Chamberlain's Men offered at court at Christmas 1594.[49] On the other hand, thanks partly to Plautus himself, the plotting in *The Comedy of Errors* is far in advance of *The Two Gentlemen* and even *The Shrew*. The play could have been further revised after 1594 (it draws on a translation of *Menaechmi* published in 1595). What the law students and their guests saw may have been a much simpler work than the one in the Folio. Indeed, because of what happened on the night of 28 December, it is not clear how much of it they saw.

The Inns of Court were accustomed to regular performances by professional companies: for example, the Inner Temple hosted performances on All Saints' Day (1 November) and Candlemas (2 February). These were the days of the most elaborate feasting, on which all members were required to be in attendance; other inns also had "sports" for the occasion, such as mock-trials and plays, some of which they wrote themselves.[50] Arthur Brooke, who wrote *Romeus and Juliet*, had been an Inner Temple man, and when he wrote and produced the masque of *Beauty and Desire* for its Christmas revels of 1561 the society rewarded him with honorary membership.[51] *The Supposes*, from which Shakespeare took the subplot of *The Shrew*, had been a Gray's Inn play in 1566. George Gascoigne, who translated it, was another of the many celebrated writers who had studied there, and its students had presented *The Misfortunes of Arthur* at court in the winter of 1588/9.

As Alan Nelson points out, "professional playwrights must always have written with the gentlemen of the Inns of Court in mind."[52] The possibility of performance at an Inn may have encouraged the playwright to choose subjects that involved trial scenes and debates. Long speeches, far from being boring, were a treat for these connoisseurs, eager to copy the *sententiae* into their tablebooks. But an invitation, however much of an honor, carried certain risks. The Inns of Court were expensive to join, and candidates for admission had to be recommended by two members, so their atmosphere was that of an exclusive club. The residents ranged from distinguished senior lawyers, aristocrats, and scholars, some of whom were there by invitation, to young men fresh from university who were supposed to be learning enough law to act as justices of the peace in their own counties. The students not only studied law but were also expected to attend some of the cases being tried at Westminster Hall. Since many of them were taking fencing and dancing lessons as part of their education, they would have been particularly critical of actors who failed to be convincing in these gentlemanly exercises. During the season of "revels" the younger spectators seem to have felt licensed to behave as wildly as they liked, especially if they had been coerced (absence was punished by a stiff fine) into attending a performance that they did not enjoy.[53] They got into fights with the Earl of Oxford's players in 1580 and the Earl of Berkeley's players in 1581.[54] Disrupting performances, Andrew Gurr suggests, "seems to have been a student fashion of sorts at this time."[55]

The 1594 festivities had an overall theme of friendship: Gray's Inn exchanged ambassadors with the Inner Temple in a parody of diplomatic negotiations that was probably hilarious to those in the know. Unfortunately, the organizers were too successful for their own good, with the result that on the second night of Revels the hall was overcrowded with excited spectators, perhaps including former Gray's Inn men like the Earl of Southampton, Thomas Hughes (the main author of *The Misfortunes of Arthur*), and John Lyly, who was admitted to membership on this occasion.[56] Three other men must have been present, unless they were busy with their own last-minute rehearsals: Francis Bacon (aged 33), a resident at the Inn for much of his life, had written some of the speeches for the previous night; Francis Davison (aged 20), a new member, had devised a highly successful masque with music by the poet and musician Thomas Campion (aged 27). It may have been the most distinguished audience before which Shakespeare had yet performed. But there were too many distinguished people, not to mention the women who had also been invited, all of them expecting to be given the best seats. Scuffles broke out; the "Ambassador" from the Inner Temple departed in a (possibly feigned) huff, and the events in his honor were cancelled. Instead, the chronicle states, there was "dancing and reveling with gentlewomen, and after such sports, a *Comedy of Errors* (like to Plautus his *Menechmus*) was played by the players. So that night was begun, and continued to the end, in nothing but confusion and errors, whereupon, it was ever after called, *The Night of Errors*."[57] Having served their turn, Shakespeare and his company would have returned their costumes and props to storage and made their way home in the early, or even late, morning.

The following night featured a mock-arraignment of the "sorcerer or conjuror" who was said not only to have caused all the troubles but to have "foisted a company of base and common fellows, to make up our disorders with a play of errors and confusions." It would be delightful to think that Shakespeare himself was present to play the part of this conjuror, pretending to be overwhelmed with guilt for something that can hardly have been his fault. However, the Gray's Inn revels were too incestuous to admit an outsider into their jokes. The arraignment probably featured one of the organizers (all were ambitious men, eager for publicity). The absent actors would not have known that they were described as base and common – a term that in any case was hardly applicable to the servants of the Lord Chamberlain. Indeed, the fact that the speaker remembered the plot of the play and referred obliquely to the role of the conjuror Dr. Pinch could be taken as a compliment. Perhaps there was more to it than one might guess. Dr. Pinch, a tiny part, is vividly described by Antipholus of Ephesus, the victim of his attempted exorcism:

> A hungry, lean-faced villain,
> A mere anatomy, a mountebank,
> A threadbare juggler and a fortune-teller,
> A needy, hollow-eyed, sharp-looking wretch,
> A living dead man.
> (5.1.238–42)

Simply making up the actor to resemble this description is enough to guarantee that his brief appearance will be remembered. It has sometimes been suggested that the role was written for an exceptionally thin member of the company, perhaps the one who would later play the half-starved apothecary in *Romeo and Juliet*. Another possibility, however, is that one of the law students – perhaps the one responsible for arranging the actors' visit – took this small part for a single performance. He could then be present for the arraignment, and the contemptuous reference to the actors would be funnier if everyone knew that some of them at least were nothing of the sort.

Lynne Magnusson has suggested that the Gray's Inn performance may have been a humiliating experience for the actors, who probably had to wait for hours before performing to an over-excited audience in no condition to listen to them.[58] The numerous play-within-a-play scenes in Shakespeare's works ring various changes on the theme of actors performing before their social superiors. As Meredith Skura notes, the Induction to *The Taming of the Shrew*, "the dream of a beggar playing in a great man's house," is an idealized depiction of the experience.[59] The Lord welcomes the players, making it clear that he knows them personally, and warns them that one of their spectators – Christopher Sly, who has never seen a play – may get out of hand. Though the actors assure him that they can handle the situation, the Lord decides that he should join them, since

> Haply my presence
> May well abate the overmerry spleen
> Which otherwise would grow into extremes
> (Induction 1.135–7)

This contrast between the politeness of an aristocrat and the boorishness of a tinker might be an implied rebuke to the Gray's Inn audience. If, on the other hand,

Shakespeare and his colleagues saw themselves as temporarily part of an upper-class social event, the precise nature of their reception might not have mattered so much. *Errors* is the shortest of all Shakespeare's published plays, and may have been designed for audiences with short attention spans, like the reveling lawyers, or for court performances, where even visitors who spoke no English would probably know the plot of *Menaechmi*. If the play performed in 1594 was anything like the one published in the Folio, Shakespeare might have been somewhat disappointed that this sophisticated audience failed to notice how much he had done to his original. "W.W.," the author of the 1595 translation, claimed to have chosen it because it was the "least harmfull, and yet most delightfull" of Plautus's comedies.[60] Although Shakespeare added dirty jokes, he made the story basically more moral: Adriana did not commit adultery and incest and Antipholus of Ephesus made the improbable claim that he had only a platonic relationship with the courtesan at whose house he dined. This self-censorship may point to its origins as a play for boys, or it may show the influence of the queen's well-known attitude to romantic plots, one that would now be seen as almost Victorian.

Not present in Plautus, Aegeon's sentence of death and his longing to be reunited with his scattered family give the play a romance framework. A softer tone is also evident in the uneasiness and bewilderment of Antipholus of Syracuse, who falls in love with his supposed wife's sister, and in the surprising loyalty of the two slaves, despite the repeated beatings they receive from their masters. The contrast between Adriana and her sister Luciana is like that between Katherine and Bianca, but more easily resolved. The most ingenious of Shakespeare's inventions is the introduction of the Abbess, whose real identity, the forgotten missing piece of the family puzzle, is revealed only after she has established herself as one of the wise women of Greek romances. If Shakespeare reread the play later in his career with a view to revision, it might have influenced his late comedies, all of which turn on the reunion of a scattered family. Ephesus – the city of Diana – reappears at the end of *Pericles*, and *The Tempest* is the only other play to obey the classical unity of time.

There were no hard feelings after the performance, since many of Shakespeare's other plays had connections with the Inns. The name of the hero in *The Two Gentlemen of Verona* might allude to the *Masque of Proteus*, while its theme of friendship may be linked to the Masque of Amity performed at Gray's Inn a week after *The Comedy of Errors*, which compared the new friendship between the Gray's Inn and Inner Temple men to other great friendships of the past, such as those between Theseus and Pirithous or Achilles and Patroclus. In *The Shrew*, Lucentio's arrival in Padua to begin a course of study, and Tranio's reminder that he should think of pleasure too, would have played well to an audience of students on holiday. Moreover, Sly's temporary status as Lord paralleled that of the Prince of Purpoole himself, whose reign was only from 20 December until Twelfth Night. In 1595, shortly after the *Comedy of Errors* evening, Thomas Greene of Stratford was admitted to the Middle Temple, with two John Marstons, father and son, as his sureties. Greene would be solicitor for Stratford in 1601 and its town clerk in 1603. Both he and his brother John (a lawyer at Clement's Inn) seem to have been friends of Shakespeare's. The younger Marston, who had become a playwright by the end of the century, may well have been one too.

Writing for the Lord Chamberlain's Men

It was in Shakespeare's interest to supply his company not only with good plays but with plays that would win invitations to prestigious venues like the Inns. The existence of these varied audiences may explain one of the puzzles about his works. By every calculation – including the likelihood that actors spoke considerably faster then than they do now – most of his plays, especially the histories and tragedies, are too long for performance not just in "the two hours' traffic of our stage" named in the Prologue to *Romeo and Juliet* but even in the longer time-frame ("two hours and a half and somewhat more") that Jonson asked his audience to allow for *Bartholomew Fair* in 1614. According to Alfred Hart, the average length of plays between 1587 and 1616 was never more than 2,500 lines. Though Shakespeare was apparently the first dramatist to write plays that exceeded the usual performance length, several of Jonson's are in fact even longer.[61] Other plays were certainly cut in performance: Webster's *The Duchess of Malfi*, published in 1623, says on the title page that it includes more than was performed, and in 1647 the publisher Humphrey Moseley assured the readers of his Beaumont and Fletcher Folio that the volume would give them "all that was acted, and all that was not."[62] By the seventeenth century, publication of plays was becoming common, but this was not the case in the 1590s, and the obvious question is why a busy dramatist would waste time writing a play too long to be performed as written.

Andrew Gurr suggests that authors deliberately submitted their plays to the licenser in the longest form, knowing that they could cut but not add after the play had been licensed.[63] Lukas Erne, reviving a view of Shakespeare as essentially a literary rather than theatrical figure, has proposed that, from the start, he envisioned both a heavily cut acting text and a longer one for a reading public.[64] It may well be that different audiences got more or less of a play, depending on the situation. Though the need for spectators to leave the theater by nightfall has been thought to be a built-in deadline, this would not have affected performances in a private house or at the Inns of Court. Michael J. Hirrel, who has found evidence that even public performances sometimes concluded after dark, also points out that a play was only one part of an entertainment that might include extra events (dances, tumbling, etc.) as needed.[65] From the beginning, Shakespeare was writing plays of varied length: both *Richard III* (3,609 lines) and *The Comedy of Errors* (1,787 lines) date from the early 1590s, while *Cymbeline*

(3,350 lines) and *The Tempest* (2,086 lines) are late works.[66] *Hamlet* exists in a very short version (Q1) and two much longer ones which themselves show different cuts to the text.

Initially, his success was due less to the poetic and dramatic quality of his plays than to his ability to create opportunities for his actors to show the full range of their talents. Habitual theatergoers behaved like sports fans discussing the respective merits of two players. John Marston, in *The Scourge of Villainie* (1598), imagines himself talking theater with a stage-struck gallant, using the names of two famous Roman actors to refer to their contemporary equivalents, Alleyn and Burbage: "Say who acts best? *Drusus* or *Roscio*?"[67] An important part of any performance was feats of skill, such as fighting and dancing, that the audience could evaluate, discuss – and attempt to recreate. Amateur actors, ranging from apprentices to aristocrats, also performed plays, or scenes from plays, both in private houses and, on at least one occasion, in a public playhouse.[68] An apprentice in *The Knight of the Burning Pestle* is described by his proud master as having nearly "played Jeronimo with a shoemaker for a wager." Someone, in other words, would have laid bets on the two amateurs, and someone else would have judged which of them came closest to the actor they had seen as Hieronimo in *The Spanish Tragedy*. It was essential for professionals to show their superiority, which no doubt is one reason why the theater loved to display hilarious examples of bad amateur acting. While plays with rapid costume changes showed off the actors' physical dexterity, the real point of disguise plays was to allow the audience to see actors doing what everyone could recognize as acting. As Robert Weimann and Douglas Bruster put it, "disguise is a practice of concealment that, in theatrical performance, allows its own process to be observed."[69] Some of the plays in the repertory of the Admiral's Men involved characters disguising themselves as other characters in the play, which would have required mimicry of known actors, like Edward Alleyn, with his distinctive "stalk." It is likely that many metatheatrical jokes lie concealed in Shakespeare's plays: apparently irrelevant characters, for example, may have been recognizable on sight as some contemporary object of ridicule.

Memorizing was another skill that many spectators had acquired in school – unlike modern ones, whose first question to an actor is usually "How do you learn all those lines?" The audience pounced eagerly on any actor who was unable to get through a speech, or who tried clumsily to ad-lib; in *Love's Labour's Lost*, the courtiers even set out to make the actors "dry" (see 5.2.166). The shouts of "out!" and the expressions "out of his part" or "beside his part" show the audience seizing control, like a referee penalizing players. Stichomythia and highly rhetorical speeches, with frequent repetition, were obviously easy to learn, but Shakespeare sometimes seems to have written speeches that draw attention to their difficulty. For instance, Biondello in *The Taming of the Shrew* lists the various diseases with which Petruchio's horse is afflicted: "possessed with the glanders and like to mose in the chine, troubled with the lampass, infected with the fashions, full of windgalls, sped with spavins, rayed with the yellows, past cure of the bots, swayed in the back and shoulder-shotten . . ." (3.2.49–55). Even spectators who had spent their childhood memorizing Latin *sententiae*, and who knew about the diseases of horses, would have recognized this speech as a tour de force of memory, only partly facilitated by its intermittent use of alliteration and assonance. In modern productions, the actor who delivers it often gets a round of applause, and I suspect that the same sometimes happened in the 1590s.

While Shakespeare, like Tilney, was becoming a "manager of mirth" in London, he could have had very little presence in Stratford. Yet this was a time when his family must have wanted his advice. In 1595, almost exactly a year after the first fire, the town suffered a second one. Again, the Shakespeare properties were spared, but many families were almost ruined. Since the fire had followed yet another bad summer and harvest, bread and ale were in short supply and Parliament had just introduced legislation against excessive malting, which was the occupation of most of the town, even the vicar and the schoolmaster. Those specifically banned from engaging in the practice included bailiff Thomas Rogers. Tempers frayed: on 28 November 1595, he was accused of having bought a cartload of barley before it came into the market and replied, according to the record, "that he will justifye yt and he careth not a turde for them all."[70] This is the same Rogers, former town clerk, from whom, some scholars argue, Shakespeare acquired his knowledge of law.

The coincidence of the two fires produced the predictable statements about God's punishment on the sins of Stratford's inhabitants. One of the sins of which Shakespeare could have been accused was the publication in 1593 of *Venus and Adonis*, a work of which many of his countrymen may not have approved. Fortunately, most of them would have known of only one work by him from 1594: *Lucrece*, unimpeachably based on history and dedicated to a peer of the realm. Shakespeare may have been glad that his name was not on the title pages of the two plays published anonymously that year – *Titus Andronicus* and *The First Part of the Contention of the Two Famous Houses of York and Lancaster* – or *The True Tragedy of Richard Duke of York*, published in 1595, since anyone who read *Lucrece* in their context would have taken the author for a political radical. Within a few years, Shakespeare had revised these plays, possibly to remove some of their implications. His exceptional productivity over the next few years suggests that he was eager to prove something – both to his sophisticated acquaintances in London and to his family and friends in Stratford.

Notes

1. Chambers, *ES*, 4: 286. Quoted in Dutton, "Censorship," 294.
2. Maclean, "Adult Playing Companies, 1583–1593," 53.
3. Freeman, *Thomas Kyd: Facts and Problems*, 38.

4. Rowland Whyte wrote to Robert Sidney (7 Dec. 1595) that, after hearing a summary of "your letters, sent by the Page," Elizabeth "demanded where the boy was, and would have let him come to her presence." Unfortunately, he was already gone and thus, Whyte lamented, "missed of that happiness; it may perchance never come so again as long as he live." *Letters and memorials of state*, ed. Collins, 1: 373.

5. Repr. in Wickham, 104 and 106.

6. Gurr, "Venues on the Verges: London's Theater Government between 1594 and 1614," 484.

7. Knutson, "What's So Special about 1594?".

8. Wickham, 361.

9. Streitberger, "Personnel and Professionalization," 348.

10. The latter is reprinted in Wickham, 181–3.

11. Marston, *The Malcontent*, ed. Eric Rasmussen and David Bevington, in *English Renaissance Drama*, ed. Bevington, Induction, 63–4, 67–9.

12. Riddell, "Some Actors in Ben Jonson's Plays."

13. Other Williams after whom these children might have been named are the fifth Earl of Derby and the third Earl of Pembroke.

14. M. Eccles, "Elizabethan Actors III."

15. See e.g. the essays by David Kathman listed below, Mary Edmond's *ODNB* entry on Nicholas Tooley, and Astington, *Actors and Acting in Shakespeare's Time*.

16. Kathman, "The Boys of Shakespeare's Company."

17. Kathman, "Players, Livery Companies, and Apprentices," 418.

18. Kathman, "Grocers, Goldsmiths, and Drapers," 8.

19. Edmond, "Tooley [Wilkinson], Nicholas," *ODNB*.

20. Belsey, "Shakespeare's Little Boys," 62.

21. McMillin, "The Sharer and His Boy: Rehearsing Shakespeare's Women"; Tribble, *Cognition at the Globe*, 134–50.

22. *The Diary of John Manningham*, ed. Sorlien, 75.

23. Schoenbaum, 205–6 and 205n. It is possible that the Manningham entry is a forgery based on the Wilkes story, since the *Diary* was found and quoted by J. P. Collier, who is notorious for his insertions into other manuscripts of the period. However, the style of Manningham's narrative, and the fact that it lacks some of Wilkes's more picturesque elaborations, makes it likely to be genuine – which does not mean that it is true.

24. Duncan-Jones, *Shakespeare: An Ungentle Life*, 151–2.

25. John Davies of Hereford, Epigram 159 from *The Scourge of Folly*, in *Complete Works*, ed. Grosart, 2: 26.

26. Chambers, *WS*, 2: 210.

27. Nelson and Altrocchi, "William Shakespeare, 'Our Roscius'"; Duncan-Jones, "Shakespeare the Motley Player."

28. Cited in Schoenbaum, 201–2.

29. Paul S. Conklin, *A History of Hamlet Criticism: 1601–1821* (London: Frank Cass, 1968), 10, n. 6, quoted in de Grazia, *Hamlet Without Hamlet*, 40; Greenfield, "Quoting Hamlet in the Early Seventeenth Century," 519.

30. Bradbrook, *The Rise of the Common Player*, 85–6.

31. Kathman, "The Boys of Shakespeare's Company"; see also id., "Players, Livery Companies, and Apprentices," 424–5.

32. Skura, *Shakespeare the Actor*, 57.

33. From *CCXI. Sociable Letters*, 1674, letter clxxiii, pp. 362–3. Quoted in Herford and Simpson 11: 510.

34. From broadside Prologue to the Revived *Alchemist*, found in Worcester College, Oxford, and dated 1660 by C. H. Wilkinson in *Oxford Bibliographical Society Papers* (i. 281–2); quoted in Herford and Simpson, 9: 227–8.

35. A strip of land at the west end, which John Shakespeare sold in 1596/7, was described as a "toft," meaning land on which a demolished building had once stood. Fripp, *Shakespeare: Man and Artist*, 402–3.

36. *Minutes*, V: xix. Fox points out that the contemporary annalist John Stow mentions the period of bad harvests, often thought to have inspired the passage in *A Midsummer Night's Dream* where Titania describes the unnatural weather (ibid., xxi).

37. "He calls his Kate, and she must come and kisse him," from Antony Shute's *Beauty Dishonoured, Written Under the Title of Shore's Wife* (Stationers' Register June 1593). See *Companion*, 110. It is possible, however, that "kiss me, Kate" was already a catch-phrase, just as it was at the time of Cole Porter's musical. Barbara Hodgdon suggests further that "Kate," because it sounds like "cate," may have been the equivalent of "honey": *The Taming of the Shrew*, ed. Hodgdon, 11–12.

38. See Marino, "The Anachronistic *Shrews*."

39. Blayney, "The Publication of Playbooks," 399.

40. Quoted from the photocopy of the 1594 Quarto printed as appendix 3 to *The Taming of the Shrew*, ed. Hodgdon, p. 372; since no act and scene numbers are given, the references are both to signatures and page numbers. Interestingly, one of the other lovers declares that he is worried that "all my labours lost" (B1^v, p. 352).

41. Baldwin, *Shakspere's "Love's Labor's Won,"* 15.

42. See McLuskie, "The Patriarchal Bard," esp. 97–8.

43. S. Roberts, *Reading Shakespeare's Poems in Early Modern England*, 178, citing Gary Taylor, "Some mss of Sh's sonnets" (*Bulletin of John Rylands Library* 68, 1985–6).

44. See Belsey, "Shakespeare's Little Boys," and Astington's chapter on "Players at Work," in *Actors and Acting in Shakespeare's Time*, 140–73.

45. See Richard Beadle, "Crab's Pedigree," in Michael Cordner, Peter Holland, and John Kerrigan, eds., *English Comedy* (Cambridge University Press, 1994), 12–25, cited in William C. Carroll's note to 2.3.01 in his edition of *The Two Gentlemen of Verona*.

46. *The Two Gentlemen of Verona*, ed. Carroll, 86–7.

47. This masque was based on material from the second part of *The Faerie Queene*. It was not published until late in 1596, but this episode shows that the contents of Books IV to VI were already well known. See Albright, "*The Faerie Queene* in Masque at the Gray's Inn Revels."

48. For the fullest account of this celebration, see *REED Inns of Court*, ed. Elliott and Nelson.

49. The date of the court performances was apparently the same as that of the Gray's Inn performance. Either the date is given wrongly in the court records or Shakespeare was not yet part of the Chamberlain's Men and it was another company that performed his play.

50. Arlidge, *Shakespeare and the Prince of Love*, 33.

51. Axton, *The Queen's Two Bodies*, 55–6; Nelson, "The Universities and the Inns of Court," 282.

52. Nelson, "The Universities and the Inns of Court," 286.
53. See Axton, *The Queen's Two Bodies*, 4–10, and *Gesta Grayorum*, ed. Bland, xiii–xv.
54. Wickham, 92.
55. Gurr, *The Shakespearian Playing Companies*, 168.
56. Hunter, "Lyly, John," *ODNB*.
57. *Gesta Grayorum*, ed. Bland, 22. See also *REED Inns of Court*, ed. Elliott and Nelson.
58. Magnusson, "Scoff Power in *Love's Labour's Lost* and the Inns of Court," 202, 208.
59. Skura, *Shakespeare the Actor*, esp. ch. 4.
60. W.W. has sometimes been identified as William Warner, author of *Albion's England*, but Katharine A. Craik thinks that he "is more likely the committed innovator of English versification William Webbe, whose Discourse of English Poetrie (1586) includes a defence of Plautus." Craik, "Warner, William," *ODNB*.
61. A. Hart, "Play Abridgement," in id., *Shakespeare and the Homilies*, 87. In fact, Hart shows, it is mainly because of the histories that Shakespeare's average is so high; if they are excluded, he averages only 2,671 lines, which is not much above the 2,500-word norm (pp. 94–5).
62. "The Stationer to the Readers," in *Works of Francis Beaumont and John Fletcher*, ed. Glover, 1: xiii.
63. Gurr, "Maximal and Minimal Texts: Shakespeare v. The Globe," esp. 70 and 77.
64. Erne, *Shakespeare as Literary Dramatist*, esp. 140, 212–44.
65. Hirrel, "Duration of Performances and Lengths of Plays."
66. Since editors vary in their lineation, all calculations of line length are approximate. These are taken from the website "Shakespeare Plays in Order of Line Length" – http://www.shakespearelinecount.com/shakespeare-plays-line-length – which bases its count on the edition by Hardin Craig.
67. *The Scourge of Villanie*, Satire xi, "Humors," in *The Poems of John Marston*, ed. Davenport, 168.
68. *The Hector of Germanie* was, according to its 1615 title page, "publickly Acted at the Red-Bull, and at the Curtayne, by a Company of Young-men of this Citie" (A1^r) and its author, William Smith, said that it was "made for Citizens, who acted it well." Since Smith had previously written a (lost) play performed by the King's Men, he may have been given exceptional privileges. See Kathman, "Smith, William," *ODNB*.
69. Weimann and Bruster, *Shakespeare and the Power of Performance*, 120.
70. *Minutes*, V: xxi, 49.

"The Strong'st and Surest Way to Get"

Histories, 1595–1596

Bolingbroke. My gracious lord, I come but for mine own.
King Richard. Your own is yours, and I am yours, and all.
Bolingbroke. So far be mine, my most redoubted lord,
    As my true service shall deserve your love.
King Richard. Well you deserve. They well deserve to have
    That know the strong'st and surest way to get.
                             (*Richard II* 3.3.196–201)

This patterned dialogue seems at first simply to play with language: "mine," "yours," "deserve." Indeed Richard's first line recalls Shakespeare's dedication of *Lucrece* to the Earl of Southampton: "What I have done is yours; what I have to do is yours; being part in all I have, devoted yours." But its silky ambiguity might make one wonder even about that dedication. It is not clear whether "Your own is yours" is a performative utterance (Richard officially returning Bolingbroke's inheritance to him) or a bitter statement of the fact that the king is no longer in a position to withhold it. Richard's final reply is unquestionably sarcastic, but it reflects a view with which many readers of the play now agree, and that was beginning to be accepted even in Shakespeare's time.

This chapter and the next artificially separate works that were probably written close together: historical plays and romantic comedies, all apparently dating from the mid-1590s. Andrew Gurr thinks that Shakespeare was under contract to write one comedy and one serious play (tragedy or history) each year, since this seems to be what Shakespeare in fact did.[1] The alternation of lighter and heavier drama made sense both as a marketing strategy and as a way of spreading the workload, though of course Shakespeare's plays were not the only ones the company was performing. In 1594 Shakespeare had a reputation outside the theater primarily for writing about

The Life of William Shakespeare: A Critical Biography, First Edition. Lois Potter.
© 2012 Lois Potter. Published 2012 by Blackwell Publishing Ltd.

love. Within the theater, he may have been best known for dramatizing English history. He seems to have enjoyed this kind of writing – no one else has ever written so many history-based plays – but he may also have been under some pressure to do so. The year 1594 was memorable to many for an anonymous publication (probably by the Jesuit Robert Parsons), *A Conference About the Next Succession to the Crowne of Ingland*, provocatively dedicated to the Earl of Essex. The title was already treasonous, since any discussion of the succession involved imagining the queen's death, which was legally equivalent to plotting her murder. The speakers, supposedly English and Irish gentlemen living abroad (i.e., Catholic exiles), discuss the history behind the current succession crisis. One points out that all controversy over the English Crown can be traced back to the wars of York and Lancaster, from whom all the contenders descend.[2] Parsons clearly intended to create the fear of civil war following the death of the queen and, while supposedly leaving the question open, to suggest that the Spanish Infanta (a direct descendant of John of Gaunt's first wife) might be the best solution to the problem. By using English history as part of his dangerous argument, he had made the writing of historical plays even more delicate than before.

Richard III

Shakespeare must always have intended to follow the popular Henry VI plays with a sequel about the legendary evil king whose defeat in 1485 had made way for the house of Tudor and thus for the reign of Elizabeth I. He may well have written some version of it before the plague closed the theaters, perhaps for Lord Strange's Men – there is some whitewashing in its treatment of Stanley, Strange's ancestor. Yet, as James Siemon points out, there are no references to this play in the pre-plague years,[3] and the Lord Chamberlain's Men did not give it during their season with the Admiral's Men at Newington and the Rose in 1594. Moreover, the title role was always associated with Richard Burbage, thanks in part to the coincidence that gave him the same first name, whereas Edward Alleyn would have been the obvious person to play it if it had been performed in the early 1590s. The play may have been taken on tour in the country at an earlier date, but it might have been as late as 1595 before London audiences saw Shakespeare's first great success, which was published in 1597.

    Richard III had a more conservative political and moral purpose than its predecessors: in it, the accession of the first Tudor king is made as legitimate as possible, considering that it was a military conquest, and all major characters at some point recognize the existence of divine justice, often based on their actions in earlier plays. The only events that are begun and ended in the play are curses and their fulfillment. Margaret's lengthy curses are the most obvious examples, but even more striking are the numerous occasions on which characters unwittingly curse themselves. Richard successfully courts Lady Anne, who has just wished misery on anyone who is fool enough to marry him; Buckingham wishes that he may be betrayed if he betrays Edward IV's heirs. Both Anne and Buckingham die miserable deaths and agree that they deserve to. Many of the characters in the play, such as Rivers, Buckingham, and Richard himself, had also appeared in the *Mirror for Magistrates*, a series of monologues by ghosts of once mighty men, now victims seen in the light of the "fall of princes" theme. As compared with the world of Marlowe's tragedies, and even the Henry VI plays, then, *Richard III* is ostentatiously Christian and moral. Yet its didactic effect is largely canceled out by the theatrical dominance of its comic and charismatic central figure. His ability to drop from the grand style to the rudely colloquial derives from the medieval character of the Vice, but his explanations of his own cleverness are characteristic of the stage Machiavel, who makes the audience his accomplice.

Shakespeare still had not only the lines but the dramatic structure of Kyd and Marlowe in his head. The play's opening, with a long, bravura speech from the title character, recalls the monologues of the heroes of *The Jew of Malta* and *Doctor Faustus*, both of whom appear to choose villainy because other courses of action are impossible for, or uninteresting to, them. Clarence's account of his nightmare journey to the underworld is obviously based on Andrea's famous speech at the beginning of *The Spanish Tragedy*. His line "Into the kingdom of perpetual night" (1.4.47) is a verbal and rhythmical echo of Marlowe's description of Lucifer as "Chief lord and regent of perpetual night" (2.1.56), and these cadences recur throughout the play, surrounding the deaths of its shady politicians with a gloomy grandeur. Like Barabas in *The Jew of Malta*, Richard is set apart from the rest of humanity and reviled by it, uses clever deception to turn his weakness into strength, and is finally destroyed when his enemies unite against him. Like Faustus, he has enemies in the supernatural realm as well as on earth. Where Faustus hears good and evil angels whispering to him, sees the seven deadly sins in person, and has visions of heaven and hell while he waits to be carried off by devils, Richard dreams that the ghosts of those he has murdered are telling him (as Faustus tells himself at 5.1.48) to "despair and die" in the next day's battle.[4] Part of the fascination of Richard is that he speaks partly from Barabas's essentially amoral position, as a comic theatrical figure outside ordinary human concerns, and partly, like Faustus, as a Christian inhabiting a moral universe in which his role is that of a damnable villain. In the theater the unifying presence of an actor can make these very inconsistencies the source of Richard's lifelikeness, but in the final act the conflict between them becomes difficult to perform. After a nightmare in which he sees the ghosts of his victims, he conducts an elaborate dialogue between these two roles:

Is there a murderer here? No. Yes, I am.
Then fly. What, from myself? Great reason why:
Lest I revenge. What, myself upon myself?
                                        (5.3.184–6)

The Christian villain declares, "I shall despair" while the amoral villain scoffs at his fears; both finally join in accepting the fact that he is neither loved nor pitied.

In one respect, however, Richard differs from his Marlovian models: he has no death speech. After depicting the deaths of so many characters in the earlier history plays, most of whom expire uttering Latin tags or surprisingly pious prayers, Shakespeare apparently decided to leave the final moments of this character's life entirely up to the actor, ending his speaking part with the shout of "A horse, a horse, my kingdom for a horse!" Curiously, the line may be a quotation of sorts. In George Peele's *The Battle of Alcazar* the villainous Moor, Muly Mahomet (an Edward Alleyn part), cries out to his boy to bring him a horse. The boy is horrified: "My lord, if you return, you die." But the Moor insists that this is not his intention:

Villain, I say, give me a horse to fly,
To swim the river, villain, and to fly.[5]

There is an obvious relationship between the two plays, since *Alcazar* includes a dumb show in which murderers strangle two young princes. It is likely that Shakespeare wrote his play not long after (or before?) he collaborated on *Titus Andronicus* with Peele, so perhaps one of the two dramatists deliberately invoked a comparison between Alleyn's Muly Mahomet and Burbage's Richard. Peele may have been debunking the concept of the heroic villain, or Shakespeare may have been demonstrating the superiority of his villain to Peele's, or they may have exploited the cross-references to give their successful plays even more publicity.

What follows Richard's line is the stage direction "*They fight. Richard is slain.*" The words give no clue as to what kind of fight was required, and if Shakespeare had ever written a death speech for Richard, he removed it before the play went to press. It posed too difficult a problem: the character he had depicted for five acts could never have repented of his actions, yet letting him remain a viciously defiant villain like Aaron risked making him admirable. The key to Richard's final state of mind is not in his words but the playing of the final combat between Richard and Richmond. Though the king apparently recovers from the effects of his nightmare as morning comes, even his oration to his army, prefaced as it is with "If not to heaven, then hand in hand to hell" (5.5.313), suggests that the curse of "despair and die," has already come true. The theater, for over three centuries, allowed Richard to show the suicidal courage of despair (the sin of Judas) in a thrilling stage fight that lived up to Catesby's description of Richard's offstage prowess ("The king enacts more wonders than a man," 5.4.2). As his leading actors went on to play other Shakespeare heroes, other villains, and other death scenes, their author continued to struggle with the need to reconcile the theatrical and moral imperatives of such moments.

Shakespeare prepared the way for a play focusing on Richard in his revisions to the Henry VI plays. Richard Gloucester seems to have been at first intended, like Cade, mainly as a comic villain, a version of "the formal Vice, Iniquity," in the moral interludes to which he himself refers (3.1.82). Perhaps the first version was written or adapted with another actor in mind. In _The Contention_ Richard runs away from Clifford; in _The True Tragedy_ he has to be rescued by Warwick and, asked by Edward IV whether he will remain loyal, he replies, like a clown:

> For why hath Nature made me halt downright,
> But that I should be valiant and stand to't?
> For, if I would, I cannot run away.[6]

The lines would later be replaced with something more dignified – "Ay, in despite of all that shall withstand you" (_3 Henry VI_ 4.1.146). Shakespeare's conception of the plays had become more epic. The sheer length of _Richard III_, and the fact that the Quarto published in 1597 differs in many details from the text printed in 1623, probably point to successive additions and revisions, perhaps designed for different audiences. There are cuts that might be due to censorship. The Folio at times has a somewhat softer tone: one of the murderers sent to kill the Duke of Clarence repents and makes a brief attempt to save him; Queen Elizabeth addresses the Tower, touchingly (or sentimentally, depending on taste) urging it to "use my babies well" (4.1.102). This text may be based on an earlier version of the play than the Quarto (generally thought to be a memorial reconstruction). Thus it is not easy to know whether the play became more or less cruel in the course of its theatrical history. In any case, neither the murderer's repentance nor Elizabeth's prayer has a happy result. In this respect, they recall the many disappointed hopes and unanswered prayers in the Henry VI plays, particularly the pious wishes of the king himself, and they announce a theme that will be much more strongly emphasized in _King Lear_.

Edward III

The years following 1594 were probably the first in which two or more London-based companies had a stable enough situation to take account of each other's repertory, and the second half of the 1590s shows something like competition, or perhaps dialogue, between them. Plays based on the chronicles seem to have been something of a specialty of the Lord Chamberlain's Men at this point. Now that they had a designated task of performing at court, someone may have suggested that they should depict more edifying reigns than those of Henry VI and his immediate successors. The most obvious choice would seem to be Henry V, whose name is nostalgically evoked throughout the plays dealing with his successor, but the popular Queen's Men play, *The Famous Victories of Henry V*, had already dramatized his life, and it might be hard to compete with a work still in many memories. King John, the opponent of the Pope and foreign invaders, was another obvious subject, but the existence of *The Troublesome Reign of King John*, published anonymously in 1591 but possibly by George Peele, would make publication of another King John play difficult. So why not focus on Edward III, the greatest of English conquerors before Henry V, with victories both in France and in Scotland? Hunsdon might have suggested this: he had spent over ten years hunting down Scottish supporters of Mary Queen of Scots and was "the privy council's Scottish expert."[7] The Lord Chamberlain might have added – but probably did not need to – that for court performances it would be a good idea to depict female characters as something other than ambitious homicides or pathetic victims.

Shakespeare seems to have had at least a hand in *Edward III*, which was entered into the Stationers' Register at the end of 1595 and published anonymously in 1596. Hall had sketched the events of this reign only lightly, since his story began with the deposition of Richard II. However, Holinshed's *Chronicles*, which Field printed, dealt with the entire period from the Norman Conquest to the beginning of Elizabeth's reign. Shakespeare and his collaborator(s?) might have borrowed Volume III, the one that dealt with English history, for a fee,[8] or perhaps at this point someone decided that it was worthwhile for the Lord Chamberlain's Men to invest in a book that was clearly going to be an indispensable source. The play's title page credits no theater company, saying only that the play "hath been sundry times played about the City of London." It may have been acted as early as 1592, since a ballad about the king's courtship of the Countess of Salisbury – the part of the play usually attributed to Shakespeare – was registered in March 1593.[9]

Edward III begins, as *Henry V* would later do, with a statement of Edward's claim to the throne of France. Here, it is based on the fact that his mother (the demonized queen of Marlowe's *Edward II*) was the sister of the late French king, all of whose children have died without issue. As with *Henry V*, too, its emphasis on the justice of the war can be read ambiguously, since the main supporter of Edward's claim is a disaffected Frenchman whose insistence that his motives are purely disinterested is hard to believe (especially since he is at once rewarded for his support).[10] The intention may be to shift the blame for the war onto a Frenchman, just as in *Henry V* it is given mainly to the Archbishop of Canterbury and hence to the Catholic Church. Though the play covers the period between Marlowe's *Edward II* and Shakespeare's *Richard II*, it dramatizes only the most glorious part of the reign, the victories of the king and his son, the Black Prince, in France. It gives no hint that the prince will die young, leaving behind only a very young son, the future Richard II, to succeed his grandfather. Indeed, the Black Prince in this play has no wife. On the other hand his mother, Queen Philippa, appears onstage in an advanced stage of pregnancy, perhaps to remind spectators of the fertility that was to be the main cause of civil war among the many descendants of Edward's seven sons.

The scenes that have been most confidently attributed to Shakespeare take place before Edward goes to France, when he attempts to seduce the Countess of Salisbury. These seem partly an expansion of Edward IV's brief and stichomythic courtship of Elizabeth Woodville in *3 Henry VI* and partly a rewriting of *Lucrece* with a happy ending. Reasons for ascribing them to Shakespeare include the extended development of this rather minor part of the plot (sheer length was beginning to be a Shakespearean characteristic), the unexpected display of graciousness and humor, and the focus on the art of writing. Edward's secretary Lodowick describes the king's telltale reactions to the Countess's charms (2.1.1–24) in terms like those of Boyet in *Love's Labour's Lost* when he tells the Princess his reasons for thinking that Navarre is in love with her. The language in which Edward tells the secretary to express his passion uses similar conceits:

> Devise for fair a fairer word than fair,
> And every ornament that thou wouldst praise
> Fly it a pitch above the soar of praise ...
> (2.1.85–7)[11]

His ecstatic praise of the Countess is in the language of *Romeo and Juliet*:

> *King Edward.* Read, lord, read,
>   Fill thou the empty hollows of mine ears
>   With the sweet hearing of thy poetry.
> *Lodowick.* I have not to a period brought her praise.
> *King Edward.* Her praise is as my love, both infinite,
>   Which apprehend such violent extremes
>   That they disdain an ending period.
>   Her beauty hath no match but my affection;
>   Hers more than most, mine most and more than more;
>   Hers more to praise than tell the sea by drops
>   Nay, more than drop, the massy earth by sands,
>   And sand by sand print them in memory.
>   Then wherefore talk'st thou of a period
>   To that which craves unended admiration?
> (2.1.127–40)

"While the best boy actors at the disposal of the playing companies were evidently superb," Katherine Duncan-Jones has written, "they were probably at their best in parts which required a good deal of shrillness and shrewishness."[12] Unlike most women in the history plays, the Countess is a mature, married woman, not only witty and eloquent but principled as well. Her replies, when the king begins to court her, show an argumentative intelligence that goes beyond anything heard yet from any of Shakespeare's female characters:

> To be a king is of a younger house
> Than to be married: your progenitor,
> Sole-reigning Adam on the universe,
> By God was honoured for a married man,
> But not by him anointed for a king.
>
> (2.1.263–7)

The action becomes melodramatic when the king persuades the Countess's father, the Earl of Warwick, to make a solemn promise to do whatever will make his sovereign happy, then reveals that he wants Warwick to act as a bawd to his own daughter. Warwick keeps his promise by speaking to her and makes the case for yielding to Edward, but changes course ("And mark how I unsay my words again," 2.1.432) once he is satisfied that she can resist temptation. His oration against corruption ends with what he calls "reasons," though they are really proverbs:

> A spacious field of reasons could I urge
> Between his glory, daughter, and thy shame:
> That poison shows worst in a golden cup;
> Dark night seems darker by the lightning flash;
> Lilies that fester smell far worse than weeds;
> And every glory that inclines to sin,
> The shame is treble by the opposite.
>
> (2.2.448–54)

This self-consciousness and redundancy are characteristic of Shakespeare at this period; "Now mark me, how I will undo myself," Richard II declares (4.1.204) before a similarly lengthy list, and in *King John* a courtier speaks seven lines of proverbs to make the point that the king has just been guilty of "wasteful and ridiculous excess" (4.2.16). It was the comparison to festering lilies (line 452) – identical with the last line of Sonnet 94 – that first alerted readers to the possibility that the scene might be by Shakespeare. The question is, of course, which came first, the play or the sonnet (not published until 1609). I think the former: the line is appropriate to its context in the play, whereas, since it is, or sounds, proverbial, its recurrence in the sonnet could be a quotation. The idea that the corruption of the best is the worst kind of corruption recurs throughout the plays, for instance in *Richard II*:

> Since the more fair and crystal is the sky,
> The uglier seem the clouds that in it fly.
>
> (1.1.41–2)

The idea recurred, strangely transformed, at about the time when the sonnets were published. Lepidus's description of Antony's larger-than-life character, as Janet Adelman brilliantly pointed out, inverts the usual moral significance of light and dark: "His faults in him seem as the spots of heaven,/ More fiery by night's blackness" (*Antony and Cleopatra* 1.4.12–13).[13]

Fortunately, in *Edward III*, the father and daughter are clever enough to convert the king back to virtue. One of Edward's soliloquies is spoken to the sound of a drum in the background, and, though (in a curious reversal of Richard III's opening soliloquy) he orders it to be silent or turn into a lute song, it accompanies the arrival of Prince Edward, whose entry reminds the king of his duties as a soldier and a father. The introspective quality shown in his surprisingly self-aware comment –

> Lust is a fire, and men, like lanthorns, show
> Light lust within themselves, even through themselves.
> (2.2.90–1)

– gives way, in the rest of the play, to the tough, overbearing figure of history. The main interest from this point on is clearly the young prince Edward, at the beginning of the career that will make him famous as the Black Prince. The scene in which he and the old Lord Audley await the start of the Battle of Poitiers has also been seen as Shakespearean. Audley, who thinks the English position hopeless, describes the enemies ranged against them in detail; the Prince notes that "Thy parcelling this power hath made it more" (4.4.41): a handful of sand is easy to grasp but if it is counted, grain by grain, it seems an overwhelming amount. In the intellectual quality of scenes like this, the play differs from other history plays of the period.

In retrospect, the Countess scenes, based not on Holinshed but Froissart, are totally irrelevant. She disappears from the action, and, though the Earl of Salisbury appears in a later episode, the plot makes no connection between his role and that of his wife.[14] Giorgio Melchiori has suggested that they were inserted as part of a never-developed theme of Edward III's institution of the Order of the Garter, since the original garter that inspired the Order was sometimes supposed to have belonged to the Countess of Salisbury, though the episode in which the king declares "Honi soit qui mal y pense" is not dramatized.[15] A major Garter investiture was held in Windsor in 1593; George Peele wrote a poem for the Earl of Northumberland, who was to receive the Order that year, and was well rewarded by him. Peele, who had already written plays about Edward I and, probably, King John,[16] and had worked with Shakespeare before, might then have been the co-author of *Edward III*. Some of the play's effects, particularly those involving offstage sounds, recall those in which he specialized. It may be that the project was never completed or that the scenes making it a Garter play were used only in a private production, not in the text that got into print.

Edward III was never officially acknowledged as the work of any author, and there is an obvious reason for this. Far more than anti-French, it is quite blatantly anti-Scottish, particularly in the Countess subplot. As soon as Edward has decided on invading France, he hears that the Scots have broken their treaty with him and are now besieging the Countess. She appears almost at once, lamenting not so much her danger as the boorishness of her enemies: "what a grief it is/ To be the scornful captive to a Scot, / Either to be wooed with broad untunèd oaths, / Or forced by rough insulting barbarism" (1.2.6–9). The Scots who enter next, though they are a king and an earl, live up to her sarcastic comments, and fly ignominiously when the king's army arrives. Later, the Countess, according to Edward, is especially witty when she is ridiculing the Scots (though the mimicry of Scots speech is given to the adult actor rather than the boy):

> What a strange discourse
> Unfolded she of David and his Scots?
> "Even thus", quoth she, "he spake," – and then spoke broad,
> With epithets and accents of the Scot,
> But somewhat better than the Scot could speak.
>
> (2.1.27–31)

The assumption that all Scots are poor, barbarous, and inarticulate is so integral to this part of the play that it is impossible to imagine any company performing it once its patrons had recognized that the Scottish king was likely to be Elizabeth's successor. In both 1596 and 1598 James protested about the treatment of events and characters related to him, some of which he must have learned from his emissaries in London.[17] Someone might even have sent him a copy of *Edward III*. When the play was reissued in 1599 it again lacked the name of a theater company; perhaps none wished to be associated with it.

King John

English history was always, of course, susceptible of romantic and patriotic inter-pretations, however unpromising the reigns of some English rulers might have been. Plays listed in Henslowe's *Diary*, of which nothing remains but the titles, may have filled what now seem odd gaps in the dramatized history of England – for instance, the foreign conquests of Richard I. The Lionheart, an obvious candidate for hero-king, is mentioned in many plays, but the surviving drama depicts him only in the context of the Robin Hood legend. He could, however, be invoked in plays on later periods, as Henry V is in the Henry VI plays, as a symbol of lost greatness. In *Look About You*, which has a tangential relation to the history of Henry II's last years, the young Richard is a likeable womanizer, attempting to seduce the wife of the elderly

Falconbridge. The play may originally have been meant as a prequel to a revival of the old Queen's Men play, _The Troublesome Reign of King John_, in which the bastard son of Falconbridge plays a major role. _The Troublesome Reign_ had been in print since 1591 and, like other Queen's Men plays, was now apparently available for anyone who wanted to adapt it. It provided an entertaining and patriotic framework for a story that was not in itself very attractive. What may have started as a simple reworking of that play became more complex with revision. Probably because _The Troublesome Reign_ could be seen as holding copyright in the subject, _The Life and Death of King John_ was first published only in 1623.

In writing a play on King John, any dramatist would be entering into controversial territory. This notably unsuccessful king lost most of his lands in France, never went on a crusade, divorced his wife, and antagonized both the nobility and the Pope, who excommunicated him and put the entire land under interdict for six years. It was this last fact – a parallel to Pius V's excommunication of Elizabeth I in 1570 – that made John a suitable case for revisionist treatment. On the theory that he had been the victim of "monkish" writers because of his defiance of the church, Reformation historians tried to claim him as a hero. In the 1530s, when it was still hoped that an extensive propaganda campaign would be sufficient to win hearts and minds, John Bale, a Protestant polemicist, took John's story as the basis for an innovative hybrid of morality play and history. Bale had to flee to the Continent after Edward VI's death, but after Elizabeth's accession he revised his play, which may have been performed before her. In both versions, John's numerous failures are blamed on the allegorical figures united against him: Sedition (the comic Vice), the wavering Nobility, the plotting Clergy, and the blind Commonalty, helplessly following orders from Clergy. There is hope only in the final scene. After John's pathetic death, in which he laments that he could not do more for England, Imperial Majesty (representing Henry VIII in the first version and Elizabeth I in the second) completes the task of reformation.

Though Bale's play was not printed until the nineteenth century, his historical works were known to later chroniclers and used by Holinshed and others. But even Holinshed, though he duly condemns John's contemporaries, "who of mere malice conceal all his virtues, and hide none of his vices," has trouble making much of someone who was "a great and mighty prince, but yet not very fortunate," "somewhat cruel of nature" and "not so hardy as doubtful in time of peril and danger."[18] Not surprisingly, the dramatists of the 1590s found it hard to rehabilitate this king. Even the _Troublesome Reign_, despite its anti-Catholic message, makes John himself comic and villainous. The play focuses on three of the many problems of John's reign: the war over the boy Arthur's claim to the throne, the papal interdict, and the temporary defection of the English barons to the French dauphin. John's struggles are interspersed with the adventures of the comic and likeable (and only vaguely historical) bastard Falconbridge, and with scenes of friars and nuns behaving badly.[19] The other members of the Catholic hierarchy consist of a cardinal who meddles in politics, a monk who decides to poison John since he has heard that "the King loves not a friar," and an abbot who, overhearing part of the monk's soliloquy, is comically terrified that the poison is meant for him instead. In a melodramatic ending, Falconbridge apparently stabs the abbot after he realizes that John has been poisoned. Shakespeare followed the emphasis of the earlier play and retained the negative depiction of Cardinal Pandulph, the papal legate, but kept the rowdy friars and the poisoning monk offstage. While this tactful treatment may reflect his own Catholic sympathies, it may also show his sense of his audience. Essex himself was strongly Protestant but in favor of toleration, and many of his followers, who happened also to be keen theatergoers, were Catholics or Catholic sympathizers. It was not in a playwright's interest to alienate them, or, for that matter, to write anything that might lead to uproar in the playhouse.

Even so, Shakespeare's King John is no more admirable than his predecessor. For one brief moment, indeed, he may look like a king, when he does what Bale praised him for doing and defies the Pope. This moment ("What earthly name to interrogatories/ Can task the free breath of a sacred king? . . . no Italian priest / Shall tithe or toll in our dominions," 3.1.147–8,153–4) was always highlighted in revivals of the play whenever England felt the threat from a Catholic pretender (the son of the exiled James II in 1715, Bonny Prince Charlie in 1745) or from Catholic France (Napoleon). But the scene in which this defiance occurs is more memorable for its depiction of the divided loyalties caused by the Pope's ultimatum. The King of France, who has just sworn peace with England and helped to arrange a marriage alliance between the two countries, begs the papal legate not to force him into breaking his oath. Blanche, who has just been married to the French Dauphin, now finds that his Petrarchan love speeches meant nothing as he drags her away into what has become an enemy army. The only one who rejoices at the Pope's action is Constance, who has persuaded France to go to war on behalf of her young son who, by most laws of succession, is the rightful heir to the English throne. Holinshed had explained Queen Eleanor's support for John against Arthur in terms of her jealousy of the power that Arthur's reign would give Constance: "So hard it is for women to agree in one mind, their natures commonly being so contrary, their words so variable, and their deeds so indiscreet" (3.158) It soon becomes apparent that all the other characters, even his devoted mother, are using the boy for their own ends. Constance's ambition for her son leads eventually to his capture and death. Shakespeare makes the young prince a child, more helpless than he was either in history or in *The Troublesome Reign*. Perhaps the older boys were needed for the two women's roles and it was important for him to be noticeably smaller. As in most of Shakespeare's earlier works, the female characters seem created mainly to afford opportunities for extreme expressions of emotion. Constance is constantly in a state either of anger or grief, and her squabbling with the more political Eleanor is vividly realized in the play. Curiously, in *King John* as in *Romeo and Juliet*, her grief over her son is expressed before his death occurs: the audience knows that

Juliet has only taken a sleeping potion and that young Arthur has been captured but not yet killed.[20]

The culmination of this proto-Machiavellian behavior comes when Pandulph consoles the dauphin Lewis for the capture of Arthur by pointing out that, when John kills the boy, Lewis will be able to take advantage of popular revulsion at the murder, invade England, and claim the throne through his wife Blanche. Just as the dauphin is beginning to warm to the idea, it occurs to him that perhaps it is based on a wrong assumption:

> *Lewis.* Maybe he will not touch young Arthur's life,
> But hold himself safe in his prisonment.
> *Pandulph.* Oh, sir, when he shall hear of your approach,
> If that young Arthur be not gone already,
> Even at that news he dies . . .
>
> (3.4.160–4)

So the dauphin, apparently forgetting that his initial grief was caused by the prospect of Arthur's death, rushes off, at the instigation of the church, to raise an army that may well bring about that very death. Unlike the earlier history plays, *King John* shows a major development occurring entirely through an extended and subtle dialogue which lets the audience perceive the moral implications for itself.

The one figure with some claim to a choric role is the bastard Falconbridge, and even he is only intermittently admirable. His curious mixture of bluff soldier and potential statesman is partly explained by his mixed origins, including one of the rare sources that Shakespeare explicitly names. When Falconbridge's mother calls him a saucy knave, he replies, "Knight, knight, good mother, Basilisco-like" (1.1.244). Basilisco, the funniest braggart soldier before Falstaff, is a character in *Soliman and Perseda*, which is almost certainly by Kyd. He derives his name from the Italian *commedia* tradition, which Kyd would have known: braggart soldiers claimed to be so frightening in appearance that, like the basilisk, they could kill with looks. Kyd paired his braggart with a small boy, Piston, who keeps undermining his boasts with asides and cheeky retorts. In the passage that Shakespeare was alluding to, Piston answers Basilisco's insistence that he should be given his title – "Knight, goodfellow, Knight, Knight" – with, "Knave, good fellow, knave, knave" (1.3.169–70). Basilisco is himself something of a mixed character, capable of nobility as well as bragging and cowardice; similarly, Falconbridge begins as a comic opportunist, but his braggart qualities are displaced onto the Duke of Austria, whom he kills. His soliloquy, "Mad world, mad kings, mad composition!" (2.1.562), is partly an intelligent description of what has just happened in a scene of phony courtship and compromise, and partly an example of gratuitous cynicism. By the end, he is the closest thing to a responsible statesman that the play can show. The emphasis of the final scenes is on the return of the disaffected lords, perhaps recalling both the Puritans who had fled to Geneva under Mary Tudor and the Catholic diaspora. The bastard's final speech, another traditional patriotic passage, insists on the need for English aristocrats to remain loyal to their own country, with all its faults, rather than trust foreigners to help them. This may not have been the King John play that the court would have liked, but no one could claim that the author had made John any worse than the chronicles had already done. If it was given at one of the Inns of Court, the young students, who were encouraged to read the English chronicles for entertainment in their spare time,[21] would probably have enjoyed its treatment of complex legal and dynastic issues.

Richard II

When Shakespeare embarked on the research and writing for *Richard II* he probably knew already that Parsons's seditious *Conference* on the English succession had suggested that the deposing of a king was not necessarily evil. The examples Parsons gave included the relatively safe cases of two kings with little to be said for them: Richard III, defeated by Henry VII (Elizabeth's grandfather), and Edward II, whose son and successor, Edward III, was not tainted with the guilt of deposition. More controversially, the *Conference* also approved of the deposition of the saintly Henry VI, because he "did suffer himself to be overruled by the Queen his wife."[22] Richard II, according to Parsons, was a particularly strong example of how good could come of a usurpation, since Richard's successor was the father of the glorious Henry V. Richard II was the king with whom Elizabeth was most often compared in the 1590s, both because of the power she gave to favorites like Essex and because it had become certain that she was going to die childless.

Though *Richard II* is usually discussed, and often performed, in conjunction with *1* and *2 Henry IV* and *Henry V*, it may not have been written with any view of a sequel. Nor is it a sequel to *Edward III*, which deals with the immediately preceding reign. When characters in *Richard II* speak of Richard's grandfather, Edward III, and of the glorious victories of the Black Prince, they do so only in general terms, as when York recalls that he and John of Gaunt once "rescued the Black Prince, that young Mars of men,/ From forth the ranks of many thousand French" (2.3.100–1). The episode is not dramatized in *Edward III*, where the prince never needs rescuing. On the other hand, references to the events of *Richard II*, and even the words spoken by its characters, abound in the two plays about the reign of his successor. The prodigal son pattern exemplified in *The Famous Victories of Henry V* – wild youth followed by repentance and redemption – is already present in *Richard II*, though it is incomplete: the king learns something, and perhaps repents, but only when it is too late. Shakespeare's play is more commonly compared with Marlowe's *Edward II* and follows the same general trajectory: the king behaves self-destructively throughout the first half of the play, undergoes a deposition scene that is both self-dramatizing and tragic, and is finally murdered in prison, after which the new king attempts to re-establish order by punishing the murderer. Yet the two works are very different. Though both Edward and Richard are willing to call upon their status to justify their actions, Richard's actions are recognizably those of a ruler, however bad, whereas Edward's are those of a delinquent schoolboy. Both Edward's tyrannical behavior and his later sufferings are extreme. Like Edward, Richard is blamed for the influence of his favorites, yet Shakespeare gives very little sense of their responsibility for what happens or, in the text at least, of the homoerotic relationship that is so important in Marlowe. Very few characters in fact flatter Richard II; most of them berate him. Perhaps Shakespeare had been warned to steer clear of possible embarrassing parallels with James VI.

Marlowe transforms the conventional imagery of the king as sun into Edward's poignant question, "But what are kings, when regiment is gone,/ But perfect shadows in a sunshine day?" (5.1.26–7) This question, and Marlowe's contrast between the luxurious poetic "complaint" of the king and the unpoetic voice of his opponent, lie behind much of Shakespeare's play. From 1.2 on, _Richard II_ is dominated by scenes of lamentation: the Duchess of Gloucester grieves for the unavenged murder of her husband and leaves the stage to die; John of Gaunt and his son exchange grief-stricken farewells and Gaunt dies in near-despair over the state of England; Richard's queen is full of grief even before she knows that she has reason to grieve; and the same is true of Richard on his return from Ireland. In _King John_ Constance's premature grief over Arthur had provoked the comment, "You are as fond of grief as of your child" (3.4.92). Shakespeare knew that despair is a branch of the sin of Sloth, and might therefore have agreed with modern critics who feel that Richard not only gives in to self-pity but even brings his misfortunes on himself by despairing too soon. Yet the play also makes it clear that nothing he could have done would make any difference. Apparently passive sufferers can, however, sometimes show a feline maliciousness and sometimes devastating accuracy – as when Henry VI confronts Richard of Gloucester (_3 Henry VI_ 5.6.2–5) or when Constance calls the Duke of Austria "Thou ever strong upon the stronger side!" (_King John_ 3.1.117). In _Richard II_ the mood of renunciation is elaborated until it seems self-indulgent even to Richard himself ("Well, well, I see/ I talk but idly, and you laugh at me," 3.3.170–1), while the sharpness seen from the start in his stichomythic exchanges with Gaunt reaches its peak when he is most clearly the underdog, as in this chapter's epigraph. Nicholas Brooke has noted that _Richard III_ is built on the contrast between a "highly formalized structure and writing" and "sudden penetrations of the mundanely human."[23] This contrast is not unique to Shakespeare – both Kyd and Marlowe frequently move between tragic and comic, or grandiose and denigrating, views of a situation – but whereas in the earlier play the "mundanely human" is confined to Richard III's character, Richard II himself combines the two modes. It is his personality, not his political situation, that dominates the play.

Repetition of motifs from the early histories was perhaps inevitable, given the nature of the chronicles themselves: exemplary and cautionary anecdotes tend to attach themselves to more than one historical character in the sources that Holinshed's authors were trying to consolidate. The repetition may, however, suggest something about Shakespeare's changing attitude toward his material or his audience. A good example is the brief passage in *3 Henry VI* when Edward IV persuades the Mayor and Aldermen of York to let him enter the city, only to be undercut by his brother Richard's aside:

> *King Edward.* Why, and I challenge nothing but my dukedom,
>   As being well content with that alone.
> *Gloucester [aside].* But when the fox hath once got in his nose,
>   He'll soon find means to make the body follow.

>   (4.7.23–6)

When the Mayor has agreed to open the gates to them, the Yorkists comment sarcastically on his willingness to be persuaded: "The good old man would fain that all were well,/ So 'twere not long of him . . ." (4.7.31–2). Their blatant deception and the Mayor's weakness become something much more ambiguous in *Richard II*. Bolingbroke sounds sincere when he claims to seek only his dukedom, and the Duke of York is as fuzzy as the Mayor of York about where his duty lies:

> It may be I will go with you, but yet I'll pause,
> For I am loath to break our country's laws.
> Nor friends nor foes, to me welcome you are.
> Things past redress are now with me past care.
>   (2.3.168–71)

As in *King John*, a complex moral situation is presented but not commented on by any authoritative figure. No one in this play explicitly tells the audience either that Bolingbroke is lying or that York is being weak. It is only in *1 Henry IV* that other characters, looking back on earlier events, accuse the king of having deceived them. Since the plays seem rarely to have been acted together, it is likely that the audience would have found it hard to remember what Bolingbroke said or what he seemed to mean by it, and would thus have been in much the same situation as the characters in the play. The same is true of the controversy that opens the play: the murder of Thomas of Woodstock, Duke of Gloucester. The issue is raised twice, each time provoking a series of denials and challenges to combat, and yet is never resolved. And so of the other questions that arise in the course of the play. Was Richard justified in banishing the two combatants? Was Bolingbroke justified in deposing him? Were Bolingbroke's supporters traitors?

Some of the confusion may be tactical. Shakespeare had to avoid any interpretation that advocated the deposition of a king, however bad. This may be why the murder of the Duke of Gloucester is never directly pinned on Richard even when it is brought up again in 4.1. The audience is told of numerous unspecified crimes but sees only the possibly curable arrogance of youth. Richard goes to war in Ireland but, like York in _The First Part of the Contention_, he is seen only when he returns, and nothing is said about what he did there. On his return, Richard is in the company of a churchman, who, though constantly urging him to action, also speaks eloquently against the deposing of a king and joins with another churchman, the Abbot of Westminster, in an unsuccessful plot against the usurper. On the other hand, the play leaves out the Archbishop of Canterbury, an important supporter of Bolingbroke. Religion seems, then, to be on Richard's side. When Richard is asked to read out the list of the crimes for which he is being deposed – a list which Holinshed prints in full – he behaves so hysterically that Bolingbroke agrees to omit this part of the ceremony. The scene in which this occurs was not present when the play was first published in 1597 or in two subsequent Quarto editions. When the fourth Quarto was published in 1608 the title page drew attention to the fact that it now contained "new additions of the Parliament Sceane, and the deposing of King Richard." There is some debate as to whether this scene had not yet been written in 1597 or whether its absence means that it was censored from the play. Like most scholars, I think the latter. It reads like an enriched and expanded version of Edward II's deposition. Whereas Edward's feeble attempts to prolong the process by hesitations and laments are treated with contempt by the emissaries from court, Richard seizes the opportunity to dominate the stage, making himself the creator of his own abdication, and thus emphasizing that no one else has the power to do it. At the end of the story, Shakespeare chooses the more sympathetic and heroic of the alternative versions accounts that Holinshed gives of Richard's death, while reinforcing the theme that regicide is damnable, a view that is immediately confirmed by the repentant killer.

Given this treatment of the sources, I find it hard to believe that Shakespeare thought, but dared not say, that Richard's deposition was a good thing for England. In the context of the plays that followed it, it would be hard to make an argument from success, as Parsons had tried to do. The reign of Henry V might justify his father's usurpation, but the Epilogue to _Henry V_ makes a point of reminding the audience of the disasters in the reign of Henry VI, "which oft our stage hath shown" (13). If followed through to the ending that Hall gave his history, in the marriage of Henry VII and Elizabeth of York, the story perhaps becomes triumphant again, but there is a great deal of violence in proportion to a small amount of happiness. Everything depends on where the narrative is stopped. "I come but for mine own," says Bolingbroke; "Your own is yours," Richard replies. In the moment, Bolingbroke may be sincere and Richard petulantly cynical. With hindsight, Richard is right about Bolingbroke's motives. Yet their characters may matter less than the cyclical pattern that was emphasized in John Barton's famous production of 1973 for the Royal Shakespeare Company, in which actors alternated the roles of Richard and Bolingbroke. One of the many striking images in the deposition scene is Richard's comparison of himself and Bolingbroke, each with a hand on the crown, to "two buckets filling one another" (4.1.186). Though Richard himself imagines that the process will end when he sinks down, filled with water (tears), while the empty Bolingbroke rises in the air, there is a sense in which they do go on filling and emptying each other, as Sonnet 64 describes the land and sea taking away from each other successively, "increasing store with loss, and loss with store" (64.7–8). Near the end of his life, Henry IV will use similar language to describe the political changes in his own lifetime (*2 Henry IV* 3.1.45–56).

Notes

1. Gurr, *The Shakespeare Company, 1594–1642*, 149–51.
2. Doleman [Robert Parsons], *A Conference About the Next Succession to the Crowne of Ingland*, B2ᵛ–B3.
3. Siemon notes the significance of Nashe's failure to mention it in *Pierce Penniless* (entered in the Stationers' Register in August 1592), where he praises the theatrical effect of *1 Henry VI*. *King Richard III*, ed. Siemon, 47–9.
4. The recurring Shakespearean rhythm, though not its Marlovian source, is pointed out in Rossiter, "The Unity of *Richard III*," in *Angel with Horns*, 10–12. Marlowe quotations come from *Doctor Faustus and Other Plays*, ed. Bevington and Rasmussen. The "perpetual night" line occurs in both the A and B texts, but "Despair and die" is only in the B text (pub. 1616).
5. Quotations are modernized from *The Battle of Alcazar*, ed. John Yoklavich, in *The Life and Works of George Peele*, gen. ed. Prouty, vol. 2.
6. I have modernized and realigned the lines.
7. MacCaffrey, "Henry Carey, first Baron Hunsdon," *ODNB*.
8. Blayney, *The First Folio*, 29.
9. Deloney, *Strange histories, or, Songs and sonnets, of kinges, princes, dukes, lords, ladyes, knights, and gentlemen . . .* (1612). This collection of ballads was first published in 1602 but the ballad on Edward III and the Countess of Salisbury appears only in the third edition.
10. Anny Crunelle-Vanrigh, "Notice" to *Edouard III* in her edition of *Edward II / Edouard III*, 1642.
11. *Edward III* is quoted from the edition of Giorgio Melchiori.
12. *Shakespeare's Poems*, ed. Duncan-Jones and Woudhuysen, 32.
13. Adelman, *The Common Liar*, 26.
14. David Rintoul, who played Edward III in the RSC production at the Swan Theatre, Stratford, in 2002, describes the efforts he made to load one line in the final scene to convey an indirect apology both to Salisbury and to his queen. See Rintoul, "King Edward III," 81. Interestingly, although Rintoul was struck by the considerable differences in power between the Countess scenes and the rest, he was reluctant to ascribe this to multiple authorship, suggesting instead that the play had originally been written by a very young Shakespeare and later revised.
15. See Melchiori, *Shakespeare's Garter Plays*.
16. See Vickers, "The Troublesome Reign."

17. See Anny Crunelle-Vanrigh's "Notice" to her edition of *Edward II / Edouard III*, 1629.
18. *The Third Volume of Chronicles*, 196a.
19. John appears again in Anthony Munday's two-part play about Robin Hood (1599), where he is both comic and villainous; in the prequel called *Look About You* (1600) he is depicted as a spoiled brat whose plans invariably go wrong.
20. In *Edward III*, too, his parents are told of the Black Prince's almost certain death in battle when the audience knows that he is in fact victorious and on his way to them. See Rintoul's comments in "King Edward III," 81–2.
21. Sir John Fortescue, *A Learned Commendation of the Politique Laws of England*, 114^v–115, quoted in Axton, *The Queen's Two Bodies*, 5.
22. Doleman [Parsons], *Conference*, 60.
23. Brook, *Shakespeare's Early Tragedies*, 50, 54.

9

"When Love Speaks"

Tragedy and Comedy, 1595–1596

For valor, is not Love a Hercules,
Still climbing trees in the Hesperides?
Subtle as Sphinx, as sweet and musical
As bright Apollo's lute, strung with his hair.
And when Love speaks, the voice of all the gods
Make heaven drowsy with the harmony.
              (Love's Labour's Lost 4.3.314–19)

"When Love speaks": Venus is love, and she had already spoken at length in Shakespeare's first published work. These lines from *Love's Labour's Lost* come near the climax of another eloquent and persuasive speech, but one that is clearly marked from the start as an example of disingenuous and extravagant oratory. The link between Shakespeare the love poet and Shakespeare the comic writer was evident to the publisher of *Troilus and Cressida*, who wrote in 1609 that the comedies "seem (for their height of pleasure) to be born in that sea that brought forth *Venus*."[1] Those who loved the poem could indeed find many of the same pleasures in his lyrical tragedies (*Richard II* and *Romeo and Juliet*) and two lyrical comedies (*A Midsummer Night's Dream* and *Love's Labour's Lost*). In the main source for *Romeo and Juliet* the heroine is 16; Shakespeare insists on the fact that she is 13, the youngest female character whose age is given in a play of this period. *Venus and Adonis* had similarly emphasized its young hero's unreadiness for love, and the creation of a composite Adonis/Juliet figure, embodied in a boy actor, could only have added to the emphasis on the precariousness of beauty. In *A Midsummer Night's Dream*, Venus's curse on lovers lies behind the lament of Hermia and Lysander that "the course of true love never did run smooth," and the flower into which Adonis was metamorphosed may also be the "little western flower,/ Before milk white, now purple with love's wound"

The Life of William Shakespeare: A Critical Biography, First Edition. Lois Potter.
© 2012 Lois Potter. Published 2012 by Blackwell Publishing Ltd.

(2.1.166–7), that is the source of the love juice in the play. *Richard II*, too, is as poetic as it is historical; it is entirely in verse, frequently falls into the rhyming quatrains and couplets that suggest the sonnet form, and includes a scene between Richard and his queen that looks not only back to the parting of Queen Margaret and Suffolk in *2 Henry VI* but forward to that of Romeo and Juliet.

The four plays are so similar in tone that they probably date from roughly the same period. Though some think that *Richard II* was written just before its sequel, the first part of *Henry IV*, the differences in style between the two histories suggest at least a brief lapse of time between them, and *A Midsummer Night's Dream* might have been even funnier for an audience that had already seen *Romeo and Juliet* a number of times. My suggested order – *Richard II, Romeo and Juliet, Midsummer Night's Dream, Love's Labour's Lost* – differs from most in placing *Love's Labour's Lost* at the end of the sequence, for reasons that will be explained. Another link between them is the influence of Chaucer, whom Shakespeare must have recently read or reread. Since the Admiral's Men had performed *Palamon and Arcite*, based on the Knight's Tale, in September 1594, it would be natural for other dramatists to look for other Chaucer stories to dramatize. Shakespeare's response was, however, rather oblique. In *A Midsummer Night's Dream*, the personality of Theseus is recognizably influenced by his depiction in Chaucer (and perhaps in the lost Palamon and Arcite play). The last book of *Troilus and Criseyde* lies somewhere behind *Romeo and Juliet*'s depiction of the pain of banishment; in *Love's Labour's Lost* the curious character of Boyet – the Princess's chamberlain or chaperone, with a prurient interest in the ladies' love affairs – may owe something to Chaucer's depiction of Pandarus. When he was researching the reign of Richard II, Shakespeare might have been reminded that Chaucer was a poet at that king's court. Gower says in *Confessio Amantis* that Richard had ordered him to write that poem, which is dedicated both to the king and to Chaucer.

Romeo and Juliet

In *A Midsummer Night's Dream*, Bottom, told that he is to play Pyramus, naturally assumes that it must be the leading role, and asks, "What is Pyramus, a lover or a tyrant?" (1.2.19). He might have been thinking of Burbage's two previous successes, the tyrant Richard III and the lover Romeo. "The lover" was an established dramatic type in Italian comedy and in English drama, but it was recognized as a difficult one to play successfully, perhaps because audience response to such characters depends on qualities, like sexual charisma, that no amount of training can give an actor. The lover, especially if male, is also expected to convey emotions exalted to the point of absurdity. Burbage was about 27 when he played Romeo, and still unmarried – hence, an ideal object for audience fantasies.

When the play appeared in Quarto in 1597, the title page said that this *"Excellent conceited Tragedie of Romeo and Iuliet" had "been often (with great applause) plaid publiquely, by the right honourable the L. of Hunsdon his Seruants."* The praise of the play's conceitedness recognizes the quality of the language that made it so quotable for contemporaries. Equally significant is the fact that the company could have been described as Lord Hunsdon's servants rather than the Lord Chamberlain's Men only between the death of the old lord chamberlain and the appointment of his son to the same office – that is, between 23 July 1596 and 14 April 1597 – and thus Q1 must have been printed quite early in 1597. So Romeo and Juliet was first acted in 1596 and written in 1595–6, during Shakespeare's first two years with the Lord Chamberlain's company.

Though the play was Shakespeare's most distinctive and original work to date, the quality that might most have impressed well-read spectators was his remarkable fidelity to his source. Arthur Brooke based his narrative poem *Romeus and Juliet* on a story that was known all over Europe, existed in several versions, and was believed by many to be true. Like the two lovers, Brooke had died young – by drowning – and this fact may have given more notoriety to his poem. Shakespeare, then, approached it as a television adapter approaches a famous novel, knowing that his success would depend both on recreating the experience of reading the work and on adding visual and aural richness to make up for what could not be dramatized. Much of what makes the play so interesting is, surprisingly, also in Brooke: the relationship of Romeo and the Friar; the Nurse's ramblings that exasperate Juliet when she is eager for news of Romeo; Juliet's fears before she takes the potion; the apothecary who sells poison because he is too poor to make a living within the law. The sonnet that forms a prologue to Shakespeare's play is obviously inspired by the sonnet that Brooke used as his preface, and the poem's final couplet,

> There is no monument more worthy of the sight
> Than is the tomb of Juliet and Romeus her knight.
> (3019–20)[2]

is echoed in the last lines of the play:

> For never was a story of more woe
> Than this of Juliet, and her Romeo.
> (5.3.279–80)

Many of Shakespeare's alterations to this story must have been made with his actors in mind. He needed, for instance, more male roles. The most important of these was developed out of a hint in Brooke's account of the ball where the lovers meet. After the dance, Juliet sits next to a gallant named Mercutio, who takes one of her hands while Romeus seizes the other. When Romeus apologizes for his presumption, she excuses him by saying that she appreciates the warmth of his hand by contrast with Mercutio's cold one. Shakespeare's imagination, perhaps recalling *Hero and Leander* ("These lovers parlèd by the touch of hands," 1.185), found in this short episode both the hint of Mercutio's character and the subject of the opening dialogue of the lovers. Though Friar Lawrence is an important character in Brooke's poem, Protestant distrust of Catholic clergymen meant that Brooke could not resist saying that the part of his cell where Romeus hides was also where in his youth the friar used to keep "his fair friends" (1273). Shakespeare makes no jokes about friars and nuns, and his treatment of Friar Lawrence is almost wholly sympathetic. The exception is in the final scene, where, by comparison with his concern for Romeo, his treatment of Juliet seems remarkably insensitive: he abruptly tells her that her husband is dead, says he will "dispose of" her in a convent (5.3.156), and then runs away, leaving her to commit suicide alone.

Romeo and Juliet gives every indication of being intended to dazzle its audience and to show off the talents not only of the title characters but of the entire company. The setting in Verona, among wealthy Italian families, requires sumptuous costumes. It is not surprising that Juliet compares her feelings as she awaits her wedding night to those of "an impatient child that has new robes/ And may not wear them" (3.2.30–1). The complex group scenes must have needed rehearsal: the taunting between two servants that develops into a fight involving at least six people; a ball with a number of masked dancers and torchbearers, where the dialogue is apparently cued by music; a fight in which a third party steps between two duelists (potentially very dangerous for all three actors); a wedding procession that turns into a funeral cortège; and a curious scene of lamentation after Juliet's supposed death, that apparently requires the actors to speak simultaneously. The play's language includes Petrarchan verse, elaborate (and now almost unintelligible) punning, and the rambling and often indecent recollections of the Nurse. In what is usually called the "balcony scene" (although Juliet appears at a window rather than a balcony), Shakespeare finally developed to its full the visual and auditory experience that he remembered from *The Jew of Malta*. Few plays of the period use the upper level so much in a context so different from that of the war plays. Romeo's "But soft, what light through yonder window breaks?/ It is the east and Juliet is the sun" (2.2.2) echoes Barabas's "But stay, what star shines yonder in the east?/ The loadstar of my life, if Abigail" (2.1.41–2). Lars Engle, in an acute analysis of this scene, has pointed out that Romeo's immediately preceding line ("He jests at scars that never felt a wound," 2.2.1) recalls Barabas's comparison of the memory of his lost wealth to a "soldier's scar."[3] Romeo also echoes the merchant Barabas when he explains his venturing into the Capulets' orchard:

> I am no pilot; yet, wert thou as far
> As that vast shore washed with the farthest sea,
> I should adventure for such merchandise.
>
> (2.2.82–4)

Just before he drinks the poison, he will recall the other aspect of the merchant's life, the adventurous voyage and shipwreck that become part of the plot of *The Merchant of Venice*, though here it is the "desperate pilot" who himself chooses to wreck his ship.

This is the first Shakespeare play for which a prologue survives. Shakespeare, or someone else, must have written a prologue for each of his plays, and an epilogue as well, though this sometimes consisted only of a couple of lines inviting the audience to applaud. Prologues may have been spoken only at the first performance of a play. If this was true of *Romeo and Juliet* it would, as Tiffany Stern notes, make a considerable difference to the audience's experience: "with the prologue, the play is heralded as a tragedy from the outset; without it, the play is comic until the death of Mercutio."[4] However, *Romeo and Juliet* may be a special case. The Brooke poem is prefaced by several sonnets and Shakespeare seems to have wanted the play to be associated with the form, since another sonnet, usually cut in performance, precedes Act 2. The change of direction is also signaled by the lovers' premonitions and Friar Lawrence's warnings about the dangers of "violent delights" that "have violent ends" (2.6.9). In any case, audiences were used to dramatic frameworks which emphasized the arbitrariness of fate, as in the repeated appearances of Love, Fortune, and Death in *Soliman and Perseda*. Love – and comedy – dominate the early part of that play, but in the final act, dominated by Death, even the comic characters die. Soliman, in love with Perseda, kills her lover; in revenge, she anoints her lips with poison so that, when Soliman kisses her, he will die too. Juliet kisses the dead Romeo because she *hopes* that there might still be poison on his lips.

Juliet's father and her nurse, both genial comic figures in the first half of the play, take on strange shapes in Act 4, as if her grief had become a distorting mirror that makes them hideous. Not only Juliet and Romeo but the spectators themselves are caught up in a confused emotional deception. In the scene where the Nurse comes to wake Juliet on her wedding morning, they know what she is about to find. As she makes her typically bawdy jokes about the forthcoming wedding night, they have to wait for her to draw the bedcurtains and, surprised, see Juliet wearing her wedding clothes. Then there is further suspense before she finally touches Juliet and "realizes" that the girl is dead. Even though they know that this is not true, they are forced to identify with the Nurse's various stages of shock and grief:

> I needs must wake her. – Madam, madam, madam!
> Ay, let the County take you in your bed;
> He'll fright you up, I'faith! – Will it not be?
> What, dressed, and in your clothes, and down again?
> I must needs wake you. Lady, lady, lady!
> Alas, alas! Help, help! My lady's dead!
> Oh, welladay, that ever I was born!
> Some aqua vitae, ho! My lord! My lady!
>
> (4.5.9–16)

As with Mercutio's death, the change from laughter to appalled grief in connection with a comic character is deliberately sudden. Though the laments that follow the Nurse's discovery differ considerably between Q1 and Q2, both versions are apparently meant to be spoken in unison by Juliet's parents, the Nurse, and Paris, another deliberately artificial effect. The Nurse disappears from the stage after this scene. The actor probably had to swell the crowd in the final scene, perhaps doubling as one of the watchmen or playing a larger role such as Montague, or perhaps he also performed in the jig. In any case, there was no way that Shakespeare could make this character react a second time to the discovery of a dead Juliet, while her absence allows the audience to experience it in a totally different way. The Nurse's absence also avoided the need to send her into banishment, as in Brooke's poem.

Brooke had felt it necessary in his preface to draw some moral from the story, pointing out the abuse of confession, which Juliet twice uses as a pretext to get out of her parents' house. Shakespeare's Romeo seems to put himself in the hands of God the pilot "that hath the steerage of my course" (1.4.112). However, most of the plot shows, as in Sophocles' *Oedipus*, how everything that the lovers and the Friar do to escape tragedy simply brings them closer to it. Moralistic readings blame all three characters for being hasty, or disobedient to parents, or devious. Fatalism and Calvinism are, however, closely linked, and the Calvinist conclusion, which the Prince endorses (5.3.291–5), is that a just God has willed everything that happened: the deaths of the lovers are God's punishment on their parents, while the deaths of his kinsmen Mercutio and Paris are meant to punish the Prince himself for not being strict enough with the feuding families. "See what a scourge is laid upon your hate," he moralizes (5.3.292). The company knew Queen Elizabeth's dislike of plays that advocated love and marriage, but they could feel comfortable about offering her one in which love turned out disastrously. At the same time, most of what went wrong could be blamed on the family feuds that were the bane of every ruler's life. Indeed, the "two households, both alike in dignity" recall those of Lancaster and York, whose strife, Hall reminded everyone, had been reconciled through marriage.

However, this is not what anyone took away from the play. It has always been remembered for the lovers' poetry and for (some of) the comic scenes; the deaths of the lovers come close to being idealized and exemplary, appealing to a secret belief that lovers should die young, before anything can spoil their image of each other. This was the first play in which Shakespeare created characters and situations for which a highly lyrical style seemed natural. Some of the lovers' lines almost sing themselves: "Arise, fair sun, and kill the envious moon" (2.2.4), "It is my lady, oh, it is my love" (2.2.10), "Believe me, love, it was the nightingale" (3.5.5). Above all, the play offered the sensuous poetic delights of the narrative poems in a more universally appealing form. *Venus and Adonis* put its most luscious writing into the mouth of a rejected goddess for whom marriage is irrelevant; in *Lucrece* the heroine's beauty is seen through the eyes of her rapist. Romeo looks at Juliet three times without her seeing him – at the Capulets' ball, as she soliloquizes at her window, and as she lies apparently dead. Each time, he puts his wonder into words, and the audience luxuriates in a guilt-free experience.

A Midsummer Night's Dream

Theseus announces at the beginning of *A Midsummer Night's Dream* that he is waiting impatiently for the new moon, at which time he and Hippolyta will be married. In the last act the three newly married couples watch another play in order to pass the three long hours until they can go to bed. It is Theseus's wedding that brings Oberon and Titania into the woods, where the feud between the fairy king and queen implicates, confuses, and finally resolves the apparently incompatible desires of the four lovers. It is for his wedding, too, that the Athenian artisans rehearse and perform their play. Not surprisingly, scholars have speculated that the play may have been written for an aristocratic wedding, whose spectators would have been in the same position as the onstage spectators of *Pyramus and Thisbe*.[5] It was, however, designed to be performed in the public theater as well, perhaps without the final appearance of the fairies to bless the bridal beds. The only obviously topical elements, all confined to the fairy characters, are a reference to the exceptionally bad weather of summer 1594 and a compliment to the queen's invincible chastity. At a court performance, there would also have been comic topicality in the anxiety of the amateur actors about how their play will be received, their speculations about the reward they might get for a court performance, and perhaps even the interruption of the play by comments from the aristocratic audience.

Sidney's account of delightful incongruity in the *Apology for Poetry* (first published in 1595) was the closest Shakespeare seems to have come to a theory of comedy: "So in Hercules, painted with his great beard and furious countenance, in a woman's attire, spinning, at Omphale's commaundement, it breeds both delight and laughter: for the representing of so strange a power in Love procures delight, and the scornfulness of the action stirreth laughter."[6] *A Midsummer Night's Dream* juxtaposes just such disparate elements: the "cross-wooing" of four confused young lovers, a practical joke played by the king of fairies on his wife, and the attempt of a group of working men to perform a play for the wedding of the Athenian hero Theseus with the Amazon Hippolyta – which is itself a marriage of contrarieties, since they have been enemies in war. The most unlikely of all the juxtapositions results from the magic by which Oberon makes his wife fall in love with a weaver wearing an ass's head. The image of Bottom with Titania derives from Apuleius's *The Golden Ass* and Ovid's *Metamorphoses*, which depict many unnatural and unlikely pairings. The comedy is not only saturated with Ovidian themes – metamorphosis, unnatural love, magic; it is also Ovidian in structure, with one story interrupting another. Sometimes, as in the

Metamorphoses, someone (usually one of the young lovers) comes running into the story; sometimes someone is "discovered" onstage. When Titania awakes to the sound of Bottom's raucous singing and cries, "What angel wakes me from my flowery bed?" (3.1.124) her line is not only delightful but funny because it is so patently ridiculous – she is looking not at an angel but at a man with the head of an ass. It also reminds the audience of a forgotten part of the plot (she has been asleep onstage for over 250 lines; even if visible, she was ignored during the previous scene). This interweaving creates the delight-in-laughter that Sidney wrote of. It goes well beyond the framework plots that may have been Shakespeare's original inspiration, such as Greene's *The Scottish History of James IV* (published 1592), where the fairy king Oberon puts on a play about a Scottish king in order to entertain a misanthropic Scot. In Shakespeare, it is not always clear what is framing what. Everything initially seems framed by the wedding of Theseus and Hippolyta, but the fairies later reveal that they have been guiding the human characters like Homeric gods. The story of the four lovers is framed by that of the fairies, but the fairies themselves are not always in complete control and seem unaware that they are being watched and judged by their human audience in the theater.

It is only at the very end that Puck breaks out of the frame to address the "real" audience and ask for its applause. He does this immediately after the conclusion of a play that has been watched by most of the characters we are watching. As has often been noticed, the hilariously bad performance of the tragedy of Pyramus and Thisbe recalls the story of Romeo and Juliet. Shakespeare probably got the idea of parodying his own very popular play from the end of *The Spanish Tragedy*, where an absurdly truncated version of *Soliman and Perseda* (probably also by Kyd) is watched by characters who are themselves being watched by a ghost and a personification of Revenge. Whatever the sequence in which the two plays were written, once they were both in the repertoire, the performance of the "reduced" *Soliman and Perseda* as part of Hieronimo's revenge plot was bound to come across as a parody. The original cast of *Pyramus and Thisbe*, as Quince describes it in 1.2, actually sounds more like *Romeo and Juliet* than like the play performed at the end of *Midsummer Night's Dream*, since it includes Pyramus's mother and Thisbe's father, though they do not in fact appear. Hieronimo, after the last body hits the stage in *The Spanish Tragedy*, informs his audience that the deaths they have been watching are real; Bottom, on the other hand, insists that the audience of *Pyramus and Thisbe* should be carefully informed that the characters in this play do not really die.

As with *The Taming of the Shrew*, the entire play emphatically defers sexual consummation, and in the play-within-a-play the lovers do not even manage to kiss each other. On the other hand, there is a dirty joke about what they kiss instead. Moreover, since Jan Kott's famous account of the play in *Shakespeare Our Contemporary* (1964), there has been considerable interest in the possibility that the short love affair between Titania and Bottom can be seen as an example of bestiality, or at least adultery, and thus that Oberon's treatment of his wife is either sadistic or masochistic. It is impossible to imagine this theory being expressed overtly in an early modern performance, but any play that deals with magic and fantasy lends itself to sexual interpretation. Attempts to find a moral in the story mostly focus on whether Titania is justified in keeping the changeling boy from Oberon and whether he is justified in tricking her into giving up the child. Their conflict is passionate and crucial in the early acts but evaporates in the heat of the plot, so that one hardly notices that Oberon has successfully tamed the fairy queen just as Theseus has tamed Hippolyta. Similarly, the apparently insoluble problem of Hermia's refusal to marry the man her father has chosen for her vanishes when that man falls in love with another woman who has been loving him in vain. As in a dream, nothing has consequences. Love is magic; magic is love; theater is magic; all depends on "imagination" or illusion, but all may equally be real because the emotions evoked are real.

Love's Labour's Lost

In January 1596 Richard Field entered into the Stationers' Register what must have been one of the most eagerly awaited books of the decade, the second part of Spenser's *Faerie Queene*. Spenser had held his audience in suspense, since the publication of the first three books in 1590, over the adventures of the Red Cross Knight, Sir Guyon, Prince Arthur, and Britomart. Arthurian knights from "Britain" (Wales) and fairy knights from Fairyland, operating in parallel universes, nevertheless occupied the same spaces in the narrative. As the 1590 volume ended, the lady knight Britomart was still in quest of her destined husband Artegall, though he had not yet entered the poem as a character. Other knights had completed their initial quests but were still wandering. Six years later, the author, a civil servant helping to administer the English occupation of Ireland, was finally publishing three new books, on the subjects of friendship, justice, and courtesy. They offered a number of surprises. In particular, Book V, on justice, turned out to be an obvious commentary on current events, with the allegorical names barely concealing recognizable contemporary protagonists, such as the Earl of Leicester, Mary Queen of Scots, Spenser's own patron, Lord Grey, and even Queen Elizabeth herself and the present King of France, Henri IV, formerly the King of Navarre.

Only two years after *Lucrece* was published, its author would still have had reason to visit Richard Field's shop in the Blackfriars, since Field continued to print new editions of the poems, though he had transferred his rights to another publisher. Perhaps by now Shakespeare could afford to buy expensive books; perhaps he devoured Field's copy of Spenser or borrowed someone else's. As Sir Walter Ralegh would later write in the preface to his *History of the World* (1614), "Whosoever, in writing a modern history, shall follow truth too near the heels, it may happily strike out his teeth" (E4^r) This nearly happened to Spenser. In one episode of the fifth book he had depicted Queen Mercilla (the merciful aspect of Elizabeth I) reluctantly agreeing to the execution of a character who, though she originally represented duplicity and Catholicism, was now clearly identified with Mary Queen of Scots, executed by Elizabeth's government in 1587. James VI, an early reader of the poem, immediately recognized the posthumous denunciation of his mother and by November 1596 had lodged an angry protest, ordered a boycott of the poem in Scotland, and demanded that the author be punished. Shakespeare knew better than to follow Spenser into the dangerous world of political commentary, since the theater, far more than the printing press, was capable of stirring people to violence. The complex multiple meanings of the poet's allegory did, however, hint at a way of playing with topicality without being destroyed by it. If everything had *several* possible meanings, could they perhaps cancel each other out, so that no one could accuse the author of subversion?

Love's Labour's Lost has always been a puzzle to readers. It is not surprising that there is no source for the plot, since there is hardly any plot. The audience might well expect topicality once it realized that the setting was Navarre and that the four young men who open the play by signing articles of agreement were the King of Navarre and three lords with names (Biron, Dumain – or du Mayenne – and Longueville) identical with those of participants in the recent French wars of religion. Their names turn up in the titles of a number of books published by Richard Field, who had inherited his French master's sympathy for the Huguenot cause.[7] Some of these men were personal acquaintances of the Earl of Essex and his English followers, who had been in France in 1591, fighting to establish Henri of Navarre on his throne.[8] In Book V, moreover, Spenser had not hesitated to touch on Henri's conversion to Catholicism in 1593, which was the price demanded by the Parlement of Paris for support of his claim. This opportunistic abandonment of his Protestant faith was depicted in *The Faerie Queene* as a romantic betrayal by Burbon (Henri IV was the first of France's Bourbon kings). Courting his lady, Fleurdelys (the lily that symbolizes France), Burbon throws away his shield (his faith) but the lady still refuses to accept him. Prince Arthur (partly an abstract ideal of Magnanimity and partly an idealized portrait of the Earl of Leicester's handling of the war in the Netherlands) reproves him for his apostasy but also chastises the lady for her fickleness and orders her to marry Burbon – that is, to accept him as her lawful king. (The marital allegory was dangerously close to the truth: not only had Henri IV's marriage been the occasion of the St. Bartholomew's Day Massacre, but his wife, Marguérite de Valois, was notoriously unfaithful, and the couple would separate in 1600.) The apostasy of the historical Navarre had been a bitter disappointment to English supporters, but many found it convenient to believe that the conversion was purely political. Suspicion of his sincerity was felt by Catholics as well as Protestants – and would result, seventeen years later, in the king's assassination by a fanatical Catholic.

The French allusions are not the only topical ones. The King of Navarre is apparently named Ferdinand, the name of the fifth Earl of Derby who had died in 1594, but the audience would not have known this, as the name is used only in a single stage direction, perhaps simply to ensure that readers would not think his name was Henry. The sixth Earl of Derby, William Stanley, had traveled in France in the 1580s, visiting Navarre's "academy" at Nérac. Derby was also a king – of the Isle of Man – and apparently something of a recluse. The masque of Russians in Act 5 would certainly have reminded Inns of Court students of the 1594/5 Gray's Inn revels at which *The Comedy of Errors* was played. As part of the "pomp" associated with the lord of misrule, the Prince of Purpoole had made a mock-voyage to Russia from which he "returned" to London with a good deal of pageantry. Rosaline's joke that the king must be "Sea-sick, I think, coming from Muscovy" (5.2.394) seems particularly apt, since the prince apologized in a letter to Queen Elizabeth that seasickness prevented him from paying his respects to her.[9] The Lord Chamberlain's Men may even have counted on the delight the law students would have felt at recognizing the expensive costumes from this occasion.

What a more general audience was meant to make of all these vague connections with real and very famous people is impossible to tell at this distance. Perhaps Shakespeare made the play more obviously political for its Inn performance and later removed some topical references. Perhaps the conflation of two different contexts – the French civil wars and the English cultural scene – was designed to keep anyone from looking too closely at either. Or perhaps the play was originally written as a romantic comedy, after which – because of the perjury theme – the characters were jokingly given names that suggested deeper meanings. The recurrence of words like "faith" and "perjury" seems designed to create an atmosphere of sophisticated tolerance, an assumption that spectators were capable of living with the knowledge that there were differing degrees of support for the official church. Some tinkering or cutting may have gone on in later performances, but the play's clowning, songs, dances, and dressing-up kept it popular. It was probably most memorable for its witty, often rude, repartee. The epigrammatist John Weever in 1599 repeated the jokes about a smallpox-affected face "full of Oos" and a woman who, having received a chain and a long letter from her lover, wished that "The chain were longer, and the letter short."[10] When the play was revived early in James I's reign, no one seems to have felt that it had become dated.

While *Love's Labour's Lost* is closer to a sex-war comedy than any of Shakespeare's other plays, in that the men and women consistently operate as competitive teams, at the end the women seem to occupy the moral high ground. It is not clear how they have won the right to it, since they are as bitter-tongued as the men, and the Princess's line, "The effect of my intent is to cross theirs" (5.2.138), makes her sound much like Katherine in *The Taming of the Shrew*. Perhaps, in fact, the two plays can throw light on each other. Petruchio works on Kate by being "more a shrew than she" (4.1.76); similarly, Rosaline, having already heard of Berowne's "gibing spirit" (5.2.848), decides to treat him as badly as she thinks he will treat her. Shakespeare seems at first to have intended Berowne to fall in love with the woman named Katherine (this is what she is called in two of their encounters in the Quarto version of 2.1), then to have changed her name to Rosaline. Since Kate had probably been established by now as the name of a witty shrew, it would have been appropriate enough for the kind of behavior she displays for most of the play, but, perhaps for this reason, or because *The Taming of the Shrew* was now part of his company's repertory, or because of the nature of the actors available to him, he made use instead of the name of another dark-eyed woman, Romeo's first love. Rosaline is also Colin Clout/Spenser's mysterious mistress in *The Shephearde's Calender*, who had reappeared briefly in "Colin Clout's Come Home Again" (1595) and in the newly published sixth book of *The Faerie Queene*. Katherine remains a character in the play, but a subdued one who comes into her own only when she engages in a rather bitter exchange of repartee with Rosaline (5.2.13–46). The Princess, who at first enjoys it ("Well bandied both; a set of wit well played," 5.2.29) calls an end to it ("I beshrew all shrews," 5.2.46) when Rosaline goes on to allude to Katherine's smallpox scars. Both names may have become standard for female characters in comedy, like Isabella in the Italian *commedia* tradition.

The title page of the first surviving edition (1598) says that *Love's Labour's Lost* was performed "before her Highnes this last Christmas"; unless there was another, lost edition before this one, the performance must be either that of 1597/8 or 1596/7.[11] Though the play is often dated earlier, it might in fact be later than *A Midsummer Night's Dream*. Both plays, of course, end with an onstage audience watching, and mocking, a performance by characters of a lower social class. Because the play scene in the *Dream* is much funnier and more elaborate, it is often thought to be later. On the other hand, if in *Love's Labour's Lost* Shakespeare was reusing a comic device that had already worked well, he tricked the audience into expecting a very different ending from the one he finally delivered. The sheer artificiality and allusiveness imply a supremely confident writer. In 1598, when the craze for humors comedy was at its height, and when the Henry IV plays were famous among theatergoers, *Love's Labour's Lost* would have been seen as a comedy of humors. What it most resembles is Chapman's *A Humorous Day's Mirth* (performed by the Admiral's Men in May 1597), though the traditional dating of *Love's Labour's Lost* would make Chapman the imitator. This comedy, also set in France, has virtually no plot except the display of a collection of odd people (humorists) who are mocked by cleverer ones. The fact that its witty protagonist is called Lemot (French for "the word") suggests a connection with Shakespeare's play, since the page Moth is also called Mot and Costard wonders why Armado has not yet "eaten thee for a word" (5.1.40). Jonson's *Every Man in His Humour* (1598) is another play that brings a number of stupid or eccentric people together in order to allow a few clever ones to see how ridiculous the others are. At the courts of Navarre and France, other people are treated simply as objects of ridicule. In the first scene of *Love's Labour's Lost*, the courtiers agree that their "recreation" during three years of academic study will consist of laughing at the absurdities of the peasant Costard and the braggart Spaniard Don Armado (his relationship with the tiny page Moth recalls that of Basilisco and his page, mentioned at about this time in *King John*). But Shakespeare's play differs from the other humor comedies in two important respects. First, even though, like them, it makes fun of affected language, it also has a strongly lyrical element: the ending dissolves into music – "the songs of Apollo" – which transcends the matter-of-fact and satiric "words of Mercury." Second, it does not exempt the witty courtiers from its mockery. Everything in the play is both enjoyable and ridiculous, whereas the ridiculous in Jonson or Chapman is often simply disgusting.

All four of the fictional French lords have sworn to study for three years and to renounce the sight of women, and their apostasy consists simply of falling in love, with suspicious symmetry, as soon as they actually see women of their own rank: the Princess of France and her three ladies. From the first scene – when Berowne caps a pair of rhyming lines with one that makes no sense but is "something then in rhyme" and an absurdly bombastic letter arrives from Don Armado, to be read aloud and enjoyed by the four men – it is clear that the play is to include extensive critiquing of styles in both verse and prose. Prose romances generally include a good many poems and letters – sometimes they were even indexed separately for readers who wanted to read them out of context – but few plays make the characters do so much writing as this one. In romances the women write as much as the men, but, because writing is being satirized here, only the men are writers. Though it is usually suggested that the young men's poems are meant to be perceived as bad, most of those who heard them probably enjoyed them. However, they are much less beautiful than the speech that Berowne makes when he is asked to "prove" that he and the other courtiers are justified in breaking their vow not to speak to a woman for three years. He has already insisted, after his friends call Rosaline too dark to be beautiful, that he will "prove her fair, or talk till doomsday here" (4.3.270). This is itself an example of double-talk, since on one level he may mean simply that he will make a case for her beauty, but on another he is claiming the ability to prove that black is white. Thus the speech that he goes on to make, arguing that love is the greatest of educators, is already set up as an example of rhetoric used in a doubtful cause. But the beauty of his argument triumphs over its own falseness. His final argument, which resembles Proteus's explanation for betraying Julia and Valentine, is:

> Let us once lose our oaths to find ourselves,
> Or else we lose ourselves to keep our oaths.
> It is religion to be thus forsworn,
> For charity itself fulfils the law,
> And who can sever love from charity?
>
> (4.3.335–9)

The reference to religion seems almost designed to recall Navarre's conversion. Moreover, as Gillian Woods points out, the open-ended conclusion, with its deferral of marriage, is potentially political: "The comic 'marriage' ending is sought specifically because it is hoped that it will solve the problems of succession, and put an end to 'war'."[12]

The poems composed by the four young men of Navarre appeared in a collection of 1599, as did two other sonnets later reprinted as 137 and 144 in the 1609 *Shakespeare's Sonnets*. The sonnets beginning with 127 ("In the old days, black was not counted fair") are often called the Dark Lady group, because some (not all) of them play with the theme of forswearing and the double meanings of fair and black, much as the play does. Even those that seem to compliment the mistress do so in a rather backhanded way. Sonnet 130 admits that the lady does not fit the usual pattern of sonnet clichés ("If hairs be wires, black wires grow on her head," 130.4), and, although the speaker ends by expressing love for her, he does so mostly in order to ridicule those who can praise their mistresses only in clichés. Sonnet 131, addressed to a woman, is spoken by someone who admits that other people do not think her beautiful enough to inspire his love. Though he argues "That black is fairest in my judgment's place," he finally explains, "In nothing art thou black save in thy deeds." Sonnet 152 begins "In loving thee thou knowst I am forsworn," which sounds like a confession of adulterous love, but which, in the context of *Love's Labour's Lost*, would refer to the promises made by the four young men to be faithful to their books.

As in these sonnets, Berowne's attitude to the woman he is supposed to love is almost antagonistic:

> Nay, to be perjur'd, which is worst of all;
> And, among three, to love the worst of all –
> A whitely wanton, with a velvet brow,
> With two pitch-balls stuck in her face for eyes;
> Ay, and by heaven, one that will do the deed
> Though Argus were her eunuch and her guard.
> (3.1.192–7)

There is no explanation as to why Berowne assumes so quickly that Rosaline is ready to "do the deed" – that is, betray her lover or husband. Shakespeare might be alluding to the notoriously unfaithful Marguérite de Valois, or to the reputation of French women for immorality. Shakespeare's sonnets give no names to the characters who appear in them, nor do they have a title identifying the mistress and/or her lover. Perhaps, as Edmondson and Wells suggest, Shakespeare wrote them as a way of trying out ideas for a play in which he intended to include sonnets as a form.[13] Perhaps the popularity of the sonnets in the play was such that he toyed with the idea of a sequence called *Berowne and Rosaline* that, like *Astrophil and Stella*, might tell a story. The question "Who is Rosaline?" had been asked since the publication of Spenser's *Shepheardes Calender,* where the anonymous annotator assures the reader that her name, being "well ordered," will reveal the real object of Colin Clout/ Spenser's love. This implies that her name is an anagram. If treated as such, it can be made to include "Elisa," one of the common poetic terms for Elizabeth, with the "R" perhaps standing for Regina. As for the use of the name in *Love's Labour's Lost,* James Shapiro writes, "It is hard to avoid the impression that this is something of a private joke on Shakespeare's part."[14] The private joke did not originate with Shakespeare and it seems to have been one that others could join in.

"Every Word Doth Almost Tell My Name"

These are the first distinctively "Shakespearean" plays – plays, that is, that one cannot imagine anyone else writing. They are more expansive, more lyrical, and even more discursive, than he had allowed himself to be before. The success of his earlier works had given him the confidence to take the time he needed to develop a thought or situation to its highest pitch. Discursiveness in the form of abstract generalization was present in the earlier plays: the Lord in the Induction to *The Shrew* comments sententiously on how the drunken tinker resembles the figure of death, and some of the lovers' speeches in *Two Gentlemen* are more elaborate than they need to be simply to convey the story. Many things need time to have their full effect – some jokes, for instance. To portray the development of a relationship, similarly, needs time – not as much time as goes into a real-world relationship, but more time than dramatists usually allowed for it. The same is true of the process of reflection. Dramatists of the early 1590s condense it, often making the speaker conduct a dialogue with himself. The Earl of Suffolk, meeting Margaret of Anjou, shows his growing attraction to her in a series of abrupt decisions, changes of mind, and rhetorical questions, one of which turns out after all to need an answer:

> Fain would I woo her, yet I dare not speak.
> I'll call for pen and ink and write my mind.
> Fie, de la Pole, disable not thyself!
> Hast not a tongue? Is she not here?
> Wilt thou be daunted at a woman's sight?
> Ay, beauty's princely majesty is such
> Confounds the tongue and makes the senses rough.
> (*1 Henry VI* 5.3.65–71)

When Richard III wakes from what he takes to be a nightmare – one which is real to the audience, since the ghosts of his victims have actually appeared on the stage

– his language also confuses dream and reality, since his rhetorical questions keep turning into real ones:

> Is there a murderer here? No. Yes, I am.
> Then fly. What, from myself? Great reason why:
> Lest I revenge. What, myself upon myself?
> Alack, I love myself. Wherefore? For any good
> That I myself have done unto myself?
> Oh no, alas, I rather hate myself
> For hateful deeds committed by myself!
> (*Richard III* 5.3.184–90)

The two speeches are theatrically exciting because the men's answers to their own rhetorical questions are not what they expected when they started to speak. But they rush toward their conclusion in a series of comic reversals – appropriate enough, since the audience is not being invited to empathize with either speaker. By contrast, the length of the speeches given to Richard II, the fairies in *The Dream*, Romeo and Juliet, and Berowne in *Love's Labour's Lost* not only allows the actor to create audience sympathy but also serves a dramatic purpose. The vestiges of early drafts that survive in *Romeo and Juliet* and *Love's Labour's Lost* show, I think, Shakespeare's developing awareness of the importance of taking time over certain situations. In the first Quarto of *Romeo* (Q1), published in 1597, Romeo's final speech concludes:

> Ah deare Iuliet,
> How well thy beauty doth become this graue?
> O I beleeue that vnsubstantiall death,
> Is amorous, and doth court my loue.
> Therefore will I, O heere, O euer heere,
> Set vp my euerlasting rest
> With wormes, that are thy chamber mayds.
> Come desperate Pilot now at once runne on
> The dashing rockes thy sea-sicke weary barge.
> Heers to my loue. O true Apothecary:
> Thy drugs are swift; thus with a kisse I dye.
> (K1ᵛ)

Scholars have argued as to whether the vast differences between Q1 and other versions of the play result from bad transmission of a text or from its shortening for particular performance conditions Interestingly, the much longer Quarto (Q2) published in 1599 apparently preserves a manuscript on which Shakespeare had made revisions. The above passage (5.3.101–20 in the modern edition) appears like this:

> Ah deare *Iuliet,*
> Why art thou yet so faire? I will beleeue,
> Shall I beleeue that vnsubstantiall death is amorous,
> And that the leane abhorred monster keepes
> Thee here in darke to be his parramour?
> For feare of that I still will staie with thee,
> And neuer from this pallat of dym night.
> Depart againe, come lye thou in my arme,
> Heer's to thy health, where ere thou tumblest in.
> O true Apothecarie!
> Thy drugs are quicke. Thus with a kisse I die.
> Depart againe, here, here, will I remaine,
> With wormes that are thy Chamber-maides: O here
> Will I set vp my euerlasting rest:
> And shake the yoke of inauspicious starres,
> From this world wearied flesh, eyes looke your last:
> Armes take your last embrace: And lips, O you
> The doores of breath, seale with a righteous kisse
> A datelesse bargaine to ingrossing death:
> Come bitter conduct, come vnsauoury guide,
> Thou desperate Pilot, now at once run on
> The dashing Rocks, thy seasick weary barke:
> Heeres to my Loue. O true Apothecary:
> Thy drugs are quicke. Thus with a kisse I die.
>
> (Q2, L3ʳ)

This Quarto was used, with very few corrections (such as "pallat" to "Pallace" in line 107), as the basis of the text in the Folio of 1623. Yet it seems clear that the first three words of the third line were meant to replace the last three of the previous line, and that the four lines beginning "Depart againe" were to be replaced by the much longer passage that follows. Modern audiences, who want everything to be as short as possible, may well feel that Shakespeare's revisions were self-indulgent, or a pandering to audience sentimentality. But they slow down the play at just the point when it needs to move more slowly. The lovers, in all their scenes together, are in a hurry. Now, as Romeo takes a last farewell to everything he is about to lose – showing how much, in spite of himself, he still loves it – his speech, which contains several "false endings," means for the audience an agonizing prolongation of the hope that Juliet will wake in time to prevent him from drinking the poison (in some modern productions she begins to move just as he raises the cup to his lips).

The plays in this group are more elaborately decorated than any of their predecessors, more rich in details that seem to invite enjoyment for their own sake rather than because they fulfill a particular plot function. The episode with the apothecary occurs in Brooke's poem, but Shakespeare could easily have omitted it, since no one would wonder where Romeo got the poison that he brings to the tomb.

Shakespeare may have kept the encounter simply because he liked it, but in performance it resonates with the rest of the play precisely because it is so unexpected. It is one more example of fate working against the lovers: if the apothecary had not been so poor, Romeo might not have been able to get a poison that killed him so quickly. When Romeo shows real or feigned sympathy for the man's poverty and reflects that gold does more harm than poison, the play gives a brief glimpse of the world outside the enclosed space of the lovers. In the tragic mode, moreover, its hero acquires some of the peculiar mental quirks of Richard II. Romeo dreams of his own death, yet thinks that the dream presages something good, because it concludes with Juliet's reviving him with a kiss. The next news he hears is that she is dead. It is left to the audience to recognize the relation of this dream to what actually does happen. His state of mind is given more attention than the plot requires. Having killed an unknown man in Juliet's tomb, he recognizes him as Paris, then reflects confusedly,

> What said my man when my betossèd soul
> Did not attend him as we rode? I think
> He told me Paris should have married Juliet.
> Said he not so? Or did I dream it so?
> Or am I mad, hearing him talk of Juliet,
> To think it was so?
>
> (5.3.76–81)

This depiction of the distorting effect of grief is not necessary to the plot, nor is Romeo's sympathy for the rival that he has just killed; he even promises to fulfill the dying man's request to be laid in the tomb with Juliet. Yet everything in a work of art becomes relevant once one has determined to treat it as art. Romeo's final touch of generosity is part of a sense, crucial to the play's ending, that love is beginning to suffuse everything with beauty. Though that ending also contains unromantic touches, such as Friar Lawrence's apparent callousness toward Juliet and concern for his own safety, and the narrow focus of the griefs expressed by the lovers' parents and the Prince, most readers and spectators hardly notice them, since by then they have become complicit in the creation of the love story. Even the Prince succumbs to it in his final words, where "never was a story of more woe" refers, not to what happened in Verona but to what Shakespeare has made of it.

It is evident that the plays' characterization was from the first what audiences responded to, even if, initially, they attributed it to the skill of the actors rather than the author. Perhaps the extent of Shakespeare's contribution became clear only when they had seen more than one actor play the same role. This may be why he drew attention to the quality of the writing by making the characters themselves self-conscious about their language. They parody each other or apologize for their style. Romeo and Juliet both make puns, in spite – or because – of their own overcharged emotions. Richard II wonders if people will laugh at him for talking "idly" and, in prison, sees his own imaginative excess as a possible sign of madness. Characters in *Love's Labour's Lost* constantly critique each others' language and Berowne, who is supposed to be French, is even laughed at for using a French word. They also point out disjunctions in tone. Bolingbroke, faced with the domestic squabbles of the York family in the middle of the revelation of a conspiracy, comments that "Our scene is altered from a serious thing,/ And now changed to 'The Beggar and the King'" (*Richard II* 5.3.79–80). Theseus, hearing the description of *Pyramus and Thisbe* as "very tragical mirth" (*Midsummer Night's Dream* 5.1.57), recognizes the concept of *concordia discors* but suspects that in this case it will be impossible to achieve. *Romeo and Juliet* warns its audience several times that the play will be a tragedy, but still shocks them with the suddenness of Mercutio's death and its consequences. *Love's Labour's Lost* is the most obviously self-conscious. A messenger brings news of the death of the King of France at the height of noise and confusion, as two comic characters are preparing for a mock-battle; Berowne tells them to leave because "the scene begins to cloud," (5.2.717), but they return to perform two songs and have the last word. He also comments that the romantic part of the story does not end "like an old play" (5.2.864). It ends in fact like a very new kind of play, one that pulls the rug out from under its audience by suggesting that they should not have enjoyed the jokes at which they have just been laughing. Berowne is given an unusual degree of verbal dominance (the text of Q1, with its several versions of the same idea, shows that a good deal of work went into giving argumentative shape to the long lyrical speech from which this chapter's epigraph is taken). Yet he is castigated by Rosaline both for the artificiality of his language and for his wit, which turns out to be irrelevant:

> A jest's prosperity lies in the ear
> Of him that hears it, never in the tongue
> Of him that makes it.
>
> (851–3)

This is the kind of knowledge that an actor-dramatist might well have acquired over many years of playing before a variety of more and less receptive audiences. It is hard to see how there could ever have been a real sequel to this play: what would be the point of an unwitty Berowne, fresh from a year in a hospital, demonstrating the kinds of jest that offend no one? But, like the sudden intrusion of death into the comedy, the reminder that not everyone thinks Berowne's jokes are funny points forward to the plays Shakespeare would write in the next few years. It is also uncannily like the next events in his life.

Notes

1. From the prefatory epistle to the 2nd edn. of *Troilus and Cressida* (1609), repr. in Chambers, *WS*, 2: 216–17.
2. Brooke's poem is quoted from Bullough, 1: 363.
3. Engle, "Watching Shakespeare Learn from Marlowe," 45. Engle adds that the hurried scene between Macbeth and his wife after Duncan's murder shows continuing recollection of the scene, though in this case Macbeth speaks from the upper level and Lady Macbeth is on the stage (p. 46).
4. Stern, "'A small-beer health to his second day'," 174, n. 8.
5. The two most likely occasions are the weddings of the Earl of Derby and Elizabeth Vere (Jan. 1595) and of Thomas Lord Berkeley with Lord Hunsdon's daughter Elizabeth in February 1596. As Honan points out (p. 213), both were Queen Elizabeth's god-daughters.
6. Sidney, *Apologie for Poetry*, p. 112.
7. Arber, ed., *A Transcript of the Registers of the Company of Stationers of London*, 1: 244b, 253, 255.
8. Bullough, 1: 428–9.
9. See *Love's Labour's Lost*, ed. Woudhuysen, 64.
10. From epigrams 9 and 8, respectively, in the "Fourth Week." Photographic facsimile in Honigmann, *John Weaver*. Cf. *Love's Labour's Lost*, 5.2.45 and 55–6. Weever's *Faunus and Melliflora* (1600) also alludes to *Venus and Adonis*, *Romeo and Juliet*, and *Love's Labour's Lost*.
11. *Companion*, 117.
12. Woods, "Catholicism and Conversion in *Love's Labour's Lost*," 120.
13. Edmondson and Wells, *Shakespeare's Sonnets*, 101–4.
14. J. Shapiro, *A Year in the Life of William Shakespeare*, 215.

10

"You Had a Father; Let Your Son Say So"
1596–1598

> *Who lets so fair a house fall to decay,*
> *Which husbandry in honor might uphold*
> *Against the stormy gusts of winter's day*
> *And barren rage of death's eternal cold?*
> > *Oh, none but unthrifts! Dear my love, you know*
> > *You had a father; let your son say so.*
> > > (Sonnet 13.9–14)

The phrase "You had a father" is used again in *The Merry Wives of Windsor*, when Justice Shallow urges his limp and unenthusiastic nephew Slender to court Anne Page. What he means, though Slender misses the point, is that the young man needs to show some of the ardor his father had shown in begetting him. A decaying house can also be compared, as in the early sonnets, with a young man who refuses to procreate, since a gentleman who failed to increase his wealth through marriage or to produce a male heir could cause a catastrophic loss to family and estate. English history had been changed by Henry VIII's desperate desire for a son; now the House of Tudor was decaying, year by year, in the person of his aging daughter. That a house could be both a building and a family becomes a joke in *1 Henry IV*, when Hotspur angrily comments on a letter from someone who has written of "the love I bear your house": "In respect of the love he bears our house! He shows in this he loves his own barn better than he loves our house" (2.3.4–6). When he had time – the pace of his writing over the past few years must have been exhausting – Shakespeare was thinking about the House of Shakespeare.

Neither he nor his acting company owned a house in 1596; both relied on rented accommodation and the lease on the Theatre was due to expire on 25 March

The Life of William Shakespeare: A Critical Biography, First Edition. Lois Potter.
© 2012 Lois Potter. Published 2012 by Blackwell Publishing Ltd.

1597. By contrast with the lyrical works discussed in the previous chapter, which deal with characters miraculously exempt from financial problems, the plays apparently written between 1596 and 1598 – *1* and *2 Henry IV*, *The Merchant of Venice*, and *The Merry Wives of Windsor* – say a good deal about hand-to-mouth living and the desperate need for money to maintain one's social status. For most dramatic characters, the safest way to get money is by making love to women who have it. In Shakespeare's own life there do not seem to have been any fairytale princesses like Portia or gullible women like Mistress Quickly. Some of his colleagues, particularly Heminges and Condell, were more fortunate in their marriages; both were already respectable London residents and established members of the parish where they would later act as churchwardens. No one seems to have thought them tainted by the theater. Cuthbert Burbage with his wife apparently provided a home for the apprentices of his brother Richard, who was still a bachelor. William Shakespeare, married but living apart from his wife during the playing season, was not a citizen of London and never would be a church-warden, either there or in Stratford. He had all the more reason, then, to translate his earnings into some universally accepted signs of status. Perhaps with the same intention, James Burbage in February 1596 paid £600 for a large room in the Blackfriars complex, which had been vacant since the boys' companies had stopped using it almost ten years ago. The ancient Dominican structure, confiscated at the Reformation and rented out piecemeal to a variety of tenants, was one of the "liberties" outside the jurisdiction of the City of London, like other former church property. For much of the rest of 1596 Burbage was busy supervising its transformation.

The year 1596 would be a bad one for Shakespeare, but it began well. The Lord Chamberlain's Men played at court four times in all, starting in late December, with a final performance on Twelfth Night. Their schedule gave them only three days in which to reach Rutland, where, on the evening of their arrival, they performed *Titus Andronicus* as part of Sir John Harington's holiday festivities at Burley-on-the-Hill. Harington's guests (over 200) were treated to morning and evening sermons by guest preachers, music during meals, and dancing after dinner. On New Year's Day he offered them both a masque by a family member and a performance of *Titus*. A French spectator wrote to Sir Anthony Bacon that "la monstre a plus valeu que le suiect" (the spectacle was worth more than the subject matter).[1] On the French stage he would certainly not have seen so much mutilation and blood. Some scholars, who doubt that the company could have managed both its court performances and the one at Burley-on-the-Hill, argue either that *Titus* was played by another company or that the Chamberlain's Men split into two groups at this period. The play was by now in print, so any company could have played it, but Harington's munificence may have extended to subsidizing the fastest and most comfortable transport. Assuming that he did, the actors probably took the direct route back to London in order to play at court on 6 January; Shakespeare is unlikely to have detoured to visit his family in Stratford, who must have spent yet another Christmas without him.

If Shakespeare visited Peele in January to report on the success of their play, he would have found his former collaborator very ill and even more hard-up than usual. It was in that month that Peele sent a copy of one of his poems to Lord Burghley with a request for help. To add to its pathos, he used as his messenger "my eldest daughter, and necessity's servant," because he was too ill to go himself. The letter was apparently ignored.[2] Since Peele was married in 1580, the daughter who was sent alone to cope with the lower levels of the Elizabethan court could have been no older than 14 or 15. Later, when Peele had become the hero of a jestbook, one story would make this precocious daughter, then said to be about 10, his helper in a swindle. *The Merry Jests of George Peele* (1607) is not reliable – most of its stories come from other jest-books – but this episode is one for which no source has been found.[3] It may, then, be true, or at least based on what someone remembered about Peele's life. If Shakespeare had ever thought of bringing his family to London, in the year when Susanna Shakespeare was 12 years old, his glimpse of the Peele household might have changed his mind.

He would remember the summer for several deaths. The first was that of the company's patron, Lord Hunsdon, who died on 23 July 1596. The Chamberlain's Men stopped playing as a sign of respect. The theaters were then closed again because of plague, and not reopened until October. The company went on tour for part of that time. Shakespeare may have wanted to go back to Stratford to write, but he needed books for the early stages of his new project, an extensive expansion and revision of *The Famous Victories of Henry V*. Fortunately, that play had not yet been published, so he could avoid difficulties with the Queen's Men, its original owners, and with the Stationers' Company. Part One of *Henry IV* sticks so closely to both the old play and to Holinshed's *Chronicle* that Shakespeare must have had them available at least some of the time while he was writing. He would not have wanted to carry the heavy and expensive third volume of Holinshed back and forth between Stratford and London. Richard Field had printed it and probably had a copy.

The Coat of Arms and Hamnet Shakespeare

While still in London, Shakespeare may have taken the opportunity to visit the College of Arms in Derby Place (now bordered by Queen Victoria Street), so as to restart the application for a coat of arms that his father had made (according to the notes preserved in the college) at least twenty years ago. This meant producing evidence of his father's income, status, and employment in the queen's service (as bailiff of Stratford and council member), as well as his connection by marriage with the noble Arden family.[4] Scholars suspect that there was some fudging in the statement that John Shakespeare was worth the remarkable sum of £500 a year (had William paid off all his debts?), and have wondered whether John himself really devised the coat of arms pictured there.[5] But there is no reason why John and a representative of the College of Arms should not have decided, between them, to depict a spear resting on a shield. As the College of Arms website states, "There is a long tradition of puns in heraldry, some of them obvious, others less so."[6] This was one of the more obvious ones. The pun is carried still further in the crest above the shield, a falcon shaking his spear. Katherine Duncan-Jones thinks that the conceit was William's rather than his father's and that he was advertising his connection with Southampton, whose coat of arms carried four falcons.[7] Whether or not for that reason, falcons were a key symbol for the early Shakespeare: they represent soaring ambition (*2 Henry VI* 2.1.5–14), a wild thing that must be tamed (*Taming of the Shrew* 4.1.178–80), and a loved one whom one wants, like a trained falconer, to call back at one's will (*Romeo and Juliet* 2.2.159–60). Above all, they stand for carefully disciplined desire.

The designing of shields and mottos was taken very seriously. By 1596 Shakespeare could have studied many examples of the genre in the Shield Gallery of Whitehall, which, as James Shapiro points out, lay on the way to the Great Chamber where he took part in court performances. Shapiro thinks that Shakespeare may even have been known for his designs, though the only record of one dates from 1613.[8] The motto *Non sans droit* (Not without right) obeys the rules by being brief and in a foreign language. Mottos are often enigmatic and can easily be misread. The clerk who originally copied this one wrote *Non, sans droit* – that is, "No, without right." Perhaps the mistake arose from his hearing the phrase quoted to him with emphasis on the *Non*, which might have made him think that a comma was needed. Shakespeare would have known two famous examples of the modest double negative, both relevant: Horace's claim that his amorous battles had been "not without honour" (*Odes* 3.26) and Jesus's statement that "A prophet is not without honour, save in his own country, and in his own house" (Matthew 13: 57). Since, ideally, neither motto nor image was meant to be fully comprehensible on its own, the motto and spear-shaking falcon, taken together, might mean that the owner of the coat of arms should not brandish his spear (or draw the sword which a gentleman had the right to wear) unless he had right on his side. If Shakespeare was rereading and revising his earlier histories at this time, he may have remembered what he had written for Henry VI, who knights his son in *3 Henry VI*: "Edward Plantagenet, arise a knight,/ And learn this lesson: Draw thy sword in right" (2.2.61–2).[9] Unlike Jonson and Chapman, he had no military career to offer as an example to his son and may have felt that this was the best "lesson" for him.

However, Hamnet Shakespeare would never inherit the status of gentleman or the sword that went with it. On 11 August 1596 he was buried in Stratford. There is no record of the cause of his death. The death rate nationwide was unusually high in the summers of 1596 and 1597, not only because of plague but also because of the bad harvests of 1594–7, which left children in particular susceptible to the illnesses spread by insects in warm, wet weather.[10] On 1 August the Chamberlain's Men were acting in Faversham, Kent. If Shakespeare was with them, news may have arrived too late for him to see the boy alive or even to attend the funeral.[11] Assuming that he returned to Stratford at some point, he was definitely back in London in the autumn, and still in the parish of St. Helen's, Bishopsgate, where he was assessed for 5 shillings' tax on a notional £5-worth of goods.[12] He may have moved into an inn called the Angel. It had just been taken over by a relative of the landlord of the Oxford tavern where he probably stopped on his journeys to and from Stratford.[13]

In October he called in again at the College of Arms, and on the 20th of that month finally received his "letters patent," drawn on a sheet of vellum, and signed by the Garter herald, Sir William Dethick. It is sometimes thought that he was embarrassed by a joke in Jonson's *Every Man Out of His Humour* (1599), where a character says that the device on his coat of arms will be "Not Without Mustard." This is, however, a reference to an anecdote also told in Nashe's *Pierce Penniless*: someone who is expecting to make a wretched meal off dried salt cod pleads, "Not without mustard, good Lord, not without Mustard."[14] Perhaps Shakespeare got in first with his own joke: at the end of *Love's Labour's Lost* Berowne, renouncing pretentious language, makes the mistake of using a French word and is told to speak "sans 'sans,' I pray you" (5.2.417). Though a number of actors were in fact gentlemen by this time, the occupation was still suspect. In 1602, the York Herald of Arms commented acerbically on the granting of arms to undeserving types, including "Shakespeare the player," whose coat he sketched (Figure 6). Other members of the College of Heralds defended their decision, and his complaint was not upheld. Shakespeare may nevertheless have decided to avoid ostentation. He did not use the motto in any of his surviving works, nor did he or anyone else advertise his gentle status there (only the title page of *The Two Noble Kinsmen*, published in 1634, names the authors as John Fletcher and William Shakespeare, bracketed together as "Gent."). As Schoenbaum points out, the coat of arms does not even appear on his Stratford monument or his daughter Susanna's gravestone.[15] Perhaps it seemed pointless, since the arms granted to John Shakespeare could pass on only through his legitimate male descendants. In late 1596 Anne Shakespeare was probably 41 and past childbearing; unless she died and he remarried, Shakespeare would be the last of his family. In 1598 Hamnet and Judith Sadler, who had been Hamnet Shakespeare's godparents, named their newborn son William. If Shakespeare was the godfather, he may have been in Stratford for the christening.

1 Henry IV

1 Henry IV, the most brilliant and comic of his historical plays, must have been completed in 1596 or early 1597 – that is, in the immediate aftermath of Hamnet's

Figure 6 The Shakespeare coat of arms as sketched, perhaps caricatured, *c*.1600. By permission of the Folger Shakespeare Library

death. Father–son relationships are crucial to all the histories, but here they are the main focus. Henry IV's son is a shadowy, unseen figure in *Richard II*, where Burbage was playing Richard, and the one passage in which the prince is mentioned may have been added later to connect the two plays. Henry IV, apparently recalling the Bishop of Carlisle's prophecy that Richard's deposition will be divinely punished, says of Hal, "If any plague hang over us, 'tis he" (*Richard II* 5.3.3), and in the sequel he continues to think of his son as a punishment. The play's elaborate structure makes the rivals Hal and Hotspur the same age and hence alternative sons to the king (in history, Hotspur was much older), while Hal's real father, Henry IV, is contrasted with his false father, Falstaff. The parallels are underlined when Hal imitates Hotspur and both Hal and Falstaff imitate Henry IV. In a still more unsettling parallel, the language of robbery clings to the political figures.[16] In *Richard II* Henry orders, "convey him [Richard II] to the Tower" and the deposed king retorts, "conveyers are you all," using "conveyer" in the sense of "thief" (4.1.317–19). The joke recurs in the confrontation between Worcester and the royal army at Shrewsbury:

> *Worcester.* I have not sought the day of this dislike.
> *King.* You have not sought it? How comes it then?
> *Falstaff.* Rebellion lay in his way, and he found it.
> *Prince.* Peace, chewet, peace!
>
> (5.1.26–9)

Falstaff's line (whether an aside or not) makes Worcester sound like a man detected with a stolen purse who refuses to admit any agency in acquiring it. Henry IV usually says that he was pushed by fate into taking the throne, but occasionally his language ("I stole all courtesy from heaven," 3.2.50) suggests the opposite.

The play's emphasis on character is clear from the title page of the Quarto published in 1598, which includes among the play's contents "the humorous conceits of Sir Iohn Falstalffe [*sic*]." This crucial word "humor" recurs in Hal's description of Falstaff as a "trunk of humors" (2.4.444) and the insistence of Hotspur's wife that her husband is "altogether governed by humors" (3.1.231). Between 1597 and 1599 the words "humor" and "humorous" frequently appear in Henslowe's list of plays in process. They refer to characters whose eccentric temperament (the result of a physical imbalance) makes them both comic and predictable.[17] The most remarkable achievement of *1 Henry IV* is its fusion of humors comedy with history. While much of the play's material comes from *The Famous Victories*, the characterization of Hotspur and his fellow-rebels is Shakespeare's own. He must have known that members of the Percy family were part of Essex's circle, and his treatment of their rebellion manages to make it both understandable (in the idealistic Hotspur) and wrong (in Hotspur's cynical father and uncle). The treatment of the Scot Douglas is curiously inconsistent: he is something of a braggart, like the Scots in *Edward III*, yet other characters frequently praise him. Their hyperboles may be last-minute additions, since the play was published in the year when James VI complained about the theater's treatment of the Scots. The Welsh, on the other hand, are sympathetically portrayed: the Tudors were proud of their Welsh descent, and Essex, who spent much of his childhood in Wales, had many Welsh followers.[18] Like the Welsh captain who appears briefly in *Richard II*, Glendower and the boy who played his daughter were probably genuinely Welsh performers. Since the Welsh lines they speak (and, in the boy's case, sing) are not written out, Shakespeare presumably expected them to make up their own. Hotspur, the "northern youth," may also have spoken with an accent. Perhaps the intention was to associate rebellion with the "foreign,"[19] but these roles are also showcases for actors, requiring gifts of impersonation and caricature.

The Famous Victories included a number of scenes depicting Hal as a robber and thug, with his wild young friends Tom, Ned, and Jockey Oldcastle. Retaining

Ned Poins as a contemporary of Hal's, Shakespeare transformed Oldcastle, perhaps because of his name, into an elderly rascal. His age differentiates him from the otherwise familiar and popular character type, the braggart soldier. Some spectators may also have heard in him, particularly in soliloquy, an echo of Lyly's Sir Thopas or of Basilisco in Kyd's *Soliman and Perseda*. Kyd's braggart had meditated on death over the body of Erastus, the romantic hero:

> *Basilisco.* I will ruminate: Death, which the poets fain to be pale and meager, hath deprived Erastus' trunk from breathing vitality, a brave cavalier, but my approved foeman. Let me see)...
>
> $$(5.3.63–9^{20})$$

He indulges in the *ubi sunt* trope ("where is that Alcides, surnamed Hercules, the only Club man of his time? dead." etc.), and continues:

> I am my self strong, but I confess death to be stronger: I am valiant, but mortal; I am adorned with Nature's gifts, a giddy goddess that now giveth and anon taketh: I am wise, but quiddits will not answer death. To conclude in a word: to be captious, virtuous, ingenious, are to be nothing when it pleaseth death to be envious.
>
> *(Soliman and Perseda 5.3.76–83)*

When Oldcastle describes his famous meditation on honor as "my catechism," he shows the same self-consciousness as Basilisco when he says, "To conclude in a word." Although the "honor" speech is spoken on an empty stage, it really ends with Oldcastle's next appearance. Like Basilisco, he stands over a dead warrior: "Soft, who are you? Sir Walter Blunt. There's honor for you" (5.3.32–3). Later, he also stands over the dead Hotspur and, in carrying him, he briefly becomes "a double man" (5.4.137).

Since *The Famous Victories* had taken Hal's career from Wild Prince to Conqueror of France, Shakespeare must have intended his Henry IV play to have a sequel. The end of Part One, therefore, had to be provisional. As in Parts Two and Three of *Henry VI*, he ended with a military victory, using it to resolve all his plot lines. Hotspur is dead and the rebellion symbolically over. Henry IV, who has achieved his throne by rebellion, declares, with no apparent sense of irony, "Thus ever did rebellion find rebuke" (5.5.1). Hal's relationship with his father has been repaired and his rehabilitation is linked with the possibility of Oldcastle's: "If I do grow great, I'll grow less; for I'll purge, and leave sack, and live cleanly as a nobleman should do" (5.4.161–3). Like Oldcastle, Shakespeare has left his options open. Those who remembered *The Famous Victories* might have expected a new play to include a deathbed scene for the old king, Hal's public reformation through the banishment of his former friends, and a glorious campaign in France interspersed with comic interludes. The last months of 1596 were dominated by the threat of another Spanish invasion, always a good time for a patriotic war play. Shakespeare might, then, have planned to move on to the famous victories in 1597.

However, he had an unexpected problem. The author of *The Famous Victories* presumably knew that the historical Oldcastle was burned at the stake as a Lollard and rebel against Henry V, but ignored facts that might spoil his story. Shakespeare had gone still farther, giving the character impertinent Scripture quotations and comments that recalled the fate of the historical Oldcastle, such as "I'll be a traitor then, when thou art king" (1.2.143–4). He transformed an episode from *The Famous Victories*, in which a clown impersonates a judge, into one in which Oldcastle impersonates Henry IV, perhaps parodying the absurdly tearful king of the old play. When Hal insists that they exchange roles, Oldcastle cries out, "Depose me?" (2.4.430), recalling Richard's deposition and hinting that Henry himself might be overthrown. Shakespeare probably assumed that no one could blame him for using a name from a previous play. But he reckoned without his own success. The orotund *miles gloriosus* voice, in which one can almost hear the speaker's physical fatness, had an edge of intelligence that made audiences long to see him fooled so that they could see him get out of his situation. He inspired affection in spite of despicable acts like stabbing the dead Hotspur, and he was too well known to be ignored by those for whom the historical Oldcastle was a revered figure.

Despite their name, the Lord Chamberlain's Men were not linked to the official responsible for organizing court functions, but to their patron, who in 1594 had also been the current lord chamberlain. After Hunsdon's death, they were taken under the patronage of his son George Carey, and thus became Lord Hunsdon's Men, but the new lord chamberlain, as of July 1596, was Henry Brooke, Lord Cobham. Cobham, a remote descendant of Oldcastle, does not appear to have been particularly hostile to theater, but he could hardly overlook this treatment of a proto-Reformation martyr and ancestor, especially since Shakespeare was writing another play about him. A less successful dramatist might have found himself accused of Catholic propaganda. Some of Falstaff's impudence could have been taken to be the dramatist's own. And maybe it was. With so many brilliant successes behind him, and perhaps unsettled by his son's death, Shakespeare may have briefly succumbed to the dangerous belief that he could do no wrong.

Now he needed to write Oldcastle out and another name in, without losing continuity with the first play. In Holinshed's chronicle he found a Sir John Fastolfe who had been a distinguished general until he disgraced himself by running away at the Battle of Patay in 1429. To be on the safe side, or for the sake of the pun, Shakespeare altered his name to Falstaff, suggesting both the unheroic False Staff and the impotent Fall Staff (not to mention Shake Spear, which is why some critics think that Shakespeare identified himself with the character).[21] *1 Henry VI* as it appears in the 1623 Folio makes a great deal of one Sir John Falstaff (not Fastolfe, as in the chronicle), who helped lose a crucial battle when he "Cowardly fled, not having struck one stroke" (1.1.134). Talbot refers to this betrayal in 1.4 and later, in what seems like overkill, the knight is seen running away yet again:

> *Captain.* What? Will you fly and leave Lord Talbot?
> *Falstaff.*   Ay,
> All the Talbots in the world, to save my life.
>
> (*1 Henry VI* 3.2.107–8)

He appears once more, in the scene where young Henry VI is crowned in France. Talbot tears the garter from Falstaff's leg, calling him unworthy of so high an honor, and Henry VI, approving the action, banishes the cowardly knight on pain of death (4.1.46). To give so much attention to such a minor character seems odd; I suspect that Shakespeare or someone else introduced him, or added to the role, after his name had become known from the Henry IV plays and the garter references in *The Merry Wives of Windsor*. These episodes hammer home the fact that, as the Epilogue to *2 Henry IV* assured audiences, "Oldcastle died a martyr and this was not the man" (29–30). As if to query the importance of names, Part Two has two Bardolphs, a lord and a lowlife (perhaps because his colleague Augustine Phillips had appropriated the coat of arms of William Phillips, Lord Bardolph).[22] *As You Like It* would have two characters named Jaques.

The Merchant of Venice

The Merchant of Venice, set in safely remote Italy, must also have been written not long after Hamnet's death, if the mention of "my wealthy Andrew" – a richly laden vessel of that name (1.1.27) – refers to a Spanish ship captured during Essex's Cadiz expedition in July 1596. Going to sea or investing in a sea voyage was traditionally a way of taking great risks in the hope of becoming rich. Sir Francis Drake's death, also in 1596, may have brought back recollections of the return of the *Golden Hind* in 1580, which made its investors rich overnight. The most famous play to deal with the dangerous glamor of the merchant's life was Marlowe's *The Jew of Malta*. The fabulous wealth of its hero, Barabas, is emphasized in the first act, when the rulers of Malta seize it. After that, he becomes a serial killer, initially justified in his desire for revenge, then a comic villain increasingly enmeshed in his need to cover up his crimes. He ends up in a boiling cauldron, gloating (like Aaron in *Titus*) over his evil deeds. Although the play had been consistently popular since 1591, some of its later revivals were probably topical. On 1 January 1594, the Earl of Essex accused Dr. Roderigo Lopez, the queen's personal physician, of plotting to poison her. Lopez did not wear a distinguishing costume, had lived in London since 1559, and had supposedly been a Christian all his life, though suspected of being a practicing Jew in private. There can hardly have been much resemblance between him and the

Jews of the ghettos of Amsterdam and Venice, which were then a tourist destination rather like modern Chinatown. Shakespeare might have seen Lopez at court, since he had been a rich man and a public figure.

If he still felt some affiliation with Southampton and hence with the Earl of Essex, Shakespeare may have believed in the poisoning plot, as Essex at least claimed to do. Physicians were generally suspected of being poisoners because of their knowledge of herbs which, as Friar Lawrence's opening speech in *Romeo and Juliet* indicates, can be both curative and deadly. The rumors about Lopez may have started because he had once been employed by the Earl of Leicester, himself the target of similar accusations. The doctor may have been taking Spanish money and playing a double game, like many of those whom the government used as intelligencers, but he was essentially a victim of Essex's determination to prove the efficiency of his intelligence network.[23] The doctor's conviction reinforced the earl's position at court and his anti-Spanish policy. The Admiral's Men gave three performances of *The Jew of Malta* between 4 February and 4 June 1594, and the closeness of the last one to Lopez's execution on 7 June was no accident.

Some two years later, when he began *The Merchant of Venice*, Shakespeare was probably thinking mainly of rivaling Marlowe's immensely popular play, which he had admired even before the opportunistic revivals. Since his own play was often called *The Jew of Venice*, it's clear that the relationship was recognized. Unlike Marlowe's play, which had some historical basis – though the siege of Malta in 1565 had ended in a decisive defeat for the Turks – Shakespeare's source was an Italian story, to which he added extensively. The emphasis on lending and charging interest inspired him to build the plot around the exchanging of material objects, as with the chain in *The Comedy of Errors*. Trade depends on borrowed money, and Bassanio's courtship depends on maintaining a presence far beyond his individual worth. What Antonio borrows from Shylock is lent, interest-free, to enable Bassanio to win Portia's hand, so that he can use her immense wealth to repay Antonio both for his past loans and for the new one. Complicated arrangements like this, with more than one lender involved and a bond signed by several parties, were common in an age where there was never enough ready money to go round. Philip Stubbes, in *The Anatomie of Abuses*, had claimed that "An Usurer is worse than a Jew, for they to this day will not take any usury of their brethren, according to the law of God."[24] Shylock, in not taking interest, treats Antonio like a fellow-Jew, and the practice of "legal fictions" meant that conditions like the one about the pound of flesh could be inserted into a bond without any intention that they should be taken literally.[25]

When Antonio recognizes that in Venice "the trade and profit of the city/ Consisteth of all nations" (3.2.30–1), Shakespeare may have been remembering March 1593 when Parliament debated a bill that would have prevented aliens from trading in London. One speaker had argued that "the riches and renown of the city cometh by entertaining of strangers and giving liberty unto them," citing Venice and Antwerp as other examples that proved the point.[26] It was the defeat of that bill that provoked the events that indirectly caused the deaths of both Kyd and Marlowe. The play's emphasis on foreign stereotypes, which begins when Portia caricatures her undesirable, non-Italian suitors and continues in the depiction of the princes of Morocco and Aragon (opportunities for the actors to caricature an African and a Spaniard), is in keeping with the depiction of Venice as a cosmopolitan yet not really welcoming city. As someone who had lived among "strangers" in London, and had begun as a stranger himself, Shakespeare was well acquainted with both sides of that world.

Even so, *The Merchant of Venice* disturbs readers, in a way that the more farcical *Jew of Malta* does not, because it seems to offer Christianity as an unequivocally good alternative to a character who is presented as typically Jewish. The play is, however, surprisingly open to other readings, and seems even to invite them. Moralistic generalizations are not necessarily validated: to Portia's "good sentences and well pronounced," Nerissa replies, "They would be better if well followed" (1.2.10–11), and Antonio responds to Shylock's biblical examples of "thrift" with "The devil can cite Scripture for his purpose" (1.3.96). Though directed against an obvious outsider-figure, the line alerts the audience to be cautious in its response to *sententiae*, and perhaps even to apparently normative characters like Bassanio. Nothing is said to indicate that the audience should disapprove of this hero's apparent willingness to live off his friend until he can live off his wife instead, or of Jessica's robbing her father when she elopes. But none of the other romantic couples in Shakespeare behave like this. No play of Shakespeare's is so full of cruel jokes (Lancelot's treatment of his father, his joking with Jessica that she is damned), and none has more racial stereotypes. Even Bassanio, as he meditates on the caskets, uses "the beauteous scarf/ Veiling an Indian beauty" as an example of how appearances may deceive, giving you, by implication, the ugly where you expect the beautiful. Ironically, he goes on to talk of the deceptiveness of wigs taken from a dead person's hair:

> So are those crisped, snaky, golden locks,
> Which maketh such wanton gambols with the wind
> Upon supposed fairness, often known
> To be the dowry of a second head,
> The skull that bred them in the sepulcher.
>
> (3.2.92–6)

The boy playing Portia, standing beside him as he speaks, would have been wearing just such a wig. When Bassanio finds Portia's portrait, a sign that he has chosen the correct casket, he rhapsodizes on her golden hair, the poetic equivalent of her unbelievable wealth, demonstrated when, hearing that Antonio needs the enormous sum of three thousand ducats, she cries, "What, no more?" Shakespeare seems to be daring his audience to remember the real conditions of his stage, where two actors are creating the illusion of rapturous love but neither the hair nor the money is real. The emphasis on wigs is all the more daring because the actor playing Portia will soon be reappearing in men's clothes (though the doctor's gown might make it relatively easy to retain part of her female costume). This is Shakespeare's first cross-dressed heroine since *The Two Gentlemen of Verona*, and her disguise role as the young lawyer Balthazar is much more sophisticated and authoritative than Julia's nervous page-boy impersonation. The reappearance of this kind of disguise in two later comedies indicates its popularity. It may also have been a good solution to the problem of how best to use a popular boy actor who was getting too big for female roles.

On one level, Shylock is a humor character, a Pantalone, or usurer, or cruel father, exploiting the same knee-jerk recourse to humor theory that would also be caricatured in Nym: "I'll not answer that./ But say it is my humor. Is it answered?" (4.1.42–3). His language, like that of the Welshman Glendower in *1 Henry IV*, is distinctive, correct, yet "foreign." Like other "humorists," he dominates the comedy. Yet he is not its center. He is ignorant of most of the plot – never knowing, for example, that the money he lent Antonio is, indirectly, the means by which the lawyer defeats him – and he is not present in the final act. There have been many attempts to continue his story. As with Richard III, audiences want a parallel universe in which the character can remain himself (dramatically interesting) and yet be admirable rather than comic or evil. Shakespeare must have sensed something of what he had done, since in both cases he avoided complete closure: Richard III has no death speech and Shylock's final lines are anticlimactic. The dramatist could not take Shylock's religion seriously enough to recognize, as later readers have, the wrongness of his forcible conversion. Yet there is a loophole. Asked whether he accepts the conditions laid on him, Shylock replies, "I am content," says he is not well, and asks the court to send him the relevant documents to sign later (4.1.391–5). One can imagine either that he will die of grief offstage (as was usually suggested when tragedians played Shylock) or that, reverting to the trickster image that he shares with Barabas, he will somehow evade the non-financial part of the penalty. After all, Petruchio's "I am content," in *The Taming of the Shrew*, turns out to mean "I am content you shall entreat me stay,/ But yet not stay, entreat me how you can" (3.2.166–7). Though the last act used to be considered an anticlimax, a landmark interpretation by John Barton (RSC 1978) made Portia's disillusionment with her new husband crucial to the play, and many productions since then have seen *The Merchant of Venice* as a play about marriage as well as about money.

No Place and New Place

The Merchant of Venice was probably performed during the Christmas season of 1596/7, when the "mercy" theme would have been particularly appropriate. Shakespeare may not have bothered to visit Stratford after receiving his coat of arms in October, as he would have needed to be in London for rehearsals in November. November 9th was the funeral of George Peele. He may have died of the pox, as Francis Meres claimed in 1598, but he had been ill for some time, and his death at 40 was the waste of a great talent. As with many other writers of that decade, his plays survive only in badly printed editions. If he had had more time, more money, and perhaps more self-discipline, he would be remembered as a brilliantly innovative writer. Instead, his posthumous life in the *Merry Jests of George Peele* outlasted his fame as a dramatist.

It was also at about this time that the Lord Chamberlain's Men learned that they would not after all be moving into the playhouse currently under construction in Blackfriars. Surprisingly, James Burbage seems not to have foreseen the reaction of local residents to his plans for their neighborhood. There was a difference between the private theater in which the boys acted, probably only once a week, until 1590, and the "common playhouse" that gave performances almost every day. In order to get to Blackfriars, visitors had to pass through some of the dirtiest streets in Westminster and London. Not surprisingly, women in particular now chose to come in coaches, a new invention. They choked the narrow city streets, inconveniencing those trying to do business. Then there were the noisy spectators arriving and leaving, the "drums and trumpets" associated with a performance, and the criminals who would be attracted to any place where crowds were gathered. A petition against the playhouse, addressed to the Privy Council in November 1596, carried the signatures of thirty-one Blackfriars residents, one of whom was the company's own patron, Lord Hunsdon. Burbage may have been devastated, left as he was with an expensive and empty property. On the other hand, it would be odd if the old man, however stubborn he was supposed to be, had not communicated with his patron before purchasing this prime city space. It may, as Roslyn Knutson suggests, have been "a real estate investment" intended for renting out to other companies.[27] When Burbage died in January 1597, his sons divided his estate: Cuthbert, the elder, inherited most of his property, but Richard kept the Blackfriars site.[28] He would lease it out to a boys' company in 1600, but before then he could have made it break even by charging rent for its use. It may also have served as a useful storage location.

The failure of the Blackfriars project may explain why a document dated 29 November 1596 shows Shakespeare on the other side of the river in Southwark, and, for perhaps the only time in his life, accused of being a physical threat to someone. One William Wayte asked for sureties of the peace against Shakespeare, Francis Langley, and two women. Nothing is known about the women, but Langley was a notorious figure, owner of the Bear Garden and the new Swan Theatre, which he had built in 1595 on land acquired by extortionate moneylending. Leslie Hotson's search among the legal documents revealed that Wayte was retaliating, since Langley had already taken out a similar surety against both Wayte and Wayte's kinsman William Gardiner, a justice of the peace for Middlesex and another unpopular moneylender; moreover, Gardiner had already sued Langley for slander three times that autumn.[29] Shakespeare seems to have been caught in the middle of an ongoing feud. Writs of attachment were common and the phrasing was standard – the complainant claimed fear of death or maiming and those named by him had to post a bond that would be forfeited if they committed any violence. Hotson takes the document as evidence that Shakespeare had by now moved to Southwark and was negotiating to perform at the Swan.[30] Langley was certainly attempting to form a company of actors, and was also offering rented accommodation. On the other hand, since the Privy Council had specifically limited playhouses to one on each side of the river, the building of the Swan was not only an infringement of this rule but also something of a threat to the two established companies. Though Shakespeare was often mixed up in bad company – he could hardly avoid it in the theater world of this period – he had no reason to be on Langley's side at this point or to leave the company in which he was a sharer. He might have been involved in some negotiation that turned nasty. But the episode is mysterious.

If Shakespeare did get to Stratford for Christmas 1596, it must have been a subdued holiday. There were more family deaths: his uncle Henry was buried on 29 December and Henry's widow followed him only two months later. Shakespeare may have been with his company in Stratford at some point, since the bailiff for 1596–7, Abraham Sturley, "rewarded four companies of players and a show of the City of Norwich."[31] Sturley knew Shakespeare and was a close friend of both Adrian and Richard Quiney. A deeply devout man, to judge from his surviving letters, he was obviously not hostile to the theater. However, many of his colleagues must have felt differently, since this was the last year in which Stratford allowed players to perform.

Up till now, Shakespeare may have had some hopes that his parents' lawsuit against the Lamberts would eventually restore the land in Wilmcote that would have been his inheritance. Though John apparently brought another suit in Chancery in 1597, probably through his son, there is no record of how it turned out. Now that the land was felt to be lost for good, Shakespeare began looking seriously for property in Stratford. What he found was something of a bargain. New Place had been built by Stratford's greatest benefactor, Hugh Clopton, who died just a hundred years before Hamnet Shakespeare. It had suffered from a series of tenants, not all of whom could afford to keep it up. The year before Shakespeare's birth, its current owner, William Bott, a Stratford alderman, had been accused of poisoning his own daughter with ratsbane as part of a scheme to inherit her husband's lands. He was never prosecuted, and the accusation may have been a slander inspired by his unpopularity: it was to his seat on the council that John Shakespeare was elected, after Bott had accused all the other members of dishonesty. By 1597 this was ancient history, and the house was owned by William Underhill, the son of a recently deceased Inner Temple lawyer whom Shakespeare might have known in Stratford or London. Oddly enough, the Underhills were also related to the owner of the Angel in Bishopsgate, Shakespeare's probable residence at this time – newcomers to London tended to stick together with people from their own part of the country. With so many Stratford residents needing to rebuild their burned houses, there may not have been much competition to buy New Place. Even so, the true price was probably double the £60 recorded in the deed of sale.[32] Legal documents in this period are not the precise evidence that their appearance would suggest. Several centuries of attempting to avoid the constricting regulations of the common law had led to financial practices of mind-boggling complexity. The purchase of New Place was a typical transaction in that it began with "friendly litigation." The legal historian J. H. Baker explains this extraordinary process:

> In its perfected form, the action of ejectment was brought by a wholly imaginary lessee, usually called John Doe, against an equally imaginary person, sometimes called Richard Roe, William Styles or Shamtitle, who was supposed to be the lessee of the person in possession and to have ejected John Doe. These fictitious creatures were puppets of the real claimant, who could pull the strings without incurring the trouble, and the possible danger, of making a physical entry, granting an actual lease, and waiting for the lessee to be personally ejected by the real defendant. The puppet defendant was made to inform the real defendant that an action had been commenced against him, asking him to intervene to defend his title. The court, of course, allowed the real defendant to intervene, but only on condition that he signed the "consent rule". This rule obliged the defendant to accept the fictions and to enter a plea of not guilty. As a result, questions of title were raised in evidence to the jury on the general issue, and the more slippery technicalities associated with pleading title were eliminated.[33]

Shakespeare is often thought of as a highly successful businessman who knew his way around practices like these. I suspect that he relied on his lawyer for advice.

He may have been in Stratford on 4 May 1597, when the house was transferred to him by deed. New Place evidently needed a good deal of work to make it comfortable, but the family had moved in by the end of the year. Shakespeare may have supervised the work himself, or he may have left it to Anne or his brothers or Anne's brother Christopher, who seems to have been supportive.[34] A book published by Richard Field in 1596 might have briefly tempted him to experiment with new technology. This was the water-closet described in *A New discourse of a Stale Subject* by Sir John Harington, better known by its short title, *The Metamorphosis of Ajax*. The idea came to Harington, he claimed, after a discussion at which the Earl of Southampton was among the participants.[35] The book was a mock-serious discourse on the subject of defecation, in the manner of Rabelais and Montaigne, complete with marginal notes and quotations in Latin. Shakespeare, who could have known Harington either through Field or through his friend Thomas Russell,[36] must have been reading his book not long after its publication, since Harington's various puns on names that sound like "jakes" (privy) apparently inspired jokes about Jaques in *As You Like It* and Ajax in *Troilus and Cressida*. The final section of the book gave a diagram of the invention and even recommended the shop from which to purchase the materials ("in Lothbery at the Bores Head").[37] Shakespeare probably decided that he couldn't afford it.

New Place – three stories high and with ten fireplaces – was big enough to house another family a decade later and its residents may have included not only Anne and the two girls but also the Shakespeare brothers (Gilbert was 30, Richard 22, Edmund 16). By 1597 Gilbert Shakespeare was in the parish of St. Bride in London, where he had set up as a haberdasher. This might have meant either that he sold hats, caps, and small wares generally, or that he was involved in the making of hats. Perhaps he hoped to profit from his brother's theatrical connections. Both men may have known the hatter William Hart, who married Joan Shakespeare some time before 1600. However, Gilbert was back in Stratford within a few years. Once New Place was ready, he may have become its unofficial manager, in which case William's writing life was made possible by the support system in his own family.[38]

He needed the time, since 1597 brought more official commissions. The company was Lord Hunsdon's Players for less than a year. When Lord Cobham died, the queen, who was as fond of George Carey as she had been of his father, appointed him to the office of lord chamberlain, and his company reassumed its old name on 14 April 1597. Carey was made a Knight of the Garter that year on 23 April, and the installation at St. George's Chapel, Windsor, took place between 22 and 24 May. Arriving for the event, Hunsdon brought with him 300 retainers on horseback, in "blue coats faced with orange coloured taffety, & orange coloured feathers in their hats, most part having chaines of gold."[39] The Lord Chamberlain's Men might have been among them. If so, the purchase of New Place, followed by these events, would have made May a busy month for Shakespeare.

The Merry Wives of Windsor

Hunsdon's new honor probably lies somewhere behind *The Merry Wives of Windsor*, which combines a farcical "jealous husband" intrigue with references to the Garter ceremony. Falstaff resides at the Garter Inn in Windsor, and in the last act the Fairy Queen (or Mistress Quickly in that role) compares flowers to the colors in the insignia of the Order and quotes its motto, *Honi soit qui mal y pense*. A possible time for the performance would have been at the Garter Feast, which in 1597 took place at Whitehall on St. George's Day. It seems plausible enough that Hunsdon commanded his players to perform a play as a thank-you offering to the queen; the current popularity of Falstaff would make him a natural center for such a plot. Clearly, Shakespeare cannot have been in much official trouble over Oldcastle, if he was invited to resurrect the character with only a cosmetic name-change. He must already have been writing the second part of *Henry IV*, where Pistol is first introduced, when he broke off to write the comedy for his patron's special occasion.

217

The Merry Wives includes no historical characters, so it needed new comic ones, and it seems that Nym was invented at this point, though he did not appear in the history plays until *Henry V*. Some links between comedy and history could have been added later. In *2 Henry IV* the king asks after Hal and is told that the prince may have gone hunting at Windsor (4.4.14). Fenton, the young man whom Ann Page loves, is disliked by her father partly because he is not rich enough and partly because "he kept company with the wild Prince and Poins" (*Merry Wives* 3.2.65–6). Fenton himself admits to Ann that his original attraction was to her father's wealth, though he assures her that he now loves her. Like Prince Hal, and unlike the rest of Hal's cronies, Fenton is abandoning his wild youth and reforming. Shakespeare already knew that his history sequence would end with Henry V marrying a French princess partly for reasons of state and partly for love.

The legend that Queen Elizabeth asked for a play about Falstaff in love is unlikely to be true, since she did not approve of plays about love and lust. Besides, as Samuel Johnson said, "Falstaff could not love, but by ceasing to be Falstaff."[40] The knight expects women to wait on him, have sex with him from time to time, and, above all, lend him money. This is one reason why the character has never been as well liked by women as by men.[41] If the queen ever did condescend to speak to Shakespeare about the subject matter for a new play (both James VI and Charles II made such suggestions to others), she might have wanted to see Falstaff being fooled by women rather than exploiting them. The basic plot of *The Merry Wives* was an old one, which probably began as a combination of two even older ones: (1) a husband learns of plots to cuckold him from the would-be lover, who does not realize who he is talking to;(2) a lover manages to elude the search of a jealous husband by hiding in a series of increasingly unlikely places. The combination of the two plots results in the dramatically satisfying scenes where the absurdly jealous Ford has to conceal his fury while Falstaff recounts his adventures with Mrs. Ford. (Though Ford's lines, on the page, often seem mean-spirited and unfunny, in performance the actor can sometimes dominate even Falstaff.) Such plots were frequent in the post-performance jigs, but those were usually based on the assumption that the wife was having, or at least wanted to have, an extramarital affair. Shakespeare makes it clear from the outset that both Windsor wives are chaste. Mrs. Page believes she would go to hell if she committed fornication (2.1.46–7), and both women find Falstaff ridiculous. The Fords and the Pages are almost Shakespeare's only portrayal of middle-class couples. The gentlemen are well off, spending much of their time hunting or birding, while the women manage their households at least to the extent of supervising the washing. As roles for boys, they are unusual in that they do not illustrate either the feminine or the unfeminine: they are simply human beings with female tasks. They are also, by Elizabethan standards, middle-aged, roles for senior boy actors; Ann Page, a small part, was probably a new member of the company.

The Merry Wives was a great and long-lasting success. By the eighteenth century, when performers of *1* and *2 Henry IV* cut out most of the politics, it was the best liked of the Falstaff plays. In the twentieth century Falstaff's role in the histories became richer as it was restored to its political context, and *The Merry Wives* started to look trivial by comparison. The Windsor Falstaff is not really a different character from Prince Hal's companion, but that intellectually demanding relationship is the most interesting part of his life. Reflecting the craze for humors (Nym's humor consists largely of his obsessive use of "humor"), the play offers many roles that can be created almost entirely by costume, appearance, and accent. The Welsh and French accents of Evans and Caius are mocked by others, including Falstaff, and so is the stupidity of Mrs. Quickly, Shallow, Slender, and Simple. Revue-like episodes (usually cut in modern productions) include a mysterious subplot in which the Host is cheated by "Germans," which once had a topical meaning and seems later to have been cut so heavily as to be unintelligible. Though the setting is still presumably the medieval, Catholic England of Henry IV, it is also post-Reformation: Parson Evans is clearly a Protestant clergyman (in itself important, since Wales was suspected of harboring many secret Catholics). Mrs. Page's pointed remark –

> We'll leave a proof, in that which we will do,
> Wives may be merry and yet honest too

– bridges the two periods. "Honest" (chaste, or faithful) wives are a product of the Elizabethan Protestant emphasis on the godly household. But "merry," a more loaded word, takes over in the final scene, as these solid Protestant middle-class characters dress up as the fairies of Merrie England's disappearing folklore.

2 Henry IV

Writing *2 Henry IV* was bound to be difficult. Quite apart from the problem of Falstaff's name, his unprecedented popularity had created expectations that would be hard to fulfill. Having reconciled the prince with his father at the end of Part One, Shakespeare could hardly make Hal as wild in Part Two. Perhaps the second volume of Spenser's *Faerie Queene* offered a model of how to get out of an ending that no longer worked. Having reunited a pair of lovers at the end of Book III (and of his first volume), Spenser simply rewrote his ending for the second volume so that the lovers were separated throughout the remaining books. Shakespeare did not change the ending of his Part One, yet in Part Two Henry IV and his son seem as far apart as before. Part Two also limits the interaction between the prince and Falstaff. They meet only once before the end, in a second tavern scene which is really a scene of melancholy comedy between Falstaff and Doll Tearsheet on which the disguised Hal and Poins eavesdrop. The darkness that broods over even the comic scenes is one of the play's great achievements. Everyone seems to be waiting for the death of the sick and aging Henry IV, and both Falstaff and the Lord Chief Justice are constantly described as old. The prince, no longer merry, first comes onstage announcing that he is "weary." The king's new opponents, the Archbishop of York and his followers, are depressed from the beginning rather than hubristically optimistic like Hotspur. Northumberland, the only survivor of the earlier conspiracy, responds to news of Hotspur's death with rage, but soon dwindles into half-heartedness. At the court, too, the Lord Chief Justice and John of Lancaster are dry and mostly humorless figures.

The only court figure of real interest is, surprisingly, the king himself, who had seemed so devoid of inner life in *Richard II* and *1 Henry IV*. Though he does not appear until the third act, *2 Henry IV* is dominated by his memories and his fears for the future under his son. In a scene (3.1) that may have been written separately – it is absent from some copies of its first printing – the king talks to the Earl of Warwick of events from Richard's II reign onwards, even quoting words that Richard II spoke when neither Bolingbroke nor Warwick was present. Fearing, perhaps, that Richard had prophetic powers, and thus that his deposition and death were crimes against God, he recalls that the deposed king had foretold much of what has since happened. Warwick applies a version of humor theory in replying that "There is a history in all men's lives" (3.1.80): men's past actions enable one to predict their future ones. Shakespeare added another level of irony to the scene by giving this Earl of Warwick (unhistorically) the family name of Neville, so that those who remembered the Henry VI plays would identify him with the Warwick who later rebelled against Henry VI. Perhaps this highly retrospective scene was intended, like the Falstaff parts of *1 Henry VI*, for a collected edition of the English history plays that never materialized.

The Merry Wives had given Falstaff a setting outside the tavern world. The description of his recruiting methods in Part One had been so popular that it was an obvious idea to show him, in Part Two, actually recruiting, with new, country-based characters. Falstaff himself, in his first scene, suggests to his page Robin that the prince intended "to set me off" by contrast with the tiny boy (1.2.13–14). His awareness of himself as a character who needs to be artistically "set off" (like other stage braggarts with their pages, including Armado and Moth) recurs when he tells the audience (5.1.75–83) that he intends to turn Justice Shallow into comic material for Hal's benefit. He knows that he needs to work harder now to avoid losing his most important audience. His comparative silence and melancholy in the wonderful scene in Justice Shallow's orchard are part of the "atmosphere" in which these mainly elderly characters are separated rather than united by drink; they also foreshadow the final scene. Just as Rosaline had chastised and banished Berowne for humor that the audience itself had enjoyed, so Henry V silences Falstaff's attempt at yet another witty retort with "Reply not to me with a fool-born jest" (5.5.55). The audience is later told that his banishment is (like Berowne's) only provisional. It turns out, however, to be perpetual.

Shakespeare's own experience of reading and writing history may be responsible for the play's unusual emphasis on the difficulty of the historian's task. Rumour's appearance as the prologue leads to rumor in action, as three messengers from Shrewsbury give wildly different accounts of the battle. Henry IV's memories in 3.1 are undercut as well as echoed in 3.2 by the half-senile Justice Shallow, indulging in memories of his "wild" youth which Falstaff describes as "every third word a lie" (3.2.305–6). History itself becomes equivalent to rumor in 4.1, when the son of Sir Thomas Mowbray claims that Richard II's decision to stop the trial by combat with Bolingbroke was the cause of all subsequent disasters. To this, the Earl of Westmorland retorts that Mowbray would certainly have lost the fight if it had taken place. The very pointlessness of this "What if" conversation emphasizes the fallibility of both memory and history. The spectators' own memories are perhaps tested at the end of Act 4 when Hal, thinking his father dead, soliloquizes briefly over the crown before taking it away. Unlike Henry IV's recollection of Richard II's words, what Hal later tells the king he said is totally different from what the audience heard him say. The play even ends with a rumor: Prince John has "heard a bird" sing that England will be invading France within a year.

Another character garbles not history but drama. Pistol, the one person even Falstaff can defeat in a fight, is the negative side of the stage-struck spectator, impartially mangling lines from *Tamburlaine*, Peele's *Battle of Alcazar*, and (probably) another lost Peele play set in Turkey. These allusions to the work of two dead colleagues occur in a play that is full of reminiscing, where Shallow gloats more than he laments: "And to see how many of my old acquaintance are dead!" (*2 Henry IV* 3.2.34–5) The same was true of Shakespeare's old acquaintance: Greene in 1592, Marlowe in 1593, Kyd in 1594, Peele in 1596. Lodge had given up the theater and gone abroad to study medicine. These men, whether friends, collaborators, or rivals, belonged to the years in which he was developing most rapidly as a writer and was most susceptible to influence. Lodge would be a major source for him in the coming years, and he would be haunted by Kyd and Marlowe for still longer. Pistol's garbling was lethal: his misquotation of Peele's line is the version that would later be quoted by others (such as Marston, in *What You Will*, 1601).

At least one version of the play's Epilogue promises that "our humble author will continue the story, with Sir John in it, and make you merry with fair Katherine of France" (26–7). This is not an accurate description of *Henry V*, where Falstaff does not appear and Katherine is a minor character. Possibly, the promise that "for anything I know, Falstaff shall die of a sweat" (27–8) was deliberately ambiguous. Audiences might have expected it to mean that the fat knight would be seen running away from Agincourt as he had from the robbery on Gadshill, where Hal gleefully declared that he "sweats to death" (*1 Henry IV* 2.2.107).[42] The Epilogue is in any case a puzzling document, now thought to consist of texts written for several different occasions and perhaps different speakers. In the paragraph usually printed first, witty and self-deprecatory, the speaker begins like the reader of a proclamation – "Be it known to you" – then breaks off to add, "as it is very well," and admits that he "was lately here in the end of a displeasing play, to pray your patience for it and to promise you a better" (7–10). Had a performance been shouted down? Which play was it? It has been suggested that the speaker, who claims that "what I have to say is of mine own making," was Shakespeare himself, yet it seems odd that he would need to tell the audience that he was speaking his own words, and "If you look for a good speech now, you undo me" (3–4) suggests someone from whom the audience would not have expected eloquence, pretending to speak as himself. He ends by throwing himself on their mercy and kneeling, making a transition into the traditional prayer for the queen. The speaker of the second Epilogue suggests that his audience might prefer his dancing to his speech, but he is sure that the women have forgiven him and hopes the men will do likewise. Given this speaker's assumption that the gentle-women are more likely to forgive him than the men, he might have been a popular boy actor, perhaps the one who would later speak a rather similar epilogue in the role of Rosalind. It is in the third paragraph – perhaps a third alternative – that the speaker makes the promises about *Henry V* which must have disappeared from the text once that play had been written. David Wiles argues that Will Kemp played Falstaff, and that the famous dancer followed this speech with a jig – so "the pain of Falstaff is simultaneously the mirth of Kemp."[43] Whether or not re-entering so soon was compatible with the normal need for the clown to be absent from the final scene, the emphasis on the uncertainty of audience response is appropriate to Shakespeare's writing at this period.

Much Ado About Nothing

Dealing with the complications over Oldcastle/Falstaff and moving into his new house in Stratford may have taken up a good deal of Shakespeare's time in 1597 and 1598. For his next comedy, probably performed in the winter of 1598/9, he chose a familiar Italian story, with absolutely no implications for English history, about a lover falsely suspecting his fiancée. He rounded it out with what must have been the most popular parts of *Love's Labour's Lost*: the sparring lovers and the comic constable. There are other parallels between the two plays: in each, a team of men is set against a team of women, with a masque as part of the wooing process. Though the betrothal of Hero and Claudio seems to bridge the gender divide, it does not in fact do so. Separate all-male and all-female groups plot against Benedick and Beatrice, deceiving them into loving each other, and at Hero's wedding Claudio and his patron unite against the slandered woman, with only Benedick making the fateful decision not to follow them.

In the opening scene, Hero's father Leonato makes the kind of sententious comment that seems designed for a commonplace book: "How much better is it to weep at joy than to joy at weeping!" (1.1.27–8). Sophisticated spectators are invited to detect the smugness in his neat phrasing of a banal idea, and Leonato himself will later recognize the uselessness of moralizing, though he now phrases his recognition more effectively: "For there was never yet philosopher/ That could endure the toothache patiently" (5.1.35–6). While *Love's Labour's Lost* had made fun of the four young men as well as the constable and braggart, schoolmaster and vicar, it maintained the social hierarchy. *Much Ado*, however, inverts the usual assumptions about who is entitled to outwit whom. Don John deceives the Prince and Claudio, the two other highest-ranking characters, but is exposed, if accidentally, by the incompetent and mostly illiterate watchmen. Claudio and Don Pedro, along with Hero and Ursula, deceive Beatrice and Benedick, but their attempts to gloat over their triumph fall flat, since, by now, Beatrice and Benedick know much more than they do.

The characterization is actor-driven. Like *The Merry Wives*, *Much Ado* requires four female characters and a boy. The most obviously comic characters – Dogberry the constable and Verges his elderly assistant – were written for Kemp and Cowley (whose names accidentally got into a stage direction of the 1600 Quarto); they had probably played Falstaff and Justice Shallow in *2 Henry IV* and *The Merry Wives of Windsor*. The prostitute Doll Tearsheet and Mistress Quickly, like the Merry Wives, could be played by boys who, in *Much Ado*, were ready to take on young men's roles. While Lady Percy resembles a comedy heroine in *1 Henry IV*, where she is seen squabbling with her husband, her brief appearance in Part Two shows her as a tragic figure, even a vindictive one. The boy who played her would have been the natural choice for Beatrice, and his ability to make the transition from comedy to deadly seriousness might have inspired Beatrice's "Kill Claudio," a moment that still takes audiences by surprise.

The title is cleverer than it seems, since "nothing" was pronounced like "noting" (looking, observing, and, in this case, eavesdropping) and had the slang meaning of a woman's sexual organ. But, like other excessively clever puns, it seems to have gone largely unnoticed, since contemporaries evidently thought of the play as "Beatrice and Benedick." Claire McEachern points out that the parallel "notings" in *Much Ado* use the same structural device as the Henry IV plays, where "rebellion in the tavern echoes rebellion in the state, the robbery of purses prefiguring the suppression of the Percies."[44] Both plays are full of misunderstandings resulting from incorrect reporting and "noting." As Lorna Hutson writes, Dogberry's characteristically nonsensical statement to the suspects brought before him – "Masters, it is proved already that you are little better than false knaves, and it will go near to be thought so shortly" (4.2.21–3) – "articulates the inherently preposterous working of suspicion itself."[45]

The spectators themselves are asked to "note" what they see, since the play implicitly teaches the importance of being what Jonson would call "understanding" playgoers. Much of the time, they can enjoy the disparity between the characters' perception of the situation and their own – for instance, drawing their own conclusions from the fact that Beatrice and Benedick constantly talk about each other, even while proclaiming their mutual dislike. Benedick's utterly mistaken belief that he can see "some marks of love in her" (2.3.240–1), once he has been told that she loves him, demonstrates the effect of preconceptions. In the wedding scene, Don Pedro and Claudio humiliate Hero in public on the basis of evidence that is deliberately not shown to the audience (so that it is possible to believe simultaneously that they found it credible and that they should not have done so).[46] Everyone in the cast looks at the young bride, attempting to read her face. Hero's father immediately assumes her guilt, arguing from the apparent sincerity of her accusers: "Would the two princes lie and Claudio lie . . .?" he asks, remembering her fiancé's obvious grief and forgetting that he ought also to be asking whether his daughter would lie. The audience, meanwhile, is probably watching the reactions of Beatrice and Benedick: Don Pedro has twice looked forward to seeing their first meeting after their deception, yet now it has happened and no one else notices. The Friar, to whom no one is paying attention, is the one whose "noting" of Hero is vindicated. On a stage where the audience has a wide choice of where to look, this scene is a test of everyone's powers of observation.

The After-Effects of Grief

Inevitably, biography wants to find evidence of Shakespeare's grief in the writings that followed the loss of his son. In fact, his most striking depictions of parental grief – in *The True Tragedy/3 Henry VI* and *King John* – pre-date Hamnet's death (though *King John*, not printed before 1623, could have been added to). As Evelyn B. Tribble points out, young boys in Shakespeare's plays are nearly always pathetic: "A young boy's towardness is often said to presage his early demise."[47] Richard III's "So wise so young, they say, do never live long," was a contemporary superstition, but if Hamnet was in fact a frail child there might have been reason why it recurs throughout the plays. On the other hand, the death of Shakespeare's 7-year-old sister Anne in 1579 might have been a still more harrowing experience for him, since he would have been 15 and living at home when it happened; his cousins Lettice and James had also died in childhood. It can hardly have escaped his notice, of course, that his historical plays were about relationships between fathers and sons, the winning and losing of honor, and, strikingly, the betrayal of sons by their fathers. This thread is not explicit in Holinshed, though it can be inferred from him. Sons' actions are dictated by filial obligation, from Bolingbroke's refusal to take back his accusations of Mowbray – "Shall I seem crestfallen in my father's sight?" (*Richard II* 1.1.188) – to Hal's promise to Henry IV that he will perform heroic deeds to prove that he *is* his father's son. Yet in *Richard II* the Duke of York gallops to court to accuse his son of treason, apparently concerned only with how the episode will reflect on him. His wife, on the other hand, pleads for her son without caring about the political consequences.

Both parents are made to look ridiculous, as if Shakespeare did not dare to give serious attention to their conflict. In *1 Henry IV* Hotspur and Mortimer fight the battle of Shrewsbury without the armies that Hotspur's father Northumberland and Mortimer's father-in-law Glendower should have brought; Hotspur's uncle, Worcester, is still more responsible for his death, since concern for "my safety" (5.5.11) makes him withhold the king's offer of mercy. Northumberland, in Part Two, is devastated by the news of Hotspur's death, yet he once again betrays the rebels who counted on his help. Ironically, it is Hotspur's widow who persuades him to do so. If one is looking for the voices of Anne and Judith Shakespeare, they might be found in the bitterness with which Lady Percy tells her father-in-law,

> Never, oh, never do his ghost the wrong
> To hold your honor more precise and nice
> With others than with him!
>
> (2.3.39–41)

Shakespeare had been absent from home while his family needed him. But, as elsewhere in his work, personal experience and feeling are diffused among several characters and are inseparable from literary influences and the demands of drama.

The plays that Shakespeare wrote in 1596–8 – *1 Henry IV*, *The Merchant of Venice*, *The Merry Wives of Windsor*, *2 Henry IV*, and *Much Ado About Nothing* – contain some of his funniest scenes. Human mortality is a joke to Beatrice, who makes it an argument against marriage: "Would it not grieve a woman to be overmastered with a piece of valiant dust?" (*Much Ado* 2.1.56–7). It is of course possible to find personal reasons for Shakespeare's choice of even his comic sources: Richard P. Wheeler suggests that plays in which a woman impersonates a man may reflect Shakespeare's longing to have his daughter become his lost son;[48] many comedies end with the reappearance of a character believed to be dead. The relation between life and art is, however, not necessarily direct, and the experience of grief may affect *Much Ado* in a more oblique way. It is essential for a comic writer or actor to be able to sense what is or is not funny to other people, and Shakespeare may still have been assimilating the discovery that his greatest comic character looked to some spectators like a tasteless travesty of a proto-Protestant martyr. He perhaps thought that the fuss over the name Oldcastle was indeed "much ado about nothing." The play is, in fact, full of episodes in which characters fail to distinguish between jest and earnest. Even when Claudio asks Benedick to be serious (1.1.159), the latter is unable to be so, and cannot tell whether his friend is joking or not. Beatrice's jokes are often not so much "merry" as embarrassing, even to her – as when she realizes that she has virtually pushed Don Pedro into a proposal (2.1.307–10). The men are so used to joking that when Claudio answers "No" to the question, "You come hither, my lord, to marry this lady?" Hero's father, assuming that the bridegroom has chosen this moment to quibble about the phrasing of the ceremony, hastily interjects, "To be married to her.

225

Friar, you come to marry her" (4.1.4–7). After the aborted wedding scene, Don Pedro and Claudio seem unable to stop joking, even when Benedick challenges Claudio: "He is in earnest," they say, astonished (5.1.191). The endings of *Love's Labour's Lost* and *2 Henry IV* had emphasized the isolation of the jester when the world turns serious, but *Much Ado* gives an equally vivid image of the person who is serious while everyone else is joking. After Hamnet's death, Shakespeare, especially when writing comedies, may have felt a similar isolation from the mood of those around him.

The possibility of another still more emotional response went unnoticed until recently. In October 1597 Edward Alleyn, aged only 31, retired from acting with the Admiral's Men. He would make a brief return to the stage when the company opened the Fortune Theatre in 1600, but no one could know that at the time. His farewell performances packed in the crowds for his great roles in *The Jew of Malta* and *The Spanish Tragedy*. Since Marlowe's play had never been printed, it remained out of reach for other actors, but Kyd's had been published in 1592. Once Alleyn retired, the Chamberlain's Men apparently felt free to adopt this popular classic as a vehicle for their own leading actor. In a play acted at Cambridge in the Christmas season of 1601 or 1602, Burbage is shown using it as an audition piece.[49] The academic author might have been misinformed about the play's ownership, but there is corroboration in the 1619 elegy on Burbage that names Hieronimo as one of his famous roles. The Induction to Marston's *The Malcontent* (1604) may give a clue to what happened. Asked how the King's Men come to have a play that originally belonged to a boys' company, an actor replies, "Faith, sir, the book was lost; and because 'twas pity so good a play should be lost, we found it and play it" (Induction, 73–4). The dialogue implies that a play could occasionally move from one company to another.

In 1602 *The Spanish Tragedy* was published in a new edition with a title page promising "new Additions of the Painter's part, and others, as it hath of late been divers times acted" (Figure 7).[50] Most of the new material expands Hieronimo's part. After initially recognizing his son's body, the father lapses into denial, wondering "how this fellow got his clothes" (first addition, line 15), before finally acknowledging the horrible truth. In another brief addition, he uses the phrase "a thing of nothing" (second addition, line 8), which occurs in *Hamlet*, in a similar context (a sarcastic hint at villainy). The depiction of grief over the death of a son dominates the scenes that follow, though even here it is expressed with an edge of self-mockery:

> My son! and what's a son? A thing begot
> Within a pair of minutes, thereabout:
> A lump bred up in darkness, and doth serve
> To ballace [ballast] these light creatures we call women:
> And at nine moneths' end creeps forth to light.
> (third addition, 4–8)

Figure 7 Title page of *The Spanish Tragedy* (1615), by Thomas Kyd. The woodcut depicts its most famous scene, in which Hieronimo discovers his son's body hanging in his orchard. *By permission of the Folger Shakespeare Library*

The scene of the "Painter's part," mentioned on the title page, was obviously memorable. Hieronimo asks a painter to depict him discovering his dead son:

> *Hier[onimo]*. There you may show a passion, there you may show a passion. Draw me like old Priam of Troy, crying, "The house is a-fire, the house is a-fire, as the torch over my head." Make me curse, make me rave, make me cry, make me mad, make me well again, make me curse hell, invocate heaven, and in the end, leave me in a trance – and so forth.

227

Paint[er]. And is this the end?
Hier[onimo]. O no, there is no end: the end is death and madness.
(fourth addition, 155–63)

The author is not credited on the title page. Henslowe in September 1601 and June 1602 recorded substantial payments to Ben Jonson for additions to the play, but there has always been some doubt as to their authorship, both because they resemble nothing else written by Jonson and also because in 1599, well before Henslowe's payments, Marston parodied the painter scene in *Antonio and Mellida* 5.1.[51] Shakespeare's authorship of the additions was suggested by Warren Stevenson in 1968; more recently, Hugh Craig and Brian Vickers have taken the same view on the basis of computer tests and verbal analysis.[52] The "additions" catch the style of Kyd's original, with its sharp transitions between the lofty and the down-to-earth. They make the play even more of a star vehicle than before, presumably to allow Burbage to outdo Alleyn in his own role. After the opening of the Fortune Theatre in 1600, the play probably received yet another revival. It would have needed new material for Alleyn to compete with the additions written for Burbage, and Jonson was so well paid for his additions that, as Edwards notes in his edition,[53] they must have been more extensive than the printed ones. Jonson did not include them in his published works, and Shakespeare's additions, if they were his, were not published in the Folio. It would not be strange if Shakespeare, the actor, found it easiest to dramatize his response to Hamnet's death by taking on another man's voice. Rereading the play, he noticed Kyd's awareness of how extreme grief absorbs everything else into itself. When the elderly Bazulto tells Hieronimo that he is pleading "for his murder'd son," Hieronimo responds, "No, sir, it was my murder'd son" (3.13.79-80); he later takes the old man to be his son ("Horatio, thou art older than thy father," 3.13.150) and then, recognizing his mistake, calls him "the lively image of my grief" (3.13.162). Shakespeare, a few years later, would make Lear take Edgar for an old man, asking him, "Didst thou give all to thy daughters? And art thou come to this?" (3.4.48–9).

Notes

1. Letter from Jacques Petit to Anthony Bacon, Lambeth Palace Library MS 654, no. 167, discovered by Gustav Ungerer and reprinted in "An Unrecorded Elizabethan Performance of *Titus Andronicus*."

2. It was filed "with others from cranks and crackpots": *The Life and Minor Works of George Peele*, ed. Horne, 108.

3. *The Life and Minor Works of George Peele*, ed. Horne, 114. Middleton used episodes from this jestbook in several of his plays, including *The Puritan*, which includes a character based on Peele. See Christian, "Middleton's Acquaintance with the Merrie Conceited Jests of George Peele."

4. See Sutherland, "The Grant of Arms to Shakespeare's Father."
5. See e.g. Duncan-Jones, *Shakespeare: An Ungentle Life*, 105, and Honan, who thinks John Shakespeare's income was stated "optimistically" (p. 228).
6. www.college-of-arms.gov.uk: "How to get a coat of arms."
7. Duncan-Jones, *Ungentle Shakespeare: Scenes from his Life*, 96.
8. J. Shapiro, *A Year in the Life of William Shakespeare*, 28–9.
9. In the play, the prince replies that he will "draw it as apparent to the crown, / And in that quarrel use it to the death" (lines 64–5).
10. Slack, *The Impact of Plague in Tudor and Stuart England*, 66–7.
11. Greer, *Shakespeare's Wife*, 197.
12. Honan, 225.
13. Edmond, *Rare Sir William Davenant*, 20–1.
14. Nash, *Pierce Pennilesse his Supplication to the Devil*, B2^r.
15. Schoenbaum, 229–32.
16. Winny, *The Player King*, 105–31.
17. See Ch. 9 above for *Love's Labour's Lost* in the context of other humors comedies of the period.
18. Lacey, *Robert Earl of Essex*, 275.
19. See e.g. Howard and Rackin, *Engendering a Nation*, 137.
20. The line numbering is that of *The Works of Thomas Kyd*, ed. Boas, but I have put the passage into prose.
21. Bloom, *Shakespeare: The Invention of the Human*, 274.
22. Honan, 229.
23. Hammer, *The Polarization of Elizabethan Politics*, 161–2.
24. Stubbes, *The Anatomie of Abuses*, lines 4772–4 (p. 182).
25. For legal fictions, see J. H. Baker, *Introduction to English Legal History*, 175–6; for bonds, see pp. 269–70. A defendant in a lawsuit in 1655 claimed that the sum of money named in a thirty-year-old bond had been a legal fiction: see Kathman, "Players, Livery Companies, and Apprentices," 422.
26. Yungblut, *Strangers Settled Here Amongst Us*, 41.
27. Knutson, "What Was James Burbage *Thinking*??," 128–9.
28. Herbert Berry, in Wickham, 502.
29. Hotson, *Shakespeare versus Shallow*, 12.
30. Ibid., 13.
31. M. Eccles, *Shakespeare in Warwickshire*, 100.
32. Honan, 237.
33. J. H. Baker, *Introduction to English Legal History*, 254–5.
34. Greer, *Shakespeare's Wife*, 185.
35. [Harington], *A new discourse of a stale subiect, called the metamorphosis of Aiax*, L4^r.
36. Russell's stepfather Sir Henry Berkeley was a friend and neighbor of Harington. See Hotson, *I, William Shakespeare, do appoint Thomas Russell, Esquire. . .*, 98.
37. This section is attributed to Thomas Combe, Harington's servant, and may well be by him, as Combe was also an artist. See *Sir John Harington's New Discourse*, ed. Donno, 12.
38. See Honan, 291, quoting Macdonald, "A New Discovery about Shakespeare's Estate in Old Stratford."

39. Quoted from Bodley Ashm. MS 1112, fo. 16ᵛ, in Green, *Shakespeare's Merry Wives of Windsor*, 43–4.

40. Note on *Merry Wives of Windsor* (5.5.223): *Johnson on Shakespeare*, ed. Sherbo, in *The Works of Samuel Johnson*, 7: 341.

41. Elizabeth Inchbald, a playwright and actress, seems to have been the first, in 1817, to state this openly. See McMillin, *Henry IV, Part One*, 30. Feminist readings have attempted to salvage Falstaff by suggesting that, because of his garrulousness, his cowardice, and his womb-like stomach – he is really a maternal rather than paternal figure. See e.g. Parker, *Literary Fat Ladies*, 43, and Traub, "Prince Hal's Falstaff." The part has in fact occasionally been played by a woman. The comedian Pat Carroll, who played Falstaff in *the Merry Wives of Windsor*, said however that she would not dream of playing the part in the histories, For a recent eulogy of Falstaff, sometimes almost religious in tone, see Bloom, *Shakespeare: The Invention of the Human*: "You define who you are by your relation to Falstaff. . . . Those who do not care for Falstaff are in love with time, death, the state, and the censor" (288).

42. Melchiori, *Shakespeare's Garter Plays*, 70–2.

43. Wiles, *Shakespeare's Clown*, 132.

44. *Much Ado About Nothing*, ed. McEachern, 61.

45. Hutson, *The Invention of Suspicion*, 342.

46. Geoffrey Bullough (2: 76–7) notes that "such a scene is found in all the analogues."

47. Tribble, *Cognition at the Globe*, 142.

48. Wheeler, "Deaths in the Family," 146.

49. *The Second Part of the Return from Parnassus, or, The Scourge of Simony*, in *The Three Parnassus Plays*, ed. Leishman, 4.4.

50. Cited from *The Spanish Tragedy*, ed. Edwards.

51. Anne Barton and David Riggs, pointing to Jonson's great stylistic range, think he was the author. See Barton, *Ben Jonson, Dramatist*, 12–15; Riggs, *Ben Jonson: A Life*, 87–91. Riggs argues that Marston's parody was inserted when the play was published in 1602 because he "knew, or suspected," Jonson's authorship (p. 91).

52. Stevenson, "Shakespeare's Hand in the Spanish Tragedy 1602," later expanded into *Shakespeare's Additions to Thomas Kyd's "The Spanish Tragedy": A Fresh Look at the Evidence Regarding the 1602 Additions*. See also Craig, "The 1602 Additions to *The Spanish Tragedy*," in Craig and Kinney, eds., *Shakespeare, Computers, and the Mystery of Authorship*, 162–80, and Vickers, "Shakespeare and Authorship Studies in the Twenty-First Century," esp. 141–2.

53. *The Spanish Tragedy*, ed. Edwards, lxii.

11

"Unworthy Scaffold"

1598–1599

> But pardon, gentles all,
> The flat unraisèd spirits that hath dared
> On this unworthy scaffold to bring forth
> So great an object
> (*Henry V*, Prologue, 8–11)

In the Prologue to *Henry V* the lack of subject-verb agreement, though common in writing of this period, makes it unclear whether the "unraisèd spirits" are those of the actors or (since the verb is singular) those of the author. Since the author was probably one of the actors, it is not surprising that he blurs the distinction. But why "unraisèd"? Perhaps because Marlowe's Faustus, though unable to raise Alexander and his paramour from the dead, had actually raised the spirits who impersonated them. In the play that follows this Prologue, Captain Fluellen, an enthusiast for ancient history, draws multiple parallels between Alexander and Henry V, as Plutarch had between Alexander and Julius Caesar. The speaker of its Epilogue goes on to call Shakespeare "our bending author," a phrase that has been variously explained as weighed down with his burden (Bevington), stooped over his desk (Norton), or bowing – either to receive applause (Folger) or humbly (Arden 3). In any case, it seems that in his Prologue Shakespeare, disclaiming any ability to bring back the English king from the dead, is apologizing for the author, the actors, and their theater. Similarly, at the end of *As You Like It* Rosalind, addressing the audience, exclaims that she is "neither a good epilogue nor cannot insinuate with you in the behalf of a good play" (7–9). It is dangerous to lean too much on the evidence of prologues and epilogues, often written for specific occasions and, as Tiffany Stern has shown, not necessarily spoken at every performance.[1] In those for the court, which are the most likely to survive, the actors were particularly likely to be humble.

The Life of William Shakespeare: A Critical Biography, First Edition. Lois Potter.
© 2012 Lois Potter. Published 2012 by Blackwell Publishing Ltd.

The last years of the sixteenth century may, however, have been a period when Shakespeare became particularly apologetic about his work, if only because his previous successes had created expectations that he was nervous about fulfilling. By comparison with his intense activity in 1594–6, the next two years seem to have resulted in only three plays. Moreover, scholars now think that it is to the years 1598–1600 that they can date the so-called "Rival Poet" sonnets, those in which Shakespeare seems to feel that his works are undervalued compared to those of someone else.

Ben Jonson

It was at this time that Shakespeare got to know someone whose highly critical approach to writing might have made him more self-conscious about his work. He probably met Ben Jonson in 1597, when Pembroke's Men produced what may have been his first play, *The Case is Altered*, with the author in the cast. Like *The Comedy of Errors*, it combined two plays by Plautus but transposed the story to a modern setting. As actor-playwrights, the two men had something in common, but Jonson, as Shakespeare would learn, had crowded a great deal of experience into twenty-four years: an excellent classical education at Westminster School, several years as an apprentice bricklayer, two years fighting in the Low Countries, marriage, and fatherhood. Acting was his latest venture; he had apparently performed some major roles with a touring company.

It did not take him long to get into trouble. In the summer of 1597 Nashe was also writing for Pembroke's Men. He later claimed that, when the plague drove him from London, he left behind the induction and one act of a play, *The Isle of Dogs*, which he had promised the company. The impatient actors persuaded Jonson to complete it, since the subject matter was topical. Ever since More's *Utopia*, islands had been associated with political satire, and this play was probably no exception. After its first performance, in July, the Privy Council suppressed it so thoroughly that no one knows what it was about. Jonson, who was acting in it, was imprisoned along with two other actors. Nashe's papers were seized, as he himself would have been if he had been in town. Then a Privy Council order of 28 July closed all the London theaters, and for a while they were threatened with demolition. In August the imprisoned actors were interrogated by, among others, Richard Topcliffe, whose brutal methods were notorious. The episode must have been frightening: Kyd's and Marlowe's papers had been seized only five years earlier and Topcliffe had tortured the Jesuit poet Robert Southwell ten times before his execution in February 1595. Jonson claimed later that two spies were sent to prison with him in order to trap him, and he was proud that he had given nothing away, though it is not clear just what he had to conceal.[2] Yet on 2 October Jonson and the other actors were released, unharmed, and the playhouses

Figure 8   Ben Jonson, by Robert Vaughan, frontispiece to the second volume of his *Works* (1640). © The British Library Board (G.11630, frontispiece)

reopened. The real casualties were Pembroke's Men, who ceased to exist as a company; Nashe, whose career as a playwright was effectively over; and the Swan Theatre, which did not function again as a playhouse until 1610. Jonson apparently gave up acting for good.

By 1597, then, everyone in the London theater world had reason to know about Jonson, who had nearly cost them their livelihood. They do not seem to have blamed him, and perhaps they had no reason to do so, since *The Isle of Dogs* had finally removed Pembroke's Men and the Swan as competitors, and that may have been the real motive behind the whole episode. Jonson offered the Chamberlain's

Men what he himself considered his first major comedy, *Every Man in His Humour*. He set it in Italy, in homage to the Italian comic tradition, and followed a new trend by building his plot around a display of humor characters. Nicholas Rowe in 1709 recorded a story that it was Shakespeare himself who recognized the play's merit when the company was about to reject it.[3] Perhaps, given Jonson's recent history, they had good reason to be nervous, and they may also have worried about the absence of an obvious leading role, but they put it on at the Curtain in the fall of 1598. The cast included Shakespeare, Burbage, and Kemp. Because Shakespeare is listed at the head of the cast, he is thought to have played Old Lorenzo, the first character to appear and the first one listed in 1601. The actors' names are given only in the 1616 Folio, which prints a heavily revised version of the play, set in London. Jonson presumably meant that Shakespeare acted in both versions, but the date of the revised text is unknown.

Whatever bond might have been created between actors and author was probably strained when, shortly after *Every Man in His Humour* opened, Jonson killed a member of Henslowe's company in a duel. He was imprisoned again and could have been sentenced to death if he had not been allowed to plead benefit of clergy. When he emerged, on 6 October 1598, he was branded on the thumb and his property had been confiscated. The branding may have been done with a cold iron, since, as David Riggs notes, none of Jonson's contemporaries taunted him with it.[4] Shakespeare might, however, have remembered it when in Sonnet 111 he said that, because of his acting, his name had received "a brand." To make matters even worse, during his two weeks in Newgate, Jonson had met a forceful Catholic priest, Father Thomas Wright, and was converted to an officially outlawed religion.

For whatever reason, Shakespeare is not listed in the cast of Jonson's next play, *Every Man Out of His Humour*, which the Lord Chamberlain's Men staged in 1599. Though this comedy is often thought to allude to Shakespeare's new coat of arms and motto (see Chapter 10 above), it is hard to imagine either that Jonson would have written lines publicly ridiculing a leading member of the company for which he wrote or that, if he had, Shakespeare's colleagues would have been willing to speak them. In fact, the play's Epilogue suggests that the two writers were on friendly terms. Macilente, the envious man who acts as surrogate author of the play, tells the audience that, if they show their approval by applauding, "you may make lean Macilente as fat as Sir John Falstaff." This was not only a compliment, carefully using the new name of his colleague's most famous character, but also a reminder that both of them were writers of the comedy of humors. *Every Man in His Humour* was in fact similar to *2 Henry IV*, which premiered in the same season, and Jonson's Bobadill might be seen as homage to Falstaff. Jonson's tavern scenes, where young gentlemen enjoy slumming with a disparate collection of humorists, owe something to Shakespeare's scenes at the Boar's Head.

The Scaffold and the Globe

What, in fact, was the "unworthy scaffold" mentioned by the *Henry V* Chorus? Just after James Burbage's death, the company's lease on the Theatre had expired, and their landlord Giles Allen had refused to negotiate a new one. The Chamberlain's Men played at the next-door Curtain, a smaller venue, where they may have performed both *As You Like It* and *Henry V*, perhaps *Julius Caesar* as well. The Chorus's apologetic tone could have been a way of lobbying for something better, which the Burbage brothers, at least, already had in mind. They may have known something of their rivals' plans. Unlike the Burbages, Alleyn and his father-in-law Henslowe held court offices, and, after Alleyn's (temporary) retirement, they were working jointly to acquire more – particularly the lucrative position of Master of the Bear Gardens, which they finally got in 1604. Meanwhile, they were also making plans for a new theater building on the other side of the Thames. and carefully prepared the way by promising a generous contribution for poor relief from their profits.[5] If the Chamberlain's Men knew of these plans, they must have become all the more aware of the need for a building of their own.

As if to make up for the absence of Alleyn, Henslowe paid for thirty-five new plays in 1598 alone. During the weeks when the playhouses were open, spectators could count on the average of a new play every week at the Rose. The Lord Chamberlain's Men, given the difficulties surrounding their move to the Globe, may have been more limited in what they could offer. Henslowe's *Diary*, which preserves the titles of many lost plays (for example *The Famous Wars of Henry I and the Prince of Wales*), suggests that he was hoping to find more successful histories to compete with the *Henry IV* plays. Shakespeare's countryman, the poet Michael Drayton, was among the authors of the two-part *Sir John Oldcastle* that opened in October 1599 with a prologue ("It is no pampered glutton we present," line 6) reminding the audience that the character had been unjustly treated with "forged invention" in Shakespeare's play.[6] Henslowe was so delighted with the result that he gave the playwrights an extra 10 shillings after the first performance.[7] But Shakespeare seems to have managed to establish Falstaff's name, since in July 1599 the Countess of Southampton wrote to her husband, then with Essex in Ireland, that "Sir John Falstaff is by his Mrs Dame Pintpot made father of a godly miller's thumb, a boye that's all head and very little body, but this is a secret."[8] Pintpot is the name that Falstaff gives to the Hostess in *1 Henry IV* (2.4.394). The allusion must be a private joke; it shows both that both Southampton and his wife knew Shakespeare's plays well and that Falstaff's name had replaced Oldcastle's among regular theatergoers.

By now, Shakespeare was obviously known to be well-off. Two Stratford aldermen, Richard Quiney and Abraham Sturley, wondered about interesting him in some investments, and corresponded on the subject in January 1598. Both men were in financial trouble at this time because of their losses in the Stratford fires of 1594 and 1595, and Quiney had run into considerable expenses on trips to London on Corporation business. In particular, he had to spend four months there, between October 1598 and February 1599, in the long process of petitioning the Privy Council and various courtiers to exempt Stratford, on account of its recent losses, from new taxes that had been voted by Parliament that year, and to grant it some financial help.[9] Early in his visit, when funding had not yet come through, Quiney wrote to Shakespeare, asking for his help in procuring money. Addressed to "my loving good friend and countryman Mr Wm Shakespeare" and dated from his inn in London on 25 October 1598, this is the one surviving letter addressed to the playwright:

> Loving countryman, I am bold of you as of a friend, craving your help with £30 upon Mr. Bushell's and my security or Mr. Mytton's with me. Mr Rosswell is not come to London as yet and I have especial cause. You shall friend me much in helpinge me out of all the debts I owe in London, I thanke God, and much quiet my mind which would not be indebeted. I am now towards the court in hope of answer for the dispatch of my business. You shall neither lose credit nor money by me, the Lorde willing, and now but persuade yourself so as I hope and you shall not need to fear but with all hearty thankfulness I will hold my time and content your friend, and if we bargain farther you shall be the paymaster yourself. My time bids me hasten to an end and so I commit this <to> your care and hope of your help. I fear I shall not be back this night from the court. Haste. The Lord be with you and with us all. Amen.[10]

Quiney was reluctant to be indebted to someone he did not know personally; he evidently hoped either that Shakespeare would lend him the £30 or, as the mention of "your friend" implies, introduce him to an honest moneylender.[11] The fact that the letter remained in Quiney's papers may mean that he never sent it or that it is a copy of one that he did send. Alderman Sturley seems to have heard from him, in a letter of the same date, that "our countryman Mr Wm Shak. would procure us money," which, Sturley added, "I will like of as I shall hear when, and where, and how."[12]

Richard Quiney's efforts at court were successful, since Stratford was exempted from the new taxes and granted a subsidy of £75. When Quiney sent his expense account to the Corporation after returning home in early February, the total came to £44, including fees to the various officers involved, and travel expenses for the journey, three days in each direction. Shakespeare's friend Hamnet Sadler was with Quiney in London for at least some of the time, and Sturley wrote from Stratford that his wife Judith was missing him badly; she was expecting another child in April.[13] These countrymen of Shakespeare's might have gone to see his plays, but Quiney did not include entertainment on his expense account.

The period of Quiney's visit was the time when the Lord Chamberlain's Men were always busiest, and in late 1598 they must have been unusually anxious. Not only did they have to prepare for their usual court performances, but Cuthbert and Richard Burbage were busy planning a dramatic and dubiously legal action. At a low point in their relations with their landlord Giles Allen, they had looked again at their lease. Allen owned the land on which their Theatre was built but not the building itself, some of which may have been erected by the late James Burbage. Burbage's sons decided to dismantle the entire structure and move it from its Shoreditch site. They chose a very cold day at the end of December 1598, when they knew Allen was out of town. The builder Peter Street and his workmen were responsible for the demolition and presumably kept note of the original locations of the timbers (so Shakespeare and the other actors did not have to pitch in, as is sometimes imagined). When Allen's neighbors and tenants protested, Street and Cuthbert Burbage pointed out some damaged bits of wood and explained that they were only taking down the building in order to repair and re-erect it.[14] They did not say *where* they intended to do this. It was only on 21 February that they signed their lease for a property on the south bank of the Thames, but they had leased the land from their new landlord in December,[15] and they delayed signing their contract until the builder had brought a second load of timber from the old site in January.[16] The building's components, stored for the rest of the winter, were eventually re-erected as a new playhouse, called "The Globe on Bankside" to distinguish it from the Shoreditch theaters. Meanwhile, the actors must have performed at other venues: the Curtain, the court, and private houses. Naturally, Giles Allen sued the company (complaining, among other things, that they had ruined his grass and terrified the neighbors), and they countersued him. The company had taken such an enormous risk that it seems likely that they knew they could count on official backing or at least tacit approval. This would explain why the court eventually found in Burbage's favor on 18 October 1599.

The Burbage brothers quickly formalized their relations in the new playing space. The lease of 21 February was in three parts: one for the owner of the ground, one for the two Burbages, and one divided among the five actor-sharers: Shakespeare, Augustine Phillips, Thomas Pope, John Heminges, and William Kemp. Shortly thereafter, Heminges arranged for two friends and neighbors to act as trustees in a deed which changed the lease from joint tenancy to tenancy in common.[17] As Schoenbaum explains, the original arrangement would have meant that as each participant died his shares would be divided among his associates; the tenancy in common allowed the rights of shareholders to pass to their heirs.[18] It would cause difficulties later, when non-theater people succeeded to membership. Curiously, Kemp sold his share almost immediately after the signing of this second lease. It has been tempting to make a story out of this decision. Anthony Burgess's novel *Nothing Like the Sun* depicts Shakespeare destroying Kemp for ad-libbing too much and he carried the idea over into his biography of Shakespeare ("Kemp had to go. There must have been acrimony…"), where it seems to have become canonized.[19]

The main reason for assuming that Shakespeare disliked ad-libbers is Hamlet's speech to the players, probably first performed two years after Kemp's departure. As published in the 1603 Quarto, it looks like an opportunity for the actor of Hamlet to impersonate well-known contemporary clowns with recognizable catch-phrases. The 1604 version reduces this exhibition to the comment that irrelevant clowning can make people miss "some necessary question of the play" (3.2.40–1). The speaker is Hamlet rather than Shakespeare, and the tone may be affectionately amused rather than hostile. If anyone had wanted Kemp out of the company, the obvious time to get rid of him would have been just after the move across the river, when the legal situation was still unsettled. Martin Butler's *ODNB* entry on Kemp suggests that the clown liked to travel and was happier being a one-man show than a company member. The players may have known that Kemp was planning to move on, and may even have devised their new tenancy in common to help him make money by selling his share when he left. In February 1600 he performed a highly publicized stunt – his "Nine Days' Wonder" – of dancing from London to Norwich, after which he wrote up the journey as a pamphlet (Figure 9) that gives the one possible portrait of him. The feat was also a money-making venture, since he had collected pledges beforehand. He went on to perform on the Continent for another year.

Possibly because of Kemp's departure, the company took on a new comic actor, Robert Armin, who had been in a touring company for the past five years. He had trained as a goldsmith but was already known as a writer too. He joined the company while they were still playing at the Curtain (on the title page of one of his books, he later called himself "Clonnico de Curtano," the Curtain Clown). He would soon take over some of Kemp's signature roles, since in 1609 he wrote in a dedication: "pardon I pray you, the boldnes of a Begger, who hath been writ downe for an Asse in his time."[20] This quotation of Dogberry's famous line indicates that he had not only played the part but played it successfully enough to erase memories of Kemp's performance. To judge from what seems to be an illustration of his performance as a Fool in one of his later plays (Figure 10), he was small and rather ugly; his publications show that he was also clever, and Shakespeare would write some of his finest roles for him.

The Globe may have been in use by May, but the earliest surviving reference to it comes from a Swiss visitor who saw *Julius Caesar* there on 21 September 1599.[21] There has been much speculation about which of Shakespeare's plays would have been most appropriate as an opening production: *As You Like It* ("All the world's a stage") or *Henry V*, in which the choruses draw the audience's attention to the theater itself. "Unworthy scaffold," however, is hardly appropriate for a new theater. *Julius Caesar*, which emphasizes the sacrificial element in Caesar's death, might have been taken as an appropriate consecration of a new building.[22] Of course, it was hardly necessary to offer a new play and a new theater at the same time, since either in itself would probably attract audiences. In fact, a number of plays of this period make puns

Kemps nine daies vvonder.

Performed in a daunce from
London to Norwich.

Containing the pleafure, paines and kinde entertainment
of *William Kemp* betweene *London* and that Citty
in his late Morrice.

Wherein is fomewhat fet downe worth note ; to reprooue
the flaunders fpred of him : many things merry,
nothing hurtfull.

Written by himfelfe to fatisfie his friends.

LONDON
Printed by *E. A.* for *Nicholas Ling,* and are to be
folde at his fhop at the weft doore of Saint
Paules Church 1600.

Figure 9 Will Kemp, with pipe and tabor, dancing his way to Norwich on the title page of his pamphlet, *The Nine Days' Wonder.* By permission of the Folger Shakespeare Library

on the name of the Globe or, after 1600, the Fortune (the new theater of the Admiral's Men).[23]

Shakespeare had acquired a new address by the end of 1598, when he joined a number of his fellow-actors in settling on the south side of the Thames, probably in anticipation of the company's move. It would eventually be nearer his place of work, but he may not have enjoyed being in this disreputable if lively part of town, especially since its location would have added an extra hour to any journeys he made back to Stratford. He was assessed for contributions in the parish of St. Helen's,

THE

Hiſtory of the two Maids of More-clacke,

VVith the life and ſimple maner of IOHN
in the Hoſpitall.

Played by the Children of the Kings
Maieſties Reuels.

VVritten by ROBERT ARMIN, feruant to the Kings
moſt excellent Maieſtie.

LONDON,
Printed by N. O. for *Thomas Archer,* and is to be ſold at his
ſhop in Popes-head Pallace, 1 6 0 9.

Figure 10 The title page of Robert Armin's *The Two Maids of Moreclacke,* possibly showing the author in costume as the fool Tutch. The long petticoat indicates the fool's childlike status. By permission of the Folger Shakespeare Library

Bishopsgate, in 1597 and 1598, but the money was not collected. Like most people, including his own debtors, he never paid anything until the last possible moment.

When the collectors came around he may have been back in Stratford, where the new house was sufficiently livable that, by 1598, someone, probably Anne, was organizing malting. The period of bad harvests had finally ended in the previous year and, like most other citizens of Stratford who could afford large quantities of grain, the Shakespeares were hoarding it with a view to having enough for malting in the

240

future and perhaps also for resale at inflated prices when there was a shortage. New Place would eventually have a grape arbor that allowed the production of sweet wines. Shakespeare might have wanted to get back to his house to deal with some of these improvements himself, but he may also have been happy to leave them to others. In 1599 he heard some disturbing news. Evidence had come to light that the man from whom he bought New Place, William Underhill, had been poisoned only two months later by his teenaged son Fulke, after his father had orally bequeathed him all his property. Although the estate of a murderer was forfeited to the Crown, Shakespeare had good title to a purchase made two months before Underhill's death. Even so, the issue remained in suspense until 1602.

Sometime before 1600 his sister Joan married a hatter named William Hart, about whom nothing else is known. The wedding apparently did not take place in Stratford. His sister's family probably counted for rather little with Shakespeare (when he was making his will he could remember the names of only two of Joan's three sons), but he felt some obligation toward them. Since hats were an important part of stagewear, he may have been under some family pressure to patronize his new brother-in-law. Hart was not a success at his business: he was sued for debt in 1600 and 1601, and his growing family lived in the Henley Street house with Joan's parents, apparently unable to afford a place of their own. Shakespeare let them stay there even after both John and Mary had died. If his brothers had moved into New Place, there would have been plenty of room in Henley Street.

Satire and Satiric Drama

Contemporaries may have taken the view, later recorded by John Aubrey, that Shakespeare and Jonson "did gather humours of men daily where ever they came" – for example, basing Dogberry in *Much Ado* on a real constable whom Shakespeare had met in the country.[24] Characters larger than life are often thought to have been copied from life, but Shakespeare's comic constables are really just improvements on an already existing stereotype. The fact that he knew a real constable – his friend Hamnet Sadler became one in 1593 – did not affect his depiction of Dull, Dogberry, and Elbow. He also knew a shepherd, Thomas Whittington, but is unlikely to have put him into *As You Like It*. Whittington's will of March 1601 mentions that Anne Shakespeare was holding 40 shillings of his. This reference has been interpreted to mean that Anne was so hard up as to be forced to borrow money from one of her own servants, but Whittington may simply have left the money with her for safe-keeping.[25] However, Shakespeare was soon to be embroiled – how seriously is hard to say – in a theatrical episode that traded on satiric exchanges between real people.

Every Man Out of His Humour was one of the first plays in what is sometimes called the *poetomachia*, or Poets' War. The other term used for it, the War of the

Theatres, ignores the fact that, for once, writers rather than actors were at the center of things. In fact, most of the war consisted of Jonson and John Marston sniping at each other, with others contributing here and there. The craze for satire was already in existence when two developments of 1599 pushed it into the theater. The first occurred in June, when the Archbishop of Canterbury and Bishop of London issued an order to the Stationers' Company for the confiscation and burning of a small group of named books, and ordered "That noe Satyres or Epigramms be printed hereafter."[26] The main targets of this "Bishops' Ban" were the verse satires of John Marston and Sir John Davies, and Marlowe's Ovid translations. Thomas Nashe and Gabriel Harvey, who had been insulting each other in print for the past seven years, were forbidden to publish ever again, and their previous publications were to be confiscated. In the tense atmosphere of the last years of Elizabeth's reign, the authorities were more than usually careful to ensure that nothing subversive could be read into published texts.

Despite, or because of, the new restrictions, satire quickly migrated to the theaters. The process coincided with a second development, the revival of the children's acting companies, dormant during most of the 1590s. In the fall of 1599 the boys of St. Paul's Cathedral began to give public performances under a new master.[27] Then Nathaniel Giles, the new master of the Children of the Chapel, joined forces with a businessman, Hugh Evans, to form another children's company. They were able to rent Burbage's now empty Blackfriars, without the opposition that had prevented the Chamberlain's men from using the theater, because they normally performed only once a week and their audiences would not be a constant nuisance to the upscale neighborhood.[28] Both companies soon became fashionable. Quite apart from the qualities of the children themselves, well educated and musically trained to a high level, a small and exclusive playhouse on the north side of the Thames had considerable appeal to the wealthier playgoers, especially women.

Some writers were instantly attracted to the idea of writing for these companies. They could deal, not with actors (a category that some of them clearly disliked), but with the children's business managers. Ben Jonson, who sent his next two comedies to the Children of the Chapel at Blackfriars, must have been delighted at the prospect of working with boys who would say his lines exactly as he told them to. The plays written for the children were usually ensemble pieces rather than star vehicles. They had complicated, almost nonsensical plots, interspersed with music. Presumably the innocent-sounding voices of the boys added extra piquancy. A private theater was a safer venue for satire – a seated audience was less likely than a standing one to be provoked into a riot – so dramatists indulged in parody and topical references, thus making their plays almost unintelligible to later readers.

Along with Jonson, the most prolific writers of satire for the private theaters were George Chapman and John Marston. Chapman, almost 40, had been a public figure for some years, and his amazing literary range made him the most respected author of his time. Like Jonson, he had fought on the Continent in the early 1590s. Shakespeare, aware of the ironic contrast between his military-sounding name and his lack of war experience, may,have felt somewhat inferior to both. On the other hand, 23-year-old John Marston may have been a friend. When Thomas Greene, Shakespeare's countryman and friend, entered the Temple in 1595, Marston, along with his lawyer father, acted as surety for him. By 1599 it was obvious that the younger Marston had no intention of practicing law (as his father admitted when he made his will that year). Instead, he had published an Ovidian poem and a collection of satires which showed considerable knowledge of the theater scene; these were among the victims of the Bishops' Ban. He wrote briefly for Henslowe's theater, but the new children's companies obviously attracted him. They offered an opportunity to show off his knowledge of Italian, his mother's language.[29] He also knew Montaigne's essays, and may have been the one who introduced Shakespeare to them. His plays have an obvious, though puzzling, relationship to some of the ones that Shakespeare was writing in the period between 1599 and 1604, as if the two playwrights were deliberately choosing the same subjects or the same genres.

At a slightly later date, Shakespeare made Hamlet ask why his favorite acting company was touring instead of residing in "the city." The three existing texts give three different replies. In the Quarto of 1603 Guildenstern explains, "'I'faith my Lord, novelty carries it away, for the principal public audience that came to them are turned to private plays, and to the humour of children." The 1604 Quarto gives Rosencrantz the vague reply, "I think their inhibition comes by the means of the late innovation." Probably the reference had become obsolete by 1604, especially if the play was to be presented before James I, who would not be interested in this particular stage quarrel. The Folio *Hamlet*, on the other hand, has a lengthy discussion of the boy actors; it may derive from a version performed when the topic was still amusing, or perhaps Shakespeare revised the play with a historian's eye, so as to leave a record of the whole episode as he now saw it. The implication is that he himself was serenely above the battle.

Yet the anonymous author of the Cambridge play of 1601–2 (see Chapter 10, above) implies that Shakespeare did enter into it himself, since his fictitious "Burbage" and "Kemp" comment, "O, that Ben Jonson is a pestilent fellow; he brought up Horace giving the poets a pill, but our fellow Shakespeare hath given him a purge that made him beray his credit."[30] The actual order of events is unclear. In 1601 Jonson apparently learned that Thomas Dekker was about to collaborate with Marston on a play attacking him, to be performed by the Chamberlain's Men. In reply, he wrote *Poetaster*, set in Rome under Augustus. Its central action is the banishment of Ovid, both for his love-affair with the emperor's daughter and for his blasphemous behavior. Paralleling this story is the attempt of a paranoid senator to destroy Horace (an obvious idealization of Jonson) by accusing him of libel. The poetasters Demetrius and Crispinus are caricatures of Dekker and Marston respectively and, although the play does not contain any discernible attack on Shakespeare himself, it does imply that some actors for the public theater are ready to do anything, however base, to make money. In the final scene, the play veers into wish-fulfillment, with Horace, as part of Augustus's inner circle, allowed to choose his own punishments for his enemies. In the episode to which the *Parnassus* author referred, the Marston character vomits up the indigestible words in his poetic vocabulary. Following one of the many legends recorded in standard biographies of Virgil, Jonson then depicted the arrival of the great poet at the court of Augustus, who invites him to read from his *Aeneid* in a chair set for him by the emperor. If audiences were looking for a topical meaning in this scene, they might have considered it an oblique reproach to the government for failing to give an adequate reward to Spenser, England's Virgil. When the poet died in London in 1599, it was the Earl of Essex, not the queen, who paid for his funeral and his burial in Westminster Abbey.

The *Parnassus* author may have thought that Shakespeare's retaliation was the production of Dekker's *Satiromastix* (the whipping of the satirist), which his company and the Children of Paul's performed in 1601. Since Shakespeare may also have acted in the play (perhaps, as Jonathan Bate suggests, playing King William [Rufus]),[31] the Cambridge author might have assumed that he wrote it. It is sometimes suggested that the "purge" took a more specific form, such as a satiric portrayal of Jonson as Jaques in *As You Like It*, Malvolio in *Twelfth Night*, or Ajax and/ or Thersites in *Troilus and Cressida*. The difficulty is that the names Jaques and Ajax – puns on "jakes" (privy) – would have made most people think not of Jonson but of Sir John Harington, so famous for *The Metamorphosis of Ajax* (1597) that he was known to his contemporaries as "Sir John, (or Ajax) Harington."[32] In their present form, none of these three plays has a great deal to do with the quarrel. *Troilus and Cressida* reduces it to mere name-calling.

Satiromastix did not appear until September 1602, perhaps because it needed rewriting after Jonson's intentions had become clear. Dekker (apparently the sole author) brought Horace anachronistically to the medieval English court and depicted him sweating over his labored verses, surrounded by possibly homosexual young men and groveling to any aristocrat who might become a patron. The actors who were planning to perform it probably went to *Poetaster* to research their impersonations. They might have seen Jonson himself on the stage, since at least one performance of his play was followed by an "Apologetical Dialogue" in the form of a conversation between the author and a friend. While it has been doubted that Jonson would have played himself in a scene with two boy actors,[33] it is equally difficult to imagine him letting another actor impersonate him; his protégé Nathan Field might perhaps have done so. After seeing Jonson's idealized Augustan court, Shakespeare may have wondered whether there was any hope that James VI of Scotland would be such a ruler.

Sonnets of Competition

The Poets' War was only the most overt kind of competition. A number of Shakespeare's sonnets allude to what seems to be a public failure in comparison or competition with other poets. They are usually called the "rival poet" sonnets, since they say that everyone else is also writing to, or in praise of, the same person, and, in some cases, having more success:

> Why is my verse so barren of new pride?
> So far from variation or quick change?
> Why with the time do I not glance aside
> To newfound methods and to compounds strange?
> (76.1–4)
> But now my gracious numbers [verses] are decayed,
> And my sick Muse doth give another place.
> (79.3–4)
> Oh, how I faint when I of thee do write,
> Knowing a better spirit doth use your name,
> And in the praise thereof spends all his might
> To make me tongue-tied, speaking of your fame!
> (80.1–4)

The phrase "tongue-tied" occurs again (85.1), with a claim that silence may be more sincere than eloquence or the "gross painting" of other writers (82.13). At one point the poet implies that the person to whom he is writing has at least two semi-official protégés:

> There lives more life in one of your fair eyes
> Than both your poets can in praise devise.
> (83.13–14)

In Sonnets 80 and 86 he and the other poet are both ships, first on the sea of their subject matter, then in competition over a "prize" – a wealthy vessel that they want to capture:

> Was it the proud full sail of his great verse,
> Bound for the prize of all-too-precious you,
> That did my ripe thoughts in my brain inhearse,
> Making their tomb the womb wherein they grew?
> Was it his spirit, by spirits taught to write
> Above a mortal pitch, that struck me dead?
> No, neither he, nor his compeers by night
> Giving him aid, my verse astonishèd.

245

> He, nor that affable familiar ghost
> Which nightly gulls him with intelligence,
> As victors of my silence cannot boast;
> I was not sick of any fear from thence.
> But when your countenance filled up his line,
> Then lacked I matter; that enfeebled mine.

Naturally, there has been much interest in the identity of the poet whose writings were apparently more modish than Shakespeare's, who was associated rather contemptuously with some kind of nocturnal inspiration – and who was apparently defeating him, if there is any significance in the placing of the following sonnet which begins, "Farewell, thou art too dear for my possessing" (87.1). In sonnets that Michael Drayton published in 1599, he several times refers to a "carping critic" of his verse and addresses "Thou leaden brain that censur'st what I write,/ And say'st my lines be dull and doe not move."[34] Perhaps some such critic was also making Shakespeare uneasy. The obvious person to play this role was Ben Jonson, who had a high profile at the end of the century. There is, however, an even better case for Chapman: in 1598 his published continuation of *Hero and Leander* staked his claim to be Marlowe's poetic and dramatic successor, while his championing of Homer in the two translations published that year was calculated to create feelings of inferiority in writers who knew no Greek. Some scholars think that the "rival poet" is a composite of Marlowe and Chapman, possibly inspired by the publication of Meres's book with all its comparisons between writers.[35] Competition may in fact have been more widespread. Both Daniel and Drayton, for example, were writing poems very similar to Shakespeare's. Drayton, in *Idea's Mirror* (1594), describes himself as "a cripple hand to write, yet lame by kind."[36] This figurative use of lameness may be compared with the expressions – "I, made lame by Fortune's dearest spite" (Sonnet 37.3) and "Speak of my lameness, and I straight will halt" (89.3) – that some readers have taken as evidence that Shakespeare himself was lame.[37] To a modern reader, the most obviously "newfound methods" would be those of the songs and sonnets that John Donne was writing in the 1590s, though they would not be published for forty years. There are, for instance, strong resemblances between the opening of Sonnet 115 –

> Those lines that I before have writ do lie;
> Even those that said I could not love you dearer;
> Yet then my judgment knew no reason why
> My most full flame should afterwards burn clearer
>
> (1–4)

– and Donne's lines in "Love's Growth," "Methought I lied all winter when I swore/ My love was infinite, if spring makes it more," as between Sonnet 146 ("Poor soul, the center of my sinful earth"), and Donne's famous sonnet beginning "Death, be not proud"; Shakespeare's ends with "And Death once dead, there's no more dying then", Donne's with "And death shall be no more; Death, thou shalt die." If they had been writing concurrently and reading their verses in public, Shakespeare might well have felt himself "outdone" by the younger poet, though he never made the puns on Donne-dun or Donne-done that are found in other poets, including Donne himself.[38]

It is likely that poets habitually read and discussed their works aloud in the 1590s, a fact that might explain the remarkable amount of "borrowing" or "echoing" found in publications of the period. Such informal discussion might have felt competitive. Could the competition have become more formal? In the song contests of the classical pastoral, often imitated later, one shepherd starts a theme; the second answers it, keeping to the same form, and they go on until they decide to ask someone else to declare a winner. Poetic competitions existed throughout medieval Europe. Charles d'Orléans (the Orleans of Shakespeare's *Henry V*) had held competitions at Blois, where the assembled poets, who apparently included both King René d'Anjou (the Reignier of *1 Henry VI*) and the disreputable François Villon, were asked to complete a poem on the basis of a first line given by the Duke.[39] In 1579 the young James VI adjudicated a flyting, a traditional Scottish exchange of poetic insults, usually involving the creation of a fictitious and unflattering genealogy for one's opponent. A similar duel of two bards took place in Wales between 1581 and 1588, producing a total of fifty-four poems.[40] Given the sixteenth-century fondness for competitions of all kinds, it is possible that the similarities among many sonnets by different authors are the result of a choice, or command, to write on the same topic.[41] Some of Shakespeare's sonnets (for example 57 and 58, 78 and 79) look like alternative expressions of the same theme, and competition might explain the appearance of not one but two versions of an epigram by Marianus (originally written in Greek but already available in translation) as the two final sonnets of the 1609 volume.[42]

Perhaps the "carping critic" mentioned by Drayton was also the judge of this competition. On the other hand, the judge might have been the addressee of some of the sonnets; there would then have been a motive for flattering him. James VI had been only 13 when he presided over the flyting at his court. The future third Earl of Pembroke, as a young teenager, may have been tutored in the early 1590s by another writer of sonnets, Samuel Daniel. Given the importance of this family as literary patrons, they might have sponsored sonnet competitions before an audience of other poets or Inns of Court men. In 1595, two expert calligraphers took part in what was literally a "writing competition," with George Chapman as the judge, and Chapman would have been the obvious choice to judge the Marianus translations. Or perhaps (if the poems are dated slightly later) James brought the taste for competition with him from Scotland, and Shakespeare was writing as an Elizabethan poet already feeling out of date in a Jacobean court. Edmonson and Wells point out the resemblance between the imagined situation of the "tongue-tied" poet in a competition for favor and that of Cordelia in the first scene of *King Lear*.[43]

As You Like It

In *As You Like It* Shakespeare briefly touched on satire: its value is debated by the banished Duke and the persistently satiric Jaques (2.7.47–87), and Celia agrees with Touchstone that "the little wit that fools have was silenced" (1.2.85–6), perhaps alluding to the Bishops' Ban – although, if Juliet Dusinberre is right in thinking that Touchstone's reference to pancakes dates the play's first performance to Shrove Tuesday (20 February) 1599, the play preceded the ban.[44] In any case, the text first published in 1623 may reflect later changes. Shakespeare returns to an older satiric mode when Sir Oliver Martext makes his brief appearance, since any character with "Mar" in his name would recall the Marprelate controversy. He may have had more lines in the original version, or perhaps he was made up as a recognizable individual. The play hints at both sides of the book-burning controversy. Jaques makes the familiar defense that his satire is general rather than particular, while the Duke retorts that Jaques does not have the moral authority to expose other people's sins. His argument that Jaques himself has been a libertine seems irrelevant, since converts were usually not reproached for their pre-conversion behavior. For much of the play, Jaques is not so much a satirist as an amiable grouch and the butt of other people's humor. Both Orlando and the disguised Rosalind make fun of his melancholy, and his claim to love solitude is contradicted by his constant search for someone to talk to.

Probably a discussion of satire was not what really interested Shakespeare in this play. By 1599 the Admiral's Men had staged several Robin Hood plays, and Shakespeare had referred to Robin Hood in the brief outlaw episode of *The Two Gentlemen of Verona*. He had read, perhaps soon after its publication, Thomas Lodge's *Rosalynde* (1590), which is based on a late medieval outlaw legend. The situation of a banished duke living in a forest is the background to a charming love story in which a disguised woman carries on conversations about love with a lover who fails to recognize her. Shakespeare could have known Lodge, who had been brought up in the household of the fourth Earl of Derby, father of Ferdinando (the fifth Earl) and had dedicated a book to the reclusive sixth Earl. *Rosalynde* itself had been dedicated to the Earl of Hunsdon, now the company's patron. At a time when Shakespeare was investigating the possibility of impaling the Arden arms with those of his father's family, he may have been reminded of the novel that takes place mainly in the forest of Ardennes, or Arden. Lodge, who like Jonson had converted to Catholicism, had been out of England from 1597 to 1598, earning a medical degree in Avignon, but he may have been back in London by 1599. He would not have expected to be paid for the use of "the book of the play," but its existence may explain why *As You Like It* was not published until 1623.

Though the play uses the Robin Hood motif – an outlaw court that represents an ideal alternative to a tyrannical court – the play's frankly unrealistic mode works against any political reading. The two characters not present in *Rosalynde*, Touchstone and Jaques, are also responsible for its metatheatricality. Touchstone, the clown, may have been the first part Shakespeare wrote for Robert Armin. The character's name alludes to Armin's profession as goldsmith, since he was still a proud member of his guild, but it has other obvious meanings, one sophisticated (a tester of the truth) and one – not stressed in the text as we have it – bawdy (since "stone" also means testicle).[45] Jaques sometimes refuses to be part of the theatrical illusion – and not only in his extended comparison between the world and the stage. When Orlando says, "Good day and happiness, dear Rosalind!" he retorts, "Nay, then, God b'wi'you, an ye talk in blank verse" (4.1.27–9). When the Duke has just spoken what sound like the last lines of the play, a rhyming couplet calling for a dance, Jaques interrupts proceedings, then opts out of the happy ending by leaving before the dancing starts. Since Shakespeare retained the name of Lodge's heroine while changing those of all the other characters, it is possible that there was still some sort of Rosalind cult. If so, Jaques' sulky comment, "I do not like her name," which inspires Orlando's retort, "There was no thought of pleasing you when she was christened" (3.2.262–4), might allude to the number of literary Rosalinds already in existence.

The play is unusually full of music. Shakespeare knew of the forthcoming reopening of the children's theaters, where singing was one of the main attractions, and his turn-of-the-century plays compete with them. Even *Julius Caesar*, probably his next play, adds a character not in the source, the boy musician Lucius. The early plays for the Chamberlain's Men had drawn on offstage instrumentalists, especially lute-players, but it is not clear whether the company had a good solo singer as well. Both *A Midsummer Night's Dream* and *The Merchant of Venice* include songs which can be sung by several voices or by a soloist. In *Much Ado About Nothing*, probably performed in 1598, an adult singer named Balthazar apologizes for his bad voice and is the object of harsh commentary by Benedick ("An he had been a dog that should have howled thus, they would have hanged him," 2.3.47–8). In later revivals, at least, Balthazar was probably an excellent performer, since he was played by John Wilson, a famous musician and composer. Though Amiens in *As You Like It* is clearly a professional singer, an odd feature of the published text is the introduction of "two of the banished Duke's pages" – who appear nowhere else in the play and have almost no dialogue – to sing the latest hit song, Thomas Morley's "It was a lover and his lass," first published in 1600. They must have been very young boys, chosen for their singing voices, or perhaps Shakespeare was not sure at the time of writing who would be available to take the parts. Armin could sing, so it is likely that at some point he and Audrey took over the performance of "It was a lover and his lass," as they generally do in modern productions.

As You Like It also seems intended to demonstrate that the Chamberlain's Men were equal to the private theater companies in performing female roles. The boy actor of Rosalind has the longest part in the play, and it is the scenes between her and Orlando that still give the most pleasure to audiences. Their complexity results not only from the situation of a boy playing a girl pretending to be a boy and then impersonating a capricious woman, but also from the fact that Rosalind, as Ganymede, pretends that she wants to cure Orlando of his love for Rosalind, while in fact she would be devastated if this happened. If Rosalind and Viola are parts that women still want to play, this is because their disguises expand their acting opportunities. As women – simple, loving, and totally devoted to the men in their life – they are the extreme idealization of an emotion. Those who have experienced happiness in love think that this is how they felt, and those who have not experienced it think that this is what it should be like. Rosalind grieves for her banished father only until she meets Orlando; Viola grieves for her supposedly dead brother until she meets Orsino. Rosalind's cry, "But what talk we of fathers, when there is such a man as Orlando?" (3.4.36–7), would be cruel if it were not funny. Viola has to forget her twin much of the time for the sake of the plot. As women, they exist on the surface because, as Rosalind reminds Celia when they are alone together, "Do you not know I am a woman? When I think, I must speak" (3.2.246–7). However, their plot situations force them into concealment, and the contrast between their "true" selves and their disguise creates the illusion of an inner life.

Julius Caesar

The Folio's division of Shakespeare's plays into comedies, histories, and tragedies gives the impression that, apart from Romeo and Juliet, he had steered clear of tragedy after Titus Andronicus. He and Peele had made some attempt to give a tragic shape to Titus by emphasizing the hero's initial errors in choosing the wrong man for emperor and in making a mortal enemy out of the Queen of the Goths. Romeo and Juliet offers several rationalizations for its events: Fate, error, and divine punishment for the feuding families. Shakespeare's historical plays could also be seen as tragedies, but after the publication of Sidney's Apology for Poetry in 1595 he may have thought again about the difference between the two. Sidney claimed that poetry was superior to history because, not being tied to what had actually happened, it could be more morally and emotionally satisfying. It was at about this time that Shakespeare, probably looking for other subjects from Roman history, started to read Sir Thomas North's translation of a French translation of Plutarch's Lives of the Noble Greeks and Romans. While there is no reason to believe that he always read a source immediately before using it – he could have taken notes and returned to them later – in this case the effect was probably immediate. The Greek writer had used an innovative biographical method: he not only wrote individual biographies of Greek and Roman figures that he considered to be in some way parallel – Alexander the Great and Julius Caesar, Alcibiades and Coriolanus – but added chapters comparing the two (though not all of these were completed). Like Holinshed's chronicles, these *Lives* often give alternative accounts of an event. Successive Roman historians had in any case offered such opposing views of figures like Julius Caesar that complexity was built into the subject matter, which is further complicated by Plutarch's tendency to stress personality as much as politics as a motive for action. The divided attitude toward the rebels in *1 Henry IV* recurs with the conspirators in *Julius Caesar*. Shakespeare probably knew that Essex's circle contained some people who could be described as republicans, but it is possible to give both republican and monarchist interpretations of the play. The center of this story is not Caesar, who, like Titus Andronicus, is a military hero who returns home to find only betrayal. Instead, Shakespeare focuses attention on the motives of the conspirators and the reasons for their ultimate failure.

Shakespeare had grown up with the belief that the Romans were superior to successive generations in everything except their religion, and he builds that superiority into the language of the characters. The result was a tragedy in the high style from the beginning, as *Romeo and Juliet* is not. Brutus and Cassius are hyper-conscious of being Roman, and the greatest moral pressure they can put on others is to accuse them of not being Roman enough. Even when they are angry with each other, there is grandeur in their rage. Details that conflict with perfect Romanness – Caesar's illness, Cassius's poor eyesight, Brutus's sleeplessness – remind us that they are human, but the characters themselves try to sweep them aside or re-gender them; Cassius attributes his "rash humour" to his mother, and sees the Roman willingness to submit to Caesar as "feminine." Portia (like Lady Percy) pleads with her husband to trust her with his secrets, yet is unable to survive the knowledge. Shakespeare might almost have written the play to prove, to those who saw him still as the author of *Venus and Adonis* and *Romeo and Juliet*, that he could avoid the subject of love altogether. Yet the play is saturated with love in the form of friendship, much of it destroyed by the political motives that make Brutus say that he "did love Caesar when I struck him" (3.1.184). Caesar's affection for Brutus and the relationship of Brutus and Cassius are casualties of political principle, but at their deaths Brutus and Cassius still have friends who love and praise them.

That the play was something of a sequel to *Lucrece* must have occurred to Shakespeare. The banishment of the Tarquins had put an end to kingship in Rome, and the conspirators' main motive for assassinating Caesar was their fear that he was about to undo this historic act by making himself king. Thanks to Plutarch, the political situation is ironically balanced: the assassination leads not to a revival of the republic but to the destruction of the conspirators and a triumvirate more unstable and tyrannical than Caesar's rule ever was. Plutarch's emphasis on the various errors made by the well-meaning Brutus made him an ideal example of the Aristotelian tragic hero, who must be "good" and yet guilty of "error." The play depicts the process by which such a man commits one error after another. His soliloquy in 2.1, with its unexplained beginning – "It must be by his death" – plunges the audience more deeply into a thinking mind than Shakespeare had previously gone. The meditation on Caesar and the mystique of royalty – "He would be crowned./ How that might change his nature, there's the question" (2.1.12–13) – was relevant: kingship, notoriously, had caused a personality change in Prince Hal. Other possible kings of England (the Earl of Essex, James VI of Scotland) might provoke the same speculation. Yet, although Brutus's conclusion – "So Caesar may./Then, lest he may, prevent" (2.1.27–8) – is an obvious example of faulty logic, it does not lead audiences to look for his unconscious motivations, as do Hamlet's and Macbeth's similar soliloquies. In fact, Shakespeare suppresses one obvious motive: the possibility that Brutus might be Caesar's illegitimate son. The play's argumentative structure – nearly every scene involves someone persuading someone else to do something – appealed to audiences used to the confrontational method of teaching. From the beginning there are comments on the effectiveness of the two most dramatic confrontations, the two orations in the forum scene and the quarrel between Brutus and Cassius. A contemporary satirist, almost certainly alluding to Shakespeare's play, showed how effectively the forum scene made its point:

> The many-headed multitude were drawn
> By *Brutus'* speech, that Caesar was ambitious.
> When eloquent *Mark Antony* had shown
> His virtues, who but *Brutus* then was vicious?
> Man's memory, with new, forgets the old,
> One tale is good, until another's told.[46]

Shakespeare probably read these verses, since they occur in *The Mirror of Martyrs*, a first-person account put into the mouth of the historical Sir John Oldcastle, who uses this analogy to show how his own heroic life has been forgotten – thanks, no doubt, to plays like Shakespeare's. The emphasis on the search for novelty and the fickleness of crowds perhaps had a personal meaning for Shakespeare if *2 Henry IV* had failed to match the success of its predecessor.

Henry V

Henry V makes an obvious comparison with the opening of *Julius Caesar* in the Chorus's description of the king's return to London after Agincourt:

> The Mayor and all his brethren, in best sort,
> Like to the senators of th'antique Rome

With the plebians swarming at their heels,
Go forth and fetch their conquering Caesar in.
(5.0.25–8)

The Chorus, however, draws attention to the moral superiority of the "Christian king" (1.2.241) who orders his troops to sing "Non nobis Domine" and refuses to allow any celebration of his personal valor, "being free from vainness and self-glorious pride" (5.0.20). It seems likely, then, that this speech was written later than *Julius Caesar*, in which Caesar's triumphal procession is condemned by Marullus and Flavius as a sign of pride and the citizens' presence as a sign of ingratitude. This does not necessarily mean that the play itself was written later, since the relation of the Chorus to the rest of the play is one of the puzzles about *Henry V*.

Because *Edward III* had been tactfully removed from the repertory, Shakespeare was able to adapt his new subject matter to what often seems like the same pattern. There is, again, an English claim to the throne through the female line and a brief discussion of how to make war in France without being distracted by a Scottish invasion at home. As Giorgio Melchiori suggests, Edward's indignant question, when his secretary pretends not to understand that he wants to write a love letter to a woman – "What thinkst thou I did bid thee praise a horse?"[47] – may reappear in the absurd scene (*Henry V* 4.2) in which the Dauphin waxes lyrical over the horse to whom he has written a sonnet. However, instead of a boorish Scottish king, there is a small role for a sympathetically depicted Scottish captain; he compares favorably with an over-emotional Irish captain and wins the approval of the obviously sympathetic Welsh captain who is the play's main comic character.

2 Henry IV had been so full of rumors and false expectations – notably Falstaff's, so crushingly defeated at the end – that its effect was to question any attempt to tell the truth about the past. In *Henry V* Shakespeare went to the opposite extreme, apparently accepting as true every legend about Henry's greatness and surrounding him with admiring followers who praise even such actions as the rejection of Falstaff and the killing of the French prisoners. The only character who soliloquizes is Henry himself, but his soliloquies do not mirror a decision-making process; he does not doubt his rightness. At some point, Shakespeare decided to give the play a still more classical structure, one that almost worked against the theatrical context with constant reminders of how much greater the reality was than the stage could ever show.

There is no Chorus in the 1600 Quarto. Either this is a shortened version of what Shakespeare had already written, or the choruses were added later. In all discussions of this question, the most controversial passage is the reference – unusually topical for Shakespeare – to a contemporary campaign against the rebels in Ireland:

Were now the General of our gracious Empress,
As in good time he may, from Ireland coming,
Bringing rebellion broachèd on his sword,

253

How many would the peaceful city quit
To welcome him! Much more, and much more cause,
Did they this Harry.

(5.0.30–5)

It is usually assumed that these lines refer to the Earl of Essex, who had left for Ireland on 27 March 1599. By September of the same year, his campaign had turned out to be a failure, and Essex, convinced that he was being maligned in his absence, made an unauthorized return to court which led to his being placed under house arrest. The lines could not, then, have been spoken on the stage after that date, but this would be no reason for cutting all of the Chorus's speeches. The fact that they appear in the 1623 Folio does not prove that the general was not Essex, since James I had been very sympathetic toward the earl and in any case the Irish expedition was now almost twenty-five years in the past. However, I incline to Warren D. Smith's suggestion that the passage that looks like a premature celebration of an Essex victory was instead inserted later, in order to congratulate Essex's successor, Lord Mountjoy, who did in fact win a decisive victory ("more electrifying than Henry's at Agincourt") over the rebels on Christmas Eve 1601.[48] As Richard Dutton points out, praising a recognizable living person for a victory that had already happened sounds more like Shakespeare than betting on a victory for someone whose career was already somewhat tarnished when he left for Ireland.[49]

In August of 1600 the play was published, though there had been an order to "stay" its printing (and that of several other plays). The title page mentions not only the Battle of Agincourt but also "Auntient Pistol," probably to distinguish this book from *The Famous Victories*, which had finally been printed in 1598, obviously in the hope of catching buyers who wanted to read the Falstaff play. *Henry V* did not, however, carry Shakespeare's name on the title page. He himself may have wanted to keep it out of print, either because he was still unsatisfied with it or because he realized that it might be politically embarrassing. *2 Henry IV* was entered in the Stationers' Register on 23 August and published later that year as "by William Shakespeare." Because their original publisher reissued *The First Part of the Contention* and *The True Tragedy of Richard Duke of York* in 1600, along with the Quarto of *Henry V*, it has been plausibly suggested that the Chamberlain's Men had performed a revised version of the old Henry VI plays as sequels to *Henry V*, which refers to them in its Epilogue as works "which oft our stage hath shown" (13).[50]

The experience of revising the early histories may have influenced Shakespeare's writing of the later ones. In particular, he seems to have designed Henry V as an antitype to Richard III, with the scene of Henry's wanderings in disguise the night before Agincourt a development from Richard's (undramatized) decision, the night before Bosworth, to "play the eavesdropper" in order to detect potential deserters. Henry's wooing of Katherine of France is a light-hearted version of Richard Gloucester's wooing of Lady Anne: both men, who are responsible for the deaths of the woman's friends and relatives, use humor to defuse her emotional response to the courtship. Having taken the trouble to make the plays more clearly unified, Shakespeare must surely have wanted them seen as a coherent whole, but the Bishops' Ban probably made this impossible. Perhaps because Sir John Hayward's *First Part of the Reign of Henry IV* (1599) had been applied to the contemporary political situation (Hayward would be committed to the Tower in July 1600), it had been ordered "That no English histories bee printed except they be allowed by some of her majesty's Privy Council." Whereas it had previously been assumed that plays already licensed for performance were also fit to print, they now had to be "allowed by such as have authority." It is unlikely that Shakespeare's history cycle was ever performed as a complete sequence until the twentieth century, so its epic sweep may have first become visible only to readers of the Folio.

Quite apart from the reference to Ireland, the choruses to *Henry V* show that Shakespeare had been thinking about the relation of the theater to history, on the one hand, and to its audience on the other. He might have done so even without the influence of Jonson, but it is likely that from this point on he was constantly aware of what his colleague was doing. Ernst Honigmann thinks that the two dramatists had an ongoing argument about how far the stage could be allowed to deal in fantasy and improbability.[51] Given Jonson's later satire on the "three rusty swords" that make up the pathetically inadequate battle scenes and the Chorus that "wafts you o'er the seas," it was Shakespeare's treatment of history in particular that divided them.[52] Jonson is not now known as a writer of history plays, but in 1599 he collaborated with Chettle and Dekker on *Robert II: The Scots Tragedy*, and in 1602 he would be paid by Henslowe for a play called *Richard Crookback*, presumably his attempt to show how *Richard III* should have been written. He did not see fit to publish either play among his acknowledged works, which may mean that he himself did not feel that he had succeeded with the genre, but he continued to experiment with it in his last years. Though there is no Jonsonian history to compare with Shakespeare's, in 1599 each dramatist wrote a play (*Henry V* and *Every Man Out of His Humour*) within a framework that allowed him to say something about theater. In Jonson, the theory is almost as important as the play. Two onstage spectators draw comparisons with classical prototypes; the straw man raises objections, which are predictably refuted by a "friend of the author." It is important, for Jonson, that the poet's intention should be understood, since he is the sole creator of his "fable" and it has no prior reality. Shakespeare's Chorus, by contrast, presents the author as someone trying – with the help of a mediating Muse – to do justice to a pre-existing story, while aware that the reality transcends his feeble attempts to recreate it. He may represent Shakespeare's views, and some like to think that Shakespeare himself played the role. But the speaker of a prologue, though he wore a black cloak and a laurel wreath, was the representative of the actors, not the author himself.[53] He refers to the author in the third person, just as Jonson's speakers do, and his apparent apology for the "flat, unraisèd spirits" who are to recreate England's greatest conquest on an "unworthy scaffold" is a reminder of the difference between lawful and unlawful magic.

Notes

1. Stern, "'A small-beer health to his second day'."
2. *Conversations*, in Herford and Simpson, 1: 217–18.
3. Rowe, "Some Account of the Life &c of Mr. William Shakespear," 8.
4. Riggs, *Ben Jonson: A Life*, 53.
5. See Cerasano, "Edward Alleyn's 'Retirement' 1597–1600," and id., "Philip Henslowe and the Elizabethan Court."
6. *Sir John Oldcastle, Part I*, in *The Oldcastle Controversy*, ed. Corbin and Sedge.
7. Entry of 1599, *Henslowe's Diary*, 126.
8. Chambers, *WS*, 2: 198, quoted from *Cecil Papers*, ci, 16, in H.M.C. iii.148.
9. This account is summarized from Fripp, *Richard Quyny*, 132–60.
10. Repr. from Chambers, *WS*, 2: 102; the insertion is his.
11. Honan, 242–3.
12. Chambers, *WS*, 2: 103.
13. Fripp, *Richard Quyny*, 160, 159.
14. Evidence of Henry Johnson and John Gossage, given 26 and 27 Apr. 1600, repr. in Wickham, 376–7.
15. Knutson, *The Repertory of Shakespeare's Company, 1594–1613*, 79.
16. Sohmer, *Shakespeare's Mystery Play*, 4.
17. M. Eccles, "Elizabethan Actors II," "John Hemminge," 458.
18. Schoenbaum, 210.
19. Burgess, *Shakespeare*, 158.
20. Robert Armin, dedicatory epistle to *The Italian Tailor and His Boy*, in *Collected Works*, A3.
21. Chambers, *ES*, 2: 364–5; *Julius Caesar*, ed. Daniell, 12.
22. *Julius Caesar*, ed. Daniell, 15–16; Sohmer, *Shakespeare's Mystery Play*, ch. 4.
23. Knutson, *The Repertory of Shakespeare's Company, 1594–1613*, 81–3, citing Chambers, *ES*, 2: 177–8.
24. Aubrey, *Brief Lives*, 2: 226.
25. Schoenbaum, 240.
26. Quoted in McCabe, "Elizabethan Satire and the Bishops' Ban of 1599," 188.
27. Wickham, 307.
28. For how often the children's companies performed, see Farley-Hills, "How Often Did the Eyases Fly?" As he points out, neither company could have made a profit, however much it charged for admission, by playing only once a week. However, this may be precisely why they went out of business. See Dutton, "The Revels Office and the Boy Companies," 331.
29. See Lawrence, *"Who the Devil Taught thee so much Italian?,"* 130–2, 142–51.
30. *The Second Part of the Return from Parnassus*, 1770–3.
31. Bate, *Soul of the Age*, 377–81.

32. John Chamberlain called him this, reporting his death to Dudley Carleton on 17 Dec 1612. Birch, *The Court and Times of James the First*, 1: 214.

33. Jonson, *Poetaster*, ed. Cain, 40.

34. Drayton, *England's Heroical Epistles*, Sonnet 46.

35. See e.g. Jackson, "Frances Meres and the Cultural Context of Shakespeare's Rival Poet Sonnets," 229–33, and Duncan-Jones, *Shakespeare: Upstart Crow to Sweet Swan, 1592–1623*, 144.

36. Amour 12, in *Idea's Mirrour, Amours in Quatorzaines*, in *The Works of Michael Drayton*, ed. Hebel, 1: 103.

37. Sir Walter Scott, who was lame himself, argued this. Most recently, René Weis, in *Shakespeare Revealed*, has made the same claim.

38. For Donne/dun, see John Davies of Hereford, Epigram 97 in *The Scourge of Folly* (in *Complete Works*, ed. Grosart): "Which doing right makes bright the name of Dunne." The most famous pun on Donne/done is Donne's own in "A Hymn to God the Father."

39. Champion, *François Villon, sa vie et son temps*, 2: 94.

40. Williams, "The Poetic Debate of Edmund Prys and Wiliam [*sic*] Cynwal."

41. Barbara Mowat and Paul Werstine cite a suggestion by Steven May "in private communication" that Shakespeare's Sonnet 99 and number 16 from Constable's *Diana* might have been written in response to "a poetic competition or challenge." *Shakespeare's Sonnets*, ed. Mowat and Werstine, 329–30.

42. *The Sonnets and A Lover's Complaint*, ed. Kerrigan, 13–14. James Hutton's classic study of translations and imitations of the Marianus epigram – "Analogues of Shakespeare's Sonnets 153–4: Contributions to the History of a Theme" – was unable to find the precise source of Shakespeare's version.

43. Edmondson and Wells, *Shakespeare's Sonnets*, 104.

44. *As You Like It*, ed. Dusinberre, 37–40.

45. In Armin's own play, *Two Maids of Moreclacke*, he doubled the part of a real fool with that of a clever servant called Tutch (Touch), perhaps alluding to his earlier role as well as to his profession.

46. Weever, *The Mirror of Martyrs*, 4.

47. *Edward III* 2.1.98: see Melchiori's note on the passage.

48. W. D. Smith, "The Henry V Choruses in the First Folio," 42. I am grateful to David Bevington for this reference.

49. Dutton, "'Methinks the truth should live from age to age': The Dating and Contexts of *Henry V*," 197, 202.

50. William Montgomery, "The Contention of York and Lancaster: A Critical Edition" (D. Phil., Oxford, 1985), xxxvi, cited in Warren, "The Quarto and Folio Texts of *2 Henry VI*," 205.

51. Honigmann, *Shakespeares's Impact on His Contemporaries*, chs. 5 and 6 (pp. 91–120). See also Bednarz, *Shakespeare and the Poets' War*, 29–131.

52. Lines 10 and 116 from the Prologue to *Every Man in His Humour* as published in 1616, perhaps written not long before that date.

53. Stern, "'A small-beer health to his second day'," 180–2.

12

"These Words Are Not Mine"

1599–1601

Claudius. I have nothing with this answer, Hamlet. These words are not mine.
Hamlet. No, nor mine now.

(*Hamlet* 3.2.94–6)

Like much of what Hamlet says during his pretense of madness, this reply is based on a proverb, which, being anonymous, illustrates his point: once words are out of one's mouth, they are no longer one's own. At the turn of the century, as Shakespeare became better known, the question of the authenticity and appropriation of his words became more complicated. 1598 was the first year in which his name appeared on the title pages of any of his published plays: the second Quartos of *Richard II* and *Richard III*, both of which had appeared anonymously in the previous year, and the first Quarto of *Love's Labour's Lost* (possibly the second, if, as the title page implies, it was a corrected version of an earlier publication). As this chapter will show, he began to be quoted out of context and recontextualized in ways that transformed his meaning; his work was treated as a means to an end that could have been dangerous for him and his fellow-actors. He was also involved with two multi-authored projects, one acknowledged (his one surviving poem praising a book by someone else) and the other anonymous (a scene for a collaborative play that had run into trouble with the Master of the Revels).

Recognition: *Palladis Tamia* and *The Passionate Pilgrim*

The turn of the century saw the publication of a series of volumes under the title *Wit's Commonwealth*. These were collections of quotations, or commonplaces, from English writers, carefully coordinated under the general editorship of John

The Life of William Shakespeare: A Critical Biography, First Edition. Lois Potter.
© 2012 Lois Potter. Published 2012 by Blackwell Publishing Ltd.

Bodenham. The project was essentially a patriotic one: "to replace the ancient canon of authors and rewrite commonplaces in the language of a new canon of modern poets."[1] The first anthology (a collection of prose extracts) appeared in 1597; it was followed by the one that is now best known, Francis Meres' *Palladis Tamia* (1598), with the third and fourth volumes appearing in 1599 and 1604.[2] Meres' book (for which his subtitle, *Wit's Treasury*, is an approximate translation) was a collection of similitudes or comparisons, perhaps inspired by Plutarch's parallel lives. His method meant that he had to compare every English writer with one in another language. When he came to Shakespeare, he of course paired him with Plautus and Seneca for comedy and tragedy respectively, and with Ovid for verse. His claim that "the sweet witty soul of *Ovid* lives in mellifluous and honey-tongued *Shakespeare*" may have been a reply to Sir John Davies, who had already said when Chapman published *Ovid's Banquet of Sense* (1595) that though the Roman poet slept in death, "his waking soul in *Chapman* lives."[3] Perhaps there was some debate at this time as to which of the two writers was more Ovidian.

Fortunately for later scholars, Meres named the works by Shakespeare that he considered proofs of his achievement. He may not have known about all of them – the Henry VI plays are not included – but, since his book was entered into the Stationers' Register on 7 September, it is certain that any play on his list must have been staged or in print by mid-1598. Several of those he names (*The Two Gentlemen of Verona*, *The Comedy of Errors*, and *King John*) were not printed until 1623. The fact that he refers only to *Henry the Fourth* leaves it unclear whether he knew of both parts of this play. In 1598 only Part One was in print; Part Two followed in 1600. It is Meres who mentions a play called *Love's Labour's Won*, thus provoking endless speculation (see Chapter 7 above). His reference to Shakespeare's "sugared Sonnets among his private friends, &c" is particularly interesting, since it indicates the existence of more than the two that were to be printed in the following year. (And what did he mean by "&c"? More room for speculation.) Michael Drayton, who in 1599 published a sonnet comparing himself to other sonneteers, mentioned Sidney, Daniel, and Constable but not Shakespeare.[4] He never republished this sonnet, probably because he knew that, after 1609, omitting Shakespeare's name might look like an insult. Was he not a "private friend" in 1599, or was he so much of one that he respected Shakespeare's desire to keep his sonnet private?

The Passionate Pilgrim was not part of the "Wit" sequence. "Passionate" had been a fashionable word since Thomas Watson's early sonnet cycle, *Hekatompathia* (1584), which means, as its subtitle says, a *Passionate Century* [100 poems] *of Love*. The word was everywhere in the 1590s. Another W.S., William Smith, published in 1596 a sonnet sequence called *Chloris, or the Complaint of the passionate despised Shepherd*. A "passionate palmer" appears in Robert Greene's *Never Too Late* (1590),[5] and in 1606 there would be a *Passionate Hermit* (the subtitle of *Dolarny's Primrose*, by John Reynolds). Perhaps more surprisingly, "pilgrim" was also a key term in love poetry, with a new topicality in 1599 because of the Pope's recent announcement of pardons for anyone who made a pilgrimage to Rome in 1600.

Shakespeare must surely have seen *The Passionate Pilgrim*, printed by William Jaggard, since, notoriously, it is ascribed to him on the title page. It contains four sonnets and a song that are undoubtedly his, along with a number of other poems, some already published by other writers and some of unknown authorship. The poems were printed only on one side of the paper. The intention may have been to make a mere twenty poems look like more. The book sold well, so people apparently did not feel cheated. They might even have welcomed the publishing gimmick as a way of leaving space for them to add their own favorite poems, or to cut pages out without losing what was on the other side.[6] Anyone looking casually into the volume would have thought it genuinely Shakespearean. It opens with two sonnets that would be published in 1609, in different versions, as 138 and 144, followed by one of the sonnets from *Love's Labour's Lost*. The collection also includes two more poems from the play, as well as a number of sonnets and other poems on the subject of Venus and Adonis and perjured or frustrated love. Two of the other authors can be identified as Richard Barnfield – whose *Lady Pecunia*, the source of one sonnet, had been published by William Jaggard's brother John in 1598 – and Bartholomew Griffin, author of *Fidessa* (1596). The collection also includes a few stanzas from Marlowe's poem beginning "Come live with me and be my love," and one stanza from a reply to it that would later be attributed to Sir Walter Ralegh. Poems 15 to 20 have a separate title page calling them "Sonnets to divers notes of musicke"; number 16 is Dumaine's song from *Love's Labour's Lost*.

Because of the Barnfield connection, Jaggard must have known that some of the poems in his book were not written by Shakespeare. *The Passionate Pilgrim* is usually described as a publishing fraud, interesting only as evidence that Shakespeare's name was considered a selling point in 1599 – perhaps, the Arden editors think, because Meres' comments about the "sugared sonnets" created a demand for them.[7] Shakespeare might have been annoyed to see his poems reprinted out of context, especially if (which is not certain) the ones from *Love's Labour's Lost* were "intentionally bad."[8] If, as Katherine Duncan-Jones suggests, Shakespeare was the "W.S." whose "certain other sonnetes," along with the "Amours" of "J.D.," were entered in the Stationers' Register early in the following January but apparently never published, there might be reason to think that he wanted to set things right.[9] However, as Patrick Cheney has shown, the book can also be seen as a tribute. Cheney points out that no one seems to have complained about it in 1599, not even Barnfield or Griffin, who had more reason than Shakespeare to be angry at the misattribution of their poems.[10] Perhaps all these writers took the phrase "by Shakespeare" to mean not only *written by* Shakespeare but also *in the persona of* or *according to* Shakespeare (as in the German *bei*).[11] The sonnets on *Venus and Adonis* are clearly inspired by Shakespeare's poem, since they all feature an amorous Venus courting a very young Adonis who either rejects or ignores her. A reader who knew the plays as well as the poem might have recognized other narrative voices. The theme of forswearing, which dominates the collection, recalls *Love's Labour's Lost*, though in the poems, unlike the play, it is women who are forsworn. Many of the poems could be put into the mouths of Navarre and his courtiers, who speak for much of the time in a mixture of quatrains and couplets that could easily be mistaken for sonnets. They seem to belong to the same cynical world as the so-called Dark Lady sonnets. Finally, the poem that opens, "Good night, good rest," and rhymes "sorrow" with "come again tomorrow" echoes *Romeo and Juliet* with its repeated goodnights and Juliets:

> Good night, good night; parting is such sweet sorrow
> That I shall say goodnight till it be morrow.
> (2.2.185–6)

Whoever assembled the poems for Jaggard's volume must have calculated that few prospective buyers would be able to resist it after seeing the opening of the first poem:

> When my love swears that she is made of truth,
> I do believe her, though I know she lies ...

This was later published as number 138 in the 1609 collection. Like it, the second sonnet (later number 144) is about a relationship with an unfaithful woman and with another man who apparently lets himself be tempted by her. Its account of a speaker torn between "a man right fair" and "a woman coloured ill" has been the starting point for most attempts to find a story in *Shakespeare's Sonnets*, published ten years later. In the context of 1599, the two poems look more like a response to Marlowe's translations of Ovid or to Donne's Ovid-inspired elegies. Michael Drayton, who claimed that he was partly imitating Ovid, had written a sonnet beginning "An evil spirit, your beauty haunts me still," first published in 1599, which concludes, "Thus am I still provoked to every evil/ By this good wicked spirit, sweet angel-devil."[12] In what later became Sonnet 144, Shakespeare may be taking Drayton's idea to its furthest extreme. Both writers depict a culture of illicit love and brothels, experienced through the persona of a sophisticated young man who despises most of the people he meets there. In Shakespeare's version, the angel and devil are embodied in a man and woman, but the conclusion, where the speaker says that he will know for certain whether his good and bad angels are betraying him only if "my bad angel fire my good one out," turns nasty by introducing the subject of venereal disease. The poem that exists in a somewhat revised version as Sonnet 138 is more urbane. Its final lines in 1599 were:

> Therefore I'll lie with love, and love with me,
> Since that our faults in love thus smothered be.

261

In 1609 the pun would be considerably sharper:

> Therefore I lie with her, and she with me,
> And in our faults by lies we flattered be.

It can be read either as sad or as wryly amused. In *Othello*, the same pun would express the hero's jealous hysteria.

Duncan-Jones and Woudhuysen wonder whether Barnfield and Griffin, both of whom had Midlands connections, might have colluded in the publication of *The Passionate Pilgrim*.[13] It is even possible that Shakespeare himself used this opportunity to test the waters before deciding whether to publish the mainly misogynistic and bawdy poems that are numbered 127 to152 in the 1609 edition. In that case, he can be called a collaborator on what – however it happened – is surely a collaborative volume. As Cheney says, it "coheres in presenting the printed voice of a single authorial persona, singing a complaint against love, beauty, and the female sex."[14] Especially after the book-burning of 1599, this was probably not the persona that Shakespeare, as he grew older, wished to present as his.

Quotation: *Belvedere, England's Parnassus,* and the Parnassus Plays

Shakespeare may have been somewhat more pleased with his representation in two new collections published in 1600. John Bodenham again sponsored these anthologies of sententiae based on English poems and (for the first time) plays: *England's Parnassus* (2,350 quotations) and *Belvedere* (4,482 quotations) were edited, respectively, by Robert Allott and Anthony Munday. Many of these quotations are attributed, though not always correctly. When they are rightly assigned, Shakespeare has a total of ninety-five quotations in *Parnassus* and 214 in *Belvedere*, which is the anthology that makes most use of plays. As the fourth most frequently quoted author in *Belvedere*, he lags only behind Drayton, Spenser, and Daniel (unless *Edward III* is counted as his, in which case he ties with the last two). His most-quoted work is *Lucrece*. Jonson, on the other hand, is represented by a mere seven entries – as against forty-seven for *Richard II* alone.[15] Admittedly, Shakespeare had been writing for the stage a good deal longer, and had put more plays into print, but even so the discrepancy must have been rather humiliating, especially since Jonson kept a commonplace book and cultivated the epigram as a genre.

The reason *Belvedere* includes so many quotations is that none of them is more than two lines long. Making them fit this pattern required some rewriting, presumably by the editor Anthony Munday, who can thus be described, with Bodenham, as one of Shakespeare's (and many other people's) early collaborators.

The object of the anthologist was to make playbook quotations as untheatrical as possible. Words that identified a speaker or a context were usually removed, so that the quotation could be generally applicable. Shakespeare, glancing through *Belvedere* to see how much of his work had been thought worth quoting, may have been relieved to find that he was no longer only the poet of "I'll be a park and thou shalt be my deer" but a source of wisdom, however conventional. Quotability was exactly what he had been aiming for ever since his schooldays, when he had learned many *sententiae* out of context. Even so, he might have been surprised at some of the entries, and still more surprised at the headings under which they had been listed. Friar Laurence's many couplets were an obvious quarry, as when he tells Romeo, "Pronounce this sentence then:/ Women may fall, when there's no strength in men" (*Romeo and Juliet* 2.3.79–80). The anthologist, seizing on the signposted "sentence," not only wrote it down but, missing the point, placed it under the heading "Of Woman." *2 Henry IV* was published too late to be used, but even *1 Henry IV* was surprisingly under-represented, with nothing at all under the heading of its obvious theme of "Honor." The one line quoted from the play comes under the heading of "Gluttonie": "Advantage feeds him fat, while men delay." Presumably the editor, given the line without context, assumed that it must be about Falstaff. In fact, it is Henry IV's metaphor for the growing threat of the Percies' rebellion (*1 Henry IV* 3.2.180). Whether Shakespeare found this blatant misreading funny or annoying, it would have drawn his attention to something he may not fully have recognized as yet – the way in which the language of one part of his play sometimes seeps into another part. Just as Henry IV's "And then I stole all courtesy from heaven" temporarily puts him on the same level as the highwayman Falstaff, so Falstaff's fatness becomes part of the texture of the play itself. As Shakespeare continued to write and revise, this kind of poetic interconnection – what the nineteenth century would call organic unity and the twentieth would study as imagery – was something he would develop still further. Reading so many *sententiae* may, however, have had a negative effect on him. Only a few years later, in *Othello*, Shakespeare would make Brabantio ridicule the "sentences" quoted at him by the Duke of Venice, on the grounds that they are "strong on both sides" and can mean anything (1.3.220). Some of the lines in which John of Gaunt attempts to console Bolingbroke on his banishment in the *Richard II* Quarto of 1597 are absent from the 1623 Folio. Perhaps seeing them in *Belvedere* made Shakespeare decide that this scene was, as it were, too full of quotations.

He may perhaps have known what students at Cambridge thought of him, as evidenced in three semi-allegorical plays, produced at St. John's College between 1599 and 1602, about the journey to Parnassus (the university degree) and the return from it into the "real world." Only the third of these was published, in 1606, as *The Returne from Pernassus, or, The Scourge of Simony*. It is, however, really a sequel to another "Return" play, the second in the series, which is full of

Shakespeare quotations. A fop quotes *Lucrece* without attribution,[16] then demonstrates how he intends to woo his mistress, beginning with a garbled version of the couplet from the first stanza of *Venus and Adonis*: "Pardon fair lady, though sick thoughted Gullio make a main unto thee, and like a bold faced suitor gins to woo thee" (983–5). The simile about Venus does not work for Gullio, since he actually *is* a bold-faced suitor, but this does not bother him. The witty Ingenioso, who has been asked to stand in for the lady, comments in an aside, "We shall have nothing but pure Shakespeare, and shreds of poetry that he hath gathered at the theatres" (986–7). Gullio goes on to throw in some lines from *Romeo and Juliet*, followed by more *Venus* and a bit of *The Spanish Tragedy*. "Faith gentleman," simpers Ingenioso, in character, "your reading is wonderful in our English poets" (1004–5).

In the final "Parnassus" play, *Belvedere* receives what amounts to a contemporary review. Judicio, a press-corrector, and Ingenioso, an aspiring author, complain of the anthologies produced by people like Bodenham, "an old goose that sits hatching up those eggs which have been filched from the nest[s] of crows and kestrels."[17] With a copy of *Belvedere* as an example, they proceed to ridicule everything about it, down to its Latin motto and printer's ornament. Then they turn to the list of authors from whom the selections were chosen, using it as the springboard for the series of encapsulated judgments (for instance, that Jonson was "the wittiest fellow of a brickmaker in England") that are the best known part of this play.[18] Judicio, however, though he praises Shakespeare's two poems and their "heart-throbbing" or perhaps "heart-robbing" lines, goes on to add that it would be better, "Could but some graver subject him content,/ Without love's foolish lazy languishment" (1.2.303–4). By the end of the century, this was a singularly uninformed comment on the author of the English history plays and *Julius Caesar*, but for anyone who had just read *The Passionate Pilgrim* it might have seemed appropriate. In a later scene, the unemployed scholars who audition with "Burbage" and "Kemp" complain that actors have become undeservedly famous for "mouthing words that better wits haue framed" (Part 2, 5.1.1927). Yet they appear not to know who framed the words of the plays (*Richard III* and *The Spanish Tragedy)* that are being used as audition pieces.

Appropriation: The Essex Rebellion

A more alarming case in which Shakespeare's words seemed to escape their context occurred at the beginning of the new century. Since his unauthorized return from Ireland in September 1599, the Earl of Essex had been in limbo while the queen and the Privy Council tried to decide what to do with him. In 1600, when they were contemplating trying him for treason, Sir Edward Coke drew up an "Analytical Abstract" of the charges that might be made against him. He included a reference to Sir John Hayward's "treasonable book of Henry IV" and to "the Earl himself being so often present at the playing thereof." Hayward's *The First Part of the Life and Reign of King Henry IV* had been published in February 1599 with a dedication to Essex, but Hayward was imprisoned only in July of 1600, clearly as part of the process of compiling evidence against the earl. Since his book was too long and detailed to be dramatized as it stood, and reading it aloud would hardly count as "playing," Jonathan Bate argues that this accusation must mean "that the Earl of Essex was often present at *a play that told the same story as Hayward*."[19] The earl's enthusiasm for the play was presumably something that could be verified from the observation of other playgoers, although Coke may not have known or cared whether what Essex really liked was a play about the deposition of Richard II, rather than Shakespeare's much more popular play about the reign of Henry IV. In the fall of 1599 two of Essex's followers, the earls of Southampton and Rutland, were said to be seeing plays every day,[20] but the earl himself was in no condition to do so, since for the rest of that year and the next he was either under arrest, confined to his house, in virtual exile in the country, or seriously ill.

However, one fact that is not in doubt is that a play about Richard II was performed by the Lord Chamberlain's Men on the afternoon of Saturday 7 February 1601, at the personal request of some of Essex's followers. That the play was Shakespeare's seems very likely; the company would not have had another Richard II play in its repertory. Interrogated later, Augustine Phillips, representing the company, assured the Privy Council that the actors had been reluctant to perform what they considered an old play that no one would want to see, and that they were paid 40 shillings extra for their trouble. Meanwhile, Essex, who did not attend the performance, had been ordered to court on the next day. Convinced that there was a plot to murder him, he imprisoned the privy councilors who had come to escort him there and rode into the City of London, shouting incoherently about danger to the state. After it became apparent that no one was going to rise on his behalf, he finally allowed himself to be arrested. His trial and execution quickly followed.

Was there any connection between *Richard II* and the attempted coup? Bate believes that Essex did in fact see himself as Shakespeare's Bolingbroke, and that this fantasy led him to a fatal mistake when he emerged from his house in the Strand:

> Why did Essex turn right into the city instead of left for the court? Because he wanted people to come to their windows and cry out in his support, as they had for Bullingbrook. Subliminally, or even overtly, he was re-enacting the play in reality. ... He wanted to be acclaimed like Bullingbrook, but ironically the popular reaction was like that which greeted Richard: "No man cried, 'God save him',/ No Joyful tongue gave him his welcome home."[21]

There would have been nothing strange in the earl's being influenced by a role model: Francis Bacon later suggested that Essex had attempted his coup in imitation of the Duke de Guise, who captured Paris in 1589 with only a small band of followers.[22] If Essex really had raised his rebellion under the influence of Shakespeare's play, his enthusiasm might have been a kiss of death to its author. In the end, it does not seem to have done Shakespeare any harm – because this interpretation must surely have been known to be false. Linking the play with Hayward's history, as Coke did, was intended to establish a parallel between Essex's motivation and Bolingbroke's. But no one who knew *Richard II* could seriously think that anyone would attend it repeatedly in order to watch Bolingbroke. How the play was remembered is evident from the heading under which most of its lines were quoted in *Belvedere*: "Of griefe, sorrowe, &c." The grief, as embodied in a great actor like Burbage, was one which all spectators (including the disgraced Essex and his followers) could make their own:

> Oh, that I were as great
> As is my grief, or lesser than my name!
> Or that I could forget what I have been,
> Or not remember what I must be now!
> (3.3.136–9)

Richard's elaborately expressed desire to exchange his regality for the life of a hermit ("I'll give my jewels for a set of beads,/ My gorgeous palace for a hermitage," 3.3.147–8) was one that several courtiers had already claimed for themselves. Essex in particular was constantly announcing his intention – as a friend put it as early as 1591 – "to retire to some cell in the country, and to live there, as a man never desirous to look a good man in the face again."[23] The most obvious parallel between Richard and Essex is the earl's fear that his departure on the Irish expedition had left him exposed to betrayal at the court. As the Duke of York tells the Queen in *Richard II*:

> Your husband, he is gone to save far off,
> Whilst others come to make him lose at home.
> (2.2.80–1)

But it is possible that the play was of much greater interest to the followers who commissioned it than it was to Essex himself. One of them, as Bate pointed out, was Sir Charles Percy, a direct descendant of the Percy family who figure so prominently in the Henry IV plays. If he had already seen the depiction of Hotspur and Northumberland in *1* and *2 Henry IV*, he might have wanted to see how they had been portrayed in the earlier play. It is interesting that the person interrogated by the Privy Council was Augustine Phillips, probably the company's usual paymaster at this period, rather than the author. This is because, clearly, no one thought that either the play or the actors could be considered treasonous, but it was important to know who had commissioned the performance. Elizabeth herself had the company play at court the night before Essex's execution.

Attribution: *Love's Martyr*

The term "commonplace," far from being pejorative, celebrated the universal applicability of an idea or expression. The commonplace book that grammar school students had been taught to keep was a collection of "places" – topics – that were available to everyone, like common fields. But, just as some landowners were starting to enclose their fields in order to make them more productive, a fact that would soon impinge on Shakespeare's Stratford existence, so some authors were beginning to resent the appropriation of their words. The belated appearance of Marlowe's unfinished *Hero and Leander* (with Chapman's completion of it) was one of the most exciting literary events of 1598. In the same year, Jonson's *Every Man in His Humour* depicted the fop Matheo trying to pass off some lines from it as his own. "Steal from the dead?" says the play's hero with horror. Jonson, a scholar given to footnoting the sources of his works, felt strongly about attribution. Though Shakespeare might have read Marlowe's poem in 1592–3, when the two poets were both working on their Ovidian tales, it was only after its publication that he felt able to refer openly to it. As if to ensure that no one thought *he* was stealing from the dead, Shakespeare made Phebe in *As You Like It* acknowledge "Whoever loved, that loved not at first sight?" as the work of a "dead shepherd." Shakespeare probably knew the authorship of the lines beginning "Come live with me and be my love," printed anonymously in *The Passionate Pilgrim*, since he made Hugh Evans sing part of it in *The Merry Wives of Windsor*. It was only in 1600 that *England's Helicon* printed a fuller text of the same poem, called (perhaps in allusion to the title of the book where it first appeared) "The Passionate Shepherd to His Love." That Phebe calls the author of *Hero and Leander* a shepherd may be due to the pastoral context of *As You Like It*, but it is also possible that Shakespeare already knew the title of Marlowe's pastoral poem – or, since *As You Like It* was published only in 1623, that he inserted the reference at a later date.

It was for a volume of 1601 called *Love's Martyr* that Shakespeare wrote one of his strangest works: the short poem beginning "Let the bird of loudest lay" that is usually called "The Phoenix and Turtle" (or turtledove). It was one of a small group of poems placed at the end of the book. The others were by three other well-known poet-dramatists, Jonson, Marston, and Chapman, and by "Ignoto" (author unknown). There may be a link with the 1599 collection, since a passionate pilgrim, figuratively speaking, *is* love's martyr. In Robert Tofte's poetic collection *Alba* (1598), the authorial persona declares that he had vowed to travel like a pilgrim, "At my sweet Saint her Shrine to sacrifice" (B6ᵛ), and he later calls himself "a Martyr for religious Love" (C6). Tofte was a theatergoer: his one well-known poem tells of going to see *Love's Labour's Lost* and losing his mistress there. Here, his imagery derives from *Romeo and Juliet*.[24] Both plays incorporated sonnets as part of their dialogue, and Tofte is returning the compliment.

Just as *Venus and Adonis* is the absent center of *The Passionate Pilgrim*, Robert Chester's poem is the center of *Love's Martyr*, and the other poems refer to it, if sometimes obliquely. Its title page claims that it is a translation of an Italian poem by Torquato Caeliano, also including the "true legend of famous King Arthur, the last of the nine Worthies," which is "the first *Essay* of a new *Brytish* [that is, Welsh] Poet." In other words, the book is presented as a combination of translation and original work, with the translation ascribed to Robert Chester and the story of King Arthur to another modern poet. Caeliano/Chester tells how Nature, seeing that the phoenix is about to die without an heir, takes her to Paphos to meet a forsaken turtledove, telling the Arthurian legend on the way, at great length. The two birds agree to burn together, and a pelican, observing, sees a new, still more beautiful, phoenix rise from their ashes. The poem's first editor established that the supposed Italian author was a fusion of the names of two poets, Torquato Tasso and Livio Celiano, whose works appeared, consecutively, in an Italian collection of 1587.[25] Like the phoenix and turtledove, they are fused in the person of Robert Chester, the author of both parts of the poem. To mystify readers still further, the poem's alternative title is *Rosalin's Complaint*. The name Rosaline had been invested with secret meaning (see p. 195) ever since *The Shepheardes Calender* (1579), so, although it is never used in the poem, it may signal some private code.

By the end of the sixteenth century, it was becoming common for authors to usher their books into print with commendatory verses by other writers, the equivalent of publishers' blurbs. Shakespeare, apparently, did not write this type of poem, which makes his participation in this volume especially interesting. Chester's poem, though no one reads it now, combined an enormous number of topics in a way that might well have impressed him.[26] But his real interest was not in Chester but in the man to whom the volume was dedicated: Sir John Salusbury of Lleweni, Wales, whom the queen had just made a baronet. Salusbury (37 years old in 1601), had inherited his title in 1586, when his elder brother, a defiant Catholic, was executed for his part in the Babington conspiracy. On his estate he had been a generous patron of Welsh bards. The family commonplace book shows that Salusbury's household in Wales went in for such verbal games as acrostics spelling out the names of female relatives.[27] Similar verses, not necessarily original, are included in *Love's Martyr* as "Cantoes Alphabet-wise to faire Phoenix made by the Paphian Doue."[28] Chester placed his name at the end of this section, but, since the poem identifies Salusbury with the turtledove, the cantos would have been understood by contemporaries as the voice of Salusbury himself.

In the mid-1590s Salusbury was in London, as an "esquire of the body" to Queen Elizabeth and a student at the Middle Temple. Marston was resident there at the same time, and this may be how Shakespeare and the other poets got to know Salusbury. A poem in Jonson's hand is among the family's manuscripts. Salusbury's friend and relative by marriage, William Stanley, Earl of Derby – also at Lincoln's Inn in the mid-1590s – was a patron and backer of the Paul's Boys, for which both Marston and

Chapman wrote. Though there are several Robert Chesters, Katherine Duncan-Jones and Henry Woudhuysen have plausibly identified a Lincoln's Inn man as the main author of this volume.[29] They point out so many possible connections between Salusbury and Shakespeare that it is tempting to see in them the reason for the plays' uniformly favorable depictions of the Welsh and even to wonder whether Salusbury or Chester might have been the author of the Welsh song that is sung in *1 Henry IV*.

The collaborative mode of the appendix, and perhaps even its riddling quality, might well have seemed appropriate as a way of celebrating an amateur poet who enjoyed what Arthur Marotti has called "social textuality."[30] Since the dramatists' poems honored Salusbury rather than Chester, they were placed in an appendix with a separate title page (Figure 11). The careful wording of this title page gives credit where credit is due, emphasizing both that the poems are new and that the names of the authors ("the best and chiefest modern writers") will follow their poems. Edward Blount seems determined not to be accused, as Jaggard could have been with *The Passionate Pilgrim*, of misleading readers about the contents and authorship of his volume. The epigram from Martial means "A known book cannot change its master," and the analogy between a misappropriated book and a runaway slave is part of Martial's ongoing complaint about others plagiarizing his works.[31]

The authors seem to have agreed on the order of their contributions, or else one of them, probably Jonson or Marston, acted as a "plotter."[32] Their different sections have learned-sounding titles – *Invocatio, Threnos, Epicidium, Perfectioni Hymnus Peristeros, Praeludium, Epos,* and *Ode ἐνθουσιαστική* – that suggest a common origin. Since the knight's marriage was too far in the past to be the subject, they seem to have taken the wedding of the two birds as an allegory, with the phoenix standing for Elizabeth, who had frequently used it as her symbol. As for "the Paphian dove," he is identified with Salusbury elsewhere in the book, and Salusbury had been favored by the queen, so depicting him as a faithful and bereaved lover is no more absurd than the other conceits of court poetry. Salusbury may also represent the love of Elizabeth's subjects in general, which is how some scholars have interpreted the poem.[33]

The appendix opens with a Chorus of Bards invoking the Muses, leading to a short section called "The Burning." This is followed by a poem on the funeral of the phoenix and turtledove. It falls into two parts: an introductory section in *abba* quatrains calls a group of birds together for a funeral ceremony, followed by a *Threnos*, or funeral song. Only the *Threnos* is followed by Shakespeare's name, but it is usually assumed that he wrote the introductory section as well. Chester had radically altered the phoenix myth by making the new phoenix the offspring of *two* parents, whose union is uniquely perfect, rather than an example of one unique perfection succeeding another. Imagining a suitable requiem for such a couple, Shakespeare's poem assembles other birds associated with love, music, and immortality, and gives them a lament for the "love and constancy" symbolized by the dead birds. Reason, who cannot understand the mystical paradox of two in one, or the idea of

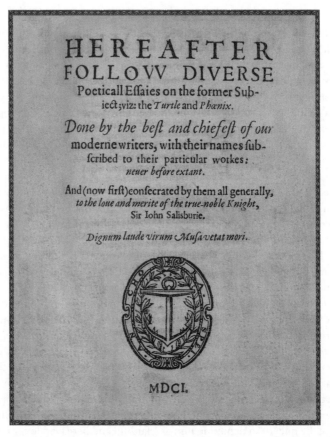

Figure 11 The separate title page for the appendix to Robert Chester's *Love's Martyr*, making it clear that the authors of the poems included here would be acknowledged. By permission of the Folger Shakespeare Library

resurrection from the dead, speaks the *Threnos* (in triplets – a three-line stanza – which might bear out David Bevington's suggestion that the poem echoes scholastic theology in its "expounding of the doctrine of the Trinity, in terms of persons, substance, accident, triunity, and the like"[34]). When Reason says that the birds are "Leaving no posterity;/ 'Twas not their infirmity,/ It was married chastity," the apparently genderless speaker directly contradicts the idea of rebirth. But the next poem, by Marston, begins, "O, 'twas a moving epicidium!" – apparently a comment on Shakespeare's poem – and goes on to deny that so much beauty and virtue could perish. Both poems are set in an imagined present, with Shakespeare depicting the apparent death while Marston focuses on the moment of rebirth and Chapman and Jonson follow with more celebration. The movement from tragedy to joy may also explain the jocular tone and rhythm of the next poem, Jonson's "The Phoenix Analysde": "Splendor! O more than mortal,/ For other forms come short all/ Of her illustrate brightness."[35]

How seriously one takes these poems depends on what one thinks the poets are writing about. William Empson thinks that they were joining in "a kind of domestic game."[36] Yet the fact that *Love's Martyr* was printed by Edward Blount and published by Richard Field – two highly respectable figures – suggests that it was seen as a serious and important gift. The writers seem to be experimenting with the kind of intellectual and obscure conceits that were becoming associated with John Donne, who might have been the writer who signed himself Ignoto.[37] Donne was another Lincoln's Inn man, and in the 1580s he had traveled with Salusbury's friend William Stanley, Earl of Derby. His coat of arms was Welsh; unlike Shakespeare, he used it in some of his portraits. The phoenix in fact is one of his many illustrations of the idea that lovers are both two and one. Duncan-Jones and Woodhuysen suggest that Donne's reference to "the Phoenix riddle" in "The Canonization" is a comment on the obscurity either of Shakespeare's poem or of the whole collection.[38] Given the date of 1601, it is not surprising that it has been suspected of being a covert tribute to Essex, but it is more likely that the poets wanted to be associated with Salusbury's recent display of loyalty to the queen, when two of his other relatives had taken part in the rebellion. They may also have wanted, as Duncan-Jones and Woodhuysen suggest, to support the knight in his struggle with local enemies in Wales who had prevented him from taking his seat in Parliament.[39] He obviously had a strong interest in protecting his reputation, and so did these writers, some of whom had Catholic connections and suspect acquaintances. Among other things, the collection, with its emphasis on praise and celebration, can be seen as a renunciation of the satiric mode that had been officially condemned in 1599. And, although it seems possible that all these poets genuinely liked Salusbury, one should not overlook the fact that the first poem, ascribed to a *Vatum Chorus* (Chorus of Bards), declares that the writers want "to gratulate/An *honorable friend*," but not out of "Mercenary hope." They protest too much; they must have been hoping for some reward from Salusbury, and they probably got it. In the following year, Shakespeare made two large purchases of land in Stratford. On the other hand, he seems never to have written any other commendatory verses – at least, not for publication.

Revision: *Sir Thomas More*

It may also have been at this time that Shakespeare agreed to help with revisions to a still unperformed play, *Sir Thomas More*. It was never printed, and any argument about its composition must depend on identifying the various hands in which the manuscript was written and reconstructing the sequence of events that followed Edmund Tilney's return of it with notes insisting on extensive alterations.

Though the play has often been dated to the early 1590s on the assumption that the anti-alien riots at the beginning refer to the ones in 1593, its most recent editor, John Jowett, argues persuasively that the subject would have been too dangerous to dramatize at all at that date. He thinks that the play was originally written around 1600 by Anthony Munday and Henry Chettle, copied out in full by Munday, submitted to Tilney, and revised in the light of his comments – initially by Chettle and Thomas Dekker, then, in 1603–4, by Thomas Heywood, Shakespeare, and Dekker, with an unknown scribe, or member of the company, doing a final tidying-up. Apart from Shakespeare, none of the dramatists identified with the manuscript was normally associated with the Chamberlain's Men or King's Men (though Dekker wrote *Satiromastix* for them in 1602). However, our knowledge of dramatists' allegiances is skewed by the fact that the only surviving records are those of Henslowe's company. It is possible that his writers (except those under contract to him) wrote for more companies than one. Jowett thinks that Munday and Chettle would have had to do so in order to survive.[40]

Henry VIII's reign was a popular subject at the turn of the century. In 1601 Henslowe paid one of his writing teams for two plays on Cardinal Wolsey, and in 1602 the anonymously published *Thomas Lord Cromwell* appeared, claiming on its title page to be by "W.S." and to belong to the Lord Chamberlain's Men. This attribution led to its finding its way into the third Shakespeare Folio (1664), but no one now thinks he had anything to do with it. However, its author or authors obviously wanted to avoid overlap with other plays on the same period: a Chorus apologizes for not dramatizing Wolsey's fall and Thomas More appears only briefly, so it is possible that someone expected a Thomas More play to appear soon. It is hard to see why so many good playwrights would have spent time on the work unless they expected it to be performed. A possible explanation is that the manuscript is a revision of an earlier play commissioned for private performance by one of More's descendants, most of whom were committed recusants. His eldest grandson Thomas, the current head of the family, was in his early sixties in 1600. When his eldest son and heir died that year, another son, Christopher Cresacre More, who had been studying for the priesthood in Douai, was ordered to come home and marry, so as to ensure the continuation of the More line.[41] His return might have been an occasion for the celebration of his great-grandfather, of whom Cresacre More later wrote a biography. In its present form, however, the play does not read like recusant propaganda. Like the Cromwell play, it is so careful to skirt political and doctrinal issues that it would be difficult for any uninformed spectator to know why the hero had to resign his office as chancellor or why he was finally executed. Even so, Tilney objected to the scene in which More refuses to subscribe to the royal supremacy. The Master of the Revels also insisted that mob violence against foreigners should only be described, not depicted.

The few pages that are now thought to be in Shakespeare's handwriting are fascinating but puzzling.[42] (A few other brief passages, not in his handwriting, have

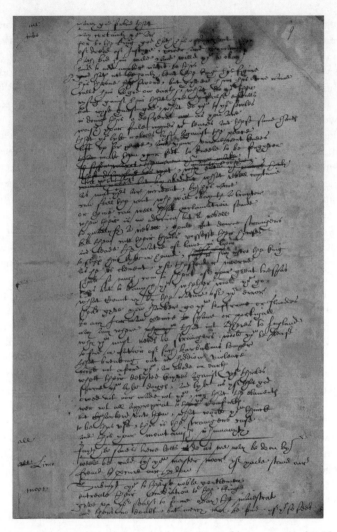

Figure 12 A page (thought to be in Shakespeare's handwriting) of the manuscript of *Sir Thomas More*, in which More addresses the crowd during the May Day riots against foreigners. Many playwrights by now were using the newer italic hand, but Shakespeare, of a slightly older generation and country background, still wrote in "secretary hand." © The British Library Board (Harley 7368, f. 9)

also been credited to Shakespeare on stylistic grounds.) The scene seems designed to satisfy Tilney's objections, since it shows Thomas More, recently made sheriff of London, exchanging repartee with the ringleaders of the mob, then calming the others in an eloquent and humane speech. As someone who was friendly both with persecuted Catholics and with French émigrés who had fled Catholic persecution (he may not have known that More himself persecuted Protestants ruthlessly), Shakespeare could easily imagine, and make More ask the crowd to imagine, the situation of the people they were attacking. How, he asks, would they feel if, as "strangers" (foreigners) in another country, they were treated "as if that God/ Owed not nor made not you . . . What would you think/ To be thus used?" (scene 6, addition I, 151–2, 154–5) The crowd's ringleaders are moved, and surrender on More's word that he will protect them. Despite his efforts, one of them is executed before the reprieve arrives, but this happens in a scene written by someone else. Did Shakespeare know when he wrote the speech that it would have these ironic consequences? Quite possibly not, since he had no historical source for the episode: it was someone else, not More, who calmed the angry citizens. The revisers seem to have been working in isolation, with the playhouse editor left to ensure coherence overall.

The year 1601 is the only one in which Shakespeare is known to have collaborated with a group of poets – in the verses on *Love's Martyr* – and, if the *Parnassus* authors knew what they were talking about, he may also have fought in the Poets' War of 1599–1601. Given these other activities in the period, he might also have been persuaded to take part in the Thomas More play. None of the other authors of the phoenix and turtle poems was involved in *Sir Thomas More*. Perhaps the topic was considered so delicate that only those known to be loyal Protestants (such as Munday, Chettle, and Dekker) could be allowed to share in the writing. The play still seems unfinished; much of what is attractive about it derives from its source material, and the various collaborators seem to have differed among themselves as to whether to treat More as a jestbook hero or a serious statesman. Shakespeare's motive for taking on extra work may have been purely financial, but, even if his involvement with the play was limited, and most of its words were not his, his awareness of the story of the most famous humanist victim of the English Reformation may have contributed to the ambiguity with which he treats the disturbing religious issues in *Hamlet*.

Notes

1. Moss, *Printed Commonplace-Books and the Structuring of Renaissance Thought*, 209–10.
2. Crawford, *"Belvedere, or the Garden of the Muses,"* 199. This essay is the main source for my information about this volume.
3. *Poems of Sir John Davies*, ed. Krueger, 201.
4. Sonnet 3 in Drayton, *England's Heroical Epistles*.
5. Dowden, introduction to *The Passionate Pilgrim*, iv, n. 2.
6. A commonplace book published in 1572, John Foxe's *Pandectae,* consisted of 600 blank pages with alphabetical headings of topics. See Kelliher, "Contemporary Manuscript Extracts from Shakespeare's *Henry IV, Part I*," 159.

7. *Shakespeare's Poems*, ed. Duncan-Jones and Woudhuysen, 83.
8. J. Shapiro, *A Year in the Life of William Shakespeare*, 194.
9. *Shakespeare's Sonnets*, ed. Duncan-Jones, 3–5.
10. P. Cheney, *Shakespeare, National Poet-Playwright*, 164.
11. John Soowthern's *Pandora* (1584), dedicated to the Earl of Oxford, contains several sonnets supposedly "by" the Countess of Oxford on the death of her son and a poem attributed to Elizabeth I, which are in fact Soowthern's own translations from the French. See R. Smith, "Southern, John," *ODNB*.
12. Drayton, *England's Heroical Epistles*, Sonnet 22.
13. *Shakespeare's Poems*, ed. Duncan-Jones and Woudhuysen, 90.
14. P. Cheney, *Shakespeare, National Poet-Playwright*, 159.
15. In *England's Parnassus* he has eleven quotations, nine of them from the two *Every Man* plays, whereas, of the ninety-five Shakespeare quotations, only twenty-five are from plays.
16. *The First Part of the Return from Parnassus*, 3.1.932–3. All three plays are published in *The Three Parnassus Plays*, ed. Leishman.
17. *The Second Part of the Return from Parnassus*, 1.2.165–71.
18. *The First Part of the Return from Parnassus*, 3.1.932–3.
19. Bate, *Soul of the Age*, 264–5 (the italics are Bate's). Bate suggests that Hayward's version of events was influenced by Shakespeare's, but if this was so Hayward must have intended his book as a rebuke to Shakespeare's comparatively sympathetic treatment of Richard. For the argument that the play in question was based on Hayward's book, see Worden, "Shakespeare in Life and Art," 32–3.
20. Rowland Whyte to Robert Sidney, 11 Oct. 1599, in *Letters and memorials of state*, ed. Collins, 2: 132.
21. Bate, *Soul of the Age*, 272.
22. [Bacon], *A Declaration of the Practises & Treasons attempted and committed by Robert late Earle of Essex and his Complices...*, H4^v–I1.
23. *The Memoirs of Robert Carey*, ed. Mares, 16–17. Carey was quoting himself at least thirty years after the event, but Whyte's letter to Sidney (see Ch. 13 n. 30 below) also speaks of Essex's intention to retire into a private country life, and in an entertainment of 1596, probably written by Francis Bacon, the earl had proclaimed his attraction to the hermit's life.
24. Duncan-Jones and Woudhuysen point out (*Shakespeare's Poems*, 86) that in John Florio's 1598 *World of Words*, an Italian–English dictionary, "Romeo" is defined as "a roamer, a wanderer, a palmer" (2E5^r). Perhaps, they suggest, Romeo was actually disguised as a pilgrim at the Capulet ball.
25. Chester, *Love's Martyr, or, Rosalin's Complaint*, ed. Grosart, lxviii–lxix.
26. See "The Narrative Poems," in Empson, *Essays on Shakespeare*, ed. Pierie, 27; 1st pub. as the introduction to *Shakespeare's Narrative Poems*, ed. William Burto (Signet Classics, 1968).
27. Christchurch Manuscript 184, repr. in *Poems by Sir John Salusbury and Robert Chester*, ed. Brown, xxxiii.
28. These "cantoes" borrow from existing collections of posies, such as those in Harleian MS 6910. See *Poems by Sir John Salusbury and Robert Chester*, ed. Brown, lv.

275

29. *Shakespeare's Poems*, ed. Duncan-Jones and Woudhuysen, 103.
30. Marotti, *Manuscript, Print, and the English Renaissance Lyric*, 135–208.
31. Fitzgerald, *Martial: The World of the Epigram*, 95–6.
32. See *The Narrative Poems*, ed. Evans, 58. Matchett, *The Phoenix and the Turtle*, 181, suggests Donne's friend Henry Goodyere, assuming that he was the H.G. who used Ignoto's line "One Phoenix borne, another Phoenix burne" in a poem in honor of Queen Anna, published in *The Mirrour of Maiestie* (1618).
33. See e.g. Axton, *The Queen's Two Bodies*, 119.
34. See *Complete Works*, ed. Bevington, 1698.
35. Chester, *Love's Martyr, or, Rosalin's Complaint*, ed. Grosart, 186.
36. Empson, "The Narrative Poems," in *Essays on Shakespeare*, 27.
37. See Maurice Evans, in his edition of *The Narrative Poems*, 58.
38. *Shakespeare's Poems*, ed. Duncan-Jones and Woudhuysen, 119–20. Of course, the phoenix is inherently a riddle, since it embodies the paradox of two in one, which is one of Donne's commonest themes.
39. Ibid., 107–9.
40. *Sir Thomas More*, ed. Jowett, 431.
41. Anderegg, "The Tradition of Early More Biography," 14.
42. The identification of "Hand D" in the play manuscript as Shakespeare's dates from 1919, when A.W. Pollard and J. Dover Wilson argued the case in the *Times Literary Supplement*. While the handwriting identification is still controversial (known examples of Shakespeare's writing being so few), MacDonald P. Jackson's "The Date and Authorship of Hand D's Contribution to *Sir Thomas More*" (2006), which compares vocabulary and phrases in the *More* passage with other plays, Shakespearean and non-Shakespearean, in the Literature Online database, has convinced most scholars of Shakespeare's authorship. See the Jowett edition, and, for a useful summary, Egan, *The Struggle for Shakespeare's Text*, 23–4, 205.

13

"Looking Before and After"

1600–1603

Sure, he that made us with such large discourse,
Looking before and after, gave us not
That capability and godlike reason
To fust in us unused.

(*Hamlet* 4.4.37–40)

Perhaps Hamlet connects rationality with the ability to look "before and after" because Shakespeare, writing in 1600, was thinking of Janus, the god who looks in both directions. No surviving play of 1599 or 1600 makes anything of the fact that a century was ending, but it was widely known that the Pope had proclaimed 1600 a year of Jubilee and that some Protestants, in return, had insisted that it was superstitious to give special significance to any one year.[1] 1300, the year of the first papal jubilee, was the year in which Dante was supposed to have made the journey described in *The Divine Comedy*: he was then halfway through the biblical lifespan and hence, as he says in his famous opening line, *Nel mezzo del camin di nostra vita* (in the middle of the journey of our life). Shakespeare in 1600 was, like Dante, halfway through his careers as actor and dramatist and might have thought that he had another thirty-five years before him, since his parents were both living, as were the siblings who had survived childhood. He probably knew something of Dante (Jonson did), and he might have been struck by the fact that the poet's guide through Hell and Purgatory was Virgil, who had himself written a famous account of an underworld journey and an encounter between a hero and his dead father. Shakespeare's personal contribution to the year 1600 was probably the writing of *Hamlet*, whose hero also takes a journey into hell.

The Life of William Shakespeare: A Critical Biography, First Edition. Lois Potter.
© 2012 Lois Potter. Published 2012 by Blackwell Publishing Ltd.

Hamlet

Shakespeare may have had practical reasons for writing his most famous play. In 1600 the Admiral's Men opened their new Fortune Theatre and Edward Alleyn returned to the stage, counting on his prestige to help establish the new venue. He took up his famous roles again, including Kyd's Hieronimo. Jonson had satirized the old play in 1598 by having an incompetent poetaster gush over its most famous lines ("Is't not simply the best that ever you heard?"),[2] but he himself wrote "additions" for the revival. If Burbage had indeed played the part after Alleyn's "retirement," the two companies may have decided to offer their spectators an opportunity to compare the two great actors. *The Spanish Tragedy* was usually known by the name of its most famous character, Hieronimo, or by his grimly enigmatic line, "Go by, Hieronymo." Kyd's Hamlet play, similarly, may have been known both as "Hamlet" and as "Hamlet, revenge" – presumably the Ghost's most famous line, since Thomas Lodge in 1595 said that the Ghost cried it "at the Theater, like an oyster wife" and a character in *Satiromastix* (1602) identified himself as "Hamlet Revenge."[3] *The Spanish Tragedy* and *Hamlet* mirrored each other, since in one a father avenges his son while in the other a son avenges his father. Kyd provided (certainly in *The Spanish Tragedy*, probably in *Hamlet*) a ghost, a hero whose grief-stricken state justifies much "antic" behavior; a villain who successfully maintains a plausible façade; a woman guilty of transgressive sexuality; a secondary female character whose madness and suicide counterpoint the hero's; and a scene where everyone watches a play that turns out to be more than pretense. If Burbage was to give up Hieronimo, temporarily, to Alleyn, he and Shakespeare may have decided to compete with the Fortune by adapting Kyd's other famous tragedy.

The Hamlet story had always been part of Danish pseudo-history, which might have been of special interest to Kyd in the early 1590s because of James VI's marriage in 1589 to the Danish princess Anna. Even before then, the sophisticated Danish court had been a venue for touring players, including Thomas Pope, now in the Chamberlain's Men.[4] Both Kyd and Shakespeare could have heard about Elsinore's fine collection of tapestries depicting kings of Denmark and the cannons at the entrance to its harbor.[5] *Hamlet* makes clear that the castle is on the sea, a fact that no visitor could have failed to mention. Otherwise, Denmark meant to Shakespeare what it meant to most Englishmen: a former invading and occupying power. For Kyd, it may have been a parallel to the threatening Spain of *The Spanish Tragedy*. The play had all too much topical relevance in any case. The atmosphere of the first scene, where the palace guards have no idea why the country is mobilizing for war, and Horatio can tell them only what "the whisper" says, suggests the secretive last years of Elizabeth's reign. Two well-known public figures had mothers who were thought to have married the murderers of their father. One was the Earl of Essex, though the allegations were made in a notorious anonymous attack on his uncle, the Earl of Leicester, and are unlikely to be true. The other was James VI of Scotland, who as a child had often been urged to take vengeance on his mother and her lover, the perpetrators of his father's murder.[6]

As Stephen Greenblatt discovered, Hamlet's question "*Hic et ubique?*" in response to the Ghost's voice from under the stage may be a recollection of a Catholic prayer that was supposed to be said on entering a graveyard: "All hail, all faithful souls, whose bodies do here and everywhere rest in the dust [*Salvete vos omnes fideles animae, quarum corpora hic et ubique requiescat in pulvere*]."[7] The play constantly refers to the dust from which human beings were made and to which they return; Margreta de Grazia has brilliantly noted the nexus of ideas around dust, dirt, lands (in the sense of kingdoms), and the grave,[8] and many have wondered whether Shakespeare, who had recently bought his first house and land, made these connections either consciously or unconsciously. Critics have wanted to link the ghost scenes with John Shakespeare, even though the play was mainly completed before his death in September 1601, and to imagine, as James Joyce did in *Ulysses*, that the poet also saw himself in the ghost and young Hamnet in the doomed prince. The play's obsession with death and the afterlife, though it may reflect a personal preoccupation, was consistent with other events of the period. If Shakespeare had asked Ben Jonson about his conversion to Catholicism in 1598, Jonson, who had been in prison for killing a man, must have told him of his fear that he would go to hell if he worshiped in the wrong faith. Thomas Wright, the priest who converted him, was a powerful writer. In 1600 he published a blistering attack on the errors of Protestantism, warning his reader, "far he leaps, and ill he lights that jumpeth into Hell, and questionless without true faith you shall never come to heaven."[9]

Among Protestant errors Wright included the view of some Puritans who took Jesus's cry, "My God, my God, why hast thou forsaken me?" to mean that he "suffered the pains of Hell upon the cross ... as if he had been afflicted and tormented with anguish of mind for his offences: for which he was deprived of the sight of God, and eternally to be deprived: all which horible punishments are included in the pains of hell."[10] The priest was referring to the controversy over whether to take literally or figuratively the statement in the Apostles' Creed that Christ had "descended into Hell" between the crucifixion and the resurrection, a subject that inspired a number of pamphlets at the turn of the century.[11] The argument had become particularly memorable in the spring of 1597, during a sermon at Paul's Cross, the pulpit outside St. Paul's Cathedral where sermons drew enormous crowds. As preacher Thomas Bilson started to explicate this passage, someone in the audience shouted that the cathedral was about to fall on them, creating near-panic in the already agitated congregation.[12] It is not surprising, then,

279

that while Hamlet, wondering about the Ghost's origins, states only the Protestant alternatives of "airs from heaven or blasts from hell" (1.4.41), the Ghost himself talks of living in "sulf'rous and tormenting flames" (1.5.3) and of a prison house which sounds like the Catholic Purgatory. *Hamlet* is the first play in which Shakespeare confronted the contradictory classical and Christian views of the afterlife, as well as the divided Christian views on the subject. *Sir Thomas More* gave him further reason to think about this religious conflict. Characteristically, he did not attempt to decide the issue. He could have written another imitation of the vivid Virgilian afterlife described by Andrea in *The Spanish Tragedy* and by Clarence in *Richard III*. Instead, Hamlet's father says that he is forbidden to speak of his "prison house" (1.5.15), reflecting the Protestant reluctance to make the supernatural visual. The world of the dead is both pagan and Christian, both Catholic and Protestant. If John Shakespeare was a Catholic, he might somehow be trapped in a Catholic Purgatory within a Protestant cosmology. The uncertainty about the Ghost's origins is part of its horror: which is more likely to be damnable – obeying a devil who is impersonating a ghost or refusing to believe that the ghost comes from a real Purgatory?

Shakespeare was, after all, adapting the play of a dead man, and a man who had been accused of atheism. Kyd's revenger had quoted Latin, but Hamlet shouts at the players in a line from the anonymous *True Tragedy of Richard III*, garbling it like Ancient Pistol. James J. Marino has pointed out references to the titles of recent Admiral's Men plays.[13] Audiences love metatheatrical jokes, and, as with Pistol's parodies, it is hard to know whether Shakespeare thought of them as anything else. Yet it is Kyd himself whose voice emerges most often from the play's "cellarage." The play scene is itself an echo of the one at the end of *The Spanish Tragedy*, but Hamlet's improvised couplet when Claudius walks out –

> And if the king like not the comedy,
> Why then belike he likes it not perdie
> (3.2.291–2)

– recalls Hieronimo's lines as he prepares *his* play-within-a-play:

> And if the world like not this tragedy,
> Hard is the hap of old Hieronimo.[14]

Other lines may be unrecognized quotations from the lost *Hamlet*. Perhaps, if Kyd's Ghost had said, Kyd's "Hamlet, revenge!" the Ghost's "Remember me" represented a deliberate rewriting. Other ghosts may haunt the play, since Shakespeare had worked with so many playwrights who were now dead. The latest of these, in 1601, was 34-year-old Thomas Nashe, the brilliant young man of the 1590s, whose literary career had been wrecked by the suppression of his writings in 1599. Jonson wrote an

elegy on his former friend and collaborator, in which there are lines that might have
been a description of Hamlet:

> When any wronged him, living, they did feel
> His spirit, quick as powder, sharp as steel;
> But to his friends her faculties were fair,
> Pleasant, and mild as the most temp'rate air.[15]

Above all, perhaps, Hamlet is a composite of everything that Burbage did best,
which is why he is everything that an actor wants to play and everything that an
audience wants an actor to be. Like Hieronimo, he has been at the university and is
even more literary than his predecessor, capable of writing in various styles: love
poems to Ophelia, "some dozen or sixteen lines" to insert into a play that has passed
the censor, and a convincing forgery of Claudius's letter to the King of England. If he
has a friend, Horatio, this is because Orestes had Pylades, rather than because he needs
a confidant; he talks to the players about acting, talks to Ophelia and to his mother
about women, talks to the gravedigger about death, and talks to the audience about
the progress of the play. A taste for philosophical generalization was coming into
vogue in the last years of the sixteenth century. Montaigne's *Essays* were the most
famous examples of it, but other writers were already attempting the genre: Bacon in
his first, small collection of *Essays* (1596), Sir John Davies in his philosophical poem,
Nosce Te Ipsum (1599), and Samuel Daniel in *Musophilus* (1599), a dialogue between a
lover of learning and a skeptic who thinks that it inhibits action ("While timorous
knowledge stands considering, / Audacious ignorance hath done the deed"). Though
Shakespeare could read French, Montaigne is not easy and he would be glad of
Florio's translation, published in 1603. *Essai*, in fact, means "attempt," and thinking
aloud on a variety of subjects, without necessarily reaching a conclusion, is built into
the text of *Hamlet*. Its many unanswered questions – did the Queen commit adultery
and was she complicit in her husband's murder? can the Ghost be believed? did
Hamlet really love Ophelia? is he really mad at any point, or only pretending madness?
– seem deliberately left open, as if to encourage discussion. The play exemplifies what
Patrick Cruttwell describes as the "new mentality" of the turn of the century:
"critical, satirical, complex, and uncertain."[16] As with Montaigne, this mentality can
be attributed to the wars of religion, whether verbal, as in England, or military, as in
war-ravaged France. It was possible for the play to digress as much as it does precisely
because the basic story was already so well known to its audience. So, while it is often
said that Hamlet is the wrong hero for his story, he is the right hero for his play.

The first version of the play (Q1) was published in 1603. In 1604 a second Quarto
(Q2) was published, its title page claiming truthfully that the text had been "enlarged
to almost as much again as it was," and perhaps less truthfully that it was based on "the
true and perfect copy." The version published in 1623 (F1) differs again: Q2 contains
some lines that are not in F1 but also lacks some of the F1 lines. Among many other

differences, Hamlet speaks of "sullied flesh" in Q2 and "solid flesh" in F. In some cases, the reason for the change is obvious: the act against profanity on the stage (1606) accounts for the transformation of "Oh God, Horatio" (Q2) into "O good Horatio" in F.

Q1 can easily be made to sound ludicrous, and has sometimes been played as a farce, but it has also been shown to act quite well when taken seriously. For anyone who can avoid comparing its language with that of Q2 and F1, it is an enjoyable, fast-moving play, focusing mainly on the revenge plot and the Hamlet–Ophelia love story. It also clarifies at least one question about Gertrude in a short scene, not present in the other two versions, where she assures Horatio that she intends to help Hamlet in his revenge. It would be satisfying to think that Shakespeare wrote this, perhaps to answer a question frequently asked by spectators, but her words at this point are those of Bellimperia to Hieronimo in *The Spanish Tragedy*. Q1 also differs in the names of two characters: Corambis (Polonius in the other texts) and his servant Montano (Reynaldo). Otherwise, it is recognizably the same play with the same plot and characters and even, at times, the same language.

Q1 might be Shakespeare's first version of the play, which he revised and expanded at a later date. Or it might be a shortened version of Q2, possibly a memorial reconstruction, used for specific occasions. The difficulty with the first argument is that much of its language does not sound like anything that Shakespeare could ever have written, or at least, that he could want anyone to think he had written. For example, Hamlet's last words in Q1 are a boilerplate death speech:

> O, my heart sinks, Horatio,
> Mine eyes have lost their sight, my tongue his use.
> Farewell, Horatio, Heaven receive my soul.

Even by comparison with the death speeches in the Henry VI plays, the lines seem flat and conventional, almost as if designed to avoid any possible accusation of atheism. Sometimes, as in Horatio's words to Fortinbras at the end, the text reads more like notes toward a speech than the speech itself:

> Let there a scaffold be reared up in the market place,
> And let the State of the world be there:
> Where you shall hear such a sad story told,
> That never mortal man could more unfold.

The first two lines do not scan, while the third and fourth form a rhyming couplet that does not exist in the two other versions. Horatio speaks at more than twice the length in Q2:

> give order that these bodies
> High on a stage be placèd to the view,

282

And let me speak to yet unknowing world
How these things came about; so shall you hear
Of carnal, bloody, and unnatural acts;
Of accidental judgements, casual slaughters,
Of deaths put on by cunning, and for no cause,
And in the upshot, purposes mistook,
Fall'n on th'inventors' heads: all this can I
Truly deliver.

F1 is largely the same, though it makes two changes to Q2 which seem like corrections.

Would any actor want to say the words of Q1 rather than those of Q2 and F? Only if he did not know any other version. Q1 seems designed for a particular market: amateur actors who wanted to perform the latest London success or touring companies taking a production abroad, where most of their audiences would be unable to follow the dialogue. Some evidence for this hypothesis is the existence of an eighteenth-century German version of the play, *Der bestrafte Brudermord* (Fratricide Punished), a late transcription of a play originally given by touring players. Since the names Corambis and Montano reappear here, it must have been based on Q1. Though by the time it was written down and printed it was so far away from the original as to be almost meaningless, it may indicate what happened when a play was adapted for touring purposes. Clowning takes up a good deal of time, and can replace dialogue in a play that emphasizes action rather than reflection. The Q1 text may have been prepared by a member of the Chamberlain's Men, or it may have been an independent venture. However, it may have been authorized by the company, since the same publisher was responsible for both quartos and may have profited from the fact that most of those who had bought Q1 would want the "corrected" text as well. Probably, the play could be longer or shorter depending on the nature of its audience. The graveyard scene, for example, can be omitted without any loss to the plot. That this must sometimes have happened seems to be indicated by Osric's telling Hamlet, "Sir, here is newly come to court Laertes" (5.2.106) – a fact that Hamlet certainly knows, since Laertes had been trying to throttle him in the previous scene.[17] Yet it is in that scene that the author most clearly intends to draw together the threads of the play: the gravedigger's answers to Hamlet's questions make it clear that the prince was born on the same day that his father killed old Fortinbras, which was also the same day that the gravedigger began working.[18] This kind of foreshadowing and patterning corresponds to what I think was happening in revisions to the history plays. The actor playing Pyrrhus both models and reflects Hamlet; Old Hamlet returns as a ghost, then dies again in the play performed before Claudius; the pre-play combat between Old Hamlet and Old Fortinbras is repeated both when Hamlet and Laertes fight in Ophelia's grave and when they engage in a more formal duel. At the end, Horatio comments on the strange coincidence that brings the ambassadors from England to Denmark just as the victorious army of Fortinbras arrives from Poland – yet another apparent ratification of Hamlet's pious comment:

> There's a divinity doth shape our ends,
> Rough-hew them how we will.
>
> (5.2.10–11)

On the other hand, the play's sheer length and its numerous digressions easily obscure these patterns and make it equally possible to argue for an absurdist interpretation.

By contrast with Hamlet's witty, outrageous, and mostly feigned madness, Ophelia's is lyrical. As if responding to the objection that his earlier heroines had been too disobedient toward their fathers, Shakespeare makes Ophelia so obedient to hers that she is finally destroyed. Unless the earlier Hamlet play anticipated him, Shakespeare was probably the first dramatist to make a madwoman sing, but the actor of this role did not need only a singing voice. At a time when boy actors in tragedy were performing mainly the roles of sexually predatory women, Shakespeare created for the first time a young woman whose brief speeches and long silences gave the sense that most of her life was an inner life. His next tragic heroines, Desdemona and Cordelia, would also be subdued women. Laertes' words show how Ophelia's madness must have been presented:

> Thought and affliction, passion, hell itself,
> She turns to favor and to prettiness.
>
> (4.5.191–2)

This might almost be Shakespeare's own comment on the kind of tragedy he had been writing since *Romeo and Juliet* – one that mitigated the sense of waste and death by surrounding them with as much beauty as possible. *Hamlet* is popular, at least partly, because it is colorful and entertaining, thanks to Hamlet's "mad" antics and the presence of the actors. Although its ending involves the deaths of virtually all the major characters, it gives the impression that the hero has "won," both in the fencing match and in the completion, however rushed, of his mission of vengeance. Like Brutus, Hamlet dies with a friend near him and achieves some kind of calm in his last moments. Moreover, Horatio makes it clear that he will be vindicated posthumously (though modern productions sometimes undercut that hope by making Fortinbras a repressive figure). In that respect it differs from the tragedies that follow, which offer almost no consolation.

The play may have premiered in 1600. After Essex's attempted coup in February 1601, the report of Laertes' attempted insurrection might have been too dangerously topical:

> The rabble call him lord,
> And, as the world were now but to begin,

284

> Antiquity forgot, custom not known,
> The ratifiers and props of every word,
> They cry, "Choose we! Laertes shall be king!"
> (4.5.105–9)

James Roberts, the printer who entered *Hamlet* in the Stationers' Register on 26 July 1602, did not print the version (Q1) that appeared in the following year, when it was described as having been acted by "his Highness' servants" (that is, the King's Men, who acquired that name only on 19 May 1603). He did however print Q2 in 1604/5 for the same publisher who had brought out Q1. Given the delicacy of the political situation at the end of Elizabeth's reign, it is possible that the company held back publication of the full text while the succession hung in the balance. Having already had so much trouble over plays about English history, Shakespeare needed to be careful with a story from Denmark, especially given that the Scots king, who had married a Danish princess and visited Elsinore in person, was very likely to be the next ruler of England. The frequent mentions of England in the play, the reminder of its recent subjection to the Danish yoke, and the presence of two English ambassadors at the end suggest that England itself will soon be in the same dangerously leaderless state as Hamlet's Denmark. At the end of the play, a foreigner, Fortinbras, unites the two often hostile kingdoms of Denmark and Norway. This conclusion seems so prophetic of the arrival of James VI that it may well have been absent from the play as performed before 1603. In Q1, Fortinbras announces his intention of claiming the Danish throne, but it is only in Q2, a year later, that Hamlet gives his vote for the foreign prince, as Elizabeth, on her deathbed, had finally done for James.

Stratford Land

When his father died in September 1601, Shakespeare inherited his status as gentleman and his property in Henley Street. In 1602 he made his last two purchases of Stratford land: in May, at a cost of £320, he bought 107 acres in the Old Town from John and William Combe, and in September he added a cottage in Chapel Lane, just opposite New Place. Where did he get the money? The size of this purchase suggests that the success of *Hamlet* was commercial as well as artistic. It might have brought him gifts from enthusiastic admirers; perhaps Sir John Salusbury had been unusually generous to the authors of the poems in *Love's Martyr*; perhaps John Shakespeare's estate was not so poor as is usually thought. Hamnet's death meant that there could be no opportunity for advancement through a wealthy marriage; now, perhaps, Shakespeare was thinking instead of his daughters' dowries. In his absence, his brother Gilbert received the deed for him, formally "entering" the land in order to have "seisin" in it.[19] This would have meant taking earth or a twig as a symbol of possession – appropriate enough, at a time when the poet had just been imagining the strange symbiosis of human bodies with the land they hope to inherit and the dust from which they are made.

Since Shakespeare was not in Stratford in May 1602, he would not have learned immediately about the brawl later that month between servants of the lord of the manor, Sir Edward Greville, and those of the bailiff, Richard Quiney. Ever since Greville had acquired the borough, he had been determined to interfere with its government, claiming as his own the right to appoint its vicar and to veto its choice of bailiff. He clearly saw Richard Quiney's election in 1601 as a provocation. Quiney by now had considerable experience of arguing in London on the Corporation's behalf and must have been Greville's main obstacle to extending his control there. With others, Quiney had attacked Greville's hedges when he enclosed them in January 1601, and had gone to London to appeal against the knight to the attorney general, Sir Edward Coke (who was at the time totally absorbed in a new emergency, the Essex rebellion). In May, a further disturbance took place in Stratford, and a drunken servant of Greville wounded the bailiff, who died within the month.[20] Shakespeare and his father had known the Quiney family all their lives, and this blatant abuse of power must have shocked everyone in Stratford. Even before this event, Shakespeare may have remembered an unpleasant fact about Sir Edward. In the last scene of *Hamlet* the hero apologizes to Laertes in a speech that most commentators have found disingenuous:

> Let my disclaiming from a purposed evil
> Free me so far in your most generous thoughts
> That I have shot my arrow o'er the house
> And hurt my brother.
>
> (5.2.239–42)

Sir Edward Greville had in fact succeeded to his family's estate, and the position of lord of the manor of Stratford, after accidentally killing his older brother with an arrow shot straight up into the air.[21] No one is likely to have made the connection at the time, and Shakespeare would probably not have introduced it later, since the words would have aligned Hamlet with a man who might also have shrugged off Quiney's death as unintended. Even so, unimpressed by Shakespeare's status as a wealthy landowner, the Stratford council in December 1602 issued an order forbidding the performance of plays in the council chamber or Guild Hall, with a 10 shilling fine for disobedience.[22]

Twelfth Night

Hamlet's success is evident from the number of imitations that it inspired in the first decade of the seventeenth century. Among the earliest was John Marston's *Antonio's*

Revenge, given by Paul's Boys in 1600 or 1601. Its hero pretends to be a fool and is visited by not one but three ghosts calling for revenge; its heroine is pathetic like Ophelia. Henry Chettle's *Hoffman, or Revenge for a Father* (the Admiral's Men, late in 1602) made the revenger a fiendishly clever villain who broods over not a skull but a complete skeleton; the mad heroine, though she sings and gathers flowers, also plans revenge. Since both plays are often comic, it is hard to tell whether they are imitations or parodies, but they are in no sense an attack on Shakespeare's play. *Hoffman*, moreover, was not published until 1631 and might have acquired some of its parodic elements later in its run.

The earliest *Hamlet* parody, however, may have been by Shakespeare himself. It can hardly be by accident that he followed a play about a man feigning madness with one in which a character is asked, "are you not mad indeed, or do you but counterfeit?" (*Twelfth Night* 4.2.114–15). Though there is no evidence that *Twelfth Night* was written after rather than before *Hamlet*, its performance at the Middle Temple Hall in 1602 was probably an early one, and may even have been the first. Candlemas was one of the two days in the year when all members of the Middle Temple were required to dine in hall.[23] Many of them were enthusiastic theatergoers and would have preferred to see a new play rather than one that they had already attended many times. Certainly, John Manningham, who wrote about it in his diary in February 1601/2, had never seen it before:

> At our feast we had a play called "Twelfth night, or what you will"; much like the comedy of errors, or Menechmi in Plautus, but most like and near to that in Italian called Inganni.
>
> A good practice in it to make the steward believe his Lady widow was in Love with him, by counterfeiting a letter, as from his Lady, in general terms, telling him what she liked best in him, and prescribing his gesture in smiling, his apparel, &c., and then when he came to practise, making him believe they took him to be mad.[24]

As Manningham recognized, Shakespeare was drawing partly on Roman comedy and partly on the Italian comic tradition. As in *The Comedy of Errors*, the confusions resulting from mistaken identity make characters wonder whether they are mad, but whereas in the earlier play it is one of the twins who is "in a dark room and bound," in *Twelfth Night* Shakespeare transferred the false diagnosis to the subplot. One mistake in Manningham's entry – seeing Olivia in black, he took her for a widow rather than a woman in mourning for her father and brother – suggests that he may have had trouble hearing the dialogue in the crowded room. However, the diarist easily understood and remembered the Malvolio plot. Sir Toby Belch has the largest role in the play; Sir Andrew is probably the funniest character, and Viola the most attractive one; yet Manningham's reaction was probably representative.

287

The character's first appearance would have made the Hamlet parody obvious. That Malvolio was a steward and not a prince would be clear from his costume, but, played by a leading actor, he would have drawn all eyes when, like Hamlet in 1.2, he entered with the rest of Olivia's court but remained silent until he was addressed. Like Hamlet, he refuses to be part of the jollity of those around him. Like Hamlet, he makes negative comments on clowns. Like Hamlet, he soon changes to an antic costume. He then is confined – as a prince could not be – in a dark room, the usual recommended cure for madness. When, in his last scene, he threatens "revenge on the whole pack of you," his attempt to turn the comedy into a revenge tragedy is the final absurd touch. Malvolio is an obvious target, since he represents the anti-holiday spirit that the players had every reason to dislike, but his humiliation is so complete that even his tormentors are embarrassed about it. There is at least some concession here to those, at the Inns of Court and elsewhere, who complained that revels frequently got out of hand. Hence, perhaps, the title of the play, which refers not only to festivity on the twelfth day of Christmas but to the point at which it has to end. The questioning about the proper use of laughter that began in *Love's Labour's Lost* continues here, assuming an audience that will recognize inappropriate as well as appropriate jesting. Jonson often makes explicit remarks about the need for an audience to use its intelligence. If more of Shakespeare's prologues had survived, it might turn out that he had also been saying this.

It was perhaps five years since the death of Hamnet, whose twin was a girl, and the plot of *Twelfth Night* calls for each twin to think the other dead until their reunion in the final scene. If Shakespeare found the subject painful, this might be why Viola is the saddest comic heroine that he had created up to this point, and why both she and Olivia are introduced grieving for the loss of a close relative. The Countess of Pembroke had gone into a long period of seclusion after her brother's death in 1586. The gratuitous addition of a brother's death as a motivation for Olivia's inaccessibility may have been a complimentary allusion to the countess as well as a way of diverting attention from the most obvious recent object of collective mourning, the Earl of Essex, often thought of as Sidney's successor. Shakespeare, who could not have made his personal grief the obvious center of a play (even Jonson, a much more self-referential dramatist, never did this), may have been able to merge it with the griefs of others. Richard P. Wheeler notes that the father of Viola and Sebastian is a constant "point of orientation" in the play, frequently mentioned by both twins in their separate plots and brought into the dialogue in which they establish their identities to each other.[25] Just as young Hamlet was born on the day of his father's victory over Fortinbras, old Sebastian died on the day that Viola (and thus also her twin Sebastian) reached the age of 13. Whether or not John Shakespeare was still alive when this play was written, this elaborate interlocking of the lives of father and children may well, as Wheeler suggests, be the result of some kind of unconscious "dream work" on Shakespeare's part.

288

The play is, however, about love, appropriately for the Inn whose Lord of Misrule was called the Prince d'Amour. The complications of the love relationships are pleasurable in their own right, but they also play with the interchangeability of male and female characters: Orsino, Olivia, and Antonio are attracted to what seems to be the same boy, though he splits into two at the end, allowing two of the three characters to satisfy their desires. Antonio, like Don Pedro in *Much Ado* and Jaques in *As You Like It*, is left alone. Whereas Don Pedro is too high-born to marry anyone in his play, Antonio is probably too low. In *As You Like It*, Jaques' line about the large number of married couples "coming to the Ark" comments on a too-neat plot resolution (and, incidentally, positions him as a critical commentator excluding himself from it). No such resolution happens in *Twelfth Night*. Sir Toby's courtship of Maria occurs mainly in casual throwaway lines, and their marriage takes place offstage. Sir Andrew, Feste, Fabian, and Antonio are not paired off with anyone. Modern productions often draw attention to these non-relationships, increasing the sense of melancholy at the play's end.

Shakespeare may originally have tilted the comedy in the direction of its heroine, who tells the sea captain in her first scene that she can not only sing to Orsino but "speak to him in many sorts of music" (1.2.58). The role was probably intended for the boy actor of Ophelia who, according to Q1, appeared in the mad scene "playing upon a lute and singing." Nothing is said about the lute in the two other texts of the play, and it is unlikely that the company would have had a steady stream of outstanding boy actors who were also gifted lutanists. Perhaps his voice broke, but someone so musically talented could also have been snatched away by one of the children's companies, which had the privilege of impressing children for service in her majesty's chapel. Fortunately, Robert Armin, the new clown, could also sing. Whereas 2.4 might originally have shown Orsino gradually falling under the disguised Viola's spell as she sang of her love, it became a scene in which Orsino and Viola, listening together to Feste's song, recognized their affinity at a deeper level than that of words. Viola's description of her supposed sister sounds like a description of Ophelia:

> *Orsino.* And what's her history?
> *Viola.* A blank, my lord. She never told her love,
> But let concealment, like a worm i'th'bud,
> Feed on her damask cheek. She pined in thought,
> And with a green and yellow melancholy,
> She sat like Patience on a monument,
> Smiling at grief.
>
> (2.4.109–15)

It may indeed indicate how Ophelia was played, with a wistful, understated beauty that allowed the audience to imagine a subtext for itself.

The chief puzzle about the role of Feste is why he is not involved in the tricking of Malvolio that occupies a good part of the play. Perhaps, once Shakespeare realized that he would have to use Armin as a singer in 2.4, he felt it was better not to over-expose him in the Malvolio plot. Although clown roles were immensely popular, they always look surprisingly short on the page. One reason is that the actor usually lengthened them with improvisations. Another possibility (not incompatible with the first one) is that the war between Feste and Malvolio reflects a real theatrical conflict and that Shakespeare dealt with it by giving each actor a scene in which he could be the center of the stage. The scene in which the three conspirators eavesdrop on Malvolio as he reads the forged letter is very much Malvolio's scene, and by placing the other characters in hiding Shakespeare required them to be relatively subdued in their responses. Fabian, who replaces Feste in this part of the plot without explanation or introduction, was probably a less experienced member of the company, less likely to engage in scene-stealing. On the other hand, in the scene where Malvolio, in the "dark house," is unable to see him, Feste not only sings but is allowed to show off his skills at impersonation, conducting a dialogue with himself and an imaginary interlocutor (Sir Thopas the Curate), perhaps a refinement of the one-man show in which Armin conversed with his baton.[26] Malvolio, either invisible or at any rate confined, is thus prevented from stealing the scene back from the clown, who, critics agree, "should have the whole stage to himself."[27] Later, when asked to read Malvolio's letter, Feste impersonates an insane Malvolio. Armin's Burbage imitation must have been hilarious, but it is so unintelligible that Olivia has to ask Fabian to take over the reading. Since these moments rely on the audience's knowledge of the actors, their apparent conflict is unlikely to have been a serious one. If Hamlet's lines about impertinent clowns who speak "more than is set down for them" had been understood as having a personal meaning, the apparent continuation of the argument in *Twelfth Night* would have given added pleasure to those who liked to feel that they knew the backstage world as well as the play. The same is true of such obvious nods to the audience as Fabian's "If this were played upon a stage, now, I could condemn it as an improbable fiction" (3.4.129–30), and perhaps Sir Andrew's telling Sir Toby that he wouldn't dare to "accost" Maria "in this company" (1.3.57–8): since only the three of them are on stage, "this company" must be the audience.

Hamlet had contained other "backstage" references, such as the little exchange between Hamlet and Rosencrantz about the popularity of boy actors, the prince's dialogue with the players, and reminders of other plays performed by the company and its rivals. *Twelfth Night* continues the game by referring to *Hamlet*. But *Twelfth Night* is a far more disciplined play than *Hamlet*, perhaps as a result of revision between its first performances and the Folio. As with *As You Like It*, Shakespeare's final scene includes a number of pointers to an offstage afterlife. The other characters will try to pacify Malvolio, if only because they need to find out what has become of the captain who has Viola's clothes, which for some reason seem to be needed before Orsino will become formally betrothed to her. Malvolio has apparently sued the captain: an Inns of Court audience would appreciate this final reference to the law, in a play that teems with them, though the line is probably also meant to amuse by drawing attention to a doubling problem that prevented the captain from appearing because he was already on stage in another role. This gratuitous complexity is the comedy's equivalent of the several "false stops" at the end of *As You Like It*.

The year 1601 was probably the most successful that Shakespeare and his company had ever known. It was also, however, the year in which the main season of revels was quickly followed by the disastrous end of Essex's short career and the imprisonment of Southampton. John Shakespeare died in September. *Hamlet* and *Twelfth Night* are companion pieces, showing the tragic and comic faces of melancholy and revenge. Given the events of the previous years, it is not surprising that they place so much emphasis on words – not only how to use them correctly, but how to use them safely. Hamlet had insisted that clowns should stick to their lines, but did not say that ad-libbing could get them into trouble. Yet whereas Philostrate is concerned mainly with quality when he screens the post-nuptial entertainments offered in *A Midsummer Night's Dream*, Claudius clearly expects Hamlet to have paid attention to the content of *The Murder of Gonzago*: "Have you read the argument? Is there no offence in't?" (3.2.230–1). During the performance, Hamlet insists on two facts that should save the play from censorship: it is a translation from the Italian and based on a historical event. In *Twelfth Night* many of the characters are in danger of being punished for their words. The precariousness of Feste's situation is made clear at the start: "to be turned away, is not that as good as a hanging to you?" (1.5.17–18). In the final scene, "Cesario" comes close to being banished from his patron's house for marrying above his station. Students at the Inns of Court would have known about the desperate situation of a former Lincoln's Inn man, John Donne, whose brilliant career had been ruined when his patron refused to reinstate him after the discovery of his marriage early in 1602.

Viola, who at one point angrily tells Olivia that "I am your fool" (3.1.144), sees the resemblance between her situation and Feste's. Both are self-conscious about their need to hold someone else's interest in order to survive, and about achieving a balance between punishable impudence and the kind that implicitly compliments the broadmindedness of the patron. As the page Cesario, Viola insists that she cannot diverge from her carefully memorized speech on Orsino's behalf: "I can say little more than I have studied, and that question's out of my part" (1.5.174–5). The joke about sticking to a text that has been passed by the licenser develops into something more serious when she compares her message to "divinity" and Olivia asks about her "text" – that is, the scriptural passage on which she is to preach. When Viola joins in the game by saying that it lies in the first chapter of Orsino's heart, Olivia replies, "O, I have read it. It is heresy" (1.5.213–23). Feste, impersonating Sir Topas the curate, interrogates Malvolio in the "dark house," finally insisting, absurdly, that the madman can't be released until he proves his sanity by adopting the heretical belief in reincarnation. In the aftermath of the interrogation of Augustine Phillips about the *Richard II* performance and with recollections of the still more frightening investigation of heresy and atheism in Marlowe and Kyd (another man turned away by his patron), these jokes are not only sophisticated but daring.

Troilus and Cressida

When *Troilus and Cressida* was published in 1609, the printer prefaced it with an epistle claiming that it was "never clapper-clawed with the palms of the vulgar." This was both an appeal to the elitist reader and an oblique statement about the play's performance history. Whereas *Hamlet* sees the Trojan story from the perspective of the *Aeneid* (it is not often realized that the First Player, telling his "tale to Dido," is actually playing the part of Aeneas), *Troilus and Cressida* is a self-conscious addition to three famous treatments of the same theme – Homer's *Iliad*, Virgil's *Aeneid*, and Chaucer's *Troilus and Criseyde* – and to the medieval works that had already conflated these tales. It was from the *Iliad* that Shakespeare got the basic framework, opening halfway through the war and comprising Achilles' refusal to fight for the Greeks, his re-entry into the war, and his killing of Hector. The *Aeneid* helps to make the play, unlike Homer, pro-Trojan, and explains the importance given to Aeneas in a plot where he has very little to do. Chaucer's poem, drawing on a long tradition that had already elaborated the Trojan theme, is an extended description of the birth and death of a love-affair destroyed by the war. It is told with great sympathy for all three parties: the lover, his mistress, and the amiable older friend who wishes well to them both. Feste, in *Twelfth Night*, makes a joke about being Pandarus and bringing a Cressida to Troilus – that is, a second coin to join the one he has already begged – and goes on to say that "Cressida was a beggar," which is true not in Chaucer's poem but in Robert Henryson's sixteenth-century sequel that was published with *Troilus and Criseyde* in the Speght collection of Chaucer's works (1598). In the 1599 play by Chettle and Dekker, according to the surviving plot, Cressida appeared with beggars. Feste's line probably assumes audience knowledge of this Admiral's Men play. Shakespeare's *Troilus and Cressida*, which might be in dialogue with it, was first entered in the Stationers' Register in February 1603 and described as "acted by my Lord Chamberlain's Men," but apparently the printer was unable to get permission to publish it. As with *Hamlet* its publication may have been disrupted by the events of late March.

The Prologue, in which the speaker says that he is wearing armor," but not in confidence/ Of author's pen or actor's voice" (23–4), alludes to the armed epilogue of Marston's *Antonio and Mellida* (1599) and Jonson's armed prologue to *Poetaster* (1601). But neither of these playwrights was Shakespeare's main target. George Chapman's name has come up before, often in the context of a comparison with

292

Figure 13 Portrait of George Chapman, from *The Whole Works of Homer* (1609).
By permission of the Folger Shakespeare Library

Shakespeare. It had been known for some years that this scholar and ex-soldier (see Figure 13) was embarked on the immense and prestigious task of translating Homer, though he spent much of the 1590s publishing shorter works and writing comedies to keep himself solvent. His translation of seven books of the *Iliad* (1–4 and a selection of later ones) appeared in 1598, as did *Achilles Shield*, a famous passage from Book 18 which he published so that readers could compare it to the description of Aeneas' shield in the *Aeneid*. These Homer translations were perhaps the most popular poems since Shakespeare's *Venus* and *Lucrece*, the more so as virtually no one in the period knew enough Greek to read Homer in the original. They were not the first translations of Homer (a free version of the first ten books was published in 1581), but Chapman's self-publicizing made them a significant publication event.[28] In *Achilles Shield* his praise of Homer was hyperbolic ("Counsellors have never better oracles than his lines: fathers have no morals so profitable for their children, as his counsels)" (B2^v–3). Noting that his previous translation had resulted in many comparisons between Virgil and Homer, he argues that Virgil is not only derivative from Homer but more labored and less inventive. In verses at the end of the book, he adds that the controversy "is made a Courtly question now" (D3^v) – presumably meaning that even the court was discussing the respective merits of the two classical authors. Jonson's *Poetaster*, contemporary with *Troilus*, restated the view of Virgil as an almost divine figure.

Shakespeare may have been among the first to read the Homer translation, which was probably his first direct encounter with the *Iliad*. One passage in Chapman's preface suggests that he might also have been among the first to critique it. Chapman comments that some have complained of his obscure vocabulary, but he sees no reason why his coinages should not be as valid as other new words, such as "swaggerers" (B2^r). As happened most notoriously in *Poetaster*, writers in those quarrelsome years often ridiculed each others' linguistic mannerisms. If the person criticizing Chapman's obscurity had been Jonson, one would expect Chapman to retort by pointing to something comparable in Jonson's own work. The word he seized on instead was "swaggerers." No theatergoer could forget that in *2 Henry IV* Falstaff, Mistress Quickly, and Doll Tearsheet had spoken variations on that word a total of twelve times (2.4.71–108). It is not clear what Shakespeare might have said to provoke this retort, unless perhaps Chapman knew of the "rival poet" sonnets and took them personally.

Even if he had no personal rivalry with Chapman, Shakespeare might have acquired a negative view of the Greek heroes from older works like Lydgate's *History, Siege and Destruction of Troy* (first printed in 1513), which, he would have noted with interest, was written at the command of Henry V. Lydgate was drawing on later retellings with a more strongly Trojan bias, but he nevertheless took issue directly with Homer's glorification of Achilles, who, he argued, had killed both Hector and Troilus unfairly.[29] Readers may have expected Chapman's translation to restore the nobility of the Greek heroes, but nothing could alter the fact that Achilles, during much of the poem, let a sense of personal injury keep him from fighting for his own country. In 1598 Chapman had dedicated both Homer translations to the Earl of Essex, praising his "Achillean vertues." The comparison was apt, since Essex, like Achilles, was a soldier and poet. It was also two-edged, since even Achilles' friends comment on his capacity for rage and resentment. The situation in the first book of the poem, when Achilles nearly attacks Agamemnon, was embarrassingly close to a court incident in July 1598, when the queen boxed Essex's ears and he had to be stopped from drawing his sword in retaliation.

Was Shakespeare's play, then, denigrating Essex or attacking Chapman's aggrandizing of both Essex and Homer? It is generally assumed that the former protégé of Southampton must have shared in the adulation of this glamorous aristocrat. At the time when Shakespeare was presumably writing *Hamlet* and *Troilus and Cressida*, however, Essex was already in disgrace and even his friends seem to have felt pity rather than admiration for him.[30] Both plays seem confused in their attitude to war: Hamlet's admiration for Fortinbras's expedition does not seem sarcastic, yet the play makes its pointlessness clear – and the soliloquy expressing this admiration disappeared from the play after Q2 was published. In *Troilus and Cressida*, Ulysses criticizes Achilles and Patroclus's contempt for their commanding officers:

> They tax our policy and call it cowardice,
> Count wisdom as no member of the war,
> Forestall prescience, and esteem no act
> But that of hand. . . .
> So that the ram that batters down the wall,
> For the great swinge and rudeness of his poise,
> They place before his hand that made the engine,
> Or those that with the fineness of their souls
> By reason guide his execution.
>
> (1.3.197–200, 206–10)

At moments like this, the play seems to privilege what Hamlet calls "capability and godlike reason" (4.4.39) over brute force. Yet it is chance rather than the "policy" of Ulysses that finally brings Achilles to the field, and he kills Hector despicably. Homer describes the scurrilous Thersites as a trouble-maker, whose beating by Ulysses wins enthusiastic approval from everyone. In the play Thersites is a fool and hence "a privileged man" as Achilles says; he expresses contempt for Ulysses, as for everyone else. The references to his appearance suggest that this was another Armin part. Though the character sometimes "fools" in the traditional sense – he creates question-and-answer games and impersonates other characters – his running commentary on the action, which reduces both war and love to their basest level, is never contradicted.

The love story is less obviously mocked than the Homeric one, and has moments of what seem real pathos, but its characters are unable to live up to it. Troilus, in his first scene, refuses to fight the enemy because he is in love. Cressida's coy and deceitful behavior, if excusable as a survival strategy, is stereotypically female in the worst sense. Chaucer's likeable Pandarus has become an elderly fusspot – Justice Shallow acting as a bawd. All three characters behave as if they have already become the versions of themselves that legend will make them. The one thing that seems to have impressed Shakespeare was their sense of mortality. There is a constant tension between the pettiness of their current existence and the pathos that results from projecting their thoughts into a future, as Cressida describes it,

> When time is old and hath forgot itself,
> When waterdrops have worn the stones of Troy
> And blind oblivion swallowed cities up,
> And mighty states characterless are grated
> To dusty nothing.
>
> (3.2.184–8)

Ironically, this haunting evocation occurs in the context of a solemn vow that the audience knows Cressida will break, since for them she has already been punished, as she says she is willing to be if she is false, by becoming a synonym for falsity. The passage recalls Brutus and Cassius's prediction that their assassination of Caesar will be dramatized in future ages; as in *Julius Caesar*, the characters are right in thinking that they will be remembered but wrong about *how*. The Epilogue, in which Pandarus addresses the audience as fellow "traders in the flesh," likewise riddled with the pox, is the ultimate reduction of a famous love story, and perhaps results from the Elizabethan view of Chaucer as above all a "bold spirit" who, according to William Webbe, constantly satirized any "enormities" he saw, "either in plain words, or else in some pretty and pleasant covert, that the simplest might espy him."[31] It is unlikely that the Epilogue would have been spoken at a public performance, but an Inns of Court audience might have liked its cynicism. *Troilus and Cressida* feels like something written at the end of a reign, looking back to the age of the great military men, and ahead to the probability that either Elizabeth or her successor would make peace with Spain.

The End of the Reign

After *Troilus and Cressida*, Shakespeare needed to find subjects less likely to alienate female spectators. Perhaps recalling the success of *The Merry Wives of Windsor*, with its Italian source, he looked again at Cinthio Giraldi's *Hecatomithi* (A Hundred Tales), Boccaccio, and Bandello for other stories about women who outwit unworthy husbands. Early in 1603 he went to the Rose Theatre, recently taken over by Worcester's Men, where his old colleague Will Kemp and a new actor, John Lowin, were playing in Heywood's *A Woman Killed with Kindness*. Lowin had just finished his apprenticeship as a goldsmith and may already have been attracting attention as a professional actor. Surprisingly, given Kemp's presence, Heywood's play turned out to be a tragedy about an adulterous wife whose husband, instead of killing her and her lover, takes what everyone regards as a merciful attitude. The wife soon dies of a broken heart, with her forgiving family around her. Either Kemp or Lowin probably played the Puritanical servant Nicholas, who reluctantly tells his master about the adultery.[32] Frankford at first strikes Nicholas, but later recognizes that "though blunt, yet he is honest."[33] The scene between the two men, which brings out the difficulty and danger involved in shattering a husband's happiness and the nastiness of the task, whether or not the woman is guilty, may have stayed with Shakespeare as he thought about his next tragedy.

He would soon have plenty of time in which to write it. Though the queen was observed to be depressed and nervous, the players gave the usual plays at court during the Christmas season, and she saw her last performance, by the Admiral's Men, on 6 March. Since Philip Henslowe added up his final reckoning with the company on the following day, it has been suggested that he may have been anticipating the closure of the theaters that would follow her death.[34] His contacts at court might have told him that the lords on the Privy Council had just been notified that she was seriously ill.[35] She seemed to be recovering a week later, but in the second half of the month Londoners recognized the familiar signs that an important public event was being kept from them. The theaters were closed on 19 March. There were arrests, particularly of vagrants and Catholics; some were even deported; then the ports were closed. Courtiers, cut off from their usual correspondents at home and abroad, apologized later for their inability to write, because all official channels were blocked "and all conveyance so dangerous and suspicious."[36] Most guessed what turned out to be true: on 24 March the queen had finally died. The diarist John Manningham, who had seen *Twelfth Night* a year ago, went on 23 March to hear a preacher at Richmond "and to be assured whether the Queen were living or dead." Only a day later, he heard the proclamation of James's succession and was surprised at the lack of emotion: "No tumult, no contradiction, no disorder in the city; every man went about his business as readily, as peaceably, as securely, as though there had been no change, nor any news ever heard of competitors."[37] There was no uprising of Catholics or Puritans, no invasion from Spain. Though Elizabeth had favored her cousin of Scotland as a successor, she refused to name him publicly until the very end, but many courtiers had for years been engaged in secret correspondence with him. At the funeral, according to custom, each court official broke his staff of office and threw the pieces into the grave. Lord Hunsdon's white staff as Lord Chamberlain went in among the rest. It was probably broken by his deputy, since Hunsdon (whose daughter, the queen's closest friend, had died in the previous month) had been too ill to attend Privy Council meetings for over a year, though he refused to resign his position.[38] Even if he lived some years longer, the Lord Chamberlain's Men did not know whether he would remain their patron and the leading purveyor of court entertainments. Everything depended on the decision of the new ruler, who was on his way to London.

Notes

1. *The Ceremonies, solemnities, and prayers, vsed at the opening of the holy gates of foure Churches, within the Citie of Rome, in the yere of Iubile.* . . . Compare *An Answere or Admonition to those of the Church of Rome, touching the Iubile, proclaimed by the Bull, made and set foorth by Pope Clement the eyght, for the yeare of our Lord. 1600.*
2. Jonson, *Every Man in His Humour*, ed. Miola, 1.3.139–40.
3. Lodge, *Wit's Miserie*, H4^v.
4. M. Eccles, "Elizabethan Actors III," 301.
5. See Holmes, *The Guns of Elsinore.*
6. See e.g. Frye, *The Renaissance Hamlet.*
7. Greenblatt, *Hamlet in Purgatory*, 16, 234–5.
8. De Grazia, *Hamlet Without Hamlet*, 23–44.
9. [Wright], *Certaine Articles or Forcible Reasons Discouering the palpable absurdities, and most notorious errour of the Protestants Religion*, D1^v.
10. Ibid., B2.
11. Among the works that debate this point are Jacob, *A Defence of a Treatise touching the Sufferings and Victorie of Christ*; [Barlow], *A Defence of the Articles of the Protestant Religion*; and Bilson, *The Effect of Certain Sermons* and *The Survey of Christ's Sufferings.*
12. See Richardson, "Bilson, Thomas," *ODNB.*
13. Marino, *Owning William Shakespeare*, 97–103.
14. See the note to 3.2.285–6 in *Hamlet*, ed. Thompson and Taylor.
15. Duncan-Jones, "Jonson's Epitaph on Nashe," 4.
16. Cruttwell, *The Shakespearean Moment*, 39.
17. Osric himself may be a late addition to the play; Marino notes (*Owning William Shakespeare*, 97, 99) that his name gets unusual emphasis because it was already familiar from two Admiral's Men plays.
18. See Paris, *Hamlet, ou les Personnages du fils*, 184, and de Grazia, *Hamlet Without Hamlet*, 81–2.
19. M. Eccles, *Shakespeare in Warwickshire*, 108.
20. Ibid., 99; see also Fripp, *Master Richard Quyney.*
21. M. Eccles, *Shakespeare in Warwickshire*, 77. Fripp suggests the connection in *Minutes*, IV: xxxi.
22. M. Eccles, *Shakespeare in Warwickshire*, 133.
23. Arlidge, *Shakespeare and the Prince of Love*, 33.
24. *The Diary of John Manningham*, ed. Sorlien, 48.
25. Wheeler, "Deaths in the Family," 151.
26. Butler, "Armin, Robert," *ODNB.*
27. *Twelfth Night*, ed. Lothian and Craik, xcvii; ed. Warren and Wells, 58.
28. See *Troilus and Cressida*, ed. Bevington, 375–6.
29. Lydgate, *The Historye, Sege, and Destruction of Troye*, 2784–2836, in Bullough, 6: 185–6.
30. See e.g. the letters of Rowland Whyte to Sir Robert Sidney in the summer of 1600, esp. those of 7 June, 11 June, and 26 July, in *Letters and memorials of state* (1746), 2: 200–8.
31. *A Discourse of English Poetrie* (1586), in *Elizabethan Critical Essays*, ed. Smith, 1: 241.
32. Rowland, *Thomas Heywood's Theatre, 1599–1639*, 147, n 145.

33. Heywood, *A Woman Killed with Kindness*, ed. van Fossen, 8.72.
34. C. Eccles, *The Rose Theatre*, 78.
35. C. Loomis, *The Death of Elizabeth I*, 14.
36. See e.g. Chamberlain, *Letters*, ed. McLure, 1: 188.
37. *The Diary of John Manningham*, ed. Sorlien, 205–6, 209.
38. Barroll, *Politics, Plague, and Shakespeare's Theater*, 33–4.

14

"This Most Balmy Time"
1603–1605

> *Not mine own fears nor the prophetic soul*
> *Of the wide world dreaming on things to come*
> *Can yet the lease of my true love control,*
> *Supposed as forfeit to a confined doom.*
> *The mortal moon hath her eclipse endured,*
> *And the sad augurs mock their own presage;*
> *Incertainties now crown themselves assured,*
> *And peace proclaims olives of endless age.*
> *Now with the drops of this most balmy time*
> *My love looks fresh, and Death to me subscribes,*
> *Since, spite of him, I'll live in this poor rhyme,*
> *While he insults o'er dull and speechless tribes;*
>   *And thou in this shalt find thy monument*
>   *When tyrants' crests and tombs of brass are spent.*
>   (Sonnet 107)

Several of Shakespeare's sonnets seem to be post-1603. Sonnets 123–5 refer to "pyramids" such as those on the triumphal arches built for James's entry into the city (123.2); to "state" (124.1) and "Policy" (124.9); and to bearing the canopy – apparently both an honor and a sign of obsequiousness to authority (125.1–4). The allusions are hardly celebratory, since the sonnets reject public success and fame in favor of the personal relationship with the person they address.

Sonnet 107 is more optimistic. Since "endured" can mean either "survived" or "suffered," the "mortal moon" has been interpreted to mean the crescent-shaped Armada of 1588, the queen's grand climacteric (the age of 63, supposedly dangerous) of 1595, and her death in 1603. The last is the most likely: before 1603, even in a

The Life of William Shakespeare: A Critical Biography, First Edition. Lois Potter.
© 2012 Lois Potter. Published 2012 by Blackwell Publishing Ltd.

privately circulated poem, it might have been risky to refer to her mortality, much less to her death. Venus, addressing Adonis in a time of plague, had rejected the gloomy prophecies of "the stargazers, having writ on death." Against the background of another plague, Shakespeare sees the "balmy time" of James's coronation as an antidote to gloomy forecasts. The abstractions of line 7 ("Incertainties now crown themselves assured") are obscure, as allegories were supposed to be. James's coronation in July 1603 had ended a long period of uncertainty; there may be a submerged suggestion that Incertainty had actually become Assurance, as a ruler might take on a new name at his coronation, or a Vice in drama assume the name of a virtue. The other possible meaning – that uncertainty was now crowned – undercuts the promises of assurance and peace.[1]

As often in Shakespeare, it is not clear whether "love" means the emotion or the person who is its object, or whether that object is also the "thou" addressed in the couplet. The lines might be relevant to either Southampton or Pembroke, since both benefited from the accession of a king who saw Essex and his followers as martyrs in his cause. Southampton, who had been in the Tower since the Essex rebellion, was released by an order of 5 April 1603 and restored to his earldom. Writers once again started dedicating books to him,[2] and poets wrote verses celebrating his release.[3] William Herbert, now Earl of Pembroke, who had suffered a brief period of imprisonment under Elizabeth, received the Order of the Garter from James in June 1603.[4] If either of these lords is "my love," the patron–client relationship must have been both longer and more public than the other evidence indicates. Or, as both Katherine Duncan-Jones and MacDonald P. Jackson have suggested, the object of these poems may be a composite of the two lords and perhaps others.[5]

Duncan-Jones points out that Michael Drayton wrote in similar terms in a sonnet published in 1605, mentioning even more public events:

> Essex' great fall, Tyrone his peace to gain,
> The quiet end of that long-living Queen,
> This King's fair entrance, and our peace with Spain,
> We and the Dutch at length ourselves to sever.
> Thus the world doth and evermore shall reel;
> Yet to my Goddess am I constant ever,
> Howe'er blind Fortune turn her giddy wheel.[6]

Drayton may have been somewhat uneasy about the "peace with Spain" which, as he says, led to a break with the Protestant states of Holland and the cause for which Sir Philip Sidney had died. Others, too, were nervous about the imminent return of so many soldiers who had been accustomed to a life of killing and looting, and about the fact that the peace treaty had effected the instant transformation of heroic privateers into lawless pirates. None of this gets into Shakespeare's sonnet. Both poets contrast their own constancy in love with the changing events around them, but in

Shakespeare's case love dominates so much that it is difficult to know exactly which events he means. While Duncan-Jones thinks that Drayton may have known Shakespeare's sonnet, it might be the other way round. Shakespeare could be less specific than Drayton if he was assuming knowledge of the earlier poem.

Welcoming the New Reign

The accession of James VI of Scotland, as James I of England, was welcomed by nearly everyone. He was 36 – a little over half the age of the late queen – with two sons, a daughter, and a pregnant wife. England had a royal family, for the first time in over fifty years, and an apparently assured succession. As John Chamberlain wrote in one of his entertaining letters, "not only protestants, but papists and puritans, and the very poets with their idle pamphlets promise themselves great part in his favor."[7] Everyone had reason to hope for something from the son of a devout Catholic mother who had been brought up by a devout Presbyterian scholar. James was an enthusiastic religious controversialist, apparently open to arguments from all sides. He had corresponded with Anglican writers and shown sympathy toward the Church of England, but on his way to London he had been polite with Puritans who were calling for further reforms. James looked good on paper and had already filled a good deal of it. His book on the art of ruling (*Basilikon Doron* [The King's Gift]) became a best-seller on his accession. The players noted that in 1601 he had allowed English actors to perform in Edinburgh despite opposition from the Kirk. Through his French relatives and the Danish ones he acquired through marriage he had links with most other European countries. His court would receive not only diplomatic missions but friendly royal visits, occasions on which court entertainments would be needed.

Ben Jonson, Samuel Daniel, and Michael Drayton all wrote congratulatory poems. Henry Chettle implicitly reproached them for forgetting Elizabeth, pointedly dedicating his own poem to "*all that loued the deceased Queene, and honor the liuing King.*" He may have been alluding to Shakespeare when he commented on the silence of "Melicert" (*mel* means honey, and sweetness was constantly associated with Shakespeare).[8] If the phrase "tyrants' crests" at the end of Sonnet 107 reflects his feelings about Elizabeth's last years, there was a reason for the poet's silence. He may have welcomed the new reign, but only in ephemeral prologues and epilogues.

James set off for his new capital on 4 April, but traveled slowly, both in order to go hunting wherever possible and to avoid arriving before the queen's funeral, which took place on 28 April.[9] The Chamberlain's Men probably marched in that procession, so they would have been in London when her successor arrived.[10] One of James's first acts was to take the company under his own patronage. In the Royal Patent of 17 May the players were listed as "Lawrence Fletcher, William Shakespeare, Richard Burbage, Augustine Philips, John Heminges, Henry Condell,

William Sly, Robert Armyn, Richard Cowley, and the rest of their Associates." They were licensed to produce "comedies, tragedies, histories, enterludes, morals, pastorals, stage plays and such others like as they have already studied, or hereafter shall use or study."[11] The prominence of Lawrence Fletcher in this list is due to his previous role as the head of a dramatic company that performed at James's court in 1599 and 1601. Perhaps the earls of Southampton and Pembroke had something to do with the king's action at a time when there were many higher priorities than the fate of a company of players.[12] James eventually gave patents to the Admiral's and Worcester's Men, who became Prince Henry's and the Queen's Men respectively. The boys' companies became the Children of the Queen's and King's Revels. Princess Elizabeth and Prince Charles would be assigned their own companies later. The players were part of the court, and in that capacity had to swear an oath of loyalty either to the lord chamberlain or to his deputy.[13]

Relief at the peaceful succession was brief, since the plague that began in May 1603 grew virulent during an unusually hot June.[14] Though the royal entry into London was put off until it was felt safe for crowds to assemble, the coronation itself took place on 25 July, a small and deliberately muted affair with admission by ticket only.[15] The King's Men probably celebrated on tour in Bath rather than in London.[16] After that, Shakespeare could have returned to Stratford, but he needed to spend much of the autumn of 1603 planning, with his colleagues, a series of plays for the new court.

Deaths caused by the plague, and the long break in public playing, meant changes in the company's personnel. Boy actors like Cooke, Gough, and Tooley graduated to male roles (the first two were married by now); Phillips's apprentices Gilburne and Sandes moved up in the hierarchy; and the company acquired new boys. This may be when John Rice, the leading boy actor of the decade, joined the company, though he is not mentioned until 1607. Other boys may have been bought from the children's companies, such as John Underwood and William Ostler, who moved on to adult roles in the next decade. An adult actor, who would eventually be the company's longest-serving one, was John Lowin: like Armin, he had been apprenticed as a goldsmith, but was probably already acting before the end of his apprenticeship in 1602, since he played leading roles from the beginning.[17] At some point, he probably took over as Falstaff. The portrait painted of him in 1640 (Figure 14) shows that he filled the stage in every sense. Jonson probably wrote the role of Sir Epicure Mammon in *The Alchemist* (1610) for him. He may have been the first Iago, or at least the second.

On 2 November 1603, "William Kemp, a Man" was buried at St. Saviour's in Southwark.[18] If this was the famous Will Kemp, one would expect the event to get more attention, even at a time of widespread mortality. The first Quarto of *Hamlet*, published this year, contains a tribute to the fictitious jester Yorick which is often thought of as a tribute to Richard Tarleton, dead since 1588. In performance, audiences might have thought of Kemp, or of Thomas Pope, who was dead by late

Nugent Sculp.

JOHN   LOWIN.

1640. Ætat. 64.

From an Original Picture in the Ashmole Museum, Oxford.

London Pub June 7 1792 by E Harding Pall Mall Street.

Figure 14 John Lowin, aged 64 in 1640. He acted with the King's Men for their entire history up to the outbreak of the Civil War. Print by Thomas Nugent, based on the painting, by an unknown artist, at the Ashmolean Museum, Oxford. By permission of the Folger Shakespeare Library

1604. Kemp may in fact have survived the plague: Katherine Duncan-Jones has found that a Will Kemp was the servant of Lady Hunsdon, widow of the former Lord Chamberlain.[19] Nothing else is heard of him, which seems odd for such a self-publicist, but he had been looking, like everyone else, for security, and perhaps he fell silent once he had achieved it.

If *Sir Thomas More* was ever performed, it might have been during the long period between the queen's death and the first court performances. It is clear from the

304

correspondence of ambassadors from Catholic countries, much of it wishful thinking, that they hoped for a change in the state religion. According to the Venetian secretary, writing in late April, "Elizabeth's portrait is being hidden everywhere, and Mary Stuart's shown instead with declaration that she suffered for no other cause than for her religion."[20] Those who met James early, such as Sir John Harington, also noticed that he spoke much of his mother's death.[21] As John Jowett suggests, there are elements in *Sir Thomas More* suggesting that, at least for some of its authors, it was really "the life and death of a martyr."[22] Someone might have thought that the play would be appropriate for the court of a man who prided himself on his learning and revered his mother's memory. At the beginning of James's reign, Jowett suggests, the mob scenes might have seemed less inflammatory, and the prospect of peace with Spain might make the subject matter "a timely renegotiation of the Catholic past and of Henry VIII's break with it."[23] Unfortunately, given the tensions between the English and the newly arrived Scots, those scenes might by now have acquired a different sort of topicality, at least in Tilney's eyes. James had not emulated Henri IV of France, and English Catholics were already beginning to feel the frustration that would lead a small group of them to become the Gunpowder plotters. It is possible that some other version of the More play ended up with a touring company, like the one that, a few years later, was accused of performing Catholic plays to sympathetic audiences in Yorkshire (see Chapter 16 below).

The 1603/1604 Season

All three companies had been invited to perform at Hampton Court during the Christmas season, but, because of the plague, none could rehearse by giving public performances in the playhouses. The court had moved to Wilton, the home of the Earl of Pembroke, and government business was being transacted at Winchester. In December 1603 someone – perhaps Pembroke – arranged for the Lord Chamberlain's Men to perform at Wilton and paid them an exceptionally large fee to cover the time and trouble of their journey. They traveled from Mortlake, where Augustine Phillips lived; they may have been using his house as their base rather than staying in London.[24] Line-learning could be done anywhere, but the spectacular effects required in a court performance needed space for rehearsal. It is possible that the Wilton visit was intended for the company not only to perform but also to rehearse the plays for Christmas.

A fascinating but undocumented possibility is suggested by something a visitor wrote from Wilton in 1865: "The house (Lady Herbert said) is full of interest: above us is Wolsey's room; we have a letter, never printed, from Lady Pembroke to her son, telling him to bring James I from Salisbury to see *As You Like It*; 'we have the man Shakespeare with us.' She wanted to cajole the King in Raleigh's behalf – he came."[25] Since the letter containing this unlikely phrase has never been found and the Victorian Lady Herbert is not always a reliable source,[26] the story sounds too good to be true; on the other hand, it is consistent with what the countess was in fact doing late in 1603, when Ralegh's trial, near-execution, and life sentence were the most discussed events of the day.[27] Shakespeare, especially if he had once been part of Pembroke's Men, could by now have been well known at Wilton.

Among the plays given when the court moved to Hampton Court was *A Midsummer Night's Dream*, performed for 10-year-old Prince Henry on New Year's Day 1604. Other Shakespeare plays must have been on the program, probably including *Hamlet*, which, according to the title page of Q1, had recently been acted in Oxford and Cambridge.[28] The company also played *The Fair Maid of Bristow* [Bristol], an anonymous comedy with many of Shakespeare's favorite themes – betrayed friendship, disguises, characters who are wrongly thought dead, and a heroine who wants to save her husband's life even though he has tried to have her poisoned. The prince may have liked it better than the *Dream* because it contains a sword fight. If Shakespeare acted in *The Fair Maid of Bristow*, he may have remembered the audience's delight at the *coup de théâtre* in the final scene, when a hooded friar casts off his disguise, revealing that he is the man for whose murder three other characters have been sentenced to death.

The other play the King's Men are known to have given during that season is Jonson's *Sejanus His Fall*, probably written in 1602–3 but postponed because of the plague and the queen's death. Like much of Jonson's work, this play is surrounded with controversy. He said many years later that it led to his being brought before the Privy Council and accused of "popery and treason," perhaps because of the resemblance between a treason trial in the play and that of Sir Walter Ralegh in November 1603.[29] Jonson published *Sejanus* in 1605 with the full trappings of a literary work: an address to the readers, commendatory poems (Chapman and Marston contributed), marginal notes identifying the sources, but *not* – "something unheard of for a stage play," as Eugene Giddens points out – any mention of the company that had performed it.[30]

Jonson himself wrote in his "Epistle to the Readers" that the published text was "not the same with that which was acted on the public stage, wherein a second pen had good share; in place of which I have rather chosen to put weaker (and no doubt less pleasing) of mine own, than to defraud so happy a genius of his right by my loathèd usurpation." Considering how much he praises this "second pen," it is odd that Jonson did not name him. If he meant that the play was originally written in collaboration, the collaborator could have been Chapman.[31] Chapman was even more fond of topical satire than Jonson, so excising his parts of the play might simultaneously have made it less offensive. On the other hand, there might be some significance in the phrase "public stage." If the play was first given at court and then, after a pause, at the reopened Globe, someone in the King's Men may have felt that it needed to be made more entertaining. The audience was, after all, used to Jonson as the author of comedies, and *Sejanus* is a bitterly satiric tragedy. It is possible that Shakespeare was involved in – even insisted on – some minor touching-up, probably to Jonson's annoyance: hence the sarcasm in "so happy a genius" and "my loathèd usurpation."

As the plague was finally considered to have ended, the king made his formal entry to London on 15 March 1604. Members of the royal household, including the players, were issued four and a half yards of red cloth each, so that the city would be filled with festive colors. Some of the speeches from the elaborate triumphal arches were made by professional actors. As Alan H. Nelson argues, Shakespeare may well have been among them.[32] The Globe reopened on 9 April, and *Sejanus*'s first public performance finally took place.[33] It became a legendary theatrical disaster. Jonson's dedication compares its fate to that of its title character, who was torn to pieces by the Roman public. Audiences apparently divided along class lines. In the commendatory verses one writer refers to "the people's beastly rage,/ Bent to confound thy grave and learned toil" while another contrasts the "wits of gentry" who applauded.[34] It is not hard to understand the reaction of a popular audience. *Sejanus* is too long, its characters are exceptionally unpleasant, and the ending leaves neither a sense of tragedy nor any belief that justice has been done. What is important here is that, if it was indeed hissed off the stage, Shakespeare, who was in the cast, was among those subjected to the hissing. As a well-known company member, he may even have spoken the Epilogue inviting the audience to applaud, in which case he would have experienced the full force of their anger at the play. It might have had a decisive effect. When biographers comment on Shakespeare's "disappearance" from cast lists after 1604, they imply the existence of many other cast lists in which he should be present but isn't, whereas in fact very few have survived. However, *Sejanus* is the last play with which he is associated as an actor, and his name does not appear in the cast of *Volpone* (1605–6), the next Jonson play performed by the King's Men. A list of fees paid to "Players of enterludes," dated 1607, names the company as "Burbage, Fletcher, Alexander Cook, Heminges, John Lowin, Armin, with others." Shakespeare was hardly so unimportant as to be one of the "others."[35]

Quite apart from the *Sejanus* fiasco, the company's new status may have made the playwright eager to shake off the image of the actor and, like Edward Alleyn, to ration his stage appearances in order to cultivate his status as a gentleman. Stubbes's moralistic question, "who will call him a wise man that playeth the part of a foole and a Vice?,"[36] may seem naive, but a surprising number of spectators believe that actors resemble the characters they play, and many scholars still think that Shakespeare played characters whose views were authorial. By the summer of 1604 he had left rowdy and unhealthy Southwark for the more fashionable area of Cripplegate, and was renting a room from Christopher and Marie Mountjoy, French Huguenot immigrants.[37] Their house in Silver Street was also the shop where they made "tires" – fancy headdresses for masques and plays, using gold and silver wires covered with lace. One attraction of its location was its proximity to the Castle Inn, from which carriers went to Stratford on their way to Worcester and Evesham. His colleagues Heminges and Condell also lived in the area, as did Richard and Jacqueline Field. It is unlikely that Shakespeare learned French from the Mountjoys, since he must already have been studying it by the early 1590s, but he might have enjoyed practicing it.

He may even have needed to use the language. In August 1604 the Constable of Castille came to London to sign the peace treaty between England and Spain. It was the first major international visit of the new reign, and James was determined to make an impression on the delegations from Spain and the Spanish Netherlands. They were lodged, respectively, in Somerset House and Durham House, now furnished with tapestries and elegant canopied chairs that had been moved from other palaces. Having to provide attendants for all the diplomats and their suites evidently stretched the capacity of James's court. Since both Southampton and Pembroke took part in the peace negotiations, it may have been one of them who suggested that the households should be temporarily supplemented by Grooms of the Chamber, consisting of twelve members of the King's and Queen's companies of actors.[38] Shakespeare was probably one of the twelve who served the Spanish delegation. While many legends have been spun around the episode (for instance, that Cervantes was in London, which he was not), it seems that the main reason for using the actors was to impress the Spaniards with the good looks and bearing of the king's servants.

Ten days of subsidized food and drink represented a considerable help to the players. They valued the opportunity to observe the famous Spanish formal manners, which they might need to imitate in the theater. While Shakespeare could have traveled back to Silver Street at night, it would have been easier to stay at Somerset House. If he talked with the visitors, he probably used French, although he may have made some attempt to learn Spanish, which was becoming fashionable. Exactly what the grooms did to earn their *per diem* is not clear. Since the Constable had kept James awaiting his arrival for months, into the start of the all-important hunting season, James remained in the country even after the Spanish party had reached London. Perhaps he expected the actors to entertain the visitors with a play during his absence. However, the Spanish reporter, who went into detail over everything else, including the splendid canopies in the state rooms that may be recalled in Shakespeare's Sonnet 125, and describes rope dancing and tumbling after the formal signing of the treaty, never mentions plays.[39] Both the Constable and the envoy from the Low Countries were in poor health and spent as much time as possible in their private apartments, gathering strength for the exhausting public events: as a courtier says in Marston's *The Malcontent*, probably satirizing these negotiations, "you know your ambassador must drink" (3.1.70–1). Illness may have been a cover for secret meetings. A secondary purpose of the Spanish delegation was to bribe influential courtiers to work on behalf of English Catholics and Spanish interests. The universal greed for Spanish gold inspired contempt at home and abroad, and the most shameless courtier of all was the Countess of Suffolk, wife of the lord chamberlain. The actors themselves profited: the budget for the Spanish embassy included not only official presents and unofficial bribes, but also a total of 6,000 ducats for "the guards, officials and lesser servants of the Royal Palace."[40] Shakespeare received a farewell present – perhaps the silver gilt bowl mentioned in his will.

Returning to the Mountjoy house, Shakespeare soon found himself drawn into his one recorded interaction with the family. He knew, perhaps from mealtime conversation, that they thought well of their apprentice Stephen Belott. It must have been shortly after his ten-day stint at Somerset House that he was asked by Mrs. Mountjoy to persuade Belott to marry their daughter Marie.[41] How much persuasion was necessary is not clear. With the apprentice, the poet discussed dowries (a subject that, given the ages of his own daughters, he must already have thought about). He may have been present at the formal betrothal and could have attended the wedding on 19 November, since he would have been in town for the court performances at the beginning of November and then for rehearsals of the Christmas ones. About six months later, the Belotts moved out of the Mountjoys' lodgings and took up residence in the house of George Wilkins, probably nearby in St. Giles, Cripplegate. Wilkins was also a writer. He and Shakespeare would soon be colleagues of sorts.

The King's Playwright?

The new royal family was proving almost embarrassingly enthusiastic about the theater. The Revels accounts speak for themselves. Elizabeth saw more plays near the end of her reign than at the beginning, reaching a maximum of eleven in 1600–1,[42] but Shakespeare had to fit into an already existing court culture and established preferences. James, on the other hand, was developing a court of his own. He was frequently absent – about half the year in fact – because of his passion for hunting,[43] but he saw plays throughout the year and subsidized performances for his family when he was not present. The season of 1604/5 is unusually well documented. It began early, like its predecessor, and went up to the beginning of Lent, perhaps to make up for the long period of plague closure. *Othello*, on 1 November 1604, was followed three days later by *The Merry Wives of Windsor* (pairing tragic and comic jealousy). The Christmas playing season began on 26 December, with *Measure for Measure*. The court also saw *Henry V*, Jonson's two *Every Man* comedies, and an otherwise unknown play called *The Spanish Maze*, chosen perhaps because it recalled the recent peace negotiations. For some reason, *The Merchant of Venice* was performed both on 10 and 12 February. Either the king liked it enough to demand a second showing or someone who had missed the first performance was being accommodated by a second one.

The company members, then, needed even more plays than usual to maintain their status as the acknowledged royal players. Already by January 1605 one of the Burbage brothers had to tell a courtier, delegated to find something with which to entertain the queen, that the company had "no new play that the queen hath not seen," but the actors "have revived an old one called *Loves Labor Lost* which for wit and mirth he says will please her exceedingly."[44] Even this play had already been booked by the Earl of Southampton, who probably knew it well. Both courtiers feasted the queen, but it is not known which of them ended up hosting the performance. Oddly enough, it was part of the celebrations for the arrival of the queen's brother, Ulric, Duke of Holstein. *Love's Labour's Lost* seems the worst possible choice for a 24-year-old prince who knew no English, but, as under Elizabeth, the players were constantly called on to perform before foreign rulers and ambassadors. The experience of these visitors must have been much like that of the typical opera-goer before the days of surtitles. The duke was in fact so enthusiastic that he attempted to create his own company of players.[45]

It is sometimes argued that the so-called Jacobean drama owed more to the patronage of James's wife and children than to him.[46] The main evidence for this view is a letter dated 15 January 1604 in which Dudley Carleton told John Chamberlain that "The first holy days we had every night a public play in the great hall, at which the king was ever present and liked or disliked as he saw cause, but it seems he takes no extraordinary pleasure in them. The queen and prince were more the players' friends, for on other nights they had them privately and have since taken them to their protection."[47] It does not seem unreasonable for James to like or dislike as he saw cause; perhaps Carleton expected him to be dazzled, as foreign visitors often were, at the sumptuous costumes and polished performances of the English players. Despite this early impression of indifference, James, in the winter of 1607/8, was recorded by Chamberlain as taking a very different view: "The King was very earnest to have one [play] on Christmas-night, (though as I take it he and the Prince received [took communion] that day) but the Lords told him it was not the fashion, which answer pleased him not a whit, but said what do you tell me of the fashion? I will make it a fashion."[48] Moreover, he compensated his men – apparently, alone among the dramatic companies – for their loss of earnings during the plagues of 1608–9 (£30) and 1609–10 (£40).[49] In 1610–11 he attended ten plays and a masque, while another twenty-six plays were given before one or more of the royal children, presumably with Queen Anna also in attendance.[50] There is, then, no evidence that, as one biographer puts it, James "fell asleep during England's most celebrated plays."[51] If this happened, it would have been in later years, when he was in poor health and drank more heavily.

Could Shakespeare have been disappointed in his expectations from the king? Katherine Duncan-Jones has seen a hint of this in two poems by John Davies of Hereford that seem to date from this period. One says of Shakespeare and Burbage that

> Fell *Fortune* cannot be excus'd,
> That hath for better uses you refus'd.

In the other, a poem about the 1603 plague, published in 1609 as *Humours heav'n on earth*, he added a marginal note, "W.S.," to a line about those that Fortune "guerdond not, to their desarts."[52] As Jackson suggests, Davies's 1603 poem may be in dialogue with the opening lines of Shakespeare's Sonnet 111:

> Oh, for my sake do you with Fortune chide,
> The guilty goddess of my harmful deeds,
> That did not better for my life provide
> Than public means which public manners breeds.

If Shakespeare is answering Davies's poem, his fourth line might end with a question mark. On the other hand, "do you" may be an imperative, in which case Davies, who could have read the sonnet before it was printed, might see himself as fulfilling a request.[53]

In 1610 Davies published another collection of epigrams that included the most intriguing verses on Shakespeare written during the poet's lifetime:

> *To Our English Terence Mr. Will: Shakespeare*
> *Epig.* 159
>
> Some say good *Will* (which I, in sport, do sing),
> Had'st thou not played some Kingly parts in sport,
> Thou hadst bin a companion for a *King*;
> And, been a King among the meaner sort.
> Some others rail; but rail as they think fit,
> Thou hast no railing but a reigning Wit:
> *And* honesty *thou sow'st, which they do reap;*
> *So, to increase their* Stock *which they do keep.*

The verses form part of a group addressed to other friends and writers with court connections, such as Samuel Daniel, Ben Jonson, and Inigo Jones. It is to "others" that Davies attributes both the unspecified "railing" and the mysterious comment that Shakespeare might have been "companion for a King" if he had not been an actor who played kings. It is not clear whether the lines mean anything more specific than that Shakespeare's gifts make him equal to anyone, however high-born.[54] Duncan-Jones has suggested that Shakespeare had hoped, as Edward Alleyn was said to have hoped, to be made a knight at James's accession.[55] Davies might have been thinking about the formation of Prince Henry's household, which was already large long before the king allowed him a separate establishment in 1610. James had a strong sense of the importance of the arts for the prestige of a country, and his plans for his children's education involved those whom he regarded as the most important representatives of English culture: Chapman, Drayton, and Daniel, all of whom were both poets and translators. Since Davies himself was a famous calligrapher and taught the prince penmanship, he knew these companions for a (future) king. None of them, of course, had ever been on the stage. Leeds Barroll notes pertinently that in *Basilikon Doron* James advised

Henry not to make friends with comedians, warning him that tyrants had often delighted in the theater.[56]

It is in fact quite likely that the players had even more contact, at least with the queen and her children, than has been recorded. As Michael Dobson notes, Hal and Falstaff's "play extempore" and Hamlet's brief performance of a speech from a favorite play are examples of the taste for amateur theatricals traditionally found in royal and aristocratic circles, though most recorded examples date from a later period.[57] James's circle of poets in Edinburgh may or may not have read plays as well as poems, but at the English court the availability of several companies of actors could have allowed the royal children to benefit from coaching by experienced professionals. In 1633, when Henrietta Maria and her ladies were preparing to perform Walter Montague's *The Shepherds' Paradise* for a private court audience, they were given intensive rehearsals by Joseph Taylor, who succeeded Burbage as the leading actor of the King's Men.[58] James's court was in touch with events in France, where amateur theatricals were popular. The physician to the future Louis XIII of France records that, after seeing a performance by visiting English actors in 1604, the 3-year-old announced that he wanted to act himself.[59] As John H. Astington suggests, quoting this example, "The training of a prince might have included the example of stage kings."[60]

By the eighteenth century, actors were often teachers of elocution: when George III made his first public speech as king, the famous actor James Quin is supposed to have exclaimed, "Ah! I taught the boy to speak"[61] There is no indication that the future Charles I, who suffered from a speech impediment, was ever tutored by Burbage, but if James's children were like other spectators of this period they probably wanted to perform plays themselves, with or without the collaboration of professionals. For those who did not have the time to learn lines, reading aloud was an alternative. The ideal audience for the plays that Shakespeare was writing from 1600 on would have been one whose members did not have to leave before dark and who could stop the reading to comment on the lines they had just heard. There is no proof that such an audience ever existed, but if it did (at court? at the Inns? among friends?), it might explain why Shakespeare continued to write both at length and in depth throughout James's reign.

Though some scholars find it distasteful to imagine a great poet writing with a view to the preferences of *Jacobus Rex*, the Jacobean players badly needed the royal largesse. Sunday performances were forbidden throughout James's reign, as they had not been under Elizabeth.[62] There were probably fewer opportunities to tour. James's letter to the university, city, and county of Cambridge, dated 26 July 1604, encouraged student performances but forbade anything "unprofitable or idle" within five miles of the city, including "interludes, comedies, and tragedies in the English tongue."[63] Combined with frequent visitations of the plague, these restrictions reduced the opportunities for public performance and made the King's Men still more dependent on the taste of the court and private patrons.

In writing his earlier tragedies, Shakespeare seems to have been mindful of the prohibitions on the discussion of religion on the stage, setting his plays either in pagan or in Catholic countries (though the clergymen in *Love's Labour's Lost*, *The Merry Wives*, *As You Like It*, and probably *Twelfth Night* are clearly Protestant and English). The references to Wittenburg and Purgatory in *Hamlet* are a cautious venture into forbidden territory. It was known in 1603 that James was planning to hold a major conference at Hampton Court about the reform of religion in England. The early Jacobean plays, both comic and tragic, seem designed for an audience that took theological questions seriously. The time of plague was another sobering influence. There was considerable controversy in 1603 as to whether it was permissible to take preventative measures against what, some Puritans argued, was not simply a disease but the hand of God.[64]

Shakespeare may have had his own reasons for thinking about hypocrisy and evil, the subjects of his next plays. It was only in the fall of 1602 that his ownership of New Place was finally confirmed, when the next heir to William Underhill came of age and Shakespeare paid the fee to clear the title.[65] Though his right to the property had not really been in danger, the transaction must have brought back memories of Underhill's murder by his older son. If Shakespeare had met the young man during the negotiations over New Place, he must have recalled his failure to recognize anything suspicious about him.

Measure for Measure

Following James's accession, several dramatists, starting with Marston in *The Malcontent*, wrote plays in which a wise ruler mingles with his people in disguise and solves everyone's problems. The energetic activity of the Duke in *Measure for Measure* is Shakespeare's main departure from his source, George Whetstone's *Promos and Cassandra* (1578). Part One of Whetstone's play shows the degeneration of a Hungarian city under a corrupt deputy, Promos, who blackmails Cassandra into sex in exchange for her brother's life. When she yields at her brother's pleading, Promos betrays her by ordering the execution to proceed, though fortunately the brother escapes from prison. The King appears for the first time only in Part Two. When his agents expose Promos's villainy, he forces the deputy to marry Cassandra, intending to execute him afterwards. Cassandra, believing that her duty as a wife supersedes her duty to take vengeance, pleads for Promos. The situation is resolved when her supposedly dead brother reveals himself. He and Cassandra have a joyful reunion and both couples appear to be happy.

313

It is not clear where or whether Whetstone's play was performed, but it was certainly written with performance in mind, perhaps at one of the Inns. Whether or not he ever saw it, Shakespeare could appreciate the potential appeal of its low-life scenes and the clashes between various clownish figures and a corrupt legal system. As if gesturing toward his source, he included deliberately archaic octosyllabic couplets (oddly enough, given to the Duke, who in Whetstone speaks blank verse). His characters, like Whetstone's, conduct intellectual arguments but respond to their situations with intense emotion. In particular, Claudio expresses a chilling fear of death ("this sensible warm motion to become/ A kneaded clod," 3.1.121–2). The debate about justice and mercy in *The Merchant of Venice* becomes the play's center in the brilliant scenes between Isabella and Angelo, but the argument ceases to matter when Isabella's very innocence awakens Angelo's desire. The questions the play asks – How far can either justice or mercy go before they become ineffectual? Is a woman damned (as Isabella believes) even if she loses her virginity for a virtuous purpose? Is a man guilty of a crime that he intended to commit, and thinks he has committed, even though he has not in fact done so? – are so interesting that it is hard to imagine any ending that would not disappoint. Though the final scene is full of brilliant comic twists, like the one that makes Lucio himself reveal the identity of the man who will prove him a liar, the Duke's manipulations evade rather than answer the major issues. People who believed in an all-powerful and all-knowing God might not find anything suspect in a ruler whose observation is compared to "power divine" (5.1.377), especially if his machinations brought about comic complications and a happy ending. On the other hand, the Duke's insistence that the "bed trick" is legitimate ("To bring you thus together, 'tis no sin," 4.1.72) would hardly be necessary unless it was controversial. In the final speech, the Duke's casual revelation that he has heard Mariana's confession in his disguise as Friar (5.1.538) seems designed to shock any Catholics in the audience.

Measure for Measure not only seems to know James's dislike of crowds (1.1.68–73) but also to assume that he will not mind having it alluded to in public. Since the play was not published until 1623, it is possible that its "Jacobean" feeling was intensified at a later date. Jonathan Goldberg has pointed out how completely the final scene recalls James's last-minute pardon in December 1603 of the convicted Main Plot conspirators, which contemporaries saw as royal theatricality.[66] Gary Taylor and John Jowett think that Thomas Middleton revised the play, perhaps in 1621, to update the political references, adding Mariana's song and developing the characters of Lucio and the two Gentlemen in order to create further opportunities for satire.[67] There is enough confusion in the play to suggest revision: two of the Duke's speeches seem to have been accidentally transposed, and the scenes preceding his official return to Vienna (4.5.12–14) prepare for something more elaborate than actually happens. The King's Men may initially have attempted to recreate the pageantry that accompanied James's formal arrival into London, removing it in later revivals when it was no longer relevant.

Othello

As Ernst Honigmann has pointed out, the relationship of Iago with his gull Roderigo in *Othello* is very close to that of Sir Toby with Sir Andrew in *Twelfth Night*, performed in 1602,[68] and the tragedy may have been written soon afterwards, though not acted until the 1603 plague was over. As I have suggested, Shakespeare had been presenting jokers more ambiguously, even negatively, with each play, and Iago is, as W. H. Auden brilliantly argued, the quintessential joker: "Practical jokes are a demonstration that the distinction between seriousness and play is not a law of nature but a social convention which can be broken, and that a man does not always require a serious motive for deceiving another."[69] It is no accident that Iago is also a dispenser of *sententiae* like "Who steals my purse steals trash" (3.3.170), which even now are often quoted approvingly. Perhaps there is no need to look further for the germ of his character than Cinthio's description of the villain in his story as an attractive and plausible scoundrel. While the spectators at *Othello* are never in ignorance of Iago's plans, their simultaneous awareness of how convincing he looks to others and how evil they know him to be makes this play the one that has always agitated audiences most violently. Nothing else in Shakespeare creates such a mixture of horror and guilty pleasure as the great scene of 3.3, in which Iago, step by step, destroys Othello's happiness. The final scene, even in the worst productions, is a harrowing experience.

Perhaps relatively few spectators worry about how, within the play's time-scheme, Othello could believe that Cassio was able to seduce Desdemona at all, much less "a thousand times" (5.2.219). Once critics started looking seriously at the question, there seemed to be two possible responses. One was to hypothesize a convention of "double time" which allows the story to operate in two different time-schemes according to its needs. The other was to treat the time-sequence realistically, rejecting the traditional view of Othello as a noble victim of deception and labeling him instead a jealous and stupid man who kills an innocent woman on the flimsiest of evidence. Shakespeare was apparently willing to risk the confusion in order to establish Othello's stature before his transformation into a murderer. While Sophocles was able to show Oedipus going from a great and confident king to a broken exile in the space of a relatively short play, Shakespeare had not yet depicted any tragic hero who was happy at the beginning of his play. Even Titus Andronicus, returning to Rome in triumph, is mourning the deaths of his sons in battle. Romeo is unhappily in love with Rosaline, Brutus is already disturbed when Cassius speaks to him, and Hamlet is in mourning for his father. Act 1 of *Othello* allows Othello to achieve a level of happiness that frightens even him, and to prove his military reputation during the Turkish threat to Venice and Cyprus. Shakespeare knew of James I's epic *Lepanto* (1591), which was republished in 1603. It celebrated the Christian victory in 1571 over "Circumsized turbaned Turks" (line 11), a retaliation for the Turks' seizure of Cyprus in the previous July.

Othello's rescue of Cyprus, thanks to a storm like the one that dispersed the Spanish Armada, is alternative history.

Shakespeare had also read Torquato Tasso's *Gerusalemme Liberata*, published in Edward Fairfax's translation in 1600. Tasso was almost legendary in England by the end of the sixteenth century: a tragic Malvolio, he was believed to have gone mad, and to have been imprisoned, for love of an aristocratic lady. The Admiral's Men had performed plays based on his epic and his supposed life story. *Tasso's Melancholy*, a lost but evidently very popular play first performed in 1594–5, was revived with additions in 1602, perhaps to compete with *Hamlet*.[70] In 1604, the mad lover in an anonymous poem, *Daiphantus*, was compared to both Hamlet and Tasso, perhaps the Tasso of the lost play.[71] Along with the Christian–Muslim conflict and the story of Tancred, who kills the woman he loves through error, an episode in Book II of the poem may have given Shakespeare the idea of further complicating the tissue of lies and deceptions on which Iago's plot is based. The Muslim ruler of occupied Jerusalem orders the entire Christian population to be put to death because an image of the Virgin and Child has disappeared from the mosque in which he had placed it. Sophronia, a young Christian woman, confesses to the theft. It is of her that Tasso uses the phrase *magnanima menzogna* – or, in Fairfax's words, "O noble lie! was ever truth so good?" (II: xxii). When she is about to be burnt, a young man who has secretly loved her springs forward and insists that he was the criminal. They are both lying, and, in the end, they are both pardoned and married.

The question whether it was permissible to lie in a good cause had haunted Christian theology at least since the time of St. Augustine, who had posed a famous dilemma: suppose that someone is gravely ill and asks whether his son, also gravely ill, is still alive. His son is dead, but you know that to tell him so will kill him. Because he has asked you a direct question, silence is not an option. Many people would have been in favor of lying in such a case, citing biblical examples (for example Joshua 2: 4–5), but the Puritan casuist William Perkins insisted that Christians were not permitted to lie, whatever the motive.[72] One reason for Puritan distrust of the virtuous lie was that its best-known practitioners were the Roman Catholic missionary priests who believed that it was permissible to use equivocation or mental reservation in the cause of true religion.

Desdemona is the play's virtuous liar: in the course of the play, she pretends to be merry while she is in fact deeply worried about her husband's safety (2.1.124–5); she says the handkerchief is not lost (3.4.85); and, reviving briefly after Othello has strangled her, she tries to save him by lying about the cause of her death:

> *Emilia.* Oh, who hath done this deed?
> *Desdemona.* Nobody; I myself. Farewell
>   Commend me to my kind lord. Oh, farewell!

(5.2.128)

Othello's "She's like a liar gone to burning hell" and Emilia's reply, "O the more angel she" (5.2.127–8), reflect the current debate about the "virtuous lie." Othello, who thinks Desdemona is lying when she tells him that she is chaste, warns her that she will be damned if she dies with a lie on her lips. In a ghastly irony, this is what she does; since suicide was damnable, she would also have been damned if she had been telling the truth. Emilia's later words to Iago –

> You told a lie, an odious, damned lie!
> Upon my soul, a lie, a wicked lie!
> (5.2.176–7)

– are not tautologous; Emilia is making a contrast with the "noble lie" told by Desdemona on her deathbed. When Othello realizes that he has killed an innocent and loving woman, he reaches for words to describe his anticipation of the Last Judgment:

> When we shall meet at compt,
> This look of thine shall hurl my soul from heaven
> And fiends will snatch at it. Cold, cold, my girl?
> Een like thy chastity. Oh, cursèd, cursèd slave!
> Whip me, ye devils,
> From the possession of this heavenly sight!
> Blow me about in winds! Roast me in sulfur!
> Wash me in steep-down gulfs of liquid fire!
> (5.2.282–9)

Now convinced that his wife is in heaven, Othello in killing himself commits what he believes to be a damnable act that will separate him from her forever. Iago is condemned to "any cunning cruelty/ That can torment him much and hold him long" (5.2.343–4) – that is, something as close as possible to the pains of hell. *The Spanish Tragedy* had ended as its victims were consigned to different parts of a classical afterlife, and Revenge reminded the audience that the story was not yet over:

> For here though death hath end their misery,
> I'll there begin their endless tragedy.

Othello, less absolute about the eternal destinations of its three protagonists, seems designed to provoke agonized questioning about their fates.

Contemporary evidence makes it clear that *Othello* was immensely successful in the public theater, and one other fact suggests that it might have been equally so at court. For her first appearance in a court masque at Whitehall, in January 1605, Queen Anna disconcerted the planners by deciding that she and her ladies would blacken their faces and arms and play African river nymphs who come to Britain to

317

be made white. Jonson duly devised the plot of *The Masque of Blackness* to accommodate this conceit, but the letter-writer Dudley Carleton thought the women looked hideous in their make-up.[73] Moors and moorish costumes had always been more popular in the Scottish court than the English one,[74] but it is at least possible that the queen was responding to the powerful romantic effect of Burbage's Othello.

King Lear

Shakespeare's next two tragedies were probably written very close to each other. Since the Admiral's Men had anticipated the new reign in two (lost) plays about Scottish history,[75] Laurence Fletcher may have suggested that his colleagues in the King's Men should attempt to repeat the success of Shakespeare's English history plays with Scottish subject matter. James's Scottish courtiers were probably not enthusiastic about English history plays, in which they frequently figured as the villains; the English needed to know more about the Scots, and the Scots, starting with James himself, probably wanted to see their own history glorified. James VI's escape from death in the 1600 Gowrie conspiracy had affected him so deeply that he made its date, 5 August, a national holiday. Somebody dramatized the event, and, in December 1604, John Chamberlain wrote:

> the tragedy of Gowrie with all the action and actors hath ben twice represented by the King's players, with exceeding concourse of all sorts of people, but whether the matter or manner be not well handled, or that it be thought unfit that princes should be played on the stage in their lifetime, I hear that some great councillors are much displeased with it, and so is thought shall be forbidden.[76]

Chamberlain, the only source of this information, had not seen the play, and his account leaves many questions unanswered. It implies that someone had impersonated the king, yet that the disapproval came from the Privy Council, not James himself. The King's Men were not punished; in fact, they were conspicuous at court in the winter of 1604/5, giving ten plays, seven of them by Shakespeare. Perhaps the Gowrie incident was overshadowed by the still bigger scandal when Samuel Daniel's classical tragedy *Philotas* was performed at court in January 1605. As Daniel wrote later, he thought that the history of ancient Greece was remote enough not to be contentious, but everyone immediately saw analogies with the career and trial of the Earl of Essex and the nervous author was questioned by the Privy Council.[77] He too, like the King's Men, seems to have continued to receive court patronage, but dramatists had been warned to be careful about their subject matter.

Whether or not he had anything to do with its initial writing, Shakespeare may have wondered about salvaging the Gowrie play. He looked into Scottish history for a story that could be dramatized with fewer problems, but most Scottish heroes owed their fame to defeating the English, something that could hardly make successful public theater drama. The Earl of Gowrie was supposed to have been influenced in his actions by witches' prophecies. Since James had a longstanding interest in witchcraft and demonic possession, and had written about it, Shakespeare took up a book first published in 1603 and popular enough to have been reissued twice, Samuel Harsnett's *Declaration of Egregious Popish Impostures*. Harsnett, an Anglican bishop who had already attacked Puritan claims to exorcise demons, here turned his attentions to a series of Catholic exorcisms of 1585–6 that had been subject to a second inquiry in 1602. Shakespeare might already have known about them, since one of the interrogators in the first trial was Lord Strange and one of the priests who took part in the exorcisms, Robert Dibdale, was born in the Stratford-upon-Avon parish some eight years before Shakespeare.[78] Harsnett's fascinating account assumes that the chambermaids diagnosed with demonic possession were picking up cues from their interrogators; since Shakespeare was presumably planning to depict deceit and conspiracy, the theatricality of the supposed devils' behavior was exactly what he wanted.

However, the exorcism material ended up in a different tragedy. In the summer of 1605, an old anonymous play arrived on the bookstalls: *The True Chronicle History of King Leir*, one of the Queen's Men plays from the 1580s. The company had probably disbanded on Elizabeth's death, which would explain why the play had only just been released for publication.[79] Shakespeare already knew it, however, and had echoed it in some of his early plays. The most obvious resemblance is with this exchange in *Leir*:

> *Ragan.* A[h], good my friend, that I should have thee do
>   Is such a thing as I do shame to speak;
>   Yet it must needs be done.
> *Messenger.* I'll speak it for thee, queen. Shall I kill thy father?
>   I know 'tis that, and if it be so, say.
> *Ragan.* Aye.
> *Messenger.* Why, that's enough.
>
> (4.5.22–8)[80]

Both Richard III, with Buckingham, and King John, with Hubert, try to get someone else to intuit what they are trying to ask for, which in each case is the murder of a child; John tells Hubert that he has "a thing to say" but cannot bring himself to utter it, though both men, in the end, have to be blunt:

> *King John.*   Death.
> *Hubert.* My lord?
> *King John.*   A grave.
> *Hubert.*   He shall not live.
>
> (3.3.75–6)

If, as has recently been argued, the author of *Leir* was Thomas Kyd, Shakespeare would probably have known this fact and it would be natural for him to look again at the play, since Kyd's *Hamlet* had inspired the biggest success of his career.[81] Burbage had played old men in his youth with great success. After young Hamlet and black, middle-aged Othello, a play whose central character was "fourscore and upward" would let him revisit his earlier triumphs as Titus and Hieronimo. Moreover, a play about a king dividing his kingdom could hardly fail to be topical at a time when a new king had just reunited it. The map on display at the start of the play would show the united Britain that James had just created.

The True Chronicle History opens with all three daughters about to be married. Leir decides to trap Cordella, who wants to marry for love, by asking all three how much they love him, since he plans to insist that Cordella prove her words by agreeing to his marriage choice. The elder daughters, tipped off in advance about the plan, find no difficulty in saying that they would do anything for him, but Cordella, revolted by their flattery, simply says that she loves as a child ought to do. The action proceeds as in Shakespeare's main plot. Leir does not go mad but undergoes many hardships before being reunited with his youngest daughter. In the scene that Shakespeare remembered best, Leir and Cordella take turns kneeling to each other – she asking for his blessing, he for her pardon. With her French husband, she invades England and restores her father to his throne. He declares that he has learned not to believe flatterers.

In some respects Shakespeare must have found the play difficult to rethink. Far from advocating a united Britain, it ridicules the Welshman Cambria (husband of one evil sister) as a coward. Too much time is spent on the conventional and old-fashioned romantic relationship of Cordella and her husband – who, as the king of France, could not in any case be seen leading a victorious invasion of England. (*Leir*, rather daringly, used the invasion to satirize incompetent local efforts at defense against Spain.) It is evident from the clumsy way in which the French king is kept off stage after Act 1 that he remained a problem in the new version. The husbands of the two older sisters became the dukes of Albany and Cornwall, equivalent to Scotland and Wales, but also the titles of James's two sons. Shakespeare might have known that Darnley, James's father, the object of a murderous plot between his wife and her lover, had also been Duke of Albany.[82] Though Leir and Cordella are triumphant in the *Leir* play, Shakespeare knew from the historians and from Spenser that after her father's death she was defeated by her sisters' sons and hanged herself in prison.

The multiple sources that Shakespeare absorbed are part of what makes *Lear* like nothing else in drama. While having Lear go mad (like Hieronimo and Titus) must have been his intention from the start, Shakespeare may also have been stuck by the coincidence of the name Cordella with that of Cordell Annesley, who became briefly famous in 1603 after taking a stand against her sister and brother-in-law, who had attempted to get their father declared insane. (There was a third daughter, but she was not involved in the quarrel.) Brian Annesley died in 1604, leaving everything to Cordell. Sir William Harvey, now husband of the Countess of Southampton, was one of the executors of the Annesley will; after the countess's death in 1607, he himself married Cordell.[83]

There was no fool in the old *Leir* play, perhaps because it had exploited Richard Tarlton's fencing skill in the role of a witty lord who is also a dashing warrior. Dwarfish Robert Armin would play a fool who sings rather than fights. Some of his speeches look like separate comic turns; they are easy to delete, and might have been optional parts of the performance. Notoriously, he disappears halfway through the play, yet no one wonders where he has gone. The King's Men are thought to have discontinued the custom of jigs by this time, but it is noticeable that the clowns in two of their other plays, *Timon of Athens* (probably 1607–8) and Wilkins's *The Miseries of Enforced Marriage* (1607), also disappear early in the play. Perhaps Armin needed time to prepare some kind of post-play entertainment.

While the Lear plot must have been shaped by political considerations – the need to show the importance of a united kingdom and the right choice of an heir – Shakespeare's replication of the situation in his subplot turned it into a story of what Lear called "filial ingratitude" and what later readers often called parental stupidity. Shakespeare remembered an episode in the *Arcadia* where travelers overhear a young man dissuading an old man from suicide. The old man is a former king who has been deceived by his bastard son into seeking the death of his legitimate son Leonatus. Once he has given his power to the bastard, retaining only the name of king, the bastard puts out the old man's eyes, leaving him alive to beg his bread. Leonatus has returned to forgive and help his father, who has asked to be led to the top of a rock, from which he intends to cast himself down. At this point, the travelers intervene; the old king is restored to his throne, sets the crown on the head of his virtuous son, and dies, "his heart broken with unkindness and affliction, stretched so far beyond his limits with this excess of comfort."[84] There is much that is dark and disturbing in the *Arcadia*, a work in which the most evil character, a woman, is also an atheist.

It is in the Gloucester story, drawing as it does on the feigned supernatural, that the play takes on its most hallucinatory aspect. Good characters disguise themselves for fun in *Leir*, but in *Lear* Edgar plays a mad beggar so covered with scars and filth as to be unrecognizable even to his own father. The title page to the 1608 Quarto of the play (Figure 15) is interesting both as an example of how a publisher had to differentiate his King Lear play from an already existing one, a point well made by James J. Marino,[85] and as evidence that feigned madness was a selling point; Edgar's role, which requires several changes of accent, was probably more central to the play than it now tends to be. As Lewis Theobald first noted in the eighteenth century, the names of the devils with whom Edgar claims to be possessed come from Harsnett's *Declaration*. Harsnett had evidently been fascinated by the chair to which the servant girl was tied while the priests questioned the devils within her; he also comments sarcastically on the way the name "Edmund" – Father Edmunds, alias Weston, the chief interrogator – kept recurring in the devils' cries.[86] In the most famous example of onstage brutality in Shakespeare, Gloucester is tied to a

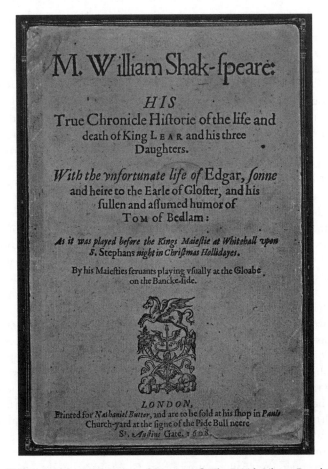

Figure 15 Title page of the 1608 Quarto of *King Lear*. © The British Library Board (C.34.k.18, title page)

chair and interrogated about his possession of an incriminating document, which he carefully describes as "a letter guessingly set down,/ That came from one that's of a neutral heart,/ And not from one opposed" (3.7.48–50). There is nothing like this in the old *Leir* or in Harsnett, and Sidney's reference to the blinding of the old king occupies less than a sentence of the *Arcadia*. It might, however, have been in Shakespeare's mind, ten years after the other great plague of 1593, when Kyd had been arrested and questioned, perhaps tortured, for possessing a dangerous document.[87] If Kyd was in fact the author of the old *Leir*, its optimistic and moralistic ending would have seemed particularly ironic. The voice of Hieronimo, who asks the heavens –

> How shall we term your dealings to be just,
> If you unjustly deal with those that in your justice trust?
> (*The Spanish Tragedy* 3.2.9–10)

– is echoed in Gloucester's bewilderment at his guests' treatment of him and his later comparison of the gods to "wanton boys" who "kill us for their sport" (4.1.36–7), as in Lear's only apparently insane questions: "What is the cause of thunder?" (3.4.153); "Is there any cause in nature that makes these hard hearts?" (3.6.76–7). An audience might have expected *Lear* to end with the prospect of a reunited Britain, but, as in *The Spanish Tragedy*, the entire royal lineage has been destroyed and Albany and Edgar, the only survivors, are too exhausted to prophesy better times.

If Shakespeare was writing *Lear* in 1605, he probably intended it for performance at the Globe in the fall and at court during that Christmas season. The theaters were closed because of plague on 5 October, and the King's Men went on an extensive tour that took them as far as Barnstaple in Devon and Saffron Walden in Essex. By November they may have known that the theaters were to open in mid-December to allow them to prepare for the court's Christmas season. Then, on 5 November, the country suffered one of the greatest shocks in its history, the revelation of the Gunpowder Plot. A small number of Roman Catholic conspirators had planned to blow up the Houses of Parliament during the opening ceremony, with the king and Prince Henry in attendance. The conspirators were within hours of succeeding when, after one ineffectual search of the cellars of Parliament house, a second search revealed an enormous quantity of powder stored there.

Shakespeare would have felt still more directly involved if he had been in Stratford, as seems likely, rather than on tour. Many of the conspirators had connections in the Midlands: Clopton House, where they had planned to meet after the explosion, was only a mile north of Stratford, and the ringleaders were killed or captured at Holbeche House in the West Midlands. Some Catholics were obviously terrified of reprisals: Hugh Holland, a friend of both Shakespeare and Jonson, left England for several years' travel.[88] Thomas Lodge, who had been practicing medicine in London since the turn of the century, spent the next three years in the Spanish Netherlands.[89] Jonson himself, though he did not officially rejoin the Anglican Church until 1610, began attending its services after he was accused of failure to take Communion and of being "by fame a seducer of youthe to popishe religion."[90] Yet the court seemed determined to spend the Christmas season of 1605/6 as usual. Ten plays were given there, and the public theaters reopened on 15 December, just in time to allow the actors to rehearse. *King Lear* was not ready for that season, though it may have been performed publicly later in 1606. The 1608 Quarto gives St. Stephen's Day 1606 as the date of its court performance. 26 December, once consecrated to the first Christian martyr, was now simply the beginning of the twelve days of Christmas, for which the King's company often gave the opening production. Neither Shakespeare nor his audience may have been satisfied with the play, since the version published in the 1623 Folio differs considerably from the 1608 Quarto. Yet the changes do not really alter the total effect. Even those not acquainted with the happy ending of the old *Leir* may have been bewildered by its pessimism and its final depiction of a Britain with no apparent hope for the future.

Macbeth

Macbeth may have been completed after consultation with Tilney or someone at court. After the suppression of the play about the Gowrie conspiracy, Shakespeare would hardly have embarked on a Scottish topic without some assurance that it would be acceptable. Returning to Holinshed, he conflated material from the reigns of several Scottish kings: very few of his audience would notice this. (A few years later he adapted another Scottish episode in *Cymbeline*.) No other play of his was written under so many constraints. If imagining the queen's death (by casting her horoscope, for example) had been a capital crime, imagining a king's murder, even in a play, was still more dangerous. Shakespeare had to make the act as horrendous as possible, and to show the murderer punished in both this world and the next. On Macbeth's first entrance, he sees the witches, and the audience never knows what he was before this encounter. He is described as heroic, but with no mention of any other qualities. When his wife later refers to him as "too full o'th' milk of human kindness" (1.5.17), she means that he lacks moral courage. He stabs a sleeping man and two bewildered servants; he orders others to murder a former comrade in arms and his young son, then a mother and her children; when finally forced into battle, he fights only those he feels sure of killing, finally achieving the courage of despair when he learns that his own actions have made him the mortal enemy of the one man capable of destroying him. By contrast, the murdered king is saintly; the son who succeeds him is equally virtuous; and the final destruction of "this dead butcher and his fiend-like queen" (5.8.70) – with Scots and English fighting side by side for a righteous cause – is the salvation of the country. A scene set in England indicates that the saintly Edward the Confessor has passed his ability to heal the sick to his successors (implicitly including James), another example of England and Scotland sharing the power to do good.

Such blatant one-sidedness, and the absence of any real characterization apart from Macbeth and his wife, ought to damage the play, but its unremitting poetic and dramatic emphasis on the palpability of evil – the modern equivalent is *film noir* – has made it one of Shakespeare's most popular works. It dwells on the uncanny, perhaps because this was something to which James was peculiarly susceptible. For example, the apparitions conjured up by the witches in 4.1 might be based on James's assertion, on his first meeting with Harington, that the execution of Mary Stuart "was visible in Scotland before it did really happen, being as he said spoken of in secret by those whose power of sight presented to them a bloody head dancing in the air."[91] Hidden evil was even more frightening, as was evil aimed at children. At the time of the Gunpowder Plot, the 9-year-old Princess Elizabeth was nearly kidnapped; her guardian, Lord Harington of Exton, sent her, just in time, to a safe hiding place in Coventry.[92] Harington, who saw the conspirators, wrote to his cousin that they bore "an evil mark in their foreheads, for more terrible countenances never were looked upon. His Majesty did sometime desire to see these men, but said he felt himself sorely appalled at the thought, and so forbare."[93]

Yet the very fact that Macbeth is so clear-sighted about the horror of his actions lends him a moral and intellectual brilliance. Cosmic catastrophe is present to him from the beginning: after the witches' prophecies the "horrid image" of what he might do makes his hair stand on end; he sees "Pity, like a naked newborn babe" (1.7.21) and "the air-drawn dagger" (3.4.62) that he will use to kill his king. Like Sophocles' *Oedipus*, the play is unremittingly ironic. As Macbeth finally recognizes, "the fiend ... lies like truth" (5.5.43–4). In the one comic scene, the Porter is pretty clearly imagining a Catholic priest being escorted into hell for just such lies: "Faith, here's an equivocator, that could swear in both the scales against either scale, who committed treason enough for God's sake, yet could not equivocate to heaven. Oh, come in, equivocator" (2.3.7–11).

In the play's most puzzling episode Malcolm gives Macduff an elaborate account of his own wickedness, until the self-portrait becomes so fiendish that Macduff declares that he is giving up all hope of overthrowing Macbeth. Malcolm, seeing that the thane will fight only on behalf of a legitimate heir, retracts his words: everything he just said was a lie and he is in fact totally virtuous. This scene is so schematic that it is often cut; it seems that Shakespeare felt he needed to balance the many evil lies with a noble one. Unfortunately, there was nothing in Holinshed that would have allowed the play to end, like *Richard III*, with a royal marriage for the young conqueror. Malcolm's announcement that he is going to give the English title "earl" to the thanes who had fought on his party hardly seems an exciting climax, and the real happy ending had to be imagined as far in the future.

H. N. Paul and Leeds Barroll have suggested that *Macbeth* might have been performed on Gowrie Day (2 August).[94] The Gunpowder Plot in any case added to its topicality, since at his trial on 28 March 1606, the Jesuit Father Henry Garnet had defended the practice of equivocation. It has been pointed out that the play generally "avoids linguistic markers of Scottish identity," with the possible exception of words like "loon" in "cream-faced loon."[95] Playing a convincing Scot would have been yet another challenge for Burbage. But it is hard to imagine what kind of production was envisaged. Did the actors try to look and sound like Scots, perhaps with advice from Lawrence Fletcher?[96] If they did, could they avoid being unintelligible to the English or insulting to James and his Scottish courtiers? None of Shakespeare's subsequent plays would come so close to contemporary events.

Notes

1. *Shakespeare's Sonnets*, ed. Booth, 347.
2. Akrigg, *Shakespeare and the Earl of Southampton*, 137–9.
3. Honan, "Wriothesley, Henry, third earl of Southampton," *ODNB*.
4. *Shakespeare's Sonnets*, ed. Duncan-Jones, 22.
5. See ibid. and Jackson, "Francis Meres and the Cultural Context of Shakespeare's Rival Poet Sonnets," 245, n. 69.
6. *The Works of Michael Drayton*, ed. Hebel, 2: 336, quoted in *Shakespeare's Sonnets*, ed. Duncan-Jones, 23–4.
7. Chamberlain to Dudley Carleton, 12 Apr. 1603, in Chamberlain, *Letters*, ed. McClure, 1: 192.
8. *Shakespeare's Poems*, ed. Duncan-Jones and Woudhuysen, 6.
9. Stewart, *The Cradle King: The Life of James VI and I*, 168. Insistence on the continuity of the body politic meant that a living ruler should not be present at the funeral of a predecessor. See C. Loomis, *The Death of Elizabeth I*, 40, citing Ernst Kantorowicz, *The King's Two Bodies: A Study in Medieval Political Theology* (Princeton, 1957), 429.
10. Royal households were more likely to march at funerals than at coronations; the King's Men marched for James's own funeral in 1625. Law, *Shakespeare as a Groom of the Chamber*, 14.
11. Repr. in Wickham, 123.
12. See Barroll, *Politics, Plague, and Shakespeare's Theater*, 37–41.
13. P. R. Roberts, "The Business of Playing," 90.
14. Giovanni Scaramelli to the Doge and Senate of Venice, 4 June 1603, *Calendar of State Papers Venetian*, 10: 42.
15. Barroll, *Politics, Plague, and Shakespeare's Theater*, 105–6.
16. Law, *Shakespeare as a Groom of the Chamber*, 8–9.
17. See Butler, "Lowin, John," *ODNB*.
18. This reference is usually quoted as "Kemp, a man," but Alan H. Nelson has found that the parish register at St. Saviour's gives his first name. In a note still unpublished at this time, Nelson documents the fact that other actors were also described in the registers simply as "a man."
19. Duncan-Jones, "Retired from the Scene: Did William Kemp Live on as 'Lady Hunsdon's Man'?," 15.
20. Scaramelli to the Doge and Senate of Venice, 24 Apr. 1603, *Calendar of State Papers Venetian*, 10: 10.
21. Harington, *Nugae Antiquae*, 2: 118–19.
22. *Sir Thomas More*, ed. Jowett, 91.
23. Ibid., 7.
24. Chambers, *ES*, 1: 218; Gurr, *Shakespearian Playing Companies*, 54.
25. Repr. in Chambers, *WS*, 2: 329.
26. Honan, 302, says that "she suffered incurably from 'Shakespeare fantasies'."
27. Letter of 27 Nov. 1603, in Carleton, *Dudley Carleton to John Chamberlain*, ed. Lee, 44.
28. See Kernan, *Shakespeare, the King's Playwright*, 30.
29. Jonson, *Sejanus His Fall*, ed. Ayres, 17–22.

30. Giddens, "Editions and Editors," 66.
31. Riggs, *Ben Jonson: A Life*, 99.
32. Law, *Shakespeare as a Groom of the Chamber*, 8–9; Nelson, "Calling All (Shakespeare) Biographers," 60–3.
33. Jonson, *Sejanus His Fall*, ed. Ayres, 9.
34. Ev. B. [possibly Edmund Bolton], "To the Most Understanding Poet" (verses prefixed to the 1605 edition); William Fennor, *The Description of a Poet* [extract], in Bradley and Adams, *The Jonson-Allusion Book*, 52, 97–8.
35. P. R. Roberts, "The Business of Playing," 88.
36. Stubbes, *The Anatomie of Abuses*, 205.
37. This period, which Alan H. Nelson dates to 1602–4 and Charles Nicholl to *c.*1603–5, is discussed in Nelson, "Calling All (Shakespeare) Biographers," 63–4, and Nicholl, *The Lodger Shakespeare*. The evidence for Shakespeare's residence with the Mountjoys was first discovered by C. W. Wallace and published as "New Shakespeare Discoveries: Shakespeare as a Man among Men," in *Harper's Monthly Magazine* 120 (1910), 489–510.
38. Akrigg, *Shakespeare and the Earl of Southampton*, 142.
39. *Relacion de la Iornada del Excelentissimo Condestable de Castilla, a las Pazes entre Hespaña y Inglaterra.*
40. A. J. Loomis, "Toleration and Diplomacy," 55.
41. Nicholl thinks that the handfasting could have been no later than 3 or 4 November (*The Lodger Shakespeare*, 257).
42. Chambers, *ES*, 1: 214.
43. Croft, "Robert Cecil and the Early Jacobean Court," 137.
44. Quoted in Chambers, *WS*, 2: 332.
45. M. Eccles, "Elizabethan Actors IV," 170.
46. Barroll, *Politics, Plague, and Shakespeare's Theater*, 26–8.
47. Carleton, *Dudley Carleton to John Chamberlain*, ed. Lee, 53.
48. Chamberlain, *Letters*, ed. McLure, 1: 250.
49. Chambers, *ES*, 1: 218.
50. Chambers, *ES*, 1: 215.
51. Stewart, *The Cradle King: The Life of James VI and I*, 183. It is, however, true that he fell asleep during a University play at Oxford in August 1605. See *REED Oxford*, ed. Elliott, 299, 321. I owe this reference to Alan H. Nelson.
52. Duncan-Jones, "A Companion for a King?"
53. Jackson, "Shakespeare's Sonnet cxi and John Davies of Hereford's 'Microcosmos'."
54. When Frankford in Heywood's *A Woman Killed with Kindness* says that he might be "companion with a King," he surely means "as good as a king." Rowland, *Thomas Heywood's Theatre, 1599–1639*, 128–9.
55. Duncan-Jones, "A Companion for a King?"; Cerasano, "Alleyn, Edward," *ODNB*. Alleyn was not knighted either; the first theater knight was Henry Irving, in 1895.
56. Barroll, *Politics, Plague, and Shakespeare's Theater*, 25–6.
57. Dobson, *Shakespeare and Amateur Performance*, 23–6.
58. Montague, *The Shepherds' Paradise*, ed. Poynting, viii–ix.
59. Journal of Jean Héroard, 29 Sept. 1604, quoted in Howarth, ed., *French Theatre in the Neo-Classical Era, 1550–1789*, no. 77, p. 88.

60. Astington, *Actors and Acting in Shakespeare's Time*, 181.
61. Dobson, *Shakespeare and Amateur Performance*, 36.
62. Wickham, 122.
63. *Letters of James VI and I*, ed. Akrigg, 231.
64. Slack, *The Impact of Plague in Tudor and Stuart England*, 231.
65. Schoenbaum, 234.
66. Carleton to Chamberlain, Dec. 11, 1603, in *Dudley Carleton to John Chamberlain*, ed. Lee.
67. See John Jowett's "genetic text" in Taylor and Lavagnino, eds., *Thomas Middleton: A Companion*, 1547–85.
68. *Othello*, ed. Honigmann, 346–7.
69. Auden, "The Joker in the Pack," in *The Dyer's Hand*, 254.
70. Knutson, *The Repertory of Shakespeare's Company, 1594–1613*, 47.
71. Tasso, *Godfrey of Bulloigne*, ed. Lea and Gang, 29. Duncan-Jones suggests, intriguingly, that the poem's description of some of his mad behavior may be a clue to some of Burbage's "business" as Hamlet (*Shakespeare: An Ungentle Life*, 207–8).
72. Perkins, *Directions for the Government of the Tongue*, B4^v–B5^r (pp. 20–1).
73. Carleton, *Dudley Carleton to John Chamberlain*, ed. Lee, 67–8.
74. Sim, *Masters and Servants in Tudor England*, 38–9.
75. *Henslowe's Diary*, 124, 199–200.
76. To Ralph Winwood, 18 Dec. 1604. Chamberlain, *Letters*, ed. McClure, 1: 199.
77. "Apology," printed after the play in Daniel, *Works*, 254.
78. See Brownlow, *Shakespeare, Harsnett, and the Devils of Denham*, 76, 108–9.
79. Knowles, "How Shakespeare knew *King Leir*," 28–9.
80. *King Leir*, ed. Stern.
81. More corroboration is still needed of the authorship studies that have been attaching Kyd's name to a number of previously anonymous works, but McDonald P. Jackson, who is dubious about other Kyd attributions, thinks that *Leir* is a possible case. See Jackson, "New Research on the Dramatic Canon of Thomas Kyd," 126–7.
82. Nixon, *Elizaes Memorial*, C3.
83. Bullough, 8: 270–1, 309–11.
84. Sidney, *The Countess of Pembroke's Arcadia*, 2: 10.
85. Marino, *Owning William Shakespeare*, 128–9.
86. Harsnett, *A declaration of egregious popish impostures*, Q4^v. Brownlow, *Shakespeare, Harsnett, and the Devils of Denham*, 111, 125, discusses passages printed in his edition on pp. 296 and 386.
87. Charles Nicholl points to the "echoes of the torture chamber" (*The Reckoning*, 43) in Kyd's wish that those who informed on him may have their lives "examined and ripped up."
88. Thomas, "Holland, Hugh," *ODNB*.
89. M. Eccles, *Brief Lives*, 83.
90. The phrase occurs several times in the records of the Consistory Court of London for 1606; quoted in Bentley, *Shakespeare and Jonson*, 2: 19–21.
91. Harington, *Nugae Antiquae*, 2:118–19.
92. Lord Harington of Exton, raised to the peerage in 1603, was the cousin of 'Ajax' Harington of Kelston. He commissioned the *Titus Andronicus* production in 1596. See

Broadway, "Harington, John, first Baron Harington of Exton," *ODNB*, and Scott-Warren, "Harington, Sir John," *ODNB*.

93. Letter to Sir John Harington, 6 Jan. 1606, in Harington, *Nugae Antiquae*, 2: 239.
94. Barroll, *Politics, Plague, and Shakespeare's Theater*, 149.
95. Highley, "The Place of Scots in the Scottish Play," 57.
96. P. R. Roberts, "The Business of Playing," 88–9.

15

"Past the Size of Dreaming"

1606–1609

> *Cleopatra.* Think you there was or might be such a man
>   As this I dreamt of?
> *Dolabella.*   Gentle madam, no.
> *Cleopatra.* You lie, up to the hearing of the gods.
>   But if there be nor ever were one such,
>   It's past the size of dreaming. Nature wants stuff
>   To vie strange forms with fancy, yet t' imagine
>   An Antony were Nature's piece' gainst fancy,
>   Condemning shadows quite.
>   (*Antony and Cleopatra* 5.2.92–9)

"Late Style"

The Antony described by Cleopatra demands hyperbole. ("In his livery/ Walked crowns and crownets; realms and islands were/ As plates dropped from his pocket"). Cleopatra agrees with Dolabella that no such person ever existed and yet insists that Antony must have been real because he was too great for anyone to dream or imagine. The language is extravagant, but perfectly suited to its context: it simultaneously undercuts Cleopatra's fantasy and sustains it.

The early plays can also be mannered, as in Juliet's elaborate series of puns on I/Ay/Eye (*Romeo and Juliet* 3.2.45–9) when she thinks the Nurse is about to tell her of Romeo's death. That people should speak more elaborately and figuratively at times of heightened tension seems counter-intuitive, but the theater thrives on eloquence: when Hamlet wants "a taste of your quality" he asks the player for "a

The Life of William Shakespeare: A Critical Biography, First Edition. Lois Potter.
© 2012 Lois Potter. Published 2012 by Blackwell Publishing Ltd.

passionate speech" (2.2.431–2). Shakespeare's Jacobean plays, from *Macbeth* onward, are more difficult linguistically than his earlier ones, and not always because, as in Cleopatra's words, they are making a complex statement. The dramatist might have been remembering his schooldays, when he discovered the clever things that could be done with Latin word order. For example, in *Macbeth* he transposes subject and verb from the beginning to the end of a line, thus making a simple statement hard to take in at first –

> Against the undivulged pretense I fight
> Of treasonous malice.
> *(Macbeth* 2.3.133–4)

– while in *The Winter's Tale* he provides a series of paired nouns, verbs, and participles, which the mind has to sort into the correct columns:

> I with death and with
> Reward did threaten and encourage him,
> Not doing it and being done.
> *(The Winter's Tale* 3.2.163–5)

Both these examples occur, like Juliet's puns, at moments of heightened tension. These plays also contain examples of moving simplicity, so it is likely that Shakespeare was developing effects of contrast for reasons that go beyond realistic characterization.

Attempts at explaining Shakespeare's "late style" have ranged from the purely literary to the socio-political and psychological. Difficulty became a literary fashion in the early seventeenth century, a fact that is sometimes attributed to the change from a female to a male ruler. As Russ McDonald has pointed out in his book on the subject, the opposition between the periodic Ciceronian manner and the terse Tacitean style was traditional, as was the tendency to think of women as talkers and men as doers.[1] Shakespeare may have been influenced by the intellectual climate, but it is also possible that he might have been working too fast. Samuel Johnson thought that he suffered from "that fulness of idea, which might sometimes load his words with more sentiment than they could conveniently convey, and that rapidity of imagination which might hurry him to a second thought before he had fully explained the first."[2] It is something like this that William Empson imagined, looking at a particularly difficult passage from *Macbeth*, as printed in the Folio:

> I am sick at heart ...
> This push
> Will cheere me ever, or dis-eate me now.
> *(Macbeth* 5.3.19–21)

Empson suggests three possible explanations. First, the printer could not read the heavily rewritten passage. Second, Shakespeare had deliberately spelled the words so as to suggest more possibilities than one (cheer or chair, dis-seat or disease or defeat or disseize). Third –and here the poet Empson imagines another creative mind working at white heat –

> he put down dis-seate because it was the first word he could drag out by the heels of an intense and elaborate speech-situation that included all the puns editors have yet devised for it; that this had at all costs to be swept out of his way to make way for the May of life and its galaxy of puns (which were evidently going to produce something better); and that it was only by being as ruthless as this that he could bear in mind the soliloquy as a whole.[3]

Ben Jonson thought his colleague needed editing: in the commonplace book that he later published as *Discoveries* he wrote that Shakespeare "had an excellent fancy, brave notions, and gentle expressions, wherein he flowed with that facility that sometime it was necessary he should be stopped. '*Sufflaminandus erat*,' as Augustus said of Haterius." The process of writing is often one of initial exuberance followed by rigorous editing, and in many cases, especially with the earlier plays, the person who corrected Shakespeare was probably Shakespeare himself. But Jonson's subsequent comment, "His wit was in his own power; would the rule of it had been so too," implies that this did not happen often enough.[4] The early eighteenth-century critic John Dennis declared that a man who wants to write well must either take a great deal of time in polishing his works or have friends who can help him; he regretted that Shakespeare lacked both time and friends.[5] The Beaumont and Fletcher collaboration was thought of in this way: Aubrey, drawing on the commendatory verses to Beaumont and Fletcher's plays, later wrote that Beaumont's "main business was to correct the overflowings of Mr. Fletcher's wit."[6] A curious fact about all the plays discussed in this and the next chapter, apart from the special case of *Pericles*, is that they were not published until 1623. Perhaps, as Lucas Erne and others have argued, they were held back from publication with a view to a later collected volume. Shakespeare may have been waiting for someone to help him with the revision. Jonson's comment suggests that he may sometimes have taken an editorial hand himself, but in the early years of James's reign Jonson was busy with the writing of both plays and masques. If there was someone else who had helped in the past (like the mysterious Hand C who, John Jowett thinks, edited *Sir Thomas More*),[7] he too must have been busy, or perhaps he had died or retired. If Shakespeare himself felt that "he should be stopped," it might explain why two of the plays that he wrote in this decade were collaborations.

It is notable that Shakespeare was able to work both with Thomas Middleton, a firm Protestant, and George Wilkins, who may have been a recusant. In 1605, when Shakespeare probably got to know them, Middleton was 25 and Wilkins nearly 30.

The two men probably knew each other through the dramatists with whom they collaborated on other plays, Thomas Dekker and William Rowley.

Middleton (Figure 16) was the son of a London citizen whose widow's disastrous second marriage blighted her and her children's lives with lawsuits and difficulties over money. Though he never became a member of his father's company, his status gave him important advantages and, eventually, commissions for the Lord Mayor's Show. He attended Oxford, though he took no degree. Shakespeare could hardly

Figure 16 Portrait of Thomas Middleton, from *Two New Playes* (1653). Chapin Library, Williams College

have failed to read the young man's first published poem, *The Ghost of Lucrece* (1600), or to notice that Middleton's first non-collaborative play, *Phoenix* (1603/4), was, like *Measure for Measure*, about a disguised prince reforming abuses in his country. The play is more obviously topical than Shakespeare's, since the abuses that the prince reforms date from the reign of his father, which happens to be of the same length as that of Elizabeth I. Like Shakespeare, Middleton married young, in 1603, and his wife, whose brother was an actor with the Admiral's Men, was somewhat older than himself. They moved out from London to Newington, not far from the site of the old Newington Butts theater, and their only child, a son, was born in 1603 or 1604.[8] The expenses of marrying and buying a house must have inspired Middleton to a frenzy of activity. In 1604–5, while Shakespeare was probably writing *King Lear*, Middleton published an account of James I's entry into London and four satiric pamphlets while writing three or four brilliantly effective comedies for the Children of Paul's, and collaborating with Dekker on one for Prince Henry's Men. In his plots, creditors and debtors cheat each other; women, ranging from courtesans to those who have lost their virtue to only one lover, trick men into marriage; young spendthrifts rescue their estates and marry heiresses. The plays' happy endings are achieved by blatantly unrealistic means such as sudden financial windfalls or conversions (the latter often caused by the former).

George Wilkins, like Middleton, had recently married and had a son, born in 1605. Like Shakespeare, he had recently lost his father, who was also a writer: he had died in the summer of 1603, probably of the plague. The Belotts, whose marriage Shakespeare had helped arrange in 1604, went to live in Wilkins's "house"– apparently an inn – shortly afterwards. Perhaps this is how the two poets met; on the other hand, he may already have known Wilkins as a writer and recommended his house to the young couple. The event that connects the work of the three dramatists occurred in 1605. On 5 August of that year, a Yorkshire gentleman named Walter Calverley was executed for attempting to murder his wife and children, apparently in a state of desperation over money. It was the fact that he was a gentleman from a respectable family that made the case so notorious. At some time that year, the King's Men performed *A Yorkshire Tragedy*, a short play based on a pamphlet account. It was published in 1608 as "by W. Shakespeare," and some of its scenes are powerful enough to make critics want to accept this attribution. For instance, its treatment of the scene in which the unnamed protagonist murders his son is, as is often noticed, very much in the "pathetic child" tradition with which Shakespeare is associated.[9] However, computer studies show that its strongest linguistic affinities are with Middleton, and it is now accepted as his work. According to its title page, it was part of *All's One*, a group of four short plays of which it is apparently the only survivor. Perhaps Shakespeare and Middleton worked together on this sequence, which may have been (as its name suggests) thematically linked. The play was probably written quickly, to capitalize on the topicality of the Yorkshire murders.

In 1606 the King's Men acted a full-length dramatization of the Calverley story, *The Miseries of Enforced Marriage* by George Wilkins. It is curious that the same company should have performed two plays on the same theme, though the two are in fact very different. Wilkins's play was much more fictionalized than Middleton's. What evidently caught his imagination was the situation of a young man who, having been forced into what he believes to be irreparable evil (marrying one woman while engaged to another, who commits suicide as a result), reacts by plunging into a life of self-destructive debauchery. This sprawling but effective piece of work is both touching and funny at times, and, like Middleton's comedies, supplies an obviously arbitrary happy ending to a story that most people must have known ended tragically. Wilkins may have wanted his readers to wonder whether his play was, as some of Robert Greene's works purported to be, the autobiographical confession of a repentant sinner. On its title page he placed the motto *Qui alios (seipsum) docet* (he who teaches others also teaches himself), and he gave the hero's long-suffering wife his own wife's name, Katherine. Wilkins's publication of his play may have annoyed the King's Men, since it was their property, not his; it may also have struck both Shakespeare and Middleton as an infringement of some agreement in connection with *The Yorkshire Tragedy*. This may be why the short play was printed the following year under Shakespeare's name and with a title that identified it with the recent sensational events.

All's Well That Ends Well

All's Well That Ends Well used to be thought earlier than *Measure for Measure*, but has recently been re-dated to the Jacobean period on linguistic grounds.[10] While no one has yet suggested that it is a collaboration, several oddities in its text indicate that it underwent considerable revision between writing and publication. The story, taken from an Italian novella, is a simple one. A young woman, Helena, works a miraculous cure on a sick ruler, is rewarded by being allowed to choose a husband, and picks Bertram, a young aristocrat whom she has secretly loved for a long time. Furious at being forcibly married to a woman whom he has always thought beneath him, he abandons her and goes off to the wars, leaving a letter in which he states the conditions on which he is willing to live with her. She meets those conditions (through a bed trick) and he agrees to love her. The play makes Bertram somewhat more excusable by emphasizing his youth and the bad influence of the braggart Parolles. Both men are subjected to public humiliation, yet are redeemed. The old courtier Lafew, who has seen through Parolles from the start, decides, for no obvious reason, to take the wretched man into his service; Helena is happy to have the disgraced Bertram as her husband, and he says that he will now love her. There is some resemblance to Portia's forgiveness of Bassanio in *The Merchant of Venice* – another play where the happy ending hinges in part on the identification of a ring – but where Bassanio is made eloquent and charming despite his evident irresponsibility, Bertram says very little and none of it is intelligent. There is an obvious moral about forgiveness and the need to accept human imperfection, but, as in other plays about wild youth, it pushes the doctrine that it is never too late to repent until it becomes hard to accept.

Helena, though Bernard Shaw called her a "lady doctor," does not really have more medical skills than those every woman of the period was supposed to have, plus a prescription that her father has left among his papers. It is her role, and the fact that she so consistently takes the initiative, that differentiate this play from Middleton's comedies, where, as in Roman comedy, the "courtesans" are the only interesting women. Yet, as Laurie Maguire has pointed out, the significance of the name of Helen of Troy can hardly have escaped Shakespeare, since Lafew, who may well have been played by the same actor who played Pandarus in *Troilus and Cressida*, compares himself to "Cressid's uncle,/ That dare leave two together" (2.1.99–100). Maguire suggests that both Cressida and Helen (in her Trojan setting) are examples of women who are victims of their own names, while the French Helen proves that it is possible to transcend hers.[11] Shakespeare might also have read Pierre de Ronsard's sonnets to the maddeningly chaste Hélène and decided that it was a safe name for a French heroine. Susan Snyder wonders whether the evident revising that went on in this play means that Shakespeare himself "had occasional qualms about the unconventional heroine he had created."[12]

Something of the play's distinctiveness may be the result of changes in the acting company. The various female characters who appear only in the second half of the play look like roles for apprentice actors. As in *Hamlet* and *Othello*, the two main female roles are for an older woman and a young one. The unusual and moving relationship between the Countess and Helena begins when, having learned of Helena's love for her son, the older woman recalls her own youth ("Even so it was with me when I was young," 1.3.125), then teasingly sounds out the young woman's feelings, finally accepting her as a daughter-in-law. The scene develops the untapped potential in Gertrude's simple words at Ophelia's funeral: "I hoped thou shouldst have been my Hamlet's wife" (*Hamlet* 5.1.244). The "willow scene" between Desdemona and Emilia, another remarkable depiction of a relationship between an older and a younger woman, may also belong to this period (or, since *Othello* was clearly revised after the early performances, it may have been added later). Lady Macbeth, Cleopatra, Volumnia, and Paulina in *The Winter's Tale* are also demanding roles for a boy actor who could convincingly depict a woman of middle age – presumably one of the older boys, such as John Rice, who left the company in 1611 to play adult male roles elsewhere. *The Merchant of Venice* had a successful revival at court in February 1605. Seeing a different boy actor as Portia, its author might have reimagined some of its effects for a new performer. Helena's elaborately heralded entrance to the French court would resemble Portia's in the court of Venice, if Gary Taylor is right in suggesting that Helena too is meant to be in disguise at this point.[13]

Just as Portia's picture in the leaden casket is the proof that Bassanio has solved the riddle, Helena's dramatic entrance at the end of the play reveals that she herself is the solution of another riddle: she has fulfilled her husband's conditions and, moreover, saved him from being charged with her murder.

One of MacDonald P. Jackson's arguments for the relatively late date of *All's Well* is Parolles' reference to a (non-appearing) character called Spurio, a name which he thinks derives from Middleton's use of it in *The Revenger's Tragedy*, which he dates to 1606–7. I am not sure about this – the fact that Parolles is a compulsive liar might have led Shakespeare to make up the "spurious" name – but other aspects of the play suggest the influence of Middleton (and perhaps also Wilkins), particularly the unusually realistic depiction of Bertram's loutishness and the perfunctoriness of his final conversion. The fact that the dramatists were known to be working closely together between 1606 and 1608 might explain why not only *A Yorkshire Tragedy* but also Middleton's *The Puritan* (written for the Children of Paul's, 1607) was attributed to Shakespeare on publication. Both *Othello* and *All's Well* are, rather unusually, plays about cruelty *within* marriage. The Cinthio story on which Shakespeare based *Othello* was itself one of a series, called "The infidelity of husbands and wives."[14] In view of the difficulty that *Othello*'s time-scheme has given critics, Ned B. Allen in 1965 suggested that Shakespeare had initially written a shorter play, set entirely on Cyprus, adding the first two acts at a later date.[15] If this ever happened, the obvious place for such a play would be as part of *All's One*, the sequence of short plays that included *A Yorkshire Tragedy*. A play about an already married couple could be vague enough about the duration of time and about Cassio and Desdemona's past relationship to make the jealousy plot more credible. It is perhaps less easy to imagine a shorter version of *All's Well*, but the influence of the Calverley murders might explain the rapidity of Bertram's degeneration from the callow youth of the beginning to the hysterical liar and slanderer of the final scene.

Timon of Athens

Presumably Shakespeare, now in his early forties, chose to collaborate with Middleton because he had been impressed by the cleverly involved plotting of the city comedies. *The Revenger's Tragedy* was performed by the King's Men at about this time. If, as the Middleton editors think, *Timon* was earlier, it may have been meant as an apprenticeship for the young playwright. On the other hand, *The Revenger's Tragedy* may have made Shakespeare want to see what the two of them could do together, now that Middleton was familiar with the company.[16] The tragedy obviously alludes to *Hamlet* (the hero, Vindice, carries a skull in the opening scene and suffers from both real and feigned melancholy), but the elaborate plot of villain outwitting villains recalls *The Jew of Malta*. Like Barabas, Vindice revels in his own cleverness and is finally caught in it. His name means simply "a revenger"; he is not so much a character as a label, like the Husband, Wife, and Child of *A Yorkshire Tragedy*. *Timon* likewise contains many unnamed characters (Poet, Painter, three Strangers) and even those who do have names are mostly indistinguishable. The play's schematic nature is both its strength and its weakness.

As the senior dramatist, Shakespeare presumably chose the subject, which was already well known. Though he had read about Timon in Plutarch, most retellings of the story derive from the second-century dialogue by Lucian of Samosata, which had already inspired several dramatizations. This dialogue takes place in Timon's wilderness. Lucian draws attention to the problematic aspect of the story from the start, making Mercury explain that Timon "was brought to this by his bounty, humanity and compassion toward all in want; or rather, to speak more correctly, by his ignorance, foolish habits, and small judgement of men."[17] Jove, pitying him, sends him wealth again, and immediately he is besieged by the same scoundrels as before. Lucian, who regarded himself as marrying comedy with philosophy, wrote dialogues that sound like radio plays: the action is vividly imagined and incorporated into the language, but much of it, like Timon's beating and throwing stones at his visitors, would be unactable on a conventional stage except as farce. That the collaborators were eager to make the story more dramatic is clear both from their decision to start the story during Timon's period as a spendthrift and from the masque that they incorporated into the banquet in Act 1. The problem of achieving a balanced attitude to riches and expenditure was one that an early modern audience would have found relevant, and Middleton's plays had depicted many examples of what not to do. The story, however, offers few hints for other characters. Since the legend said that Timon had approved of Alcibiades' war on Athens, the collaborators developed his story as a parallel to Timon's. Banished from the city, he returns to besiege it, and the senators ask Timon for help (he apparently has a military reputation, hitherto unmentioned); he refuses, and dies before Alcibiades decides, perhaps to differentiate himself from Timon, that he will spare the city after all. There is a fool in the play, but he appears in only one scene and seems to be a false start. The dramatists probably decided that Robert Armin should instead play Apemantus, a "churlish philosopher" as he is called in the dramatis personae. He rails at Timon when others flatter him, yet comes to the wilderness to make sure that his former host isn't copying his own brand of misanthropy. The equivalent character in Lucian is as greedy as all the others, but the dramatists give this philosopher a touch of gruff kindness.

Apparently, both Shakespeare and Middleton were closely involved in the opening section of the play, but "the middle scenes are mostly Middleton, and the remainder is mostly Shakespeare."[18] Middleton's talent for depicting second-rate, morally obtuse characters was ideally suited to the first half, where Timon is a host with a passion for giving gifts to his hypocritical and ungrateful "friends." Middleton also developed the play's one virtuous character, the steward Flavius, and the scene in which Flavius and the other servants divide up the remaining money and leave the ruined house shows his characteristic awareness of the wider repercussions of individual prodigality. Shakespeare, on the other hand, seems to have wanted to invest Timon with the generosity that would later characterize his Antony. Plutarch's account of the society that Antony and Cleopatra tried to create around them – its Greek name is translated by North as "no life comparable"[19] – may have been at the back of his mind, since Timon, like Antony, conflates drunken reveling with mystical experience. The second half of the play takes place in Timon's wilderness. Though his misanthropic tirades are based on Lucian, their emphasis on ingratitude makes them sound like Lear on the heath, and Shakespeare seems to have wanted to orchestrate Timon, Alcibiades, and Apemantus like Lear, Edgar, and the Fool in the storm scenes of *Lear*. Instead of rising to tragedy, however, the play falls apart in the fourth act, as if the dramatists had stopped paying attention to each other's work. There are inconsistencies and non sequiturs. The crucial event, Timon's death, is never explained; his epitaph, when it is read out, consists of two incompatible inscriptions: the first insists on his anonymity, the second names him. The satire on the human race is so effective that it is hard to believe the characters who, near the end, start saying that it isn't really so bad after all.

If Shakespeare and Middleton had revised the play they could have dealt with the more obvious inconsistencies or made it clear that the play was meant to be self-contradictory. But for some reason they seem to have left it unfinished. Perhaps each dramatist became more interested in finishing another play – *Antony and Cleopatra* for one, *The Revenger's Tragedy* for the other – and never got back to the joint work. If it remained with Shakespeare's, or the company's, papers, it may have been awaiting a final revision. Given the self-contained nature of the scenes between Timon and his visitors in the wilderness, which resemble those in Lucian's dialogue, it is even possible that the play was at one time short enough to be part of *All's One*. John Jowett has noticed echoes in it of the murder pamphlets that inspired *The Yorkshire Tragedy*.[20] Perhaps, however, the play was abandoned after the dramatists had an unpleasant discussion with Tilney or Buc in the Revels office. The suppression of the play about Gowrie suggests that the king and his advisers were anxious to avoid sponsoring works with a strongly personal application, and in this case the application was obvious: James was a lavish spender, excessively generous to his friends, and even before he left Scotland he had been warned not to follow the example of Timon.[21] It should have been possible to slant the story to make it more universal, or to compliment the king's generosity while blaming those who exploited it, but in its present form the play seems to satirize both Timon and his flatterers. Middleton might not have minded the topicality: unlike Shakespeare, he wrote pamphlets on political and religious subjects and gives the impression of enjoying controversy. It is not even certain that the play was ever intended for publication: it was added to the 1623 Folio at the last minute, to fill a gap caused during the printing by some difficulty in obtaining *Troilus and Cressida*. By then, Middleton was a highly prolific and successful writer, author (and co-author) of two of the finest tragedies of the period. He may have been involved in revising some Shakespeare plays, but this would have been a case of consecutive rather than concurrent collaboration. It is a pity that their one attempt at working together was apparently unsuccessful.

Guarini and Tragicomedy

Both the story of Timon and the relationship of Antony and Octavius Caesar (as described in *Macbeth*) are mentioned in Plutarch's life of Antony, so it is likely that Shakespeare was thinking about *Antony and Cleopatra* while writing *Macbeth* and *Timon*. This play, which is not quite like anything else of his, may have taken him some time, which might explain his search for collaborators to help him finish other plays more quickly. Perhaps for the first time, he had started to think seriously about dramatic theory. Everyone already knew the term tragicomedy, which Plautus used and explained in the Prologue to his *Amphytruo*. Giovanni Battista Guarini's pastoral tragicomedy, *Il Pastor Fido* (the faithful shepherd), had been phenomenally successful in 1590 and was published in English translation in 1602. Still more important for European drama than this tragicomedy is the fact that, in his *Compendio della Poesia Tragicomica* (1602), Guarini went on to defend and analyze what he had done. Although the *Compendio* was one of the most influential works of the period, no translation was published in Shakespeare's lifetime, so he probably worked his way through it in Italian during one of the many periods of plague closure.

Guarini seems to have been the first to ask some important questions about the longstanding deference to Aristotle's theory of tragedy. Why were Christian dramatists writing as if, like the ancient Greeks and Romans, they believed in punitive supernatural beings instead of a merciful God? How could the sight of terrible events purge, rather than increase, terror in the spectators? Why did they need to be terrified in order to be good, when they had the Scriptures for their guide? Aristotle, Guarini insisted, could not have meant that the spectators should purge themselves of all pity, a vital Christian virtue, but only of the wrong kind.[22] Both tragedy and comedy, in the classical sense, dealt with extremes of human behavior. He defined tragicomedy as a blend, not a juxtaposition, of the two: it was a serious drama in which death was sometimes threatened and sometimes even seemed to have occurred, but which nevertheless ended happily. To illustrate this point, *Il Pastor Fido* rewrote the story of Oedipus. At its climax, the shepherd Mirtillo is about to be executed by a priest, when the latter discovers that the victim is his own son. It turns out that Mirtillo was sent away when young because an oracle – conditional, rather than cruelly ambiguous – had said that if he remained he *might* die by his father's hand. Though the coincidences that enable the last minute rescue may seem fantastic, for Guarini the ending was true to the Christian emphasis on the availability of salvation up to the last moment. One could say that he was simply offering a theoretical justification for the happy endings that most people have always preferred. Or one could argue that he was being as revolutionary as the dramatists of the Theatre of the Absurd when they decided that writers who did not believe that there was a purpose to life should not write purposeful plays.

Though Guarini did not advocate realism in the modern sense, his emphasis on mirroring the audience's real beliefs had wide consequences. For some it meant a drama largely focusing on the gentry (the class to which most spectators belonged), with love stories often resolved by the discovery of the true origins of one or both of the lovers. Shakespeare had of course been writing tragicomedies for years, and nearly all his comedies put at least one character in danger of death. Unlike many of his contemporaries, he continued to write roles for the fools and clowns of the popular tradition, but these characters now became part of a gentrified world rather than reminders of what existed elsewhere. The Act to Restrain Abuses of Players, which came into effect on 27 May 1606, was, as Peter Roberts points out, "the first and indeed only time that parliament legislated on matters relating to the content and performance of plays."[23] It was particularly concerned with profanity on stage; its influence can be seen in works printed after this date, where suspiciously unmetrical lines result from the substitution of "Heaven" for "God." Whatever Shakespeare thought of this attempt to purify the theater, he seems to have been attracted by the poetic unity of atmosphere that Guarini described. He may also have thought seriously for the first time about the fact that most of the sources of his tragedies belonged to an alien religious culture. Perhaps J. L. Simmons exaggerates in thinking that Shakespeare meant his audiences to contrast the secular love of Antony and Cleopatra and the suicidal self-sacrifice of Coriolanus with the transcendent love and sacrifice of Christ.[24] On the other hand, it is hard to see why else *Antony and Cleopatra* twice mentions "Herod of Jewry" and shows Octavius looking forward to a "time of universal peace" after Antony's defeat, or why the military culture of *Coriolanus* should be full of imagery of blood and milk, and reach its climax in a mother's plea to her son to use mercy.

Antony and Cleopatra

Any play about the Roman empire was potentially topical. Virgil had used the story of Antony and Cleopatra as an implicit contrast both to the self-denial of Aeneas and to the self-control of his own patron, the emperor Augustus.[25] Though the *Aeneid* had not yet been written when Antony committed suicide, Shakespeare makes him foresee it, imagining that he and Cleopatra will draw away the "troops" that surround those two famous lovers (4.14.53–4). It is perhaps his most daring allusion to the desire to rival Virgil, and daring, too, because plays about the love of two great world leaders were bound to evoke memories of both Elizabeth I and Mary Queen of Scots. It has often been suggested that James I, whose motto was *Beati Pacifici* and who was the first British monarch to portray himself as a Roman emperor on his coins,[26] might have identified himself with Octavius, creator of the *Pax Romana*.[27] James would equally, however, have credited himself with some of Antony's qualities, which are like Timon's in their extremity but here appear as virtues: generosity and the capacity for passionate love. The king might also have responded to the play's emphasis on the conflict between a ruler's personal desires and political duties, since it is clear from *Basilikon Doron* that (though perhaps no one else agreed) he believed himself to be sacrificing the first for the second.

Though in *Timon of Athens* and *Antony and Cleopatra* the title characters die, both plays are better understood as tragicomedies than tragedies. While *Timon* seems almost accidentally to fall into this category when Alcibiades decides to show mercy to the Athenians, *Antony and Cleopatra* is a masterpiece of the new genre – though, judged as a tragedy, it is often considered a failure. Guarini never dreamed that a historical tragedy could adopt the genre that he associated with shepherds, but the emphasis on love in his theory reduces the political to the personal, cutting greatness down to size. Bernard Shaw was right, though not in the way he meant, when he commented on the inadequacy of sexual infatuation as a tragic theme: "Experience proves that it is only effective in the comic spirit. We can bear to see Mrs Quickly pawning her plate for love of Falstaff, but not Antony running away from the battle of Actium for love of Cleopatra."[28] Antony himself feels that even the land on which he treads is "ashamed to bear me" (3.11.2), and his sense of shame can be as unbearable for the audience as it is for him. Uncertainty as to whether the play depicts sexual infatuation or love, and whether it is in fact tragic or comic, is part of its continuing fascination. Its boundaries constantly dissolve like the clouds to which Antony compares himself (4.14.2–8), or like Cleopatra's description of Antony's mood, "nor sad nor merry ... O heavenly mingle!" (1.5.55, 62).

Cleopatra herself is even more mingled. The boy actor of Rosalind acts out the part of a girl acting a boy acting a capricious female, and compares "boys and women," as "effeminate, changeable, longing and liking, proud, fantastical, apish, shallow, inconstant, full of tears, full of smiles, for every passion something and for no passion truly anything" (3.2.399–402). Yet the audience can believe that this is simply a performance. The capricious creature Rosalind describes does, however, seem to be the "real" Cleopatra, whose "infinite variety" is her essence. Like Rosalind, she alludes to the relation between boy actor and histrionic woman when she refers contemptuously to the boy who will caricature her in Rome. Plutarch provided much of the best material, like the description that became Enobarbus's famous account of Cleopatra on the River Cydnus, but it was Shakespeare's own idea to make her refer back to that moment as she prepares to commit suicide:

> Show me, my women, like a queen. Go fetch
> My best attires. I am again for Cydnus
> To meet Mark Antony.
>
> (5.2.227–9)

Her recreation of a remembered triumph is set against the brief and painful cry of her waiting woman: "Finish, good lady. The bright day is done,/ And we are for the dark" (5.2.192–3). As in *Troilus and Cressida*, the characters are seen simultaneously as ordinary mortals and as creatures of legend, constantly watched and commented on by others; but, as the exchange quoted at the beginning of this chapter shows, the contrast between reality and legend does not reduce them to objects of satire. The ultimate effect is triumphant.

Criticism that merely ridicules and blames the protagonists – as if to succumb to the poetry necessarily means adopting their views – has to reject almost everything in the play. On the other hand, the idea that love matters more than anything else is so close to being an orthodoxy now that the protagonists' outrageous claims may not be sufficiently recognized as dangerous and controversial. That the play's language is so different from that of *Timon* and *Macbeth* may well result from a conscious exploration of the gendered styles that Russ McDonald identifies (see above, p. 331). The equation of Rome and Egypt with the masculine and the feminine, respectively, lends itself to Jungian archetypes of gender. Jung's "Perfection is a masculine desideratum, while woman inclines by nature to completeness," though a wild generalization, works remarkably well as an account of the duality of this play. Jung went on to insist that, "just as completeness is always imperfect, so perfection is always incomplete, and therefore represents a final state which is hopelessly sterile."[29] *Macbeth* may be the most perfect of Shakespeare's plays, in the sense of being self-contained and atmospherically unified, but its power comes from the evocation of a universe that eventually shrinks to the dimensions of Macbeth's obsessed mind (and his marriage is, at least in the play's present, famously sterile). In *Antony and Cleopatra*, on the other hand, Shakespeare emphasizes the fertility of the Nile and "All the unlawful issue" of the two lovers, while never mentioning the children that the historical Antony had by Octavia. He also stresses the vast expanses that the characters travel and the equally vast distance between their best and worst moments. In *Poetaster* Augustus conferred fame and glory on Horace and Virgil. In Shakespeare's play, it is not clear whether Octavius, in his final speech, is similarly conferring fame on the two lovers or only recognizing something that is out of his control:

> She shall be buried by her Antony.
> No grave upon the earth shall clip in it
> A pair so famous.
>
> (5.2.358–60)

There is no evidence that *Antony and Cleopatra* was a popular play, and there are no contemporary references to it (though Fletcher's *The False One, c.*1620, may have been intended as a prequel). Tragicomedy was still a controversial genre and the frequently absurd and ignoble behavior of the central characters might have irritated audiences (as it still does). Mark van Doren, after writing that "Line for line it is probably the richest poetry Shakespeare wrote," added that "The peculiar greatness of the poetry defeats any conceivable dramatic end."[30] Its greatness may well be the result of careful revision, and while there is no evidence for this, I wonder whether the revision had a different theater in mind – perhaps the kind of circle that had read aloud the *Antony* of the Countess of Pembroke and the *Cleopatra* of Samuel Daniel. Readers and audiences, amateur or professional, could enjoy the luxuriant language without being distracted by the rapid entrances and exits of Acts 3 and 4 and the notoriously difficult business of drawing the dying Antony up to Cleopatra's monument.

Pericles

What the King's Men needed most, after a long period of inactivity, was a highly successful play that would recoup their losses. This is exactly what they got with *Pericles*, probably first performed in 1608 between two visitations of plague. Like *Hamlet* it appealed to both popular and elite audiences, and became almost a synonym for theatrical success. When the French and Venetian ambassadors went together to see it at the Globe that year, it must have been because it offered so many visual pleasures that could be enjoyed without a good knowledge of English.[31] Prince Hamlet had been scathing about groundlings who care for nothing but "inexplicable dumb shows and noise" (3.2.12), but *Hamlet* itself includes a dumb show. *Pericles* has more of them than any other Shakespeare play, as well as an exercise in visual interpretation, the scene (2.2) in which knights present their shields to Thaisa, while she and her father explicate their devices, none of which are in English. Dudley Carleton describes a court performance on New Year's night 1604, in which each masquer presented the king with an escutcheon along with a letter explaining it. The king and his party found the emblems easy to interpret, apart from one: "It was a fair horse-colt in a fair green field, which he [the masquer] meant to be a colt of Bucephalus' race and had this virtue of his sire that none could mount him but one as great at least as Alexander. The king made himself merry with threatening to send this colt to the stable."[32] Shakespeare might have shared James's enjoyment, though Carleton obviously felt that the joke was being run into the ground.

Shakespeare's choice of Wilkins as collaborator may have been inspired by a play that the latter wrote for another company, with two other dramatists, in 1607. *The Travels of Three English Brothers*, as its title indicates, was a story of sea travel, in which the three Sherley brothers (real people, but highly fictionalized) visit different exotic locations, some of them containing real people such as the actor Will Kemp. The brothers are separated even at the end, where the audience is apparently meant to imagine them seeing each other through the perspective glass offered by the play. *Pericles* stretches over some fifteen years, and over much of the eastern

Mediterranean, as the hero journeys from one court to another, first in flight from an enemy and then in search of his lost family. Shakespeare may have known that the *Confessio Amantis*, his main source, had been commissioned by the young Richard II. Book 8, the story of Apollonius of Tyre, uses the incest of the King of Antioch and his daughter as a starting point for the hero's travels; one shipwreck brings him to a court where he finds his wife; another near-shipwreck leads to her apparent death in childbirth and burial at sea, though she is later revived and lives as a vestal. The father and his newborn daughter are separated for the next fourteen years, and she, like her mother, is believed to be dead. She is in fact carried off by pirates and sold to a brothel, but manages to save herself from it by using her numerous accomplishments as a teacher of other women. Gower emphasizes both Apollonius's role as the school-master to his future wife and his daughter's role as a popular teacher, which gets more attention than her brief stay in the brothel.

Perhaps because Shakespeare was still working on something else, Wilkins wrote the first two acts of *Pericles*. Collaboration was relatively easy in such an episodic story, since, apart from the Chorus, the hero and his aged adviser Helicanus are the only characters present throughout the play. Thaisa, whom Wilkins depicted charmingly in her first two scenes, apparently dies between Acts 2 and 3 and can credibly seem like a different person after she is revived. Wilkins may have had a hand in other scenes as well, particularly those set in the brothel, and some of his scenes may have been revised by Shakespeare.[33] This was, in other words, a close collaboration, which suggests that the two writers got on well. Although everyone who writes on the play notices Wilkins's poetic inferiority, this is much less noticeable in performance or in casual reading. Wilkins had a good theatrical sense, and a number of scenes in the first two acts, especially the comic ones, are highly effective. The play retains much of the symmetry of Gower's original, though not much of his educational emphasis. Apollonius was renamed Pericles, perhaps because of the influence of *The Arcadia*, in which Pyrocles is one of the heroes. The play may have been intended as a companion piece to *Mucedorus*, which is named after Sidney's other hero. One of the most popular plays in the repertory of the King's Men, it was first published in 1598; its reprint in 1610 contains additions, mostly to the Clown's role, that have sometimes been attributed to Shakespeare.[34]

Pericles, like Guarini's *Pastor Fido*, reverses the Oedipus story: the hero begins by solving a riddle but avoids the crime of incest, and his destiny leads him to a reunion that is happy rather than horrified.[35] The Chorus figure, Gower, reminds the audience of his antiquity by speaking in deliberately archaic English and using various rhyme schemes, including the octosyllabic couplets in which he wrote his master-piece. The plot is equally archaic – the kind of thing that Sidney had ridiculed in his *Apology for Poetry*, with its flouting of the unities of time, place, and action. It is hard to know how naive the total effect was meant to be. The pirates who appear out of nowhere for a few seconds in 4.1 parody the romance genre; the owners of the brothel into which Marina is sold are depicted with comic realism; on the other hand,

345

the scenes where Thaisa is brought back from apparent death and Pericles gradually lets himself believe in the reality of his supposedly dead daughter Marina are extraordinarily moving.

Pericles and *Antony and Cleopatra* share the loose temporal structure of romance, in which ships cross the Mediterranean with amazing speed. They also convey a strong sense of the numinous, particularly through music with no identifiable origin. Four of Antony's soldiers hear mysterious music from under the stage (*Antony and Cleopatra* 4.3.13–31); Pericles, after his reunion with Marina, hears, though apparently no one else does, "the music of the spheres" (*Pericles* 5.1.233). They are stylistically anomalous among Shakespeare's works; in fact, one startling revelation of MacDonald P. Jackson's study of the authorship of *Pericles* is that computer analysis of *Antony and Cleopatra*, a play that no one can imagine anyone else writing, does not show it as unambiguously "Shakespearean."[36] Its peculiar quality may be partly a result of Shakespeare's attempt to assimilate Guarini's concept of stylistic harmony, sometimes producing a uniformity of diction quite different from the strong linguistic characterizations of his earlier plays.

Another influence may also be at work, this time a lyrical one. John Donne was at one time said to be "a great frequenter of plays," probably during his residence at Lincoln's Inn from 1593 to 1595 or 1596. He was also a friend of Ben Jonson, with whom he exchanged verses. After his clandestine marriage and the loss of his court position early in 1602 he lived outside London for some years, but by 1607 he was at Lincoln's Inn again, trying to rebuild his career. He seems to have been part of a club that met at the Mermaid Tavern; Shakespeare was probably not among the members, mainly Inns of Court men, but he knew some of them, including William Johnson, who eventually became the tavern's landlord. Whether or not Shakespeare and Donne knew each other, their poems certainly did (see Chapter 11 above); Janet Adelman links the plays both to Donne's poetry and to the paradoxes of "The Phoenix and Turtle."[37] If Donne's dramatic tone is the result of his theatergoing, Shakespeare's increasing lyricism may have been affected by Donne's "strong lines" (difficult images, impossible hyperboles, riddles, and paradoxes) and his religious eroticism. Donne's "Canonization" and his "Valediction: Forbidding Mourning"–

> So let us melt and make no noise,
> No tear floods or sigh tempests move;
> 'Twere profanation of our joys
> To tell the laity our love.

– recall, in both tone and imagery, the pervading language of *Antony and Cleopatra*. Enobarbus jokily comments that "We cannot call [Cleopatra's] winds and waters sighs and tears; they are greater storms and tempests than almanacs can report" (1.2.154–6); in the two last acts both lovers imagine themselves as melting or dissolving, and they sometimes claim that their love is transcendental. Pericles, too, in his reunion with Thaisa after fourteen years' separation, tells the gods,

> You shall do well
> That on the touching of her lips I may
> Melt and no more be seen.
> (5.3.42–4)

Such moments transcend the obvious absurdities of the story, just as Donne's hyperboles ridicule themselves and yet insist on their emotional truth.

The stationer Edward Blount, who had already published *Love's Martyr* in 1601, was perhaps aware of the resemblance between these two plays, since he entered them together into the Stationers' Register in 1608. He did not, however, publish either of them. In the case of *Pericles*, this was because Wilkins got in first with a prose narrative, *The Painful Adventures of Pericles* (1608; Figure 17), which states on the title page that it is "the True History of the Play of Pericles, as it was lately presented by the worthy and ancient poet John Gower." The mention of Gower was designed to establish the identity of the pamphlet with the play (much like the title page of the *King Lear* Quarto). Since the peculiar practices of the Stationers' Company (see p. 145 above) could allow a publisher to block the publication of another work that might interfere with his own work's sales, Wilkins and his publisher could have acquired something like internet domain rights even though *The Painful Adventures* is not even a play.

Coriolanus

It would be convenient for this biography if *Antony and Cleopatra* and *Pericles* could be shown to be later than *Coriolanus*, since, as Russ McDonald says, *Antony and Cleopatra* "serves as the hinge that permits Shakespeare to move from tragedy to romance."[38] But if, as is generally assumed, *Coriolanus* was the later play, we need instead to imagine a Shakespeare who could turn back to a heavily "masculine" style for the hero, contrasting it with Volumnia's longwindedness, which is almost a parody of a female stereotype. He was now recreating the atmosphere of a republican state that had to deny itself the poetry of absolutism. *Coriolanus* begins not long after the period of *Lucrece*; its hero had fought, while still a boy, against the Tarquins. But the Roman republic, idealized in *Julius Caesar* by Brutus and Cassius, is shown in this later play to be a sordid political arena. Some spectators might have identified the contemptible Junius Brutus of the play with the Brutus of *Lucrece*, whom Marcus Brutus, in *Julius Caesar*, is always being told to emulate.

Coriolanus has a splendid theme: the problem of the great man who is unfit for society. He is both too good and too bad for his own country, and when he is exiled

347

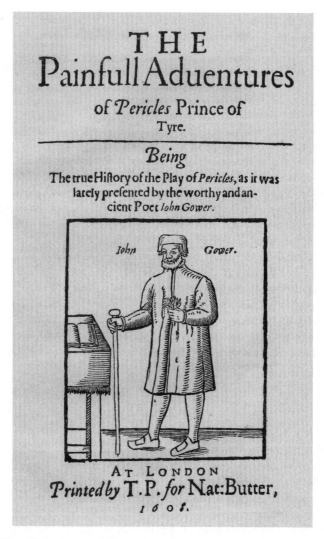

Figure 17   Title page of *The Painful Adventures of Pericles*, by George Wilkins.
By permission of the Folger Shakespeare Library

from it his story repeats itself in another setting. Though much of what he says is intelligent, it is vitiated by his inability to achieve any rapport with others except in the context of war. He exasperates even his admirers. When he wants to be generous, he is unable to remember the name of the man he wants to help. From the beginning, those who dislike him claim that he is not really serving his country, only trying "to please his mother." The line has been the starting point for many psychoanalytical readings of the character, but it is also comic, and comedy is rarely absent from *Coriolanus*. Volumnia's advice to her son is consistently bad. She urges him to compromise with his own beliefs in order to obtain power; later she urges him to have mercy on Rome, somehow imagining that he can do this and still look after his own interests. He yields to her, but chooses to go back to Corioles and face the Volscians rather than return to Rome. This should be a heroic act, but it is also muddled. He seems to know that he will not survive his decision, but what he tells his mother ("Most dangerously you have with him prevailed,/ If not most mortal to him. But let it come," 5.3.188–9) is so brief that its meaning could easily be missed. In Corioles, he behaves as if he does not know what is going to happen, and seems to let himself be provoked into yet another outburst of anger that gives his enemies an excuse to cut him down. He has no death speech, and the words that follow his death are bathetic. This is tragicomedy in the full sense of the word: the desire for tragic grandeur is constantly undercut by an apparent inability to believe in it.

Antony and Cleopatra, though it constantly gives the impression that fighting is taking place just offstage, does not require any battle scenes. *Coriolanus* is unusual in devoting so much time to them. The first part of the play seems designed to allow the hero to establish himself as a figure of prodigious energy and courage, and to show war as he himself sees it, a world of pure unselfishness where there is no doubt about who deserves reward. But, whereas Falconbridge in *King John* contrasts "a just and honourable war" with "a most base and vile concluded peace" and Falstaff refers to the largely criminal class from which he takes his recruits as "the cankers of a calm world and a long peace," *Coriolanus* does not promote this view. It is one that must frequently have been stated after the Treaty of London, as court corruption became notorious, but Shakespeare puts the pro-war sentiments into the mouths of servants who, once they find out who the disguised Coriolanus really is, claim to have recognized his true greatness all along. Their ideas about war and peace are equally discredited:

> *First Servingman.* . . . Peace is a very apoplexy, lethargy; mulled, deaf, sleepy, insensible; a getter of more bastard children than war's a destroyer of men.
> *Second Servingman.* 'Tis so. And as wars in some sort may be said to be a ravisher, so it cannot be denied but peace is a great maker of cuckolds.
> *First Servingman.* Ay, and it makes men hate one another.
> *Third Servingman.* Reason: because they then less need one another. The wars for my money!
>
> (4.5.232–41)

It is something of a caricature of the views of the war party in both Elizabeth's and James's reign. In a sermon preached just after Essex's execution, William Barlow quoted Plato's dictum that great men are "either excellently good, or dangerously

349

wicked," adding that it had also been applied by Plutarch to Coriolanus, "a gallant, young, but a discontented Roman, who might make a fit parallel for the late Earl, if you read his life."[39]

In fact, Coriolanus is utterly unlike Essex in his inability to achieve "popularity." The behavior that Richard II describes in Bolingbroke – "Off goes his bonnet to an oyster-wench;/ A brace of draymen bid God speed him well/ And had the tribute of his supple knee" (*Richard II* 1.4.31–3) – is the kind of thing that Richard, himself an actor, can parody. Volumnia, no less contemptuous of the popular audience, urges her son to give this kind of performance:

> I prithee now, my son,
> Go to them, with this bonnet in thy hand,
> And thus far having stretched it – here be with them –
> Thy knee bussing the stones – for in such business
> Action is eloquence, and the eyes of th'ignorant
> More learnèd than their ears – waving thy head . . .
> (3.2.74–9)

And so on. But it is Volumnia who acts at this point, as she does earlier when she imagines her son shouting at the soldiers on the battlefield (1.3.30–5). The fact that Coriolanus is never able to act is a source of both admiration and exasperation. In his final confrontation with Volumnia he compares himself to "a dull actor" who has forgotten his lines and is "out,/ Even to a full disgrace" (5.3.41–2), perhaps because at the climax of the scene he will stand in silence holding his mother's hand, and it is essential that the audience not spoil this moment by triumphant shouts of "Out!"[40]

Theatrically speaking, then, the play is puzzling. The most interesting dramatic characters are usually those who draw attention to an actor's own ability. Because Coriolanus is defined as someone who cannot act, he risks being unvaried and uninteresting. There are dramatic gains: when, after being forced to suppress his contempt for the plebeians, he finally has nothing to lose by expressing it, his outburst is deeply satisfying:

> You common cry of curs, whose breath I hate
> As reek o'the rotten fens, whose loves I prize
> As the dead carcasses of unburied men
> That do corrupt my air, I banish you!
> (3.3.130–3)

But, with a character who has so little capacity to articulate his feelings, the actor has to work hard in the final scenes to be anything other than "the rock, the oak not to be wind-shaken" (5.2.111–12) that he is thought to be. The protean qualities of Burbage seem wasted on the role, particularly given the amount of fighting that the actor, now about 40, would have been required to do. It is possible that the part was written for someone who could make an impression as a fighter – for instance, John Lowin, now in his early thirties, who would become famous as an impersonator of blunt soldiers. This might explain a good deal about the play's difference in tone. Lowin, oddly enough, may have managed to be both an actor and something of a Puritan. A pamphlet attacking dancing, first published in 1607 as the work of "I.L., Roscio" (that is, J.L., actor), has been attributed to him.[41] Shakespeare might, then, have built the contradiction into his part.

Events in Stratford, Events in London

The period 1606 to 1608, to which these plays belong, was one of frequent plague closures in London, and many events of great importance to Shakespeare were happening in Stratford during that time. Pointing out that the next explicit record of his presence in London is in 1612, Jonathan Bate argues that the dramatist may in fact have spent those years in Stratford, because of ill health or "some scandal" – or both, if his illness happened to be syphilis.[42] The possibility that Shakespeare may have been syphilitic has been raised by many scholars.[43] They are struck by the vivid images of the disease in Falstaff's brothel jokes in *2 Henry IV* and Lucio's in *Measure for Measure*, in the vicious image, "Till my bad angel fire my good one out" (Sonnet 144.14), and, above all, in the language of Timon and Lear: "There's hell, there's darkness, there is the sulfurous pit, burning, scalding, stench, consumption. Fie, fie, fie! Pah, pah!" (*King Lear* 4.6.128–30). Like other unattached men in London, Shakespeare must sometimes have visited the brothels and would have known that he was at risk from virulent illness. However, there is no comment on a pox-ridden Shakespeare in Jonson's writings or in the gossip picked up later by Aubrey. It also seems unlikely that Puritan Stratford would have been more tolerant of an obviously syphilitic resident than London, or that Shakespeare would have written so much about the disease if he in fact was suffering from it.

There were some Stratford events at which he would certainly have wanted to be present in this decade, and others at which perhaps he should have been. One of his main concerns was his daughter Susanna. Easter was on 20 April in 1606, and he could have learned within a week that the young woman had got into trouble for not taking communion on that day. She probably did not realize the risk involved. Everyone was supposed to attend church at least three times a year, one of these times being Easter. One consequence of the Gunpowder Plot was a tightening of such restrictions, with enormous fines for those who ignored them.[44] The intention was to isolate "church papists" – Catholics who were willing to conform by attending church but abstaining from communion, a compromise often allowed for the sake of peace. Stratford's current vicar, John Rogers, had taken office only in 1605 and may not have realized that he was supposed to overlook the behavior of the daughter of a well-to-do townsman. Or perhaps he wanted to leave his parish in no doubt that a new minister had arrived. There were numerous arrests of non-communicants in 1606. Susanna failed to put in an appearance at the consistory court, held in the church, probably because she was unwilling to pay a fine or do penance for her behavior. This is one of only three recorded glimpses of Susanna's character, and two of them have to do with court cases, but of course this is how most sixteenth- and seventeenth-century human beings have come down to posterity. Shakespeare's daughter may have been cynical about religion; she may have been casual in her church attendance; or she may have been expressing a genuine sympathy for Catholicism. The recusants in Stratford included some of her relatives and perhaps her parents' friends, Hamnet and Judith Sadler, who were cited to attend the same tribunal. Was she perhaps influenced by them, and was Shakespeare annoyed with them for causing trouble? This might explain the fact that, eight years later, he would mention Hamnet in his will only at the last minute. However, Susanna's case was later dismissed, probably because she had agreed to take communion in the meantime. It may have helped, too, that her uncle Bartholomew Hathaway had become a churchwarden in 1605.

As usual, the King's Men were busy in the early part of the year, so it is unlikely that Shakespeare rushed back to Stratford to extricate his daughter from this situation, but, aware as he must have been of the anti-Catholic mood in the country, he may have urged her to conform. He may also have become even more eager to marry her to someone who could give her an impregnable social position. She was nearly 23, a little younger than the average age for marriage in middle-class families, but it would take some time to arrange the kind of match he wanted. Nothing is known about other suitors, but since she was an heiress there may well have been some, perhaps including the man whose name would be connected with hers in a later court case, the hatter Ralph Smith, who was about 30. John Lane would also figure in that case; he was the younger son of a gentleman of Alveston Manor, too young in his mid-teens to be a possible bridegroom in 1605–7. The man that Shakespeare (and, one hopes, Susanna) chose was John Hall, a physician halfway between her father's age and hers. Hall was a Cambridge graduate who took his MA in 1597 and probably studied medicine in Montpellier during his European travels. Though he does not appear to have had a doctor's degree, his reputation had already won him a large practice. His father, also a physician, had dabbled in astronomy, astrology, and alchemy. When he died at the end of 1607, the senior Hall bequeathed his books on astronomy and astrology to his servant Matthew Morris on condition that Morris should teach these arts to John Hall if he wanted to learn them. The alchemy books were left to Morris unconditionally: the younger doctor must already have made his skepticism on this subject plain. Morris moved to Stratford with Hall, married there in 1613, and was closely involved with his family thereafter.[45] It would be interesting to know whether he continued to practice alchemy and other "secret studies."

John Hall is first heard of in Stratford in 1607, the year of his father's death and his marriage. He may have been living there earlier, but it is also possible that

Shakespeare met him elsewhere and persuaded him to settle in the borough. Hall was in any case obliged to travel extensively, since his patients came from as far away as Ludlow and Worcester. Physicians were rare, especially outside London, and much in demand. Judging from his later behavior he had Puritan sympathies, so if *Sejanus* did not make Shakespeare decide to leave the theater, his future son-in-law may have done so. Hall seems to have got on well with Anne's brother Bartholomew, the churchwarden, who would eventually make him overseer of his will.[46] Marrying late in life, Hall could afford to be particular, and he may well have hesitated over linking himself with the family of an actor, even a rich one. He probably had no objection to dramatists as such – he later treated Michael Drayton, whom he called "an excellent Poet."[47] Shakespeare went to considerable trouble to provide his son-in-law with a good estate to compensate for any potential disgrace. The 107 acres in Old Stratford, bought in May 1602, were to be Susanna's dowry. At some point in 1605 Shakespeare made the last of his major purchases in Stratford, paying £440 for a share of about a fifth of its tithes (these now went to the Corporation rather than the church). It was the equivalent of buying an annuity, since he received £60 a year in return. Even though he had to pay someone for "farming" (gathering) the tithes, and it would take some time to see a return on the investment, it probably seemed worth disposing of an enormous sum of money (again, where he got it is unknown) in order to buy financial security. The year 1603 had been all too reminiscent of the plague closures of 1593. Along with his land purchases, this new investment made his daughters substantial heiresses.

With plague keeping the public theaters closed for much of 1607, Shakespeare would have had no difficulty in being in Stratford for Susanna's wedding on 5 June of that year. It took place against a disturbed background. The common land, normally available for the peasants to graze their animals, was being enclosed with hedges or fences and turned into pasture for sheep-rearing. Since a landowner needed fewer farmhands to rear sheep than to plow his fields, the result was often depopulation. There had been a statute against enclosure since 1533, and Parliament had revived it in 1597, after four years of bad harvests, but by the end of the century the practice had been largely accepted in many parts of the country, and sometimes even initiated by peasants themselves.[48] The government was thus alarmed in May 1607 when an anti-enclosure riot in Northamptonshire spread to Leicestershire and to Hillmorton in Warwickshire, some 30 miles northeast of Stratford, where 3,000 people are said to have assembled. Investigation then and now has concluded that the riots were genuinely popular in origin.[49] They happened, however, so soon after the Gunpowder Plot, and in the same part of the country where the plotters had been cornered, that they were suspected of being a cover for something else. At the end of May, both the king and the Privy Council ordered the lords lieutenant of these counties to put down the rebellion with as much force as necessary. The king was angry with the sheriff of Warwickshire, who had attempted to reason with the rebels and sent a list of their grievances to the Privy Council.[50] Enclosure was not a simple class struggle; the Privy Council was in fact opposed to it, and Shakespeare, though a landowner, might not necessarily have supported the practice.[51] The 1607 riots were over by 14 June, but anyone traveling to Susanna's wedding would have heard about them, and they must have been much discussed. Their influence on *Coriolanus* may be present only in the uncertainty as to whether it was better to meet popular dissent with harsh measures or, like the sheriff of Warwickshire, with an attempt to understand it.

What, meanwhile, was Shakespeare doing about his younger daughter? Unlike Susanna, Judith apparently could not write her name and perhaps could not read either; she witnessed a deed in 1611 only with a mark, which, Germaine Greer thinks, shows that she was unused to holding a pen.[52] She did not marry until 1616, when she was almost 30. Perhaps Shakespeare had overstretched himself financially in providing for Susanna, but it could hardly have taken him another nine years to get a second dowry together. There is a surprising amount of scholarly enthusiasm for the idea that Shakespeare's dramatization of incest in *Pericles* (and his brief hint of it in *The Winter's Tale*) indicates darker reasons for his reluctance to let his youngest daughter marry.[53] But there are other possible explanations. Perhaps Judith simply did not wish to marry and her parents accepted her wishes, glad to have her presence in the house. Or she may have wanted, against their wish, to do what she eventually did: marry Thomas Quiney.

Shakespeare was probably still in Stratford when, on 12 August 1607, an infant, baptized the previous month, was buried in St. Giles without Cripplegate, London, as "Edward Shakespeare, son of Edward Shakespeare, player, base-born." The mother's name is unknown. Most biographers assume that the second Edward was Edmund, brother of William Shakespeare. If he was known to be the child's father, either he or the mother (who would have been under immense pressure to name him) must have confessed to fornication. The actor did not marry her, either because the child's death prevented it from being a charge on the parish or because the mother herself died in childbirth. He would have been punished, however, with public penance or a fine, which William might have had to pay for him. He was probably furious at his brother for disgracing the family and the acting profession, just as he was trying to make himself into a respectable father-in-law. The plague of 1607 culminated in the famous winter when the Thames froze over, lasting most of December and the first half of January. If Shakespeare was in London for the court performances of 1607/8, he must have been rushing about even more than usual – to rehearsals, to the court, then to Edmund's lodgings. The young man, sick perhaps of the plague or simply as the result of an exceptionally hard winter, died sometime near the end of the year, and on 31 December was buried in St. Mary Overy's (now Southwark Cathedral). Except for the "plot" of 1597 mentioned above (p. 139), the burial records of this year are the only evidence that Edmund Shakespeare was an actor. His funeral took place in the morning, and someone paid to have the church's great bell rung. Schoenbaum wonders, "Did Shakespeare arrange for a morning rather than (as customary) afternoon service so that his fellows could attend on that bitterly cold day, when children played and men and women promenaded on the frozen Thames?"[54] If he did, his action confirms that Edmund was a member of the King's Men, though not, clearly, one of its leading actors or sharers. It is hard to resist speculating about Shakespeare's feelings toward this brother, but it is a relationship about which nothing is known.

Other events might have made him want to be in Stratford in 1608. Susanna's first and (as it turned out) only child, Elizabeth, was baptized on 21 February. On 1 July William's brother Richard appeared before the church court. He confessed – the records do not say to what – and was ordered to pay a fine of twelvepence for the poor. In August Shakespeare sued the otherwise unknown John Addenbrooke (not resident in Stratford) for an unpaid debt of £6 (damages would have brought the total to over £7, more than an unskilled laborer's annual wages). There may be reasons why Shakespeare was determined not to let this particular debtor get away; the case went on for nearly a year.[55] When it finally came before a jury in June 1609, Addenbrooke, like many defendants, failed to turn up, and the records come to an end.

Shakespeare might have been in Stratford in August 1608 because he knew his mother was dying. Or, since she died on 2 September, the fact that her funeral was not until 9 September may mean that it was delayed until he could return from out of town. Critics often link her death with the writing of *Coriolanus*, though nothing known about either mother or son suggests any resemblance to the characters in the play. What might perhaps have struck him is how the disappearance of the older generation of one's family creates the state that Coriolanus wishes for himself: "As if a man were author of himself/ And knew no other kin" (5.3.36–7). He was now the most senior member of his family.

Shakespeare was probably also in Stratford on 16 October 1608, as godfather to the son of the bailiff, Henry Walker. Earlier that year, Walker had authorized Stratford's only recorded payment to players between 1597 and 1618.[56] In December 1602 the town had forbidden plays to be performed on any Corporation property, so Walker was taking a stand on behalf of his friend's profession. William Walker (who himself would be bailiff in 1649) is the only godson mentioned in Shakespeare's will; there may have been others who died young. Only two days before the christening, the names of his sister Joan and her husband, William Hart, appear in the records of the church court, but with no specific charge.[57] It almost looks as if someone was targeting the Shakespeare family, or perhaps they were victims of the increased nervousness after November 1605. Peter Ackroyd makes an important point: for Shakespeare to act as godfather, he would have had to take communion before the ceremony and otherwise conform to the Church of England.[58] Perhaps Walker was giving him an opportunity to draw attention to his orthodoxy.[59]

Once Susanna had moved out of New Place, the Shakespeares apparently took in lodgers – the lawyer Thomas Greene, his wife Lettice, and their two young children (named William and Anne) – while Greene looked for a suitable house in Stratford. He found one, but when its current owner took some time to move out Greene was not much worried, since, as he wrote in 1609, "I perceived I might stay another year at New Place."[60] Perhaps Anne welcomed the company of the Greene family after Susanna left home.

The London playhouses reopened in March 1608 but were closed again from either July or August to December and remained closed for the whole of 1609.[61] The evidence might, then, suggest that Shakespeare, no longer an actor, spent much of this period quietly writing in his study or in the pleasant garden and orchard of New Place. In a court case of 1612 (discussed in Chapter 17 below), he was identified as a resident of Stratford-upon-Avon. Yet it is likely that he wanted to be in London for the rehearsals at least of his own plays, as well as for the performances at court. Tiffany Stern's studies of early modern rehearsal practice indicate that, although two-person scenes could have been rehearsed privately, group rehearsal time was so limited that many of the actors, until the first performance, may not have known anything of the play except their lines and cues.[62] Most of her examples, however, come from the Elizabethan period. As spectacle became more important, the company may have needed more rehearsals and Shakespeare's presence may have become more rather than less necessary. Calling public performances rehearsals for court performances was of course a fiction, but the absence of opportunity to perform in public for most of 1607–10 may have meant that rehearsals became something more like their modern equivalent, with only the actors and perhaps a few privileged friends present. In 1609 the King's Men were paid an extra £40, on top of the fee for the twelve court performances they had given in the previous Christmas season, "by way of his Majesty's reward for their private practice in the time of infection that thereby they might be enabled to perform their service before his Majesty in Christmas holidays [1608/]1609."[63] The same thing happened in the following year. It would be interesting to know what happened in this "private practice" and where it took place. Was this where Shakespeare explained some of the lines that are so difficult for actors to grasp at first reading? Is this why the text of *All's Well That Ends Well* gives the impression of being worked over? What, moreover, happened in the case of the plays written in collaboration? Did Wilkins have any further input after the first reading of *Pericles* to the actors?

Antony and Cleopatra and *Coriolanus* are plays that polarize critics, who quote the same lines to prove diametrically opposite views, and productions can likewise choose either to glorify or ridicule the central characters or to attempt a balance between the two. Shakespeare could perhaps count on the actor of Coriolanus to decide for himself whether in the final scene the hero intends to provoke the Volscians into killing him or reverts to his usual pattern of losing his temper at crucial moments. But what about the play's crowd scenes, precisely the kind that had given trouble to the authors of *Sir Thomas More*, and had required careful handling in *2 Henry VI*? In the opening lines, the First Citizen asks the other plebeians, "You are all resolved rather to die than to famish?" and they all shout, "Resolved, resolved" (1.1.2–3). Their endorsement of this self-contradictory proposition can be played to show that they are too stupid to take seriously. On the other hand, they can be making a consciously paradoxical statement of their "desperation."[64] There is no such thing as a "straight" reading in a case like this, and Shakespeare is unlikely to have left it up to his actors to decide how to say lines that could be inflammatory if wrongly handled.

Unlike most of Shakespeare's earlier work, these are also plays with subtexts. Both clearly require pauses – the most famous one is actually written into *Coriolanus*, perhaps because onstage silence was so rare. The scene in *Antony and Cleopatra* when four soldiers hear what they decide is the god Hercules deserting Antony depends for its effect on the ability of four presumably minor actors to speak against a musical background and to make the most of their understated exchange:

> *First Soldier.* Music i'th'air.
> *Third Soldier.* Under the earth
> *Fourth Soldier.* It signs well, does it not?
> *Third Soldier.* No.
>
> (4.3.16–19)

Cleopatra's mysteriousness is partly due to her deliberately unfinished sentences: "Then Antony – but now – Well, on" (4.4.38), is meaningless without the actor's sense of what she is not saying. (Pericles, in the scene of his reunion with Marina, also speaks like this.) When one of Caesar's followers, trying to persuade Cleopatra to betray her lover, tells her that Caesar "knows that you embrace not Antony/ As you did love, but as you feared him," she replies simply, "Oh" (3.13.36–7). Enobarbus, who is present, thinks she is about to betray Antony, and it is never made absolutely clear whether he is right. It is customary to say that Shakespeare's plays have no subtext and that the lines themselves will do all the work if the actor simply says them clearly. It is also true that by 1606 Shakespeare must have known his actors well and been able to trust them. Even so, he would surely have wanted to work with the boy who had to say Cleopatra's "Oh."

Notes

1. McDonald, *Shakespeare's Late Style*, 244–8.
2. *Johnson on Shakespeare*, ed. Sherbo, in *The Works of Samuel Johnson*, 7: 54.
3. Empson, *Seven Types of Ambiguity*, 83. Empson adds in a footnote, "the Bard is not to be praised for the result in the present case, and the actor ought to choose some intelligible emendation."
4. *Timber, or Discoveries* (1630), in Herford and Simpson, 8: 584.
5. Dennis, Letter III in "On the Genius and Writings of Shakespeare," 42.

6. Aubrey, *Brief Lives*, 1: 96.

7. *Sir Thomas More*, ed. Jowett, 28–9.

8. Taylor, "Lives and Afterlives," in Middleton, *Collected Works*, ed. Taylor and Lavagnino, 38–9.

9. Katherine Duncan-Jones thinks that this play is at least partly by Shakespeare. See *Shakespeare: An Ungentle Life*, 242–4.

10. See e.g. the discussion in *Companion*, 126–7, and Jackson, "Spurio and the Date of *All's Well That Ends Well*," 298–9.

11. Maguire, *Shakespeare's Names*, 104–9.

12. *All's Well that Ends Well*, ed. Snyder, 55.

13. *Companion*, 495. As Taylor points out, the disguise explains both Lafeu's initial description of her simply as "Doctor She" and his otherwise puzzling reaction of surprise when she reappears as herself with the recovered king.

14. Bullough, 8: 241.

15. Allen, "The Two Parts of *Othello*," 13–26.

16. I should add that the editors of the Middleton *Complete Works* place *The Revenger's Tragedy* after *Timon*.

17. Lucian of Samosata, *The Dialogue of Timon*, trans. Geoffrey Bullough from N. da Lonigo, *Il Dilletevoli Dialogi* (1536). In Bullough, 6: 265.

18. John Jowett, "Timon of Athens," in Taylor and Lavagnino, eds., *Thomas Middleton: A Companion*, 357.

19. *Plutarch's Lives*, 6: 27.

20. *The Life of Timon of Athens*, ed. Jowett, 6.

21. Bevington and Smith, "James I and *Timon of Athens*," 63.

22. Guarini, *Il Pastor Fido*, ed. Brognoligo, 245, 235–6.

23. P. R. Roberts, "Elizabethan Players and Minstrels," 55.

24. Simmons, *Shakespeare's Pagan World*, chs. 2 and 4.

25. See Brower, *Hero and Saint*: "*Antony and Cleopatra* is an imaginative sequel to the *Aeneid*: what might have happened had Aeneas stayed in Carthage and not fulfilled his fate" (351).

26. Peck, "The Mental World of the Jacobean Court: An Introduction," in id., ed., *The Mental World of the Jacobean Court*, 5.

27. Kernan, *Shakespeare, the King's Playwright*, 121. He also cites the suggestion by H. Neville Davies that the visiting ruler, Christian IV of Denmark, might have been seen as an Antony figure.

28. Shaw, Preface to *Three Plays for Puritans*, 38–9.

29. Jung, *Answer to Job*, 71.

30. Van Doren, *Shakespeare*, 273.

31. Chambers, *WS*, 2: 335.

32. Letter to John Chamberlain, 15 Jan. 1604, quoted in Kernan, *Shakespeare, The King's Playwright*, 45.

33. The most thorough discussion is Jackson, *Defining Shakespeare: Pericles as Test Case*.

34. As is often pointed out, *Mucedorus* was the most reprinted play of its time. One reason is that it was popular with amateur actors.

35. Marrapodi, "The 'Woman as Wonder' Trope," 194.

36. Jackson, *Defining Shakespeare*, 207–8.

37. Adelman, *The Common Liar*, 112–15.
38. McDonald, *Shakespeare's Late Style*, 244.
39. Barlow, *A Sermon Preached at Paul's Crosse*, C3ᵛ.
40. See Potter, "Nobody's Perfect," 97.
41. *Conclusions upon Dances, both of this age, and of the olde.* A note on the title page says, "By Jhon Lowin witnesseth Tho. D. 1610." This has been suspected of being a Collier forgery, but Rick Bowers, in *John Lowin and Conclusions upon Dances (1607)*, his edition of the pamphlet, accepts it as genuine on the basis of a test of the ink (p. 14).
42. Bate, *Soul of the Age*, 358–9.
43. It is assumed in both Anthony Burgess's novel *Nothing Like the Sun* and Christopher Rush's *Will.*
44. Brinkworth, *Shakespeare and the Bawdy Court of Stratford*, 44–5.
45. M. Eccles, *Shakespeare in Warwickshire*, 112.
46. Honan, *Shakespeare*, 232.
47. Lane, *John Hall and His Patients*, 40.
48. Thirsk "Enclosing and Engrossing," 254.
49. Ibid., 232–3.
50. Letter from the Earl of Shrewsbury to the Earl of Kent, repr. in appendix II of Gay, "The Midland Revolt and the Inquisitions of Depopulation of 1607," 240–1.
51. See *Coriolanus*, ed. Parker, 36–7.
52. Greer, *Shakespeare's Wife*, 270.
53. Bevington, *Shakespeare and Biography*, 140–2, summarizes and discusses views on this subject.
54. Schoenbaum, 29.
55. Ibid., 241.
56. M. Eccles, *Shakespeare in Warwickshire*, 143.
57. Brinkworth, *Shakespeare and the Bawdy Court*, 110.
58. Ackroyd, *Shakespeare: The Biography*, 472.
59. A curious episode from French theater history suggests that he may have needed to give such proof. In December 1619 the actor and writer Matthieu Lefebvre, wishing to retire to his home town and fearing that he would be ostracized there, got an official royal document rehabilitating him. See Howarth, ed., *French Theatre in the Neo-Classical Era*, entry for December 1619.
60. M. Eccles, *Shakespeare in Warwickshire*, 31–2.
61. Barroll, *Politics, Plague, and Shakespeare's Theater*, 173.
62. Stern, *Rehearsal from Shakespeare to Sheridan*; Stern and Palfrey, *Shakespeare in Parts*.
63. Barroll, *Politics, Plague, and Shakespeare's Theater*, 181 (citing *Malone Society Collections* 6: 47).
64. *Coriolanus*, ed. Parker, 37. Parker argues that this line echoes the "Stratford labourers who, told that grain cost nine shillings a bushel, declared they would rebel since 'they were as good be slain in the market place as starve'" (1.1.4–5n., citing J. M. Martin, *Midland History*, 7 [1982], 30).

16

"Like an Old Tale"

1609–1611

This news which is called true is so like an old tale that the verity of it is in strong suspicion.

(*The Winter's Tale* 5.2.28–30)

Like the dialogue in *Antony and Cleopatra* that served as epigraph to the previous chapter, this line comments on the fact that truth can be stranger than fiction. The difference, however, is that Cleopatra and Dolabella are discussing a historical character about whom difference of opinion is possible, while *The Winter's Tale* is presented as fiction from the beginning. Moreover, whereas Cleopatra and Dolabella have their reasons for thinking as they do, the speaker here is only a Second Gentleman and he is talking to a Third Gentleman; they exist only for the purpose of saying that the most important event in the plot as the audience knows it – Leontes' discovery of his long-lost daughter – has just taken place offstage. It was, they insist, absolutely unmissable, but the audience has missed it. They also insist that it was unbelievable, yet the audience can easily believe it since it has seen things that these characters do not know about. Three complete nonentities thus prepare the audience for Leontes' visit to the statue of his dead wife Hermione, which will be the most unbelievable scene in the play. But first Autolycus has a short comic scene with the Old Shepherd and his son, the Clown: those, as he says, "I have done good to against my will" (5.2.125). In a gesture toward Guarini's kind of tragicomedy, even the Clown is a pastoral figure; at this point he and his father are finely dressed so that no one in the final scene will disgrace the elegant stage picture. Nor are the two characters out of keeping with the tone of the play: they hope that they may live to shed many more "gentlemanlike tears" (5.2.145) and they believe that "We must be gentle now we are gentlemen" (5.2.153–4). The episode teases by

The Life of William Shakespeare: A Critical Biography, First Edition. Lois Potter.
© 2012 Lois Potter. Published 2012 by Blackwell Publishing Ltd.

deliberately delaying the visit to the statue, which, the audience must begin to suspect, is to be the real climax.

In 1608 the King's Men had a theatrical opportunity for which they had probably been waiting for some time. In March, the boys in the Blackfriars company finally got themselves into so much trouble that James ordered them to be suppressed. Chapman's plays about the recent conspiracy and execution of Henri IV's former friend, the Duc de Biron, depicting a reigning monarch on stage, would have made the French ambassador protest even if Chapman had not also written a scene between Henri's queen and his mistress. Apparently learning nothing from this experience, the Blackfriars company went on to act another play, too dangerous to get into print, ridiculing a project for a silver mine in Scotland. It probably satirized the Scots by depicting them – and, by implication, the king himself – as poor, greedy, and drunk. Furious, James let the Privy Council know that the company "should never play more, but should first beg their bread."[1] What is more surprising than the punishment is the crime: dramatists and actors had been making assumptions, about either the king's tolerance or his inefficiency, that would have been inconceivable during the previous reign.

Because the theaters were closed at the time, the demise of the Children of the Chapel at Blackfriars was perhaps not noticed outside the theater world.[2] However, it created considerable excitement for the King's Men, who had probably been hoping for an opportunity to move into the playhouse. If they had been planning it for some time, this might explain why Shakespeare, Heminges, and Condell had chosen to live in that part of London since the early years of the century. In August 1608, a month after the Children's affairs had been wound up, and probably through the collusion of Edmund Tilney, Richard Burbage obtained the lease of the theater. Perhaps because of the plague, the neighbors who had objected so strongly to an adult company in 1597 were unable to stop the new development.

With two playhouses at their disposal, the King's Men could now perform at the Globe in the summer, when the gentry retired to their country estates, and move into Blackfriars in the winter months, using it also as a safe place to store their costumes and playtexts. Even though entrance to the Globe was cheaper, the Blackfriars held only a third of the numbers that could be crammed into the public theater. Since during the plague years the company was already giving most of its performances in private houses, it is likely that, even before the company began using Blackfriars, Shakespeare was already thinking in terms of small performance spaces and audiences willing to listen to complex language. Jonson wrote *The Alchemist* specifically for this location, with several references to its abbreviated name, "the Friars," though the plague postponed its first performance until 1610. Shakespeare wrote only a few plays specifically for Blackfriars, but may have adapted some early ones to make more use of the theater's resources, especially its musicians. *Coriolanus* would have been a very different experience if music was played between the acts to supplement its alarms, retreats, and processionals.

Plague kept the public theaters closed from August 1608; they apparently did not reopen at all in 1609, and in 1610 they were closed for at least half the year. Somewhere around 7 May 1610, news reached England that a fanatical Catholic had assassinated Henri IV of France, the king after whom Prince Henry had been named. The court went into mourning for the rest of the month, and the playhouses may have been closed as well.[3] Although the company gave a number of court performances and the king again compensated the players for some loss of earnings, they must have suffered from such a long period without the opportunity to play for their largest public. It was only after the end of March 1611 that plague ceased to be a problem, though by then it may have become such a constant threat that it took some time for everyone to readjust. Freelance dramatists may have had trouble selling new plays to the actors, who did not need as large a repertory when the only places they could perform to the general public were touring venues unaffected by sickness. If the King's Men were less willing than before to take a chance on new writers, this might explain why Wilkins wrote his prose version of *Pericles* and why his theatrical career ended just after he had been involved in such a great success.

In September 1609 Shakespeare's friend John Marston – once a satiric poet and dramatist with a reputation for obscurity and obscenity – became a deacon in the Church of England. He was only 30, but he had married a clergyman's daughter in 1605 or 1606 and seems to have stopped writing for the theater shortly afterwards. Thirty was the age at which wild young men traditionally reformed, and he was financially independent, so playwriting had been only a hobby for him. Since he said in 1609 that he had been studying philosophy for three years, he may have sold his shares in the Blackfriars company even before it was dissolved, and seems to have spent the rest of his life outside London.[4] It was probably the end of his friendship with theater people, and may have been something of a personal loss for Shakespeare, who, now 42, had every reason to wonder whether he ought likewise to change course. He probably remembered that Virgil, too, had intended to spend his final years studying philosophy and revising the *Aeneid*.

The year 1609 also seems to have been the one when Francis Beaumont and John Fletcher moved from the children's companies to write for the King's Men. They had written plays separately, but their collaborations were so seamless that they became known as models of exemplary friendship. Other dramatists, even the difficult Jonson, seem to have liked these two young gentlemen, who made playwriting look like a respectable activity. *Philaster* was the first of their distinctive contributions, probably performed in May 1609, just before another plague closure. Its plot offered outrageous situations that evidently provoked laughter and delight, as well as genuine surprise. Philaster is the rightful king of Sicily, whose throne has been unlawfully usurped; the usurper's daughter, Arethusa, is in love with him. Their situation is complicated when Philaster is led to believe that his page, acting as a go-between for them, has become her lover. His jealousy is made more credible because it is whetted not only by a malicious woman but also by the lies of a supposedly normative "honest" soldier/courtier who fears that Philaster's love for Arethusa will prevent him from leading a rebellion against the usurper. To some extent, the play depends on the audience's knowledge of *Othello*, since this blunt soldier role was almost certainly written for John Lowin, who had played both sympathetic blunt courtiers like Kent and villains like Iago. Like Othello, Philaster prepares to kill Arethusa after urging her to pray for forgiveness, and, like Desdemona, she later lies in order to save him. Arethusa is only wounded, however, and the dramatists used the boy-heroine convention to produce a happy ending, when the page finally reveals herself to be a woman in disguise. The situation resembles the end of *Twelfth Night*, when Orsino seems on the point of killing the disguised Viola out of jealousy, but in *Twelfth Night* the audience knows from the start that Viola cannot marry Olivia and there is more laughter than suspense at her plight. In *Philaster*, the audience is given hints of the truth, but does not know for certain until the end.

Fletcher knew both *Il Pastor Fido* and the *Compendio*. His attempt to introduce pastoral tragicomedy to the stage through his *Faithful Shepherdess* (1608–9) had, however, been a failure; he published the play in 1609 with a preface complaining that the audience didn't understand the new genre. From this point on, he abandoned the pastoral setting but seems to have decided that tragicomedy should deal with characters too noble for comedy but too weak and faulty (particularly when jealous) to achieve tragic dignity. That they should be forgiven at last was an implicitly Christian doctrine, but he and Beaumont also tended to emphasize the improbability of their own endings, thus relieving audiences from the necessity to believe them. Shakespeare was attracted to this kind of drama, and may have started to write it at once. Since the playhouses were closed, however, the works associated with his name in 1609 were those that appeared from the press. They were of a very different kind.

Embarrassments of 1609: *Troilus and Cressida,* *"Shakespeare's Sonnets,"* and *Pericles*

Troilus and Cressida had first been entered in the Stationers' Register in 1603 but not printed. It was re-entered in January 1609 by two publishers, who probably hoped to exploit the forthcoming publication of the second installment of George Chapman's Homer translation, consisting of the first twelve books of the *Iliad*. Entitled *The Prince of Poets*, it was dedicated to "The High-Born Prince of Men," Prince Henry, and everything about it indicated Chapman's status. Though the Prince of Poets was obviously Homer, the reader might have imagined that the translator was making an implicit bid for the same position himself. Like Spenser in *The Faerie Queene*, Chapman included sonnets to distinguished courtiers. His prefatory material, mostly in verse, insisted still more on the greatness of Homer, though he did not republish the argument for his superiority to Virgil. Naturally, he removed his earlier comparison of Achilles with the Earl of Essex; instead, in a sonnet, he praised the "Ulyssean policies" of James's most trusted adviser, Robert Cecil, the Earl of Salisbury. If the King's Men were desperate for ready money, they might have thought this a good time to sell a play in which both Achilles and Ulysses figured.

Something odd seems to have happened even while *Troilus* was being run off, since the title page of the copies first printed states that the play was performed at the Globe by the King's Men while the later copies omit any reference to the company and include a peculiar dedication, presumably by one of the two publishers, headed "A never writer, to an ever Reader. News." Its praise of Shakespeare is the most fulsome tribute published in his lifetime: "you have here a new play, never staled with the stage, never clapper-clawed with the palms of the vulgar, and yet passing full of the palm comical, for it is a birth of your brain that never undertook anything comical vainly." If "your" is not a misprint, he must be addressing the play's author, but his determination to be witty, as in the double meaning of "palm" (symbol of triumph, or applauding hands), makes him obscure. He contradicts the earlier title page in saying that the play was never performed, at least not in front of "the Vulgar." He also implies that the publication is unauthorized, "Since by the grand possessors' wills I believe you should have prayed for them rather than been prayed [that is, prayed to buy them, though there may also be a pun on "preyed"]." By now, it seems, the King's Men had something of a reputation for unwillingness to publish their most popular works. If they really were keeping Shakespeare's plays from the press, this may mean that either they or their author had already planned to publish a collected edition. Or it may simply have been a way of forcing up the price paid by the publisher. The current view of this dedication is that the publishers were being disingenuous in order to avoid punishment for publishing someone else's property. They may have been protecting others as well. In the context of 1609 the play might have been seen as an attack on Chapman's translation; its depiction of Achilles could have been taken as an oblique reference to the Earl of Essex; its unusually explicit references to homosexuality would have been embarrassing at a time when a play satirizing James's court had just been suppressed. Perhaps someone paid the publishers to dissociate it from any public stage performance and to insist that the author and actors had nothing to do with its publication.

A similar appeal to the desire for forbidden fruits may lie behind the small volume that appeared some months later with the rather odd title *Shakespeare's Sonnets never before imprinted*. Thomas Thorpe, the publisher, entered it in the Stationers' Register on 20 May and published it before 19 June. In calling the book *Shakespeare's Sonnets*, Thorpe was setting Shakespeare in the category of writers, like Greene, whose names alone could sell a book. In drawing attention to the fact that the sonnets had never been printed before, Thorpe probably hoped to imply that some of them had previously been considered unprintable. He obtained no commendatory verses, and, like the publisher of *Troilus*, wrote the dedication himself, signing with his initials a statement whose other initials have been a source of endless speculation:

TO.THE.ONLY BEGETTER.OF
THESE.ENSUING.SONNETS.
Mr. W.H. ALL.HAPPINESS.
AND.THAT.ETERNITY
PROMISED.
BY.
OUR.EVER-LIVING.POET.
WISHETH.
THE.WELL-WISHING.
ADVENTURER.IN.
SETTING.
FORTH.
T.T.

Willoughby His Avisa had used the initials H.W. and W.S. to indicate two characters in a *roman à clef*. Was Thorpe playing the same game with W.H.? He is often assumed to be addressing the anonymous young man who, in the sonnets, is promised that he will live "so long as men can breathe or eyes can see." Yet, as Jonathan Bate says, "the only begetter of these ensuing sonnets" ought surely to be the person who wrote them.[5] The dedicatee is promised the same kind of "eternity" that has been promised in the sonnets – not necessarily promised to him, and not necessarily by the poet. Perhaps "our ever-living poet" is Chapman, who had promised eternity to those who patronized poets. His dedicatory poem to Prince Henry concludes that princes should reward poetry because

Who raise her, raise themselves, and he sits sure
Whom her wing'd hand advanceth; since on it
Eternity doth (crowning Virtue) sit.
(A2)

Moreover, the poet signs himself: "By him that most ingenuously wishes your highness all the virtues and royalties eternized by your divine Homer, George Chapman."

The identity of Mr. W.H. is only one of the numerous puzzles created by this small publication. It has no preface, dedication, or other personal statement by its author – in contrast to the careful presentation of the two narrative poems in 1593 and 1594 – and it also contains some odd misreadings. The publisher would have wanted to recoup his money as soon as possible, so he might have rushed the book into print without waiting for the author to do the necessary proofreading. This does not necessarily mean that it was published against Shakespeare's will: perhaps he left town in a hurry because of the plague and sold the poems to a publisher in order to get ready money. James's reign, unlike Elizabeth's, might have seemed a good time to bring out a book that consistently devalues relationships with women compared to those with men. James was particularly interested in the sonnet form and had written sonnets himself, as had his courtiers. Among them was William Alexander of Menestrie. Shakespeare could have read his *Aurora*, which was published in 1604 by Edward Blount and printed by Richard Field. He might have been pleased to see that Alexander's Sonnet 44 developed a theme of his *Love's Labour's Lost*:

> O, now I think, and do not think amiss,
> That th'old Philosophers were all but fools,
> Who us'd such curious questions in their schools,
> Yet could not apprehend the highest bliss.
> Lo, I have learn'd in th'Academe of Love,
> A maxim which they never understood:
> To love and be belov'd, this is the good,
> Which for most sov'reign all the world will prove.

Alexander's Sonnet 84, moreover, was a plea to marry, addressed to an unknown beloved and phrased more matter-of-factly than Shakespeare's Sonnets 1–17:

> Ah thou, my Love, wilt lose thyself at last,
> Who can to match thy self with none agree:
> Thou ow'st thy father nephews, and to me
> A recompense for all my passions past.[6]

If Alexander had seen any of the Shakespeare sonnets, they must already have been in circulation in Scotland, since his own poems mainly date from before 1603 and he does not appear to have traveled south with James's other courtiers. Another Scottish poet, Drummond of Hawthornden, in an unfortunately undated note, mentions Shakespeare and Alexander together, as the writers who have most recently published their sonnets.[7]

Whoever determined the shape of the volume, its order is certainly not random: the first seventeen sonnets and the last two are clearly different from the rest, and only those from 127 on are explicitly about, or to, a woman. After the initial group on marriage and procreation, addressed to a young man, most of the sonnets are about love, often brooding on the threats to it in the form of – for example – time, death, infidelity, rivalry, a sense of unworthiness. Many of them are obviously connected, with a word like "So" or "But" beginning the sequel. The famous poems have long since transcended their apparent context. They are sometimes astonishing in their self-abnegating devotion ("Being your slave, what should I do but tend/ Upon the hours and times of your desire?," 57) and in their ability simultaneously to express deep hurt and to excuse the person who has caused it ("Farewell! thou art too dear for my possessing," 87). It is tempting to think of such poems as sarcastic, because it is so hard to imagine that anyone could seriously mean them, but a sonnet catches the tone of a single moment and makes no promises for the future. References to the seasons and to the apparent passing of three years create a framework for these moments, showing the effects of time on a relationship where the partners in turn wrong each other, forgive, and enjoy moments of peace and mutual trust. In 120, for example, the speaker harks back to past betrayals by the friend, and recognizes his own crimes against love: "For if you were by my unkindness shaken/ As I by yours, y'have passed a hell of time" (120.5–6).

Some of the poems seem to need explanation in terms of a context that is no longer retrievable: they may have been attached to the plays, or (as I suggested earlier) part of a poetic competition, friendly or otherwise. Some of those addressed to women are affectionate though patronizing, others vicious. It is of course possible that they have the same imagined recipient, but few poetic lovers imagine themselves taking the Petrarchan cliché of the cruel mistress to the point of treating her with contempt and hatred. In 1599 the sonnets from 127 on might have been seen, like the two printed in *The Passionate Pilgrim*, in the context of *Love's Labour's Lost* and *Romeo and Juliet*. Ten years later, however, a reader who knew the violent sexual language of *Timon of Athens* and *King Lear* might have thought of them as revelations of Shakespeare's own experience. As Ben Jonson later wrote,

> No poet's verses yet did ever move,
> Whose readers did not think he was in love.
> (*Underwoods*, LX, "An elegy")

That the two final poems were translations of a Greek epigram about Cupid (see above, Chapter 12) might be seen as a further link with *Troilus and Cressida*, another work about the falsity of women and a homoerotic or homosexual male friendship. The two publications, appearing so close together, are unlikely to have done Shakespeare's reputation much good. If readers then as now wanted to believe that the poet-lover of the sonnets was also the poet of *Venus and Adonis*, *Romeo and Juliet*, and *Hamlet*, they may have been bewildered by the range of emotions, many of them disturbing, depicted in the collection. There is surprisingly little contemporary comment on this volume, considering that its title page suggests that it was eagerly awaited. In a copy of Lope de Vega's *Rimas*, published in Madrid in 1613, Leonard Digges wrote a note to the friend to whom it was being sent as a gift, recommending "this book of sonnets, which with Spaniards here is accounted of as in England we should of our Will Shakespeare."[8]

The collection ends oddly, with *The Lover's Complaint*, a long poem in rhyme-royal (the form of *Lucrece*). As in other complaint poems, there is an elaborate frame: the narrator, who plays no part in the story, sees a forsaken woman tearing up what are obviously love letters and gifts, then hears her telling her tale to a sympathetic older man. She describes the irresistibly charming, good-looking, and gifted young man who courted her, quoting at length the words that he used. The poem ends with her admission that he succeeded in seducing her; it does not say that he abandoned her, though the reader infers this, and it breaks off with her admission that she would commit the same sin again if he were there. Brian Vickers considers her lack of remorse "an indictment of female sexuality and an attack on the pleasure principle, simultaneously moralizing and misogynistic."[9] Agreeing with C. S. Lewis, who also thought the poem "dialectically unlike Shakespeare,"[10] he argues that it is by John Davies of Hereford and that it resembles other works of Shakespeare only because it is heavily influenced by them. Davies has been mentioned before, since several of his poems are either to or about Shakespeare, who may have been a friend. He was a writing-master, poet and epigrammatist who moved from Oxford to London in 1605, and his profession makes his relationship to Shakespeare more intriguing. He might at some time have made fair copies of the sonnets, perhaps for presentation purposes, and might therefore have been the person who gave them to Thorpe. It could be that, as with *The Passionate Pilgrim* and *Love's Martyr*, the publisher included *The Lover's Complaint* to give the book its shape, whether or not he thought it to be by Shakespeare. Given the misogynistic tone of some of the sonnets to women, it might have seemed wise to follow them with the complaint of a woman betrayed by a male lover similar to the man in the sonnets.

However, everyone who has edited *The Lover's Complaint*, a task that requires close acquaintance, has been convinced that, though deeply formulaic, and thus much less interesting than the sonnets, it is Shakespeare's work. As was first noticed by Edmond Malone in 1780, Daniel's *Delia* (1592) had already followed a sonnet sequence with anacreontic poems and a poem of complaint put into the mouth of a woman.[11] He was followed, between 1593 and 1596, by five other poets. If stylistic analyses have any value, however, *The Lover's Complaint* belongs to a later period than these sequences. It also seems unfinished. One would expect the narrator to take some part in the story, and for the old man in whom the girl confides to attempt some sort of consolation. The forsaken maiden by a stream not only recalls Ophelia but anticipates the Jailer's Daughter in *The Two Noble Kinsmen*. In 4.1 of that play, a scene that has been attributed to both Shakespeare and Fletcher, an observer describes hearing an unhappy lamenting maiden (the victim more of delusion than of abandonment) who finally throws herself into the water, from which he rescues her.

Like *Troilus*, *Pericles* had already been registered but not printed. It may have surprised Shakespeare and his company when, at some point in 1609, a publisher with no previous experience of printing plays, Henry Gosson, brought it out. How Gosson got hold of it is unknown, but there may be a clue in the fact that one of his previous publications was a pamphlet by George Wilkins. The play's title page calls *Pericles* "the late, and much admired Play" that had been performed by "his Majesty's Servants, at the Globe on the Bankside," and gives only William Shakespeare as its author, perhaps to differentiate it from the Wilkins novel. Faced with a play written in both verse and prose, the inexperienced compositors had difficulty estimating how many lines could fit on a page. As a result, prose is printed as verse and vice versa; there are misattributed speeches and errors that sometimes make both the plot and the lines unintelligible. The state of the Quarto has been attributed to various sorts of criminality, but it may well result only from an unusually complicated manuscript transmission. Suzanne Gossett summarizes the various possibilities: "two authors, one of whom may have attempted with difficulty to copy the handwriting of the other; reporting of the script by actors; dictation, possibly involving shorthand; additions and revisions to the resulting text," and the prose/verse problems already mentioned.[12] Whether because of the difficulties over ownership, or because the play continued in any case to be profitable in the theater, the King's Men made no attempt to publish a corrected version. In any case, the playtext, despite its errors, sold well; the publisher brought out another edition toward the end of 1609, and there were four others before 1642.

The episode had a curious sequel. In the Christmas season of 1609/10 a local company belonging to Sir Richard Cholmley toured the North and West Ridings of Yorkshire with a repertory consisting of four plays: a lost one about the life of St. Christopher, *The Travels of the Three English Brothers* (by three authors, including Wilkins), *King Lear*, and *Pericles*. Sir Richard was a recusant, as were the owners of most of the houses at which his players performed. Though very little is known about most provincial touring companies, this one drew attention when it was accused of having performed, in a private house, a version of the St. Christopher play including a virulently anti-Protestant interlude. The case went to the Star Chamber in London, where the records reveal, like most legal proceedings of this period, that a surprising number of people were willing to lie under oath. As Barbara D. Palmer dryly puts it, "of the ninety-some people who testified in the Star Chamber trial, fifty swore such a play never was performed, thirty offered hearsay evidence, several said that it was another play, and only eight allowed they had seen it" – two of them, in fact, locating the performance at the house of someone else whom they presumably hoped to get into trouble.[13]

If the King's Men knew of this episode it could only have added to their annoyance with Wilkins. Shakespeare might have been embarrassed at having two of his plays in the repertory of a recusant company. The players must have used the *King Lear* Quarto published in 1608, a version riddled with printing errors. Wilkins, who may have been a recusant himself, might have had something to do with getting both plays into print and into the possession of the touring company. He may have been deliberately getting back at the King's Men, if he felt insufficiently paid for his part in a play from which they were making a good deal of money. The company's refusal to send its plays to the press, commented on by the publisher of *Troilus and Cressida*, may have seemed unfair to him. *Jests to Make You Merry* (1607), a pamphlet on which he collaborated with Thomas Dekker, includes as Jest 44 an account of a country fellow who was so taken with the tricks of the lunatics at Bedlam that he asked someone how to go mad. It's easy, replied the other: "do but marry with a whore, or else have to do with players, and thou shalt quickly run mad."[14] Even after the worst of the plague period ended, Wilkins had nothing further to do with the King's Men or the theater. Perhaps he was angry; perhaps they boycotted him. His life from 1610 until his death in 1618 seems to have been as self-destructive as that of the hero of *Miseries of Enforced Marriage*,[15] but it may be too simplistic to associate this with the end of his playwriting career.

Perhaps it was now that Shakespeare decided to revise *King Lear*, to ensure that he was not permanently represented by something so garbled. There are no records of performances apart from the ones at court and in Yorkshire, so it is not known whether the King's Men actually did revive it "with additions" (or, in some cases, deletions). In the version published in the Folio there is less stress on the French character of the invasion, less obvious madness, perhaps somewhat less flowery language. One of the other changes most often noticed is the greater emphasis on Edgar, as opposed to Albany. This might result from a desire to reward the Edgar actor, whose importance was already indicated on the Q1 title page. Henry Condell, who had created the roles of Mosca and Surly for Jonson, was at the peak of his career; he would have been a likely actor for Edgar, and he was also a friend of Shakespeare's. Unlike *Lear*, *Othello* is known to have been acted at this time: a spectator in Oxford in 1610 wrote that the Desdemona actor moved audiences even after death simply by her appearance.[16] Perhaps because a new boy actor was playing the part, Shakespeare revised this play as well. The differences between the two surviving texts – one published in 1622 (Q1) and one in the 1623 Folio – suggest real uncertainty about how to make Desdemona at once sexually attractive and innocent. It is only in the Folio that Desdemona and Emilia converse (in 4.3) about marital unhappiness: Desdemona sings the willow song and Emilia defends wives who commit adultery in retaliation for mistreatment by their husbands. Was Shakespeare improving the roles of two exceptionally good boy actors (if so, F is a revision of Q), or had the scene offended spectators by its explicit proto-feminism (if so, Q is a somewhat censored version of F)?[17] Perhaps the two versions are contemporary, played at different times for different audiences. A mainly female group around Queen Anna or the Countess of Pembroke might have liked the "willow scene". On the other hand, a theater dominated by male tragedians would shorten that scene from the late seventeenth century on, omitting it entirely for virtually the whole of the nineteenth century.

The Masque

Shakespeare's writing of this period shows heightened awareness of what could be done with the non-verbal elements of theater. His early plays suggest that he had always been fond of music, but Blackfriars had resident musicians, and his company's status now gave him the opportunity to see court masques, the most prestigious artistic form of the day. It is these that are described, often in detail, in the personal letters and diplomatic reports of the Jacobean period, which say almost nothing about the plays performed at court. The masques were moral and political allegories; their chief performers had not only a social but a political role. John Chamberlain's letters, for example, clearly take the richness of courtiers' dress as an index of their current status. Masques were also enjoyed, like some television programs, because they showed off the dancing of people who were better known in other contexts. When the queen and the royal children were among the dancers interest was particularly high. Rehearsals for these elaborate spectacles began early and were intensive. Increasingly, however, the excitement also came from the quality of the stage decoration, the costumes, and the music, designed to evoke a sense of enchantment and wonder. Inigo Jones, who had worked for Queen Anna's father in Denmark and apparently came to England at her persuasion, had traveled in Italy, where theater architecture was at its most sophisticated, and introduced the latest improvements in stage machinery.[18]

Shakespeare was one of the relatively few distinguished writers who never wrote a masque. This probably had something to do with his obligations to the King's Men, since Fletcher and Massinger, who succeeded him as chief dramatists for the company, never wrote masques either. Jonson, on the other hand, took great pride in his frequent commissions to supply the textual part of these entertainments. Although he eventually came to resent the dominance of the visual over the verbal, he was initially delighted with the form, which allowed him to use his immense learning to create a new, transcendent, multi-media art. In his typical scenario, the performance began with some comic or villainous group plotting against the event itself. They were called antimasquers, either from "ante" (before the main masque) or "anti" (in opposition to it). There was no question of asking aristocrats to play such characters, so professional performers like the King's Men were brought in for the purpose. While major dancing and singing roles were probably taken by specialists, there were also parts for comedians and other members of the company. The songs and dances associated with these figures – satyrs, witches, figures who had been enchanted by Circe into animals – could be very demanding; for instance, the witches in Jonson's *Masque of Queens* (2 February 1609) danced backwards, indicating their unnaturalness. Clearly, not all members of the company were involved in the antimasque; even so, preparations must have taken up a good deal of time that would otherwise have been spent on rehearsing new plays, and this in itself might account for Shakespeare's writing less at this period. The masque's theatrical climax came when some higher power appeared and banished or destroyed the antimasquers. A spectacular set change led to the entry of the aristocratic performers – discovered on a mountain, entering in chariots, or (in the later, more spectacular masques) descending in a cloud. James himself did not take part in the dancing but this part of the performance often involved a speech addressed to his throne by a professional actor in some allegorical role. The rest of the evening consisted of the dances that the chief masquers had practiced for the occasion, followed by general dancing with the spectators and a banquet, often going on until morning.

Attending a court masque was the privilege of only a few, and to recreate such an occasion added to the appeal of a play. As occasional antimasque performers, the King's Men had the opportunity to see how some of the spectacular effects were achieved. If, as happened sometimes, they were allowed to keep their costumes, they would naturally want to use them again on the popular stage, while their resident musicians could reuse the music. Dramatists increasingly made room for situations in which masque elements would be appropriate: embedded entertainments, visions, dreams, and scenes of conjuring. *Cymbeline* stages a dream or vision of Jupiter descending on an eagle, and a procession of Posthumus's ancestors. In *The Winter's Tale*, the dancers who appear in Bohemia dressed as satyrs, three of whom are said to have "danced before the King" (4.4.338), are probably using a dance and costumes from the antimasque by the King's Men in Jonson's *Masque of Oberon the Fairy Prince*, performed at court on New Year's Day 1611. Prospero in *The Tempest* uses his magic arts to conjure up a wedding masque for Ferdinand and Miranda (one that could easily have been used on some other occasion, though there is no proof that it was). These episodes are detachable: they could have been added or omitted depending on the intended audience. Above all, they seem intended to reproduce the dreamlike atmosphere in Jonson's account of his *Hymeneai* (5 January 1606): "to surprise with delight, and steal away the spectators from themselves."[19] By now, the King's Men may even have considered the possibility of giving plays with more spectacular "scenes" (that is, sets) such as were in use on the Continent and some private houses in England. Two decades later, a few court productions would use masque-type scenery, but the Civil War delayed this development until after 1660.

Many of the surviving masques of the period were written for marriage festivities. One way in which James differed totally from Elizabeth was in his enthusiasm for marrying off his courtiers, especially when the result was an Anglo-Scottish alliance.[20] This was the most visible effect of his unsuccessful campaign for the union of the two countries under the name of Great Britain. He was also increasingly absorbed in the idea of using the marriages of his children to create alliances on a still larger scale between Protestant and Catholic countries. Neither of these projects aroused much enthusiasm among his subjects, but in the plays that Shakespeare wrote at this period the marriage of two young people often puts an end to painful and longstanding hostilities.

Cymbeline

Shakespeare may have written both *Cymbeline* and *The Winter's Tale* during the enforced idleness of 1609–10, perhaps in Stratford. He would not have needed many books around him, as with some earlier plays. The two plays were performed in the same season, April–May of 1611, when the astrologer Simon Forman saw both at the Globe, making notes on the lessons he learned from them.[21] (There is no evidence that Forman and Shakespeare were acquainted, but many of Shakespeare's acquaintances consulted this self-taught doctor, including the boy Nicholas Tooley and many women: Winifred Burbage, Marie Mountjoy, and Jennet Davenant.) Though both plays are often thought of as influenced by conditions at the Blackfriars playhouse, they would have moved between it and the Globe, depending on the season. Most scholars place *Cymbeline* earlier, but the Oxford editors may be right in thinking it the later of the two. The relatively simple way in which *The Winter's Tale* plays with audience emotion may be seen either as a development from the complexity of *Cymbeline* or as an earlier and more cautious experiment. There was probably not much time between the two of them anyway. The influence of *Philaster* might have been immediate, or it might have taken some time for Shakespeare to decide exactly how to make his own contribution to this kind of dramaturgy. After the success of *Pericles*, it is not surprising that the King's Men continued to look for plays of travel and family loss and rediscovery, even apparent resurrection, or that Shakespeare chose to write them. There have been many attempts to relate these plots to Shakespeare's own life: they assuage his guilt at having left his wife and children in Stratford-upon-Avon, or his difficulty in relinquishing his daughters to their husbands (though Susanna lived within easy walking distance); they continue to work out his grief over Hamnet's death, or his mother's, or his brother's. His situation was hardly unique: in an age of plague and high infant mortality, the theme of return from the dead would be moving and personally meaningful to virtually everyone. More important to the plays, though difficult to appreciate in reading, is the opportunity that they offer for music, dance, and dumb show.

   Cymbeline combines a fairytale story with a theme of enmity leading to reconciliation. The political plot sets ancient Rome against ancient Britain, in a pre-Christian era where Roman does not yet mean Catholic. By setting the play in such a remote past, Shakespeare makes the history equally relevant to Scots and English. James's attempts to get Parliament to use the term Great Britain for the united kingdoms of England, Scotland, and Wales had so far met with resistance, but the play's action assumes a union of England and Wales, with Milford Haven as important a location as Dover was in *King Lear*. Rome is ruled by Augustus Caesar, but at times it seems more like modern Italy, since it produces an Italianate villain, Iachimo, as well as a stoic Roman general, Lucius. This is the background to a romantic Italian tale about a husband who is tricked into suspecting his wife's virtue, a wife who disguises herself as a boy to escape death, a wicked queen with a stupid son, a sleeping potion, and two long-lost brothers who are reunited with their sister in the final scene. Shakespeare may have been remembering or rereading his own *Lucrece*, since several episodes recall the early poem: Posthumus's bragging about his wife's chastity dramatizes an episode that the poem mentions only in passing, but

Iachimo's reaction to Imogen recalls Tarquin's, and when he gazes at her asleep he compares himself to Tarquin waiting to wake Lucretia. On a stage that is supposed to be imagined as Imogen's bedchamber, he makes notes on its furnishings: "Such and such pictures; there the window; such/ Th'adornment of her bed; the arras, figures,/ Why, such and such; and the contents o'th' story" (*Cymbeline* 2.2.25–7). The vagueness is deliberate, since the spectator sees none of this, only a bare stage with a bed and the chest in which Iachimo has been hidden. The notes become visual only later, when he describes the room to Posthumus to corroborate his claim to have seduced Imogen. The subjects depicted in its decor recall Shakespeare's earlier classical models: a tapestry shows the meeting of Cleopatra and Antony, the subject of Enobarbus's great speech, while the mantelpiece has a sculpted relief of "Chaste Dian bathing" (the spectator is cast as the voyeur Actaeon) and the silver andirons represent Cupids. As Warren Chernaik points out, the subject matter places Imogen in the company both of the chaste woman that she actually is and the whore that Posthumus will soon think her.[22]

It is important that the characters, and indeed the play, are pre-Christian. Caesar Augustus remains, unseen, in Rome throughout the play, never identified with the chilly young man of *Antony and Cleopatra*, or with the patron of Virgil and Horace. If there is any attempt to flatter the Stuart king it is extremely oblique. The royal family of the play, reunited only in the final scene, consists, like James's, of two sons and a daughter. Since Princess Elizabeth, brought up at Combe Abbey near Coventry, had come to court only at the end of 1608, this passing allusion might have been noticed even in a scene which is something of a tour de force of dénouements. As one revelation follows another, Cymbeline himself, comically bewildered, becomes a parody of the "chief spectator" at a performance. There is surely self-parody in the language with which Iachimo begins the elaborate unknotting of the plot relating the deception he practiced on Posthumus:

> Upon a time – unhappy was the clock
> That struck the hour! – it was in Rome – accurst
> The mansion where! – 'twas at a feast – Oh, would
> Our viands had been poisoned, or at least
> Those that I heaved to head! – the good Posthumus –
> What should I say? He was too good to be
> Where ill men were . . .
>
> (5.5.155–61)

And so on, while his listeners are trembling with impatience. This is writing that draws attention to its own artificiality. As in Shakespeare's earlier comedies, the play comments on itself for comic effect yet allows the characters' feelings to be taken seriously. Its most astonishing scene – Imogen's awakening from supposed death to find herself lying on the headless body of a man in her husband's clothes – is pure theatricality. It requires the boy actor to play tragic grief in a situation that the audience knows to be false, since it knows the contrivance that got the stupid Cloten into Posthumus's clothes in the first place. In *Romeo and Juliet* the Nurse's discovery of Juliet's (supposedly) dead body required a comic actor to make a transition to grief that the audience knew to be based on error, although the plot would make Romeo, with tragic effect, repeat this failure to tell a living body from a dead one. Imogen, on the other hand, risks being comic, because she is so convinced that she is recognizing the body of her adored husband. The potential comedy is, however, enclosed within a plot that will itself turn out happily.

Shakespeare's multiplying of theatrical effects like this may be his way of avoiding the risky political implications of Beaumont and Fletcher's play. While the plot of *Cymbeline* resembles that of *Philaster* – in both, a princess loves a noble and persecuted hero, whose jealousy nearly destroys her, and both women are improbably forgiving – Philaster is the rightful heir to the throne, which Posthumus is not. The collaborators had depicted the tyrannical king angrily (if comically) shouting at a courtier, "Thou traitor, that dar'st confine thy king to things/ Possible and honest."[23] Shakespeare's king is well-meaning but, until the final scene, deceived by a wicked queen (something no one could say of James, who by now was living apart from his wife), and Imogen's marriage becomes irrelevant at the end, since the discovery of her two brothers means that she is no longer heir to the British throne. That Cymbeline should win the war, but agree to continue paying tribute to Rome, involves some odd contortions, but makes sense in terms of the paradoxical theme of reconciliation through empire. The sight of Roman and British flags waving side by side would have implicitly reinforced James's claim to an empire of three kingdoms. Here, too, however, there is ambiguity. The final scene reveals the meaning of an oracle, always a key element in romance, but the Soothsayer (whose name, Philharmonus, shows what his real function is) gives an explanation riddled with false Latin and blatant hindsight when he reinterprets the vision that in 4.2 portended Roman victory (349–55) as the union of "Imperial Caesar" with "radiant Cymbeline." Like him, the author has things both ways at once. Stressing the absurdity of all these coincidences allows the audience to have both the naive pleasure of a providential happy ending and the sophisticated awareness that it is really an artificial creation.

The Winter's Tale

The Winter's Tale is the last of Shakespeare's plays to be based on a work by a dead author whom he had known personally: Robert Greene, whose *Pandosto* was popular enough to go through eight reprints before 1636. In view of the attack in *Greene's Groatsworth of Wit* in 1592, it has been suggested that Shakespeare's use of the novel was either a private vengeance or an act of forgiveness comparable to others depicted in the play. Shakespeare, however, may not even have identified the *Groatsworth* attack with Greene himself, and he had already modeled Hero's epitaph in *Much Ado About Nothing* on the one for Bellaria in *Pandosto*. He may have known Greene's novel too well to bother rereading it. He remembered that someone was married to the daughter of the emperor of Russia, but forgot who. His reversal of the two locations – in the novel, the jealous husband reigns in Bohemia and his friend in Sicily – may have been deliberate rather than accidental, since, as some critics have pointed out, Sicily is associated with Proserpina and myths of return from the dead. Jonathan Bate also suggests that Shakespeare was drawing on his knowledge of the two countries: Sicily was Catholic and under Spanish domination, while Bohemia was both Protestant and hospitable to English artists and scientists.[24] Though Shakespeare was certainly mistaken in making a ship land on the coast of landlocked Bohemia, in this respect he was merely following Greene.[25]

In 1610 Edmund Tilney finally died (at 74, he had outlived most of those who had once competed for his job). The new Master of the Revels, Sir George Buc, had been his intended successor since 1603 and had been licensing plays for the press since 1607.[26] This change seems to have made no immediate difference to the company, but it resulted in one odd episode that may or may not be relevant here. Buc was interested in establishing the authorship of the older anonymous plays in his possession and seems to have talked to theater people who remembered the 1590s. On the title page of one of them, *George à Greene* (published 1599), he noted that Shakespeare had told him that the play was by a "minister" who had played the leading role himself. Someone else gave Buc very different information, attributing the play to Robert Greene. This sounds more likely. Was Shakespeare, then, suppressing what he knew about Greene's authorship, or was he joking, or did he make up the idea of a minister-actor to illustrate the bad old days when the church was full of unworthy servants, by contrast with the present when acting was a professional activity?[27]

Anyone who knew Greene's novel would have been surprised at the ending of *The Winter's Tale*. It is possible, however, that, since Shakespeare changed the names of all Greene's characters, he wanted to keep audiences from recognizing the story, at least until late in the play. Greene had stated unequivocally that Bellaria (Hermione) died, although earlier in the book she had been recovered after she fainted. At the end of the novel, moreover, Pandosto (Leontes) abruptly develops an incestuous passion for his unknown daughter; later, remorse for his past actions leads him to commit suicide. Shakespeare hints at this possibility in Leontes' initial reaction to Perdita, which Paulina sharply reproves ("your eye hath too much youth in't," 5.1.225). *Pericles*, however, had already exploited the incest theme and its divine punishment. *The Winter's Tale* instead provides a happy ending after a harrowing first half caused by the hero's irrational jealousy. The appearance of Time as Chorus, at the play's halfway point, hints that the tone is about to change.

Autolycus, played presumably by Robert Armin, brings not only clowning but music into the play, and the fourth act, with its songs and dancing, is qualitatively different from anything that has gone before. Perdita, like Marina, is associated with flowers. She and her lover Florizel are symbols of youth and spring, images of their parents, and only occasionally credible human beings. The apparently resurrected Hermione is first presented to Leontes as a marvelously lifelike work of art. His gradual realization that she is real, and that happiness and forgiveness are still possible for him, is intensely moving, the more so because the audience, like Leontes, can hardly believe what it sees.

Forman's account of the play does not include the statue scene: he is unlikely to have read Greene's novel and thus would not have had as much reason as some of his fellow-spectators to be surprised at it. However, this fact has led some scholars to suggest that the play's original ending was tragic. There is some precedent for plays with alternative endings – Nathaniel Woods's *The Conflict of Conscience*, a play of the 1570s, although based on the life of a real person, had one ending in which he commits suicide and is damned and another in which he is saved at the last minute. Later, Sir John Suckling would supply two endings to his *Aglaura* (1637). Some biographers have imagined that the happy ending was somehow inspired by Shakespeare's return to Stratford and the need to reconcile himself with his wife. Modern productions, which take much more interest in the dynamics of married relationships than Shakespeare's contemporaries seem to have done, have sometimes ended the play with Leontes and Hermione looking nervously at each other, as if beginning their relationship afresh. But, unless both Will and Anne were spiritually outside their socioeconomic world, it is hard to see why there would have been any need for such a reconciliation. They seem, between them, to have done very well in Stratford. Parents did not expect to see their children constantly. Though in the opening scene Polixenes gives an affecting description of his relationship with his son ("he's all my exercise, my mirth, my matter," 1.2.166), he has in fact been away from his family for nine months when he says this. Leontes does not hesitate to accuse Mamillius's mother in front of him and, hearing of the boy's serious illness, does not go to him (Shakespeare probably knew that royal parents were usually kept away from dying children).

Some spectators may also have recognized that, as with Guarini's *Pastor Fido* and with *Pericles*, the play was deliberately rewriting a famous classical prototype.[28] Euripides' *Heracles* is a strange comi-tragedy which, like *The Winter's Tale*, falls into two parts. In the first half, Hercules returns home in time to save his wife from a predatory suitor. This provisional happy ending, however, is followed by a brief interlude where the divine messenger Iris appears with a personification of Madness. They explain that Juno, Heracles' enemy since birth, now intends to take vengeance on him. The second half of the play consists of her vengeance: he goes mad and kills his wife and children, mistaking them for animals, then, reawakened to sanity, is left in a frenzy of despair and self-loathing. As Eugene Waith says, rage is a quality that Antony shares with Heracles;[29] shame is another, and, in his reactions after his last battle, he had already imagined himself re-enacting one episode from Euripides' play:

> Teach me,
> Alcides, thou mine ancestor, thy rage.
> Let me lodge Lichas on the horns o' th' moon
> And with those hands that grasp'd the heaviest club
> Subdue my worthiest self.
> *(Antony and Cleopatra* 4.12.43–7)

Shakespeare's play, like Euripides', separates the tragic and comic modes by an allegorical figure, Time (*Pandosto* is subtitled *The Triumph of Time*). Although *The Winter's Tale* is set in a world dominated by Apollo, its characters achieve a kind of forgiveness that seems impossible for the gods in classical drama.

The Tempest

Shakespeare must have been in Stratford in the fall of 1611, since he contributed, along with seventy other Stratford citizens, to the costs of bringing a bill in Parliament for the improvement of the highways, a subject that would naturally interest anyone who did as much traveling as he did. Schoenbaum notes that his name was added on the right, near the top, and speculates, "Perhaps he was in London when the sponsors first canvassed support."[30] He may have gone there to deliver the manuscript of the play that his company would be performing in the next Christmas season.

The Tempest was printed as the first play in the 1623 Folio of *Comedies, Histories and Tragedies*. It has sometimes been suggested that this was because it was a relatively easy one for the compositors to set. It would have been a clean text, since it was the first of the six plays that the capable scribe Ralph Crane transcribed for the Folio. It might also have been one of the few that Shakespeare had time to revise between its first performance in 1611 and its publication. It is relatively short, to allow for an unusual amount of music and dance, and its language rarely falls into the habit of "overflowing" that Jonson associated with Shakespeare. The play is also very much a court entertainment, for which rich-looking costumes were a necessity: characters draw attention to the fact that they are well dressed, even though Prospero and Miranda have been living in isolation for twelve years and the Neapolitan courtiers have just survived a shipwreck. Had someone made objections on the grounds of realism? The company had performed Jonson's *The Alchemist* in 1610 and *Catiline*, his second and last tragedy, in the current season. Perhaps they had the benefit of Jonson's views on costume: did the three cheaters in *The Alchemist* look as tawdry as one would expect, or were they impressive in borrowed finery? Was the Roman costume for *Catiline* more authentic than usual? *The Tempest* is, more than any other Shakespeare play, a series of excuses for spectacle: a magician and his assistant spirit perform tricks and put on a wedding masque for an aristocratic audience. The characterization is thin in comparison to earlier works, but the richness of the language and spectacle, along with its multiple levels of allusion and illusion, give it the kind of depth usually found in opera rather than drama.

Prospero is a composite of every kind of symbolism associated with the figure of the magus. As Donna Hamilton writes, "the first association of the magus figure for the Jacobean court audience would no doubt have been with the tradition of the philosopher-king."[31] The Prospero of the past, so "rapt in secret studies" and so indifferent to the welfare of his state that his brother is able to depose him, might have been recognized as an allusion to Rudolf II, Holy Roman Emperor, who had been a great patron of the arts and occult sciences, but, after being forced to cede much of his power to his younger brother in 1605, was finally deposed in all but title in 1611. (In 1609 Rudolf had granted freedom of worship to Bohemian Protestants, so he was a sympathetic figure in English eyes.) As Martin Wiggins points out, the hierarchy of rulers and usurping rulers, from Prospero to the ultimately repentant Alonso to the unrepentant Antonio, replicates that of Marston's *Malcontent*.[32] The Prospero of the present, who overcomes his enemies by mental rather than physical power, and who forgives them, however grudgingly, was close enough to James I's ideal role model to be a compliment without excessive flattery. The most obvious verbal imitation is that of Ovid's Medea, who must have been recognized by many spectators as the source of Prospero's great speech renouncing his magic, but the play evokes the *Aeneid* when Gonzalo surprises the courtiers with the information that the country they have just visited has a history – "This Tunis, sir, was Carthage" (2.1.85). Ariel's disguise as a harpy (3.3.53–82) repeats the episode in Virgil's Book II when harpies destroy the banquet of Aeneas's men and prophesy that the Trojans will be punished for their crimes. Moreover, losing a kingdom in one place and finding it in another is the epic's main theme.[33]

In the year when Chapman finally published his completed translation of Homer's *Iliad*, printed by Richard Field, Shakespeare was not only returning to Virgil the author, he was also drawing on legends of the necromantic Virgil of medieval tradition, who had the power, like Prospero, to raise the dead and make himself invisible. Faustus mentions seeing not only the poet's "golden tomb" (*Doctor Faustus* 3.1.13) but also

> The way he cut, an English mile in length,
> Thorough a rock of stone in one night's space . . .
> (3.1.14–15)

In sailing to Naples at last, Prospero will visit the city where Virgil was buried, and of which he was taken to be a kind of patron saint.[34] The play never makes clear

379

whether the books that matter so much to Prospero are written by others or by himself. He promises to drown only one of them, but the echo of Faustus's final cry, "I'll burn my books," has often been noted. Had there been revivals of the Marlowe play? It had opened with Faustus reading from a Latin translation of the Bible and using its wording to justify his turning to magic. The scene would have acquired new meaning in 1611, with the new Bible translation (often named after the king who had commissioned it). In the last months of 1611, as the King's Men were preparing their Christmas season, a high-profile heresy trial was taking place in Lichfield, soon to be followed by the imprisonment of another heretic in London. Both men denied the divinity of Christ, the same heresy of which Kyd and Marlowe had been accused, and both, apparently at the king's instigation, would in the spring of 1612 become the last heretics to be burned in England.[35] Many scholars think that the revised *King Lear* published in the Folio, in which the Fool satirically prophesies a utopian England where there are "No heretics burned but wenches' suitors [from venereal disease]" (3.2.84), must be earlier than these events. Either that, or the joke was in deliberately bad taste.

The *Tempest* invites many kinds of allegorical readings, one of which is religious. Ferdinand, when given Miranda's hand in 4.1, sees himself as Adam in Paradise; Prospero has to fend off a rebellion led by one that he considers "a born devil" (4.1.188). At the end, the other human characters see all as having happened for the best, even though it has included long periods of grief and even madness, and even though they are unsure how much is due to Prospero and how much to Providence. Critics once took him to be a wholly good figure who might say, like Jupiter in *Cymbeline*, "Whom best I love I cross, to make my gifts,/ The more delayed, delighted" (5.4.101–2). Now, most readers and spectators are so accustomed to distrusting authority figures that it is rare to see a wholly sympathetic Prospero in a professional production. Little touches like the irritability of an aging man toward inattentive listeners, perhaps intended as humanizing traits, are taken for indications of his essentially tyrannical nature. In *Cymbeline* Jupiter appeared only near the end, an obvious allusion to the classical *deus ex machina*, but Prospero makes clear from the start that he intends Ferdinand and Miranda not only to love each other but to think that they are doing so in spite of him. This is the fate of mortals in a Calvinist universe, where freedom of the will is only an illusion. When they are "discovered" in the final scene, the young couple are playing chess – a suitable game for princes, but also an image of their own roles as pieces in Prospero's game. Prospero's final renunciation of his magic would hardly be necessary if it were a completely good thing. The play's design incorporates uneasiness about the nature of any absolute power that is not divine. Antonio and Sebastian point out that Gonzalo's plan to establish an ideally egalitarian commonwealth can be accomplished only if he himself becomes king and forces equality on everyone. In their brief reappearance at the end, Caliban, Stephano, and Trinculo seem chastened by their experiences. They contrast with the silence of Antonio and Sebastian, the last of Shakespeare's inveterate and annoying jokers, who had been prepared to commit regicide. That the two nobles have no lines of repentance is usually taken to mean that they do not repent, and that Prospero has only contained their threat, not destroyed it. Shakespeare may have left it to the actors to devise some business to indicate their state of mind, as happens in modern productions, or he may have wished to leave their feelings ambiguous.

Since Britain was an island, it was natural to look at fictitious islands as political allegories – as with More's *Utopia*, Jonson and Nashe's *The Isle of Dogs* (1597), and John Day's *The Isle of Gulls* (1606). The inhabitants of the play's island debate their rights to it in terms of inheritance, priority, and moral superiority. Though Prospero's island is clearly in the Mediterranean, somewhere between Tunis and Naples, it is often discussed as if it were Bermuda, to which the Virginia Company had sent an expedition, thought lost in 1609, which miraculously reappeared in 1610. The schematic plot, particularly the relation of Prospero to his two servants, the spirit Ariel and the "thing of earth" Caliban, asks to be given more than a literal interpretation. Ariel and Caliban are like the light and dark sides of Puck in *A Midsummer Night's Dream*. One is associated with fire and air, the other with earth and water – complementary elements that a magus has to control. For the poet W. H. Auden, they are complementary aspects of aesthetic creation, the ideal and the uncomfortably real, that the artist has to understand and hold in balance.[36] In a political reading they can be the "good" and "bad" colonial subject, either colluding with or rebelling against the invader. Robert Armin presumably played either the delicate Ariel or the grotesque Caliban, and his performance might have affected the balance of audience sympathy between the two characters.

Yet, as elsewhere in Shakespeare, the existence of so many possibilities seems intended to prevent easy (and dangerous) explanations. One of the few loose ends of the play is the discussion in 2.1 of Claribel's marriage to the king of Tunis, the ostensible reason why the Neopolitans are at sea in the first place. Since Claribel never appears in the play, it seems excessive for Antonio and Sebastian to remind Alonso at such length of everyone's opposition to the marriage. To a contemporary audience, however, it would probably recall the continuing controversy over James's own plans for his children. A marriage between Prince Henry and the Spanish Infanta had been contemplated ever since the signing of the Treaty of London in 1604, and any husband chosen for Princess Elizabeth was bound to live on the other side of the Channel. Claribel's marriage to a bridegroom whose kingdom was "Ten leagues beyond man's life" (2.1.248) turns out at last to have been the cause of lasting happiness for her father and brother, yet the play leaves it uncertain whether she herself will be happy.

The play is like an old tale, and yet it is not (it has no obvious source). In the final scene, Prospero's revelations, first of his identity and then of Ferdinand and Miranda, do not make the audience hold its breath, like the revelation of Hermione's statue. Unlike Leontes, Prospero is not going to be reunited with anyone; rather, he will lose his daughter and say farewell to Ariel; only Caliban, possibly, will remain in his service. The Epilogue, in which Prospero not only begs the audience to waft him to Naples with their applause, but also to forgive him, is another version of the *plaudite*, like Puck's "If you pardon, we will mend" (5.1.425), but, unlike the earlier epilogue, it also allows for a serious religious interpretation. Treating *The Tempest* as Shakespeare's last play, which it was not, critics have looked in it for a definitive statement of its author's philosophy and attempted to identify his views with those of Prospero. It is hard to see why Prospero's return to Milan, via Naples, would make anyone think of Shakespeare's intention to leave London for Stratford, since he had been moving for some time between the two locales and would continue to do so. Moreover, there is no reason to believe that the dominant role of Prospero would have been played by Shakespeare rather than Burbage, or that his final speeches would have been applied to anyone except their speaker, especially since the author himself went on to write more plays.

Notes

1. Sir Thomas Lake to the Privy Council, 11 Mar. 1608, repr. in Wickham, 515.
2. For a full account, see Dutton, "The Revels Office and the Boy Companies," 339–40.
3. Barroll, *Politics, Plague, and Shakespeare's Theater*, 184.
4. Knowles, "Marston, John," *ODNB*.
5. Bate, *The Genius of Shakespeare*, 61. Bate suggests that perhaps W.H. is a misprint for W. S., and that "only begetter" might be meant to contrast with the multiple authorship of *The Passionate Pilgrim* (pp. 62–3).
6. Sonnet 84, in *English and Scottish Sonnet Sequences of the Renaissance*, ed. Klein, 360.
7. *Shakespeare's Sonnets*, ed. Duncan-Jones, 35.
8. Morgan, "'Our Will Shakespeare' and Lope de Vega," 118.
9. Vickers, *Shakespeare, A Lover's Complaint, and John Davies of Hereford*, 6.
10. Lewis, *English Literature in the Sixteenth Century*, 502.
11. Spenser also wrote *two* epigrams on Cupid and the bee. See *The Sonnets and A Lover's Complaint*, ed. Kerrigan, 13–14.
12. *Pericles*, ed. Gossett, 27–8.
13. Palmer, "Playing in the Provinces," 103–4.
14. Dekker and Wilkins, *Jests to Make You Merry*, C3^v.
15. Roger Prior, "The Life of George Wilkins," suggests that the play was prophetic. See also Prior's "George Wilkins and the Young Heir" for another story of financial ruin, tangentially connected with Wilkins, that resembles the material of city comedy.
16. The account of this performance, described in Latin by Henry Jackson, was first published by Geoffrey Tillotson: "*Othello* and *The Alchemist* at Oxford in 1610," 494.
17. See Potter, "Editing Desdemona."
18. Wickham, 125.
19. Herford and Simpson, 7: 229, lines 571–2.
20. See the chapter on "Inventing a Language of Union" in Curran, *Marriage, Performance, and Politics at the Jacobean Court*, 17–56.

21. Extracts are printed in Rowse, *Simon Forman*, 303–7.
22. Chernaik, *The Myth of Rome in Shakespeare and His Contemporaries*, 236.
23. Beaumont and Fletcher, *Philaster*, ed. Gossett, 4.4.35–6.
24. Bate, *Soul of the Age*, 304.
25. See *The Winter's Tale*, ed. Pitcher, 102. Though Pitcher notes that belief in the sea coast of Bohemia was a byword for stupidity, his examples postdate the play and may derive from Jonson's ridicule of it.
26. Dutton, *Mastering the Revels*, 302.
27. Much depends, of course, on when Buc made his note. Alan H. Nelson believes that it was shortly after *George a Greene* was published, and that, since that play was performed at the Rose in the same season as *Titus Andronicus* (1593/4), Shakespeare probably did know what he was talking about. See Nelson, "George Buc, William Shakespeare, and the Folger *George a Greene*."
28. For evidence that Shakespeare could have known Euripides from any number of early modern texts, see Maguire, *Shakespeare's Names*, 98–104.
29. Waith, *The Herculean Hero*, 127.
30. Schoenbaum, 280.
31. Hamilton, *Virgil and "The Tempest,"* 108.
32. Wiggins, *Shakespeare and the Drama of His Time*, 109.
33. See the Introduction and notes to Hamilton, *Virgil and "The Tempest,"* for a useful summary of earlier writers on this subject.
34. Comparetti, *Vergil in the Middle Ages*, 48–9, 149.
35. On 18 March 1612 Bartholomew Legate was burned in Smithfield, followed by Edward Wightman at Lichfield a month later. See their biographies in *ODNB* by David R. Como and Stephen Wright, respectively.
36. Auden, *The Sea and the Mirror: A Commentary on Shakespeare's "The Tempest."*

17

"The Second Burden"

1612–1616

If there be nothing new, but that which is
Hath been before, how are our brains beguiled,
Which, laboring for invention, bear amiss
The second burden of a former child!

(Sonnet 59.1–4)

The hideous idea of a mother miscarrying the same child she has already borne is a grotesque result of the Elizabethan equation of artistic creation with childbirth. Shakespeare probably did not visualize the image at all, since his main purpose in this sonnet was to wonder aloud how he and his poetic addressee compared with those of the past. Nevertheless, the sense of advancing age had preoccupied his poetry for at least ten years. As Robert Ellrodt points out, Shakespeare and Montaigne had in common "the same sense of ageing and being already near death in their thirties."[1] In the version of Sonnet 138 that was published in 1599, the speaker asks rhetorically, "Wherefore say not I that I am old?" (10). The logical reply would have been, "Because you are only thirty-five." In 1609 the slightly revised sonnet asks the same question, while Sonnet 62 describes the author as "beated and chapped with tanned antiquity" (10). These speakers are as fictitious as the elderly Prospero who plans to devote "every third thought" to his grave. In 1612–13, although he was only 46, Shakespeare began to behave as if he was old. "Labouring for invention," he may have felt that his Muse was simply repeating itself. Further, his life was beginning to show the elements of repetition and recurrence that, in music, mean something is drawing to a close.

Whether or not he had been annoyed by *The Passionate Pilgrim* in 1599, he cannot have been happy when its printer Isaac Jaggard brought out an enlarged edition early in 1612, with a new subtitle that was bound to link it with

The Life of William Shakespeare: A Critical Biography, First Edition. Lois Potter.
© 2012 Lois Potter. Published 2012 by Blackwell Publishing Ltd.

Shakespeare: *Certaine Amorous Sonnets, betweene Venus and Adonis, newly corrected and augmented. The third edition. Where-unto is newly added two Loue-Epistles. The first from Paris to Hellen, and Hellens answere backe againe to Paris.* Just as Jaggard's 1599 volume had relied on the relationship of its poems to *Romeo and Juliet* and *Love's Labour's Lost*, in his 1612 version he obviously meant the Love Epistles, which constituted something like half the book, to look like spin-offs from *Troilus and Cressida*. They were in fact unacknowledged extracts from Thomas Heywood's *Troia Britannica*, published in 1609. Heywood was probably furious, but he knew better than to direct his anger at Shakespeare. In a letter to his printer, added to his *Apology for Actors* when he published it later that year, he claimed to be afraid that he would be thought to have stolen the epistles from Shakespeare. His tone is very respectful – Heywood knows his lines are "not worthy his patronage, under whom he hath published them" ("his" seems to mean Shakespeare's and "he" is the printer), but it is odd that he refers to Shakespeare only obliquely, as "another" and "the author"; in fact, his vague use of pronouns makes the whole passage rather obscure.[2] Perhaps Shakespeare had asked to have his name kept out of the controversy. As the father of two daughters, at least one of whom could read and write, not to mention a well-educated and very moral son-in-law, he could not have wanted to be associated with a book that included jaunty retellings of favorite sex scandals from Ovid. Of the two extant copies of the 1612 edition, one has Shakespeare's name on the title page and one does not, so Jaggard may have altered it after the two writers protested.

Another episode from the past resurfaced in May 1612, when he was called to give evidence at the Court of Requests in Westminster Hall. Since he was described in the record as a resident of Stratford-upon-Avon he may have made a special journey for this occasion, staying in Westminster rather than his more usual haunts in the city. Being near Whitehall may have been convenient, since it was also in May that a visiting delegation from the Rhineland was at court, arranging the details of the marriage contract between James's daughter Elizabeth and Frederick V, the Count Palatine and an Elector of the Holy Roman Empire. This was the sort of occasion on which the King's Men might be called on for a court performance, though as the records of this year are incomplete there is no way of knowing whether they were. Once the contract was signed, Shakespeare and his fellow-actors were eager to learn the date of the marriage, since they were sure to be wanted for the celebrations surrounding that event.

In an ironic parallel, the case in which Shakespeare found himself implicated was the result of the marriage of Mary Mountjoy and Stephen Belott, which he had helped to negotiate. After the death of his wife in 1608, Mary's father Christopher had (so the couple claimed) reneged on his promised dowry, and Stephen finally sued him in January 1612. Son and father-in-law totally contra-dicted each other in their initial statements, each claiming that the other owed him money and that the initiative for the marriage had come from the other.

The question of whether Mountjoy had sent one or more persons to talk Belott into the marriage was important, since doing so implied that he was prepared to be generous in order to make his talented apprentice part of the family. Shakespeare was one of the witnesses asked to remember exactly what had been said at the time of the betrothal. The fact that he was unable to do so does not mean that his memory was failing. Mountjoy's own deposition is confusing: he insists that he of course intended to be good to his only child, but that he had been assuming that the couple would continue to live and work with him; besides, he was really thinking of what he would leave them in his will rather than give them on their marriage. He refused to name a sum, on the grounds that he had no idea how much he would be worth at his death or whether the couple would deserve anything.[3] If he was this evasive in 1604, it is not surprising that the two first witnesses were equally unsure about what had been said, or when the money was to be paid, though one of them thought he remembered that Shakespeare had been more specific. Shakespeare, the third and last witness on that day, was firm in remembering that the Mountjoys had thought well of Belott ("he hath hard the def[endant] and his wyefe diuerse and sundry tymes saye and reporte that the said compl[ainant] was a very honest fellowe"), and "that the said def[endant's] wyeffe did sollicitt and entreat this deponent to moue and perswade the said Complainant to effect the said Marriadge and accordingly this deponent did moue and perswade the complainant thervnto." Shakespeare thought that Mountjoy had made some promises but did not know how much money was involved or when it was to be paid; he also pointed out (perhaps somewhat acerbically) that, since the master and apprentice were living in the same house, they had had plenty of time to discuss it among themselves.[4]

His evidence apparently felt so final that the court did not recall him for its second sitting on 19 June, when he may well have been back in Stratford. He was quoted by another witness as having corroborated a new accusation of Belott's: that Mountjoy had not only wanted the marriage but had threatened to disinherit his daughter if she did not consent. Interestingly, a 19-year-old apprentice who had known Mountjoy and Belott for only a few years also quoted Shakespeare's recollections of these negotiations, which suggests that Shakespeare, though no longer living in Silver Street, still had some contact with people in the house.[5] Given the absence of hard facts, the court handed the case over to the ministers of the French church in London, who felt equally negative about both parties. Belott may finally have made his peace with them, but Mountjoy never did. Christopher Mountjoy was known as a troublemaker, seems to have been unreasonably harsh to his daughter and son-in-law, and certainly emerges as the villain in the most thorough account of the affair, Charles Nicholl's *The Lodger: Shakespeare in Silver Street*. He had fathered two illegitimate children, and his wife Marie had paid him back: she told the doctor Simon Forman in 1597 that she was having an affair and feared that she might be pregnant. Given this background of mutual infidelity,

Christopher may have suspected – perhaps even known, if his wife had made a deathbed confession – that Mary was not his child. There is an obvious parallel with Leontes' jealousy in *The Winter's Tale,* and his rejection of his child as a bastard, but Shakespeare had of course developed this subject-matter from Greene's novel. If he thought about the relationship between the passions that tear apart the fictitious court of Sicily and those that were making Mountjoy's family take each other to court, it could only have heightened his awareness that life is never really "like an old tale," though his characters keep validating the plot's improbabilities by saying that it is.

He would have been all the more reminded of the difference between life and romance because George Wilkins was another of the witnesses called in the case. The court record gives Wilkins's profession as "victualler"; he was living in one of the worst parts of the city and apparently not only did his inn double as a brothel but his prostitutes may have stolen for his benefit. He had already been in court several times, most recently in 1611 for "abusing" a man and kicking a pregnant woman on the belly (probably intending to cause a miscarriage). He lost his license as a victualler in 1612, and the rest of his life, until his death in 1618, aged about 42, is recorded only in a series of criminal charges. The lawsuit may have brought the former collaborators together again, though, as they were not called on the same day, Shakespeare may not have had to see what had become of the talented but vulnerable young man who had worked with him on *Pericles.*

In the familiar theater world he must also have had a sense of déjà vu. Many of the plays currently being submitted to the King's Men or performed by other companies were obviously influenced by his work. This did not prevent them from being impressive and even original. Cyril Tourneur's *The Atheist's Tragedy,* published in 1611/12, deliberately echoes iconic moments from *Hamlet* (the hero and heroine meet in a graveyard and sleep with their heads pillowed on skulls) and gets farcical comedy out of characters dressing up as ghosts, but rewrites the story in terms of what ought to happen in a Christian culture. The play's most unusual feature is the exemplary behavior of Charlemont, a young man whose father is murdered and whose role, conventionally, should be that of a revenger. When the father's ghost appears to his son, however, it tells him to "Leave revenge unto the king of kings." The hero obeys, and is rewarded when the murderer dies in a freak accident, making a full confession. Nothing is known of the play's performance history, which is a pity, since its effect would be quite different depending on whether it was played in the same repertory as *Hamlet* or by a rival company.

Shakespeare may have been most gratified, or perhaps most worried, by a new tragedy from John Webster, who until 1612 seems to have written only in collaboration. Like Marston, who was probably a friend, he had been a law student at the Middle Temple at the end of the 1590s, and apparently started writing plays in 1602, when he was in his early twenties. The King's Men would have known him through his lively Induction for their adaptation of Marston's *The Malcontent* in 1605. A confessedly slow writer, he had spent some time on an ambitious tragedy called *The White Devil*, which paid homage to *The Winter's Tale* and *Hamlet* – in both cases, by inverting the Shakespearean situation. Hermione, on trial, is an innocent woman who makes an eloquent and moving defense before a powerful accuser who is also her judge; in *The White Devil* the woman who is brilliantly eloquent in the same situation is an accessory to murder. Later, an old woman grieving over the death of her son offers flowers to the standers-by in virtually the same words that Ophelia uses when grieving over the death of her father: "There's rosemary for you, and rue for you" (*White Devil* 5.4.75).[6] A moment later, a ghost enters, carrying a pot of flowers with a skull beneath them, probably alluding to the scene in *Cymbeline* where Imogen finds a dead body strewn with flowers and moralizes that "These flowers are like the pleasures of the world,/ This bloody man the care on't" (*Cymbeline* 4.2.299–300). Despite Webster's frequent and wide-ranging quotations,[7] the play is totally original in its feverish atmosphere, its eccentric wit, and its moments of lyrical pathos.

The White Devil was produced in the winter of 1612/13 at the Red Bull. The timing was unfortunate, since the winter was one of the worst on record, with high winds and torrential rains; audiences were sparse, and the play was unsuccessful. Webster had his play printed almost at once. In the Preface, bristling with Latin quotations, he not only complained of the stupidity of his audience, in Jonsonian style, but also named the dramatists whom he most admired, something that Jonson was never inclined to do:

> For mine own part, I have ever truly cherished my good opinion of other men's worthy labors, especially of that full and heightened style of Master Chapman, the labored and understanding works of Master Jonson, the no less worthy composures of the both worthily excellent Master Beaumont and Master Fletcher, and, lastly, without wrong last to be named, the right happy and copious industry of Master Shakespeare, Master Dekker, and Master Heywood, wishing what I write may be read by their light . . .

The order in which he names these dramatists has often been taken as evidence of poor judgment on his part, but the only name that modern critics would consider an obvious omission is Middleton's, which is odd since Webster had collaborated with him – perhaps he was still known mainly for comedies and pamphlets and Webster was thinking of authors of tragedies. Chapman's pre-eminence is a tribute to his reputation for immense learning and his position in Prince Henry's household, while Jonson is credited with his "understanding" (a key word for him). Webster probably left Marston out because he knew that the former dramatist, now a clergyman, wanted his theatrical career to be forgotten. His comment that the last three dramatists are "lastly, without wrong last to be named" is the equivalent of "last, not least" rather than a claim that they deserve to be at the end of the list. Shakespeare

388

is keeping company here with two very prolific dramatists who wrote both alone and, like Webster, in collaboration.

John Fletcher and *Cardenio*

To be imitated, echoed, and parodied was flattering but it must also have created doubts in Shakespeare's mind about his own ability to avoid imitating himself. In Sonnet 76 he had asked, with mock-dismay, "Why write I still all one, ever the same?" (5). Now he may have wondered whether it was true. Perhaps, as has been suggested half-jokingly,[8] his fellow-actors were finding his style too elliptical and wanted him to work with someone who could write more plainly. Perhaps he was finding it literally harder to write. The cause might have been anything from arthritis to difficulties with his vision. Middle age often brings on presbyopia, or long-sightedness. Sometimes it actually corrects mild cases of myopia, but for someone already very short-sighted the result is a condition which now can be corrected with bifocals or surgery, but which, in the seventeenth century, would have made reading and writing, especially the latter, very difficult. Perhaps there is some connection between this fact (if it is one) and his apparent acquaintance with the writing-master Davies of Hereford. I have sometimes wondered whether the parenthetical style of some of the late plays could be due (as with the late novels of Henry James) to the fact that they were dictated.

For whatever reason, Shakespeare, after *The Tempest*, worked again with a collaborator. Though John Fletcher (Figure 18) was some fourteen years younger, he was already an experienced playwright who with his friend Francis Beaumont had written several successful King's Men plays after moving from the children's theater. Although he wrote many plays on his own, he seems to have preferred collaboration, and Beaumont's retirement on marriage to an heiress in 1613 probably provided the opportunity for him and Shakespeare to work together. Surprisingly little is known about him, considering that his family was so distinguished. His father, Richard Fletcher, had been favored by both Queen Elizabeth and Essex. For a brief period he had been Bishop of Worcester, and was in fact hosted by the Stratford Corporation in January 1595,[9] but he moved on almost immediately to the more prestigious post of Bishop of London. When he died suddenly in 1596 he left so many debts that John may have had to leave Cambridge, where he was probably preparing for an ecclesiastical career, like many of his relatives. The Fletcher family was strongly Protestant – Richard Fletcher had tried unsuccessfully to convert Mary Queen of Scots in her last hours – but this fact apparently created no problem in Fletcher's collaborations with Beaumont, who came from a recusant family. In fact, neither dramatist seems to have shared the strong convictions of his relatives.

The royalist authors of the commendatory verses to the 1647 edition of Beaumont and Fletcher's *Comedies and Tragedies* had political motives for praising a dramatist whose father was a bishop, when Parliament had so recently abolished

Figure 18   Portrait of John Fletcher. By permission of the Folger Shakespeare Library

the Church of England and executed the Archbishop of Canterbury. Nevertheless they seem largely agreed in the few comments they make on his personality. Richard Brome, who had been Jonson's servant and knew Fletcher, writes,

> You that have known him, know
> The common talke that from his Lips did flow,
> And run at waste, did savour more of Wit,
> Then any of his time, or since have writ[10]

390

Another writer says that, far from bragging of his work, he "slighted every thing he writ as naught,"[11] which suggests that he was either modest or playing at gentlemanly indifference. He might not have been the ideal collaborator if, as his friends suggest, he too had a "wit" that needed curbing, but that he was a pleasant and accommodating man is borne out by the fact that he is apparently the only playwright with whom Shakespeare worked more than once.

Fletcher may have paid Shakespeare the compliment of writing a sequel to *The Taming of the Shrew*, called *A Woman's Prize, or, the Tamer Tamed*, which was first produced in 1611. While the King's Men would have been the obvious company to perform it, especially since Fletcher had already been responsible for several of their biggest successes, its many roles for women seem intended for a boys' company. Perhaps Fletcher planned that two companies would join forces to put it on.[12] However, he makes no effort at continuity in the names of any characters except Petruchio. The links with *The Shrew* may have been introduced at a later date, maybe even after the publication of the Folio. At the play's opening, Kate has died and Petruchio is about to marry again. His new wife, Maria, has pretended to be as meek as Bianca, but after marriage reveals herself to be determined to hold her own. The difference is that she is not an isolated eccentric like Kate. Other women help her in the deceptions that reduce Petruchio to a nervous wreck. Since Fletcher's practice is to keep his audience guessing, he does not let either Maria or Petruchio indicate anything in their relationship except antagonism. As the play's title indicates, the woman is playing for a prize, as in a fencing competition, but, having received her husband's abject surrender, Maria promises to be a model wife. The audience is asked to believe that all she wanted was for him to give her the choice.

By 1633 *The Woman's Prize* was being performed in repertory with *The Taming of the Shrew*, and a possible reference to another Fletcher play in the *Shrew* Induction suggests that perhaps some late changes were made in Shakespeare's play as well as in Fletcher's.[13] Fletcher returned to the sex war in several later plays. While it is tempting to imagine an enlightened Shakespeare sighing at their sexual stereotyping, he may have found their basic message quite congenial: two opposing parties can achieve mutual respect and love within the status quo, once the stronger one stops assuming that power is his (or hers) by right. This is, after all, the conclusion of *Cymbeline*, where the king agrees to continue paying tribute to Augustus Caesar after winning a war fought over precisely that issue. The ideology bears some relation to James I's theory of monarchy, which likewise assumes that the ruler will always act in the subject's interest once he is given his proper respect, but it is not easy to decide whether Jacobean dramatists intend to reinforce or critique this view. Certain accepted doctrines of the period (that it is never too late to repent, that women are unpredictable) and certain stereotypes (lawyers, schoolmasters, stepmothers) were so useful for early modern drama that it hardly matters whether their authors actually believed in them.

At some point in the 1612/13 season, a play listed both as *Cardenno* and *Cardenna* (and *Cardenio*, when it was finally entered in the Stationers' Register) was performed at court and repeated during the visit of the Duke of Savoy's ambassador on 8 June 1613. Given this context, it must have been an elaborate production. Its title suggests that it was based on one of the subplots of Part One of *Don Quixote*, involving a hero (Cardenio) who goes temporarily mad after a friend's treachery and a broken engagement. Cervantes' novel had been an international sensation almost from the moment of its publication in 1605, which was also the year when the peace treaty with Spain was ratified in Valladolid. Spanish culture became fashionable at court. Though the English translation by Thomas Shelton was published only in 1612, English playwrights were alluding to Quixote as early as 1607 (George Wilkins was one of the first), and Fletcher's friend Beaumont wrote *The Knight of the Burning Pestle*, obviously influenced by Cervantes, sometime before 1613.[14] Fletcher knew Spanish; some of his plays draw on sources not available in translation. The young man going mad for love was already a signature character for him, so it is likely that he was either the author or co-author of *Cardenio*. Shakespeare could read Italian and might have been able to manage Spanish even if he had not studied it. He might have seen the Shelton translation through its publisher Edward Blount, who also published *Love's Martyr* in 1601 and entered *Pericles* in the Stationers' Register in 1608.

This play is the Lost Atlantis of Shakespeare studies, and a number of scholars have been tempted to recreate it.[15] It is appealing to imagine the greatest English dramatist helping to adapt a novel by the greatest Spanish novelist. However, everything about this play, and especially about Shakespeare's connection with it, has been questioned. It was first attributed to the two dramatists in 1653 by the publisher Humphrey Moseley, who never printed the play and may never have had it in his possession; it has since disappeared. The only proof that the play was based on *Don Quixote* is the hero's name. In 1728 the scholar and playwright Lewis Theobald published a play, *Double Falsehood*, which he claimed was based on a manuscript by Shakespeare in his possession. If it is indeed based on a Jacobean original, its authors ignored the most original and popular part of Cervantes' novel, the characters of Quixote and Sancho Panza, focusing instead on one of its embedded narratives. Theobald may have attempted to restore what he took to be the original version of a play already adapted during the Restoration. As Tiffany Stern has pointed out, he was himself enthusiastic about *Don Quixote* and, as an editor of both Fletcher and Shakespeare, was so thoroughly steeped in their works as to be quite capable of writing lines that sound like theirs.[16]

Henry VIII and Its Aftermath

One practical reason for collaboration was that the King's Men were stretched very thin in the autumn of 1612. James I wanted to celebrate England's first royal wedding in over fifty years, that of his daughter Elizabeth, on a princely scale. Her German fiancé was due to arrive from Heidelberg in October and the wedding was to end the Christmas celebrations, for which the court scheduled even more plays than usual. Assuming that they did write *Cardenio* in 1612, Fletcher and Shakespeare probably began planning *Henry VIII* shortly afterward. James's accession had made it possible to present the Tudor monarchs on the stage, and there had already been a number of plays depicting both Henry VIII and Elizabeth I. By 1612, as the two writers probably knew, Prince Henry had become interested in history, especially when it was relevant to his aspirations. In 1609 he had commissioned scholars to find precedents allowing him to be created Prince of Wales as early as possible,[17] and Sir John Harington, at his request, sent him material from his family archives, including verses and sayings attributed to Henry VI and Henry VIII.[18] Since the prince wanted to know about rulers named Henry, Fletcher and Shakespeare must have felt that it was a brilliant idea to present the future Henry IX with a play about his predecessor, emphasizing the great achievement of the English Reformation and its connection with Germany, home of Princess Elizabeth's bridegroom. The play would take the place of the poems that both dramatists had failed to write in 1603: it would celebrate the late queen, whose christening is its final event, look forward to the glorious reign of her successor, and, by implication, compliment his attractive and popular children, the new Henry and Elizabeth. Given the interest taken in the subject by the royal family, the company could probably obtain authentic court robes and give the play with the utmost splendor.

Remembering the problems with *Sir Thomas More*, Shakespeare knew that they would have to take care with the subject matter. To explain the English Reformation, they needed to depict the divorce of Henry VIII from Catherine of Aragon (or Katherine, as the dramatists call her). In fact, the temptation to do so must have been irresistible, since the proceedings had taken place in the Parliament Chamber at Blackfriars, the location of the company's theater. No other performance of the period would offer such a frisson of authenticity (hence the alternative title, *All Is True*). Though Henry's character could be read very darkly, Shakespeare and Fletcher did their best to give a sympathetic but recognizable view of someone who was on record as a violent and changeable man, capable of recognizing his wife's goodness and attracted by the simple virtue of Thomas Cranmer, but equally capable of punishing someone unjustly. Katherine's situation in the courtroom scene recalls Hermione's in *The Winter's Tale* as well as Vittoria's in *The White Devil*, where the accuser is also a Cardinal. Both Katherine and Cardinal Wolsey were of course Catholics, but the dramatists portray him conspiring against her on behalf of Rome, while she, as his victim, transcends the religious schism. She dies after a deathbed vision of dancing spirits (carefully not called angels). Her daughter Mary, who never appears, is excluded from the final vision of the future and, with her, England's brief return to Catholicism; Anne Boleyn has only a small and ambiguous role. Although Thomas More does appear, most readers and spectators are unaware of the fact.

393

Wolsey is told that More has replaced him as Lord Chancellor (3.2.394–5), but the Chancellor who appears in 5.3 is a colorless figure who bears no resemblance to the More of history or jestbook. Both dramatists used Holinshed's *Chronicles* and Foxe's *Acts and Monuments* extensively, and the differences between the two sources account for the play's subtler moments, like the scene (4.2) in which Katherine of Aragon and her gentleman-usher Griffith give two contrasting summings-up of the dead Cardinal Wolsey. This careful dealing with history is mirrored in the play's depiction of the difficulties involved in telling the truth to monarchs. When the Old Lady comes to Henry from the delivery room, he urges her to say that the child is a boy. She obediently does, then tells the truth: "'Tis a girl/ Promises boys hereafter" (5.1.165–6). The final scene relies on the absurd idea that Henry is delighted when Cranmer prophesies not only the greatness of Elizabeth's reign but the fact that she will die unmarried. The familiar phoenix imagery, now applied to James's succession, hardly compensates for the statement that, despite Henry's desperate struggle for a male heir, the Tudor line will be extinct within one generation. The implications would not have displeased James: in his *Basilikon Doron* he had contrasted his own marital fidelity with Henry's lasciviousness and implied that he had been rewarded with his three healthy children while none of Henry's had left issue.[19]

However, the many projects built around Prince Henry came to an end in November 1612. Those close to the prince recalled that he had seemed unusually agitated for some months. Being strongly Protestant, he disliked his father's master plan for pacifying Europe, which required him to maintain the religious balance by taking a Catholic bride. Some thought that Henry had made secret plans to leave the country with the wedding party and look for a bride in Germany. By mid-October 1612, when his future brother-in-law arrived, he was visibly altered; his absence from the Lord Mayor's Show at the end of the month made the seriousness of his condition obvious, and he finally died on 6 November. The Privy Council at once banned plays and other shows within the city and liberties. Henry had been a charismatic, energetic, outgoing young man, with none of his father's off-putting intellectual arrogance. While a few sober commentators recognized that any 18-year-old prince will be a focus for popular fantasies, most of the country was devastated. Ralegh, a prisoner in the Tower for ten years, gave up writing his *History of the World* when he heard the news. The prince had been a friend and might have set him free.

Henry must also have been known to the King's Men, but Shakespeare must now have realized how lucky he was not to be part of the prince's household. Its disbanding was disastrous for Chapman and Drayton, its leading poets, who never received their promised pensions. Prince Charles, now the heir to the throne, was only 12 and the king was in no hurry to give him a household like his brother's, which had been a drain on royal finances. It would be years before this prince, after years of being overshadowed by Henry, developed a personality of his own. The court now had to decide what to do about Elizabeth's wedding and how to entertain their guests from Germany, many of whom were eager to return home. James finally postponed the wedding until Valentine's Day 1613.

Between Christmas and May the King's Men were paid for performing twenty plays, including at least seven by Shakespeare. No one seems to have worried about the potential topicality of the interrupted wedding in *Much Ado About Nothing*, the jealous husbands in *Othello* and *The Winter's Tale*, or the scene in *The Winter's Tale* in which Leontes is told of the sudden death of his son, who will later be replaced by a royal son-in-law. There is no evidence that the young couple had a chance to see *Henry VIII* before they set off for Heidelberg on 26 April, but a private performance at Whitehall would have given a special resonance to the play's reference to the transfer of York Place after the fall of Wolsey: "'Tis now the King's, and call'd Whitehall" (4.1.95).[20] Because it was summer, *Henry VIII*, apparently under the title *All Is True*, opened in June 1613 at the Globe rather than the historically appropriate Blackfriars. The elaborately costumed production drew a large audience. Sir Henry Wotton wrote to a friend that the play was "set forth with many extraordinary Circumstances of Pomp and Majesty, even to the matting of the Stage; the Knights of the Order, with their Georges and Garter, the Guards with their embroidered Coats, and the like."[21] It may be, in fact, that the play's opening had been delayed because it took so long to collect and refurbish these liveries, which had been needed for the many public events surrounding Elizabeth's marriage. The stage at the Globe, much larger than the one at Blackfriars, could accommodate impressive processions.

Not only spectacle but "noise" – trumpets and the sound of gunpowder going off – was part of the audience's pleasure. Shakespeare and Fletcher had noticed that in Holinshed's *Chronicles* the author, Abraham Fleming, emphasizes the *loudness* of the cannons fired when the king visited Wolsey's banquet.[22] This concern for sound and spectacle turned one of the company's biggest triumphs into a disaster. During the performance on 29 June, when this moment was dramatized, a spark from a cannon landed in the thatch on the roof. Flames were soon flickering round the whole roof. Astonishingly, everyone got out safely, but the theater was quickly consumed. Letters and ballads described the fire as a major event, and Jonson, only half-joking, commented in verse, "See the world's ruins."[23] The only consolation was that the players still had Blackfriars. Not only was it a playing space, but it was probably where they stored their costumes, props, and playbooks. If those valuable objects had been destroyed in the Globe fire the newswriters would have said so.

Within a few days the sharers met to discuss what to do. The two Burbages, Heminges, and Condell decided to rebuild the Globe. Andrew Gurr claims that their decision to retain two playhouses was a sentimental one.[24] It may have been economically sound as well. The Globe could be rented to other companies, amateur actors, and fencers. It might have been useful as a rehearsal space, when the special effects for court performances required large numbers of hired performers from outside the company. Besides, although the higher admission costs of the Blackfriars made it relatively more profitable, the number of people willing to pay these costs may not have been great enough to sustain it over an entire season. The one penny admission for groundlings at the Globe, which remained constant throughout the period, was roughly equivalent to the £5 currently charged for standing room at "Shakespeare's Globe" in London. Even well-off spectators who wanted to see a play more than once might have preferred to pay less for their admission and witness it in a larger space. Rebuilding the Globe was expected to take at least the £700 that the company had spent on the first Globe (in the end it cost twice as much).[25] This meant that each shareholder would need to contribute £100. Two of them chose not to be involved in this expense. One, not a company member, had inherited his share from Augustine Phillips after the remarriage of Phillips's widow. The other was Shakespeare.

The timing could not have been worse for him: 1613 had been a year of upheavals. In the midst of the frenetic preparations for the royal wedding, he had heard of the death of his last surviving brother, Richard, shortly before his thirty-ninth birthday. The funeral on 4 February was at just the wrong time, but he may have left the final rehearsals to make a quick trip to Stratford. All that now remained of John Shakespeare's once large family was William and his married sister Joan. Richard is unlikely to have left any money; more likely, he may have cost his brother money, as Joan and her family probably did. Yet in March 1613 Shakespeare seems to have felt like spending. The company had probably received a substantial present for its Christmas and wedding performances, and its author may have been separately rewarded. He was soon to receive 44 shillings in gold for devising an impresa, painted by Burbage, for the shield carried by the Earl of Rutland (brother of Southampton's friend) at the accession day tournament on 24 March. Though there is no record of it, he may have written a sonnet to accompany the impresa, as was sometimes done.[26] (Sir Henry Wotton saw the tilting and admired two imprese, but found some of the other devices unintelligible.[27])

Shakespeare's first and only London property was a gatehouse in Blackfriars (now Ireland Yard, which leads into Playhouse Terrace, the site of the theater). Before passing to its current owner, the house had belonged to one Fortescue, whose daughter had married John Beaumont, the older, devoutly Catholic brother of Francis Beaumont the dramatist. Fortescue had been notorious for harboring priests on those premises, conveniently near an escape route at Puddle Wharf, but this part of its history had ended ten years ago and the house's tenant since 1604 had been a haberdasher. Though Shakespeare eventually chose to rent out the house, and the new tenant was still there in 1616, it seems unlikely that he would have spent £140 on this residence if he had expected to cut all his ties with the King's Men and his London life. He may have been thinking of the desirability of living nearby during the forthcoming Blackfriars performances of *Henry VIII* and work on his next project. Perhaps he even thought of bringing his family – or at least John and Susanna Hall – to London for the season, giving them the coveted opportunity to attend a court performance.

Or perhaps the house had nothing to do with Shakespeare himself. This might explain the peculiar way in which he bought it. On 11 March he paid down £80 in cash, with another £60 remaining on mortgage until September of that year. For reasons that are not clear, his title deed lists three other purchasers, though they were in fact trustees. One was William Johnson, the landlord of the Mermaid Tavern; the others were a London citizen about whom nothing is known and "John Hemmynge," probably Shakespeare's colleague. The main function of trustees in land purchases was to ensure that the real wishes of the purchaser would be carried out, regardless of the restrictions imposed by common law. The biographer Sidney Lee cites a legal opinion that the purpose of the trusteeship was to prevent Anne from inheriting this piece of her husband's property,[28] but Shakespeare may not have intended so much to exclude his wife (or his Hathaway relatives) as to help his daughter and son-in-law, who might have found it convenient to have a London base. His Globe shares do not figure in his will, so he probably sold them either in order to buy the Gatehouse or to rid himself of company responsibilities. No one seems to have felt that he was being disloyal. He and his colleagues remained on good terms: he left bequests to three of them, and the work of Heminges and Condell on the 1623 Folio is ample evidence that they still cared about him.

The Two Noble Kinsmen

Shakespeare and Fletcher collaborated one last time, probably in 1613, on a play based on Chaucer, an author they both admired. The Knight's Tale, from *The Canterbury Tales*, with its noble cast of characters and a story that would be familiar to European visitors from Boccaccio's earlier version, was an obvious choice to dramatize for a royal entertainment. In the winter of 1612/13 the conjunction of funerals and nuptials (frequently rhyming in the verses written for the occasion) gave an eerie appropriateness to a story in which the death of one young man is followed by the marriage of another. The opening song, supposedly for a wedding, echoes the funeral verses Shakespeare wrote for *Love's Martyr* in 1601 (the book was republished in 1611).[29] Even the play's title, *The Two Noble Kinsmen*, would remind spectators of the short-lived friendship between Henry Frederick and his sister's fiancé, Frederick Henry. The dramatists further emphasized its aristocratic context by borrowing a country morris dance from Beaumont's *Masque of the Inner Temple and Gray's Inn*, which had been performed at court after the wedding in February. Theseus and his court watch the dance and its inept introduction, much as they had once watched "Pyramus and Thisbe." Theseus is generally the voice of reason in Greek tragedies, and it was his capacity for urbane, tolerant amusement, as depicted by Chaucer, that Shakespeare had used for his portrayal in *A Midsummer Night's Dream*. In *The Kinsmen*, too, he is generally treated with respect, but, as in Chaucer,

397

he is tragically powerless against the workings of fate, and comically unable to control the irrational desires of the lovers. His attempts to see the outcome as an example of divine justice are as ineffectual as all attempts at consolation had been after the recent public loss.

With the theater's affairs in chaos, Shakespeare may have decided to leave London soon after the burning of the Globe. If he did, he arrived in Stratford in time for another crisis. In May or June 1613 his daughter Susanna learned that one John Lane had accused her of committing adultery and of having "running of the reins," or gonorrhea. Odd as it sounds, the period was one in which people frequently accused each other of having the pox, and actions of slander, a relatively new development, had become common.[30] The accusation had to be combated immediately, and Susanna or her representative brought the case to the bishop's consistory court in Worcester. As often happened in the early stages of a lawsuit, Lane failed to turn up for the preliminary hearing, and she won by default. Consistory courts did not award financial damages, but Lane could have been forced to do penance. He probably settled out of court.

If Shakespeare felt obliged to stay in Stratford during this episode, he may have written his part of *The Two Noble Kinsmen* there, sending his scenes to Fletcher for revision. In performance the resulting play can be coherent, but closer examination shows that the initial plotting must have been rather rushed. The two men do not seem to have discussed how to pronounce the name of Theseus's friend Pirithous (perhaps Fletcher knew some Greek and Shakespeare did not – or perhaps, as Eric Rasmussen suggests, they were using different sources: "Shakespeare was writing in his chamber where he had a Folio of North's Plutarch; Fletcher was writing in another location where he had a Chaucer Folio").[31] They may also have differed as to how much to emphasize Chaucer's humor, on the one hand, or his philosophical seriousness on the other. The plot starts from what might have been a comic event: Palamon and Arcite, both cousins and friends, fall in love with the same woman. They engage in a formal combat for her, but the winner is killed in a freak accident and the loser, after (in the poem) many years of mourning, finally marries her. The two playwrights seem to accept the courtly love tradition (only death can end the men's commitment to Emilia), but they are also aware that Chaucer himself often subverts it by his tone. Some critics have seen the *Kinsmen* as a sequel to *A Midsummer Night's Dream*,[32] in which rivalry is settled through a magical change of affections. The dramatists offer the tantalizing possibility of a similar happy ending through the presence of a new character, the Jailer's Daughter, who falls in love with Palamon. (She is never named, perhaps because the two dramatists never got round to discussing names for the non-Chaucerian characters.) Instead of changing Chaucer's tragic ending, Fletcher and Shakespeare exploited the Daughter's unusually explicit display of frustrated sexuality for both pathos and comedy. Her story reaches a resolution of sorts when a doctor persuades her former suitor that the best way to cure her is to impersonate the man she loves. Apparently believing that she is speaking to Palamon, she takes the initiative:

> *Jailer's Daughter.* And then we'll sleep together.
> *Doctor [to the Wooer].*   Take her offer.
> *Wooer [to the Jailer's Daughter].* Yes, marry, will we.
> *Jailer's Daughter.* But you shall not hurt me.
> *Wooer.* I will not, sweet.
> *Jailer's Daughter.* If you do, love, I'll cry.
>
> (5.2.109–14)

The spareness of this dialogue may be meant to characterize the speakers as unimaginative and simple or, on the contrary, to give them a subtext of shy tenderness. The dramatists apparently leave it for the actors themselves to decide how far the daughter is deceived at this point – or else Shakespeare expected to attend rehearsals.

Other unusual features of this play made it attractive in the late twentieth century. Hippolyta, though happily married to Theseus, recognizes that his relationship with his friend Pirithous is different from, and as deep as, his love for her. The two kinsmen of the title, though sadly aware that they must forever be mortal enemies, cannot shake off their lifelong affection. In the final moments Palamon sums up the agonizing result:

>   Oh, cousin,
> That we should things desire which do cost us
> The loss of our desire! That naught could buy
> Dear love but loss of dear love!
>   (5.4.109–12)

In one of the most intriguing Shakespearean additions, the heroine Emilia recalls the childhood girlfriend who died when they were both 11. In a play where both dramatists play on the words "twinning" and "twining" to describe close relationships,[33] it may be relevant that Emilia's friend died at the same age as Hamnet Shakespeare, and that Emilia says she never expects to love any man as much as she loved this friend. *The Duchess of Malfi*, whose protagonist has a twin brother, may have made Shakespeare think again about his unmarried daughter, now nearly 30.

The language of the parts generally ascribed to Shakespeare is often even more extreme than in *Cymbeline*. Its grotesqueness sometimes works against the speaker's apparent intention, as when Hippolyta is asked to kneel no longer "than a dove's motion when the head's plucked off" (1.1.98). Arcite prays to Mars while evoking the hideousness of war; Palamon prays to Venus in a speech that veers into satiric examples of the absurd matches made by sexual desire. Pirithous's account of how Arcite's horse goes mad and finally falls backward on to him is elaborately parenthetical at a point where everyone is breathlessly waiting for information. In performance, the most effective scenes are usually the ones attributed to Fletcher, such as the young men's first sight of Emilia. Within moments of swearing eternal friendship, they are quarreling over which of them is entitled to love her, and Palamon's "I saw her first" (2.2.163) – childish, yet a valid argument in the courtly love ethos – invariably arouses affectionate laughter. By contrast, the Shakespearean lines are often laden with more emotion than the context seems to require, as if he were writing without much sense of where the play was meant to go. Fletcher, reading his collaborator's scenes, was probably too impressed with their poetic quality to revise them in Shakespeare's lifetime. He may, however, have felt that the play was essentially his own, since it was not included in the Folio of 1623. There is some evidence that it was revised for a performance in the 1620s. It may initially have been given an elaborate production and scaled down later, when it turned out to appeal only to Blackfriars audiences.

Unlike Jonson, Fletcher, and Webster, whose published prefaces continue to argue with their audiences, Shakespeare was quiet in print about his theatrical failures, so nothing is known about the reception of his final play. Its Prologue – which is probably by Fletcher and may not belong to the time of its first performance – refers to the company's "losses" and the desire to make "dull time" pass more quickly for both actors and audience. John Chamberlain grumbled that the plays given in the Christmas season of 1613/14 were "for the most part such poor stuff, that instead of delight, they send the auditory away with discontent. Indeed, our poets' brains and inventions are grown very dry, inasmuch that of five new plays there is not one pleases, and therefore they are driven to furbish over their old, which stand them in best stead, and bring them most profit."[34] Chamberlain did not get to the theater very often and his critique is probably secondhand. Perhaps the negative response to new plays included *The Two Noble Kinsmen*; modern productions usually receive only polite applause.

Shakespeare was ceasing to be his company's one indispensable playwright. The previous decade had seen many dramatic successes, including Fletcher's, and he must have been impressed with the brilliance of Jonson's *The Alchemist*, which the King's Men acted in 1610, and Middleton's *A Chaste Maid in Cheapside*, a Queen Elizabeth's Men play, which opened at the Swan in spring 1613. Still more unsettling was the success of Webster's *Duchess of Malfi*. It was probably rehearsed alongside *The Kinsmen*, which lacks major roles for Burbage and Lowin, the Wolsey and Henry VIII of the previous collaboration. The two great actors were needed instead for Webster's Ferdinand and Bosola. Webster's play became a classic, revived even after the Civil War. Shakespeare must have recognized his own influence, still more than in *The White Devil*. Webster had seized on such moments as Lear's "I am bound/ Upon a wheel of fire, that mine own tears/ Do scald like molten lead" (4.7.47–9) and much of his play conveys that atmosphere, as in the Duchess's bleak description of her life in prison:

> I'll tell thee a miracle:
> I am not mad yet, to my cause of sorrow.
> Th' heaven o'er my head seems made of molten brass,
> The earth of flaming sulfur, yet I am not mad.
> I am acquainted with sad misery
> As the tanned galley-slave is with his oar.
> (4.2.23–8)

Recognizing the source of Desdemona's morally ambiguous lie on her deathbed (see p. 316 above), Webster made the Duchess speak of what "Tasso calls *Magnanima menzogna*, a noble lie" (3.2.182–3). Strangled like Desdemona, she revives to murmur her husband's name and it is her murderer, Bosola, who replies with a lie, in a desperate (noble?) attempt to give her a reason to live.

It has been argued that Webster's remarkable fusion of verbal and physical imagery shows that he "was compelled to imitate intellectually a process which in Shakespeare was mainly intuitive."[35] Shakespeare's image patterns were not purely intuitive: in the course of revision, he probably developed and enriched what he found already there. Webster's play could, however, have made him more aware of what he had been doing. This may not have been a good thing. If Shakespeare is one of the few major dramatists who made no attempt to preface his published plays, this may not be simply because such prefaces became common only near the end of his career. The self-protective instincts that every writer must develop may have told him that he would be better off if he did not say too much, or know too much, about his writing.

Last Years

Whether Shakespeare saw it as a success or a failure, *The Two Noble Kinsmen* is the last play in which he is known to have been involved. In other words, he stopped writing for the stage at the age of 49 or 50. His "retirement" could have had many different motives, including fatigue and a desire to escape the unhealthy air of London. Marston, at 30, had given up playwriting. Henry Constable (who died in 1613) had stopped writing sonnets when he "found that such vain poems as I had by idle hours writ did amount just to the climacterical number 63."[36] What Constable meant was the "grand climacteric" of 63, nine times seven. In April 1613 Shakespeare would reach the age of 49, or seven times seven, a "minor climacteric," and might have thought it significant. Others stopped writing in these years: Ralegh ended his *History of the World* after Prince Henry's death and John Donne, concluding an elegy on another young man, declared that his Muse would write no more. I have written of Shakespeare's brothers as if they were nonentities, but they are only victims of history's dependence on the written record. For all we know, they may have been an important part of the poet's life, and Richard's death early in 1613 could have been some sort of catalyst. Whereas in 1600 Shakespeare could have seen himself midway in a Dantesque journey, the deaths of his three younger brothers may have given him the sense that he was now nearing the end of it.

To Henry James, totally defined by his life as an artist, the relevant question was not why but *how* someone of such apparently inexhaustible imaginative energy could suddenly turn it off: "What became of the checked torrent, as a latent, bewildered presence and energy, in the life across which the dam was constructed?"[37] This is of course a modern perspective, assuming that "The creative individual comes to love his work – indeed, cannot thrive without it."[38] James's question would be meaningless in a period that had no concept of retirement because it had no concept of a "career" – a word derived from "cursus," a horse race."[39] One likely if unexciting answer is that Shakespeare had planned to use his imaginative energy in revising his works for publication.[40] He must have known of Ben Jonson's plans for what became the 1616 Folio. Jonson evidently saw it as a stopping point, since it was ten years before his next play was performed.[41] The reluctance of the King's Men to publish Shakespeare's Jacobean plays may mean that he wanted to revise them with the care that he knew Jonson was giving to his own works. Neither dramatist wanted to leave behind the unfinished drafts or notes that fascinate the modern student. For them, the task of the writer was to produce a "perfect" – complete and finished – work, not to draw attention to the nature of the creative process.

In Jonson's *Poetaster*, as in Donatus, Virgil is praised for his scrupulous perfectionism. This fact was enough to convince Jonson's early twentieth-century editors that the Virgil of *Poetaster* could not possibly be modeled on the Shakespeare whose carelessness Jonson himself pointed out several times.[42] But what if Shakespeare himself thought of the parallel? Donatus's biography says that Virgil read the *Georgics* aloud to the Emperor Augustus, who admired them so much that he set aside four days for the reading, with Maecenas filling in whenever the poet's voice gave out. Sometimes, while reading, the poet improvised half-lines and his listeners ordered him to write them into the poem.[43] If Shakespeare had been reading his plays and poems aloud – at court, at the Inns, or to friends in Stratford – he must have found that the experience of re-voicing them, and perhaps hearing comments on them, made him want to rewrite. In 1611, the Stratford council had raised the penalty for allowing plays to be performed on council property from 10 shillings to £10,[44] making publication even more desirable. After years of working quickly, relying on the opportunity to make changes during rehearsal and performance, a quiet year or two at Stratford might allow him to decide on his canon and polish his works to his own satisfaction.

On the other hand, the answer to Henry James's question about the "checked torrent" of imagination may be that Shakespeare could not sufficiently check it. A deadline is an excuse for imperfection: it makes writing possible for writers who otherwise could never finish anything to their own satisfaction. Rereading early work may have been painful for someone who had moved on so far that rewriting would probably have meant total rethinking: when Sidney revised his *Arcadia*, the new material no longer matched the old. Unlike Jonson, Shakespeare may have been uncertain whether to retain alterations by others that had become part of the received performance version. Perhaps he destroyed some early works, as Jonson apparently did, to prevent them from becoming an embarrassment to the canon. In the end, reading and rewriting may have been too much for his imagination as well as his eyes.

As usual, he is almost invisible in the Stratford records. Anne Shakespeare was used to running the household and he probably let her continue to supervise the garden, the vines, the orchard, and the malting, relying increasingly on her brother and his family. Even so, Stratford may not have been the quiet retreat that is sometimes imagined. The sheer size of New Place may have made its inhabitants feel that they had a duty to entertain, something that would have taken away from his writing time. In 1614, with the help of a gift of wine from the Corporation, he hosted the visiting clergyman who preached in the Guild Chapel across the street at Easter or Whitsuntide.[45] In July, another fire burned fifty-four houses to the ground and looked at one time as if it would destroy the whole town. Again, the Shakespeares were lucky to escape it. Alderman Sturley, an acquaintance, and Judith Sadler, an old friend, died in this year.

The absence of theater in Stratford was an incentive to revisit London. In November 1614 Shakespeare and John Hall went there together. They probably inspected the Blackfriars property and the new Globe, which had opened in July, and attended the Christmas productions at court. Jonson's innovative Aristophanic comedy *Bartholomew Fair* may still have been playing at the Hope Theatre, "stinking" (as Jonson said in the Induction) from its other use as a bear garden. Shakespeare probably made himself attend, since he knew the play contained jokes at his expense: a speaker in the Induction tells the audience that the author won't show them "a servant-monster" (like Caliban, perhaps already the favorite character of *The Tempest*), since "He is loath to make Nature afraid in his plays, like those that beget tales, tempests, and suchlike drolleries" (Induction, 126, 127–9). *Bartholomew Fair* even satirizes the theme of rival friends in love and makes a young fortune-hunter briefly adopt the name Palamon "out of the play" (4.3.70). Shakespeare, aware that Jonson was more inclined to make fun of a success than a failure, was probably pleased that his last play was considered worth noticing. He must have talked to Burbage and his other friends in the company; perhaps they discussed future projects.

A less optimistic interpretation of this visit may be inferred from the diary of Thomas Greene, Shakespeare's former lodger and Stratford's lawyer, who was now in London for the legal term. On 17 November he wrote, "At my cousin

Shakespeare coming yesterday to town I went to see him how he did."[46] This may mean only a polite social call, but, if Greene was seriously concerned about his cousin's health, it might explain why Shakespeare and the doctor had traveled together. Thomas Greene had good reason for wanting to see this prominent Stratford citizen. William Combe, son of the Thomas Combe from whose brother John Shakespeare had bought his Old Stratford lands, was proposing to enclose a substantial area for sheep farming. The Stratford council prepared to resist. Shakespeare and Greene may have feared, like other townsmen, that enclosure would affect their tithe lands, because "sheep pastures would pay less in tithes than fields of grain and hay."[47] Yet Shakespeare was a friend of the Combes so he and Greene may have been at cross-purposes. He and Hall assured Greene that (as the latter summarized it) "they think there will be nothing done at all."[48] It is not clear whether they were mistaken (the Combes may have lied to them) or disingenuous. Greene later heard from his brother John that Shakespeare was supposed to have said, "I was not able to beare the encloseinge of Welcombe." The best explanation of this mysterious note is Mark Eccles's suggestion that Greene, who crossed out "he," originally meant to write "barre" – in other words, Shakespeare thought it would be impossible for Greene, or anyone else, to stop Combe's depopulation of Welcombe. Through his lawyer, Shakespeare got his own lands and Greene's exempted from the enclosure proposal, but Greene continued to oppose it, as he had promised the council to do.[49] Their differences on this point may have caused an irreparable breach between the two men. Shakespeare left Greene nothing in his will, whereas he bequeathed his sword to William Combe's brother Thomas, who had called the Stratford councilmen "dogs & curs." The case against Combe went to Chief Justice Edward Coke in 1615, and in 1619 to the Privy Council; both sided with Stratford council. But in 1617, perhaps tired of dealing with the Stratford bureaucracy, Greene resigned as town clerk, sold his property, and moved to Bristol. William Combe's behavior, as described by Greene, Stratford council, and Coke, seems thoroughly obnoxious, and it is depressing to find Shakespeare on his side. The poet clearly felt a strong loyalty to the family, and it is clear from his other bequests that his friends in Stratford were largely confined to the gentry. Francis Collins, who had acted for Shakespeare in 1605 when he bought the tithes, drew up both John Combe's will and Shakespeare's.

During 1615 Shakespeare was probably arranging a marriage for his younger daughter, but the final decision may have been hers rather than his. Thomas Quiney, now 26, was one of the nine children left fatherless in 1602 after Richard Quiney's fatal beating by servants of the lord of the manor. The family was wealthy enough to survive the disaster: Thomas's older brother Richard became a successful grocer in London, and his younger brother George took a degree at Oxford, then became a curate at Stratford. Thomas, who became a vintner, was a grammar school product who could write French and Latin. The Quineys lived in the High Street, five minutes' walk from New Place. In 1611 Judith, along with the Greenes, witnessed a legal document for Richard Quiney's widow, signing only with a mark. The two families had known each other all their lives and there seems no reason why Shakespeare should have objected to a Quiney as son-in-law, but he may have had doubts about Thomas.

In January 1616, at the beginning of the year in which he would turn 52, Shakespeare sent for Francis Collins and drafted the first version of his will. If he had died intestate, as many did, his estate would have been divided into three parts: one to his wife, one to be divided between his daughters, and the "dead man's third" – the one part of his personal property that he was historically entitled to dispose – would have been administered, according to the decision of a church official, by his wife or one of his daughters. His land would also have been divided between his daughters, although if they had been sons the elder would have been sole heir.[50] Many people put off making a will because of a superstition that it hastened one's death, with the result that they had to dictate from their deathbed, as did, for example, Philip Henslowe and Richard Burbage.[51] Shakespeare must have had a reason for planning ahead. One reason was Judith's forthcoming marriage, though he may not have known yet how soon it would be. Although the document's opening sentence includes the formulaic claim that the testator is "in perfect health and memory, God be praised," he may have been ill already. At the back of his mind, there may have been another reason. According to Donatus, Virgil died at 52.

Most of the will is concerned with his immediate family and reflects the period's anxiety over the transmission of property. Legislation in the reign of Henry VIII, much of it designed to prevent the Crown from losing its feudal rights over land, had been manipulated through a series of devices with a view to making it possible for a landowner not only to bequeath property but to retain it in the family for several generations. Shakespeare's problem was the absence of a male heir to his eldest daughter, after nearly eight years of marriage. Her younger sister was about to be married and might well have a son. What should be their relative status as heirs to his estate? His future son-in-law had probably enquired exactly this, and Susanna and John Hall were nervous about the potential injustice to their child.

The will that Shakespeare devised was not calculated to improve relations between his daughters. Any sons Susanna might have in the future would take precedence over her daughter Elizabeth, but Elizabeth took precedence not only over Judith but also over any future sons of hers. He did, however, give a marriage portion of £150 to Judith, of which £100 was to be paid within a year of his death; any delay would accrue 20 percent interest – perhaps he remembered the confusion over Christopher Mountjoy's promise to the Belotts. The remaining £50 would be paid to Judith only if she renounced her right to any of his lands in favor of her sister Susanna. There was to be a further £150 "if she or any issue of her body be living at the end of three years next ensuing the day of the date of this my will." This money, however, was to be administered by his executors so that she received only the interest on it while she was married, and then only if "such husband as she shall at the end of the said three years be married unto or attain after" was willing to assure her and her children lands of comparable value. She was also given a "broad silver & gilt bowl," presumably something of sentimental value, since it is (with one significant exception) the only household object specifically named. The convoluted language suggests both affection for his daughter and lack of confidence in her husband. He may even have contemplated the possibility that Judith might divorce Thomas.

The rest of Shakespeare's family, for the most part, was well treated. He allowed his sister and her children to continue living in the Henley Street house for a nominal rent of twelvepence a year, giving Joan an additional £20 and all his clothes, which she should have been able to sell for a considerable amount. The bequest might have included hats made by her husband, who was perhaps terminally ill when Shakespeare was conferring with Collins. The only specific bequest to Anne was, famously, "my second best bed with the furniture [i.e., hangings, coverlet, etc.]." Thomas Greene had been left a second-best bed by his father in 1590 and beds were valuable objects, often named in wills,[52] but this one was probably mentioned simply in order to ensure that Anne was named somewhere. She may have been entitled to her "dower right" – one-third of her husband's real estate – but in any case she was now 60, an old lady by Jacobean standards, and no one was going to turn her out of her house. Whatever else Shakespeare felt for her would go without saying.

Several friends got small sums of money; others memorial rings. He left £10 to the poor of Stratford, which was relatively generous for the period. Patrick Collinson, who studied wills made in Cranbrook, Kent, between 1565 and 1612, found that "only three out of 122 testators in this community of fluid and disposable wealth made any religious or charitable bequests whatsoever apart from the common formal gift of a few shillings for distribution to the poor, sometimes in the form of bread." Most of them felt that they had already given enough, having subsidized everything "from the two shillings paid annually to the man who whipped the dogs out of church to charges for repair of the fabric, payment of clerk, sexton and schoolmaster and the relief of the poor."[53] Shakespeare's comparative generosity may have been meant to make up for the long periods when he had been absent from Stratford. There is no mention of books. He might have given them to John and Susanna Hall or to friends in London, especially if reading was becoming difficult for him. Relatively few wills, even those of clergymen and schoolmasters, mention books,[54] and Collinson's study found that only twenty out of 138 probate inventories mentioned a Bible, though most testators must have had one.[55]

The will was not completed or signed in January. Perhaps Judith's plans suddenly interfered, since her wedding took place on 10 February. It was Lent, but (like William and Anne Shakespeare in 1582) Quiney was in a hurry, even though the church excommunicated the couple for marrying without a license. The reasons became clear when, early in March, a young unmarried woman named Margaret

Wheeler died, with her child, in childbirth. The midwives, as was their duty, probably extracted from her the name of the father, Thomas Quiney. The church court promptly went into action, though Thomas, who confessed, managed to avoid doing penance in a sheet. No one in the Shakespeare family would have found it easy to live with the idea that Thomas had been seducing Margaret Wheeler at the same time that he was courting Judith Shakespeare, or that he may have proposed to Judith in order to avoid being compelled to marry Margaret.

Shakespeare revised his will on 25 March, the day before Thomas made his confession. Crossing out "son-in-law" on the first page, Collins, or his clerk, wrote "daughter Judith" and Shakespeare took care to leave everything in her name, not her husband's. He may have known that Judith suspected that she was pregnant (her first child was born on 25 November). In the list of persons to receive money for memorial rings, he had Collins cross out Richard Tyler and replace him with Hamnet Sadler. He may have been influenced by rumors about Tyler's mishandling of funds collected for victims of the recent fire,[56] but he may simply have realized he had forgotten his old friend Sadler and chose to make the substitution rather than a more complicated revision. He added other names, including Burbage, Condell, and Heminges, his three oldest and closest friends from the King's Men.

By the time he signed the revised will, handwriting experts think, Shakespeare was definitely ill. The only tradition about this last illness is a very late one: William Ward, vicar of Stratford in 1662, wrote that "Shakespeare, Drayton, and Ben Jonson had a merry meeting, and it seems drank too hard, for Shakespeare died of a feaver there contracted."[57] Ward knew at least that Drayton was a Warwickshire man, but Jonson's presence seems less likely, unless he already knew that Shakespeare was seriously ill. The year 1616 was the first of three in which burials in Stratford exceeded baptisms.[58] Since Shakespeare's brother-in-law William Hart died only a week before him, both men may have succumbed to some epidemic. Typhoid, caused by bad water, is one possibility. So is typhus, which had killed others in that warm spring. Since it was borne by lice, it was most prevalent in the winter, "when people huddled together for warmth in unventilated living conditions."[59] It would have been a wasting and feverish illness, so perhaps the fever that Ward heard about was a vague memory of the truth. On the other hand, Shakespeare may have been suffering for some years from an ongoing and worsening condition; this might explain Greene's concern in 1614 and the gap between the first draft of the will and his death. Hall, who must have been the attending physician, recorded his successful treatment of another patient in 1616 – Thomas Greene's 12-year-old daughter – but the notes that he prepared for publication do not describe the cases he could not cure.[60] After making the will, Shakespeare lived until 23 April, which was either his fifty-second birthday or close to it. He had survived, though only barely, to the age at which, according to the biographies he knew, Virgil had died. Later biographers would note that Miguel Cervantes died on the same day – but he was living by a different calendar.

407

No one in Stratford thought of recording Shakespeare's last words. Seventeenth-century tradition insisted that he himself wrote the crude verses found in Holy Trinity church:

GOOD FREND FOR IESUS SAKE FORBEARE,
TO DIGG THE DUST ENCLOASED HEARE!
BLEST BE YE MAN YT SPARES THES STONES,
AND CVRST BE HE YT MOVES MY BONES.

If he was indeed responsible for them, they were the most effective he ever wrote: one late seventeenth-century visitor to Stratford was told that "for fear of the curse" no one dared touch the gravestone, "though his wife and daughters did earnestly desire to be laid in the same grave with him."[61] Placing a curse on anyone who "moves my bones" might have been motivated, as another visitor was told, by fear of being tossed into the church "bone-house."[62] It also ensured that his body could never be removed to Westminster Abbey. Perhaps it never occurred to Shakespeare that he would be considered worthy of burial near Chaucer and Spenser, but the possibility must have arisen soon after his death, since a poem attributed to William Basse imagines their dead bodies moving over to make room for him, while Jonson's famous elegy rejects the idea as unnecessary. The poet might have been anxious to avoid an honor he no longer felt he deserved, since he had failed to perfect his writings. As E. A. J. Honigmann points out, after comparing many other wills, Shakespeare left no bequest to the church and no request to have an annual sermon or a monument erected in his memory.[63] He might have been demonstrating his anger over the church's treatment of Judith and Thomas, or he might have left it to posterity to decide what he deserved. The most extreme interpretation would be that he wished to be forgotten. In that case, he might also have destroyed any imperfect manuscripts in New Place. Such acts are usually thought of as post-Romantic,[64] but Sidney had commanded that his manuscripts of the *Arcadia* and *Astrophil and Stella* should be burnt, while the dying George Herbert, in 1633, gave his friends the choice between burning or printing his manuscript poems. Virgil, on his deathbed, is supposed to have commanded the burning of the still-imperfect *Aeneid*, an order countermanded by Augustus himself. If Shakespeare made a similar request to Susanna and John Hall, it is all too likely that they obeyed him.

The Survivors

John Hall went to London in June 1616 in his capacity as executor, in order to "prove" the will and provide an inventory of goods (now lost). He may have made further arrangements for the Blackfriars gatehouse, since in February 1618 the trustees conveyed it into the joint possession of Matthew Morris, former assistant of

Hall's father, and John Greene (Thomas Greene's brother, a lawyer of Clement's Inn).[65] In so doing, the trustees declared, they were carrying out "the true intent and meaning of the last will and testament of the said William Shakespeare." There is no way of knowing whether Shakespeare's true intent and meaning differed from their interpretation. Since Hall's own will refers to a house in London, it is possible that the trusteeship was an indirect way of conveying the property to him and Susanna. The mention of John Greene may mean that Shakespeare, despite the enclosure controversy, had remained on friendly terms with Thomas.

Hall's medical practice continued to thrive. He refused a knighthood in 1626, paying a £10 fine instead. He also refused repeated invitations to sit on Stratford council, finally accepting in 1632. Predictably, its demands clashed with his need to visit patients, and he frequently had to pay fines for missing meetings. He was also at odds with other council members, in part because of his enthusiastic support of the town's Puritan vicar. A lawsuit by fellow-councilman Baldwin Brookes left him with a debt of over £77, still unpaid when he died in November 1635. His death was probably unexpected, since he was able to make only an oral will, expressing regret at the absence of a friend to whom he had hoped to leave his manuscripts. In the end, he gave them to his son-in-law Thomas Nash, saying that he could "burn them or else do with them what you please." Was he remembering Shakespeare's words?

The aftermath of Hall's death was messy and unpleasant. He had appointed no executor; Susanna and Nash argued over their respective rights; still, two years later, no one had taken an inventory. They told Brookes that its absence made it impossible to value the estate and Susanna insisted that the Stratford and Blackfriars properties belonged to her by virtue of her father's will. (Hall, in his oral will, had left them to her, obviously thinking that they belonged to him.) Brookes finally took the law into his own hands. Officers broke into the Stratford home, where they seized "Divers bookes boxes Deskes moneyes bonds bills and other goods of greate value," thus making it, as Susanna protested, still harder for her to produce the promised inventory.[66]

Nothing further is known about this lawsuit or the consequences of the home invasion. Nash insisted that some of the stolen property was his, not Hall's. No one said anything about drafts of plays, notebooks, or letters by Susanna's father. What Hall's family may have been most eager to retrieve were his medical manuscripts: the doctor's mixtures and methods were carefully guarded secrets intended for publication only after his death. In 1644 Susanna had a visitor, the physician James Cooke. He records his argument with her over the handwriting of two manuscripts that he recognized as Hall's hand but that she did not.[67] She might have been confused by Hall's habit of writing in Latin and French, perhaps using different hands for different purposes. Cooke bought the two medical manuscripts and in 1657 translated and published extracts from them. His preface does not mention that Hall's wife was also Shakespeare's daughter, though the fact is commemorated on his tomb.[68]

Susanna lived through the Civil War. When Henrietta Maria stayed at New Place for two nights in 1643, one of the queen's officers is said to have borrowed a book from its library; it was a hostile biography of the French Queen Catherine de Medicis and sounds more like Hall's taste than Shakespeare's. When Susanna died in July 1649, her epitaph indicated that she might have had some role in Hall's medical practice. It asks the passer-by

> To weep with her that wept with all;
> That wept, yet set her self to cheer
> Them up with comforts cordial.

Hall in his notes occasionally refers to his recipes for "our milk water" or "our Antiscorbutic Julep,"[69] which might mean that Susanna and Elizabeth had been involved in making it, though it is more likely that, as was common when writing in Latin, he avoided the first person singular. The more interesting part of the epitaph is its opening:

> Witty above her sex, but that's not all,
> Wise to salvation was good Mistris Hall,
> Something of Shakespeare was in that, but this
> Wholely of him with whom she's now in bliss.[70]

The phrase "wise to salvation" is biblical (2 Timothy 3: 15),[71] but there is something puzzling about the distinction between her spiritual wisdom and the "wit" that she inherited from her father. There may have remained some suspicion about Shakespeare's religious faith, or perhaps, as Germaine Greer suggests, Hall had converted Susanna from Catholicism.[72]

Their daughter Elizabeth had a comfortable life. Her father recorded, interestingly, that she went to London (perhaps with her parents) for the first three weeks of April 1624.[73] Since he was writing about the illness from which he cured her on her return, he gave no other information, but the dates are suggestive. The Folio had appeared in the previous November and Elizabeth returned to Stratford on 22 April: was there any commemoration of her grandfather in either London or Stratford? Her wedding took place on 22 April 1626, a date perhaps chosen as another tribute to him,[74] and her first husband, Thomas Nash, was the son of one of Shakespeare's friends. She became a widow in 1647 and on 5 June 1649, only a month before her mother's death, married a widower, John Barnard. Barnard was later made a baronet by Charles II – probably for his services to the royalist cause, but perhaps also because the king remembered his father's admiration for the plays of Lady Barnard's grandfather. The couple owned but did not live at New Place, which was eventually sold to a series of owners, and finally pulled down in 1752.

Judith and Thomas Quiney stayed together into old age. The Corporation made him chamberlain in 1622–4, but he did not rise higher in local government, and he was not a success at his business. One detail that scholars often hold against him – he misquoted some French verses on the statement of accounts that he presented in 1622–3 – suggests at least that he knew them more or less by heart and thus may have had literary tastes that endeared him to a poet's daughter.[75] In 1633 the lease of his tavern was taken over by John Hall and others in trust for Judith and her sons, presumably because he was not considered financially responsible. Though Shakespeare had never cut Judith out of his will altogether, trying only to ensure that her husband did not cheat her, it may be that the rest of the family disowned her. As Peter Holland points out, her mother's tomb names only Susanna as her child, and Màiri Macdonald has found a legal note only twenty years after Shakespeare's death implying that Shakespeare had only one daughter.[76] Hall's case-book records the treatment he prescribed in 1623 to Thomas Quiney's consumptive younger brother George,[77] but he never mentions giving medical attention to the family of his sister-in-law. Yet it was Judith and Thomas who had the son that Shakespeare had wanted, born on 23 November 1616; the couple named him Shakespeare Quiney. The child however died in the following May. Two more sons, Richard and Thomas, lived to the ages of 21 and 19 before dying of unknown causes in 1639, apparently within weeks of each other. Their deaths effectively removed any claim Judith might have had to part of her father's estate. Shakespeare's will and those of his heirs continued to inspire litigation for much of the rest of the century.[78] Thomas Quiney is last heard of in 1655, when he would have been 66; Judith died, aged 70, in 1662. At Elizabeth Barnard's death in 1670, "the whole direct line – male and female – was now extinct."[79] Elizabeth left the Henley Street properties to the Hart family, still living there for a peppercorn rent, and Shakespeare Hart inherited both in 1694. They remained in the family until 1806.[80]

Notes

1. Ellrodt, "Self-Consistency in Montaigne and Shakespeare," 148.
2. "To my approved good Friend, Mr. Nicholas Okes," in Heywood, *An Apology for Actors*, ed. Perkinson, [G4^v].
3. Nicholl, *The Lodger Shakespeare*, reprints the legal documents. My account summarizes Bellot's initial Bill of Complaint, 28 Jan. 1612 (pp. 279–81), Mountjoy's Answer, 3 Feb. 1612 (pp. 281–4), Bellot's Replication, 5 May 1612 (pp. 284–5), and Mountjoy's Rejoinder, which is undated (pp. 285–6).
4. Deposition of William Shakespeare, repr. in Nicholl, *The Lodger Shakespeare*, 289–90: 290.
5. Ibid., 292–3.
6. Webster's *White Devil* and *Duchess of Malfi* are quoted from the editions by David Bevington in *English Renaissance Drama*, ed. Bevington.
7. See Dent, *John Webster's Borrowing*.
8. Dawson, "Tempest in a Teapot."
9. Accounts of 11 Jan. 1594. *Minutes*, V: 19n.

10. *Works of Francis Beaumont and John Fletcher,* ed. Glover, 1: lv.
11. Ibid., xix.
12. Thomas Heywood's *The Four Ages* was, according to his prefatory epistle, performed in this way between 1610 and 1612/13.
13. Among others, the Royal Shakespeare Company and the American Shakespeare Center in Staunton, Virginia, have performed the Shakespeare and Fletcher plays in repertory.
14. Brean Hammond, introduction to *Double Falsehood,* 36.
15. Gary Taylor, Stephen Greenblatt (with Arthur Mee), and Gregory Doran have written recreations of the play. In *Miguel-Will,* by Carlos Somoza, Shakespeare tries in *Cardenio* to achieve the mixture of tragic and comic that he sees in *Don Quixote,* but the play is such a failure that he insists on its omission from all editions of his works.
16. For a convincing presentation of the skeptical arguments, see Stern, "'The Forgery of Some Modern Author'?".
17. Sutton, "Henry Frederick, Prince of Wales," *ODNB.*
18. Harington, *Nugae Antiquae,* 2: 143–8.
19. *Basilikon Doron,* in James VI and I, *Political Writings,* ed. Sommerville, 39.
20. Kernan, *Shakespeare, the King's Playwright,* 52.
21. Letter to Sir Edmund Bacon, *Reliquiae Wottonianae,* 426.
22. Holinshed, *The Third Volume of Chronicles,* Ssss3.
23. Jonson, "Execration upon Vulcan," in Wickham, 500.
24. "The Economics of the 1613 Decision," paper delivered at Blackfriars Conference, Staunton, Virginia, 24 Oct. 2009.
25. Herbert Berry, in Wickham, 607.
26. In a letter of 15 Jan. 1604 Dudley Carleton mentions a masquer who presented "an impresa in a shield with a sonnet in a paper to express his device": *Dudley Carleton to John Chamberlain,* ed. Lee, 53–4.
27. Letter to Sir Edmund Bacon, March 1613, in *Reliquiae Wottonianae,* 405–6.
28. Schoenbaum, 274.
29. *Shakespeare's Poems,* ed. Duncan-Jones and Woudhuysen, 115n., 120.
30. J. H. Baker, *Introduction to English Legal History,* 367–70.
31. Rasmussen, "Collaboration," 231.
32. Wickham, "*The Two Noble Kinsmen,* or, *A Midsummer Night's Dream,* Part II?".
33. *The Two Noble Kinsmen,* ed. Potter, 55–6.
34. Chamberlain to Carleton, 5 Jan. 1613–14, in Birch, *Court and Times of James I,* 1: 290.
35. Frost, *The School of Shakespeare,* 155.
36. *The Poems of Henry Constable,* ed. Grundy, 179.
37. Henry James, Introduction to *The Tempest.*
38. Gardner, *Art, Mind, and Brain,* 355.
39. Patrick Cheney, in Cheney and de Armas, eds., *European Literary Careers,* 8.
40. See, Erne, *Shakespeare as Literary Dramatist,* 110: "Few writers beside him would have been in a better position to contemplate the possibility of an ambitious collected edition of thier writings."
41. Herendeen, "Introduction: On Reading the 1616 Folio," 16.
42. Herford and Simpson, 1: 433–7.
43. *The whole xii. Bookes of the Aeneidos of Virgill,* trans. Phaer, C1^v.

44. M. Eccles, *Shakespeare in Warwickshire*, 132–3.
45. Schoenbaum, 280–1.
46. Chambers, *WS*, 2: 142.
47. M. Eccles, *Shakespeare in Warwickshire*, 136.
48. Ibid., 137.
49. Ibid., 136–8.
50. Clarkson and Warren, *The Law of Property*, 193–6, 218.
51. Honigmann and Brock, eds., *Playhouse Wills*, 17.
52. Clarkson and Warren, *The Law of Property*, 241–2 and n. 70.
53. Collinson, "Cranbrook and the Fletchers," 186–7.
54. Honigmann and Brock, eds., *Playhouse Wills*, 4–5.
55. Collinson, "Cranbrook and the Fletchers," 188.
56. M. Eccles, *Shakespeare in Warwickshire*, 124, 136.
57. From C. Severn, *Diary of John Ward* (1839), 183, quoted in Chambers, *WS*, 2: 250.
58. Lane, ed., *John Hall and His Patients*, xxi.
59. Ibid., xxii.
60. Ibid., xxxix–xl, 126–9.
61. "Mr. Dowdall," letter of 10 Apr. 1693, quoted in Chambers, *WS*, 2: appendix C, xviii, 259.
62. William Hall, letter in Bodleian MS Rawlinson D. 377, fo. 90; repr. in Chambers, *WS*, 2: appendix C, xix, p. 181. This author also says that Shakespeare was buried 17 feet deep, which Chambers thinks "most improbable so near the Avon."
63. Honigmann, "Shakespeare's Will and Testamentary Traditions," 127–8.
64. See Nebel, *The Dark Side of Creativity*.
65. Arlidge, *Shakespeare and the Prince of Love*, 43.
66. Marcham, *William Shakespeare and his Daughter Susannah*, 70. The relevant documents are reprinted on pp. 58–76.
67. Joseph, *Shakespeare's Son-in-Law*, 105.
68. Honan, 398, notes that his arms are impaled with Shakespeare's.
69. Lane, ed., *John Hall and His Patients*, 225, 244.
70. Chambers, *WS*, 2: 12.
71. Fripp, *Shakespeare: Man and Artist*, 185, n. 5.
72. Greer, *Shakespeare's Wife*, 140.
73. Lane, ed., *John Hall and His Patients*, 67.
74. First suggested by Thomas De Quincey, cited in Chambers, *WS*, 2: 2.
75. See Schoenbaum, 294–5, and Fripp, *Master Richard Quyny*, 206–7.
76. Holland, "William Shakespeare," *ODNB*; Macdonald, "A New Discovery about Shakespeare's Estate in Old Stratford," 89.
77. Lane, ed., *John Hall and His Patients*, 35–6.
78. Chambers, *WS*, 2: 179–80.
79. Schoenbaum, 319.
80. M. Eccles, *Shakespeare in Warwickshire*, 143.

18

"In the Mouths of Men"
1616 and After

Or I shall live your epitaph to make,
Or you survive when I in earth am rotten,
From hence your memory death cannot take,
Although in me each part shall be forgotten.
Your name from hence immortal life shall have,
Though I, once gone, to all the world must die;
The earth can yield me but a common grave,
When you entombèd in men's eyes shall lie.
Your monument shall be my gentle verse,
Which eyes not yet created shall o'erread,
And tongues to be your being shall rehearse
When all the breathers of the world are dead.
You still shall live – such virtue hath my pen –
Where breath most breathes, even in the mouths of men.

(Sonnet 81)

Though at first sight Sonnet 81 looks like the many others that promise immortality to the recipient, it speaks only of immortalizing his or her "name." And, as is often pointed out, that name is never given. Though contemporary sonneteers populated their world with lovers called Astrophil, Parthenophil, Stella, Delia, and Idea, the only names that appear in Shakespeare's sonnets are Adonis, Helen, Mars, Saturn, Philomel, Eve, Cupid, Diana, and Time – and the one non-mythical figure, the author, "Will." This poem uses "shall" throughout for the future tense, as if determined to avoid the pun on his name. But, despite the stated contrast between the fate of the speaker, who will be forgotten, and that of the recipient, who will be remembered, it is really entirely about its author. He is worth only "a common

The Life of William Shakespeare: A Critical Biography, First Edition. Lois Potter.
© 2012 Lois Potter. Published 2012 by Blackwell Publishing Ltd.

grave" and yet his verse is "gentle." The promised immortality will be that of silent reading ("men's eyes") and of what was more common in this period, reading aloud or acting ("tongues to be" and "the mouths of men"). The promise is meaningful only in context – either a biographical one that is now unrecoverable or a theatrical one, where a fictitious speaker and recipient make the words their own. Shakespeare, who died knowing that his name would not survive in his family, might be addressing another person of the same name – father, mother, brother, wife – or, since he himself is both a mortal body and the source of "immortal" words, he might be speaking to himself. John Marston had after all dedicated one of his books "To his most esteemed, and best beloved Selfe" and "to Everlasting Oblivion"; his epitaph in 1634 would be *Oblivioni Sacrum*.

This sonnet, then, may be the only one in which Shakespeare recognizes that his dramatic works will be the source of his fame. If he had written only the sonnets and the two narrative poems, he would still be remembered as a poet on the level of Spenser, but his readership would be as limited as Spenser's. Despite public contempt for the theatrical profession, despite his awareness that breath is merely "air," he can imagine future ages hearing his words as they are breathed out of the mouths of future actors and readers. He could never have foreseen that his right to fame would be questioned, not because there was any doubt as to the value of his works, but because they were so highly valued that some people would not believe that he had written them. This chapter traces the process by which the occupant of the "common grave" acquired the monuments by which he would be remembered. It then looks (with absurd brevity) at the various forms that memory has taken.

The Folio of 1623

Shakespeare's death in Stratford might have been reported in London by the beginning of May 1616. The sonnet by Hugh Holland printed in the 1623 Folio sounds like an immediate reaction:

> Those hands which you so clapped, go now and wring,
> You Britons brave, for done are Shakespeare's days;
> His days are done, that made the dainty plays,
> Which made the Globe of heav'n and earth to ring.

Holland and his friend Ben Jonson may have originally planned to publish a volume of poetic tributes, then decided to save their contributions for a bigger project, a collection of Shakespeare's plays. The memorial rings that Shakespeare bequeathed to Heminges, Condell, and Burbage would remind them of the need to preserve the works of their company's greatest author. Late in 1616, they received a further reminder with the appearance of the magnificent Folio edition of Jonson's *Works*, over 1,000 pages in length. Richard and Winifred Burbage may have commemorated Shakespeare privately when they gave the name William to their child born in November 1616, but they may also have been honoring the lord chamberlain, William Earl of Pembroke, who later referred to Burbage as "my old acquaintance."[1]

The production of the Folio was a long process, as indicated by the opening of the commendatory poem by Leonard Digges:

> Shake-speare, at length thy pious fellowes give
> The world thy works . . .

Had there been some complaint of the delays? It had probably been planned by 1619, when the King's Men used their influence with Pembroke (now lord chamberlain) to stop William Jaggard from printing a collection of quartos that seemed intended to be bound together as a single volume. If Burbage had been working on the project, it may have been held up by his death on 9 March 1619. He was only 51 and had been acting up to the end. His will was oral, perhaps indicating an unexpected death. Given his reputation as a painter, it is tantalizing to think that there might once have been some thought of engraving the Folio frontispiece (illustrated in Figure 19) from a portrait of Shakespeare by his leading actor. The frontispiece must have been based on an existing painting, though the engraver need not have copied it exactly.

A large project like the Folio was going to tie up a number of presses, since printing and publishing were, like most guild activities, intended to employ as many members as possible. The syndicate of publishers who took it on was dominated by Edward Blount, who had published *Love's Martyr* in 1601, and William Jaggard. The latter may seem an unlikely choice, after his involvement with *The Passionate Pilgrim* and the abortive 1619 project, but he evidently had access to a number of copyrights and was both printer and publisher. Since he had been blind since 1612, and in fact died late in 1623, the printing was mainly supervised by his son Isaac.[2]

Jonson's 1616 Folio had included plays, poems, and masques. Since Shakespeare's narrative poems were still in print, the 1623 editors decided to collect only what they called Shakespeare's *Comedies, Histories, and Tragedies*. The effort and expense of acquiring good texts of the plays, and paying off those who already owned the rights to them, must have been considerable. Mary Edmond has found that "Mr John Hemmings of London" – quite probably the Heminges of the King's Men – contributed 10 shillings in 1620 toward the clock and chimes of St. Martin's, Carfax, in the center of Oxford. He was there, she suggests, on his way to Stratford to look for more of Shakespeare's papers, and might have called in at the tavern run by John Davenant.[3] Shakespeare knew Davenant from the days when, as a vintner in London, he was famous for his love of poets and plays. He and his wife Jennet must have loved living in London, but their first six children, conceived and born there, either died young or were stillborn. After their move to Oxford in 1601, Jennet had

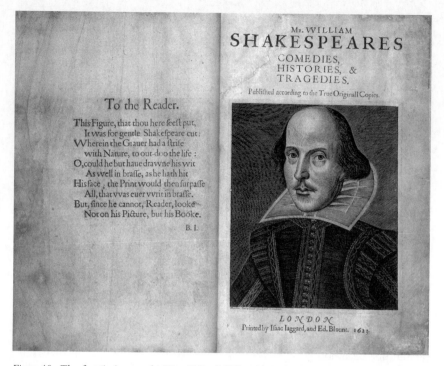

To the Reader.

This Figure, that thou here seest put,
It was for gentle Shakespeare cut;
Wherein the Grauer had a strife
with Nature, to out-doo the life :
O, could he but haue drawne his wit
As well in brasse, as he hath hit
His face ; the Print would then surpasse
All, that vvas euer vvrit in brasse.
But, since he cannot, Reader, looke
Not on his Picture, but his Booke.

B. I.

Mr. WILLIAM
SHAKESPEARES
COMEDIES,
HISTORIES, &
TRAGEDIES.
Published according to the True Originall Copies.

LONDON
Printed by Isaac Iaggard, and Ed. Blount. 1623.

Figure 19 The frontispiece to the First Folio (1623), with Jonson's verses on it. © The British Library Board (C.39.k.15, dedication and frontispiece)

seven more children, all of whom lived to adulthood. Shakespeare had stayed with this family as a guest (the tavern was not a hostelry) on his trips between Stratford and London.[4]

Probably the search did not produce any revised manuscripts. There may, however, be significance in the fact that the printing of the Folio was interrupted at one point, apparently because of some problem with obtaining the text of *Twelfth Night*. As Keir Elam points out, this play had never been printed before, so the difficulty cannot have been one of copyright, but rather "physical access to the manuscript, or the need to have a transcript made for the use of the printer."[5] It is tempting to think that a revised *Twelfth Night* manuscript was fetched at the last moment from Stratford, since this play, despite some minor inconsistencies, feels exceptionally "finished." The name Orsino has been linked to the official visit of Don Virginio Orsini to Elizabeth's court in 1601, and the performance of a play before him on 6 January (Twelfth Night). One argument against this connection is the fact that the visiting duke would hardly have been flattered to see his name used for a lovesick count.[6] In revision, however, Shakespeare might have introduced the name as a reminiscence of the 1601 performance, just as he had

417

used the names of real French courtiers in *Love's Labour's Lost*. He might have been reminded of the Orsini visit because Webster made Orsini's ancestor, Paulo Giordano Orsini, Duke of Bracciano, a central character in *The White Devil*, published in 1612.

Several plays were omitted. The absence of *Pericles*, one of the King's Men's biggest successes, might be due to the existence of the Quarto and the Wilkins novel on the same subject. A similar copyright problem might explain the difficulty in obtaining *Troilus and Cressida*. It had been meant to follow *Romeo and Juliet*, but *Timon of Athens* was substituted at the last minute and *Troilus* was finally placed after *Henry VIII*. There was no attempt to identify collaborators. Middleton and Fletcher were the only ones still living, and Middleton was probably not sorry to have his name omitted from the obviously unfinished *Timon*. Obviously bearing no hard feelings, in 1624 he gave the King's Men his political satire *A Game at Chess*, which had the longest run in their history, though he may have spent some time in prison for it. Despite the play's huge success, he was apparently not well off when he died three years later, aged 47. In the case of Fletcher, now the company's leading playwright, Heminges and Condell may have reached a compromise. Fletcher would have recognized the logic of including *Henry VIII*, the last of the English histories, but might have insisted on retaining *The Two Noble Kinsmen* and *Cardenio* for a collection of his own works. He died aged 49, in the 1625 plague, and his own canon is still disputed: the "Beaumont and Fletcher" Folio of 1647 contains much that is neither by him nor Beaumont.[7]

The Shakespeare Folio was on sale at least by 5 December 1623, when the first recorded purchase was made.[8] While the price varied according to the bookseller, it would typically have cost 15 shillings in an unbound copy, compared with the Jonson Folio which was 9 or 10 shillings in 1616 (rising to as much as £1, depending on the quality of the binding).[9] Heminges and Condell dedicated the volume to the Pembroke brothers, stating as a well-known fact that they had honored the plays "and their Author living." Sir Henry Salusbury – son of the Sir John Salusbury for whom Shakespeare had written his poem on the phoenix and turtledove – copied into his commonplace book a short poem of which he probably sent the original to "my good friends" Heminges and Condell: "you have pleased the living, loved the dead," he told them.[10] Shakespeare's tomb in Holy Trinity Church – by Gheerart Janssen, who had already created a monument for John Combe – must have been known by 1623, since verses in the Folio refer to "thy Stratford monument." The Latin inscription below the bust is remarkable in the claims that it makes for its author:

> Judicio Pylium, Genio Socratem, Arte Maronem:
> Terra tegit, populus maeret, Olympus habet.

This is one of those elegant Latin constructions that the dramatists of Shakespeare's youth enjoyed replicating in English: three objects in the first line, three subjects and

418

verbs in the second: "The judgment of Nestor, the genius of Socrates, the art of Maro [Virgil]/ Earth covers, the people mourn, Olympus/ heaven possesses."

As the verse-writers in the Folio noted, borrowing a common classical motif, the book itself was also a monument. Despite its high production cost, it was successful enough to justify another edition in 1632. Charles I owned a copy, which he took with him to prison in 1647. It contained a poem by the young John Milton who, seventeen years later, would quote from "one whom we well know was the Closet Companion of these his solitudes, William Shakespeare," to attack the king's posthumous image as a serious and religious monarch.[11] It is possible that by 1632 there was talk of erecting something in Westminster Abbey's Poets' Corner (as finally happened in 1740). This might explain why Milton's poem begins by asking why Shakespeare should need "The labor of an age in pilèd stones."

A few other poems, most of which could be anyone's work, were ascribed to Shakespeare shortly after his death. At present, a number of scholars think it possible that he wrote the simple and dignified epitaphs on the tomb of Sir Thomas Stanley in Tong Church, Shropshire. The one beginning "Not monumental stone preserves our fame,/ Nor sky-aspiring pyramids our name" may be echoed in Milton's verses, which refer to "a star-ypointing pyramid."[12] In 1640 those who wanted more Shakespeare could buy *Poems: written by Wil. Shake-speare. Gent*, a compilation by John Benson based on the 1609 *Sonnets* and the 1612 edition of *The Passionate Pilgrim*, and thus – though he may not have known this – full of non-Shakespearean works. Benson grouped the poems, rather randomly, under the kinds of headings used in poetic miscellanies: Sonnet 20, for instance, is called "The Exchange." The volume contains a poem by Leonard Digges, expanding on the one he wrote for the 1623 volume. He had already insisted that no scenes could ever be more theatrically effective than those in *Romeo and Juliet* and *Julius Caesar*. In the longer poem he again mentions *Caesar*, contrasts audiences' lukewarm response to *Sejanus* with their enthusiasm for "honest Iago, or the jealous Moor," says that the theater was always full for Falstaff, and records the immense popularity of *Much Ado* and *Twelfth Night*:

> Let but *Beatrice*
> And *Benedick* be seen, lo in a trice
> The cockpit, galleries, boxes, all are full
> To heare *Malvolio* that cross-gartered gull.[13]

The poem may indicate how these two plays were known to most spectators – including Charles I, who in his copy replaced their titles in the table of contents with the names of their most memorable characters.

Early readers used the Folio in different ways. Sir Edward Dering, who held amateur dramatic performances in his home, bought two copies, despite the expense, perhaps to allow more rapid copying of parts.[14] Reading the plays in succession also led to the discovery of their inconsistencies. A letter from the Bodleian librarian Richard James, thought to date from 1625, relates that "A young Gentle Lady" asked him how Falstaff "could be dead in the time of Harry the Fifth and again live in the time of Harry the Sixth to be banished for cowardice." James told the young lady that Falstaff had originally been Oldcastle and that Shakespeare's use of Falstaff's name for a comic character was as reprehensible as his original choice.[15] Probably no one had ever been able, in the theater, to follow Falstaff from play to play.

The King's Men must have had their own copy of the Folio, and some of their house dramatists benefited from being able to read it. Philip Massinger, whose father was a trusted servant of the second Earl of Pembroke and a member of the countess's household, was Fletcher's most frequent collaborator, and the Folio's influence has been traced in much of his work after 1623. The play that most startlingly reworks Shakespearean material, John Ford's *'Tis Pity She's a Whore* (published 1633), was not performed by the King's Men. Perhaps they did not want a play that depicted two star-crossed lovers, a friar, and a comic nurse, but in which the lovers are a brother and sister whose sexual liaison ultimately causes multiple deaths. Jonson's later plays are more genial, less satiric, than his early ones: Anne Barton contends that his involvement with the Folio led to his belated realization of the genius of his former colleague and "affected him profoundly."[16] He lived to be 65, becoming something of a legend by the time of his death in 1637; some of the young poets who gathered round him in the London taverns liked to be called his sons.

If there were any Sons of Will, the most obvious candidates are Sir John Suckling and Sir William Davenant, who, in the years before the Civil War, wrote exclusively for the King's Men. Suckling was too young to have known Shakespeare, though his father (a Gray's Inn man and courtier) might well have done so, His plays are strongly influenced by Shakespeare and he chose to be painted by Van Dyck (Figure 20), probably in 1637/8, holding a copy of the Folio open to *Hamlet*, as if to advertise his self-identification with the title character. He was about 28 at this time and had only a few more years to live.[17]

Davenant, son of the tavern-keeper in Oxford with whom Shakespeare is said to have stayed during his visits to the city, was so eager to be a "son" of Shakespeare that, according to John Aubrey, he was willing to hint at an affair between his mother and the poet. The idea has appealed to many biographers, although it would mean that Shakespeare had cuckolded, under his own roof, a man who was supposedly one of his greatest admirers. After 1660 Davenant, as manager of one of the theater companies established by Charles II, adapted five Shakespeare plays. Since he must have seen them in performance before the theaters were closed in 1642, his textual readings and stage directions have been of interest to later editors.

Figure 20 Sir John Suckling, by Anthony Van Dyck (1637/8). Copyright the Frick Collection, New York

Actors, Biographers, and Editors

It was Nicholas Rowe, a dramatist, who in 1709 produced the first one-volume edited text of Shakespeare's plays. For it, he also compiled the first biography of Shakespeare, recording most of the early anecdotes. Some of them came from other theater men like the Restoration actor Thomas Betterton, who made a trip to Stratford in search of information. Betterton had known Davenant, who had known

Shakespeare, insofar as someone born in 1606 could know someone who died in 1616. John Aubrey, the other major source of early anecdotes, has already been quoted. Aubrey worked on his ambitious biographical project between 1669 and 1696, but by the time he got to Shakespeare and his fellow-dramatists it was too late to find many survivors of the pre-war literary scene.

The messy state of Aubrey's papers sometimes makes them difficult to read, and this is particularly true of what he writes about Shakespeare. Some of his comments begin with "I thinke I have been told" and some are now known to be inaccurate: Shakespeare's father was not a butcher, so William could not have "exercised his father's trade";[18] he did not leave his sister £200 or £300 a year. Aubrey came across one first-hand source, William Beeston, whose father Christopher had acted with the Chamberlain's Men, and who had himself managed one of the children's companies before the war. Though he made a note to ask the old man, "who knew all the old English poets," about Shakespeare and Jonson, the only detail specifically credited to him is the statement that Shakespeare had once been "a schoolmaster in the country."[19] Another comment has been extensively quoted: "Would not be debauched: and if invited to court he was in paine." Andrew Clark's edition of 1898 gives this reading, attributing the statement to Beeston talking about himself.[20] E. K. Chambers and Samuel Schoenbaum examined Aubrey's manuscript and concluded that Beeston was probably talking about Shakespeare rather than himself; their reading is "if invited to, writ: he was in paine."[21] Much speculation has been based on this glimpse of a Shakespeare who was constantly using illness or pain as an excuse to stay home (and write?). To me, it sounds more like something that Beeston would say of himself (especially to Aubrey, who was frequently invited to be "debauched" and had trouble saying no) than something that he would have remembered about someone else.

The Restoration Shakespeare was essentially someone who belonged to the theater. After Charles II ordered the new companies to follow the practice of the rest of Europe and replace boy actors with female performers, numerous adaptations of the old plays improved the female roles, complied with new concepts of decorum, and fitted them for a stage that had begun to use localizing "scenes." A few of these adaptations were so successful that they continued to be performed for a century or more, although further adaptations sometimes restored more of the original text. The most obvious example is the *King Lear* by Nahum Tate (1681), which made Cordelia a major role, omitted the discordant character of the Fool, and satisfied the demands of poetic justice by restoring Lear to the throne, after which he abdicates in favor of Cordelia, who marries Edgar.[22] Cibber's adaptation of *Richard III* (1699) was popular with both actors and audiences because it made the title role even more of a star vehicle, and more sympathetic, than it had originally been. Some American actors were still performing it in the twentieth century.

The separation of scholarship from the theater began early, as editing became a more specialized activity. Rowe's edition was entirely based on the Folio, the only text known to the first generations of readers. By the eighteenth century early play quartos were scarce and owned only by collectors (a few unique copies were in fact discovered only in the twentieth century). Editorial practice was gradually transformed by awareness of their existence: editors now had to choose between two versions of a passage as well as correcting what looked like printers' errors. Early editors often omitted passages they disliked, attributing them to additions by the actors. (Pope, Theobald, and Johnson had themselves written plays and their works had been altered by the actor-playwrights Cibber and Garrick.) The greatest of the Romantic critics, Coleridge, also blamed "the players" for incongruous elements such as the Porter's monologue in *Macbeth*. The assumption was that the real Shakespeare was somehow hidden behind, and frustrated by, the theatrical demands of his age.

By the twentieth century, bibliographical research found a new set of villains. It was becoming clear that much of what happened to a published text might be the result of scribal and printing-house practices and that it was essential to distinguish these from authorial habits. Comparing multiple copies of the same volume – as Charlton Hinman was able to do on the basis of some 55 of the 80 + copies of the 1623 Folio in the Folger Shakespeare Library – resulted in the discovery that any given volume might contain both corrected and uncorrected sheets, which meant that, ideally, an editor should examine all available copies. An increasingly elaborate list of criteria – preferred spellings and typographical habits, the use of type that could be seen to deteriorate in the course of printing – seemed to make it possible to know which compositor set which pages (or "formes," the large sheets which held several pages that would be cut and folded after printing) and to identify some compositors as more accurate than others, thus determining which pages were more likely to need emendation. This kind of scholarship produced fascinating reconstructions of what might have been going on while Shakespeare's words were taking printed form, and sometimes led to the demonizing of certain compositors, printers, and publishers. Further bibliographical study has, however, suggested that printing house practices were often too inconsistent to allow this kind of certainty.

While it might seem obvious that the most important thing to do for an author is to establish an accurate record of what he or she wrote, in the case of a dramatist the question of a definitive text is more problematic. If "the players" made changes to Shakespeare's text during his lifetime, they were probably doing what he expected them to do, and the result can therefore be called authorized if not authorial. The same could be said of printing house changes based on spelling and punctuation conventions that authors then, as now, let others decide. When editors restore oaths that they think were omitted because of the 1606 Act against profanity onstage, they do so on the assumption that these represent what Shakespeare really wanted the characters to say; it would be equally possible to imagine that the older playwright might himself have wanted to tone down his language for a supposedly more refined audience. It is not clear, moreover, that anyone involved in the publishing process – even the author – was as strongly concerned with absolute verbal accuracy as modern scholars are.

Despite attempts to make editing a scientific process, editorial practice and critical assumptions still seem inseparable. Although Edmond Malone's 1780 *Supplement* to his edition of the plays was not the first to reprint the 1609 sonnets rather than Benson's heavily adapted 1640 edition, it was the first to make Shakespeare widely known as a poet as well as a dramatist – and, for those who read closely, a poet of strongly erotic feelings for both sexes. The implications for both biography and criticism were not fully realized until the late twentieth century. Including the poems and sonnets in editions of Shakespeare's works helped to separate him from a purely theatrical context and to justify reading and performing the plays in the light of the sonnets. Appreciation of *1 Henry VI*, *Titus Andronicus*, *Timon of Athens*, *Pericles*, and *The Two Noble Kinsmen* has always depended on whether they were considered to be by Shakespeare alone. A reaction against the early twentieth-century "disintegrationists" who attributed "inferior" lines to other authors led to the search for an aesthetic that could explain the presence of apparently contradictory elements. When the taste for "organic unity" gave way to a preference for inconsistency and conflict, deconstructionists revived disintegrationist approaches. *The Division of the Kingdoms* (1983), edited by Gary Taylor and Michael Warren, is the best known of a number of studies arguing that plays of which there are two different versions – in this case, *King Lear* – might differ, not because both texts were inaccurate reproductions of a common original, but because one text was a revision of the other. In this case, Shakespeare is thought to have revised his own work, but the landmark Oxford edition of the *Complete Works* (1986) took the view that Middleton had revised both *Macbeth* and *Measure for Measure*, while in the 2008 Oxford edition of Middleton's works, Gary Taylor and John Jowett, the editors, respectively, of *Macbeth* and *Measure for Measure*, attempt to reconstruct the "original" Shakespeare version. The editing of Shakespeare is the flagship for editorial practice in general: conservative editions prefer to leave a line unintelligible rather than choose an emendation, while more radical ones not only make but act on assumptions about collaboration and revision.

Performance

For some two centuries after Shakespeare's death, what spectators saw in the playhouse was very different from what editors were attempting to reconstruct. By the mid-eighteenth century the plays were becoming known outside Britain, and their unconventional dramaturgy was perceived as symbolic of British liberty, often by contrast with French classicism and the *ancien régime*. Yet when foreign visitors came to England to see the plays that they had been admiring in translation, or which they had painfully studied English in order to read, they found themselves watching Tate's *King Lear,* Cibber's *Richard III,* and Garrick's *Romeo and Juliet* (which, because it allowed Juliet to awaken in time for a last love scene with Romeo before his poison took effect, became the basis of most operas and ballets). They also saw very much shortened versions. Charles II had licensed only two London theaters in 1660 – a legacy of the Privy Council's attempts to restrict the number of playhouses in London. As London grew, these theaters could only become larger and larger, but acting to enormous audiences inevitably meant a more operatic style, with emphasis on the leading actor, on the plays' big "arias," and on visual effects. An early nineteenth-century image of Shakespeare and his characters (Figure 21) is only one example of the interdependence of the playwright and the theater. Shakespeare is frozen in time, in a position based on the Westminster Abbey statue designed by William Kent; it is his characters, in performance, who remain alive.

Even after the Theatres Act of 1843 ended their monopoly, the major theaters continued to affirm their importance by performing Shakespeare with the greatest possible visual splendor. The great theater managers – William Macready, Samuel Phelps, and Henry Irving – felt that it was their duty to produce Shakespeare with the kind of visual beauty that he himself would have wished. The availability of illustrated books on costume and architecture made it possible to achieve historically accurate productions. and new kinds of lighting, first gas and then electric, created poetry and magic of their own. At times, the visual and verbal seemed at odds. On the one hand, as critical admiration for Shakespeare grew, performers were persuaded to restore more of the unadapted text (Macready reunited the Fool and King Lear in 1836). On the other hand, as sets became more elaborate, the plays had to be cut again in order to allow time to create the beautiful scenic effects.

When at the end of the century Bernard Shaw and other writers of the "new drama" attacked Shakespeare, it was because they saw his dominance, and the theater's emphasis on visual pleasure, as a disincentive to write or produce more innovative and intellectual work. Eventually, however, the drama of the early twentieth century had its own influence on Shakespearean acting. The rise of the non-acting director meant a taming of the actors, whose performances could be subordinated to a single concept. Smaller theaters allowed low-key, "psychological" or "Chekhovian" readings, with emphasis on unspoken feelings. Symbolic sets and props could become actors in the play. Pauses could give almost any text a subtext, and body language could play "against the lines." The psychological, character-based interpretation still dominates western Shakespearean production. The plays, however, belong to a period when there was still a strong emphasis on external signs of class, which makes them equally susceptible to non-mimetic presentational methods: Brechtian theater (itself inspired by Brecht's particular concept of Elizabethan theatrical style), various Asian theatrical traditions, the eastern European mime and marionette theater, and so on – all have been drawn on in eclectic modern productions.

425

Figure 21 Images of Shakespeare with scenes from his plays, by H. Heath (*c.* 1820). The large central compartment is the age's great actor, Edmund Kean, in the favorite role of Richard III; the other compartments show, clockwise from the upper right, Romeo and Friar Lawrence, Macbeth and Lady Macbeth, Othello, Falstaff and his crew, Prospero, Miranda and Caliban, Hamlet and the Ghost, Brutus and the Ghost of Caesar, and the drinking scene from *Twelfth Night*. By permission of the Folger Shakespeare Library

To a large extent, too, scholarship and the theater are now collaborating. One example of their interaction is the decision of the editors of the Oxford *Complete Works* to prefer what they took to be playhouse versions of the texts to those possibly derived from the original authorial papers. As Gabriel Egan points out, their view had its origin in the work of the Shakespeare Institute in Stratford, which was founded "to build a scholarly relationship with the Shakespeare Memorial Theatre."[23] The availability of good editions of the plays, some of which even indicate alternative readings of the lines, has empowered actors and directors to make their own decisions about interpretation; some in fact prefer to work from unedited texts, effectively becoming editors themselves. Theatrical technology is now so good that directors in major theaters no longer have to choose between sumptuous staging and the playing of a full text.

Interest in knowing and reproducing the conditions of the Elizabethan theater began with nineteenth-century German scholars and was later taken up in England, at the end of the century, by William Poel. His experiments, initially marginal, included all-male productions, Elizabethan dress, a stage without scenery, and fuller (though expurgated) texts. Later "Elizabethan" productions were largely confined to universities and to summer festivals like North America's Ashland, Oregon, and Stratford, Ontario, but became almost mainstream at the end of the twentieth century. "Shakespeare's Globe" on London's South Bank, a careful reconstruction of the first Globe near its original site, enables the general public sometimes to see productions with what are now called "original practices": all-male casts (though not boy actors), authentic costuming, and music played on reproductions of early instruments. The indoor Blackfriars Theatre in Staunton, Virginia, is also a repro-duction; though fire regulations prevent the use of candlelight, the electric lighting remains constant throughout. Those who predicted that these would be "museum theaters" were wrong. Both theaters have been used for a variety of production styles, but the one constant factor in "original practices" productions is their exploitation of the immediacy of theater. Actors address their lines to audience members whenever possible. The fact that groundlings at the Globe are able to move around changes them from passive spectators to active participants. Blackfriars audiences do not stand, but some spectators sit on stools on stage, where they are often drawn into the action. Since no "early modern" theater is ever very comfortable (the benches at the Globe are backless), the audiences tend to be young and/or scholarly, and the atmosphere is often carnivalesque – probably not exactly what the King's Men would have wanted, but certainly close to the popular and participatory tradition that was one source of their repertoire.

Theater is affected by critical interests, and vice versa. *Measure for Measure*, unplayable for most of the nineteenth century because of its explicitness about sexual behavior, had many successful revivals in the late twentieth century. Like *The Taming of the Shrew* it is a key text in feminist criticism: whereas it was once assumed that Isabella would silently and happily accept the Duke's last-minute proposal, some productions now make her silently reject him, while others leave the audience in suspense as to her reaction. *Titus Andronicus*, another once unplayable work, appeals variously to a taste for the gothic or for black comedy. A tendency to suspect all authority figures means that in many productions the victorious Richmond and Malcolm are shown to be just as bad as Richard III and Macbeth, while Henry V is either a cold-blooded war-machine or a figure tormented by the suffering that he is obliged to inflict. "Resistant readings" – deliberately opposing what is taken to be the author's intention – try to prevent Shakespeare's authority from being used to justify racism or misogyny. Multi-racial casting has opened up many plays to re-examination. The disabled Richard III, Shylock the Jew, the Moors Aaron and Othello, and many female characters, arouse anger in those who feel that they are not presented fairly and yet make actors want to embody them in order to recreate them, in all-male companies, all-female companies, companies restricted by ethnicity, companies of disabled actors.

Though there is now a wide consensus, especially among those who teach Shakespeare, about the importance of his theatrical context, not all critics agree. Those who have strong views on the characters or on the plays' political meanings do not like the power of performance to influence audiences with the "wrong" view. Harry Berger, Jr. argues from the opposite position: since performance can offer only one reading of a play at a time, he prefers the "imaginary audition" that allows the reader to explore multiple performances simultaneously.[24] Theater practitioners are sometimes equally uneasy about the dominance of the theater by such a highly verbal dramatist. As Robert Weimann put it, turning Shakespeare into a national shrine creates an obligation "to preserve inviolate the literary art of the poet vis-à-vis the irreverent zest, the game, the craft and craftiness of the performer."[25]

Cornucopian Shakespeare: Criticism – and Everything Else

The history of Shakespearean criticism is almost identical with the history of literary criticism since 1660, but those who have adapted and interpreted his works in the other arts often seem more sensitive to them than those who have written about him in his own verbal medium. This is because his words are generally better than those that try to replace or explicate them. Restoration critics recognized his power, but their emerging critical vocabulary had difficulty in describing it. Jonson's elegy had credited him with both "art" and "nature," and the two terms remained the basis for critical discussions well into the nineteenth century. When Dryden wrote in 1667 that "All the images of Nature were still [always] present to him" he was trying to explain the lifelikeness, or believability, of Shakespeare's characters. It was these characters that the earliest critics praised; they were what everyone wanted, and still wants, to recreate in new contexts.

Something not often enough considered is the sheer length and complexity of the Shakespeare canon and the belief that it is all in some way important. Even scholars know only a fraction of it – "know" in the sense of being able to recall it, not necessarily verbatim, without a text – and thus any critical approach will ignore much of what he wrote. Another way to put this is that almost any critical approach can offer new insights. Because the plays often set opposing views in conflict, they can easily be shown to contain whatever most interests the commentator, to justify almost any opinion, and to exemplify whatever literary or theatrical qualities are most favored in any given period. Samuel Johnson admires Shakespeare's naturalness of language, praises his characterization for being "general" rather than specific, but condemns him for not inculcating moral values more clearly. A twenty-first-century critic would be more likely to find Shakespeare's language difficult, his characterization vividly individual, and his occasional didacticism irritating. In the nineteenth century, he was admired for his vivid awareness of the natural world, a quality barely noticed in the previous century, while the twentieth century was interested in his depiction of the political complexities that had struck the two previous centuries as boring. Though Johnson recognized that Shakespeare's plays were "neither tragedies or comedies, but compositions of a distinct kind," both criticism and the theater, in the nineteenth century and much of the twentieth, tended to homogenize the genres, ignoring or deleting whatever worked against the nobility of tragedy or the innocent pleasure of comedy. Late twentieth-century postmodernism emphasized instead the plays' mixture of theatrical styles and their metatheatricality. So did the theater itself.

Adaptation is criticism, though often unconscious criticism, of the source text. Critics and ordinary readers since the nineteenth century have taken pleasure in treating the plays like detective fiction, piecing together the clues as to what the characters were doing before the play, between the scenes, and in their dreams. The fact that so many Shakespeare characters remember things that happened before the play began – one of the secrets of their lifelikeness – has encouraged imaginative writers to fill in the blanks. *Hamlet* has inspired prequels (John Updike's *Gertrude and Claudius*, 2000), sequels (Alithea Hayter's *Horatio's Version*, 1972), and versions set in a parallel universe (W. S. Gilbert's travesty *Rosencrantz and Guildenstern*, 1874, Tom Stoppard's *Rosencrantz and Guildenstern Are Dead*, 1966, and Jasper Fforde's *Something Rotten*, 2004). Making the plays visual is a way of memorializing them. This must surely explain the large number of silent Shakespeare films from the early days of cinema, even though, with only the briefest of captions, they might seem as intelligible as photographic negatives. Opera and musical comedy can use only a fraction of the words of a Shakespeare play, but they can express the feelings of several characters simultaneously. Historically, the focus has often been on the romantic and melodramatic (not surprisingly, *Romeo and Juliet* and *Othello* have been most frequently and successfully adapted), but as music itself has changed the range of works that it can adapt has also become greater.

Film adaptations are mainly responsible for the global impact of Shakespeare, and filmic Shakespeare is probably the most popular field of study, since, unlike theater, it is theoretically accessible to everyone. The sense that Shakespeare was "high art" affected most early filmmaking and can be seen in the choice of black and white for Olivier's *Hamlet* and Orson Welles's *Othello*, as well as in camera effects that draw attention to themselves. The alternative, populist type of film, like nineteenth-century theater, offers gorgeous costumes, views of exotic places, and star performances from famous actors. Once television had "covered" all the plays (the BBC television Shakespeare series, 1978–85, made all except *The Two Noble Kinsmen* available in deliberately conventional interpretations), the way was open for more freely adapted versions. In the fifteen years between 1989 and 2004 there were more than thirty film adaptations of Shakespeare – more than twice as many as in the thirty previous years.[26] While some have been faithful to the (heavily cut) words, others have rewritten the stories in new genres, such as the gangster film or the teen romance. It has often been predicted that film, and then television, and then electronic media, would kill the theater. In fact, the cyber-media are still exploring Shakespeare's potential, with YouTube, for example, allowing anyone to perform Shakespeare at virtually no cost, and transmit the result to an invisible but potentially enormous audience.

Memorializing Shakespeare: National and Global

For two centuries, the monuments to Shakespeare in London and Stratford were his only obvious memorials, though Stratford was already a tourist attraction in the eighteenth century, with enterprising locals offering souvenirs for sale. The famous Stratford jubilee celebration by David Garrick in 1769 is sometimes ridiculed, both because much of it was rained out and because it included no performances of the plays, but the fact that it featured original literary and musical works and the opportunity to take part in a procession in the costume of Shakespeare characters shows the extent to which the public could make the dramatist their own. By the twentieth century, however, there was a sense in Britain that the national poet was perhaps being taken too much for granted. As World War I approached, Germany, where scholarship on Shakespeare's language and theater was well in advance of that in the English-speaking world, began to claim him for her own. In return, the British press began to quote Jonson's lines from the First Folio –

> Triumph, my Britain; thou hast one to show
> To whom all scenes of Europe homage owe

– with a new, nationalistic emphasis. There had been considerable discussion of how best to commemorate the 300th anniversary of Shakespeare's death in 1916 (another monument and a national theater were the favorite suggestions). Since the event arrived in the middle of the war, it received a relatively muted celebration. But by the next significant anniversary, 1964, the Shakespeare festivals at Stratford had led to a theater that performed year-round. In 1961 the Shakespeare Memorial Theatre became the Royal Shakespeare Theatre. When London's National Theatre, which opened in 1963, also became Royal, England had returned to something like the situation created by the Privy Council in 1594 and by the royal patronage of James I, though of course these two theaters were no longer the exclusive homes of

Shakespearean drama. The Festival of Britain in 1951 saw the first of several revivals of a history play cycle at Stratford (the *Richard II–Henry V* sequence) and in 1964 the Royal Shakespeare Theatre performed *Henry VI–Richard III* (adapted by John Barton and Peter Hall and reducing four plays to three), followed soon after by the more familiar second tetralogy. The practice of rethinking the histories as a whole, roughly every ten years, became a trademark of Stratford Shakespeare for the rest of the century and a kind of unofficial memorial. It is something that only a subsidized repertory company can do, and something that only a widely educated public would want to see.

As tourism became increasingly important in the late twentieth century, the combination of Shakespeare and the theater became one of Britain's most important attractions. Shakespeare sometimes became the accidental victim of the hostility of those who did not want Britain to become a playground for the rich, who found "Bardolatry" embarrassing, or who suspected the relationship between "author" and "authority." Yet, as in the Romantic era, he was seen simultaneously as an Establishment figure in Britain and as a force for subversion in countries where, because of state censorship, only recognized classics could be performed. *Richard III* was hugely popular in countries living under totalitarian regimes, but almost any play could become subversive. Martin Hilský has described the relieved laughter at his Czech translation of *Love's Labour's Lost*, played in Prague in 1987 under the Soviet occupation when the four young men in their Russian disguise were told to "be gone." It was, he writes, "a re-enactment of desire that could not yet be realized in practical politics."[27]

Many enthusiasts outside the Anglophone world first met Shakespeare's works in translation, which can never reproduce all his poetic effects, especially those of sound; blank verse, for example, is not effective in languages lacking a strong stress pattern. Heavy cutting often destroys the Shakespearean cornucopia effect. Puns and jokes are lost or reinvented to make them funnier. Each language creates different problems for the translator and a different experience for the audience: Japanese has separate vocabularies for male and female speakers, and can put the verb only at the end of a sentence;[28] the French preference for abstract nouns over verbs made André Gide, famously, translate "Seems, madam? Nay, it is" as "Apparence? Eh! non, Madame. Réalité."[29] But there are gains as well. Since there were no complete and accurate translations before the Romantic period, most of those now heard on the stage are modern; thus, paradoxically, audiences outside the English-speaking world are now those who find the plays easiest to understand.

Conclusion: Myth and "Genius"

Maurice Morgann in 1777 brilliantly evoked Shakespeare's exceptionalism: "Him we may profess rather to feel than to understand; and it is safer to say, on many occasions, that we are possessed by him, than that we possess him."[30] A. C. Bradley called the "Poor naked wretches" passage from *King Lear*, "one of those passages which make one worship Shakespeare."[31] Harold Bloom, still more uncompromisingly, writes, "I preach Bardolatry as the most benign of all religions. . . . To me, Shakespeare is God."[32] Many reasons have been offered for the collective Shakespeare-worship of four centuries: nationalism, globalism, and the determination to have a "best" even in categories where comparison is irrelevant. There are obvious mythic elements in this worship. Take the story about Shakespeare's early life that is supposed to have been told by Davenant to Betterton, who told Rowe, who told Pope, until it finally turned up in Johnson's Shakespeare edition. The young Shakespeare, it says, began his career by looking after gentlemen's horses outside the London theaters, something that apparently he did exceptionally well.[33] Donatus, whose biography of Virgil has already been mentioned several times, tells a similar tale about the poet's early years as a lowly member of Augustus's household; the emperor asked to meet him after learning of his almost magical ability to cure horses and dogs, and was so impressed that he became his patron. Other stories that Rowe recorded – that Shakespeare was given £1,000 by the Earl of Southampton, and that he was commanded by the queen herself to write about Falstaff in love – recall the immense wealth and reputation that Virgil is supposed to have achieved in Augustus's Rome. Donatus even records an "authorship controversy": when some verses were falsely claimed by another, Virgil proved his authorship by writing half-lines that no one else was able to complete.

The point of this comparison is that the Donatus "biography" represents what people for a thousand years felt a great poet's life should be. It is an example of what E. M. Butler has called the "myth of the Magus": human, not divine, these geniuses are characterized by humble birth, chance discovery by someone of high rank, unjust denigration or misattribution of their achievements, great rewards, and a death that is unusual, violent, or sometimes only early.[34] Virgil was, according to a translation published in 1573, "of so gentle nature, that there was no man, unless he were over-stubborn and malicious, that not only favoured him, but also heartily loved him. He seemed to have nothing private to himself. His library stood as ready open to other men as to himself, and he oftentimes used the saying of Euripides: *All things amongst friends are common.*"[35] It is not hard to see the Virgilian model behind descriptions of Shakespeare, from Chettle's brief comment on his "uprightness of dealing" and "facetious grace in writing" to Jonson's later reference to his "open and free nature" and the recurring epithet of "gentle." The early lives of Virgil apparently read backwards from the works into the life: because he wrote the *Georgics*, Virgil is assumed to have come from a farming family; because he wrote the *Eclogues*, he is said to have been homosexual.[36] I have sometimes suggested that Shakespeare thought of himself as following Virgil's path, because he might have needed some such fantasy (to write at all, you have to believe that you are good). Some scholars have felt that he was essentially a country man, happiest when in Stratford; others see him as a man whose real life was in London. I prefer Peter Ackroyd's suggestion that "His life as a dramatist, and his life as townsman, were separate and not to be compared."[37] This also means, I think, that when he wrote a play he was totally committed to the world of that play, regardless of what he believed about the world outside it, just as he was committed to the viewpoint of each speaker while that person was speaking. Machiavelli, another compartmentalizer, changed into his court robes when he went into his library; his reverence for his friends in books was quite separate from his feelings about mankind.

The writers of imaginative literature sometimes have insights into the life of an imaginative writer but they too show the power of the myth. Few fictitious Shakespeares are downright unpleasant, though Edward Bond's *Bingo* (1973) depicts his political and social views as evil and his final state as despair. The problem, for more of them, is excessive awe. "Why is it," a character in a novel of 1838 asks the teenage Shakespeare, "that I feel this veneration on so short a acquaintance with a mere boy?"[38] It is hard to think what Shakespeare could possibly say to justify this reaction. The mythical magus must of course meet royalty, and Queen Elizabeth duly turns out to be an admirer of Shakespeare both as actor and author. She is seen many times in these fictions, in a role like that of Athene for Odysseus or Venus for Aeneas; she quarrels with him in Bernard Shaw's *Dark Lady of the Sonnets* (1910) and puts him down verbally in the Marc Norman and Tom Stoppard film, *Shakespeare in Love* (1998). (It is not surprising that one of the wilder anti-Stratfordian myths makes the "real" Shakespeare her son; sometimes he is imagined as her lover as well, thus turning him into Sophocles' great archetype.) Fiction is usually less interested in James I, but Clara Longworth de Chambrun (1935) effectively weaves quotation with imagination when the dramatist pays a short visit to Scotland: "Mon, I ken ye weel, the sovereign is in touch with the seats of learning and the master-works of our sister kingdom. . . . A King who's but a poor prentice in the divine art of poetry should vail his bonnet to our English Ovid! Right welcome are ye to our kingdom! Body o' my soul, ye shall lack nothing James Stewart can command."[39]

Probably because it is hard to imagine dialogue suitable for the author of so many brilliant words, a surprising number of writers have created a fictional Shakespeare who is virtually inarticulate – as in Shaw's play, where he keeps writing down the poetic things that others say, in the comic novel *No Bed for Bacon*, by Caryl Brahms and S. J. Simon (1941), and in *Shakespeare in Love*. When he appears in the famous *Doctor Who* episode (2007), his first words, eagerly awaited by the Doctor, are a deliberate anticlimax. However, Anthony Burgess in *Nothing Like the Sun* (1964) bravely rises to the challenge of recreating the Shakespeare voice –for example, in a supposed diary entry on the genesis of *A Midsummer Night's Dream*:

> Snow falling as I sat to work (I cannot have Plautus twins for most will have seen C of
> E but I can have the Pouke or Puck confound poor lovers) and the bellman stamped

433

his feet and cursed, blowing on his fingers. Yet with my fire made up I sweated as midsummer, and lo I got my title.[40]

Shakespeare makes a brief but convincing appearance in one chapter of John Arden's *Books of Bale* (1988), in which the heroine (mother of the Dark Lady, as it turns out) discovers the connection between the *King Johan* play by her father John Bale and the one that Shakespeare will eventually write. Christopher Rush's *Will* consists mostly of the dying Shakespeare's internal monologue, interspersed with brief dialogue as his lawyer draws up the will. Though it sometimes falls back on making Shakespeare quote himself, it gives him a *copia* of rich language, perhaps more like Dylan Thomas than an Elizabethan poet, as when he recalls his early obsession with Anne Hathaway:

> So I sighed away the last of April and all of May and June. Violets died like greensick girls, the elves evacuated the cowslips, the harebells' blue music was heard no more. But the Milky Way, always in blossom, dusted the huge skies, the stars dripped on the elder trees and the trees on the fields, showering them with the strong white scents of life.[41]

"To stay on now ... this would be death," Will thinks, as he flees from Stratford, with his wife and children running after him in vain. The scene is modeled on *Pilgrim's Progress*: "he had not run far from his own door, but his wife and children, perceiving it, began to cry after him to return; but the man put his fingers in his ears, and ran on crying, 'Life! life! eternal life'."[42] Unfortunately, this Shakespeare, by the end of his life, is burned out, contemptuous of his fellow-actors and playwrights, as well as his wife and children, and interested only in words and in sex. Grace Tiffany's first Shakespeare novel, *My Father Had a Daughter*, told by Judith Shakespeare, depicts someone who neglects his family for his work but is preoccupied and chilly rather than unkind. Her second, another mammoth work called *Will*, ends with a burned-out poet – literally so, since it is after the Globe fire that he finally achieves an exhausted reconciliation with his wife: "In her arms, he became human, and wept."[43] The myth implied in both *Will*s is that of the Faustian bargain: one has to pay for great creative gifts by the loss of common humanity.

Within some fifty years of Shakespeare's death, there seems already to have been a feeling that his fame was somehow unfair. John Aubrey was told by some Stratford residents that their town had held another prodigy contemporary with Shakespeare, "that was held not at all inferior to him for a natural wit, his acquaintance and coetanean, but died young."[44] There have been other attempts to show that someone else really deserves fame more than he did, including recent fictions suggesting that he murdered or otherwise destroyed his equally gifted contemporaries. As James Shapiro remarks in *Contested Will* (2010), doubts that Shakespeare could have written the works attributed to him arose as a result of his deification and of the Romantic assumption that writers could write only about what they had personally experienced: the "unbearable tension ... between a deified Shakespeare and a depressingly mundane one" led to the search for a more interesting author.[45] Yet attributing his works to another human being – Francis Bacon, Edward Earl of Oxford, or someone else – does not solve the problem; it merely requires one to hypothesize an elaborate deception and to explain why so many people consented to it. *Contested Will* is such a good study of the "authorship debate" that I shall not make this book even longer by dwelling further on the subject.

Those disappointed by the Folio engraving and the Stratford bust have often tried to find a more attractive image. Some of these are shown in Figure 22. This engraving shows (in the oval at lower right) the Stratford bust as it appeared in the nineteenth century, after it had been painted white on the advice of Edmond Malone. (It was later repainted, but the new colors cannot be relied on as authentic.) The monument as a

Figure 22 A composite of images of Shakespeare as they were known in the nineteenth century. By permission of the Folger Shakespeare Library

435

whole was restored in 1749, and at least some of its features clearly belong to that period. In its present form, it does not resemble the drawing made by William Dugdale for Wenceslas Hollar, who was to engrave it for Dugdale's *Antiquities of Warwickshire* (1656), and it is not certain whether the image ever showed the poet, as he now appears, his mouth open, as Schoenbaum thinks, "to declaim his just-composed verses,"[46] and his eyes blank, presumably to indicate inspiration.[47] On the upper right is the engraved frontispiece to the 1640 *Poems* by William Marshall, which uses the same pose that he later gave Milton in the frontispiece to his 1645 *Poems*; it is based on a reversal of the 1623 Droeshout engraving, seen on the upper left. The largest frame is given to a copy of the so-called Flower Portrait, now known to be a nineteenth-century forgery. The two images at the bottom date from the seventeenth century but are no longer thought to be of Shakespeare. Some of the portraits are copies of each other, and some (it was later discovered) were altered, usually by creating a more receding hairline, to make them like the Folio engraving. Rumors that a Burbage portrait once existed date from the early eighteenth century. It has been suggested that the "Chandos portrait" (Figure 23) was copied from a Burbage original.[48]

The "Cobbe portrait" (Figure 24) that may have belonged to the Earl of Southampton is apparently the original from which several others were copied, and it is close in appearance to the Chandos portrait; so if the one is a portrait of

Figure 23 The Chandos portrait, so called because it was owned by the Duke of Chandos before becoming the first portrait in the National Portrait Gallery (attributed to John Taylor, oil on canvas, feigned oval, *c*.1610). © National Portrait Gallery, London

Figure 24 The Cobbe portrait, once thought to be of Sir Thomas Overbury, now believed by some to represent Shakespeare and to have been owned by the Earl of Southampton. Cobbe Collection (reproduced under copyright held by a private trust)

Shakespeare, the other may be too. Its inscription, *Principum amicitias!* (the alliances/ friendship of princes), is tantalizing.[49] In its context (Horace's *Odes* 2.1), it could refer to the danger expressed in the last words of the dying Antonio in *The Duchess of Malfi*, "And let my son fly the courts of princes," and it would be particularly appropriate to Sir Thomas Overbury, sometimes said to be the subject of the portrait, since his death by poisoning in the Tower was the result of his involvement with several extremely powerful people. But the motto would be equally appropriate to someone writing on historical subjects (like the person Horace was addressing), or simply to a man who was the friend of princes. Neither of these portraits can be authenticated, but both are attractive and plausible images: the Chandos suggests the writer who worked with people like George Wilkins, the Cobbe is more like the man who dedicated his first poems to a young earl and whose last years show a concern with his status among the Stratford gentry. A Shakespeare for our time must have sex appeal; he cannot be the balding, overweight figure of the Stratford bust or the coolly remote, mask-like face of the Folio.

The "anti-Stratfordian" movement has had some good effects, giving a serious impetus to "authorship studies." The development of computer databases to supplement traditional stylistic analysis promises, and to some extent has delivered,

437

greater certainty on the dating and authorship of many works. Already this research has destroyed some widespread myths about Shakespeare, such as the number of words that he created. It turns out that, compared with his contemporaries, "Shakespeare has a larger vocabulary because he has a larger canon."[50] Many words have been credited to him as first user only because the compilers of dictionaries knew him better than any other author. In fact, his famous variety, and much of what seems distinctive or puzzling in him, is due to the wide range of sources that he used. More attention is finally being given to the dramatists who collaborated with Shakespeare and who, this book has argued, were an important part of his life. Reading his contemporaries is a good antidote to the belief in his uniqueness. In most cases they wrote less, or less of their work survives; those who were most productive were less able or willing to give their writing the kind of attention that he gave his. There are no portraits of many of them. His superiority may have been much less evident in his own day, however, because good actors can give a "Shakespearean" depth to the characters in the drama of his contemporaries. Gary Taylor has written, rightly, that "There's nothing in Shakespeare's early work that competes with Marlowe's *Tamburlaine* or *Doctor Faustus*. And if you asked me to name the best play of 1610, I'd have to concede that Ben Jonson's *The Alchemist* out-classes Shakespeare's *Cymbeline* or *The Winter's Tale*. For 1613, Thomas Middleton's *A Chaste Maid in Cheapside* would certainly beat *The Two Noble Kinsmen*."[51] The plays he mentions, and many others, still exist only in a sort of half-life, needing more theatrical productions to test their quality. Though the tragedies contain some superb acting opportunities, there are only a few roles – Marlowe's heroes, Volpone, the Duchess of Malfi, Vendice in *The Revenger's Tragedy*, Beatrice and De Flores in *The Changeling* – that have become well known as parts that leading actors want to play. The comedies have many good parts, but none for a star actor. Even the plays that have received some good criticism and a few major productions are not haloed by the long years of conflicting yet mutually enriching interpretations which, more than we realize, make up our experience of a Shakespeare play. Taylor has shown his belief in the constructed nature of literary value by bringing out an impressive edition of Middleton's works that showcases a still greater and more varied productivity (at least, in terms of the genres in which he worked) than Shakespeare's. The availability of well-edited texts should encourage more productions of this writer's plays (his other works are unlikely ever to be popular), but it will take at least fifty years to show whether they have the Shakespearean ability to seem relevant to an era other than the one that rediscovered him, which shares Middleton's fascination with the relation between sex and money.

One effect of situating Shakespeare among other writers may be to make the anti-Stratfordian argument irrelevant. If he can be seen as an author like any other, there is no need to talk about his "genius" and no need to displace him with someone else. "Genius" is a term unpopular in scientific circles because it makes no distinction between potential and achievement. It is however a term that people like to use about Shakespeare, and perhaps the main reason people like to read books about Shakespeare is that they hope to discover some cause of "genius" that they themselves can imitate. Yet what they most need to imitate is his productivity. As Dean Simonton writes, "the single most powerful predictor of eminence within any creative domain is the sheer number of influential products an individual has given the world."[52] As I have already indicated, it is the sheer number of Shakespeare's surviving plays and poems, and the fact that few people can claim both breadth and depth of knowledge in them all, that makes them an inexhaustible field of study. We are all, forever, trying to remember him.

In Henry James's short story "The Birthplace" (1903), the protagonist is offered the post of resident guide to the birthplace of someone who, though never named, is obviously Shakespeare. The reaction of this typically sensitive and educated Jamesian character perfectly captures what might be called the Shakespearean imaginarium at a time when Shakespeare was still a matter for private reading rather than study in school: "He felt as if a window had opened into a great green woodland, a woodland that had a name, glorious, immortal, that was peopled with vivid figures, each of them renowned, and that gave out a murmur, deep as the sound of the sea, which was the rustle in forest shade of all the poetry, the beauty, the colour of life."[53] This response to the name of Shakespeare is not innocent of the knowledge that he is a famous and revered author. The characters are already "renowned": an educated Englishman can no longer meet Juliet or Hamlet, or hear an actor say "So this is the Forest of Arden" for the first time. Aura, however, is only part of James's description, which condenses into one dreamlike impression the "green world" of the early comedies, a general sense of music and the sea that suggests the late romances, and the "vivid figures" for which Shakespeare has always been famous. It is both visual and verbal, though without specific recollection of a single word of the poetry that it evokes.

What James leaves out, however, is the theatrical instinct – how much time to spend on each episode, how to use suspense and surprise, how to orchestrate vivid characterizations and styles of speech, how to give the actors their opportunities. The theatrically effective line is often very simple: Cordelia's "No cause, no cause," when Lear has finally admitted that she has every reason to hate him, or Leontes' "O, she's warm," when he touches the hand of the wife he has not dared to believe is alive. Falstaff's "By the lord, I knew ye as well as he that made ye," is a great comic climax because the audience has to wait for it, after a long series of lies on his part and knowing comments from the other characters. It is absurdly obvious, and yet it also justifies Harold Bloom's praise of "an intelligence without limits."[54] The plays' intellectual pleasures are not confined to the debates in *Troilus and Cressida* or the cosmic questioning in *King Lear*. They can be found in Biondello's maddeningly logical reply to the question, "When will he [Petruchio] be here?" – "When he stands where I am and sees you there" (*Taming of the Shrew* 3.2.39–41), and even in Rosalind's apparently anti-intellectual debunking of Jaques' claim to have gained

439

experience by his travels: "And your experience has made you sad. I had rather have a fool to make me merry than experience to make me sad – and to travel for it too!" (*As You Like It* 4.1.24–6). All these moments depend on characters listening to each other and remembering what they hear. If the audience is equally intelligent, it will have the pleasure of recognizing, for example, that Iago, after ridiculing Roderigo for talking of Desdemona's "blessed condition" – "Blessed fig's end! ... Blessed pudding!" (2.1.252–5) – stores away that very word and uses it, perhaps searches for it, when urging Cassio to sue to Desdemona because "She is of so free, so kind, so apt, so blessed a disposition" (2.3.313–14).

People were quoting Shakespeare early, because they found him easy to remember. By the eighteenth century they often did not bother with attribution. In the nineteenth century he was still more widely known: when Rochester in *Jane Eyre* casually asks, "Was that the head and front of his offending?" (chapter 13), Jane expresses no surprise at a phrase (from *Othello* 1.3.82) that most readers now probably find mysterious. Even now, when there are constant complaints about the break-down of the "common culture," Susan Baker points out that the solution of the classic detective story often depends on the recognition of the sources of Shakespeare quotations. They are considered "fair" clues – that is, something that an educated reader should be able to recognize.[55] Shakespeare is quotable, and hence memorable, because he intends to be. No other dramatist so persistently veers from the particular to the general. When one of Octavius Caesar's advisers pronounces his movingly understated epitaph on Mark Antony –

> A rarer spirit never
> Did steer humanity, but you gods will give us
> Some faults to make us men
>
> (5.1.31–3)

– the words are not only a judgment on a particular historical and theatrical character; they are words that one will want to use many times in the future – not merely to show off, but for the pleasure of saying them.

And that is the main point about the passages I have been quoting. Whether spoken in a neutral tone or in a persona, they allow the speaker to achieve the highest common denominator. Speaking Prospero's "The cloud-capped towers, the gorgeous palaces" is not the same as making a pessimistic statement about the brevity of life. Orsino can be played as a lovesick fool, but his words about the woman he loves – "O when mine eyes did see Olivia first,/ Methought she purged the air of pestilence" – are joyous. "Shakespearean insults" are popular on tea towels, mugs, and refrigerator magnets because they are fun to say. An example of how to transform a negative statement into a positive one is Fluellen's retort to Gower, who has just said that there is no point in the English army keeping quiet, when the nearby French one is so loud – "If the enemy is an ass and a fool and a prating coxcomb, is it meet, think you, that we should also, look you, be an ass and a fool and a prating coxcomb?" (*Henry V* 4.1.78–80). Finally, many of Shakespeare's most famous lines are those in which characters praise others. The sonnets do this magnificently. Among many other examples, one might cite Romeo's "O, she doth teach the torches to burn bright," Lady Percy remembering Hotspur with "by his light/ Did all the chivalry of England move," Horatio's "Good night, sweet prince," Enobarbus saying that Cleopatra's appearance "beggared all description," Florizel's "What you do/Still betters what is done." It is good to praise others. By showing how to do it, Shakespeare has earned the right to be praised himself, and has made the writing of this book a pleasure.

Notes

1. Quoted in *Shakespeare's Sonnets*, ed. Duncan-Jones, 67–8.
2. Wells, "Jaggard, William," *ODNB*.
3. Edmond, "Heminges, John," *ODNB*.
4. Summarized from Edmond, *Rare Sir William Davenant*, ch. 1.
5. *Twelfth Night*, ed. Elam, 362.
6. See Hotson, *The First Night of Twelfth Night*, and *Twelfth Night*, ed. Elam, 93–4.
7. See Hoy, "The Shares of Fletcher and his Collaborators."
8. Blayney, *The First Folio*, 25.
9. Ibid., 28, 32.
10. Quoted in Chambers, *ES*, 2: 234. According to Israel Gollancz, who discovered the poem in the archives of the Salisbury family, it follows entries dating from 1622 and is thus an early response to the Folio.
11. *Eikonoklastes* (1649), ed. Hughes, 361. Milton goes on (ibid., pp. 361–2) to suggest that Charles I was as hypocritical as Shakespeare's Richard III.
12. See *Shakespeare's Poems*, ed. Duncan-Jones and Woudhuysen, 438–45, and Campbell, "Shakespeare and the Youth of Milton."
13. Freehafer, "Leonard Digges, Ben Jonson, and the Beginning of Shakespeare Idolatry," argues that this poem was originally intended for the 1623 Folio.
14. Holland, "Theatre without Drama: Reading *REED*," 50–1.
15. Chambers, *WS*, 2: 241–2.
16. Barton, *Ben Jonson, Dramatist*, 258.
17. Clayton, "Suckling, Sir John," *ODNB*. Clayton translates the motto on the stone, "NE TE QUAESIVERIS EXTRA," as "seek not outside thyself" (Persius, *Satires* 1.7). The *Hamlet* allusion may be significant: though there are conflicting accounts of Suckling's death, it is generally thought that he committed suicide in 1641.
18. Duncan-Jones, however, suggests that the reference was originally to Shakespeare's godfather, the butcher William Tyler: *Shakespeare: Upstart Crow to Sweet Swan, 1592–1623*, 3.
19. Aubrey, *Brief Lives*, 2: 227.
20. Ibid., 1: 97.
21. Chambers reprints the relevant page in *WS* 2, facing p. 252. See also Schoenbaum, 255.

22. When James II was overthrown in 1688 by his daughter Mary and her husband William of Orange, the accidental parallel with Tate's ending was so obvious that the play went unperformed during the whole of their reign.
23. Egan, *The Struggle for Shakespeare's Text*, 167.
24. See Berger, *Imaginary Audition: Shakespeare on Stage and Page.*
25. Weimann, "Ideology and Performance in East German Versions of Shakespeare," 343.
26. Helbig, "Cinematic Intertextuality in Contemporary Shakespeare Films," 144.
27. Hilský, "Translations of Politics/Politics of Translation," 219.
28. Kishi, "'I know not what you mean by that': Shakespeare in Different Cultural Contexts."
29. *Hamlet*, trans. Gide, 27. It is only fair to add that Gide's translation of the next sentence – "Qu'ai-je affaire avec le 'paraître'?" – does replicate the odd grammar of the original.
30. [Morgann], *An Essay on the Dramatic Character of Sir John Falstaff*, 66.
31. Bradley, *Shakespearean Tragedy*, 287.
32. Bloom, *The Anatomy of Influence*, 77.
33. Versions of this anecdote are quoted in Chambers, *ES*, 2: by "Anon." (p. 284), Robert Shiels (pp. 285–6), and Johnson (pp. 287–8).
34. See Butler, *The Myth of the Magus*, 3, 4, and, for Virgil, 97–8.
35. *The whole xii. Bookes of the Aeneidos of Virgill,* trans. Phaer, C3.
36. Stok, "The Life of Vergil before Donatus," 113.
37. Ackroyd, *Shakespeare: The Biography*, 409.
38. Curling, *The Forest Youth*, 66.
39. De Chambrun, *My Shakespeare, Rise!*, 297.
40. Burgess, *Nothing Like the Sun: A Story of Shakespeare's Love-Life*, 144.
41. Rush, *Will*, 131.
42. Rush, *Will*, 169; *Pilgrim's Progress*, ed. Pooley, 14.
43. Tiffany, *Will, a Novel*, 403.
44. Aubrey, *Brief Lives*, 2: 226.
45. J. Shapiro, *Contested Will*, 69. The final chapter makes the case for Shakespeare's authorship. See also Matus, *Shakespeare in Fact*, and David Bevington's brief remarks in *Shakespeare: The Seven Ages of Human Experience*, 8–12.
46. Schoenbaum, 310.
47. See the *TLS* correspondence from Peter Beal (16 June 2006), Brian Vickers (30 June 2006), Jonathan Bate and Stanley Wells (7 July 2006), and Peter Beal (14 July 2006), and Vickers's essay, "The Face of the Bard?," 17.
48. See Duncan-Jones, "Fame in a Feigned Oval" (a review of the National Portrait Gallery's "Searching for Shakespeare" exhibition and catalogue), 16; Cooper, *Searching for Shakespeare*, 54–61; Cobbe, "Shakespeare to the Life."
49. Cobbe, "Shakespeare to the Life," 11.
50. Craig, "Shakespeare's Vocabulary," 63.
51. Taylor, "True Is It That We Have Seen Better Plays."
52. Simonton, *Origins of Genius*, 6.
53. James, "The Birthplace," 405.
54. Bloom, *Shakespeare: The Invention of the Human*, 271.
55. S. Baker, "Shakespearean Authority in the Classic Detective Story," 437.

Bibliography

Place of publication is London unless otherwise stated.

Shakespeare Editions

The Complete Works of Shakespeare, ed. David Bevington. 5th edn. New York: Longman Pearson, 2004.

The Complete Works of Shakespeare, ed. Stanley Wells, Gary Taylor, John Jowett, and William Montgomery. Oxford: Oxford University Press, 1986.

Shakespeare's Plays in Quarto: A Facsimile Edition of Copies Primarily from the Henry E. Huntington Library, ed. Michael J. B. Allen and Kenneth Muir. Berkeley: University of California Press, 1981.

The Complete Sonnets and Poems, ed. Colin Burrow. Oxford: Oxford University Press, 2002.

The Narrative Poems, ed. Maurice Evans. Harmondsworth: Penguin, 1989.

Shakespeare's Poems, ed. Katherine Duncan-Jones and H. R. Woudhuysen. Arden 3. 2007.

Shakespeare's Sonnets, Edited with Analytic Commentary, ed. Stephen Booth. New Haven: Yale University Press, 1977.

Shakespeare's Sonnets, ed. Katherine Duncan-Jones. Arden 3. 1997.

Shakespeare's Sonnets, ed. Barbara A. Mowat and Paul Werstine. New York: Washington Square Press, 2004.

The Sonnets and A Lover's Complaint, ed. John Kerrigan. Harmondsworth: Penguin, 1986.

All's Well that Ends Well, ed. Susan Snyder. Oxford: Clarendon Press, 1993.

Antony and Cleopatra, ed. David Bevington. Cambridge: Cambridge University Press, 1990.

As You Like It, ed. Juliet Dusinberre. Arden 3. 2009.

Coriolanus, ed. R. B. Parker. Oxford: Clarendon Press, 1994.

Edward II/Edouard III, ed. Anny Crunelle-Vanrigh, in Jean-Michel Déprats and Gisèle Venet, gen. eds., *Shakespeare: Histoires*, vol. 1. Paris: Gallimard, 2008.

Edward III, ed. Giorgio Melchiori. Cambridge: Cambridge University Press, 1984.

The Life of William Shakespeare: A Critical Biography, First Edition. Lois Potter.
© 2012 Lois Potter. Published 2012 by Blackwell Publishing Ltd.

Hamlet, trans. Jean-Michel Déprats, in Jean-Michel Déprats and Gisèle Venet, eds., *Œuvres complètes de William Shakespeare*, vol. 1 (2002). Paris: Gallimard, 2002–8.

Hamlet, trans. André Gide. Paris: Gallimard, 1946.

Hamlet, ed. Harold Jenkins. Arden 2. 1982.

Hamlet, ed. Ann Thompson and Neil Taylor. Arden 3. 2006.

Hamlet. The Texts of 1603 and 1623, ed. Ann Thompson and Neil Taylor. Arden 3. 2007.

1 Henry VI, ed. Edward Burns. Arden 3. 2000.

2 Henry VI, ed. Ronald Knowles. Arden 3. Walton-on-Thames, 1999.

3 Henry VI, ed. John D. Cox and Eric Rasmussen. Arden 3. 2001.

Julius Caesar, ed. David Daniell. Arden 3. 1998.

King Richard III, ed. James Siemon. Arden 3. 2009.

Love's Labour's Lost, ed. Henry Woudhuysen. Arden 3. 1998.

Much Ado About Nothing, ed. Claire McEachern. Arden 3. 2006.

Othello, ed. E. A. J. Honigmann. Arden 3. Walton-on-Thames, 1997.

Pericles, ed. Suzanne Gossett. Arden 3. 2004.

Sir Thomas More, ed. John Jowett. Arden 3. 2011.

The Taming of the Shrew, ed. Ann Thompson. Cambridge: Cambridge University Press, 1984; rev. edn., 2003.

The Taming of the Shrew, ed. Barbara Hodgdon. Arden 3. 2010.

The Tempest, ed. Alden Vaughan and Virginia Vaughan. Arden 3. 2000.

The Life of Timon of Athens, ed. John Jowett. Oxford: Oxford University Press, 2004.

Timon of Athens, ed. Anthony B. Dawson and Gretchen E. Minton. Arden 3. 2008.

Titus Andronicus, ed. Jonathan Bate. Arden 3. 1995.

Troilus and Cressida, ed. David Bevington. Arden 3. 1998.

Twelfth Night, ed. Keir Elam. Arden 3. 2008.

Twelfth Night, ed. J. M. Lothian and T. W. Craik. Arden 2. 1975.

Twelfth Night, ed. Roger Warren and Stanley Wells. Oxford: Oxford University Press, 1994.

The Two Gentlemen of Verona, ed. William C. Carroll. Arden 3. 2004.

The Two Noble Kinsmen, ed. Lois Potter. Arden 3. 1997.

The Winter's Tale, ed. John Pitcher. Arden 3. 2010.

Early Texts and Other Editions

An Answere or Admonition to those of the Church of Rome, touching the Iubile, proclaimed by the Bull, made and set foorth by Pope Clement the eyght, for the yeare of our Lord. 1600 [1600].

Arber, Edward, ed. *A Transcript of the Registers of the Company of Stationers of London; 1554–1640 A.D*, vol. 1: *Text*. Repr. Mansfield Center, CT: Martino Publishing, 2006.

Armin, Robert. *The Collected Works of Robert Armin*. 2 vols. Introd. J. Feather. New York: Johnson Reprint Corp., 1972.

Aubrey, John. *Brief Lives, Chiefly of Contemporaries, set down by John Aubrey, between the Years 1669 & 1696*, ed. Andrew Clark.2 vols. Oxford: Clarendon Press, 1898.

[Bacon, Francis]. *A Declaration of the Practises & Treasons attempted and committed by Robert late Earle of Essex and his Complices.....*1601.

[Barlow, William]. *A Defence of the Articles of the Protestant Religion, in aunsweare to a libell lately cast abroad, intituled Certaine Articles* ... 1601.

Barlow, William. *A Sermon preached at Paules Crosse, on the first Sunday in Lent.* 1601.

[Barnfield, Richard]. *The Affectionate Shepheard. Containing the Complaint of Daphnis for the loue of Ganymede.* 1594.

Barnfield, Richard. *Cynthia, with Certaine Sonnets, and the Legend of Cassandra.* 1595.

Beaumont, Francis, and John Fletcher. *Comedies and Tragedies.* 1647.

Beaumont, Francis, and John Fletcher. *The Dramatic Works in the Beaumont and Fletcher Canon,* gen. ed. Fredson Bowers. 10 vols. Cambridge: Cambridge University Press, 1966–96.

Beaumont, Francis, and John Fletcher, *Philaster,* ed. Suzanne Gossett. Methuen, 2009.

Beaumont, Francis, and John Fletcher. *The Works of Francis Beaumont and John Fletcher,* ed. Arnold Glover. 10 vols., vol. 1. Cambridge: Cambridge University Press, 1905.

Bel-vedere, or The Garden of the Muses. 1600.

Bilson, Thomas. *The Effect of Certain Sermons.* 1599.

Bilson, Thomas. *The Survey of Christ's Sufferings.* 1604.

Birch, Thomas. *The Court and Times of James the First.* 2 vols. 1849.

The Book of Common Prayer 1559: The Elizabethan Prayer Book, ed. John E. Booty, Washington, DC: Folger Shakespeare Library, 1976.

Bradley, Jesse Franklin, and Adams, Joseph Quincy, eds. *The Jonson Allusion-Book.* New Haven: Yale University Press, 1922.

Brinsley, John. *Ludus Literarius, or, The Grammar School.* 1612.

Brinsley, John. *A Consolation for Our Grammar Schooles* [1622]. Facsimile edn., introd. Thomas Clark Pollock. New York: Scholars' Facsimiles & Reprints, 1943.

Bullough, Geoffrey, ed. *Narrative and Dramatic Sources of Shakespeare.* 8 vols. Routledge & Kegan Paul. 1957–75.

Bunyan, John. *The Pilgrim's Progress, From This World to That Which Is To Come,* ed. Roger Pooley. Harmondsworth: Penguin, 2008.

Calendar of State Papers Venetian, vol. 10: *1603–1607,* ed. Horatio R. Brown. 1900; repr. Liechtenstein: Kraus, 1970.

Camden, William. *Remains Concerning Britain,* ed. R. D. Dunn. Toronto: University of Toronto Press, 1984.

Carey, Robert. *The Memoirs of Robert Carey,* ed. F. H. Mares. Oxford: Clarendon Press, 1972.

Carleton, Dudley. *Dudley Carleton to John Chamberlain 1603–1624: Jacobean Letters,* ed. Maurice Lee, Jr. New Brunswick, NJ: Rutgers University Press, 1972.

The Ceremonies, solemnities, and prayers, vsed at the opening of the holy gates of foure Churches, within the Citie of Rome, in the yere of Iubile... 1600.

Chamberlain, John. *The Letters of John Chamberlain,* ed. Norman Egbert McClure. 2 vols. Philadelphia: American Philosophical Society, 1939.

Chandler, Wayne A.ed., *An Anthology of Commendatory Verse from the English Renaissance.* Lewiston, NY: Edwin Mellen Press, 2005.

Chapman, George. *Achilles Shield*. 1598.

Chapman, George. *Homer Prince of Poets, Translated According to the Greek in Twelve Books of the Iliads*. 1609.

Chapman, George. *Seaven Bookes of the Iliades of Homer, Prince of Poets*. 1598.

Chapman, George. *The Shadow of Night: Containing Two Poeticall Hymnes*. [1594].

Chaucer, Geoffrey. *The Riverside Chaucer*, ed. F. N. Robinson, rev. L. D. Benson. Oxford: Oxford University Press, 1987.

Chester, Robert. *Love's Martyr, or, Rosalin's Complaint* (1601), ed. Alexander B. Grosart. New Shakspere Society. N. Trübner, 1878.

Chester, Robert. *Poems by Sir John Salusbury and Robert Chester*, ed. Carleton Brown. Early English Text Society, Kegan Paul, and Oxford University Press, 1914.

Cicero. *Marcus Tullius Ciceroes thre bokes of duties, to Marcus his sonne, turned oute of latine into english, by Nicolas Grimalde*, ed. Gerald O'Gorman.Renaissance English Text Society. Washington, DC: Folger Shakespeare Library; Associated University Presses, 1990.

Clement, Francis. *The Petie Schole, with an English Orthographie* (1587), repr. in *Four Tudor Books on Education*, introd. Robert D. Pepper. Gainesville, FL: Scholars' Facsimiles & Reprints, 1966.

Constable, Henry. *Diana, or the excellent conceitful Sonnets of H.C. Augmented with diuers quatorzains of honorable and lerned personages. Deuided into viij. Decads*. 1584.

Constable, Henry. *The Poems of Henry Constable*, ed. Isobel Grundy. Liverpool: Liverpool University Press, 1960.

Corderius, Maturinus [Maturin Cordier] (trans. T.W.). *Principia Latine Loquendi. A very necesssary and profitable entraunce to the speakyng and writyng of the Latin tongue*. 1575.

Cordier, Maturin. *Corderius Dialogues Translated Grammatically. For the more speedy attaining to the knowledge of the Latine tongue, for writing and speaking Latin. Done chiefly for the good of Schooles....*[trans. John Brinsley]. 1636.

Coryate, Thomas. *Coryat's Crudities; reprinted from the Edition of 1611. To which are now added, His Letters from India, &c. And Extracts Relating to Him from Various Authors*. 3 vols. 1776.

Covell, William. *Polimanteia or, The meanes lawfull and vnlawfull, to iudge of the fall of a commonwealth, against the friuolous and foolish coniectures of this age*. 1595.

Culman, Leonard. *Sententiae Pueriles pro primis Latinae Linguae Tyronibus, ex diversis Scriptoribus collectae. Hic accesserunt pleraeque veterum Theologorum Sententiae de vera religione*. 1639.

Cunningham, W. *A new Almanach and Prognostication, seruynge the yere of Christ M.DL.X.III, faithfully calculated for the longitude of London, and pole articke of the same*. 1564.

Cunningham, W. *A Prognostication for the Yeare of our redemption, 1564, in which is manifestly set out the vengeaunce of God, [?] to fall on the inhabitantes of Europe for their vyle and abbominable lyvynge, so farre as by natural disposition of the celestiall bodyes, may be gathered, and for that cause published as a warnyng unto all*. 1563.

Daniel, Samuel. *The Whole Works of Samuel Daniel*. 1623.

Davies, John. *Poems of Sir John Davies*, ed. Robert Krueger. Oxford: Clarendon Press, 1975.

Davies, John, of Hereford. *Complete Works*, ed. Alexander Grosart. 2 vols. Edinburgh: Edinburgh University Press, 1878.

Davies, John, of Hereford. *Wits Pilgrimage.* [1610–11].

Dekker, Thomas, and George Wilkins, *Jests to Make You Merry.* 1607.

Deloney, Thomas. *Strange histories, or, Songs and sonnets, of kinges, princes, dukes, lords, ladyes, knights, and gentlemen and of certaine ladyes that were shepheards on Salisburie plaine: very pleasant either to be read or songe, and a most excellent warning for all estates.* 1612.

Dennis, John. "On the Genius and Writings of Shakespeare" (1711). In *Eighteenth-Century Essays upon Shakespeare,* ed. D. Nichol Smith. Glasgow, 1903.

Doleman, R. [Robert Parsons]. *A Conference About the Next Succession to the Crowne of Ingland, divided into two partes.* Imprinted at N. with Licence [i.e., printed illegally in Amsterdam], 1594.

Double Falsehood, ed. Brean Hammond. Arden 3. 2010.

Drayton, Michael. *England's Heroical Epistles, newly enlarged, with Idea.* 1599.

Drayton, Michael. *Peirs Gaueston, Earle of Cornwall, his life, death, and fortune.* [1593?].

Drayton, Michael. *The Works of Michael Drayton,* ed. J. William Hebel. 5 vols. Oxford: Blackwell, 1931.

Elizabethan Critical Essays, ed. G. Gregory Smith. 2 vols. Oxford, 1904.

Englands Parnassus, compiled by Robert Allot, 1600, ed. Charles Crawford. Oxford: Clarendon Press, 1913.

English Renaissance Drama, ed. David Bevington. New York: Norton, 2002.

English and Scottish Sonnet Sequences of the Renaissance, ed. Holger Klein. 2 vols. Hildesheim: Georg Olms, 1984.

Fletcher, Giles. *Licia. Or Poemes of Loue, in Honour of the admirable and singular vertues of his Lady, to the imitation of the best Latin Poets, and others. Whereunto is added the Rising to the Crowne of Richard the third* [1593].

Fuller, Thomas. *The Worthies of England,* ed. (and abridged) John Freeman. George Allen & Unwin, 1952.

Gager, William. *The Complete Works,* ed., with translation and commentary, Dana F. Sutton. 4 vols. New York: Garland, 1994.

Gascoigne, George. *The Complete Works of George Gascoigne,* ed. John W. Cunliffe. 2 vols. Cambridge: Cambridge University Press, 1910.

Gesta Grayorum, or the history of the High and Mighty Prince Henry Prince of Purpoole Anno Domini 1594, ed. Desmond Bland. Liverpool: Liverpool University Press, 1968.

Gower, John. *Confessio Amantis.* In *The English Works of John Gower,* ed. G. C. Macaulay. 2 vols, vol 2. K. Paul, 1901; repr. 1957.

Greene, Robert, and Henry Chettle. *Greene's Groatsworth of Wit, Bought with a Million of Repentance,* ed. D. Allen Carroll. Binghamton, NY: Medieval & Renaissance Texts and Studies, 1994.

Greene, Robert. *The Life and Complete Works in Verse and Prose of Robert Greene, M.A.,* ed. Alexander B. Grosart. 12 vols. 1881–3.

Greene, Robert. *Menaphon: Camilla's Alarm to slumbering Euphues, in his melancholie Cell at Silexedra.* 1589.

Greene's Groatsworth of Wit Bought with a Million of Repentance (1592), attributed to Henry Chettle and Robert Greene, ed. Carroll, D. Allen. Binghamton, NY: Medieval & Renaissance Texts and Studies, 1994.

Greg, W. W. *A Bibliography of the English Printed Drama to the Restoration.* 4 vols. Oxford University Press, 1939–59.

Guarini, Gianbattista. *Il Pastor Fido e Il compendio della Poesia Tragicomica*, ed. Gioachino Brognoligo. Bari: Gius. Laterza & Figli, 1914.

Guy of Warwick (1661), ed. HelenMoore.Malone Society. Manchester: Manchester University Press, 2007.

Hall, Edward. *Hall's Chronicle.* 1809.

[Harington, John]. *A New Discourse of a stale subiect, called the metamorphosis of Aiax: vvritten by Misacmos, to his friend and cosin Philostilpnos.* 1596.

Harington, John. *Sir John Harington's A New Discourse of a Stale Subject, Called the Metamorphosis of Ajax*, ed. Elizabeth Story Donno. Routledge & Kegan Paul, 1962.

Harington, John. *Nugae Antiquae, being a miscellaneous collection of original papers, in prose and verse*, ed. Henry Harington. 2 vols. 1792.

Harsnett, Samuel. *A declaration of egregious popish impostures to with-draw the harts of her Maiesties subiects from their allegeance, and from the truth of Christian religion professed in England, vnder the pretence of casting out deuils.* 1603.

Harvey, Gabriel. *Foure Letters and Certeine Sonnets, especially touching Robert Greene and other parties by him abused* (1592), ed. G. B. Harrison. Bodley Head quartos. New York: E. P. Dutton; John Lane, the Bodley Head, 1923.

Hausted, Peter. *The Rival Friends.* 1632.

Henslowe, Philip. *Henslowe's Diary*, ed. R. A. Foakes. Cambridge: Cambridge University Press, 2002.

Herring, Francis. *A Modest Defence of the Caveat Given to the Wearers of Impoisoned Amulets, as Preseruatiues from the Plague. . .* 1604.

Heywood, Thomas. *An Apology for Actors* (1612) and I.G., *A Refutation of the Apology for Actors* (1615), ed. Richard H. Perkinson. New York: Scholars' Facsimiles and Reprints, 1941.

Heywood, Thomas. *A Woman Killed with Kindness*, ed. R. W. van Fossen. Revels Plays Cambridge, MA: Harvard University Press, 1961.

[Holinshed, Raphael.] *The Third Volume of Chronicles, Beginning at Duke William the Norman, commonlie called the Conqueror: and descending by degrees of yeeres to all the Kings and queenes of England on their orderlie successions. First compiled by Raphael Holinshed, and by him extended to the yeare 1577. Now newlie recognized, aumented, and continued (with occurrences and accidents of fresh memorie) to the yeare 1586.* [1587].

Holyband, Claudius[Claude Sainsliens]. *The French Littelton: The Edition of 1609*, with introduction by M. St. Clare Byrne. Cambridge: Cambridge University Press, 1953.

Holyband, Claudius [Claude Sainsliens]. *The French Schoole-maister, wherin is most plainlie shewed, the true and most perfect way of pronouncinge of the frenche tongue.* 1573.

Injunctions given by the Queenes Maiestie anno Dom. 1559. Repr. Robert Barker, 1600.

Jacob, Henry. *A Defence of a Treatise touching the Sufferings and Victorie of Christ in the Worke of our Redemption*. 1600.

James VI and I. *Letters of James VI and I*, ed. G. K. V. Akrigg. Berkeley: University of California Press, 1984.

James VI and I. *The Poems of James VI of Scotland*, ed. James Craigie. 2 vols. Edinburgh: W. Blackwood, 1955, 1958.

James VI and I. *Political Writings*, ed. Johann P. Sommerville. Cambridge: Cambridge University Press, 1994.

James VI and I. *Selected Writings*, ed. Neil Rhodes, Jennifer Richards, and Joseph Marshall. Aldershot: Ashgate, 2003.

Jonson, Ben. *Ben Jonson*, ed. C. H. Herford, Percy Simpson, and Evelyn Simpson. 11 vols. Oxford: Clarendon Press, 1925–63.

Jonson, Ben. *Every Man in His Humour*, ed. Robert S. Miola. Revels Plays. Manchester: Manchester University Press, 2000.

Jonson, Ben. *Poetaster*, ed. Tom Cain. Manchester: Manchester University Press, 1995.

Jonson, Ben. *Sejanus His Fall*, ed. Philip J. Ayres. Manchester: Manchester University Press, 1990.

Jonson, Ben. *The Workes of Beniamin Jonson*. William Stansby, 1616.

King Leir, ed. Tiffany Stern. Nick Hern Books, 2002.

Kyd, Thomas. *The Spanish Tragedy*, ed. Philip Edwards. Methuen, 1959.

Kyd, Thomas. *The Spanish Tragedie*, ed. Emma Smith. Harmondsworth: Penguin, 1998.

Kyd, Thomas. *The Works of Thomas Kyd*, ed. Frederick S. Boas. Oxford: Clarendon Press, 1901.

Lane, John. *Tom Tel-Troths Message*. 1600.

Letters and memorials of state, ed. Arthur Collins. 2 vols. 1746.

[Lily, William.] *An Introduction of the Eight Partes of Speche and the Construction of the same, compyled and set for the by the commaundement of our most gracious soueraygne lorde the kyng*. 1544.

Lodge, Thomas. *The Complete Works of Thomas Lodge [1580–1623?] now first collected*, ed. Edmund W. Gosse. 4 vols. The Hunterian Club. 1883.

Lodge, Thomas. *Wit's Miserie, and the Worlds Madnesse*. 1596.

Lyly, John. *Campaspe*, ed. George K. Hunter. Manchester: Manchester University Press, 1991.

Lyly, John. *Gallathea and Midas*, ed. Anne Begor Lancashire. Lincoln: University of Nebraska Press, 1969.

Manningham, John. *The Diary of John Manningham of the Middle Temple 1602–1603*, ed. Robert Parker Sorlien. Hanover, NH: University Press of New England, 1976.

Marlowe, Christopher. *The Complete Poems and Translations*, ed. Stephen Orgel. Harmondsworth: Penguin, 1971; rev. edn., 2000.

Marlowe, Christopher. *Doctor Faustus and Other Plays*, ed. David Bevington and Eric Rasmussen. Oxford: Oxford University Press, 1995.

Marston, John. *The Poems of John Marston*, ed. Arnold Davenport. Liverpool: Liverpool University Press, 1961.

Marston, John. *The Selected Plays of John Marston*, ed. MacDonald P. Jackson and Michael Neill. Cambridge: Cambridge University Press, 1986.

May, Steven, ed. *Elizabethan Courtier Poets: The Poems and Their Contexts*. Columbia: University of Missouri Press, 1991.

Meres, Francis. *Francis Meres's Treatise "Poetrie": A Critical Edition*, ed. Don Cameron Allen. University of Illinois Bulletin, no. 21. Urbana: University of Illinois Press, 1933.

Meres, Francis. *Palladis Tamia: Wits Treasury*. 1598.

Middleton, Thomas. *Collected Works of Thomas Middleton*, ed. Gary Taylor and John Lavagnino. Oxford: Clarendon Press, 2007.

Milton, John. *Eikonoklastes* (1649), ed. Merritt Y. Hughes, in *Complete Prose Works of John Milton*, vol. 3. New Haven: Yale University Press, 1962.

Minutes and Accounts of the Corporation of Stratford-upon-Avon and other records 1553–1620. Transcribed Richard Savage. Introduction and notes by Edgar I. Fripp. Vol. 1 (1553–66), Oxford: Dugdale Society, 1921. Vol. 2 (1566–77), Dugdale Society, 1924. Vol. 3 (1577–86), Dugdale Society, 1926. Vol. 4 (1586–92), ed. Levi Fox, Dugdale Society, 1929. Vol. 5 (1593–8), Hertford: Dugdale Society, 1990.

Montague, Walter. *The Shepherds' Paradise*, ed. Sarah Poynting. Malone Society. Oxford: Oxford University Press, 1998.

Montgomerie, Alexander. *Poems*, ed. David J. Parkinson, 2 vols. Edinburgh: Scottish Text Society, 2000.

Nash, Thomas. *Pierce Pennilesse his Supplication to the Devil*. 1592.

[Nesbit, E.]. *Caesar's Dialogue, or a Familiar Communication containing the first Institution of a Subiect, in allegiance to his Soueraigne*. 1601.

Nixon, Anthony. *Elizaes Memorial, King James His Arrival, and Romes Downfall*. 1603.

The Oldcastle Controversy, ed. Peter Corbin and Douglas Sedge. Manchester: Manchester University Press, 1991.

Ovid. *Heroides and Amores*, trans. Grant Showerman. 2nd edn., rev. G. P. Gould. Cambridge, MA: Harvard University Press; William Heinemann, 1977.

Ovid's Metamorphoses, trans. Arthur Golding, ed. John Frederick Nims. Philadelphia: Paul Dry Books, 2000.

Peele, George. *The Life and Minor Works of George Peele*, ed. David H. Horne. New Haven: Yale University Press, 1952.

Peele, George, *The Life and Works of George Peele*, gen. ed. Charles Tyler Prouty. 3 vols. New Haven: Yale University Press, 1952–70.

Perkins, William. *Directions for the Government of the Tongue according to God's word*. Printed by John Legate, sold by Abraham Kitson. Cambridge, 1593.

Perkins, William. *Two Treatises: I. Of the nature and practise of repentance. II. Of the combat of the flesh and spirit*. Cambridge, 1593.

Pettie, George, trans. *The Ciuile Conuersation of M. Stephen Guazzo* [Book 4 trans. Bartholomew Young], introd. Sir Edward Sullivan. Tudor Translations. Constable; New York: Alfred A. Knopf, 1925.

Playes written by the thrice noble, illustrious and excellent princess, the Lady Marchioness of Newcastle. 1662.

Plutarch's Lives of the Noble Grecians and Romans, Englished by Sir Thomas North, ed. W. E. Henley. 6 vols. 1896.

Proctor, John. *The Fall of the Late Arrian.* 1549.

Publilius Syrus. In *Minor Latin Poets*, ed. and trans. J. Wight Duff and Arnold M. Duff. Heinemann; Cambridge, MA: Harvard University Press, 1934.

Quintilian, *The Institutio Oratoria of Quintilian*, trans. H. E. Butler. 4 vols. Heinemann; Cambridge, MA: Harvard University Press, 1969.

REED Cambridge, ed. Alan H. Nelson. 2 vols. Toronto: University of Toronto Press, 1989.

REED Inns of Court, ed. John R. Elliott and Alan H. Nelson. Cambridge: D. S. Brewer, 2010.

REED Oxford, ed. John R. Elliott et al. 2 vols. Toronto: British Library/University of Toronto Press, 2004.

Relacion de la Iornada del Excelentissimo Condestable de Castilla, a las Pazes entre Hespaña y Inglaterra, que se concluyeron y juraron en Londres, por el mes de Agosto, Año M. DC. IIII. Milan, 1605.

Roscio, I. L.[John Lowin?]. *Conclusions upon Dances, both of this age, and of the olde. Newly composed and set forth, by an Out-landish Doctor.* John Orphinstrange, 1607; ed. Rick Bowers as *John Lowin and Conclusions upon Dances (1607).* Garland Publishing, 1988.

Rowe, Nicholas. "Some Account of the Life &c of Mr. William Shakespear," in D. Nicol Smith, ed., *Eighteenth Century Essays on Shakespeare.* Glasgow, 1903.

Savage, Francis. *A Conference betwixt a Mother a Devout Recusant, and her Sonne a zealous Protestant, seeking by humble and dutifull satisfaction to winne her vnto the trueth, and publike worship of god established nowe in England.* Cambridge, 1600.

Selimus (The Tragical Reign of Selimus), ed. W. Bang. Oxford: Malone Society Reprints, 1908.

The serpent of deuision VVherein is conteined the true history or mappe of Romes ouerthrowe, gouerned by auarice, enuye, and pride, the decaye of empires be they neuer so sure. Whereunto is annexed the tragedye of Gorboduc, sometime king of this land, and of his two sonnes, Ferrex and Porrex. Set foorth as the same was shewed before the Queenes most excellent Maiesty, by the Gentlemen of the Inner Temple. 1590.

Shakespeare in the Public Records Office, ed. David Thomas. HMSO, 1985.

Sidney, Philip. *An Apology for Poetry, or the Defence of Poesy*, ed. Geoffrey Shepherd, rev. R. W. Maslen. Manchester: Manchester University Press, 2002.

Sidney, Philip. *The Countess of Pembroke's Arcadia*, in *The Prose Works of Sir Philip Sidney*, ed. Albert Feuillerat. 1912; Cambridge: Cambridge University Press, 1965.

[Southwell, Robert]. *Saint Peter's Complaint, with other Poëms.* Edinburgh [1600].

Spenser, Edmund. *Poetical Works.* Oxford University Press, 1961.

Stratford-upon-Avon Inventories 1580–1699. Vol. 1: *1538–1625*, ed. Jeanne Jones. Dugdale Society, in association with the Shakespeare Birthplace Trust, 2002.

Stubbes, Philip. *The Anatomie of Abuses*, ed. Margaret Jane Kidnie. Tempe, AZ: Renaissance English Text Society, 2002.

Surrey, Henry Howard, Earl of. *Certain Bokes of Virgiles Aenaeis turned into English meter by the right honorable lorde, Henry Earle of Surrey.* 1557.

The Taming of a Shrew: The 1594 Quarto, ed. Stephen Roy Miller. Cambridge, 1998.

Tasso, Torquato. *Godfrey of Bulloigne*, trans. Edward Fairfax, ed. Kathleen M. Lea and T. M. Gang. Oxford: Clarendon Press, 1981.

The Three Parnassus Plays (1598–1601), ed. J. B. Leishman. Ivor Nicholson & Watson, 1949.

Tofte, Robert. *The Poetry of Robert Tofte 1597–1620: A Critical Old-Spelling Edition*, ed. Jeffrey N. Nelson. New York: Garland, 1994.

Tottel's Miscellany (1557–87), ed. Hyder Edward Rollins. 2 vols. Cambridge, MA: Harvard University Press, 1928, 1929.

Virgil. *Aeneid*, trans. H. R. Fairclough. Loeb Classics. Cambridge, MA: Harvard University Press, 1978.

Virgil. *The Pastoral Poems*, trans. E. V. Rieu. Harmondsworth: Penguin, 1949.

Virgil. *The whole xii. Bookes of the Aeneidos of Virgill*, trans. Thomas Phaer. 1573.

W.W. (trans.). *The Menaechmus*.

Wallace, C. W. *C. W. Wallace Papers*. San Marino, CA: Huntington Library.

Webbe, William. *A Discourse of English Poetrie, together with the Authors Iudgment, touching the reformation of our English Verse* (1586). In *Elizabethan Critical Essays*, ed. G. Gregory Smith. 2 vols. Oxford, 1904. 1: 226–302.

Whetstone, George. *The right excellent and famous historye, of Promos and Cassandra deuided into two commicall discourses*. 1578.

Weever, John. *Faunus and Melliflora, or, the Original of Our English Satyres*. 1600. *See also under* Honigmann *below*

Weever, John. *The Mirror of Martyrs, or, The Life and Death of that Thrice Valiant Captaine, and Most Godly Martyre, Sir John Oldcastle, Knight, Lord Cobham*. 1601.

[Weever, John]. *The Whipping of the satyre*, ed. A. Davenport. Liverpool: University Press of Liverpool, 1951.

Willobie His Avisa, ed. Charles Hughes. Sherratt & Hughes, 1904.

Wilson, Robert. *The Cobler's Prophecy* (1594), ed. A. C. Wood, Malone Society Reprint, 1914.

Wotton, Henry. *Reliquiae Wottonianae*, 4th edn. 1685.

[Wright, Thomas]. *Certaine Articles or Forcible Reasons Discouering the palpable absurdities, and most notorious errour of the Protestants Religion*. Antwerp, 1600.

Critical and Historical Scholarship

Acheson, Arthur. *Mistress Davenant: The Dark Lady of Shakespeare's Sonnets*. Bernard Quaritch; New York: Walter M. Hill, 1913.

Ackroyd, Peter. *Shakespeare: The Biography*. Chatto & Windus, 2005.

Adelman, Janet. *The Common Liar: an Essay on Antony and Cleopatra*. New Haven: Yale University Press, 1973.

Akrigg, G. P. V. *Shakespeare and the Earl of Southampton*. Hamish Hamilton, 1968.

Albright, Evelyn May. "*The Faerie Queene* in Masque at the Gray's Inn Revels," *PMLA* 41 (1926), 497–516.

Alcock, N. W., with Robert Bearman. "Discovering Mary Arden's House: Property and Society in Wimcote, Warwickshire," *SQ* 53 (Spring 2002), 53–94.

Alexander, Peter. *Shakespeare's Henry VI and Richard II.* Cambridge: Cambridge University Press, 1929.

Allen, Ned B. "The Two Parts of *Othello,*" *SS* 21 (1968), 13–26.

Anderegg, Michael A. "The Tradition of Early More Biography", in R. S. Sylvester and G. P. Marc'hadour, eds., *Essential Articles for the Study of Thomas More.* Hamden, CT: Archon Books, 1977.

Arlidge, Anthony. *Shakespeare and the Prince of Love: The Feast of Misrule in the Middle Temple.* DLM, 2000.

Astington, John H. *Actors and Acting in Shakespeare's Time: The Art of Stage Playing.* Cambridge: Cambridge University Press, 2010.

Auden, W. H. *The Dyer's Hand and Other Essays.* New York: Random House, 1962.

Auden, W. H. *The Sea and the Mirror: A Commentary on Shakespeare's "The Tempest",* in *Collected Longer Poems.* Faber & Faber, 1968.

Axton, Marie. *The Queen's Two Bodies: Drama and the Elizabethan Succession.* Royal Historical Society, 1977.

Baker, J. H. *An Introduction to English Legal History.* 2nd edn. Butterworths, 1979.

Baker, Susan. "Shakespearean Authority in the Classic Detective Story," *SQ* 16 (1995), 424–48.

Baldwin, T. W. *Shakspere's "Love's Labor's Won": New Evidence from the Account Books of an Elizabethan Bookseller.* Carbondale: Southern Illinois University Press, 1957.

Baldwin, T. W. *William Shakespeare's Small Latine & Lesse Greeke.* 2 vols. Urbana: University of Illinois Press, 1944.

Barroll, Leeds. *Politics, Plague, and Shakespeare's Theater: The Stuart Years.* Ithaca, NY: Cornell University Press, 1991.

Barton, Anne. *Ben Jonson, Dramatist.* Cambridge: Cambridge University Press, 1984.

Bate, Jonathan. *The Genius of Shakespeare.* Picador, 1997.

Bate, Jonathan. *Soul of the Age: The Life, Mind, and World of William Shakespeare.* Viking Penguin, 2008.

Bearman, Robert. "John Shakespeare: A Papist or Penniless?," *SQ* 56/4 (2005), 411–33.

Bednarz, James P. *Shakespeare & the Poets' War.* New York: Columbia University Press, 2000.

Belsey, Catherine. "Shakespeare's Little Boys: Theatrical Apprenticeship and the Construction of Childhood," in Brian Reynolds and William N. West, eds., *Rematerializing Shakespeare: Authority and Representation on the Early Modern Stage.* Houndmills: Palgrave Macmillan, 2005.

Benbow, R. Mark. "Dutton and Goffe versus Broughton: A Disputed Contract for Plays in the 1570s," *REED Newsletter* 3 (1981), 3–9.

Bentley, Gerard Eades. *Shakespeare and Jonson: Their Reputations in the Seventeenth Century Compared.* 2 vols. in 1. 1945; Chicago: University of Chicago Press, 1965.

Berger, Harry, Jr. *Imaginary Audition: Shakespeare on Stage and Page.* Berkeley: University of California Press, 1990.

Bergeron, David M. *King James & Letters of Homoerotic Desire.* Iowa City: University of Iowa Press, 1999.

Bevington, David. *Shakespeare and Biography*. Oxford: Oxford University Press, 2010.

Bevington, David. *Shakespeare: The Seven Ages of Human Experience*. Oxford: Blackwell, 2002.

Bevington, David, and David L.Smith. "James I and *Timon of Athens*," *Comparative Drama* (1999), 56–87.

Blayney, Peter W. M. "'The Booke of Sir Thomas Moore' Re-Examined," *Studies in Philology* 69/2 (1972), 167–91.

Blayney, Peter W. M. *The First Folio of Shakespeare*. Washington, DC: Folger Shakespeare Library, 1991.

Blayney, Peter W. M. "The Publication of Playbooks," in John D. Cox and David Scott Kastan, eds., *A New History of Early English Drama*. New York: Columbia University Press, 1997.

Bloom, Harold. *Shakespeare: The Invention of the Human*. Fourth Estate, 1999.

Bloom, Harold. *The Anatomy of Influence: Literature as a Way of Life*. New Haven: Yale University Press, 2011.

Bolgar, R. R. *The Classical Heritage and its Beneficiaries*. Cambridge: Cambridge University Press, 1954.

Boughner, Daniel C. "Sir Toby's Cockatrice," *Italica* 20/4 (1943), 171–2.

Bradbrook, M. C. *The Rise of the Common Player: A Study of Actor and Society in Shakespeare's England*. Cambridge, MA: Harvard University Press, 1962.

Bradley, A. C. *Shakespearean Tragedy*. Macmillan, 1951.

Brady, Jennifer, and W. H. Herendeen, eds., *Ben Jonson's 1616 Folio*. Newark: University of Delaware Press, 1991.

Brau, Lorie. "The Women's Theatre of Takarazuka," *Tulane Drama Review* 34/4 (Winter 1990), 79–95.

Braunmuller, A. R. *George Peele*. Boston: Twayne, 1983.

Brennan, Michael J., and Noel J. Kinnamon. *A Sidney Chronology 1554–1654*. Houndmills: Palgrave Macmillan, 2003.

Brinkworth, E. R. C. *Shakespeare and the Bawdy Court of Stratford*. Phillimore, 1972.

Bromley, G. W. *Baptism and the Anglican Reformers*. Lutterworth Press, 1953.

Brooke, Nicholas. *Shakespeare's Early Tragedies*. Methuen, 1968.

Brooks, C. W. *Pettyfoggers and Vipers of the Commonwealth: The "Lower Branch" of the Legal Profession in Early Modern England*. Cambridge: Cambridge University Press, 1986.

Brower, Reuben. *Hero and Saint: Shakespeare and the Graeco-Roman Heroic Tradition*. New York: Oxford University Press, 1971.

Brownlow, F. W. *Shakespeare, Harsnett, and the Devils of Denham*. Newark: University of Delaware Press and Associated University Presses, 1993.

Burgess, Anthony. *Nothing Like the Sun: A Story of Shakespeare's Love-Life*. New York: Norton, 1964.

Burgess, Anthony. *Shakespeare*. New York: A. A. Knopf, 1970; repr. Chicago: Elephant Paperbacks, 1994.

Burkhart, Robert E. "The Playing Space in the Halls of the Inns of Court," *South Atlantic Review* 56/4 (Nov. 1991), 1–5.

Butler, E. M. *The Myth of the Magus*. Cambridge: Cambridge University Press, 1948; repr. Westport, CT: Hyperion, 1979.

Campbell, Gordon. "Shakespeare and the Youth of Milton," *Milton Quarterly* 33 (1999), 95–105.

Capp, Bernard. *When Gossips Meet: Women, Family, and Neighborhood in Early Modern England*. Oxford: Oxford University Press, 2003.

Carney, James. *The Irish Bardic Poet: A Study of the Relationship of Poet and Patron as Exemplified in the Persons of the Poet, Eochaidh O hEoghusa (O'Hussey) and his Various Patrons, Mainly Members of the Maguire Family of Fermanagh*. Dublin: Institute for Advanced Studies, 1967.

Carroll, D. Allen."Who Wrote *Greenes Groats-worth of Witte* (1592)?," *Renaissance Papers 1992*, ed. George Walton Williams and Barbara J. Baines (1993), 69–77.

Carson, Neil. *A Companion to Henslowe's Diary*. Cambridge: Cambridge University Press, 1988.

Cerasano, S. P. "Edward Alleyn's 'Retirement' 1597–1600," *Medieval and Renaissance Drama in England* 10 (1998), 98–112.

Cerasano, S. P. "Philip Henslowe and the Elizabethan Court," *SS* 60 (2007), 49–57.

Chambers, E. K. *The Elizabethan Stage*. 4 vols. Oxford: Clarendon Press, 1923.

Chambers, E. K. *William Shakespeare*. 2 vols. Oxford: Clarendon Press, 1930.

Chambers, E. K., and W. W. Greg, eds. "Dramatic Records from the Lansdowne MSS," in *Collections 1:2*. Oxford: Malone Society, 1908.

Champion, Pierre. *François Villon: Sa vie et son temps*. 2 vols. Paris: Honoré Champion, 1933.

Cheney, C. R., ed. *A Handbook of Dates for Students of British History*. New edn., rev. Michael Jones. Cambridge: Cambridge University Press, 2000.

Cheney, Patrick. *Shakespeare, National Poet-Playwright*. Cambridge: Cambridge University Press, 2004.

Cheney, Patrick. *Shakespeare's Literary Authorship*. Cambridge: Cambridge University Press, 2008.

Cheney, Patrick, and Frederick A. de Armas, eds., *European Literary Careers: The Author from Antiquity to the Renaissance*. Toronto: University of Toronto Press, 2002.

Chernaik, Warren. *The Myth of Rome in Shakespeare and His Contemporaries*. Cambridge: Cambridge University Press, 2011.

Christian, Mildred Gayler. "Middleton's Acquaintance with the Merrie Conceited Jests of George Peele," *PMLA* 50 (1935), 753–60.

Clarkson, Paul S., and Clyde T. Warren. *The Law of Property in Shakespeare and the Elizabethan Drama*. Baltimore: Johns Hopkins University Press, 1942.

Clayton, Tom, Susan Brock, and Vicente Forés, eds. *Shakespeare and the Mediterranean: The Selected Proceedings of the International Shakespeare Association World Congress, Valencia, 2001*. Newark: University of Delaware Press, 2004.

Cobbe, Alec, Alastair Laing, and Stanley Wells. "Shakespeare to the Life," in Stanley Wells, ed., *Shakespeare Found! A Life Portrait at Last: Portraits, Poet, Patron, Poems* (Stratford-upon-Avon: Cobbe Foundation/Shakespeare Birthplace Trust, 2009).

Collinson, Patrick. "Cranbrook and the Fletchers: Popular and Unpopular Religion in the Kentish Weald," in Peter Newman Brooks, ed., *Reformation Principle and Practice: Essays in Honor of Arthur Geoffrey Dickens*. Scolar Press, 1980.

Collinson, Patrick. *The Religion of Protestants: The Church in English Society 1559–1625*. Oxford: Clarendon Press, 1982.

Comparetti, Domenico. *Virgil in the Middle Ages* (1885), trans. E. F. M. Benecke, introd. Jan M. Ziolkowski. Princeton, NJ: Princeton University Press, 1997.

Cooper, Helen. "Guy of Warwick, Upstart Crows and Mounting Sparrows," in Takashi Kozuka and J. R. Mulryne, eds., *Shakespeare, Marlowe, Jonson: New Directions in Biography*. Aldershot: Ashgate, 2006.

Cooper, Tarnya. *Searching for Shakespeare*. Yale University Press, 2006.

Cox, John D., and David Scott Kastan, eds. *A New History of Early English Drama*. New York: Columbia University Press, 1997.

Craig, Hugh. "Shakespeare's Vocabulary: Myth or Reality?" *SQ* 62/1 (2011), 53–74.

Craig, Hugh, and Arthur F. Kinney, eds. *Shakespeare, Computers, and the Mystery of Authorship*. Cambridge, Cambridge University Press, 2009.

Crane, Mary Thomas. *Framing Authority: Sayings, Self, and Society in Sixteenth-Century England*. Princeton, NJ: Princeton University Press, 1993.

Crawford, Charles. "*Belvedere, or the Garden of the Muses*," *Englische Studien* 43 (1910–11), 198–228.

Cressy, David. *Birth, Marriage, and Death: Ritual Religion, and the Life-Cycle in Tudor and Stuart England*. Oxford: Oxford University Press, 1997.

Cressy, David, ed., *Education in Tudor and Stuart England*. New York: St. Martin's Press, 1975.

Croft, Pauline. "Robert Cecil and the Early Jacobean Court," in Linda Levy Peck, ed., *The Mental World of the Jacobean Court*. Cambridge: Cambridge University Press, 1991.

Cruttwell, Patrick. *The Shakespearean Moment and its Place in the Poetry of the 17th Century*. Chatto & Windus, 1954.

Culliford, S. G. *William Strachey 1572–1621*. Charlottesville: University Press of Virginia, 1965.

Curling, [Henry], Captain. *The Forest Youth, or, Shakspere as He Lived*. Eli Charles Eginton, 1838.

Curran, Kevin. *Marriage, Performance, and Politics at the Jacobean Court*. Farnham, Surrey: Ashgate, 2009.

Davidson, Clifford. *The Guild Chapel Wall Paintings at Stratford-upon-Avon*. New York: AMS Press, 1988.

Dawson, A. B. "Tempest in a Teapot," in Maurice Charney, ed., *Bad Shakespeare: Revaluations of the Shakespeare Canon*. Rutherford, NJ: Fairleigh Dickinson Press, 1988.

De Chambrun, C. Longworth. *My Shakespeare, Rise! Recollections of John Lacy, one of his majesty's players*. Stratford: Shakespeare Press; J. B. Lippincott, 1935.

De Grazia, Margreta. *Hamlet without Hamlet*. Cambridge: Cambridge University Press, 2007.

De Grazia, Margreta, Maureen Quilligan, and Peter Stallybrass, eds., *Subject and Object in Renaissance Culture*. Cambridge: Cambridge University Press, 1996.

de Luna, B. N. *The Queen Declined: An Interpretation of Willobie His Avisa*. Oxford: Clarendon Press, 1970.

De Young, Jim, and John Miller. *London Theatre Walks: Thirteen Dramatic Tours through Four Centuries of History and Legend*. New York: Applause Books, rev. edn. 2003.

Dent, R. W. *John Webster's Borrowing*. Berkeley: University of California Press, 1960.

Dobson, Michael. *Shakespeare and Amateur Performance*. Cambridge: Cambridge University Press, 2011.

Doran, Susan. *Monarchy and Matrimony: The Courtships of Elizabeth I*. Routledge, 1996.

Dowden, Edward.Introduction to *The Passionate Pilgrim* facsimile by William Griggs. W. Griggs, 1880–91.

Dubrow, Heather. "'Incertainties now crown themselves assur'd': The Politics of Plotting Shakespeare's Sonnets," *Shakespeare Quarterly* 47/3 (1996), 291–305.

Duncan-Jones, Katherine. "A Companion for a King? Shakespeare's Status Anxiety," *TLS* (14 Apr. 2006), 14–15.

Duncan-Jones, Katherine. "Fame in a Feigned Oval," review of "Searching for Shakespeare" exhibition and catalogue, National Portrait Gallery, *TLS*, 17 Mar. 2006, 16–17.

Duncan-Jones, Katherine. "Jonson's Epitaph on Nashe," *TLS*, 7 July 1995, 4–6.

Duncan-Jones, Katherine. "Much Ado with Red and White: The Earliest Readers of Shakespeare's *Venus and Adonis* (1593)," *RES* 44 (Nov. 1993), 479–501.

Duncan-Jones, Katherine. "Retired from the Scene: Did William Kemp Live on as 'Lady Hunsdon's Man'?," *TLS*, 13 Aug. 2010, 13–15.

Duncan-Jones, Katherine. *Shakespeare: An Ungentle Life*. Arden Shakespeare, 2010.

Duncan-Jones, Katherine. "Shakespeare the Motley Player," *RES* 60 (2009), 723–43.

Duncan-Jones, Katherine. *Shakespeare: Upstart Crow to Sweet Swan, 1592–1623*. Arden Shakespeare, 2011.

Duncan-Jones, Katherine. *Ungentle Shakespeare: Scenes from His Life*. Arden Shakespeare, 2001.

Dutton, Richard. "Censorship," in John D. Cox and David Scott Kastan, eds., *A New History of Early English Drama*. New York: Columbia University Press, 1997.

Dutton, Richard. *Mastering the Revels: The Regulation and Censorship of English Renaissance Drama*. Iowa City: University of Iowa Press, 1991.

Dutton, Richard. "'Methinks the truth should live from age to age': The Dating and Contexts of Henry V," *Huntington Library Quarterly* 68/1–2 (2005), 173–204.

Dutton, Richard, ed. *The Oxford Handbook of Early Modern Theatre*. Oxford: Oxford University Press, 2009.

Dutton, Richard. "The Revels Office and the Boy Companies, 1600–1613: New Perspectives," *English Literary Renaissance* 32/2 (2002), 324–51.

Dutton, Richard, "Shakespearean Origins," in Takashi Kozuka and J. R. Mulryne, eds., *Shakespeare, Marlowe, Jonson: New Directions in Biography*. Aldershot: Ashgate, 2006.

Eccles, Christine. *The Rose Theatre*. Nick Hern Books, 1990.

Eccles, Mark. *Brief Lives*, special issue of *Studies in Philology* 79/4 (1982), 1–135.

Eccles, Mark. "Elizabethan Actors I: A–D," *N&Q* (Mar. 1991), 38–49.

Eccles, Mark. "Elizabethan Actors II: E– J," *N&Q* (Dec. 1991), 454–61.

Eccles, Mark. "Elizabethan Actors III: K–R," *N&Q* (Sept. 1992), 293–303.

Eccles, Mark. "Elizabethan Actors IV: S to End," *N&Q* (June 1993), 165–76.

Eccles, Mark. *Shakespeare in Warwickshire*. Madison: University of Wisconsin Press, 1961.

Edmond, Mary. *Rare Sir William Davenant*. Houndmills: Palgrave Macmillan, 1987.

Edmondson, Paul, and Stanley Wells. *Shakespeare's Sonnets*. Oxford: Oxford University Press, 2004.

Egan, Gabriel. *The Struggle for Shakespeare's Text: Twentieth-Century Editorial Theory and Practice*. Cambridge: Cambridge University Press, 2010.

Ellrodt, Robert. "Self-Consistency in Montaigne and Shakespeare," in Tom Clayton, Susan Brock, and Vicente Forés, eds., *Shakespeare and the Mediterranean: The Selected Proceedings of the International Shakespeare Association World Congress, Valencia, 2001*. Newark: University of Delaware Press, 2004.

Empson, William. *Essays on Shakespeare*, ed. David B. Pierie. Cambridge: Cambridge University Press, 1986.

Empson, William. *Seven Types of Ambiguity*. New York: New Directions, 1947.

Engle, Lars. "Watching Shakespeare Learn from Marlowe," in Peter Kanelos and Matt Kozusko, eds., *Thunder at a Playhouse: Essaying Shakespeare and the Early Modern Stage*. Selinsgrove: Susquehanna University Press, 2010.

Erne, Lukas. *Beyond "The Spanish Tragedy": A Study of the Works of Thomas Kyd*. Manchester: Manchester University Press, 2001.

Erne, Lukas. *Shakespeare as Literary Dramatist*. Cambridge: Cambridge University Press, 2003.

Farley-Hills, David. "How Often Did the Eyases Fly?," *N&Q* 38/4 (Dec. 1991), 461–6.

Faucit, Helena, Lady Martin. *On Some of Shakespeare's Female Characters*. Edinburgh: William Blackwood & Sons, 1891.

Fitzgerald, William. *Martial: The World of the Epigram*. Chicago: University of Chicago Press, 2007.

Freehafer, John. "Leonard Digges, Ben Jonson, and the Beginning of Shakespeare Idolatry," *SQ* 21/1 (1970), 63–75.

Freeman, Arthur. *Thomas Kyd: Facts and Problems*. Oxford: Clarendon Press, 1967.

Fripp, Edgar I. *Master Richard Quyny*. Oxford: Oxford University Press, 1924.

Fripp, Edgar I. *Shakespeare: Man and Artist*. Oxford: Oxford University Press, 1938.

Fripp, Edgar I. *Shakespeare Studies, Biographical and Literary*. Oxford: Oxford University Press, 1930.

Fripp, Edgar I. *Shakespeare's Haunts Near Stratford*. Oxford University Press, 1929.

Frost, David L. *The School of Shakespeare: The Influence of Shakespeare on English Drama 1600–42*. Cambridge: Cambridge University Press, 1968.

Frye, Roland Mushat. *The Renaissance Hamlet: Issues and Responses in 1600*. Princeton, NJ: Princeton University Press, 1984.

Gardner, Howard. *Art, Mind, and Brain: A Cognitive Approach to Creativity*. New York: Basic Books, 1982.

Gay, Edwin F. "The Midland Revolt and the Inquisitions of Depopulation of 1607," *Transactions of the Royal Historical Society*NS 18 (1904), 195–244.

Giddens, Eugene. "Editions and Editors," in Julie Sanders, ed., *Ben Jonson in Context*. Cambridge: Cambridge University Press, 2010.

Gill, Roma. "Christopher Marlowe," in A. C. Hamilton, ed., *The Spenser Encyclopedia*. Toronto: University of Toronto Press, 1990.

Goodare, Julian, and Michael Lynch, eds. *The Reign of James VI*. East Linton, East Lothian: Tuckwell Press, 2000.

Gray, J. W. *Shakespeare's Marriage, His Departure from Stratford, and Other Incidents in His Life*. Chapman & Hall, 1905.

Green, Martin. *Wriothesley's Roses in Shakespeare's Poems, Sonnets and Plays*. Baltimore: Clevedon Books, 1992.

Green, William. *Shakespeare's Merry Wives of Windsor*. Princeton, NJ: Princeton University Press, 1962.

Greenblatt, Stephen. *Hamlet in Purgatory*. Princeton, NJ: Princeton University Press, 2001.

Greenblatt, Stephen. *Shakespearean Negotiations: The Circulation of Social Energy in Renaissance England*. Berkeley: University of California Press, 1988.

Greenblatt, Stephen. *Will in the World: How Shakespeare Became Shakespeare*. New York: Norton, 2004.

Greenfield. Sayre N. "Quoting Hamlet in the Early Seventeenth Century," *Modern Philology* 105/3 (2008), 510–34.

Greer, Germaine. *Shakespeare's Wife*. Bloomsbury Books; New York: HarperCollins, 2007.

Greg, W. W. *A Bibliography of the English Printed Drama to the Restoration*. 4 vols. Bibliographical Society. Oxford University Press, 1939–59; repr. Scolar Press, 1970.

Gurr, Andrew. "The Date and the Expected Venue of *Romeo and Juliet*," *SS* 49 (1996), 15–25.

Gurr, Andrew. "Maximal and Minimal Texts: Shakespeare v. The Globe," *SS* 52 (1999), 68–87.

Gurr, Andrew. "Privy Councillors as Theatre Patrons," in Paul Whitfield White and Suzanne Westfall, eds., *Shakespeare and Theatrical Patronage*. Cambridge University Press, 2002.

Gurr, Andrew. *The Shakespeare Company, 1594–1642*. Cambridge: Cambridge University Press, 2004.

Gurr, Andrew. "Shakespeare's First Poem: Sonnet 145," *Essays in Criticism* 21 (1971), 221–6.

Gurr, Andrew, *The Shakespearian Playing Companies*. Oxford: Clarendon Press, 1996.

Gurr, Andrew. "Venues on the Verges: London's Theater Government between 1594 and 1614," *SQ* 61/4 (2010), 468–89.

Hamilton, A. C., ed. *The Spenser Encyclopedia*. Toronto: Toronto University Press, 1990.

Hamilton, Donna B. *Virgil and "The Tempest": The Politics of Imitation*. Columbus: Ohio State University Press, 1990.

Hammer, Paul E. J. *The Polarization of Elizabethan Politics: The Political Career of Robert Devereux, 2nd Earl of Essex, 1585–1597*. Cambridge: Cambridge University Press, 1999.

Hannay, Margaret P. *Philip's Phoenix: Mary Sidney, Countess of Pembroke*. New York: Oxford University Press, 1990.

Harbage, Alfred. *Annals of English Drama, 975–1700*, revised Samuel Schoenbaum; 3rd edn. revised Sylvia Stoller. Wagonheim. Routledge, 1989.

Harris, Jonathan Gil, and Natasha Korda, eds. *Staged Properties in Early Modern English Drama*. Cambridge: Cambridge University Press, 2002.

Hart, Alfred. *Shakespeare and the Homilies and Other Pieces of Research into the Elizabethan Drama*. Melbourne: Oxford University Press, 1924.

Hart, Moss. *Act One, an Autobiography*. New York: Random House, 1959.

Hattaway, Michael. *Elizabethan Popular Theatre: Plays in Performance*. Routledge & Kegan Paul, 1982.

Hebel, J. William. "The Surreptitious Edition of Michael Drayton's *Peirs Gaueston*," *The Library* (1923), 151–5.

Helbig, Jörg. "Cinematic Intertextuality in Contemporary Shakespeare Films," in *Sh@kespeare in the Media: From the Globe Theatre to the World Wide Web*. Frankfurt am Main: Peter Lang 2004; 2nd edn. 2010.

Herendeen, W. H. "Introduction: On Reading the 1616 Folio," in Jennifer Brady and W. H. Herendeen, eds., *Ben Jonson's 1616 Folio*. Newark: University of Delaware Press, 1991.

Highley, Christopher. "The Place of Scots in the Scottish Play," in Willy Maley and Andrew Murphy, eds., *Shakespeare and Scotland*. Manchester: Manchester University Press, 2004.

Hilský, Martin. "Translations of Politics/Politics of Translation: Czech Experience," in Irena R. Makaryk and Joseph G. Price, eds., *Shakespeare in the Worlds of Communism and Socialism*. Toronto: University of Toronto Press, 2006.

Hindle, Steve. "Dearth, Fasting and Alms: The Campaign for General Hospitality in Late Elizabethan England," *Past and Present* 171 (2001), 44–86.

Hirrel, Michael J. "Duration of Performances and Lengths of Plays: 'How Shall We Beguile the Lazy Time?'," *SQ* 61/2 (2010), 1–182.

Holland, Peter. "Theatre without Drama: Reading *REED*," in Peter Holland and Stephen Orgel, eds., *From Script to Stage in Early Modern England*. Houndmills: Palgrave Macmillan, 2004.

Holmes, Martin. *The Guns of Elsinore*. Chatto & Windus, 1964.

Honan, Park. *Shakespeare: A Life*. Oxford: Oxford University Press, 1998.

Honigmann, E. A. J. *John Weever: A Biography of a Literary Associate of Shakespeare and Jonson, together with Photographic Facsimile of Weever's "Epigrammes" (1599)*. Manchester: Manchester University Press, 1987.

Honigmann, E. A. J. *Shakespeare: The "Lost Years."* Manchester: Manchester University Press, 1985; 2nd edn. 1998.

Honigmann, E. A. J. "Shakespeare, *Sir Thomas More*, and Asylum Seekers," *SS* 57 (2004), 225–35.

Honigmann, E. A. J. *Shakespeare's Impact on His Contemporaries*. Houndmills: Macmillan, 1982.

Honigmann, E. A. J. "Shakespeare's Will and Testamentary Traditions," in Tetsuo Kishi, Roger Pringle, and Stanley Wells, eds., *Shakespeare and Cultural Traditions: The Selected Proceedings of the International Shakespeare Association World Congress, Tokyo 1991*. Newark: University of Delaware Press, 1994.

Honigmann, E. A. J., and Susan Brock, eds. *Playhouse Wills, 1558–1642: An Edition of Wills by Shakespeare and his Contemporaries in the London Theatre*. Manchester University Press, 1993.

Hope, Jonathan. *Shakespeare and Language: Reason, Eloquence and Artifice in the Renaissance.* Methuen, 2010.

Horne, David H. *The Life and Minor Works of George Peele.* New Haven: Yale University Press, 1952.

Hotson, Leslie. *The First Night of Twelfth Night.* Rupert Hart-Davis, 1954.

Hotson, Leslie. *I, William Shakespeare, do appoint Thomas Russell, Esquire . . .* Jonathan Cape, 1937.

Hotson, Leslie. *Shakespeare versus Shallow.* Nonesuch Press, 1931.

Houlbrooke, Ralph, ed. *James VI and I: Ideas, Authority, and Government.* Aldershot: Ashgate, 2006.

Howard, Jean E., and Phyllis Rackin. *Engendering a Nation: A Feminist Account of Shakespeare's English Histories.* Routledge, 1997.

Howarth, William D., ed. *French Theatre in the Neo-Classical Era, 1550–1789.* Cambridge: Cambridge University Press, 1997.

Howe, Michael J. A. *Genius Explained.* Cambridge: Cambridge University Press, 1999.

Hoy, Cyrus. "The Shares of Fletcher and his Collaborators in the Beaumont and Fletcher Canon," *Studies in Bibliography* 13 (1960), 77–108.

Hutson, Lorna. *The Invention of Suspicion: Law and Mimesis in Shakespeare and Renaissance Drama.* Oxford: Oxford University Press, 2007.

Hutton, James. "Analogues of Shakespeare's Sonnets 153–4: Contributions to the History of a Theme," *Modern Philology* 38/4 (May 1941), 385–403.

Ife, Barry W. "Cervantes and Shakespeare: Asymmetrical Considerations," in José Manuel Gonzalez and Clive A. Bellis, eds., *Cervantes and Shakespeare: New Interpretations and Comparative Studies.* Aldershot: Ashgate, forthcoming.

Ingram, William. *The Business of Playing: The Beginnings of the Adult Professional Theater in Elizabethan London.* Ithaca, NY: Cornell University Press, 1992.

Ingram, William. "Laurence Dutton, Stage Player: Missing and Presumed Lost," *Medieval and Renaissance Drama in England* 14 (2001), 122–43.

Jackson, MacD. P. "The Date and Authorship of Hand D's Contribution to *Sir Thomas More*: Evidence from 'Literature Online'," *SS* 59 (2006), 69–78.

Jackson, MacD. P. *Defining Shakespeare: Pericles as Test Case.* Oxford: Oxford University Press, 2003.

Jackson, MacD. P. "Francis Meres and the Cultural Context of Shakespeare's Rival Poet Sonnets," *RES* 56 (2005), 224–46.

Jackson, MacD. P. "New Research on the Dramatic Canon of Thomas Kyd," *Research Opportunities in Medieval and Renaissance Drama* 47 (2008), 107–27.

Jackson, MacD. P. "Shakespeare's *Richard II* and the Anonymous *Thomas of Woodstock*," *Medieval and Renaissance Drama in England* 14 (2001), 17–65.

Jackson, MacD. P. "Shakespeare's Sonnet cxi and John Davies of Hereford's 'Microcosmos' (1603)," *Modern Language Review* 102/1 (2007), 1–10.

Jackson, MacD. P. "Spurio and the Date of *All's Well That Ends Well*," *N&Q* 48/3 (2001), 298–9.

461

James, Henry. "The Birthplace," in *The Complete Tales of Henry James*, vol. 11 (1900–3), ed. Leon Edel. Philadelphia: J. B. Lippincott, 1954.

James, Henry. Introduction to *The Tempest*, in Sidney Lee, *Complete Works of William Shakespeare*. 1907.

Jenkins, Harold. *The Life and Work of Henry Chettle*. Sidgwick & Jackson, 1934.

Johnson, Samuel. *Johnson on Shakespeare*, ed. Arthur Sherbo. *The Works of Samuel Johnson*, vols. 7–8. New Haven: Yale University Press, 1968.

Jones, Emrys. *Scenic Form in Shakespeare*. Oxford: Clarendon Press, 1971.

Joseph, Harriet. *Shakespeare's Son-in-Law: John Hall, Man and Physician. With a Facsimile of Hall's "Select Observations on English Bodies."* Hamden, CT: Archon Books, 1964.

Jowett, John. "Notes on Henry Chettle," *RES* 45 (Nov. 1994), 517–22.

Jung, Carl G. *Answer to Job*, trans. R. F. C. Hull. Cleveland: World Publishing, 1960.

Kathman, David. "The Boys of Shakespeare's Company," in David Scott Kastan, ed., *A Companion to Shakespeare*. Forthcoming.

Kathman, David. "Grocers, Goldsmiths, and Drapers: Freemen and Apprentices in the Elizabethan Theater," *SQ* 55/1 (2004), 1–49.

Kathman, David. "Players, Livery Companies, and Apprentices," in Richard Dutton, ed., *Oxford Handbook of Early Modern Theatre*. Oxford: Oxford University Press, 2009.

Kathman, David. "Shakespeare's Stratford Friends," http://shakespeareauthorship.com/.

Kay, Dennis. *Shakespeare*. Sidgwick & Jackson; New York: William Morrow, 1992.

Kelliher, Hilton. "Contemporary Manuscript Extracts from Shakespeare's *Henry IV, Part I*," *English Manuscript Studies, 1100–1700* 1 (1989), 144–81.

Kelliher, Hilton. "Francis Beaumont and Nathan Field: New Records of Their Early Years," *English Manuscript Studies* 8 (2000), 1–42.

Kendall, R. "Richard Baines and Christopher Marlowe's Milieu," *English Literary Renaissance* 24 (1994), 507–52.

Kernan, Alvin. *Shakespeare, the King's Playwright: Theater in the Stuart Court 1603–1613*. New Haven: Yale University Press, 1995.

Kishi, Tetsuo. "'I know not what you mean by that': Shakespeare in Different Cultural Contexts," In Tetsuo Kishi, et al., eds., *Shakespeare and Cultural Traditions*.

Kishi, Tetsuo, Roger Pringle, and Stanley Wells, eds. *Shakespeare and Cultural Traditions: The Selected Proceedings of the International Shakespeare Association World Congress, Tokyo 1991*. Newark: University of Delaware Press, 1994.

Knowles, Richard. "How Shakespeare knew *King Leir*," *SS* 55 (2002), 12–35.

Knutson, Roslyn L. *The Repertory of Shakespeare's Company, 1594–1613*. Fayetteville: University of Arkansas Press, 1991.

Knutson, Roslyn. "What Was James Burbage *Thinking*??," in Peter Kanelos and Matt Kozusko, eds., *Thunder at a Playhouse: Essaying Shakespeare and the Early Modern Stage*. Selinsgrove: Susquehanna University Press, 2010.

Knutson, Roslyn L. "What's So Special about 1594?," *SQ* 61/4 (2010), 461–2.

Kott, Jan. *Shakespeare Our Contemporary*, trans. Bolesław Taborski. Methuen, 1967.

Kozuka, Takashi, and J. R. Mulryne, eds., *Shakespeare, Marlowe, Jonson: New Directions in Biography*. Aldershot: Ashgate, 2006.

Kuriyama, Constance. *Christopher Marlowe: A Renaissance Life*. Ithaca, NY: Cornell University Press, 2002.

Lacey, Robert. *Robert Earl of Essex: An Elizabethan Icarus*. Weidenfeld & Nicolson, 1971.

Lake, Peter. *Anglicans and Puritans? Presbyterianism and English Conformist Thought from Whitgift to Hooker*. Unwin Hyman, 1988.

Lamb, Charles. "The Sanity of True Genius," in *Elia and The Last Essays Of Elia*, ed. Jonathan Bate. Oxford: Oxford University Press, 1987.

Lane, Joan, ed. *John Hall and His Patients: The Medical Practice of Shakespeare's Son-in-Law*, with medical commentary by Melvin Earles. Shakespeare Birthplace Trust. Stratford-upon-Avon: Alan Sutton, 1996.

Law, Ernest. *Shakespeare as a Groom of the Chamber*. G. Bell & Sons, 1910.

Lawrence, Jason. *"Who the Devil Taught thee so much Italian?": Italian Language Learning and Literary Imitation in Early Modern England*. Manchester: Manchester University Press, 2005.

Leggatt, Alexander. "Shakespeare and Bearbaiting," in Tetsuo Kishi, Roger Pringle, and Stanley Wells, eds., *Shakespeare and Cultural Traditions: The Selected Proceedings of the International Shakespeare Association World Congress, Tokyo 1991*. Newark: University of Delaware Press, 1994.

Lewis, C. S. *English Literature in the Sixteenth Century, Excluding Drama*. Oxford: Clarendon Press, 1959.

Loomis, Albert J. "Toleration and Diplomacy: The Religious Issue in Anglo-Spanish Relations,1603–1605," *Transactions of the American Philosophical Society* NS 53/6 (Sept. 1963), 1–60.

Loomis, Catherine. *The Death of Elizabeth I: Remembering and Reconstructing the Virgin Queen*. Houndmills: Palgrave Macmillan, 2010.

Macdonald, Màiri. "A New Discovery about Shakespeare's Estate in Old Stratford," *SQ* 45 (1994), 87–9.

Mack, Peter. "Early Modern Ideas of Imagination: The Rhetorical Tradition," in Lodi Nauta and Detlev Pätzold, eds., *Imagination in the Later Middle Ages and Early Modern Times*. Louvaine: Peeters, 2004.

Mack, Peter. *Elizabethan Rhetoric: Theory and Practice*. Cambridge: Cambridge University Press, 2002.

Maclean, Sally-Beth. "Adult Playing Companies 1583–1593," in Richard Dutton, ed., *The Oxford Handbook of Early Modern Theatre*. Oxford: Oxford University Press, 2009.

Magnusson, Lynne. "Scoff Power in *Love's Labour's Lost* and the Inns of Court: Language in Context," *SS* 57 (2004), 196–208.

Maguire, Laurie. *Shakespeare's Names*. Oxford: Oxford University Press, 2007.

Makaryk, Irena R., and Joseph G. Price, ed. *Shakespeare in the Worlds of Communism and Socialism*. Toronto: University of Toronto Press, 2006.

Maley, Willy, and Andrew Murphy, eds. *Shakespeare and Scotland*. Manchester: Manchester University Press, 2004.

Manley, Lawrence. "From Strange's Men to Pembroke's Men: *2 Henry VI* and *The First Part of the Contention*," *SQ* 54/3 (2003), 253–87.

Marcham, Frank. *William Shakespeare and his Daughter Susannah*. Grafton, 1931.

Marino, James J. "The Anachronistic *Shrews*," *SQ* 60/1 (2009), 25–46.

Marino, James J. *Owning William Shakespeare: The King's Men and Their Intellectual Property*. Philadelphia: University of Pennsylvania Press, 2011.

Marotti, Arthur. *Manuscript, Print, and the English Renaissance Lyric*. Ithaca, NY: Cornell University Press, 1995.

Marrapodi, Michele. "The 'Woman as Wonder' Trope: from *Commedia Grave* to Shakespeare's *Pericles* and the Late Plays," in Michele Marrapodi, ed., *Shakespeare and Renaissance Literary Theories: Anglo-Italian Transactions*. Farnham, Surrey: Ashgate, 2011.

Martin, Randall, and John D. Cox, "Who is 'Somerfille' in *3 Henry VI*?," *SQ* 51 (2000), 332–52.

Masten, Jeffrey. "Playwriting: Authorship and Collaboration," in John D. Cox and David Scott Kastan, eds., *A New History of Early English Drama*. New York: Columbia University Press, 1997.

Matchett, William H. *The Phoenix and the Turtle: Shakespeare's Poem and Chester's Love's Martyr*. Paris: Mouton, 1965.

Mateer, David. "New Sightings of Christopher Marlowe in London," *Early Theatre* 11/2 (2008), 13–38.

Matus, Irvin. *Shakespeare in Fact*. New York: Continuum, 1994.

Maus, Katharine Eisaman. *Inwardness and Theater in the English Renaissance*. Chicago: University of Chicago Press, 1995.

Maxwell, Baldwin. *Studies in the Shakespeare Apocrypha*. New York: Columbia University Press, 1956.

McCabe, Richard A. "Elizabethan Satire and the Bishops' Ban of 1599," *Yearbook of English Studies* 11 (1981), 188–93.

McCarthy, Jeanne H. "The Queen's 'Unfledged Minions': An Alternate Account of the Origins of Blackfriars and of the Boy Company Phenomenon," in Paul Menzer, ed., *Inside Shakespeare: Essays on the Blackfriars Stage*. Selinsgrove: Susquehanna University Press, 2006.

McDonald, Russ. *Shakespeare's Late Style*. Cambridge: Cambridge University Press, 2006.

McLuskie, Kathleen. "The Patriarchal Bard: Feminist Criticism and Shakespeare: *King Lear* and *Measure for Measure*," in Jonathan Dollimore and Alan Sinfield, eds., *Political Shakespeares: Essays in Cultural Materialism*. Manchester: Manchester University Press, 1985; 2nd edn. 1994.

McMillin, Scott. "Casting for Pembroke's Men," *SQ* 23 (1972), 141–59.

McMillin, Scott, ed. *Henry IV, Part One*. Shakespeare in Performance. Manchester: Manchester University Press, 1991.

McMillin, Scott. "The Sharer and His Boy: Rehearsing Shakespeare's Women," in Peter Holland and Stephen Orgel, eds., *From Script to Stage in Early Modern England*. Houndmills: Palgrave Macmillan, 2004.

McMillin, Scott, and Sally-Beth MacLean, *The Queen's Men and Their Plays*. Cambridge: Cambridge University Press, 1998.

McMullan, Gordon. *The Politics of Unease in the Plays of John Fletcher*. Amherst: University of Massachusetts Press, 1994.

Melchiori, Giorgio. *Shakespeare's Garter Plays: "Edward III" to "Merry Wives of Windsor"*. Newark: University of Delaware Press; Associated University Presses, 1994.

Menzer, Paul, ed. *Inside Shakespeare: Essays on the Blackfriars Stage*. Selinsgrove: Susquehanna University Press, 2006.

Morgan, Paul. "'Our Will Shakespeare' and Lope de Vega: An Unrecorded Contemporary Document," *SS* 16 (1963), 118–20.

[Morgann, Maurice]. *An Essay on the Dramatic Character of Sir John Falstaff*. 1777.

Moss, Ann. *Printed Commonplace-Books and the Structuring of Renaissance Thought*. Oxford: Clarendon Press, 1996.

Muldrew, Craig. *The Economy of Obligation: The Culture of Credit and Social Relations in Early Modern England*. Houndmills: St. Martin's Press, 1998.

Nebel, Cecile. *The Dark Side of Creativity: Blocks, Unfinished Works and the Urge to Destroy*. Troy, NY: Whitston Publishing, 1988.

Nelson, Alan H. "Calling All (Shakespeare) Biographers! or, A Plea for Documentary Discipline," in Takashi Kozuka and J. R. Mulryne, eds., *Shakespeare, Marlowe, Jonson*. Aldershot: Ashgate, 2006.

Nelson, Alan H. "George Buc, William Shakespeare, and the Folger *George a Greene*," *SQ* 48 (Spring 1998), 74–83.

Nelson, Alan H. *Monstrous Adversary: The Life of Edward de Vere, 17th Earl of Oxford*. Liverpool: Liverpool University Press, 2003.

Nelson, Alan H. "The Universities and the Inns of Court," in Richard Dutton, ed., *The Oxford Handbook of Early Modern Theatre*. Oxford: Oxford University Press, 2009.

Nelson, Alan H., and Paul H. Altrocchi, "William Shakespeare, 'Our Roscius'," *SQ* 60/4 (2009), 460–9.

Nettle, Daniel. *Strong Imagination: Madness, Creativity and Human Nature*. Oxford: Oxford University Press, 2001.

Newcomb, Lori Humphrey. *Reading Popular Romance in Early Modern England*. New York: Columbia University Press, 2002.

Newdigate, Bernard H. *Michael Drayton and His Circle*. Oxford: Basil Blackwell, 1941.

Newton, Diana. *The Making of the Jacobean Regime: James VI and I and the Government of England 1603–1605*. Royal Historical Society. Woodbridge: Boydell, 2005.

Nicholl, Charles. *A Cup of News: The Life of Thomas Nashe*. Routledge & Kegan Paul, 1984.

Nicholl, Charles. *The Lodger Shakespeare: His Life on Silver Street*. New York: Viking, 2007.

Nicholl, Charles. *The Reckoning: The Murder of Christopher Marlowe*. Jonathan Cape, 1992.

Nuttall, A. D. *Shakespeare the Thinker*. New Haven: Yale University Press, 2007.

Orrell, John. "The Theatres," in John D. Cox and David Scott Kastan, eds., *A New History of Early English Drama*. New York: Columbia University Press, 1997.

Palmer, Barbara D. "Playing in the Provinces: Front or Back Door?," in S. P. Cerasano, ed., *Medieval and Renaissance Drama in England* 22. Madison: Fairleigh Dickinson University Press, 2009.

Paris, Jean. *Hamlet, ou les personnages du fils*. Paris: Éditions du Seuil, 1953.

Parker, Patricia. *Literary Fat Ladies: Rhetoric, Gender, Property*. Methuen, 1987.

Pearlman, E. "The Invention of Richard of Gloucester," *SQ* 43/4 (1992), 410–29.

Peck, Linda Levy, ed. *The Mental World of the Jacobean Court*. Cambridge: Cambridge University Press, 1991.

Peck, Linda Levy. *Northampton: Patronage and Policy in the Court of James I*. George Allen & Unwin, 1982.

Pointon, Marcia. "National Identity and the Afterlife of Shakespeare's Portraits," in Tarnya Cooper, ed., *Searching for Shakespeare*. National Portrait Gallery, 2006.

Pollard, A. W. *Shakespeare's Folios and Quartos*. 1909.

Potter, Lois. "Editing Desdemona," in Ann Thompson and Gordon McMullan, eds., *In Arden: Editing Shakespeare: Essays in Honour of Richard Proudfoot*. Arden Shakespeare, 2003.

Potter, Lois. "Nobody's Perfect: Actors' Memories as a Factor in Shakespeare's Plays of the 1590s," *SS* 42 (1989), 85–97.

Pressly, William L. *A Catalogue of Paintings in the Folger Shakespeare Library*. New Haven: Yale University Press, 1993.

Prior, Roger. "George Wilkins and the Young Heir," *SS* 29 (1976), 33–9.

Prior, Roger. "The Life of George Wilkins," *SS* 25 (1972), 137–52.

Prockter, Adrian, and Robert Taylor. *The A to Z of Elizabethan London*. Lympne Castle, Kent: Harry Margary; Guildhall Library, 1979.

Puddlephat, Wilfrid. "The Mural Paintings of the Dance of Death in the Guild Chapel of Stratford-upon-Avon," *Transactions of Birmingham Archeological Society* 76 (1956), 29–35.

Rasmussen, Eric. "Collaboration: The Determination of Authorship," in Suzanne Gossett, ed., *Thomas Middleton in Context*. Cambridge: Cambridge University Press, 2011.

Reed, Henry. "The Great Desire I Had," in *The Streets of Pompeii and Other Plays for Radio*. BBC, 1971.

Rhodes, Neil. "'Wrapped in the strong arms of the Union': Shakespeare and King James," in Willy Maley and Andrew Murphy, eds., *Shakespeare and Scotland*. Manchester: Manchester University Press, 2004.

Richmond, Velma Bourgeois. *The Legend of Guy of Warwick*. New York: Garland, 1996.

Rickard, Jane. *Authorship and Authority: The Writings of James VI and I*. Manchester: Manchester University Press, 2007.

Riddell, James A. "Some Actors in Ben Jonson's Plays," *Shakespeare Studies* 5 (1969), 285–98.

Riggs, David. *Ben Jonson: A Life*. Cambridge, MA: Harvard University Press, 1989.

Riggs, David. *The World of Christopher Marlowe*. Houndmills: Macmillan, 2006.

Rintoul, David. "King Edward III," in Robert Smallwood (ed.), *Players of Shakespeare 6*. Cambridge: Cambridge University Press, 2004.

Roach, Joseph. *The Player's Passion: Studies in the Science of Acting*. Newark: University of Delaware Press, 1985.

Roberts, Peter R. "The Business of Playing and the Patronage of Players at the Jacobean Courts," in Ralph Houlbrooke, ed., *James VI and I: Ideas, Authority, and Government*. Aldershot: Ashgate, 2006.

Roberts, Peter R. "Elizabethan Players and Minstrels and the Legislation of 1572 against Retainers and Vagabonds," in Anthony Fletcher and Peter Roberts, eds., *Religion, Culture and Society in Early Modern Britain: Essays in Honour of Patrick Collinson*. Cambridge: Cambridge University Press, 1994.

Roberts, Sasha. *Reading Shakespeare's Poems in Early Modern England*. Houndmills: Palgrave Macmillan, 2003.

Robertson, Jennifer. "The Politics of Androgyny in Japan: Sexuality and Subversion in the Theater and Beyond," *American Ethnologist* 19/3 (Aug. 1992), 419–42.

Rossiter, A. P. *Angel with Horns and Other Shakespeare Lectures*, ed. Graham Storey. Longmans, 1961.

Rowland, Richard. *Thomas Heywood's Theatre, 1599–1639: Locations, Translations, and Conflict*. Farnham, Surrey: Ashgate, 2010.

Rowse, A. L. *Simon Forman: Sex and Society in Shakespeare's Age*. Weidenfeld & Nicolson, 1974.

Rush, Christopher. *Will*. Beautiful Books, 2008.

Salingar, Leo. *Dramatic Form in Shakespeare and the Jacobeans: Essays by Leo Salingar*. Cambridge: Cambridge University Press, 1986.

Salingar, Leo. *Shakespeare and the Traditions of Comedy*. Cambridge: Cambridge University Press, 1974.

Sams, Eric. *The Real Shakespeare: Retrieving the Early Years, 1564–1594*. New Haven: Yale University Press, 1995.

Sanders, Chauncey. "Robert Greene and His 'Editors'," *PMLA* 48/2 (June 1933), 392–417.

Sanders, Julie, ed. *Ben Jonson in Context*. Cambridge: Cambridge University Press, 2010.

Schoenbaum, Samuel. *William Shakespeare: A Compact Documentary Life*. Oxford: Oxford University Press, 1977.

Scodel, Joshua. *The English Poetic Epitaph: Commemoration and Conflict from Jonson to Wordsworth*. Ithaca, NY: Cornell University Press, 1991.

Senger, Matthias Wilhelm. *Leonhard Culmann: A Literary Biography and an Edition of Five Plays as a Contribution to the Study of Drama in the Age of the Reformation*. Bibliotheca Humanistica & Reformatorica 35. Nieuwkoop: B. de Graaf, 1982.

Shapiro, James. *Contested Will: Who Wrote Shakespeare?* New York: Simon & Schuster, 2010.

Shapiro, James. *A Year in the Life of William Shakespeare: 1599*. New York: HarperCollins, 2005.

Shapiro, Michael. *Children of the Revels: The Boy Companies of Shakespeare's Time and Their Plays*. New York: Columbia University Press, 1977.

Shaw, Bernard. Preface to *Three Plays for Puritans* (1900), in *The Bodley Head Collected Shaw, II*. Max Reinhardt, 1971.

Shaw, Bernard. *Shaw on Shakespeare*, ed. Edwin Wilson. New York: E. P. Dutton, 1961.

Sillars, Stuart. *Painting Shakespeare: The Artist as Critic, 1720–1820*. Cambridge: Cambridge University Press, 2006.

Sim, Alison. *Masters and Servants in Tudor England*. Stroud, Glos.: Sutton Publishing, 2006.

Simmons, J. L. *Shakespeare's Pagan World: The Roman Tragedies*. Charlottesville: University of Virginia Press, 1973.

Simonton, Dean Keith. *Genius, Creativity and Leadership: Historiometric Inquiries*. Cambridge, MA: Harvard University Press, 1984.

Simonton, Dean Keith. *Origins of Genius: Darwinian Perspectives on Creativity*. New York: Oxford University Press, 1999.

Simpson, A. W. B. *A History of the Land Law*. 2nd edn. Oxford: Clarendon Press, 1986.

Sisson, C. J., with Mark Eccles and Deborah Jones. *Thomas Lodge and Other Elizabethans*. Cambridge, MA: Harvard University Press, 1933.

Skura, Meredith. *Shakespeare the Actor and the Purposes of Playing*. Chicago: University of Chicago Press, 1993.

Slack, Paul. *The Impact of Plague in Tudor and Stuart England*. Oxford: Oxford University Press, 1990.

Smallwood, Robert, ed. *Players of Shakespeare 6*. Cambridge: Cambridge University Press, 2004.

Smith, Charles G. *Shakespeare's Proverb Lore: His Use of the Sententiae of Leonard Culman and Publilius Syrus*. Cambridge, MA: Harvard University Press, 1963.

Smith, D. Nicol, ed. *Eighteenth-Century Essays upon Shakespeare*. 1903; repr New York: Russell & Russell, 1962.

Smith, Warren D. "The *Henry V* Choruses in the First Folio," *Journal of English and Germanic Philology* 53/1 (1954), 38–57.

Sohmer, Steven. *Shakespeare's Mystery Play: The Opening of the Globe Theatre in 1599* Manchester: Manchester University Press, 1999.

Staub, Susan C. "'A Poet with a Spear': Writing and Sexual Power in the Elizabethan Period," in George Walton Williams and Barbara J. Baines, eds., *Renaissance Papers 1992*. Durham, NC: Southeastern Renaissance Conference, 1993.

Steele, Mary Susan. *Plays and Masques at Court during the Reigns of Elizabeth, James, and Charles*. New Haven: Yale University Press, 1926.

Stern, Tiffany. *Documents of Performance in Early Modern England*. Cambridge: Cambridge University Press, 2009.

Stern, Tiffany. "'The Forgery of Some Modern Author'? Theobald's Shakespeare and Cardenio's Double Falsehood," *SQ*, 62/4 (Winter 2011), 555–93.

Stern, Tiffany. *Rehearsal from Shakespeare to Sheridan*. Oxford: Clarendon Press, 2000.

Stern, Tiffany. "'A small-beer health to his second day': Playwrights, Prologues, and First Performances in the Early Modern Theater," *Studies in Philology* 101/2 (Spring 2004), 172–99.

Stern, Tiffany, and Simon Palfrey. *Shakespeare in Parts*. Oxford: Oxford University Press, 2007.

Stevenson, Warren. *Shakespeare's Additions to Thomas Kyd's "The Spanish Tragedy": A Fresh Look at the Evidence Regarding the 1602 Additions*. Lewiston, NY: Edwin Mellen Press, 2008.

Stevenson, Warren. "Shakespeare's Hand in the *Spanish Tragedy* 1602," *Studies in English Literature* 8 (1968), 307–21.

Stewart, Alan. *The Cradle King: The Life of James VI and I, the First Monarch of a United Great Britain.* New York: St. Martin's Press, 2003.

Stok, Fabio. "The Life of Vergil before Donatus," in Joseph Farrell and Michael C. J. Putnam, eds., *A Companion to Vergil's Aeneid and Its Tradition.* Oxford: Wiley-Blackwell, 2010.

Stone, Lawrence. *The Family, Sex and Marriage in England 1500–1800.* Weidenfeld & Nicolson, 1977.

Streitberger, W. R. "Personnel and Professionalization", in John D. Cox and David Scott Kastan, eds., *A New History of Early English Drama.* New York: Columbia University Press, 1997.

Sutherland, Raymond Carter. "The Grant of Arms to Shakespeare's Father," *SQ* 14/4 (1963), 379–85.

Swanson, Heather. *Medieval Artisans: An Urban Class in Late Medieval England.* Oxford: Basil Blackwell, 1989.

Taylor, Gary. "Shakespeare and Others: The Authorship of *Henry the Sixth, Part One*," *Medieval and Renaissance Drama in England* 7 (1995), 145–205.

Taylor, Gary. "The Transmission of *Pericles*," *Publications of the Bibliographical Society of America* 80 (1986), 193–217.

Taylor, Gary. "True Is It That We Have Seen Better Plays," *Time* (Europe) (19 Mar. 2006).

Taylor, Gary, and John Lavagnino, eds. *Thomas Middleton and Early Modern Textual Culture: A Companion to the Collected Works.* Oxford: Clarendon Press, 2007.

Taylor, Gary, and Michael Warren, eds. *The Division of the Kingdoms: Shakespeare's Two Versions of King Lear.* Oxford: Clarendon Press, 1983.

Thacker, Jonathan. *A Companion to Golden Age Theatre.* Tamesis, 2007.

Thirsk, Joan. "Enclosing and Engrossing,", in H. P. R. Finberg, ed., *The Agrarian History of England and Wales*, vol. 4: *1500–1640*. 8 vols. Cambridge: Cambridge University Press, 1967–2000.

Thomas, David, ed. *Shakespeare in the Public Records.* HMSO, 1985.

Tiffany, Grace. *My Father Had a Daughter.* New York: Berkley, 2003.

Tiffany, Grace. *Will, a Novel.* New York: Berkley, 2004.

Tillotson, Geoffrey. "*Óthello* and *The Alchemist* at Oxford in 1610," *TLS*, 20 July 1933.

Times Literary Supplement. Correspondence from Peter Beal (16 June 2006); Brian Vickers (30 June 2006); Jonathan Bate and Stanley Wells (7 July 2006); Peter Beal (14 July 2006).

Tiner, Elza C. "Patrons and Travelling Companies in Warwickshire," *Early Theatre* 4 (2001), 35–52.

Traub, Valerie. "Prince Hal's Falstaff: Positioning Psychoanalysis and the Female Reproductive Body," *SQ* 40/4 (1989), 456–74.

Tribble, Evelyn B. *Cognition at the Globe: Attention and Memory in Shakespeare's Theatre.* New York: Palgrave Macmillan, 2011.

Tronch-Perez, Jesus. "Playtext Reporters and *Memoriones*: Suspect Texts in Shakespeare and Spanish Golden Age Drama," in Tom Clayton, Susan Brock, and Vicente Fores, eds.,

Shakespeare and the Mediterranean: The Selected Proceedings of the International Shakespeare Association World Congress, Valencia, 2001. Newark: University of Delaware Press, 2004.

Trousdale, Marion. *Shakespeare and the Rhetoricians.* Chapel Hill: University of North Carolina Press, 1982.

Ungerer, Gustav. "An Unrecorded Elizabethan Performance of *Titus Andronicus,*" *SS* 14 (1961), 102–9.

Unwin, George. *Industrial Organization in the Sixteenth and Seventeenth Centuries.* Oxford: Clarendon Press, 1904; repr. Cass, 1957.

Van Doren, Mark. *Shakespeare.* New York: Henry Holt, 1939.

Veale, Elspeth M. *The English Fur Trade in the Later Middle Ages.* Oxford: Clarendon Press, 1966.

Vickers, Brian, "The Face of the Bard?," *TLS*, 18 and 25 Aug. 2006.

Vickers, Brian. "Shakespeare and Authorship Studies in the Twenty-First Century," *SQ* 62/1 (2011), 106–42.

Vickers, Brian. *Shakespeare, Co-Author: A Historical Study of Five Collaborative Plays.* Oxford: Oxford University Press, 2002.

Vickers, Brian. *Shakespeare, A Lover's Complaint, and John Davies of Hereford.* Cambridge: Cambridge University Press, 2007.

Vickers, Brian. "Thomas Kyd, Secret Sharer," *TLS*, 18 Apr. 2008, 13–15.

Vickers, Brian. "The Troublesome Reign, George Peele, and the Date of King John," in *Words that Count: Essays on Early Modern Authorship in Honor of MacDonald P. Jackson.* Newark: University of Delaware Press, 2004.

Wade, Nicholas J. *A Natural History of Vision.* Cambridge, MA: MIT Press, 1998.

Waith, Eugene. *The Herculean Hero in Marlowe, Chapman, Shakespeare and Dryden.* New York: Columbia University Press; Chatto & Windus, 1962.

Ward, Bernard M. *The Seventeenth Earl of Oxford, 1550–1604, from Contemporary Documents.* John Murray, 1928; repr. 1979.

Warren, Roger. "The Quarto and Folio Texts of *2 Henry VI*: A Reconsideration," *RES* 51 (May 2000), 193–207.

Warren, Roger. *Staging Shakespeare's Late Plays.* Oxford: Clarendon Press, 1990.

Watt, Tessa. "Piety in the Pedlar's Pack: Continuity and Change, 1578–1630," in Margaret Spufford, ed., *The World of Rural Dissenters, 1520–1725.* Cambridge: Cambridge University Press, 1995.

Weimann, Robert. "Ideology and Performance in East German Versions of Shakespeare," in Irena R. Makaryk and Joseph G. Price, eds., *Shakespeare in the Worlds of Communism and Socialism.* Toronto: University of Toronto Press, 2006.

Weimann, Robert, and Douglas Bruster. *Shakespeare and the Power of Performance: Stage and Page in the Elizabethan Theatre.* Cambridge: Cambridge University Press, 2008.

Weis, René. *Shakespeare Revealed: A Biography.* John Murray, 2007.

Wells, Stanley. *Shakespeare & Co.* New York: Pantheon Books, 2006.

Wells, Stanley, ed. *Shakespeare Found! A Life Portrait at Last: Portraits, Poet, Patron, Poems.* Stratford-upon-Avon: Cobbe Foundation/Shakespeare Birthplace Trust, 2009.

Wells, Stanley, Gary Taylor, John Jowett, and William Montgomery. *William Shakespeare: A Textual Companion.* Oxford: Oxford University Press, 1987; corrected edn., Norton, 1997.

Wheeler, Richard P. "Deaths in the Family: The Loss of a Son and the Rise of Shakespearean Comedy," *SQ* 51/2 (2000), 127–53.

Wickham, Glynne, ed. *English Professional Theatre 1530–1660.* Cambridge: Cambridge University Press, 2000.

Wickham, Glynne. "*The Two Noble Kinsmen,* or, *A Midsummer Night's Dream,* Part II?," in G. R. Hibbard, ed., *Elizabethan Theatre VII.* Waterloo, 1980.

Wiggins, Martin. *Shakespeare and the Drama of His Time.* Oxford: Oxford University Press, 2000.

Wilde, Oscar. *The Portrait of Mr. W.H.* Hesperus Press, 2003.

Wiles, David. *Shakespeare's Clown: Actor and Text in the Elizabethan Playhouse.* Cambridge: Cambridge University Press, 1987.

Williams, Gruffydd Aled. "The Poetic Debate of Edmund Prys and Wiliam [*sic*] Cynwal," *Renaissance Studies* 18/1 (2004), 33–54.

Willoughby, Edwin Eliott. *A Printer of Shakespeare: The Books and Times of William Jaggard.* Philip Allan, 1934.

Wilson, F. P. "Marston, Lodge, and Constable," *The Modern Language Review,* 9/1 (Jan. 1914), 99–100.

Wilson, Richard. *Secret Shakespeare: Studies in Theatre, Religion, and Resistance.* Manchester: Manchester University Press, 2004.

Winny, James. *The Player King: A Theme of Shakespeare's Histories.* Chatto & Windus, 1968.

Woods, Gillian. "Catholicism and Conversion in *Love's Labour's Lost,*" in Laurie Maguire, ed., *How To Do Things with Shakespeare: New Approaches, New Essays.* Oxford: Blackwell Publishing, 2008.

Worden, Blair. "Shakespeare in Life and Art: Biography and *Richard III,*" in Takashi Kozuka and J. R. Mulryne, eds., *Shakespeare, Marlowe, Jonson.* Aldershot: Ashgate, 2006.

Wrightson, Keith. *English Society 1580–1680.* Hutchinson, 1983.

Yates, Frances A. *The French Academies of the Sixteenth Century.* Warburg Institute, 1947; Routledge, 1988.

Yates, Frances A. *John Florio: The Life of an Italian in Shakespeare's England.* Cambridge: Cambridge University Press, 1934.

Yungblut, Laura Hunt. *Strangers Settled Here Amongst Us: Policies, Perceptions and the Presence of Aliens in Elizabethan England.* Routledge, 1996.

Online Sources

For views of St. Helen's, the parish church that Shakespeare presumably attended in the 1590s, see www.themcs.org/churches/Bishopsgate%20St%20Helen.html
www.college-of-arms.gov.uk

For discussions of the Cobbe portrait, see Anthony Holden, *Observer*, 21 Apr. 2002; available online, with a link to the portrait, at http://books.guardian.co.uk/departments/classics/story/0,6000,688633,00.html#article_

"Shakespeare Plays in Order of Line Length": http://www.shakespearelinecount.com/shakespeare-plays-line-length

The following entries were accessed from the online edition of the *Oxford Dictionary of National Biography* (*ODNB*) (Oxford University Press, 2004):

Bergeron, David. "Munday, Anthony"

Berry, Herbert. "Brayne, John"

Broadway, Jan. "Harington, John, first Baron Harington of Exton"

Butler, Martin. "Armin, Robert"

Butler, Martin. "Kemp, William"

Butler, Martin. "Lowin, John"

Cerasano, S. P. "Alleyn, Edward"

Clayton, Tom. "Suckling, Sir John"

Colclough, David. "Donne, John"

Como, David R. "Legate, Bartholomew"

Cox, John D. "Barnes, Barnabe"

Craik, Katharine A. "Warner, William"

Daugherty, Leo. "Stanley, William, sixth Earl of Derby"

Donaldson, Ian. "Jonson, Ben"

Dutton, Richard. "Tilney, Edmund"

Edmond, Mary. "Burbage, Cuthbert"

Edmond, Mary. "Burbage, James"

Edmond, Mary. "Burbage, Richard"

Edmond, Mary. "Condell, Henry"

Edmond, Mary. "Heminges, John"

Edmond, Mary. "Tooley [Wilkinson], Nicholas"

Finkelpearl, P. J. "Beaumont, Francis"

Finkelpearl, P. J. "Davies, John [of Hereford]"

Gair, Reavley. "Percy, William"

Gunby, David. "Webster, John"

Gurr, Andrew. "Beeston [Hutchinson], Christopher"

Gurr, Andrew. "Beeston [Hutchinson], William"

Halasz, Alexandra. "Lodge, Thomas"

Holland, Peter. "Shakespeare, William"

Honan, Park. "Wriothesley, Henry, third Earl of Southampton"

Hunter, G. K. "Lyly, John"

Ingram, William. "Langley, Francis"

Kathman, David. "Heywood, Thomas"

Kathman, David. "Smith, William"

Kathman, David. "Thorpe, Thomas"

Kathman, David. "Wilson, Robert"
Kincaid, Arthur. "Buck, Sir George"
Knowles, James. "Marston, John"
Lock, Julian. "Brooke, William, tenth Baron Cobham"
MacCaffrey, Wallace T. "Henry Carey, first Baron Hunsdon"
McMullan, Gordon. "Fletcher, John"
Mulryne, J. R. "Kyd, Thomas"
Nicholl, Charles. "Marlowe, Christopher"
O'Connor, Desmond. "Florio, John"
Parr, Anthony. "Day, John"
Pettegree, Andrew. "Vautrollier, Thomas"
Pitcher, John. "Daniel, Samuel"
Prescott, Anne Lake. "Drayton, Michael"
Reid, David. "Alexander, William, first Earl of Stirling"
Richardson, William. "Bilson, Thomas"
Scott-Warren, Jason. "Harington, Sir John"
Smith, Emma. "Chettle, Henry"
Smith, Rosalind. "Southern, John"
Stater, Victor. "Radcliffe, Robert, fifth Earl of Sussex"
Sutton, James M. "Henry Frederick, Prince of Wales"
Thomas, Arthur Spencer Vaughan. "Holland, Hugh"
Thomson, Peter. "Knell, William"
Thomson, Peter. "Phillips, Augustine"
Thomson, Peter. "Tarlton, Richard"
Thornton Burnett, Mark. "Chapman, George"
Wells, Stanley. "Jaggard, William"
Wright, Stephen. "Wightman, Edward"

Index

Page numbers in **bold** refer to illustrations. Works by Shakespeare (WS) are listed alphabetically by title. Works by other authors are listed under the author's name; names mentioned only in the notes aren't listed below.

The Life of William Shakespeare: A Critical Biography, First Edition. Lois Potter.
© 2012 Lois Potter. Published 2012 by Blackwell Publishing Ltd.